SUNDAYS

AND

SEASONS

2000

Augsburg Fortress

ABOUT THE ART

The most significant Christian symbol is the cross, reflecting the mystery of God's sacrificial love of creation given through Christ Jesus. The cover cross for *Sundays and Seasons* is meant to represent this mystery in a primal, direct, and rugged way. Exploding off the cover edges, this cross symbolizes the boundless and powerful life it gives while its metallic quality represents the sacred and precious nature of the Christian way.

The images in *Sundays and Seasons* symbolize the various and many beliefs and practices of the church. Some symbols are from of old, some newer. Some symbolize Christian truths, some Christian festivals, and still others Christian rituals. Primal and rugged in style, all the symbols form a family of imagery that, whatever their source or place, speaks anew of the power, beauty, and wonder of Christ Jesus and the church.

Nicholas T. Markell is a liturgical artist from Minneapolis, Minnesota. In 1984 he earned a bachelor of visual arts degree at the University of Saint Thomas in Saint Paul, Minnesota, and in 1987 chose to respond more fully to his religious yearnings by studying for Christian ministry, earning a master of arts degree in theology and a master of divinity degree from the Washington Theological Union in Washington, D.C. Among his many studies was that of ancient Christian art and symbolism. Working in a variety of media and recognized for his artistic excellence, Nicholas's original art has won national awards and has been published, exhibited in shows, galleries, academic institutions, and installed in numerous churches across the country.

SUNDAYS AND SEASONS
2000, Cycle B

ACKNOWLEDGMENTS

Copyright © 1999 Augsburg Fortress. All rights reserved. Except for brief quotations in critical articles or reviews, no part of this book may be reproduced in any manner without prior written permission from the publisher. Write to: Permissions, Augsburg Fortress, Box 1209, Minneapolis, MN 55440-1209.

Scripture quotations, unless otherwise noted, are from the New Revised Standard Version Bible © 1989 Division of Christian Education of the National Council of the Churches of Christ in the United States of America. Used by permission.

The prayers (printed in each Sunday/festival section) may be reproduced for one-time, congregational use, provided copies are for local use only and the following copyright notice appears: From *Sundays and Seasons*, copyright © 1999 Augsburg Fortress. May be reproduced by permission for use only between November 28, 1999 and December 2, 2000.

Art: Markell Studios, Minneapolis, MN
Book Design: The Kantor Group, Inc., Minneapolis, MN

Editors: Dennis Bushkofsky, Eric Vollen

Manufactured in the U.S.A.   0-8066-3626-2   3-1204

CONTRIBUTORS

Annual Materials: Introduction, Dennis Bushkofsky; An Overview of Mark's Gospel, Virgil Thompson; Children and Worship, Margaret Krych; The Millennium, Richard Jeske; Praying at the Eucharist, Theodore Asta; Shape of Worship for the Season, Worship Planning Checklist, Dennis Bushkofsky.

Seasonal Materials: Images of the Season, Catherine Ziel; Environment and Art for the Season, Samuel Torvend; Preaching with the Season, Ronald Roschke, Donald Kreiss, Robert Rimbo, Adele Stiles Resmer, Barbara Lundblad; Shape of Worship for the Season, Dennis Bushkofsky; Assembly Song for the Season, Martin Seltz; Alternate/Seasonal Liturgical Texts, Dennis Bushkofsky.

Weekly Materials: introductions to the day, introductions to the readings, Craig Mueller; the prayers, James Boline; calendar for lesser festivals and commemorations, D. Foy Christopherson; Images for Preaching, Ronald Roschke, Donald Kreiss, Robert Rimbo, Adele Stiles Resmer, Barbara Lundblad; Worship Matters, Kent Burreson, Craig Satterlee, Rhoda Schuler, Jeffrey Truscott; Let the Children Come, Beth Schlegel; Service Music, Martin Seltz.

Music Materials: mainstream hymnody, Marilyn Stulken; mainstream choral, Linda Kempke; classical choral, Teresa Bowers; popular choral, David Ellison; children's choirs, Kathy Lowrie; keyboard/instrumental, Naomi Rowley; handbell, Lee Afdahl; praise ensemble, Robin Cain.

Contributing Editors: Norma Aamodt-Nelson, Carol Carver, Lynn Joyce Hunter, Linda Parriott, Martin Seltz, Frank Stoldt.

RELATED RESOURCES

Worship Planning Calendar, 2000, Cycle B (AFP 23-2009)
Words for Worship, 2000, Cycle B (AFP 3-4025)
Living and Learning, 1999–2000, Cycles A/B (AFP 15-6050)

TABLE OF CONTENTS

INTRODUCTION

Introduction	5
Key to Music Publishers	27
Music for Worship Key	28
Key to Hymn and Psalm Collections	29
Selected Publishers	30

ADVENT

Introduction to the Season		34
Alternate Worship Texts		43
Seasonal Rites		44
First Sunday in Advent	Nov 28, 1999	46
Second Sunday in Advent	Dec 5	49
Third Sunday in Advent	Dec 12	52
Fourth Sunday in Advent	Dec 19	55

CHRISTMAS

Introduction to the Season		60
Alternate Worship Texts		70
Seasonal Rites		71
The Nativity of Our Lord/Christmas Eve	Dec 24	74
The Nativity of Our Lord/Christmas Dawn	Dec 25	77
The Nativity of Our Lord/Christmas Day	Dec 25	80
St. Stephen, Deacon and Martyr	Dec 26	83
First Sunday after Christmas	Dec 26	85
New Year's Eve	Dec 31	89
The Name of Jesus	Jan 1, 2000	90
Second Sunday after Christmas	Jan 2	92

EPIPHANY

Introduction to the Season		98
Alternate Worship Texts		106
Seasonal Rites		107
The Epiphany of Our Lord	Jan 6	109
The Baptism of Our Lord	Jan 9	111
Second Sunday after the Epiphany	Jan 16	115
Third Sunday after the Epiphany	Jan 23	118
Fourth Sunday after the Epiphany	Jan 30	121
Fifth Sunday after the Epiphany	Feb 6	125
Sixth Sunday after the Epiphany/Proper 1	Feb 13	127
Seventh Sunday after the Epiphany/Proper 2	Feb 20	130
Eighth Sunday after the Epiphany/Proper 3	Feb 27	134
The Transfiguration of Our Lord	Mar 5	137

LENT

Introduction to the Season		142
Alternate Worship Texts		150
Seasonal Rites		151
Ash Wednesday	Mar 8	153
First Sunday in Lent	Mar 12	156
Second Sunday in Lent	Mar 19	159
Third Sunday in Lent	Mar 26	162
Fourth Sunday in Lent	Apr 2	165
Fifth Sunday in Lent	Apr 9	168
Sunday of the Passion/Palm Sunday	Apr 16	171

THE THREE DAYS

Introduction to the Season		176
Alternate Worship Texts		186
Seasonal Rites		187
Maundy Thursday	Apr 20	190
Good Friday	Apr 21	193
The Resurrection of Our Lord/Vigil of Easter	Apr 22	195
The Resurrection of Our Lord/Easter Day	Apr 23	199
The Resurrection of Our Lord/Easter Evening	Apr 23	202

EASTER

Introduction to the Season		204
Alternate Worship Texts		213
Seasonal Rites		214
Second Sunday of Easter	Apr 30	215
Third Sunday of Easter	May 7	219
Fourth Sunday of Easter	May 14	221
Fifth Sunday of Easter	May 21	225
Sixth Sunday of Easter	May 28	228
The Ascension of Our Lord	June 1	231
Seventh Sunday of Easter	June 4	234
Vigil of Pentecost	June 10	237
The Day of Pentecost	June 11	239

SUMMER

Introduction to the Season		244
Alternate Worship Texts		251
Seasonal Rites		252
The Holy Trinity	June 18	253
Second Sunday after Pentecost/Proper 7	June 25	256
Third Sunday after Pentecost/Proper 8	July 2	259
Fourth Sunday after Pentecost/Proper 9	July 9	262
Fifth Sunday after Pentecost/Proper 10	July 16	265
Sixth Sunday after Pentecost/Proper 11	July 23	268
Seventh Sunday after Pentecost/Proper 12	July 30	272
Eighth Sunday after Pentecost/Proper 13	Aug 6	274
Ninth Sunday after Pentecost/Proper 14	Aug 13	277
Tenth Sunday after Pentecost/Proper 15	Aug 20	281
Eleventh Sunday after Pentecost/Proper 16	Aug 27	284

AUTUMN

Introduction to the Season		288
Alternate Worship Texts		295
Seasonal Rites		296
Twelfth Sunday after Pentecost/Proper 17	Sep 3	299
Thirteenth Sunday after Pentecost/Proper 18	Sep 10	302
Fourteenth Sunday after Pentecost/Proper 19	Sep 17	305
Fifteenth Sunday after Pentecost/Proper 20	Sep 24	308
Sixteenth Sunday after Pentecost/Proper 21	Oct 1	312
Seventeenth Sunday after Pentecost/Proper 22	Oct 8	315
Day of Thanksgiving (Canada)	Oct 9	318
Eighteenth Sunday after Pentecost/Proper 23	Oct 15	321
Nineteenth Sunday after Pentecost/Proper 24	Oct 22	324
Reformation Sunday	Oct 29	327
Twentieth Sunday after Pentecost/Proper 25	Oct 29	330

NOVEMBER

Introduction to the Season		334
Alternate Worship Texts		341
Seasonal Rites		342
All Saints Sunday	Nov 5	344
Twenty-first Sunday after Pentecost/Proper 26	Nov 5	347
Twenty-second Sunday after Pentecost/Proper 27	Nov 12	350
Twenty-third Sunday after Pentecost/Proper 28	Nov 19	353
Day of Thanksgiving (U.S.)	Nov 23	356
Christ the King/Proper 29	Nov 26	359

Bibliography	362
Preparing for Worship	Inside back cover

INTRODUCTION

Welcome to the fifth year of *Sundays and Seasons*. This resource has clearly established a strong and loyal readership in a short amount of time. Several writers within this volume explore some of the issues appropriate for the threshold of a new millennium. Richard Jeske's article, "The Millennium," will help many people gain a solid theological perspective on the calendar changes occurring this year. Writers providing preaching resources have also incorporated this topic within their reflections—but in subtler ways than much of the media seems to be treating the year 2000.

Careful readers of this resource may detect a greater attention to New Year's Eve and the Name of Jesus (January 1) than we have given either of these occasions in previous volumes. We have also included a vigil for New Year's Eve in the seasonal rites section for the Christmas season. Prayers for several of the weeks toward the beginning of this volume also acknowledge the millennial turn.

In addition to the significance of the millennium itself we can find further importance and interest in the fact that the year 2000 celebrates the 250th anniversary of the death of Johann Sebastian Bach, often called the "Fifth Evangelist." Although the performance of Bach never needs a rationale, the millennium and the anniversary offer an excellent reason to explore his choral, keyboard, and instrumental music throughout the year. To this end, consider the new choral collection from Augsburg Fortress, *Bach through the Church Year* (AFP 3-5854), which offers movements from cantatas and oratorios presented with carefully reconstructed keyboard parts and fresh English texts.

While the dated aspect of *Sundays and Seasons* allows us the possibility of making special reference to things that are unique about *this* year, other materials here might be used this year or marked for reference at a later time. Articles about the place of children within worship, the Gospel of Mark, or the importance of eucharistic prayers have a greater relevance than this year alone. Some of the suggestions about environment and art in this volume may be tried now, but will also be worth reading in future years as congregations grow in their ability to celebrate the seasons in more meaningful ways.

RELATED RESOURCES

By now, many people may have discovered that *Sundays and Seasons* is really the keystone of a whole range of lectionary-based resources produced by Augsburg Fortress. Introductions to the day, introductions to the readings, and prayers are repeated in the *Celebrate* lectionary inserts and in *Words for Worship* (an annual CD-ROM containing the full texts of lectionary readings and alternate texts for worship). Furthermore, the *Worship Planning Calendar* is intended to be the workbook for *Sundays and Seasons*, providing a place to list decisions and choices about celebrating each Sunday and festival throughout the year.

Additional lectionary-based resources will be introduced in 1999 under the common title Life Together. These are primarily educational materials designed to support the patterns of the liturgical year and the lectionary. A key to opening up the Life Together series is a volume titled *Living and Learning*, which serves as a companion to *Sundays and Seasons* in providing an overview to several other resources for virtually all other aspects of congregational ministry.

Finally, the mission for *Sundays and Seasons* is to be useful for all who have primary responsibility for liturgical leadership in congregations. In order to fulfill this task, we need your feedback regarding what you find most helpful, and what additional materials you would like to see us cover. Please feel free to call or write me with your suggestions at any time.

Dennis Bushkofsky, editor
Phone: (800) 426-0115, ext. 558
E-mail: bushkofd@augsburgfortress.org

AN OVERVIEW OF MARK'S GOSPEL

According to the usual liturgical approach, the gospels are read within the framework of the church year. John the Baptist makes his scheduled appearance in Advent. The Christmas season features stories of the birth and infancy of Jesus. Epiphany culminates with the light of the transfiguration. Similarly, in the Easter cycle readings are chosen for their appropriateness to the seasons of Lent, Easter, and Pentecost.

While this program of readings works relatively well for Luke and Matthew, both of which provide material nicely accommodating the seasons of the church year, the approach does not suit Mark nearly so well. Mark lacks material traditionally associated with the seasons of the church year—for example, neither birth nor infancy stories for Christmas; and no resurrection appearances, but only the disappointing performance of his disciples, for Easter. Thus, for more than one-third of the Sundays in cycle B the lectionary compensates for Mark's "deficiency" with readings from John.

In the interest of guarding the integrity of Mark's literary and theological program, one is tempted to propose a radical revision of the scheduled readings. That tack would be somewhat impractical; some might even say impious as well. Instead, what we propose here is merely a reversal to the usual approach. Instead of reading Mark in the framework of the church year, we consider the church year in light of Mark's story of Jesus. To that end we will first sketch an overview of Mark's story and purpose. Second, we will suggest ways in which cycle B may more appreciably be observed as the year of Mark.

AN OVERVIEW OF THE STORY

In the first verse of the gospel, Mark announces that his story is about "the beginning of the good news of Jesus Christ, the Son of God." In other words, Mark declares Jesus the fulfillment of God's messianic promise to David, "I will raise up your offspring. . . . I will establish the throne of his kingdom forever. I will be a father to him . . ." (2 Sam. 7:12b, 13b-14a). What is clear to Mark is not, however, so clear to the characters in his story. Among them the identity of Jesus is the subject of considerable controversy.

The scribes consider Jesus a blasphemer (2:7) possessed by the devil (3:22). They are partly correct. Jesus is possessed, not by the devil, but by the Holy Spirit (1:10). At his baptism the Holy Spirit of God tore apart the heavens, came down, and entered *into* Jesus (1:10). The events of the baptism—declaration of the heavenly voice and the descent of the Spirit—have taken place in secret, unbeknownst to the human contemporaries of Jesus. As with the scribes, it is clear to ordinary observers that Jesus possesses extraordinary power. To their utter amazement Jesus heals the sick (e.g., 2:3-12), casts out demons (1:27-28), and teaches with authority unlike anything they have previously encountered among the usual teachers of faith (1:22; 11:18). Still, people were uncertain what to make of it. His family "went out to restrain him, for [they] were saying, 'He has gone out of his mind' " (3:21). Even his own disciples are uncertain what to make of him (4:41).

The only ones in the story who seem to get Jesus' true identity right are the demons, and clearly to them it is not good news (1:24). The only human exception is Peter in chapter 8. There it is reported that on the way to Caesarea Philippi Jesus had been quizzing his disciples, "Who do people say that I am?" (8:27). They answer, "John the Baptist; and others Elijah; and still others, one of the prophets" (8:28). Under the pressure of Jesus' continuing interrogation Peter declares the truth: "You are the Messiah" (8:29).

Generally, readers assume that the truth of Jesus' identity had been revealed to Peter by the Holy Spirit of God. The narrative however does not encourage such a conclusion. By the end of the episode the reader is left to wonder whether Peter has not in fact come by the truth of Jesus' identity in the same way the demons have come to know the truth about Jesus. Clearly Peter is not seeing Jesus as God sees Jesus. Following his objection to the prophecy regarding the destiny of the Messiah, Jesus rebukes him, "Get behind me, Satan! For you are setting your mind not on divine things but on human things" (8:33). Even though readers are permitted to see more than Peter is able to see, still we sympathize with him. From the human point of view, by the end of the story nothing seems more ridiculous than Mark's claim that Jesus is the Messiah. While Jesus seems possessed of impressive powers, he appears nothing like the messiah of traditional expectation. In the final days as the movement surrounding him collapses, Jesus becomes the object of universal mockery. His Roman judge, Pilate, was at a complete loss to see in his wildest imagination how Jesus was a threat to anyone or anything, especially to the Holy Roman Empire (15:1-15). The soldiers who carried out the execution openly ridiculed him (15:16-20). The assembled crowd at the crucifixion did likewise (15:25-32a). Even those executed with him taunted him (15:32b).

Against the weight of the overwhelming earthly verdict against him, Mark introduces just one piece of evidence in support of his claim. As the angel explained to the women at the tomb, "You are looking for Jesus of Nazareth, who was crucified. He has been raised [by God]; he is not here" (16:6). From this point of view, the resurrection vindicates Jesus as the true Messiah, against the verdict of the world.

In what sense, then, can it be said, as Mark announces at the beginning of his story, that the reported events form the "beginning of the good news about Jesus, Messiah, Son of God"? What appears by the end of the story is that humanity—both friends of Jesus and enemies of Jesus—has, on the basis of their performance in connection with the Messiah's coming, burned their bridges toward God, "the stone that the builders rejected has become the cornerstone; this was the Lord's doing . . ." (12:10). From that standpoint would it not be more fitting to characterize these events as the beginning of the bad news?

So how is the preacher to proceed? Is one to admonish the congregation to learn from the negative performance of the characters in the story and strive to do better? The story does not provide much basis to support such a preaching strategy. In fact the story does not put much stock in the capacity of humanity—enlightened or not—to act in concert with the saving purpose of God. In response to the question of his exasperated disciples, "Then who can be saved?" (10:26), Jesus declares flatly, "for mortals it is impossible" (10:27a). But all is not lost. Salvation may prove an impossible do-it-yourself project for humanity, "but not for God; for God all things are possible" (10:27b). Salvation depends on God alone. And just so, as Jesus makes the point in his farewell sermon, humanity is justified to hold out hope of salvation. God has promised that before all is said and done the elect will be gathered from the four winds (13:26-27) under the power and glory of God's saving rule (13:26). This promise is the truth that preachers are given to proclaim in the year of Mark. The promise of such preaching is that, like the sown seed (4:26-29), it will of its own accord create faith in the saving power of Jesus, Messiah and Son of God.

ADVENT IN THE VIEW OF MARK

If the traditional themes of Advent—preparation and expectation—are to be observed in a fashion that respects Mark's way of telling the story of Jesus, then the Advent congregation must be prepared to expect the unexpected. The proclamation of Mark is that while God's promises may be trusted, specifically the promise to David that one day a Savior would arise to redeem faith's fortunes, God fulfills them in a surprising way. The days unfold one after another in what seems an endless drudgery in which evil appears so often to have the creation in a death grip. But God will not allow it to go on forever. Keep alert. Do not sleep life away in resignation and accommodation. For God will, as John has promised in his wilderness sermon, send the "one who is more powerful" (1:7). But who is the promised one more powerful than? More powerful than John? Yes. But he is also more powerful than Satan, as the reader learns in the story of Jesus' wilderness temptation (1:12-13).

While the lectionary requires the congregation to wait until Lent to hear the story of the wilderness showdown, believers may begin to anticipate the victory of the Lord. As Jesus explains his demonstrated power over the demons, "No one can enter a strong man's house and plunder his property without first tying up the strong man; then indeed the house can be plundered" (3:27). The congregation can do nothing to hurry along or help the promise of Christ's victory. It can, however, continue to go about its earthly affairs, keeping awake to the promise, waiting and praying, for God's promises may be trusted, even if they are fulfilled in surprising, unexpected ways.

CHRISTMAS IN THE VIEW OF MARK

Even though Mark offers no stories of either the birth or the infancy of Jesus, it would be interesting all the same to search the gospel for lections fitting for the Christmas season. For example, one might consider looking at Mark 1:1, raising the questions: In what sense is the story of Jesus good news and to whom? In what sense does Mark's story narrate only the beginnings of the good news? What does it mean to name Jesus Messiah, Son of God? Once the questions have been formulated, hearers can be encouraged to put them to the story itself. They will find that the story offers surprising answers.

Take, for example, that remarkable account of Jesus' encounter with an army of particularly fierce demons in the Gerasene cemetery (5:1-20). This legion of demons had taken possession of a local man and driven him over the edge: "Night and day among the tombs and on the mountains he was always howling and bruising himself with stones" (5:5). Subduing, let alone casting out the demon, was quite beyond the conventional resources of the community; "chains he wrenched apart, and the shackles he broke in pieces; and no one had the strength to subdue him" (5:4). As a consequence, for the sake of peace and order and to protect the public good, the man had been banished to the cemetery (5:3). Jesus—without so much as working up a sweat—destroys the demon, restoring the man previously possessed to sanity and life (5:15). The incident, however, proves so unsettling to the former demoniac's neighbors that they "beg Jesus to leave their neighborhood" (5:17).

The report casts Christmas and the coming of the Christ in an altogether different light from the usual. This Jesus is not so gentle, meek, and mild that you have to look twice just to make certain someone is actually there. The Jesus of Mark's story is possessed of power the likes of which are unprecedented in what we know. From that standpoint, Jesus appears dangerous. Can he be trusted to use his power for the public good?

As the episode in the Gerasene cemetery illustrates, he came and set to the work of saving the lost, but it proved too overwhelming to those in charge of peace and order. If a person imagines, to borrow from Paul Scherer (*The Word of God Sent,* Grand Rapids: Baker Books, 1977, p. 131), that God in Christ comes with a feather duster to keep what we already are and have in apple-pie order, then such a person is in for a considerable surprise when viewing Christmas according to Mark's version.

EPIPHANY IN THE VIEW OF MARK

Mark illuminates the first Sunday of the Epiphany season with the stunning story of Jesus' baptism. As reported by Mark, the scene raises a number of questions. What, for example, is the meaning of it when Mark describes the heavens being torn asunder *(schizomenos)* as the Spirit of God descends to take possession of Jesus? The only other time the word occurs in the gospel is during the crucifixion narrative, where it is used to describe what happened to the curtain of the temple when Jesus died. It was torn asunder *(schizomenos).* What perspective does the peculiarly Markan description of these events provide the hearer of the story? Donald Juel proposes, "the image may suggest that the protecting barriers are gone and that God, unwilling to be confined to sacred spaces, is on the loose in our own realm. . . . Mark's narrative is about the intrusion of God into a world that has become alien territory—an intrusion that means both death and life" (*A Master of Surprise,* Minneapolis: Fortress Press, 1994, pp. 35–36).

The season of Epiphany then unfolds with stories that flesh out the theme. Jesus sweeps responsible, productive citizens from their lives as they were and into life as it is defined solely by the call of Jesus' mission: "Follow me and I will make you fish for people" (1:17). The fishermen, without so much as a second thought, leave everything and follow, never knowing exactly what or who has hit them. With his new disciples Jesus sets out on a preaching tour that gets remarkable results. At his word, sickness is healed (1:29-31) and demons are cast out (1:23-26). The people who hear Jesus' sermon are astounded by the unprecedented authority of his teaching (1:22). The demons, when they encounter him, surrender without resistance (e.g., 1:24 and following). Despite the attempt of people to hold on to him Jesus keeps on the move under the pressure of the mission to which he is driven (1:38-39). In this sense it may be said that Jesus belongs not to the need of the people, but to the purpose of God's Holy Spirit.

By the end of Jesus' Epiphany preaching tour, the initial success he enjoyed along the way meets with reservation and resistance. Opposition comes from a surprising source. In the judgment of the authorities, Jesus' success is fine and well, but he has taken a good thing too far, in their estimation. As the readings scheduled for the last two Sundays of the season illustrate, he has crossed over the line, violating boundaries established to maintain religious and social solidarity, and thus the public good. According to the one episode, Jesus forgives sins (2:1-12). When the authorities point out that only God can forgive sins, Jesus does not argue the point, bringing down on himself the charge of blasphemy (2:7). In the other episode (2:13-32), Jesus is charged with enjoying the company of tax collectors and other sinners too much (2:16). Jesus answers the charge, "Those who are well have no need of a physician, but those who are sick; I have come to call not the righteous but sinners" (2:17). One does not imagine that Jesus' answer will be the end of the controversy. It serves only to fan the flames of opposition. As we turn our attention to the Easter cycle, Mark's story continues to attest to the floundering of his disciples, and to heat up with conflict between Jesus and the authorities. What is taken as established truth in heaven does not receive universal affirmation on earth as it makes its worldly debut. Even when God plainly reveals the truth to the inner circle of Jesus' disciples, they seem unable to grasp it (see 9:2-8; compare 9:32; 10:32-45). The authorities no longer even pretend to entertain an open mind toward Jesus (3:6).

LENT IN THE VIEW OF MARK

Satan and his minions pose relatively little opposition to Jesus. Mark's report of the wilderness encounter between Jesus and Satan ends somewhat ambiguously (1:9-15), but the ensuing narrative leaves no doubt that Jesus has proven the stronger one (see e.g., 1:24), who, having bound Satan, is now free to plunder his house (see 3:27 for Jesus' interpretation of his ministry). The more troublesome opposition arises from the established religious authority of the community, and even from his own disciples.

The narrative following Peter's confession, scheduled for the second Sunday of the Lenten season, illustrates the nature of the unwitting opposition that arises from his friends. Peter is not openly hostile toward the Lord, setting out to oppose or hinder his saving mission. His opposition arises from a mind set on human things and blind to the thoughts of God (8:31-38). Such opposition will not go unanswered, as Jesus responds, "Get behind me, Satan!" (8:33). What is most noteworthy to faith is the way in which Jesus addresses it. He does not admonish Peter to get busy, open his eyes, and stretch his mind to think the thoughts of God. The narrative recognizes that just as it has been impossible for those who are physically blind to heal themselves (8:22-26; 10:46-52), and impossible for the demon-possessed to free themselves (5:1-20), so it is impossible for the spiritually blind to heal themselves. Yet we sense the hope that they will have their eyes opened to the truth of God. The promise lies in the same one who has helped those who are physically blind and the demon-possessed. The way in which the cure will be administered is altogether surprising. Peter's story is found in the strong undercurrent to the surface flow of events as reported in the latter chapters of the gospel. In them Peter distinguishes himself as exactly the kind of sinner for whom Christ has given himself in forgiveness all the way to death and back (see 2:17). If Peter is to have a future with God, it lies only through the portal of forgiveness.

While the lectionary reserves the entire story of the final events to Passion Sunday, preachers and worship planners might profitably consider spreading the story out over the entire season either in midweek worship or Bible study. In this way more attention can be given to these crucial events of Jesus' saving mission. One week could, for example, be devoted to following Peter's experience of these events. Another week could be spent examining the nature of the opposition mounted by the temple establishment against Jesus. Another week could be dedicated to reviewing the place of faith, as represented by the disciples, in these events. Such an approach to the biblical narrative promises to engage the imagination of the congregation with the thematic development of the narrative.

EASTER IN THE VIEW OF MARK

Easter raises the question of the ending. The end of Mark's story is by no means what one might have expected. Whatever one might have expected, it was probably not, "So [the women] went out and fled from the tomb, for terror and amazement had seized them; and they said nothing to anyone, for they were afraid" (16:8). The unsettling nature of the ending among historic audiences is verified by the shorter and longer endings that have been nervously attached early on to provide a more satisfying resolution of the reported events. The evidence all points to the fact that the story of Mark concludes exactly at 16:8.

What is to be made of the ending as it is? We may begin sorting it out by admitting that the women were not expecting to find what they did. They made preparations and went to the tomb to complete the job of providing a proper burial for Jesus. Contrary to expectation, they discovered that he was not there.

If not in the tomb, where was he? Up and living. Death was not the end of him. The verdict in the court of world opinion was overturned by the higher court. Against the verdict of his accusers (14:63-65), God vindicated Jesus, true Christ, just as God had declared at the baptism (1:11) and at the transfiguration (9:7).

As the resurrected, vindicated Savior, Jesus returned to keep his promises (16:7), which makes the sermon of chapter 13 perhaps of special interest in the season of Easter. In the sermon Jesus makes promises about the future. The gist of it is that he will return to complete the job of redeeming the world (13:26-27).

PENTECOST IN THE VIEW OF MARK

Given the promise of the risen Jesus to keep his word, it is entirely fitting that the attention of the Pentecost congregation be focused on the earthly ministry of Jesus. Thus far, the year of Mark has taught the congregation that one dare not judge Jesus by our opinions and traditions. It did not work well for Peter or the religious leaders in the story, and it will not work well for readers. Instead Jesus judges our opinions and traditions. It is a reality that makes for surprises, of which the narrative of the gospel begins to tell (see 1:1).

Space permits by way of illustration only the briefest examination of several pericopes from the narrative. Inasmuch as faith's hope according to Mark lies not in the believer, but in the crucified and risen Jesus, our primary interest in the narrative will be with respect to what it tells about him. The narrative of the earthly Jesus authorizes what we may expect from the risen Jesus.

Mark's narrative of Jesus' earthly career provides faith and plenty of encouragement to trust the power and the fidelity of Jesus to keep his promises. His word has power to bring about that of which it speaks. Jesus speaks about salvation, but that is not the end of the matter; at his word the disciples were saved from physical peril more than once (4:35-41; 6:45-52). The word of Jesus has strength enough to heal the sick (5:21-34; 7:24-37; 8:22-26), cast out demons (9:14-29), and raise the dead (5:35-43). Faith is justified to trust the word of Jesus to establish the kingdom of God's saving rule, just as he promised (13:26-27, 31).

CONCLUSION

The year of Mark promises to blow fresh breezes into the congregation's experience of the church year. It promises as well to engage the congregation's imagination with the particular proclamation of Mark's gospel, "The beginning of the good news of Jesus Christ, the Son of God." The value of the project for faith could never be overestimated, for as Ernst Käsemann has said, "Our faith rests on ... the question, Do we know Jesus? and on nothing else, whatever the volumes of dogmatics and creeds may consider necessary. [He alone] forms the basis for deciding who God is and who is a false god, what God did and did not do, and how he revealed himself, as being for or against our wishes and ideas about him" (Ernst Käsemann, *Jesus Means Freedom*, Philadelphia: Fortress Press, 1968, p. 21).

INTRODUCTION

CHILDREN AND WORSHIP

We rightly welcome and encourage the presence and participation of children in the gathered worshiping assembly. As baptized children of God they are part of the whole people of God. But it is important to remember that children do not worship in exactly the same way adults do. Through abstract thinking and experience, adults and teenagers have vast resources of remembrance at their disposal on which to draw as they prepare to worship: sitting in church, saying a prayer, reading a psalm, listening to a prelude—such triggers flood adult memories with thoughts of God. But children need more time to reflect and learn about God before they are ready to worship. They do not have vast stores of experiences to draw on nor many years of using particular prayers, Bible verses, or hymns that can direct their thinking. Even if written materials are provided, children will often attend to the task of reading rather than focusing on God and preparing to worship.

Children, in fact, best respond to God on the basis of things they have recently learned or done. So singing and praise will occur most naturally for children at the end (or in the middle) of a learning session. But public worship does not often afford such intensive learning and expressive activities. In addition, children find intriguing many factors that adults screen out automatically: a figure depicted in stained glass, a stain on the floor, the texture of the pew-cushion. It may take the child some time before he or she is ready to attend to the things of God in the ways adults expect.

Because children do not participate in public worship in the same way that teenagers and adults do, we need to ask, "How can we enhance children's experience in worship?" To begin, it will be helpful to consider children's cognitive development.

THE WAY CHILDREN THINK

Over the past thirty-five years, and following the lead of Jean Piaget, research the world over has made clear the fact that children think qualitatively differently from adults. As the brain develops to maturity, children move through six stages of brain cell development with concomitant changes in the way they think. The first three stages are often grouped simply as "sensorimotor" and appear during the first two years. The subsequent three stages develop sequentially and are roughly associated with age levels. We call these stages the "preoperational stage" (about two to seven years, usually), the "concrete thinking stage" (about seven to eleven or twelve years), and the final stage of thinking typical of mature persons is termed the stage of "abstract thinking" or "formal operations."

In the preoperational stage, children are developing many wonderful capacities for thinking and communication but are not yet able to reason logically. They cannot relate parts to the whole nor can they reverse their thinking to check the accuracy of reasoning. Therefore, their thinking may appear to an adult to be distorted or amusing.

Preoperational children can see things only from their own point of view; they simply cannot be expected to understand that adults may be upset by their humming in the service or may find their staring distracting. Preoperational thinking also reasons from particular to particular, while most public worship assumes adult-type thinking that reasons from particulars to generalizations or vice versa; so young children have difficulty comprehending that they are included in groups such as "sinful people." And preoperational thinking cannot distinguish between fact and fantasy; the child under seven is simply puzzled when the pastor states, "Jesus was real!" since "real" and "fantasy" are indistinguishable in the child's thought.

Concepts of space, time, causality, and speed do not develop until the concrete thinking stage (during the years from seven to eleven or twelve). "Two thousand years ago the early Christians were killed for loving Jesus!" says the preacher—and the four-year-old who attends the "early" service wonders if her family might soon be killed just like the people the pastor mentioned.

Two thousand years, two thousand months, or weeks, or days, are all pretty similar!

In the concrete thinking stage from approximately age seven to eleven or twelve, children progressively develop the ability to generalize, and to conceive of time, space, speed, and causality. They begin to see the viewpoint of others and to grasp simple concrete similes (the likeness of characteristics that can be perceived through the senses). At nine or ten years of age children begin to take into account intentionality in judging right and wrong, and so develop more mature moral concepts and the capacity to grasp forgiveness in a new way. Concepts of death mature gradually through the concrete period, and fact is increasingly distinguished from fantasy. All these developments mean that concrete thinkers are able to grasp a great deal more of the Bible, traditional Christian teaching, and liturgical phrases than preoperational thinkers can.

However, keep in mind an important limitation: the concrete-thinking child is limited to thinking about things that *in principle* are perceivable through the senses—anything that could (given the appropriate circumstances) be seen, touched, tasted, smelled, or heard, is able to be reasoned about by the concrete-thinking child. And, consequently, concrete thinkers give sensory referents to things that are not in principle perceivable through the senses. Because of this limitation, much that adults say in metaphor is taken literally and misunderstood. Object lessons that use objects with sensory referents to refer metaphorically to entities that do not have such referents are totally lost on children younger than twelve. Somewhere around eleven or twelve usually, the child's brain matures to the point where he or she is able to use formal operations (or abstract thinking). The most important characteristics of abstract thinking that relate to worship are the ability to reason about that which, in principle, cannot be perceived through the senses, to apply principles in theory, to reason about ideals and the future, to reason about that which is contrary to fact, to grasp universal generalizations, and to use metaphor.

Abstract thinking is typical of teenagers and adults of all races and centuries. It is typical of normal brain cell development. And it clearly is presupposed by biblical writers, hymnwriters, and liturgiologists. The worship service is full of such concepts. It is simply not possible to rewrite the Bible for children conceptually. Similarly, we cannot rewrite all hymns or every part of the liturgy so that they will be comprehensible to children. Therefore, we cannot tailor the service to children in the way that we can a session in Sunday church school. The omission of abstract concepts would impoverish our liturgy beyond measure, and major points of the Christian faith would never be celebrated.

IMPLICATIONS FOR WORSHIP

Lutherans sometimes have a problem in taking the child's development seriously. We value the spoken word and pay particular attention to the way in which the gospel is *heard*. Our catechetical mind-set includes understanding. We often ignore children who cannot understand the service or we try to include doses of verbalization "just for the children." Neither approach is helpful. Much better is to consider ways in which to enhance aspects of the whole worship experience that most influence children.

Children usually respond to the "nonintellectual" aspects of the service more readily than to the cognitive. Even the youngest children may enjoy the service because of these aspects. Of course, adults are also deeply influenced by these factors. So let us consider the social and emotional aspects of the service that may help children sense God's presence and love and mercy, and may help them share in the joy of belonging to God's people.

Children respond to atmosphere. In public worship, the child experiences an atmosphere conducive to awe. Silence, music, architecture, furnishings, rich liturgical phrases—all contribute to a sense of mystery and wonder. The child may sense the greatness of God and respond with adoration or rapt amazement.

Children experience being part of the people of God. They want to learn the words of creed and prayers so they can "join in." They want to do and say what the people of God do and say, to share in the cultic ritual of God's people. Singing, reciting prayers and psalms and creeds, moving together, even saying an enthusiastic "amen" after prayers are all experiences of "we the people of God" for the child.

Children often enjoy being part of a large crowd of all age levels. It is a different experience from being in a class group and helps children appreciate the people of God as an inclusive throng with differences of many kinds who all share in the good news of God in Jesus Christ.

Children may often, in today's society, enjoy the experience of being together as a family that loves and praises God. Encouraging families to sit together may be more important than splitting them up to ensure that the choir has sufficient altos or that all children have equal turns at being acolyte. Let families remain together rather than asking children to "come forward" at particular points. (Of course, if the whole family is coming forward for a baptism, then the principle holds in reverse—the child will come forward as part of the family.) Children whose families do not attend often appreciate a "surrogate family" to sit with in church.

On the affective level, many sights and sounds in the service appeal to children: music, noise, movement (kneeling, sitting, standing, as well as the movement of the pastor, lectors, ushers, and acolytes), processions, colors (in paraments, clothing, windows, banners), singing, textures (smoothness of pews, roughness of kneelers), smells (flowers, furniture polish). Persons responsible for worship could consider how the congregation may enrich the worship through these means.

The sense of drama is present in the service. Age-old traditions in liturgy and sacraments call to children as to adults. Most children will strain to see what is going on in a baptism or at the communion. For this reason it is important that children sit where they can see. Certainly a baby who cries easily or a child who prefers to wander may better be situated near an exit. But, for the most part, children are much better behaved when seated by an aisle or near the front where they can see everything.

In worship, children have a sense of being more equal with adults—not a small thing for children who are reminded hourly that they are not yet grown-up. In the worshiping assembly children say the same words that adults do, read grown-up sounding phrases (even if they don't understand them!), and sing genuinely grown-up songs.

Children (and youth) appreciate being welcomed by congregational members and greeted by name. Adults may need to be reminded to be as hospitable to children week after week as they are to adults and visitors.

Children (and youth) appreciate hearing that the gospel is as relevant to their daily experience as it is to that of adults. Pastors need to keep all age levels in mind when preaching and use illustrations and phrases relevant to the everyday experience of children and youth as well as adults—"when going out to recess" and "when hanging out at the mall"—as frequently as the more common "when at work" and "when at the store."

AN ALTERNATIVE

Now, bear in mind that sitting in rows facing in one direction and barely moving for an hour or more is a distinctively adult activity. Contemporary schooling rarely requires children to engage in such experiences. Also, children's attention spans are much shorter than those of adults. Some children will simply find the worship service boring and will resist attending. And the younger the child, the more likely is such restlessness to be the case.

By the age of about ten, children are usually tall enough so that their feet touch the floor, and they are capable of sitting for an hour quietly. Usually, they are capable of reading well enough to participate without difficulty in the liturgy and in singing the hymns. Therefore, one can expect that fifth-graders and up will feel more comfortable in the context of public worship. Under this age children vary. While some children love the service, others resist attending regularly. Such children should not be deemed irreligious or the product of poor parenting; they are probably on a developmentally different timetable from classmates who enjoy attending regularly.

Because of individual differences, a good alternative to participation in the assembly is essential. A clean, safe nursery, staffed with mature adults, is a must if parents are to feel comfortable leaving children during the service. Young teenagers may function well as assistants, but not as senior nursery attendants. Good nurseries do not have to be expensive, but they should be clean, warm, and safe. Ideally, small babies will be kept safely separate from older youngsters.

LEADERSHIP ROLES

Children can take genuine leadership roles in several areas of public worship: one of these is in music. Such leadership by a children's choir or instrumental ensemble will help the whole assembly praise and worship. Children should not be made to perform so that adults feel entertained. The children themselves can and ought to be genuinely worshiping God in their music. This sense of worship means that music and words should be chosen from the children's point of view. A simple song that has arisen out of lessons the children have learned and enjoyed will mean most to youngsters. Choir directors need to work closely with church school teachers so that the most appropriate music is chosen. The younger the children, the more a choir's function may simply be to learn and enjoy music rather than having to prepare to "sing well for the service." If the children are old enough to participate in the entire service, then they are ready to lead in singing as a choir with appropriate instruction. Needless to say, such a choir is a wonderful opportunity for education: the children learn not only songs but a great deal about the history and practice of liturgy and worship, which will stay with them for decades.

Older children may also function as acolytes, book bearers, torchbearers, greeters, ushers, and so on. Careful training is essential, and the roles of greeting and ushering will benefit from adult mentorship.

THE FOCUS OF ATTENTION

The focus of attention in worship should be on God, not on children. Public worship is for all age levels, all races, all the baptized to gather around word and sacraments, to hear law and gospel, to receive forgiveness of sins, and to respond in faith to the word. To focus on any one age level is inappropriate. Certainly, the worship experience should be as comfortable and welcoming as possible for children. But this focus on inclusion does not mean it is necessary to set aside a few minutes "just for the children," which raises questions about the practice in some congregations of "children's talks" or "children's sermons." Consider the following suggested questions for thought.

Is the children's "sermon" genuinely a sermon? That is, is it an exposition of one or more of the passages of scripture for the day? If not, drop the pretentious title. Moreover, may not one sermon addressed to the whole gathered community be sufficient, just as there is one celebration of the eucharist within the service?

If the talk is not a sermon, then does it contribute to or does it break the unity of the service? Contributing to the unity is not at all an easy matter if the theme of the day is simply beyond the concrete-thinking child, let alone the preoperational thinker. Of course sometimes the theme may indeed be appropriate. An incident in the life of a saint, for example, might enrich a service in which that particular saint is remembered. Or a piece of furniture might warrant a brief word (e.g., the font at a baptism). But such opportunities cannot be counted on to occur weekly.

Which age level would be addressed? It is simply not possible to address both preoperational and concrete thinkers in the same way: either one group will be confused or the other will be bored. And in either case, if one genuinely speaks to children, teenagers and adults will be bored. If adults say they love children's talks, one may suspect (unless they are professional storytellers or children's psychologists, in which case they may be passing a professional judgment) that they are being excessively polite or (far more common) are reflecting that the "children's" talks are in fact appropriate for adults, not children at all. And the adults are really saying that they wish the pastor would put more stories into sermons or speak more clearly!

How about the notion that a children's talk will "tell" children they are wanted in the service? Well, children think literally. So it is better simply to say (in the announcements or at some other time, or perhaps best of all, individually while shaking hands at the door), "I am so glad to see you today; I really like to have boys and girls in our worship."

What will show respect for children? Respect is an aspect of love. Avoid at all costs any suggestion that children are in worship to entertain adults or to be laughed at. Asking children to make comments or answer questions in front of the assembly is inappropriate—the preoperational or concrete thinker tries to make sense of adult questions that require an abstract answer, and their answers seem "cute" and "funny" to adults. Such a practice teaches some children that the church is a place to perform, and these youngsters play to the audience every time. For more children the practice teaches that the church is a cruel place where, when you do your best to give a sensible answer, adults laugh at you as if you were stupid. We want rather to teach that the whole assembly welcomes and respects children and that all ages together attend joyfully to the good news of God in Jesus Christ.

RICH POSSIBILITIES

We need to help adults develop sensitivity to the difficulties children may experience in understanding; but, in addition, we need to deal with the great possibilities for increasing emotional and social and aesthetic dimensions of worship to which children may readily respond. Congregations will find that adults, as well as children, will appreciate a renewed concern for the quality of atmosphere, architecture, music, singing, dramatic action, color, and movement in the service. Beyond these elements, we can encourage congregations to rejoice that persons of all ages worship together and to welcome children as they respond in their own ways to God's presence and mystery.

FOR FURTHER READING

Nurturing Faith through the Stages of Life (1998). AFP 15-7241.
A reproducible resource book providing understandings of age-level characteristics affecting faith development at all ages.

THE MILLENNIUM

"The day of the Lord will come like a thief, and then the heavens will pass away with a loud noise, and the elements will be dissolved with fire, and the earth and everything that is done on it will be disclosed." That ominous note is sounded in 2 Peter 3:10 and read throughout the churches on the second Sunday in Advent (cycle B). Only weeks before that, on the twenty-fifth Sunday after Pentecost (proper 28, cycle A), we hear similar language, "the day of the Lord will come like a thief in the night. When they say, 'There is peace and security,' then sudden destruction will come upon them . . . and there will be no escape!" (1 Thess. 5:2-3). The Old Testament prophet Malachi had called that day "the great and terrible day of the LORD" (4:5), when God will come to vindicate God's people and exact judgment on the wicked.

When the worshiping congregation hears such words, it may wonder whether the day of the Lord is something to look forward to or not. Of course, the apocalyptic framework of such biblical passages may seem remote from today's world. On the other hand, the activities of apocalyptic or millennialist groups may be well known to Christians today. Groups use such biblical statements to inspire fear and motivate change; that change usually being to join their ranks in view of the conflagration now awaiting the world at the end of the current millennium and the beginning of the new.

In popular culture, apocalyptic terminology and symbols are in revival as the world draws closer to the year 2000. John Updike's novel *Toward the End of Time* depicts a world limping through the aftermath of nuclear cataclysm, and offers the earth's capacity for renascence as a metaphor for resurrection. The movie *Deep Impact* envisions the catastrophe awaiting this planet as it finds itself in the direct path of a meteor the size of New York City. Yet another film explores the same theme given the biblical name *Armageddon*, this time with an earthbound asteroid the size of Texas. Popular imagination is stimulated as the end of an era approaches, now not only a century but a millennium, and biblical symbols and texts take on a more strident tone for vivid effect.

THE 1,000TH YEAR

The 1,000th year has always stimulated human imagination, and not only in Christian cultures. The word *millennium* is a combination of two Latin words, *mille* (1,000) and *annus* (year), and the word *millennialism* is generally defined as belief that looks forward to the return of Christ and his subsequent reign of one thousand years, inspired largely by a particular reading of Revelation 20:1-7. The word *chiliasm*, based on the Greek word for one thousand, is a synonym for millennialism.

Revelation 20:1-7 is the only reference in the New Testament to a 1,000-year period at the end of world history in which the binding of Satan, the return of Christ, and the resurrection of the faithful are combined. In fact, millennialists themselves are not in agreement concerning the timetable suggested by this passage: "premillennialists" are those who believe the return of Christ will precede the beginning of the 1,000 years of messianic rule, while "postmillennialists" believe that the return of Christ will come at the end of the 1,000-year messianic age, which in itself refers to the flowering and maturation of the true Christian church on earth.

The intriguing concept of millennium has its beginnings long before Christianity. The Greek philosopher Plato (circa 429–347 B.C.) related a popular tale about the thousand-year journey on which the souls of the dead embarked after the judgment of their deeds in this life, a blissful journey for the just and a woeful journey for the unjust (*Republic*, lines 614–615, 621). The author Virgil (70–19 B.C.) refers to the notion of a thousand-year purification that the souls of the dead must undergo before they, purged of former sins, can be reborn into earthly existence (*Aeneid*, lines 739–751). The philosopher and biographer Plutarch (died circa A.D. 120) knows of a fourth-century B.C. Iranian wisdom tradition that divided world history into a 3,000-year period of God's rule followed by a 3,000-year period of struggle between good and evil, which again is to be followed by a shorter (probably 1,000-year) epoch of peace and prosperity in which the powers of Hades are bound and humanity enjoys total bliss and contentment (*Moralia*, line 370). This 7-by-1,000 periodization of world history, based on the days of the week, emerges in the writings of postexilic Judaism, and may well be reflected in the statement of Psalm 90:4, "A thousand years in your sight are like yesterday when it is past," a thought repeated in 2 Peter 3:8, "with the Lord one day is like a thousand years, and a thousand years are like one day."

At the time of the writing of Revelation at the end of the first century A.D., several themes associated with the 1,000-year end-time period are evident in the literature of apocalyptic Judaism, most prominently in Fourth Ezra and in Second Baruch. Universal judgment, a new world with a designated period of messianic rule, resurrection, and the eternal salvation of the just are themes that occupy these writings. The Testament of Isaac, written before A.D. 70, foresees the participation of God's people in a 1,000-year period of celebration, and Rabbi Eliezer ben Hyrkanos (circa A.D. 90) sees in Psalm 90:15 the promise of a messianic kingdom lasting 1,000 years. On the basis of the seven-day creation, including the seventh day of rest, rabbinic tradition continued to speculate about the history of the world within a 7,000-year framework, the final millennium constituting the messianic age.

All this background is to indicate that the concept of a 1,000-year period of bliss and/or judgment at the end of world history belongs to the range of concepts used in popular speculative imagination about the future within cultures previous to and contemporary with the rise of Christianity. It is a feature within the body of writing called "apocalyptic" literature and a part of the field of study called "apocalyptic" theology. The word *apocalyptic*, employed as a technical term only since the nineteenth century, is particularly used in reference to movements and thought disposed toward presenting a timetable of events that will occur at the end of world history, mostly cataclysmic in nature.

In Christianity after the first century, such speculation about the return of Christ and his reign, and about the end of the world and the final denouement of human history, continued, with such major names as Justin Martyr, Irenaus, and Tertullian all championing a millennium of earthly rule by the blessed. But St. Augustine spiritualized the concept, rejected a futuristic millennium, and held that the period of 1,000 years had already begun with the incarnation and would culminate upon Jesus' return. This teaching of Augustine dominated Christian thought on the subject for subsequent centuries until the passing of the year A.D. 1000, when a new appraisal of the biblical texts was necessitated. Joachim of Fiore (circa 1132–1202) accepted Augustine's spiritualistic interpretation and intensified it by speaking of a period of spiritual renewal in view of a church gone materialistic.

This combination of spiritualism and church criticism had its influence among Reformation radicals like Thomas Münzer, whose apocalyptic preaching stressed the end-time judgment of the wicked and who called believers to active struggle to bring in the messianic age, the Peasants' War being a facet of that struggle. The mainstream Reformers tabbed such movements "enthusiasticism" and rejected the notion that the messianic age would be brought about by human endeavor, with the Augsburg Confession rejecting the notion that the godly would take possession of a worldly kingdom and annihilate the godless (XVII.5). Although Luther felt that the corrupt church was a sign of the last days, he studiously avoided all attempts to engage in apocalyptic speculation about the end of the world, the timing of Jesus' return, and dawn of the messianic age.

The eighteenth century, however, brought renewed energy to millennialist thinking, largely due to the work of the Lutheran theologian and exegete Johann Albrecht Bengel, whose influence made academic and parish theologians take up the subject again. In the early nineteenth century the word apocalyptic became a formal term used in biblical scholarship to refer to a number of biblical and nonbiblical writings that contained characteristics similar to those found in Revelation, among them Ezekiel, Daniel, the apocryphal books of Fourth Ezra and Second Baruch, and others. In the meantime, popular speculative movements continued, basing their predictions on literalist renderings of biblical passages taken out of context and pieced together arbitrarily. For instance, the Swedish scientist Emanuel Swedenborg taught that the last judgment took place in 1757 and that the church of the New Jerusalem had actually been formed both in heaven and on earth.

In the U.S. millennialism played a role in the foundation of Mormonism, whose adherents call themselves "Latter Day Saints" to indicate that movement's belief in the near approach of the last day. The founder of Seventh Day Adventists, William Miller, held that biblical references pointed to 1843 as the year of Christ's return, and the Jehovah's Witnesses, founded by C. T. Russell (although they trace their denominational existence back to Adam), announced that the second coming of Christ had begun in 1874 when a theocratic kingdom was established and reserved only for Russell's followers, who were to reject all existing religious institutions as part of the evil world that would be destroyed at Armageddon when their 1,000-year reign would begin. The notes in the popular *Schofield Reference Bible* divided world history into seven epochs again, with the return of Christ to inaugurate the messianic age scheduled for the year 2000.

THE RETURN OF CHRIST

Christ has died.
Christ is risen.
Christ will come again.

The acclamations of the eucharistic meal remind every believer that Christian faith is eschatological; however, it is not to say that Christian faith is apocalyptic. *Eschatology* is a topic within theology that deals with "the last things"—the world beyond our world and life beyond our lives—eternity. That world is God's world, which had its beginnings before time and human history, and will also succeed time and human history. All Christian preaching and teaching is therefore eschatological, in that it speaks of God's world, earth included, and the implications of God's world for our lives in the present time. Christian preaching is eschatological in that it brings us a word from the beyond, God's word, which enters our world in terms of challenge and gift, command and promise, law and gospel. The acclamations of the eucharist bring the believer in touch with the fact that God's world is not coterminous with our world, and calls us to live out the implications of God's world in the present.

The season of Advent is that time in the Christian church year that focuses on what God has done in past, does do in the present, and will do in the future. The sacraments accent these themes as well, when God's creating activity, the redemption offered to us through the work of Christ, and the gifts and presence of the Spirit are communicated and celebrated in the lives of all believers. All these themes are eschatological; however, they are not "apocalyptic," and do not ask us to engage in predictions of end-time events and timetables. The time and shape of the future is up to God, as Luke has the risen Jesus tell his disciples, "It is not for you to know the times or periods that the Father has set by his own authority" (Acts 1:7).

It is interesting that so little of the New Testament engages in apocalyptic speculation, especially since the earliest Christian generation believed that Jesus' return would occur within their own lifetime. Paul himself had to deal with that expectation in his own theology, as his earlier writings reflect belief in Christ's imminent return (1 Thess. 4:13-18), while his later writings have come to understand that the timetable for Christ's return (and even for his own death) is not up to him (Phil. 1:22-26). Once in a while Paul uses apocalyptic language to express his main point that the future is in God's hands (compare 1 Cor. 15:23-28). But the function of such expression is not to disturb his readers, but to give them hope: they are to "encourage one another with these words" (1 Thess. 4:18).

Even as that earliest generation looked forward to Christ's return, they transmitted the clear teaching of Jesus, which urged avoidance of predicting the time of the end. The most vivid examples are the parables with a wise/foolish comparison: it is always the fool who predicts God's future. The foolish maidens are the ones who give the bridegroom only until midnight to arrive, while the wise maidens have prepared themselves with enough light to last through the dark night of waiting (Matt. 25:1-12). The rich fool has a conversation with himself about tomorrow and what he will do in the future, but that night God enters the conversation and requires his life of him (Luke 12:16-20). The wise builder will not set the limits of the future (Matt. 7:24-27; Luke 6:47-49), nor will the wise slave predict the time of the master's homecoming (Matt. 24:45-51; Luke 12:42-46). The teaching of Jesus is consistent: to predict God's future is an attempt to control it, which is foolish. So in Jesus' parables it is the foolish who predict God's future, while the wise prepare for God's future, with all its surprises, by living active lives of faithful trust and patient waiting.

When the faithful congregation at eucharist affirms that "Christ has died. Christ is risen. Christ will come again," they are affirming that their past, present, and future have all been secured by God's own action. God's future is not under their control, so they will not try to usurp it by setting timetables for God. They are recipients in past and present of God's gifts of creation, redemption, and sanctification, and they will use those gifts now as signs of active Christian hope in God's future. Not only one future day but every new day belongs to God, and it is given to us to live out each day as a sign of God's giving. For only as recipients of God's giving are we able to respond in thanksgiving, which is what the word eucharist means.

When the faithful congregation confesses its faith by means of the ancient creeds, they await the day when "he will come again in glory to judge the living and the dead." That confession holds no fear whatsoever. It is a part of the active hope that the one who is to come has already been here, and is known in word and sacrament as the one who gathers his own and sends them out in his name. The one whom Christians await at the end of history is already known as the one who meets sinners with open arms, forgives them their wrongs, restores them to partnership with God, and gives them a future beyond all human imagination. The one who is to come is one who has given them his name, so that their lives reflect the waters of baptism, where they were "marked with the cross of Christ forever."

THE DAY OF THE LORD

"The day of the Lord will come like a thief . . . the heavens will pass away . . . the elements will be dissolved with fire, and the earth and everything that is done on it will be disclosed" (2 Pet. 3:10). Such is the language of apocalyptic expression, and even though infrequent in the New Testament it does occur in the relatively later writings of the Christian canon (compare Jude 6), and should be properly understood.

The "day of the Lord" is an expression received by Christian writers from their Old Testament heritage. It represents a decisive day, when God acts to vindicate God's people and set things right again (e.g., Jer. 50:31; Ezek. 32:10). It may also be a "day" when God judges God's people as well (e.g., Amos 2:13-16; Micah 2:4). God's action may come by means of a battle or in the form of a cosmic catastrophe (e.g., Amos 1:14; Joel 2:1-2). Some sixty occurrences, however, speak of the "day of the Lord" as the time when God would deliver either Israel and/or the nations to restoration and renewal. The emphasis is always on the decisiveness of God's actions and a total break with the past for God's people, even the redemption of all humanity (e.g., Isa. 2:2-4; Zech. 2:11).

"The day of the Lord" therefore means that time when God enters human existence to shape it anew, and things will never be the same again. The Christian witness is that the end of the world is not the end of God's creation, but a break with the old and the beginning of the new creation. This thought can be expressed in apocalyptic language, with a vivid depiction of the end of the earthly signifying the total break in continuity with the old. The resurrection of Jesus is not the simple continuation of the earthly, but the beginning of a new existence now made available to all those who call upon his name. The same thought can be expressed in nonapocalyptic language as well, as Paul did in 2 Corinthians 5:17: "If anyone is in Christ, there is a new creation; everything old has passed away; see, everything has become new!" It is the meaning of the pre-Pauline baptismal liturgy as well: "As many of you as were baptized into Christ have clothed yourselves with Christ. There is no longer Jew or Greek, there is no longer slave or free, there is no longer male and female; for all of you are one in Christ Jesus" (Gal. 3:27-28).

Toward the end of the first century, the first day of the week came increasingly to be celebrated as "the Lord's day," the day of Jesus' resurrection. That was the decisive act of God by which the world was redeemed, an act that was communicated through the word of preaching. But one became attached to that act of God at any time, on any day, whenever the gospel was proclaimed. Quoting the prophet Isaiah (49:6), Paul invited all who would receive that proclamation into the community of those reconciled to God: "Now is the acceptable time; see, now is the day of salvation!" (2 Cor. 6:2).

So John of Patmos receives his "revelation" on "the Lord's day" (Rev. 1:10), and immediately engages in writing a manifesto of hope to his churches. They are to read it in their worship assemblies (1:3), and to encourage each other by his words in the face of external pressure. The symbolic imagery John uses belongs to the Old Testament prophetic heritage, which they also read in their assemblies, where it functioned as code language unrecognizable to their oppressors. The time of John's readers is a dangerous time for them, but it will not last forever. At the decisive time of God's own choosing there will be a break with this earthly tribulation, and the new age will come. Because it is a new age, and not a simple continuation with the earthly, symbolic imagery is congenial for John's use, even the traditional symbol of the "1,000 years," to signify a special time for Christ and his martyrs who are never forgotten (20:4). Their death in this world is no defeat either for them or for God, for their future is secure in God's own time and in God's own way. That future is recalled each week on "the Lord's day," the first day of the week, when God's victory in Christ is celebrated in word and sacrament, and God's community at worship is renewed, refreshed, and restored. From eucharistic meal to daily family meal, Christians of today join John of Patmos and his churches (22:20) to celebrate Christ's presence among them: "Come, Lord Jesus!"

PRAYING AT THE EUCHARIST

The liturgy for the day is full: a baptism, a children's message, many communicants, and announcements. Why also use that *long* prayer at communion? This question is often asked by pastors and members concerned with the length of the service, especially when Sunday school or another liturgy is scheduled immediately following it. While this concern is understandable in our frenetic culture, some very compelling reasons motivate the use of a prayer of thanksgiving or eucharistic prayer as a part of the normal structure for us as we approach the Lord's table.

When *Lutheran Book of Worship* was compiled, it was the strong preference of the Inter-Lutheran Commission on Worship that some eucharistic prayer be used at each celebration of the sacrament. For various historical and theological reasons, the common Lutheran practice of using only the so-called words of institution was retained as an option. Since that time, most worship books produced by mainline churches have included eucharistic prayers and encouraged their use. The prayer of Hippolytus (ca. A.D. 215), the oldest complete eucharistic prayer available to us, is now used by many Christian churches at their eucharistic celebrations. To give thanks to God in this way is to locate ourselves among the broad spectrum of Christians within the catholic tradition.

When the earliest Christians gathered for worship on the Lord's day, they did so by focusing on two actions: (1) hearing God's word through the scriptures of Israel and the writings of the apostles; and (2) giving thanks to the creator of all through Jesus Christ, the crucified and risen Lord, in the power of the Holy Spirit. This prayer and praise, the early Christians believed, was the only sacrifice possible for the followers of Christ. This thanksgiving, made over the common meal foods of bread and wine, was so central to Christian faith and life that the entire gathering soon was named for this giving of thanks: eucharist.

Giving thanks to God at meals, of course, was the common practice for Jesus and his Jewish disciples. It was the sign that they remembered at each meal their dependency on God, from whom all good gifts come. They knew that—baptized and gathered in the name of Jesus—their greatest offering to God was their lives (Rom. 12:1), given in thanks for all that God had done in the life, death, and resurrection of Christ. The importance of this twofold gathering around scripture spoken and the thanksgiving made is found in all the ancient eucharistic liturgies. The response to the spoken word is the listening ear and the moved heart; the response to the thanksgiving centered in Christ is the communal eating and drinking of the bread of life and the cup of salvation.

While Luther excised the Roman canon from his reforms of the mass, he never denied the centrality of thanksgiving to the purpose for which Christians gather at the supper. His concern was to eliminate a corrupted understanding of the mass as propitiatory sacrifice, as well as to return to a celebration of the mass as he believed Christ had instituted it. Just as Christ gave thanks to his Father and then distributed the meal to his disciples, so the church now offers thanks to the Father through Christ who feeds us with his very life.

Unlike the Roman canon in use in Luther's day, prayers of thanksgiving in use today—like that of Hippolytus (*LBW* Ministers edition, Eucharistic Prayer IV)—center around praise and thanksgiving to God for the work of Christ. They give voice to the congregation's reason for gathering and center all that has been heard and sung around the one who is the Alpha and Omega of our lives. Hearing Jesus' words at the last supper in the context of such prayer also sets the tone for our coming to the table, correcting any sense of the eucharist that is extremely penitential or individualistic. The prayer of thanksgiving roots our worship in the soil of God's creation of the world, election of Israel, liberation in Christ, and empowering of the church by the Spirit. We cannot hear this story—this good news—too often! As our forebears in the faith knew so well, the story of God's love for our broken world belongs at the heart and center of our assembly, as this same love is made visible for us in the bread and the wine.

To reduce the action at the table to a mere recitation of Christ's words of institution is to narrow the context for the sacrament to Jesus' last meal with his disciples, and to give the impression that these words alone provide the magic moment of consecration. Though general Lutheran practice through the centuries has focused on the words of institution, modern scholarship has helped us see that it is not reflective of the catholic tradition, East and West, prior to the time of the Reformation. The ELCA 1997 statement, *The Use of the Means of Grace,* says it well: "The biblical words of institution declare God's actions and invitation. They are set within the context of the Great Thanksgiving. This eucharistic prayer proclaims and celebrates the gracious work of God in creation, redemption, and sanctification" (principle 43). In recent years many Protestant churches have again returned to the ancient, biblical pattern of offering thanksgiving to God over the bread and wine as the assembly's central action.

Besides the theological appropriateness of this practice, a pastoral purpose is also served by a prayer of thanksgiving at the eucharist. It helps worshipers, especially those less knowledgeable about the faith, to place praise and thanksgiving for all God's gifts at the center of their faith and life. Even the custom of praying before meals, no longer to be taken for granted in our day, is reinforced by our praying—our giving thanks, praising and remembering God—at the church's weekly meal. This ancient catholic and evangelical form provides the norm for our faith and our life, within the assembly and in our daily lives.

What about the time factor, the length of the service? Often this question is asked from a point of view that sees the eucharistic prayer as an option, somewhat like using both the Kyrie and the hymn of praise during the gathering rite of the liturgy, or the decision to sing a departure hymn. It is important for Lutherans to acknowledge that—from a historical, theological, and ecumenical standpoint—the evangelical eucharistic prayers of which we speak are not options in the same way. Rather, they are central to our Christian self-understanding and help to define who we are as a people redeemed by God in Christ. Understanding the eucharistic prayer this way will not ask, "Do we have the time for this prayer?" but rather, "How do we shape our liturgy this day so that the two central reasons for our gathering—to speak God's word to one another and to share the holy meal as our great thanksgiving and praise to God—are made clearly visible to all?" It is also crucial from a Lutheran perspective that we not forget that the "divine service" of which we speak is first and foremost *God's* service to us, God's speaking the word of forgiveness and acceptance in Christ, and God's feeding us with the healing body and blood of our Lord. This grace of God always precedes our ability or even motivation for worship. But saying that does not mean we ought to downplay our response of faith, for an active faith always expresses itself in praise and thanksgiving to God, not to gain anything from God (everything is ours already!), but merely out of love for God. To be evangelically catholic for Lutherans is to hold these two aspects of our faith—what God does to and for us and our response of faith—in proper tension. The eucharistic prayer, in the context of the whole liturgy and solidly biblical preaching, can help us do just that.

The eucharistic prayers in *LBW* Ministers edition are all full prayers following the ancient and ecumenical patterns. *With One Voice* has gone the next step by offering seasonal prayers that correlate with the themes and images of each particular season. These prayers are shorter than the ones in *LBW*, following the example of the prayer used in *Occasional Services* for communion of the sick. These prayers keep the ancient pattern of praise and thanksgiving for creation and for the coming of Christ, contain the words of institution, remember before God Christ's reconciling work, invoke the power and presence of the Spirit, and conclude with a trinitarian doxology. The use of these prayers in place of the words of institution alone adds less than a minute to the entire service. Surely the positive value of the ecumenical use of this form of the eucharistic prayer and its focus on the central acts of our salvation are worth these extra seconds in our worship!

If the length of the liturgy remains a factor, other ways are available to address the issue. Besides taking care that the sermon is not too long, one can choose to omit the post-communion canticle and make sure that the distribution of communion is done efficiently. The prayer of Hippolytus, if done historically, is prayed without a proper preface and Sanctus, thus also shortening the great thanksgiving. If time and other factors make the regular use of the eucharistic prayer difficult, perhaps its use on festivals is a way to expose the congregation to them. Adult forums on the topic of praying at the eucharist would also go a long way in helping congregations to appreciate the nature of Christian worship and the central role that our thanksgiving to God can take.

FOR FURTHER READING

Book of Common Worship (Presbyterian). Louisville: Westminster/John Knox Press, 1993. Offers many examples of eucharistic prayers.

Jasper, R. C. D. and G. J. Cuming. *Prayers of the Eucharist: Early and Reformed.* Third revised edition. New York: Pueblo Publishing Co., 1987. A helpful source for understanding the historical development of prayer at the eucharist.

Senn, Frank C. *Christian Liturgy: Catholic and Evangelical*. Minneapolis: Fortress Press, 1997. See especially chapter 3 for a discussion of eucharistic prayer in the early church and part 2 for information about Luther and Lutheran practice in both Germany and Scandinavia.

SHAPE OF WORSHIP FOR THE SEASON

As the pattern of providing meals for a household or for entertaining guests experiences certain rhythms and seasonal changes, so may we detect similar nuances in the order of congregational worship. While certain types of foods will be reserved for special occasions, attention to the basic food groups is essential every day in order to provide balanced nutrition throughout the year. The order of worship also has ingredients that are more or less important, depending on the type of celebration desired. The key challenge is for worship planners to know which elements are at the core of our worship life, and which elements are more flexible according to the dictates of a particular day or season.

SHAPE OF WORSHIP

In the space of two pages, *With One Voice* (pp. 8–9) has presented a clear pattern for worship, which demonstrates a basic fourfold shape. The following outline of worship is adapted from that basic shape. (Baptism is another element that may at times be added to this shape.)

Confession and Forgiveness

GATHERING
 Entrance Hymn
 Greeting
 Kyrie
 Hymn of Praise
 Prayer of the Day

WORD
 First Reading
 Psalm
 Second Reading
 Gospel Acclamation
 Gospel
 Sermon
 Hymn of the Day
 (Baptism)
 Creed
 The Prayers

MEAL
 Greeting of Peace
 Presentation of the Gifts
 Great Thanksgiving
 Lord's Prayer
 Communion
 Canticle
 Prayer

SENDING
 Blessing
 Dismissal

The elements common to the simplest as well as the most festive gatherings for worship are indicated in regular type, while those elements that may be included as a gathering grows in festivity are indicated in italics. A liturgy that includes all of these elements would most likely be reserved for principal festivals throughout the year, whereas a liturgy that includes only the bare minimum of these elements would probably be a midweek or lesser festival observance, and likely not ever experienced as the primary Sunday liturgy of the congregation.

This assessment of the significance of the various elements relates primarily to their theological and historical importance in the order of worship.

GATHERING

Confession and forgiveness, while an important element in communal worship, is not absolutely essential prior to each celebration of communion. Its use may be dictated more according to seasonal patterns and congregational preferences. Elements of confession may also be included in the prayers of the congregation, without having a specific order prior to the service itself.

Though an *entrance hymn* is a common way to begin worship, it might not be used at a midweek service conducted in a chapel with a small number of people in attendance. In fact such a service might be entirely spoken.

The *greeting* and the *prayer of the day* would be key elements for any gathering. The *Kyrie* and the *hymn of praise* may be used or omitted, depending on the season and context.

WORD

All elements of the word portion of the liturgy might be routinely included for all Sundays and principal festivals; however, some elements could still be omitted after careful thought and planning. The *gospel* is central for the celebration of communion, yet another *reading* (either the *first* or *second reading* appointed for the day) could be used even for the most abbreviated of services. When at least one other reading precedes the gospel, it is desirable to have some musical response, either in the form of a *psalm* or *gospel acclamation*.

The *sermon* is an essential element for the liturgy, even if it needs to be shortened to two or three minutes for a brief service. The sermon proclaims the scriptures to a contemporary congregation in a particular location and time. The *hymn of the day* is an important congregational response within the entire liturgy of the word, and should only be eliminated for those services where no music is possible.

Use of the *creed* might be omitted at the briefest of services, or on occasions when time is a major consideration. Use of the creed in the context of weekly worship was introduced later into the liturgy, probably owing more to the need for people to be instructed in the central beliefs of the church during periods of doctrinal controversy, rather than to a particular need of the worshiping assembly itself.

The prayers are a significant part of the order of worship. Intercessions for the world, the universal church, the parish, those in need, and remembering those who have died, are customarily included.

BAPTISM

Baptisms ordinarily occur within the context of the weekly worship of the congregation. The seasonal notes in this volume indicate certain days when congregations may plan for *baptismal festivals* (namely, the Easter Vigil, Pentecost, All Saints Sunday, and the Baptism of Our Lord). These would be opportunities for the entire congregation to affirm their baptisms, even when no candidates are presented.

Having baptismal festivals helps baptism to become a highpoint of the service at various times in the year. Baptismal festivals also allow for specific opportunities to preach about baptism, and affords the possibility for more consistent catechetical preparation for baptism, as well as congregational involvement in a reception or other form of welcoming the newly baptized following the liturgy itself. Days other than the four mentioned could also be celebrated as baptismal festivals (some congregations may have a need for such festivals virtually every month). While parishes having designated baptismal festivals may also have requests for baptisms on other occasions because of pressing family needs and schedules, these can become the exception—rather than the rule—for the congregation's regular experience of baptism.

MEAL

The *greeting of peace* is an ancient part of the eucharistic liturgy, observed at least since the second century. It is hard to imagine the liturgy without at least the presiding minister exchanging the peace with the entire congregation. Its regular use among worshipers themselves as well is significant.

The *presentation of gifts* includes both monetary offerings as well as the bread and wine for communion. Even if the bread and wine have been placed on the altar prior to the service, the elements themselves need to be uncovered for the prayer of thanksgiving which follows.

The *great thanksgiving* includes everything from the preface dialog through what is commonly referred to as the eucharistic prayer itself. Here is great opportunity for variation according to the seasons and to the degree of festivity desired for the given occasion. The *words of institution* are best used within the context of a prayer in which God's gifts from creation, through the death and resurrection of Christ, and the sending of the Holy Spirit are proclaimed. *Lutheran Book of Worship* and *With One Voice* provide several options for this type of prayer.

The *Lord's Prayer* is fundamental to each eucharistic celebration, and indeed to virtually every order of worship in the church.

Various options for *distribution* of the elements of communion, as well as for accompanying music or silence, exist. Congregations will be guided here by principles 44 and 45 of *The Use of the Means of Grace*, the ELCA's 1997 statement on word and sacrament practices.

The sacrament may conclude briefly with a *blessing*, a *canticle*, and a *prayer*. These elements may be used according to seasonal or local needs, although not including a prayer following the reception of the sacrament is hard to imagine.

SENDING

No extended good-byes are needed at this point, though it may be the time to give announcements related to parish opportunities for witness and service. The *blessing* and the *dismissal* conclude the liturgy. These elements may be given a seasonal flavor through the use of special seasonal texts provided in the following sections of this volume. Special dismissals may also be used, particularly for those who are sent to distribute the eucharistic elements, and for those sent to perform specific ministries in daily life (see "Affirmation of the Vocation of the Baptized in the World" in *Welcome to Christ: Lutheran Rites for the Catechumenate*, Augsburg Fortress, pp. 59–61).

SHAPING WORSHIP ACCORDING TO SEASON

Each of the seasonal sections in this book provide pages on the "shape of worship for the season." These pages will provide worship planners with seasonally appropriate ways to adjust the basic shape of worship throughout the year. Because this crafting of the worship service is more of an art form than an exact science, the editor of this volume is eager to learn of your thoughts and "recipes" for living through the year.

WORSHIP PLANNING CHECKLIST

ADVENT
- Purchase materials needed for the Advent wreath (four candles and enough greens to cover the wreath—perhaps more than one wreath will be desired for your congregation if Sunday school openings and other groups gather for worship in multiple locations during the season)
- Arrange for the setup of the Advent wreath one or two days prior to the first Sunday in Advent (November 28 this year)

CHRISTMAS
- Arrange for purchase/donation of a Christmas tree
- Locate any decorations in storage from previous years for the Christmas tree, crèche, the chancel, other interior and/or exterior areas
- Repair or replace decorations as needed
- Decide on a date and time for Christmas decorating and solicit volunteer help needed
- Prepare for extra communion elements and communionware that may be needed for additional worshipers at Christmas services
- Prepare a sign-up list for additional flowers or poinsettia plants to be sponsored at Christmas
- Plan for removal of Christmas decorations following the twelve days (on or near January 6)
- If handheld candles are used by worshipers on Christmas Eve, determine how many candles and holders can be used from previous seasons, and how many new candles and holders will be needed
- Order special bulletin covers if needed for services on Christmas Eve and/or Christmas Day

EPIPHANY
- Determine what (if any) Epiphany decorations are needed
- If incense is to be used for a service on the festival of the Epiphany, purchase a small quantity of it (along with sufficient charcoal)
- If the Baptism of Our Lord (January 9) is to be observed as a baptismal festival, publicize the festi-

val through congregational newsletters and bulletins in advance, arrange for baptismal preparation sessions with parents, sponsors, and candidates, and when the day arrives set out the following:
- Towel (baptismal napkin) for each person baptized
- Baptismal candle for each person baptized
- Shell (if used)
- Oil for anointing
- Baptismal garment for each person baptized (if used)
- Fresh water in a ewer (pitcher) and/or the font

LENT

- If ashes are used on Ash Wednesday, arrange for someone (perhaps one or two altar guild members) to burn palms from the previous Passion Sunday (ask members to bring in their own if they also saved them at home); or contact a church supply store for a supply of ashes (a small quantity of ashes mixed with some olive oil will go a long way)
- Determine whether any Lenten decorations are to be used other than Lenten paraments
- If crosses or images are draped in purple during the Lenten season, recruit volunteers to do this between the Transfiguration of Our Lord (March 5) and Ash Wednesday (March 8)
- Order enough palm branches to distribute to worshipers on Passion Sunday (additional palm branches or plants may be used as decorations that day)
- Reserve leftover palm branches to be burned for ashes next Ash Wednesday
- Order worship participation leaflets if used for the Ash Wednesday liturgy and/or Passion Sunday processional liturgy
- Order additional bulletin covers if needed for any special Lenten services (especially midweek liturgies)

THE THREE DAYS

- Locate one or more sets of basin and pitcher to be used for the Maundy Thursday liturgy (also needed: towels for drying the feet of participants)
- If the altar and the rest of the chancel is to be stripped on Maundy Thursday, recruit helpers (perhaps an altar guild, or even children) for this task
- If procession/adoration of the cross is to be used on Good Friday, find or construct a rough-hewn cross, and determine how it will be placed in the chancel ahead of time or carried in procession
- If handheld candles are to be used by worshipers at an Easter Vigil, determine how many candles and holders can be used from previous seasons, and how many new candles and holders will need to be purchased
- Purchase a paschal candle (or arrange to make one) prior to the Easter Vigil
- Prepare materials needed to start a fire at the beginning of the Easter Vigil (kindling, wood, brazier, matches, etc.); also, recruit someone to start and extinguish the fire properly
- Place the paschal candle stand in the chancel prior to the Easter Vigil for use throughout the fifty days of Easter
- Prepare for extra communion elements and communionware that may be needed for additional worshipers at Holy Week and Easter services
- Order worship participation leaflets if used for the Maundy Thursday, Good Friday, or Easter Vigil liturgies
- Order bulletin covers if needed for any Holy Week liturgies
- If the Easter Vigil (or Easter Sunday) is to be observed as a baptismal festival, publicize the festival through congregational newsletters and bulletins in advance, arrange for baptismal preparation sessions with parents, sponsors, and candidates, and when the day arrives set out the following:
  - Towel (baptismal napkin) for each person baptized
  - Baptismal candle for each person baptized
  - Shell (if used)
  - Baptismal garment for each person baptized (if used)
  - Fresh water in a ewer (pitcher) and/or the font
  - Evergreen branches for sprinkling

EASTER

- Prepare a sign-up list for Easter lilies or other flowers to be sponsored on Easter Day (and throughout the season of Easter)
- Order extra bulletin covers for additional worshipers on Easter Day
- Determine whether special flowers are to be used

on Pentecost (some churches order several red geraniums to be placed around the church grounds or given away following Pentecost services)
- If Pentecost is to be observed as a baptismal festival, publicize the festival through congregational newsletters and bulletins in advance, arrange for baptismal preparation sessions with parents, sponsors, and candidates, and when the day arrives set out the following:
  - Towel (baptismal napkin) for each person baptized
  - Baptismal candle for each person baptized
  - Shell (if used)
  - Oil for anointing
  - Baptismal garment for each person baptized (if used)
  - Fresh water in a ewer (pitcher) and/or the font

SUMMER

- If the worship schedule changes, notify local newspapers and change listings on exterior signs and church answering machines
- Consider ways to make worshipers cooler during warm weather (fans, windows, air conditioning settings, etc.)
- If the congregation worships outside one or more times during the summer, how will worshipers know where to gather? (Are worshipers to bring their own chairs? What if some do not or cannot bring chairs?)

AUTUMN

- For worship schedule changes, notify local newspapers and change listings on exterior signs and church answering machines
- If a harvest festival (or harvest home) is scheduled, determine what (if any) additional decorations are to be used and who is to do the decorating
- If one or more food collections are to be received, notify the congregation about it in advance, and also arrange to deliver food to the appropriate agency within a day or two after its collection

NOVEMBER

- Provide a book of remembrance or another way to collect the names of those who have died and who are to be remembered in prayers this month (or just on All Saints Sunday)
- If All Saints is to be observed as a baptismal festival, publicize the festival through congregational newsletters and bulletins in advance, arrange for baptismal preparation sessions with parents, sponsors, and candidates, and when the day arrives set out the following:
  - Towel (baptismal napkin) for each person baptized
  - Baptismal candle for each person baptized
  - Shell (if used)
  - Oil for anointing
  - Baptismal garment for each person baptized (if used)
  - Fresh water in a ewer (pitcher) and/or the font

KEY TO MUSIC PUBLISHERS

ABI	Abingdon	DUR	Durand (Presser)	MCF	McAfee Music Corp. (Warner)
AFP	Augsburg Fortress	ECS	E C Schirmer	MEA	Meadowgreen
AG	Agape (Hope)	EV	Elkan-Vogel	MFS	Mark Foster
AGEHR	AGEHR Inc.	FLA	Flammer (Shawnee)	MSM	Morning Star Music
ALF	Alfred	GAL	Galaxy	NGP	New Generation (ColorSong)
AMC	Arista	GIA	GIA Publications	NMP	National Music Publishers
AMSI	AMSI	GS	GlorySound	NOV	Novello (Shawnee)
AUR	Aurole	GSCH	G Schirmer	NPH	Northwestern Publishing House
BBL	Broude Brothers	GVX	Genevox	OCP	Oregon Catholic Press
BEC	Beckenhorst	HAL	Hal Leonard: G Schirmer	OXF	Oxford University Press
BEL	Belwin (Warner)	HIN	Hinshaw	PAR	Paraclete
BNT	Brentwood–Benson Music	HOP	Hope	PET	Peters
B&H	Boosey & Hawkes	HWG	H W Gray (Warner)	PLY	Plymouth
BOR	Bornemann	INT	Integrity (Word)	PRE	Presser
BRD	Broadman	ION	Ionian Arts	PVN	Pavanne (Intrada)
BRE	Breitkopf	JEF	Jeffers	RIC	Ricordi
BRN	Bourne	KAL	Kalmus	RME	Randall M Egan
BST	Boston	KIR	Kirkland House	SCH	Schott (European American)
CAL	Calvary Press	KJO	Kjos	SCM	Shattinger
CCF	Changing Church Forum	LAK	Lake State	SEL	Selah
CEL	Celebration Press	LAW	Lawson-Gould Publishing	SGM	Stained Glass Music
CFI	Carl Fischer	LB	Lutheran Brotherhood	SHW	Shawnee
CFP	C F Peters	LED	Leduc	SMP	Sacred Music Press (Lorenz)
CG	Choristers Guild (Lorenz)	LEM	Lemoine (Presser)	VIV	Vivace
CHA	Chantry (Augsburg Fortress)	LIL	Lillenas (Royal Marketing)	WAL	Walton
CHE	Chester	LIN	Lindsborg Press	WAR	Warner (Plymouth)
CLP	Warners: CCP/Belwin	LOH	Live Oak	WJK	Westminster/John Knox
CPH	Concordia	LOR	Lorenz	WLP	World Library
DOV	Dover	LUD	Ludwig	WRD	Word Music
		MAR	Maranatha		

MUSIC FOR WORSHIP KEY

acc	accompaniment	hc	handchimes	qrt	quartet
bar	baritone	hp	harp	rec	recorder
bng	bongos	hpd	harpsichord	sax	saxophone
bsn	bassoon	hrn	horn	sop	soprano
cant	cantor	inst	instrument	str	strings
ch	chimes	kybd	keyboard	synth	synthesizer
cl	clarinet	M	medium	tamb	tambourine
cong	congregation	MH	medium high	tba	tuba
cont	continuo	ML	medium low	tbn	trombone
cym	cymbal	mxd	mixed	timp	timpani
DB	double or string bass	narr	narrator	trbl	treble
dbl	double	ob	oboe	tri	triangle
desc	descant	oct	octave	tpt	trumpet
div	divisi	opt	optional	U	unison
drm	drum	orch	orchestra	vc	violoncello
eng hrn	English horn	org	organ	vcs	voices
fc	finger cymbals	perc	percussion	vla	viola
fl	flute	picc	piccolo	vln	violin
glock	glockenspiel	pno	piano	ww	woodwind
gtr	guitar	pt	part	xyl	xylophone
hb	handbells	qnt	quintet		

KEY TO HYMN AND PSALM COLLECTIONS

CW	*Christian Worship: A Lutheran Hymnal* (Wisconsin Evangelical Lutheran Synod). Milwaukee: Northwestern Publishing House, 1993.
DATH	*Dancing at the Harvest: Songs of Ray Makeever*. Mpls: Augsburg Fortress, 1997.
GS2	*Global Songs 2: Bread for the Journey*. Mpls: Augsburg Fortress, 1997.
H82	*The Hymnal 1982* (Episcopal). New York: The Church Pension Fund, 1985.
LBW	*Lutheran Book of Worship*. Mpls: Augsburg; Philadelphia: Board of Publication, LCA, 1978.
LLC	*Libro de Liturgia y Cántico*. Mpls: Augsburg Fortress, 1998.
LW	*Lutheran Worship* (Lutheran Church–Missouri Synod). St. Louis: Concordia Publishing House, 1982.
NCH	*The New Century Hymnal* (United Church of Christ). Cleveland: The Pilgrim Press, 1995.
OBS	*O Blessed Spring: Hymns of Susan Palo Cherwien*. Mpls: Augsburg Fortress, 1997.
PCY	*Psalms for the Church Year.* 8 vol. Chicago: GIA Publications.
PH	*The Presbyterian Hymnal* (PC-USA). Louisville: Westminster/John Knox Press, 1990.
PS	*Psalm Songs.* 3 vol. Mpls: Augsburg Fortress, 1998.
PW	*Psalter for Worship.* 3 vol. (Cycles A, B, C.) Mpls: Augsburg Fortress.
SPW	*Songs for Praise and Worship.* Nashville: Word Music, 1992.
STP	*Singing the Psalms.* 3 vol. Portland: OCP Publications.
TFF	*This Far by Faith.* Mpls: Augsburg Fortress, 1999.
TP	*The Psalter: Psalms and the Canticles for Singing.* Louisville: Westminster/John Knox Press.
UMH	*The United Methodist Hymnal.* Nashville: The United Methodist Publishing House, 1989.
W3	*Worship: A Hymnal and Service Book for Roman Catholics.* Third ed. Chicago: GIA 1986.
WOV	*With One Voice.* Mpls: Augsburg Fortress, 1995.
W&P	*Worship & Praise.* Mpls: Augsburg Fortress, 1999.

SELECTED PUBLISHERS

AMSI
3706 East 34th Street
Minneapolis MN 55406
612/724-1258 General
612/729-4487 Fax

ABINGDON PRESS
201 8th Avenue South
PO Box 801
Nashville TN 37202
800/251-3320 Customer Service
800/836-7802 Fax

AGEHR, INC.
1055 E. Centerville Station
Dayton OH 45459
800/878-5459
937/438-0085

ALFRED PUBLISHING CO, INC
Box 10003
16380 Roscoe Boulevard
Van Nuys CA 91410-0003
800/292-6122 Customer Service
800/632-1928 Fax
818/891-5999 Direct

AMERICAN LUTHERAN PUBLICITY BUREAU
PO Box 327
Delhi NY 13753-0327
607/746-7511 General

ARISTA MUSIC
PO Box 1596
Brooklyn NY 11201

AUGSBURG FORTRESS
PO Box 1209
Minneapolis MN 55440-1209
800/328-4648 Ordering
612/330-3300 General

BECKENHORST PRESS
PO Box 14273
Columbus OH 43214
614/451-6461 General
614/451-6627 Fax

BOOSEY & HAWKES INC
35 East Twenty-first Street
New York NY 10010
212/358-5300 General
212/358-5301 Fax

BOSTON MUSIC CO.
172 Tremont St.
Boston, MA 02111
617/426-5100 Retail
617/528-6199 Fax

BOURNE COMPANY
5 West 37th Street
New York NY 10018
212/391-4300 General
212/391-4306 Fax

BRENTWOOD-BENSON MUSIC, INC.
One Maryland Farms #200
Brentwood TN 37027
800/846-7664

BROUDE BROTHERS LTD
141 White Oaks Road
Williamstown MA 01267
413/458-8131

BROADMAN HOLMAN GENEVOX
Customer Accounts Center
127 Ninth Avenue North
Nashville TN 37234
800/251-3225 General
615/251/3870 Fax

C F PETERS CORPORATION
373 Park Avenue South
New York NY 10016
212/686-4147 General
212/689-9412 Fax

CHANGING CHURCH FORUM/
PRINCE OF PEACE PUBLISHING
200 E. Nicollet Blvd.
Burnsville, MN 55337
800/874-2044

CHESTER MUSIC
Music Sales Corporation
257 Park Ave. South
New York, NY 10003
212/254-2100

CHURCH HYMNAL CORPORATION
445 5th Avenue
New York NY 10016-0109
800/223-6602 General
800/242-1918 Customer Service
212/592-1800 General
212/779-3392 Fax

COLORSONG PUBLICATIONS
2533 7th Ave E
North St. Paul, MN 55109
612/773-5371
800/352-6567
612/773-4053 Fax

CONCORDIA PUBLISHING HOUSE
3558 South Jefferson Avenue
Saint Louis MO 63118
800/325-3391 Sales
800/325-3040 Customer Service
314/268-1329 Fax
314/268-1000 General

E C SCHIRMER MUSIC CO
138 Ipswich Street
Boston MA 02215
800/777-1919 Ordering
617/236-1935 General
617/236-0261 Fax
614/236-1935

EUROPEAN AMERICAN MUSIC DIST.
PO Box 850
Valley Forge, PA 19482
610/648-0506

CARL FISCHER, INC
62 Cooper Square
New York, NY 10003
212/777-0900
212/477-4129 Fax

MARK FOSTER MUSIC CO
28 East Springfield Avenue
Champaign IL 61820
217/398-2760 General
217/398-2791 Fax
800/359-1386

GIA PUBLICATIONS, INC
7404 South Mason Avenue
Chicago IL 60638
800/442-1358 General
708/496-3800 General
708/496-3828 Fax

GALAXY COMMUNICATIONS
PO Box 101
Blaine WA 98230
800/333-7279 General
604/522-7955 General
604/522-7799 Fax

INTRODUCTION

HINSHAW MUSIC CO, INC
PO Box 470
Chapel Hill NC 27514-0470
919/933-1691 General
919/967-3399 Fax

HAL LEONARD CORP
PO Box 13819
7777 West Bluemound Road
Milwaukee WI 53213
414/774-3630 General
800/637-2852 Music Dispatch

HOPE PUBLISHING CO
380 South Main Place
Carol Stream IL 60188
800/323-1049 General
630/665-3200 General
630/665-2552 Fax

ICEL (INTERNATIONAL COMMISSION ON ENGLISH IN THE LITURGY)
1275 K Street Northwest
Suite 1202
Washington DC 20005-4097
202/347-0800 General

IONIAN ARTS, INC
PO Box 259
Mercer Island WA 98040-0259
206/236-2210 General

THE LITURGICAL CONFERENCE
8750 Georgia Avenue
Suite 123
Silver Spring MD 20910-3621
800/394-0885 Ordering
301/495-0885 General
901/495-5945 Fax

THE LITURGICAL PRESS
St. John's Abbey
PO Box 7500
Collegeville MN 56321-7500
800/858-5450 General
800/445-5899 Fax
320/363-2213 General
320/363-3299 Fax

LITURGY TRAINING PUBLICATIONS
1800 North Hermitage Avenue
Chicago IL 60622-1101
800/933-1800 Ordering
800/933-4779 Customer Service
800/933-7094 Fax

LIVE OAK HOUSE
3211 Plantation Rd.
Austin, TX 78745-7424
512/282-3397

THE LORENZ CORPORATION
PO Box 802
Dayton OH 45401-0802
800/444-1144 General

LUDWIG MUSIC PUBLISHING CO
557 East 140th Street
Cleveland OH 44110-1999
800/851-1150 General
216/851-1150 General
216/851-1958 Fax

MARANATHA!
30230 Rancho Viejo Rd
San Juan Capistrano, CA 92675
800/245-7664 Retail
800/251-4000 Wholesale

MASTERS MUSIC PUBLICATIONS, INC
PO Box 810157
Boco Raton FL 33481-0157
561/241-6169 General
561/241-6347 Fax

MORNINGSTAR MUSIC PUBLISHERS
1727 Larkin Williams Road
Fendon, MD 63026
800/647-2117 General
314/305-0100 Ordering
314/305-0121 Fax

MUSICA RUSSICA
27 Willow Lane
Madison, CT 06443
800/326-3132

NORTHWESTERN PUBLISHING HOUSE
1250 N. 113th Street
Milwaukee WI 53226-3284
800/662-6093

OREGON CATHOLIC PRESS
5536 Northeast Hassalo
Portland OR 97213
800/547-8992 General
800/462-7329 Fax

OXFORD UNIVERSITY PRESS
2001 Evans Road
Cary NC 27513
800/451-7556 General
919/677-1303 Fax

PARACLETE SOCIETY INTERNATIONAL
1132 Southwest 13th Avenue
Portland OR 97205

PLYMOUTH MUSIC CO
170 Northeast 33rd Street
Fort Lauderdale FL 33334
954/563-1844 General
954/563-9006 Fax

RANDALL M EGAN, PUBLISHERS
2024 Kenwood Parkway
Minneapolis MN 55405-2303
612/377-4450 General
*51 Fax

SHAWNEE PRESS
PO Box 690
49 Waring Drive
Delaware Water Gap PA 18327-1699
800/962-8584 General
570/476-0550 General
570/476-5247 Fax

THEODORE PRESSER CO
1 Presser Place
Bryn Mawr PA 19010
610/527-4242 Retail
610/527-7841 Fax

WARNER BROTHERS PUBLICATIONS
15800 Northwest 48th Avenue
Miami FL 33014
800/327-7643 General
305/621-4869 Fax

WESTMINSTER/JOHN KNOX PRESS
100 Witherspoon Street
Louisville KY 40202-1396
800/523-1631 General
800/541-5113 Fax

WORD MUSIC CO
Thomas Nelson Company
P.O. Box 14100
Nashville, TN 37214
800/483-0014

WORLD LIBRARY PUBLICATIONS
3825 North Willow Road
Schiller Park IL 60176
800/621-5197 General
847/678-0621 General
847/671-5715 Fax

ADVENT

CHRISTMAS

EPIPHANY

ADVENT

Waiting is faith

IMAGES OF THE SEASON

Of all the seasons of the liturgical year, Advent is probably the one least acknowledged by the world. Indeed, secular culture does not simply ignore Advent; it actively contradicts it. While the church tries to cling to a season of preparation and expectation, the world rushes on—prematurely, it seems to Christians—to a time of arrival and fulfillment. This determined avoidance of Advent is at least partly because the theme of the season is one with which our world is profoundly uncomfortable: waiting.

WHY DO WE WAIT?

Modern life regards waiting as a negative act, something to be avoided. Waiting is idleness. Time must be filled, used, made productive. While we wait for a plane, we make calls from our cell phones and work on our laptop computers. Or waiting is a frustration of our desires to get and to have. We do not want to wait to save up for a purchase, so we whip out our gold cards and run up our credit balances. Or waiting is a time of apprehension. We wait for the phone to ring with the results of tests or the mail to come with a response to our application. In all of these cases, we dislike the wait. We want to hurry on, get to the point, get something done.

But consider another side to waiting. In every instance, waiting speaks of our incompleteness, our need for someone or something outside of ourselves. We wait for a plane or a bus or our carpool because we cannot reach our destination alone. We need transportation. We wait for news because others know what we do not. We need their wisdom, their skills. Waiting is needing. More than that, it is trusting that someone will meet our need. Waiting is faith.

ADVENT WAITING

We wait for the coming of Christmas, of course. Those with even the least faith can understand that aspect of the season. But the Advent readings point to our needs—to that in which we have faith, that for which we wait—yesterday, today, and tomorrow.

This season points us back to the time when God broke into history and the glory of the Lord was revealed (Isa. 40:5). We wait for the revelation of God in a manger in Bethlehem. We need to know that God has acted, and so we wait for what once was.

But this waiting is not a commemoration of history. We need God in our lives now. The promise is given to Mary: the kingdom of her child will have no end (Luke 1:33). The promise is given to us: the one who comes will give us the Holy Spirit (Mark 1:8). We need God with us now; we have faith in Immanuel.

Our need goes beyond today. We long for assurance for tomorrow as well. Advent reminds us that the promise is for all time, even to the end of time. While the schedule is not ours to know (Mark 13:24-37), the reality is, for we are to be part of a new creation (2 Peter 3:13-14). We need hope for the future, and we have faith in the one who comes again.

For most people, what the church calls Advent is simply the pre-Christmas season. It is a time that exists only because of what comes next. For many, in fact, it has meaning only when it is practically a part of Christmas, a time to fit in all of the shopping, mailing, and partying before the season *ends* on December 25. What are these weeks about? They are a time of *getting* and *controlling*. Advertisers and marketers make it clear that it is the time of year to make our wishes known, to present our lists, and to be sure that we get what we want.

What makes Advent so profoundly countercultural is its insistence that it is a season about *depending* and *trusting*. For this reason we wait: because we can do nothing else. We wait because our needs are so deep. We wait because we have faith that those needs will be met.

ADVENT

ENVIRONMENT AND ART FOR THE SEASON

If blue were a sound, you would hear it in a minor key: the intense longing heard in the Yiddish folk tune of "Light one candle" (WOV 630) or the persistent cry of hope that builds in "Savior of the nations, come" (LBW 28). It's not surprising that singing the blues is the darker, more plaintive sound of jazz. Any voice that would express a glimmer of hope in the midst of sorrow, and would do so truthfully, arises out of the depths, the depths of a deep blue soul.

While many of us in the Northern Hemisphere relish the warmth and brightness of summer's weeks, the cooler days and colder nights of November and December can make lingering outdoors difficult. But that is what we must do if we would see blue, the deeper blue that fills the sky some minutes after the sun has set. Look westward as the wide expanse begins to darken. The faint whiteness of the departing sun may still linger as a line marking the horizon. But, then, look up. The heavens will be a deep azure parament flecked with stars, an Advent chasuble of blue, open and stretched from west to east.

It is fitting, then, that Advent's lectionary readings point the church to the one who comes from the east with a justice as wide and high as the sky, as deep and broad as the ocean ("People, look east," WOV 626). Some will say, "Let us be done with blue; it is too cool, too distant for our warm and happy gatherings." Indeed, the lords of commerce would agree. After all, they have clothed our land with a Victorian holiday of lively red and shiny gold. Clearly the eye—the buying eye—is drawn to the brighter colors and the false promise they hold forth: if you buy this bobble, dear consumer, you will be happy. Christian faith is far more realistic and truthful.

When we wrap ourselves in Advent's blue, we give color to the deep longing so frequently muffled in our land and in our churches. We give voice to our yearning for a world marked by a deeper justice, a land resting under a blue mantle of peace. Without such a color, indeed without the blues, we are left with the overwhelming and endlessly manipulative sounds and colors of an artificial and transitory happiness. Alas, the gospel is transformed into one more law: you must be jolly. It is true: glitter sells well for a few weeks. The blue of the early night sky, however, lets the imagination hope for something greater and more enduring than a red-nosed reindeer. A garment of salvation, perhaps? A robe of justice?

For theological reasons, Christians of the sacramental churches cherish the gifts of creation. The ancient maxim—the human is capable of bearing the divine—is a primary truth celebrated in the season of the incarnation. God comes to us through real things. Consequently, the church uses real, authentic, natural things in its worship: candles that burn down, beautiful cut flowers that will surely wither and die, living plants and trees that need water to survive, bread and wine created from harvested wheat and grapes, natural fabric, sweet-smelling oil pressed from olives. In all these things, we see the mystery of death and resurrection.

For this theological reason the church avoids the use of many artificial and manufactured goods. Or, to say it this way: preference is always given to the natural over the artificial. "Electric" candles (an oxymoron if there ever was one), plastic garlands, silk flowers, and artificial trees will not do. As congregations make preparations for the seasons and festivals of the year, it may be helpful to keep in mind this simple principle and prepare a budget accordingly.

The days of Advent, while bearing their own grace, move the church toward the celebrations of the nativity, epiphany, and baptism of the Lord. Like a path of days spread out before the worshiping assembly, the Advent season is one of simple yet steadfast growth into the incarnation; that is, God's future with us, our future with God. It is the opportunity for the people of God to welcome the one who comes with the promise of peace and justice, the one who leads this people to continue the ministry of bringing good news to the poor and liberation to the oppressed.

In contrast to much frantic social activity, the worship environment can be an oasis of peace and deliberate calm. Oh, some church people will want to jump the gun and begin celebrating Christmas on the first or second Sunday in Advent. But then consider this: what bride would ever wear her wedding dress to family dinners a month before her wedding day? The church rightly forms us in the discipline of patient and faithful preparation.

How will you signal to passersby that this community is celebrating an alternative to the retail industry's carefully calculated winter holiday sales pitch? Deep blue or purple weatherproofed cloth hangings or bunting silently suggest that something different within is happening. Simple wreaths (with no decoration) made of real evergreens or other natural branches, or plant stock native to a region and hanging on doors are a gesture of welcome.

For these four weeks, clear the clutter of racks, posters, and unnecessary furnishings from the gathering area or narthex. Bulletin boards that say "Welcome!" work well on the first day of elementary school. But for those who are followers of the one who called disciples by name, the most effective "welcome" is gracious attentiveness to the stranger.

Prepare an Advent wreath with real greens, proportionate to the size of the worship space. A one- or two-foot wreath on a table or stand may be appropriate in a home (where this custom began). But in a public space, such smallness is a seemingly inconsequential sign. In some congregations, the wreath may be three to six feet in diameter, perhaps hanging over a central aisle, a great evergreen crown floating over the worshiping assembly. Suspended over the space, a large wreath with tall white candles will not be forgotten. Simply lower the wreath on a pulley and light the candles before the people arrive. Convincing people of the value of such a large wreath, constructing it, and using it beyond the Advent season takes some planning. Its use, however, is memorable, versatile, and imaginative.

As the deep blue of night gives way to the limpid whiteness of the dawn, so this season gives way to the next. Perhaps this reality can do away with the need to have a sudden and startling switch to a new "Christmas" environment. Some congregations now use a large tailored cloth hanging of deep blue that is placed behind the altar as a "frame." Gradually but gradually, the deep blue is transformed by the addition of white sheer overlays or is framed by the addition of first narrow, then wider, white panels.

In other congregations, this sense of growth is enhanced by the placement of one or a number of undecorated evergreen trees in the space. On the third or fourth Sunday in Advent, the trees might receive a few garlands of white lights, the final decorating of the tree or trees taking place after the last Advent service. Finally, if the space holds images of David, Isaiah, John the Baptist, Gabriel, and Mary, a simple garland of evergreens can draw attention to these Advent figures who lead us to "the Child of ecstasy and sorrows, the Prince of peace and pain" (WOV 628).

ADVENT

PREACHING WITH THE SEASON

Begin at the end. That is the wisdom gleaned from two millennia of Christian liturgical development. Beginning at the end in Advent not only places us on the trajectory that will bring us to Christmas, it also helps us negotiate the darkness that will lead us to light and life. Transitions are always difficult, risky times—the terrible twos, arduous adolescence, weddings and divorces, celebrating the big "five-o," and funerals. Each poses a specific threat as it disrupts the pattern of life-as-usual. Each demands new creativity and requires us to define new habits fit for a new day.

The beginnings with which we are concerned at Advent are three:
- The beginning of a *new liturgical year* within weeks of the date at which the secular calendar rolls over
- The beginning of the *story of salvation* through the birth of Jesus of Nazareth
- A renewal of the possibility of *beginnings in our own lives*—individual and corporate—here and now

The weeks of the particular Advent we are about to enter "this time around" are especially weighty, for we begin a new church year as the chronometer of the world prepares to roll over not only a century but a millennium. All four numbers are going to change, and no one this side of the event knows what that might do to us. As the weeks of Advent unwind this time, the magi of electronic culture should have addressed most of the issues of the "Y2K problem," fixing computer bugs that would crash our aircraft and halt our Social Security checks when befuddled electronic chips no longer know what year it is. It is our own peculiar version of millennial hysteria, and it gives us an especially powerful way to reflect on the resources of Advent this year. The calendar purists among us will insist that the current century does not technically come to an end until midnight December 31, 2000, but the only thing we will do *that* night is talk about the parties we were at a year earlier. The rock musician formerly known as Prince already was singing about this New Year's Eve seventeen years ago.

Beginning at the end is difficult business. Beginnings are hard enough by themselves, but endings are extremely impenetrable. We cannot see even tomorrow, and so the endings of our stories are veiled in mystic unknowing. To grasp the significance of the millennial shift, the best we seem to be able to do is to reflect on what has happened during the past thousand years. The last time the chronometer turned four digits, what was going on? In the church and the West the Roman Empire was gone already for half a millennium, and the Holy Roman Empire was less than one hundred years old. Christian expansionism was moving into Hungary and Scandinavia, while Vikings were colonizing Greenland and trying to establish a beachhead in North America. *Beowulf* was being composed, and Macbeth had not yet murdered Duncan. Spain was under Arab control, and Seljuk Turks would bring a new and difficult era to life in Jerusalem. The strains between the church in the East and West were growing intense, and the great schism was only decades away. In Africa, culture flourished at Ethiopia and great Zimbabwe. And far away in China, while the Sung dynasty was consolidating power, gunpowder was being developed. The world was a wildly different place one thousand years ago. So, when we think not even about endings but merely about the future, it is almost impossible to try to imagine the way the world will be December 31, 2999—especially when we consider that human culture probably changed more in the last two hundred years than in the previous eight hundred.

Where are we heading? What is our future? It might be more conceivable to imagine that human life will end on earth in the next thousand years than to visualize the world humans will create in the new millennium. Carl Sagan had wondered that if, as it appears, nature seems geared toward the creation of intelligent life, why then has no advanced form of intelligence made a clear contact with us? A chilling possibility is that once intelligent beings achieve the technology that makes them capable of reaching out toward the stars, they also possess the terrible power to destroy themselves. Perhaps no one survives intelligence. Gunpowder eventually is replaced by nuclear weapons, and penicillin gives way to genetically engineered viruses. Can we survive our own future?

A darkness hovers over us at this millennial shift: it is the power lurking behind the rage that poisons our roads and pollutes our air; the conviction that we are being cheated out of the promise of our future, the golden world that was to be. Our own nightmares of global computer crashes, nuclear meltdowns, and Ebola outbreaks *do* have their counterparts in fears our ancestors experienced a thousand years ago. What makes this millennial pass uniquely chilling is that we now possess the technological power to make our own nightmares come true. It is the particular darkness into which we plunge this particular December. And into this dark, the church brashly, boldly declares the word of hope!

The word of hope comes to us out of the future, and the liturgies of Advent suggest that this future is the appropriate starting point for the new year (whether sacred or secular), the new millennium, and the new possibilities for life in the present. The future out of which this hope comes is something other than our own technological cleverness, our belief in progress, or our conviction that the same minds that create problems can also solve them. The hope announced to us in Advent is more profound than the belief in a happy ending—a day of peace beyond our current ecological, economic, familial headaches, and disaster scenarios. *The church begins at the end because we are utterly convinced the future is already in our past.* It came to us here in the middle of things when the world was a confusing buzz, and in the midst of all our contradictions the Future became Now and was laid in the straw. All our Advents come together in this most incredible, this joyously contradictory, holy season.

The clue to our Advent preaching will finally come from the wonder of the incarnation itself, and the preacher would be well advised to look at the accompanying article for "Preaching with the Season: Christmas," to peek ahead and learn the secret in the manger before Advent preparations begin. After all, reading the end of the novel first is what you have to do if you are going to begin with the end!

Meanwhile, for this season, we plunge into the darkness, and the darkness really needs to be savored. This writer's home congregation has wonderfully kept the discipline of midweek Advent vespers all these years, and it is worth your while to reintroduce them if they have disappeared from your community's piety. Advent requires watching, waiting, patience, and darkness. These disciplines are more difficult to acquire every year as the world becomes increasingly frenetic. Midweek silence breaks the spiral of the world's noise created to hide us from our own darkness. Gertrude Mueller Nelson has made a wonderful suggestion that our Advent wreaths should be made by bringing indoors the right front tire of our automobiles to stop us dead in our tracks and to give us space to "attend to our precarious pregnancy" (Gertrude Mueller Nelson, *To Dance with God*, Paulist Press, 1986, p. 63). This marvelous image deserves homiletic reflection, an image to suggest that at its heart Advent implies forsaking one kind of journey in order to make another.

The readings of Advent fall into two distinct subseasons. From its beginning through December 16, Advent calls the church to eschatological vigil, awaiting the future that is about to crash in upon us. The themes of these weeks will sound familiar to those who have passed through the final days of the Sundays after Pentecost. Such is the twisted topology when beginnings and endings are joined in a circle. The Anglican Church's experimental suggestion to fuse endings and beginnings into one "season of darkness" extending from All Saints to Candlemas still invites exploration nearly a decade after its initial proposal. (See, *The Promise of His Glory* in the bibliography.)

The origins of our Advent vigil are undoubtedly shaped by that northern European descent toward the winter solstice, but even in a world where night is turned into day by electrification, we should still explore the territories of our own particular darkness. In many ways, the first readings for these weeks set the tone for the days. The time of Second Isaiah was also a season of darkness for those living in the shadow of the destruction of Jerusalem and the dark night of the soul when the Lord did not seem to come to save the people. In that darkness the prophet announces the coming of the Lord, not simply as some distant possibility or as a strategic plan to see us through our current crises, but rather as the heraldic trumpet blast meant to rouse us from sleep/death and mobilize us into action in the present.

The gospel for the first Sunday in Advent suggests the end will come before "this generation" passes away. Either Jesus was wrong or else one way or another the world is always ending right in front of our noses; Judgment Day stares out at us from the mirror. John the Baptist strides onto the stage, announcing the end of the world as we know it and inviting us—here! now!—to step into the future. John knows that for a new world to come into being, the old world needs to be undone.

The preacher could benefit by paying attention to the art of science fiction and the genre of disaster cinema. The most successful examples of such genres are able to reflect the megadisaster in the particular suffering of individuals. The sinking of the *Titanic* is seen in the loss of a personal relationship; the comet crashes into earth, but we measure its true impact in the disruption of individual lives. The cosmic mirrors the personal, and the personal reflects the cosmic.

The stories of darkness—millennial, communal, familial, and personal—all need our attention this season, and each level will inform the other. But over it all will be announced the coming of God into our present. If it is proclaimed correctly, that Advent gospel will sound preposterous, unbelievable, disruptive; if our preaching is not infected with such qualities, chances are we are hoping too small. Through all of December (and even before) the world will sing familiar carols to set the mood of consumerism—a Christmas designed to rob you of your money so someone else can get rich. But in the poverty of our darkness, we discover the riches of the future—riches that refuse to wait for a better day.

Advent turns a sudden corner December 17, as preparation for the festival of the nativity takes center stage. The Great O Antiphons carry on the themes of waiting and expectation, but the labor contractions are already beginning, and the future can be held back no longer.

It is a wonderful dilemma to celebrate this season in the year of Mark, since this earliest of the gospel writers has no Christmas story as Luke and Matthew do, no glorious cosmic proem as John spins to get the narrative underway. But Advent and Christmas certainly are not missing from this gospel. Rather, Mark, who pays such radical, close attention to beginnings and endings, invites us to redefine not only our understanding of the Jesus story but of reality itself. Mark begins his gospel, as we shall hear on the second Sunday in Advent, by declaring it to be "The beginning of the good news of Jesus Christ, the Son of God."

In a very real sense, then, Mark's entire narrative is his Christmas story. And as we shall hear come Easter, Mark seems to leave the ending of the gospel strangely with intentionality, uncomfortably open-ended, thus extending his narrative into the future and even into the lives of his readers. That means that we, too, are part of "the beginning of the good news." Could our lives be expressions of God's advent? The darkness that fills the story of Jesus is tied not only to the universal trials that beset humanity but to the peculiar challenges and disasters that confront our present age and we who live here. The future is waiting. God is hurling toward us. As we prepare to plunge into the darkness, it is time for us to greet the light!

SHAPE OF WORSHIP FOR THE SEASON

BASIC SHAPE OF THE EUCHARISTIC RITE IN ADVENT

Confession and Forgiveness: see alternate worship text for Advent in *Sundays and Seasons*

GATHERING

- Greeting: see alternate worship text for Advent in *Sundays and Seasons*
- Use the Kyrie
- Omit the hymn of praise

WORD

- Use the Nicene Creed
- The prayers: see alternate forms and responses for Advent in *Sundays and Seasons*

MEAL

- Offertory prayer: see alternate worship text for Advent in *Sundays and Seasons*
- Use the proper preface for Advent (see *LBW* Ministers edition, and *WOV* Leaders edition for each musical setting of the liturgy)
- Eucharistic prayer: in addition to the four main options in *LBW*, see "Eucharistic Prayer A: The Season of Advent" in *WOV* Leaders edition, p. 65
- Invitation to communion: see alternate worship text for Advent in *Sundays and Seasons*
- Post-communion prayer: see alternate worship text for Advent in *Sundays and Seasons*

SENDING

- Benediction: see alternate worship text for Advent in *Sundays and Seasons*
- Dismissal: see alternate worship text for Advent in *Sundays and Seasons*

OTHER SEASONAL OPTIONS

BLESSING OF THE ADVENT WREATH

The gathering rite for either the first week or all the weeks in Advent may take the form of lighting the Advent wreath. Following the entrance hymn and the greeting, one of the prayers of blessing in the seasonal rites section may be spoken. A candle on the Advent wreath may then be lit during the singing of an Advent hymn, such as "Light one candle to watch for Messiah" (WOV 630). The service then continues with the prayer of the day. On the second, third, and fourth Sundays in Advent, the number of candles lit prior to the service would be the total number lit the previous week. One new candle is then lit each week during the service.

Alternatively, candles of the Advent wreath may simply be lit before the service, without any special prayer of blessing. Candles may also be lit during the singing of an entrance hymn, the Kyrie, or the psalm for the day, without any special accompanying prayers or music.

PROCESSIONAL OFFERINGS

If gifts in kind and other special offerings have been brought by worshipers during this season, they may be brought forward and set before the altar during an offertory procession. Such gifts may also simply be left in a gathering space or social hall prior to worship.

LECTIONARY OPPORTUNITY FOR HEALING SERVICES

- Third Sunday in Advent (first reading)

ASSEMBLY SONG FOR THE SEASON

In human society, singing is an important way to pass the time. As the church and the western world approach a rare calendar milestone, this Advent—a season ever conscious of marking time—offers a singular opportunity to sing as we wait.

A principle that might be called "progressive brightening," illustrated by the growing light on the Advent wreath, may be applied also to the music of the season. As the season progresses, songs of lament and awareness of this old world's creakiness increasingly give way to songs that celebrate the incoming of the Christ and hope for the world renewed. Not only the selection of hymns, but the use of instrumentation, the choices of incidental music, the participation of choirs—all can reinforce this principle of progressive brightening as applied to the season's music.

GATHERING

Advent is one of two seasons (with Lent) that give an important place to the Kyrie in the entrance rite, as the hymn of praise is omitted. Litanic forms (as in the *LBW* settings and *WOV* setting 4) stand up well independently due to their fuller textual content. Of various non-litanic settings, the Russian Orthodox Kyrie (WOV 602) offers a rich harmonic texture that holds up to repetition; "Have mercy, O Lord/Señor, ten piedad" (LLC 184) uses a soaring, plaintive melody; and "Lord, have mercy/Nkosi, nkosi" (TFF 22) offers an intriguing harmonic sound from South Africa.

WORD

As a season, Advent is just the right length to introduce the congregation to a new seasonal hymn by having a choir or cantor sing it the first week and including it as hymn of the day or communion hymn in succeeding weeks. Consider learning "As the dark awaits the dawn" by Susan Palo Cherwien (in *O Blessed Spring,* Augsburg Fortress, 1997; also available as a choral anthem with reproducible congregational page). This hymn evokes the "blue expectant hour" of Advent, and includes this fitting prayer: "Shine your future on this place . . ."

MEAL

Although the harvest is past in most places, "Let the vineyards be fruitful" continues to be useful as an offertory canticle with its Advent prayers: "Gather the hopes and dreams of all . . . give us a foretaste of the feast to come." Or, replace the canticle with an offertory hymn such as "Now we offer" (WOV 761), which includes an awareness that we offer "all our struggles and our time" and of "all the people who are yearning for the freedom still ahead."

SENDING

Seasonal possibilities for a sending song or post-communion song include "Shalom" (WOV 724), to which additional stanzas can be improvised (God's peace be with you; God's light be with you; etc.). Another option, growing out of the second reading for the first Sunday in Advent but appropriate throughout Advent, is "He who began a good work in you" (W&P).

MUSIC FOR THE SEASON

VERSE AND OFFERTORY

Cherwien, David. *Verses for the Sundays in Advent*. MSM 80-001. U, org, opt hb.

Hillert, Richard. *Verses and Offertory Sentences, Part 1: Advent–Christmas.* CPH 97-5501. U, kybd. Acc ed. 97-5509.

Krentz, Michael. *Alleluia Verses for Advent*. AFP 11-02564. SAB, org.

Weber, Stephen. "Verse for Advent 1." CPH 98-2886. U, kybd.

Wetzler, Robert. *Verses and Offertories: Advent 1 through Baptism of Our Lord*. AFP 11-09541. SATB, kybd.

CHORAL MUSIC FOR THE SEASON

Cherwien, David M. "O Savior, Rend the Heavens Wide." CPH 98-3209. 2 pt, org.

Erickson, Richard. "Light One Candle to Watch for Messiah." AFP 11-10887. SATB, Org.

Hopson, Hal H. "Advent Prayer." AFP 11-10950. 2 pt mxd, kybd.

Hurd, Bob. "Await the Lord with Hope." OCP 10579. SATB, cong, cant, kybd, gtr, ob.

Keesecker, Thomas. "All Earth Is Hopeful." AFP 11-10877. U/2 pt/ 3 pt, kybd.

Larsen, Libby. "Canticle of Mary." OXF ISBN 0 19 385985 8. SSA, small orch/2 pno.

Manz, Paul. "E'en So Lord Jesus, Quickly Come." MSM 50-0001. SATB.

Niedmann, Peter. "Lift Up Your Heads, Ye Mighty Gates." AFP 11-10774. Also in *The Augsburg Choirbook*. 11-10817. SATB, org.

Rutter, John, arr. "Angelus ad Virginem" in *Dancing Day*. OXF 0-19-338065-x. SSA.

Sirett, Mark. "Thou Shalt Know Him." AFP 11-10645. SATB.

Webster, Richard. "Adam Lay Ybounden." AFP 12-400002. SATB.

CHILDREN'S CHORAL MUSIC FOR THE SEASON

Christopherson, Dorothy. "Come, Lord Jesus, We Are Waiting." CG CGA592. U, cong, 3 oct hb, sop glock, kybd.

Handel/arr. Hopson. "Come, Jesus, Holy Son of God." FLA A-5623. 2 pt mxd, kybd.

McRae, Shirley. "A Litany for Advent." CG CGA570. U/2 pt, sop rec/fl, sop glock/alto glock, kybd.

Melby, James. "The King Shall Come When Morning Dawns." CPH 98-2660. SA, ob/vln, org.

Pote, Allen. "An Advent Prayer." HIN HMC-765. 2 pt mxd, kybd.

Schalk, Carl. "Light the Candle." MSM 50-0006. U, org.

Wold, Wayne. "Advent Candle Song." AFP 11-2408. U, opt cong, kybd, fl/C inst.

Yarrington, John. "Fling Wide the Door." AFP 11-2394. SATB, kybd, hand drm, opt fl.

INSTRUMENTAL MUSIC FOR THE SEASON

Bonnet, Joseph. "Magnificat." CPH 97-5483. Org.

Carter, Andrew. "Chanson de la Vierge Pensive: An Aria for Organ" in *Seasons: Advent/Christmas, Vol. I*. PVN P7001. Org.

Carter, Andrew. "Toccata on 'Veni Emmanuel' " in *The Oxford Book of Christmas Organ Music*. OXF. Org.

Guilmant, Alexandre. "March Upon Handel's 'Lift Up Your Heads.' " SCH 11311. Org.

Lasky, David. "Advent Triptych." WAR GB9605. Org.

Pachelbel, Johann. "Magnificat Fugues." KAL ed. Org.

Scheidemann, H. "Magnificats." Barenreiter ed. Org.

HANDBELL MUSIC FOR THE SEASON

Behnke, John. "Suite for Advent." CPH 97-6248. 2-3 oct.

Mason/arr. R. Haan. "Watchman Tell Us of the Night." CPH 97-6593. 2 oct, kybd, opt choir.

Moklebust, Cathy. "Savior of the Nations, Come." CG CGB 173. 2-3 oct, opt perc.

Nelson, Susan T. "Largo." AFP 11-10556. 3 oct.

Tucker, Sondra. "Meditation on 'Hyfrydol.' " CG CGB 182. 3 oct.

ADVENT

ALTERNATE WORSHIP TEXTS

CONFESSION AND FORGIVENESS
In the name of the Father, and of the ☩ Son,
and of the Holy Spirit.
Amen

As we await the fullness of Christ's coming,
let us acknowledge our sins and failures before God.
Silence for reflection and self-examination.
Our impatience for your coming,
we confess to you, Lord.
Our desire to control time and seasons,
we confess to you, Lord.
Our failure to be alert to signs of your presence in our midst,
we confess to you, Lord.
Our lack of concern for those who come after us,
we confess to you, Lord.
Our injustices toward all the people you came to save,
we confess to you, Lord.

In the mercy of almighty God, I declare to you the forgiveness of
your sins, and the grace to know joy in the Savior's coming.
Amen

GREETING
Christ comes to lighten our darkness.
Come, Lord Jesus.
May the light of God's glory be with you always.
And also with you.

PRAYERS
Walking in the light of the coming Savior, let us pray for the church,
the world, and all who await the dawn of God's justice.
A brief silence.

Each petition ends:
We pray to the Lord:
show us your light.

Concluding petition
Show us your light, O God, and bring us to see the day of our
redemption, through Jesus Christ our Lord.
Amen

OFFERTORY PRAYER
Gracious God,
**we come to your table
with gifts of heart and hand.
Fill us with your love,
so that our lives
may bear the fruit of your Word,
Jesus Christ our Savior. Amen**

INVITATION TO COMMUNION
The door to God's banquet hall is open.
Enter into the joy of the feast.

POST-COMMUNION PRAYER
In this meal, O God,
we have seen the light of Jesus, your Son,
and feasted upon him in glory.
Help us always to be alert
to your gifts in our midst;
through Christ our Lord.
Amen

BENEDICTION
May the God of peace sanctify you entirely;
and may you be kept sound and blameless
at the coming of our Lord Jesus Christ.
Amen

DISMISSAL
Go in peace.
Bear witness to the light.
Thanks be to God.

SEASONAL RITES

LESSONS AND CAROLS FOR ADVENT

Stand
ENTRANCE HYMN
LBW 32   Fling wide the door
LBW 34   Oh, come, oh, come, Emmanuel
WOV 631   Lift up your heads, O gates

DIALOG
The Spirit and the church cry out:
Come, Lord Jesus.
All those who wait his appearance pray:
Come, Lord Jesus.
The whole creation pleads:
Come, Lord Jesus.

OPENING PRAYER
The Lord be with you.
And also with you.
Let us pray.
Eternal God, at the beginning of creation you made the light that scatters all darkness. May Christ, the true light, shine on your people and free us from the power of sin and death. Fill us with joy as we welcome your Son at his glorious coming; for he lives and reigns with you and the Holy Spirit, one God, now and forever.
Amen

Sit
LESSONS AND CAROLS
First Reading: Isaiah 40:1-11
LBW 29   Comfort, comfort now my people
LBW 556   Herald, sound the note of judgment
WOV 629   All earth is hopeful (Toda la tierra)

Second Reading: Isaiah 35:1-10
LBW 384   Your kingdom come, O Father
WOV 633   Awake, awake, and greet the new morn

Third Reading: Baruch 4:36—5:9
WOV 626   People, look east

Fourth Reading: Isaiah 11:1-9
LBW 87   Hail to the Lord's anointed
WOV 762   O day of peace

Fifth Reading: Isaiah 65:17-25
LBW 33   The King shall come
WOV 744   Soon and very soon

Sixth Reading: 1 Thessalonians 5:1-11, 23-24
LBW 31   Wake, awake, for night is flying
WOV 630   Light one candle to watch for Messiah
WOV 649   I want to walk as a child of the light

Seventh Reading: Luke 1:26-38
LBW 28   Savior of the nations, come
WOV 632   The angel Gabriel from heaven came

Stand
RESPONSIVE PRAYER
Blessed is the one who comes in the name of the Lord.
Hosanna in the highest.
Show us your mercy, O Lord,
and grant us your salvation.
Give peace, O Lord, in all the world;
for only in you can we live in safety.
Let not the needy, O Lord, be forgotten,
nor the hope of the poor be taken away.
Shower, O heavens, from above,
and let the skies rain down righteousness.
Come, O Lord, at evening, with light,
and in the morning, with your glory,
to guide our feet in the way of peace.

THE LORD'S PRAYER

BLESSING AND DISMISSAL
Let us bless the Lord.
Thanks be to God.
May Christ, the Sun of righteousness, shine upon you and scatter the darkness from your path. Almighty God, Father, ✠ Son, and Holy Spirit, bless you now and forever.
Amen

SENDING HYMN
LBW 26   Prepare the royal highway
LBW 27   Lo! He comes with clouds descending

BLESSING OF THE ADVENT WREATH

FIRST SUNDAY IN ADVENT
We praise you, O God, for this evergreen crown
that marks our days of preparation for Christ's advent.
As we light the first candle on this wreath,
rouse us from sleep that we may be ready to greet our Lord
when he comes with all the saints and angels.
Enlighten us with your grace
and prepare our hearts to welcome him with joy.
Grant this through Christ our Lord
whose coming is certain and whose day draws near.
Amen
Light the first candle.

SECOND SUNDAY IN ADVENT
We praise you, O God, for this circle of light
that marks our days of preparation for Christ's advent.
As we light the candles on this wreath,
kindle within us the fire of your Spirit,
that we may be light shining in the darkness.
Enlighten us with your grace
that we may welcome others as you have welcomed us.
Grant this through Christ our Lord
whose coming is certain and whose day draws near.
Amen
Light the second candle.

THIRD SUNDAY IN ADVENT
We praise you, O God, for this victory wreath
that marks our days of preparation for Christ's advent.
As we light the candles on this wreath,
strengthen our hearts as we await the Lord's coming in glory.
Enlighten us with your grace,
that we may serve our neighbors in need.
Grant this through Christ our Lord
whose coming is certain and whose day draws near.
Amen
Light the third candle.

FOURTH SUNDAY IN ADVENT
We praise you, O God, for this wheel of time
that marks our days of preparation for Christ's advent.
As we light the candles on this wreath,
open our eyes to see your presence in the lowly ones of this earth.
Enlighten us with your grace
that we may sing of your advent among us
in the Word made flesh.
Grant this through Christ our Lord
whose coming is certain and whose day draws near.
Amen
Light the fourth candle.

NOVEMBER 28, 1999

FIRST SUNDAY IN ADVENT

INTRODUCTION

The days of Advent point the people of God toward the three comings of the Lord Jesus. He came among us at Bethlehem. He comes among us now in the scriptures, the waters of baptism, the eucharistic meal, and the community of faith. He will come again in glory to judge the living and the dead. Keep awake, for his coming is certain and his day draws near.

PRAYER OF THE DAY

Stir up your power, O Lord, and come. Protect us by your strength and save us from the threatening dangers of our sins, for you live and reign with the Father and the Holy Spirit, one God, now and forever.

READINGS

Isaiah 64:1-9

This communal lament comes from a people who have had their hopes and dreams shattered. The great visions of a restored Jerusalem and a renewed people of God, spoken of in Isaiah 40–55, have not been realized. Instead, the people experience ruin, conflict, and famine. This lament calls God to account—to be the God who has brought deliverance in the past.

Psalm 80:1-7, 16-18 (Psalm 80:1-7, 17-19 [NRSV])

Show the light of your countenance, and we shall be saved. (Ps. 80:7)

1 Corinthians 1:3-9

Paul's first letter to the Corinthians addresses many problems that had arisen in the early church. Still, he sets these problems within the context of thanksgiving for the grace and faithfulness of God.

Mark 13:24-37

In today's reading, Jesus encourages his followers to look forward to the day when he returns in power and glory to end all suffering.

COLOR   Blue *or* Purple

THE PRAYERS

Walking in the light of the coming Savior, let us pray for the church, the world, and all who await the dawn of God's justice.

A BRIEF SILENCE.

Your people long for the light of your presence, O God. Enlighten your church with servants who yearn to lead your people in love. We pray to the Lord:

Show us your light.

The world longs for the light of your presence, O God. Illumine your creatures with care for one another and all creation, that righteousness and peace may prevail in our land and among the nations. We pray to the Lord:

Show us your light.

The peoples of the earth long for the light of justice and truth, O God. Shed your soothing light on the sick and suffering, on the homeless and unemployed, on the lonely and forgotten (especially . . .). We pray to the Lord:

Show us your light.

This household of faith longs for the light of hope and healing, O God. Send the brightness of your mercy to all who worship here this day, that our darkness might be banished and our burdens lightened. We pray to the Lord:

Show us your light.

The whole company of heaven lives in the joy of your endless light. May we with all the faithful departed one day behold you in the light of your unveiled glory. We pray to the Lord:

Show us your light.

HERE OTHER INTERCESSIONS MAY BE OFFERED.

Show us your light, O God, and bring us to see the day of our redemption, through Jesus Christ our Lord.

Amen

IMAGES FOR PREACHING

It's about time. God is coming and we are waiting. "Stir up your power, O Lord, and come," the prayer of the day intones. That coming is a cosmic event, with heavens torn open to make a door. Quaking mountains, darkened sun. But the real signs of God's coming are in the empty darkness within. It is easier for God to arrive into a waiting vacuum than to try to squeeze the divine self into lives already filled with a million distractions. "You have hidden your face from us," the prophet complains. "You were angry, and we sinned," almost as if it were God's fault!

Or perhaps as if the darkness in which God-is-not becomes so deep that there is no hope of our being able to find our own way. Here in the dark Advent can begin.

It's about time! Come, God . . . now! We begin with our sense of longing rather than setting timetables based on signs and wonders. The darkness within is what counts. How do you long for God? What does your particular emptiness feel like? Does it have a name?

Do not fear the darkness or the emptiness—not if it is the place into which our God will come. As Paul reminds us, God comes to us with grace and peace, and so in that coming we lack nothing, not even while we wait.

It's about time. Some things last and some things do not. Heaven and earth will pass away, leaving a big vacuum. But if it is a vacuum into which love comes, then the emptiness is holy and all the waiting is delicious.

WORSHIP MATTERS

How can the church's worship awaken those assembled? Such awakening begins with a serious attentiveness to the planning and conduct of worship, reflecting the expectation that the master comes among his people when they gather. Such attentiveness results in worship that is fully attuned to the human experience, that makes the fullest use of the various worship symbols: bread and wine, water, incense, light, cloth, and fabric. Attentiveness results in preaching and intercessions that address the gospel to the specific needs of the assembly, the community in which it gathers, and the broader nation and world. So the assembly is awakened to its own condition and prepared to receive a master who will come again.

LET THE CHILDREN COME

During Advent, consider building a crèche, adding townspeople this week, shepherds the second week, angels the third, and Joseph and Mary the fourth. Reserve the use of magi and camels for Epiphany. Place the crèche where children can see it. Have the children place the figures in the crèche, giving children an opportunity to arrange them. All the people, in their various occupations, are waiting for Jesus. The children, too, are waiting for Jesus as they do their chores, go to school, obey their parents, and live out their daily lives. The children are part of Jesus' story.

MUSIC FOR WORSHIP

SERVICE MUSIC

See "Assembly Song for the Season" in the seasonal materials at the beginning of this section for service music suggestions that can be carried throughout the season of Advent.

GATHERING

| LBW 25 | Rejoice, rejoice, believers |
| WOV 631 | Lift up your heads, O gates |

PSALM 80:1-7, 16-18

Callahan, Mary David. PW, Cycle B.

Furlong, Sue. "God of Hosts, Bring Us Back" in PS, vol. 1.

Haugen, Marty. "Psalm 80/85" in *Gather*. GIA.

Hopson, Hal H. "Psalm 80" in *Eighteen Psalms for the Church Year*. HOP HH3941.

Marcus, Mary. "First Sunday in Advent" in *Psalm Antiphons-1*. MSM 80-721. U, hb, cong.

Smith, Tim. "Lord, Make Us Turn to You" in STP, vol. 1.

HYMN OF THE DAY

| LBW 27 | Lo! He comes with clouds descending |
| | HELMSLEY |

VOCAL RESOURCES

Boehnke, Paul. "Lo! He Comes with Clouds Descending." MSM 50-8300. SATB, kybd.

INSTRUMENTAL RESOURCES

Callahan, Charles. "Lo, He Comes with Clouds Descending" in *Advent Music for Manuals, set 2*. MSM 10-011. Kybd/org.

Held, Wilbur. "Lo, He Comes with Clouds Descending" in *Four Advent Hymn Preludes, Set 1*. MSM 10-010. Org.

Osterland, Karl. "Fanfare and Trio on 'Lo! He comes with clouds descending'" in *I Wonder as I Wander: Seasonal Hymn Preludes*. AFP 11-10858. Org.

ALTERNATE HYMN OF THE DAY

| WOV 627 | My Lord, what a morning |
| LBW 38 | O Savior, rend the heavens wide |

COMMUNION

| LBW 312 | Once he came in blessing |
| WOV 705 | As the grains of wheat |

SENDING

| LBW 332 | Battle Hymn of the Republic |
| WOV 790 | Praise to you, O God of mercy |

ADDITIONAL HYMNS AND SONGS

GS2 50	Come now, O Prince of Peace
OBS 46	As the dark awaits the dawn
H82 640	Watchman, tell us of the night
TFF 38	Soon and very soon
W&P	He who began a good work

MUSIC FOR THE DAY

CHORAL

Bach, J. S. "Jesu, Joy of Man's Desiring" in *Favorite Sacred Classics for Solo Singers*. ALF 11482 (ML); 11481 (MH).

Beck, John Ness/tr. Craig Courtney. "The King Shall Come When Morning Dawns" in *Hymn Settings of John Ness Beck*. BEC VC4. Med voice.

Brahms, Johannes. "O Saviour Rend the Heavens Wide," Op. 74, No. 2 (O Heiland, reiss Himmel auf). GSCH HL 50300310. SATB. Eng/Ger.

Keesecker, Thomas. "Hark! A Thrilling Voice Is Sounding." CPH 98-3228. SATB, pno.

Schafer, Martin J. "A Canticle for Advent." AFP 11-10880. SAB, kybd, opt cong.

Sirett, Mark. "Thou Shalt Know Him." AFP 11-10645. Also in *The Augsburg Choirbook*. 11-10817. SATB.

Thomas, André. "Keep Your Lamps." HIN HMC-577. SATB, conga drm.

CHILDREN'S CHOIRS

Clyde, Arthur. "Advent Candle Song." AFP 11-2408. U, fl, opt cong.

Sleeth, Natalie. "O Come, O Come, Emmanuel." CG CGA273. U with desc, kybd.

Sleeth, Natalie/Marshall. "O Come, O Come, Emmanuel." CG CGA721. SAB, kybd.

KEYBOARD/INSTRUMENTAL

Diemer, Emma Lou. "My Lord! What a Morning" in *Praise: Eight Pieces for Organ*. SMP 70/1069 S. Org.

Harbach, Barbara. "Fantasy and Fugue on Swing Low, Sweet Chariot." VIV 338. Org.

Young, Jeremy. "Conditor alme siderum" in *Gathering Music for Advent*. AFP 11-10798. Pno, 2 inst, opt vc.

HANDBELL

Larson, Katherine Jordahl. "Wake, Awake, for Night Is Flying." AFP 11-10634. 4-5 oct.

McFadden, Jane. "Rejoice, Rejoice, Believers." AFP 11-10632. 2-3 oct.

PRAISE ENSEMBLE

Chepponis, James. "Advent Gathering Song." GIA G-4131. SATB, cant, cong, kybd, gtr, C inst.

Cloninger, Marti/Cason. "While We Are Waiting Come" in *Songs For Praise and Worship*. WRD.

Crouch, Andrae/arr. John Helgen. "Soon and Very Soon." KJO Ed 8889. SATB, pno.

Espinosa, Eddie and Bob Kilpatrick/arr. Wilson. "Change My Heart/Lord, Be Glorified." HOP GC992. SATB, kybd.

Kellner, Mark. "O Come, O Come, Emmanuel." HOP A711. SATB, pno.

McGee, Bob. "Emmanuel" in *Songs For Praise and Worship*. WRD.

Ylvisaker, John. "You Are the Potter" in *Borning Cry*. NGP.

TUESDAY, NOVEMBER 30
ST. ANDREW, APOSTLE

Andrew is known as a fisherman who left his net to follow Jesus, and fish for people. As a part of his calling, he brought others to meet Jesus, including his brother, Simon Peter, and the boy with five loaves and two fish. Throughout the world, various countries celebrate Andrew, whose missionary travels were legendary.

How are we called to invite others to the light of Christ that we celebrate during Advent and Christmas? How do you publicize your services during December, and how do you encourage your members to invite their unchurched friends and neighbors to join them for worship and other special events during this time of year?

FRIDAY, DECEMBER 3
FRANCIS XAVIER, MISSIONARY TO ASIA, 1552

Francis Xavier (Francisco Javier), considered a great missionary, helped form the religious order known as the Society of Jesus (the Jesuits). As he traveled throughout India, Southeast Asia, Japan, and the Philippines, Francis learned the native languages, wrote on the indigenous spiritual traditions, and drew connections between Christian and Asian religious practices.

To honor Francis, consider singing "In a lowly manger born" (LBW 417, Japanese) or "Lord, your hands have formed" (WOV 727, Philippines). You may want to discuss how some people today are turning to Eastern spiritual practices to deepen their Christian experience of prayer. Pray for churches and missionaries in Asia.

DECEMBER 5, 1999
SECOND SUNDAY IN ADVENT

INTRODUCTION

John, the Advent prophet, stands by the waters of baptism and calls the church to see that "our God is here." In baptism God has made us sisters and brothers of the Lord Jesus. God has clothed us with the Holy Spirit, a fire to warm what is cold within us and to kindle our hearts with love. Fed by word and meal we go forth ourselves to prepare the way of the Lord by proclaiming the good tidings that Christ is coming.

PRAYER OF THE DAY

Stir up our hearts, O Lord, to prepare the way for your only Son. By his coming give us strength in our conflicts and shed light on our path through the darkness of this world; through your Son, Jesus Christ our Lord, who lives and reigns with you and the Holy Spirit, one God, now and forever.

READINGS

Isaiah 40:1-11

In grand, flowing, poetic lines, the prophet known as Second Isaiah announces that the exile of God's people in Babylon is over. The Lord will deliver Israel in an exodus more magnificent than the exodus from Egypt. This word can be trusted, because the only enduring reality in life is the word of the Lord.

Psalm 85:1-2, 8-13

Righteousness and peace shall go before the LORD. (Ps. 85:13)

2 Peter 3:8-15a

The Second Letter of Peter is written to Christians who believed that Jesus would return very soon and were perplexed by this seeming delay. The author reminds the readers that the certainty of God's promise is more important than the timing.

Mark 1:1-8

The Gospel of Mark does not begin with a story of Jesus' birth but with the voice of one crying out in the wilderness: Prepare the way of the Lord.

COLOR   Blue *or* Purple

THE PRAYERS

Walking in the light of the coming Savior, let us pray for the church, the world, and all who await the dawn of God's justice.

A BRIEF SILENCE.

O God, your tender voice of love reaches all who sit in deepest gloom. Speak to all peoples throughout the world, lifting those who live among dark valleys of division and despair. We pray to the Lord:

Show us your light.

Your strong voice of assurance gives hope in the midst of the changes and chances of life. Guide your church, O God, as it seeks to speak words of faith to a world seeking stability and comfort. We pray to the Lord:

Show us your light.

Your piercing voice of light breaks through the silence to give strength and hope. Grant that bishops, pastors, diaconal ministers, associates in ministry, and all who serve in positions of leadership in the church will be guided by your voice, so that together we may carry your word to those who await its coming. We pray to the Lord:

Show us your light.

Your soothing voice of comfort brings balm to the broken spirit. Lift up the hearts of all whose courage falters, whose heads are bowed down in sickness or addiction, and whose ears are unable to hear a word of hope in this holy season (especially . . .). We pray to the Lord:

Show us your light.

Your eternal voice of glory rings through the courts of heaven. Give us voices to praise your name with all who have gone before us, whose voices join with ours in the endless song of praise in your light-filled presence.

HERE OTHER INTERCESSIONS MAY BE OFFERED.

Show us your light, O God, and bring us to see the day of our redemption, through Jesus Christ our Lord.

Amen

IMAGES FOR PREACHING

"What sort of person ought you to be?" is the question raised by today's second reading, and coming as it does in the final hours of these 1900s, it is particularly poignant. "With the Lord one day is like a thousand years, and a thousand years are like one day." So maybe the millennial rollover is no big deal to God. But the question tugs at us just the same—"What sort of person?"

The end of the 1900s (and even more, the millennium) urges us toward weighty and extremely significant questions. What sort of persons do we need to be if life is to exist on this planet a thousand years from now? What do we have to do here and now if we are to be able to hand on to our great-grandchildren what was given us by ancestors?

The word of comfort spoken by the prophet is not an invitation to sit back and do nothing, as if we had another thousand years to get our act together. Hardly! This word of comfort is proclaimed even as the voice announces the arrival of God out of the desert! When? In a day? In a thousand years?

Does it matter? Or rather, as the Baptizer suggests, is *now*—*this* day—the important hinge on which eternity swings? John injected the future into the present, as if God's imminent arrival already had changed everything. What kinds of persons ought we to be? What kind of church ought we to be? With passion for the moment, we are in it for the long haul. How many institutions other than the church can claim to have been around a thousand years ago? How many are planning to be here a thousand years from now? What kinds of persons?

Make the path straight. Now!

WORSHIP MATTERS

For humanity to see God's glory, valleys must be raised and mountains made low. The liturgy provides a level place to see the incarnate Christ's glory, a glory revealed by his bearing of human burdens and weaknesses and rejoicing in those things that bring life.

This ministry of Christ is expressed through the assembly's liturgical service to one another. The sharing of the peace is more than an opportunity for a quick hello and a handshake. It allows the assembly to reveal the valleys and mountains within their personal lives. So the assembly learns to bear one another's burdens and to rejoice in things that bring fulfillment to life.

LET THE CHILDREN COME

Children learn best by repetition. In Advent, sing "Oh, come, oh, come, Emmanuel" (LBW 34) so that the youngest children can join in the refrain. Older children will enjoy learning that this hymn has five of the seven traditional Great O Antiphons used in the ancient church (see *LBW*, pp. 174–75). Have children draw pictures of the vivid images to help them learn and remember who is coming and what happens when he comes. Be sure to hang the pictures where the children can see them.

MUSIC FOR WORSHIP

GATHERING

| LBW 35 | Hark, the glad sound |
| WOV 626 | People, look east |

PSALM 85:1-2, 8-13

Callahan, Mary David. PW, Cycle B.
Harbor, Rawn. "O Lord, Let Us See Your Kindness" in *This Far by Faith*.
Haugen, Marty. "Psalm 85: Let Us See Your Kindness" in PCY.
MacAller. "Let Us See Your Kindness" in STP, vol. 4.
Makeever, Ray. "Dancing at the Harvest" in DATH.
Marcus, Mary. "Second Sunday in Advent" in *Psalm Antiphons-1*. MSM 80-721. U, hb.
Smith, Alan. "Let Us See, O Lord, Your Mercy" in PS, vol. 1.

CHILDREN'S PSALM SUGGESTIONS

Christopherson, Dorothy. "The Lord Is My Salvation." AFP 11-10254. U, fl, opt perc.

HYMN OF THE DAY

| LBW 26 | Prepare the royal highway |
| | BEREDEN VÄG FÖR HERRAN |

VOCAL RESOURCES

Laster, James. "Prepare the Royal Highway." CPH 98-2852. SATB, kybd.

INSTRUMENTAL RESOURCES

Afdahl, Lee J. "Prepare the Royal Highway." AFP 11-10723. Hb.
Cherwien, David. "Prepare the Royal Highway" in *Interpretations, Book IV*. AMSI OR-9. Org.
Dengler, Lee. "Prepare the Royal Highway" in *Advent Piano Variations*. CPH 97-6749. Pno.
Oliver, Curt. "Prepare the Royal Highway" in *Advent Keyboard Seasons*. AFP 11-10724. Pno.
Ore, Charles. "Prepare the Royal Highway" in *Eleven Compositions for Organ, Set V*. CPH 97-6107. Org.

ALTERNATE HYMN OF THE DAY

LBW 29 Comfort, comfort now my people
WOV 629 All earth is hopeful

COMMUNION

LBW 29 Comfort, comfort now my people
LBW 320 O God, our help in ages past
WOV 722 Hallelujah! we sing your praises

SENDING

LBW 35 Hark, the glad sound!
WOV 725 Blessed be the God of Israel

ADDITIONAL HYMNS AND SONGS

GS2 18 Come to be our hope, O Jesus
PH 409 Wild and lone the prophet's voice
TFF 49 On Jordan's stormy banks I stand
W&P The King of glory

MUSIC FOR THE DAY

CHORAL

Bach, J. S./arr. Hal H. Hopson. "The Lord Will Soon Appear." AFP 11-10888. SATB, kybd.

Ellingboe, Bradley. "Soul, Adorn Yourself with Gladness." AFP 11-10949. SATB.

Goudimel, Claude/A. Heider. "Comfort, Comfort Ye My People." GIA G-2893. SATB.

Handel, G. F. "And the Glory of the Lord" in *Messiah*. NOV 07 0137. SATB, org.

Hurd, David. "Carol of the Advent." AFP 11-10489. SATB, 2 oct hb.

Keesecker, Thomas. "All Earth Is Hopeful." AFP 11-10877. U, 2 or 3 pt, kybd.

Larkin, Michael. "O Child of Promise Come." AFP 11-10952. SATB, kybd.

CHILDREN'S CHOIRS

Higbe, James. "Happy Advent, Glad New Year." CPH 98-2777. U, 2 oct hb, org.

Pote, Allen. "Prepare!" CG CGA705. 2 pt mxd, kybd.

Wold, Wayne. "Every Valley, Every Mountain" in *Three Songs for Advent*. AFP 11-9949. U, kybd.

KEYBOARD/INSTRUMENTAL

Dengler, Lee. "Prepare the Royal Highway" in *Advent Piano Variations*. CPH 97-6749. Pno.

Fedak, Alfred V. "Freu dich sehr" in *A Collection of Hymns*. CLP DM9601. Org.

HANDBELL

Dobrinski, Cynthia. "Comfort, Comfort Ye My People." HOP 1689. 3-5 oct, fl, drm.

Moklebust, Cathy. "People Look East." AFP 11-10805. 3-5 oct.

PRAISE ENSEMBLE

Chepponis, James. "Advent Gathering Song." GIA G-4131. SATB, cantor, cong, kybd, gtr, C inst.

Clarke, Richard/arr. Jeffrey Honoré. "Advent Song: Lead Us from Darkness." GIA G-3902. SATB, cong, kybd, fl, hb.

Cooney, Rory. "Psalm 85: Your Mercy Like Rain." GIA G-3971. SATB, cong, pno, gtr, fl, sax.

Handel, G. F./arr. Hart. "Every Valley Shall Be Exalted" in *Handel's Young Messiah*. WRD 3010184018. SATB & trio, orch.

Olson, Larry. "Build Up." Dakota Road Music.

Tunney, Dick and Melodie/arr. Larson. "Seekers of Your Heart." GS A-6292. SATB, orch.

MONDAY, DECEMBER 6
NICHOLAS, BISHOP OF MYRA, C. 342

Nicholas, fourth-century bishop in Asia Minor, is one of the most beloved saints, but we know little of his life apart from legend. According to tradition he devoted his life to good works, was generous to the poor, and died peacefully. His gift-giving exploits are legendary.

In some countries gifts are given on this day, perhaps with a visit from St. Nicholas himself. Families, committees, parish staff, or other leadership could observe this day by giving simple gifts.

TUESDAY, DECEMBER 7
AMBROSE, BISHOP OF MILAN, 397

While a catechumen, Ambrose was elected bishop and was baptized, ordained, and consecrated as a bishop on the same day! He was a respected and deeply loved bishop, as well as a famous preacher and defender of orthodoxy. With Jerome, Augustine, and Gregory the Great, Ambrose is considered one of the four doctors (teachers) of the Western church.

Ambrose was one of the first to write Latin metrical hymns. The most famous of these is an Advent hymn, "Savior of the nations come" (LBW 28). Use this hymn sometime during this week. Like Luther centuries later, Ambrose wrote hymns as a means of strengthening faith during periods of hardship and distress.

SATURDAY, DECEMBER 11
LARS OLSEN SKREFSRUD, MISSIONARY TO INDIA, 1910

When Skrefsrud was in prison for bank robbery at age nineteen, he devoted his life to Christ while reading religious books and after talking with a visiting pastor. After attending a mission institute he went to India to minister to the Santals, a people of northern India who suffered terribly from social and political oppression.

Consider raising up the ways Skrefsrud is an Advent prophet in the same manner as Isaiah and John the Baptist. How are we called to point the way to Christ by working for justice and equality among all people?

DECEMBER 12, 1999
THIRD SUNDAY IN ADVENT

INTRODUCTION

The ancient name for this day is *Gaudete*, or "Rejoice Sunday," inspired by the opening words of the second reading, "Rejoice always." In the midst of our preparations and longings we rejoice that the faithful one who brings good news to the oppressed and brokenhearted is already in our midst, helping us hold fast to what is good. With John the Baptist we point the way to the coming light that brings great joy to all the world.

PRAYER OF THE DAY

Almighty God, you once called John the Baptist to give witness to the coming of your Son and to prepare his way. Grant us, your people, the wisdom to see your purpose today and the openness to hear your will, that we may witness to Christ's coming and so prepare his way; through Jesus Christ our Lord, who lives and reigns with you and the Holy Spirit, one God, now and forever.
or
Lord, hear our prayers and come to us, bringing light into the darkness of our hearts; for you live and reign with the Father and the Holy Spirit, one God, now and forever.

READINGS

Isaiah 61:1-4, 8-11

The people returned to Jerusalem from their exile in Babylon as the prophet had said. What they now face, however, is unforeseen hardship and oppression. Through the prophet, the Lord announces the good news of impending healing, restoration, and transformation. This good news of joy is both unexpected and inexplicable.

Psalm 126

The LORD has done great things for us. (Ps. 126:4)

or Luke 1:47-55

The Lord has lifted up the lowly. (Luke 1:52)

1 Thessalonians 5:16-24

First Thessalonians is believed to be the earliest of Paul's letters. He concludes his first epistle with joyful admonitions and blessings grounded in the hope of Christ's coming.

John 1:6-8, 19-28

John's gospel describes Jesus as the "light of the world." John the Baptist is presented as a witness to Jesus, as one who directs attention away from himself to Christ, the true light.

COLOR Blue *or* Purple

THE PRAYERS

Walking in the light of the coming Savior, let us pray for the church, the world, and all who await the dawn of God's justice.

A BRIEF SILENCE.

O God, the preparer of the way, make us ready to receive the Light of lights, and enable us to continue our Advent waiting with courage. We pray to the Lord: **Show us your light.**

Anoint the whole church with your Spirit so that we may proclaim your freedom where we see captivity and oppression. We pray to the Lord:
Show us your light.
Make us sensitive to the needs of the whole human family, the unemployed, the homeless, and all who are ill or who are grieving losses in this season of celebration (especially . . .). We pray to the Lord:
Show us your light.
Give us strength to cry out into the wilderness of our world that in Jesus you have come to bind up, to heal, and to forgive. We pray to the Lord:
Show us your light.
United with those who have gone before us in the communion of saints, may we with all the blessed dead walk in the light of your eternal presence now and forever. We pray to the Lord:
Show us your light.

HERE OTHER INTERCESSIONS MAY BE OFFERED.

Show us your light, O God, and bring us to see the day of our redemption, through Jesus Christ our Lord.
Amen

IMAGES FOR PREACHING

The servant-prophet strides more deeply into our consciousness as we prepare to turn the corner in this season. That deeper awareness, after all, is what this season is all about: a turning of corners in our hearts and minds. It is the root meaning of the repentance (*metanoia* or "new mind") to which the baptizer calls us.

The readings invite us to view this scene from two perspectives: as one who proclaims and as one who hears the proclamation. The gospel reminds us that in Advent, as in counseling or spiritual direction, these two are intimately entwined. You cannot do a good job of proclamation if you yourself have not heard the message. And if you have heard the message, you are compelled to proclaim it. This sense of urgency springs from these readings. It is what happens when the spirit of the Lord God comes upon us. It is what happens if we get our Advent/Christmas wish and God comes into our midst!

John knows what to say because he knows who he is and who he isn't. To be "the voice" means you cannot be Messiah or even Elijah. To be the voice means that you are not the message. We point beyond ourselves. "The one you do not know" is the object of our longing, and even when we know this one's name and story, he still stands beyond us as the unexpected surprise.

In the meantime, we take up our Advent disciplines of rejoicing, praying, and giving thanks. With passion for the moment but in it for the long haul, we keep what is good and save it for the future, and let go of the rest.

Travel light! It's a long road to Bethlehem, but it is the path that leads us to the new day.

WORSHIP MATTERS

Anointed with the Holy Spirit at his baptism, Christ came to anoint all people. Oil, the purificatory and healing properties of which are seldom recognized in Western society, is intended to be used with prayers for healing and with acts of blessing and consecration.

Throughout the church year, the assembly must be given ample opportunity to experience the flow of oil and to voice prayers of intercession and blessing. Regular use of the service of "Laying on of Hands and Anointing the Sick" (*Occasional Services,* pp. 99–102) is encouraged. Worship leaders should provide the people of God opportunity to voice their intercessions for healing. These opportunities may involve daily prayer, prayer chains, allowing members of the assembly to voice their own petitions during worship and special services of prayer. Such a practice requires accessibility on the part of the worship leaders. Coupled with oil, the increased utterance of prayers for healing encourages the assembly to minister in the same healing way as its anointed Lord.

LET THE CHILDREN COME

John the Baptist was a messenger for God. Messengers need to speak clearly for the message to be heard. Remind lectors to speak slowly and distinctly when reading God's word, so that all might hear. The congregation is also a messenger of God's word as it prays the liturgy together. Children just learning to read need things done slowly so they can follow along. Encourage the people to pray the psalm and confess the creed slowly and deliberately so children are better able to hear, pray, and confess.

MUSIC FOR WORSHIP

GATHERING

LBW 265	Christ, whose glory fills the skies
WOV 649	I want to walk as a child of the light

PSALM 126

Callahan, Mary David. PW, Cycle B.

Mahnke, Allan. "Psalm 126" in *Seventeen Psalms for Cantor and Congregation*. CPH 97-6093.

Roff, Joseph. *Psalms for the Cantor, vol. III*. WLP 2504.

Smith, Alan. "The Lord Has Done Great Things" in PS, vol. 1.

Stewart, Roy James. "The Lord Has Done Great Things" in PCY, vol. V.

HYMN OF THE DAY

LBW 87 Hail to the Lord's anointed
FREUT EUCH, IHR LIEBEN

VOCAL RESOURCES

Bender, Mark. "Hail to the Lord's Anointed." CPH 98-2888. SAB, 1-3 tpt, cong, kybd.

INSTRUMENTAL RESOURCES

Bender, Jan. "Freut euch, ihr lieben" in *Twenty-three Hymn Introductions, Vol. V*. CPH 97-5788. Org.

Burkhardt, Michael. "Hail to the Lord's Anointed" in *5 Christmas Hymn Improvisations, Set 1*. MSM 10-111. Org.

Wolff, S. Drummond. "Hail to the Lord's Anointed" in *Hymn Descants, Set I*. CPH 97-6051. Org, inst.

ALTERNATE HYMN OF THE DAY

WOV 628 Each winter as the year grows older
LBW 37 Hark! A thrilling voice is sounding!

COMMUNION

LBW 203 Now we join in celebration
WOV 701 What feast of love

SENDING

LBW 394 Lost in the night
WOV 723 The Spirit sends us forth to serve

ADDITIONAL HYMNS AND SONGS

OBS 79 Sweet coming for which we long
H82 74 Blest be the King whose coming
W&P Lift up your heads

MUSIC FOR THE DAY

CHORAL

Erickson, Richard. "I Want to Walk as a Child of the Light." AFP 11-10957. SATB, org.

Nystedt, Knut. "I Will Greatly Rejoice." HIN HMC 226. SATB.

Schaefer, Martin J. "A Canticle for Advent." AFP 11-10880. SAB, kybd, opt cong.

Schalk, Carl. "As the Dark awaits the Dawn." AFP 11-10951. SATB, org.

Susa, Conrad. "El Desembre Congelat" (On December's frozen ground) in *Carols and Lullabies*. ECS 4839. SATB, org or hp, gtr, mar.

Weiland, Brent. "Christ Is Coming." AFP 11-10578. SATB, opt fl.

CHILDREN'S CHOIRS

Anderson, Norma Sateren. "There Once Was a Man." CG CGA576. U/2 pt, kybd, opt hb/glock.

Cool, Jayne Southwick. "With the Help of the Spirit of the Lord." CG CGA508. U/2 pt, kybd.

Lindh, Jody. "An Advent Carol." CG CGA648. U, kybd.

KEYBOARD/INSTRUMENTAL

Organ, Anne Krentz. "Rejoice, Rejoice, Believers" in *Advent Reflections*. AFP 11-10864. Trbl inst, pno.

Osterland, Karl. "Light One Candle to Watch for Messiah" in *I Wonder as I Wander: Seasonal Music for Organ*. AFP 11-10858. Org.

HANDBELL

Clarke/arr. Jeffrey Honore. "Advent Song: Lead Us from Darkness." GIA G-3902. SATB, solo, cong, kybd, opt fl, hb.

Hopson, Hal H. "Advent Carol" (Veni, Emmanuel). CG CGB154. 3-5 oct.

White, Jack Noble. "The First Song of Isaiah." HWG CMR3347. SATB, cong, hb, opt gtr, perc, dance.

PRAISE ENSEMBLE

Chepponis, James. "Advent Gathering Song." GIA G-4131. SATB, cant, cong, kybd, gtr, C inst.

Cull, Bob. "Open Our Eyes Lord" in *Songs For Praise and Worship*. WRD.

Hanson, Handt. "Prepare the Way of the Lord" in *Spirit Touching Spirit*. CCF.

Moen, Don/Brooks and Rouse. "For All You've Done" in *Let Your Glory Fall*. INT 12106. SATB, orch.

Moen, Don. "God Will Make a Way" in *Come & Worship*. INT.

TUESDAY, DECEMBER 14
JOHN OF THE CROSS, RENEWER OF THE CHURCH, 1591
TERESA OF AVILA, RENEWER OF THE CHURCH, 1582

John and Teresa both were members of the Carmelite religious order during the sixteenth century. Teresa wrote of the states of prayer between meditation (quiet) and ecstasy (union). John's writings focus on his mystical thought and personal experience, rooted both in scripture and in psychological insight. John and Teresa believed that authentic prayer leads to a greater love of neighbor and service to those in need.

The recent interest in spirituality has led many

people to discover the depth of Teresa's and John's spiritual writings. Because Advent is a time to emphasize contemplation and prayer, consider using readings by them at an Advent prayer service, retreat, or other gathering.

THURSDAY, DECEMBER 16
LAS POSADAS

For the next nine days many Mexican families observe the custom of *Las Posadas*, which means "lodgings." Groups of people wander through the neighborhood to mark the journey of Mary and Joseph to Bethlehem. They knock on doors, asking to come in, but a rude voice says there is no room. The visitors either respond that Mary is about to give birth to the king of heaven, or they sing an Advent carol foretelling his birth. Eventually the door is opened, and everyone is welcomed into a great party of traditional Mexican holiday food and singing.

Youth groups or other congregational gatherings could include this tradition as a part of a pre-Christmas party. The traditional songs of this celebration are included in *Libro de Liturgia y Cántico* (pages 284–86). Prepare a special care package or offering for a shelter or halfway house. Las Posadas can be a strong reminder of Christ's humble birth among the poor, and the importance of sharing hospitality.

DECEMBER 19, 1999

FOURTH SUNDAY IN ADVENT

INTRODUCTION

With Mary, the church hears these words: Do not be afraid, you have found favor with God. You, the people of God. You, the baptized Christian. In an anxious and uncertain world, you need not be fearful, the Lord is with you. With these words of consolation, we also hear Mary's response: I am the servant of the Lord. Baptized into the Lord's death and resurrection, and strengthened by his body and blood, we are sent into the world to witness to God's favor for all creation.

PRAYER OF THE DAY

Stir up your power, O Lord, and come. Take away the hindrance of our sins and make us ready for the celebration of your birth, that we may receive you in joy and serve you always; for you live and reign with the Father and the Holy Spirit, now and forever.

READINGS

2 Samuel 7:1-11, 16

Instead of David building a house (temple) for the Lord, the Lord promises to establish David's house (dynasty) forever. Centuries later, after the Babylonian exile, no king sat on the throne. Even then, however, the people of Israel remembered this promise and continued to hope for a king, the messiah, the Lord's anointed.

Luke 1:47-55

The Lord has lifted up the lowly. (Luke 1:52)

or Psalm 89:1-4, 19-26

Your love, O LORD, forever will I sing. (Ps. 89:1)

Romans 16:25-27

These final words from Paul's letter to the Romans offer a doxology, or prayer of praise to God, whose wisdom and strength are the basis for hope in the gospel.

Luke 1:26-38

In this annunciation, Luke makes clear that God comes with good news for ordinary people (Mary) from little-known places (Nazareth). This king will not be born to royalty in a palace, but to common folk in a stall. Here Luke highlights the role of the Spirit, a special emphasis in his gospel.

COLOR Blue *or* Purple

THE PRAYERS

Walking in the light of the coming Savior, let us pray for the church, the world, and all who await the dawn of God's justice.

A BRIEF SILENCE.

O Root of Jesse, through the house of David you came to flower as the world's prince of peace. Grant safety for those who travel in the coming days, that we might all find ourselves at home in your peaceful presence. We pray to the Lord:

Show us your light.

O Key of David, your humble rule opens all that is closed. Grant wisdom and compassion to all who guide the nations of the world. Lead them in peaceful ways so your saving justice will be made known among all people. We pray to the Lord:

Show us your light.

O Dayspring from on high, illumine with your healing presence those who are grieving losses and suffering from anxiety or illness in this season (especially . . .). Give to all in need an assurance of your nearness to them in the midst of their pain. We pray to the Lord:

Show us your light.

O Ruler of the nations, you call all people of the world to the light of your love. Help the people of your church, and especially this congregation, to be faithful proclaimers of this message of hope. We pray to the Lord:

Show us your light.

O Immanuel, your abiding presence with us dispels our darkness and transforms it into light and life. May we, with all those who have fallen asleep peacefully in you, at length be brought to the bright courts of heaven and into endless day. We pray to the Lord:

Show us your light.

HERE OTHER INTERCESSIONS MAY BE OFFERED.

Show us your light, O God, and bring us to see the day of our redemption, through Jesus Christ our Lord.

Amen

IMAGES FOR PREACHING

"Now!" The word repeats itself in our ears from each of today's readings. "Now when the king was settled in his house. . . ." "Now to God who is able to strengthen you. . . ." "Now you will conceive. . . . Now your relative Elizabeth. . . ." The word so easily rolls off our tongues, as if it were a mere connective, some ancient form of "You know . . ." But it is hardly that at all! It is a little word pregnant with implication. *Now!*

The weight of those three letters escapes us because, like the king, we *do* get settled in our houses. We arrange our affairs and make ourselves comfortable. We bring out our holiday mementos and all the curios that make us feel warm and cozy inside. How little we know that even now God is preparing a revolution! Our Advent prayer will come true: God will tear open the heavens and come down. Such a divine disruption of the everyday! And it is hanging over our heads heavy, weighty with promise, ready to come crashing in upon us. *Now!*

God making homes. God turning the tables on David and making for him a house. God choosing to make a home in a virgin's womb. How disruptive! Do they have any idea how their lives are going to be turned inside out by God's coming? Do we?

Through the prophet, Yahweh assures David that once the divine dwelling is established and the people are planted, they will be "disturbed no more." Oh, yeah? And what about the exile? And what about Masada? And what about the twisted, tortuous trail that seems to keep unwinding its way through all our histories? And what about Golgotha?

Is there perhaps a peace surpassing understanding that even in the midst of the hectic hubbub—even when the heavens are being torn open as God descends—that there might be that quiet place within that could become a cradle for our God?

WORSHIP MATTERS

The primary business of the church is assembly for worship, centered in the Sunday eucharist. In this meal, in this feast with God's people, Christ himself gives his life in the bread and wine. As this meal is celebrated regularly and with devotion, so our houses of worship become the dwelling places of God.

The house of worship is a meeting house for the people of God because they share this family meal together, the meal that ushers in the kingdom of God. Emphasis belongs on gathering for worship throughout the church year. All other meetings of God's people are secondary. Meals are intended to engender common conversation and mutual support. When such common conversation and support develops out of the family meal, especially at the sharing of the peace and after the sending, then our houses of worship truly become meeting houses for God's people.

LET THE CHILDREN COME

The annunciation is rich in themes. Mary is the one to whom this word of God comes as an alien word—a word that must be prefaced, "Do not be afraid"—a word outside of Mary. As she hears it, this word of God is conceived by the Holy Spirit and quickens in her womb. Now is a good time to use the traditional formulation of Luke 1:40, 42 as an acclamation before the announcement of the gospel: "Hail! Mary, full of grace. Blessed are you among women, and blessed is the fruit of your womb, Jesus."

MUSIC FOR WORSHIP
SERVICE MUSIC

A long-standing practice for the last days of Advent is to sing the Great O Antiphons (*LBW*, pp. 174–75). An entrance processional (with optional handbells) that incorporates these ancient prayers is in *Praise God in Song* (GIA, 1979).

GATHERING

LBW 34	Oh, come, oh, come, Emmanuel
WOV 633	Awake, awake, and greet the new morn

PSALM 89:1-4, 19-26

Callahan, Mary David. PW, Cycle B.

Mahnke, Allan. "Psalm 89" in *Seventeen Psalms for Cantor and Congregation*. CPH. Cant and cong.

Ogden, David. "I Will Sing" in PS, vol. 1.

Ridge, R. D. "Forever Will I Sing" in STP, vol. 3.

Trapp, Lynn. "Four Psalm Settings." MSM 80-701. U, cong, opt SATB, org.

Whitaker, Howard. "I Will Sing of the Mercies." AFP 11-10093. SATB.

Weber, Paul. "I Will Sing the Story of Your Love." AFP 11-10839. SATB, kybd.

HYMN OF THE DAY

LBW 28	Savior of the nations, come
	NUN KOMM DER HEIDEN HEILAND

VOCAL RESOURCES

McIntyre, John. "Advent Procession on Savior of the Nations, Come." AFP 11-10577. SATB, org, 3 oct hb, opt ch/fc.

Wolff, Stephen. "Savior of the Nations, Come." GIA G-2685. Cong, SAB, acc.

INSTRUMENTAL RESOURCES

Albright, William. "Savior of the Nations, Come" in *A New Liturgical Year*. AFP 11-10810. Org.

Manz, Paul. "Savior of the Nations, Come" in *Improvisations for the Christmas Season, Set 1*. MSM 10-100. Org.

Rose, Richard. "Savior of the Nations, Come" in *Hymnal Companion for Woodwinds, Brass and Percussion, Series 1*. CPH 97-6710. Org, inst.

Wasson, Laura E. "Savior of the Nations, Come" in *A Christmas Season Tapestry*. AFP 11-10861. Pno/kybd.

ALTERNATE HYMN OF THE DAY

LBW 34	Oh, come, oh, come, Emmanuel
WOV 634	Sing of Mary, pure and lowly

COMMUNION

LBW 42	Of the Father's love begotten
WOV 709	Eat this bread (Taizé)

SENDING

LBW 39	Joy to the world
WOV 799	When long before time

ADDITIONAL HYMNS AND SONGS

GS2 46	Canticle of the Turning
H82 266	Nova, nova
H82 437/8	Tell out, my soul
W&P	King of kings

MUSIC FOR THE DAY
CHORAL

Distler, Hugo. "Maria Walks Amid the Thorn." CPH 98-2306. SAB.

Jennings, Carolyn. "A New Magnificat." AFP 11-10479. Also in *The Augsburg Choirbook*. 11-10817. SATB, org, S solo, A solo, opt cong.

Levine. "Mary Heard the Angel's Voice" in *Western Wind Songbook, vol. I*. FLA GA 5041. SATB.

Schalk, Carl. "My Soul Gives Glory to the Lord." MSM 50-1058. SATB, children's choir, fl/hb, org.

Thoburn, Crawford R. "The Linden Tree." AFP 11-10408. SA, U, kybd.

CHILDREN'S CHOIRS

Algozin, Charlotte. "How Will We Know Him?" CG CGA634. U, kybd, opt fl.

Kemp, Helen. "Calling All Angels." CG CGC28. A chancel drama for U choir(s), soloist(s), cong.

KEYBOARD/INSTRUMENTAL

Lovelace, Austin. "Fantasy, Trio, and Toccata on 'Oh, Come, Oh, Come, Emmanuel.'" CPH 97-6724. Org.

Organ, Anne Krentz. "The Angel Gabriel from Heaven Came" in *Advent Reflections*. AFP 11-10864. Trbl inst, pno.

Schroeder, Hermann. "Sleeper Awake." Haas Musikverlag 016-7. Org.

HANDBELL

Dobrinski, Cynthia. "O Come, O Come, Emmanuel." AG 1399. 3-5 oct.

Nelson, Susan T. "Czechoslovakian Carol." AMSI HB-27. 3-5 oct.

PRAISE ENSEMBLE

Allen and Nystrom. "We Will Wait" in *Hosanna! Music Songbook 7*. INT.

Chepponis, James. "Advent Gathering Song." GIA G-4131. SATB, cant, cong, kybd, gtr, C inst.

Harrah, Walt. "The Lord Is My Light" in *Maranatha! Music Praise Chorus Book, 3rd ed*. WRD/MAR.

Kellner, Mark. "O Come, O Come, Emmanuel." HOP A711. SATB, pno.

McRae, Shirley. "The King of Glory Comes" in *Lift Up Your Voices*. CG CGA622. U/2pt, Orff.

Unknown. "I Will Sing of the Mercies" in *All God's People Sing*. CPH.

TUESDAY, DECEMBER 21
ST. THOMAS, APOSTLE

Thomas is perhaps most remembered as "doubting Thomas," the disciple who needed to place his hand in the wounded side of the crucified and risen Lord. Yet Thomas also made one of the strongest confessions of faith in the New Testament: "My Lord and my God."

The observance of Thomas occurs on the winter solstice, the shortest day and longest night of the year. In the same way that Thomas needed to see in order to believe, we also long to see the return of the sun and the increase of daylight hours. Thomas is an Advent saint who invites us to name our doubts and fears as we yearn for the coming of the light. As Christmas draws near, it is a day to gather around the four candles of the Advent wreath and sing of the coming light. Consider using "Light one candle to watch for Messiah" (WOV 630).

ADVENT

CHRISTMAS

EPIPHANY

CHRISTMAS

Could there be a finer gift?

IMAGES OF THE SEASON

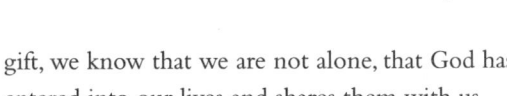

If Advent is the season most neglected by the world, then surely Christmas is the one most fervently embraced and enthusiastically celebrated. Our city streets shine with lights for the occasion. Every store window seems stuffed with packages tucked under trees. Even the government joins in, giving us our choice of Madonnas or holly leaves to stick on our mail.

A TIME OF GIFTS

Ask people walking down those sparkling streets to identify the essence of the season and quite a few are likely to point to gifts. For children, of course, gifts are clearly the heart of the holiday. The television ads begin long before Thanksgiving. The catalogs clog the mailbox while autumn is still with us. Lists are made, hints are dropped, letters are dispatched to the North Pole. The excitement of Christmas morning is tinged with apprehension, almost with anxiety. Will the right gifts appear under the tree? Will the hoped-for item really be there?

For adults, no doubt, some of that hopeful longing lingers. Certainly a great joy comes from receiving a well-chosen gift. But for adults Christmas means giving as well as getting. The concern is to find that fervently-wished-for toy, the item that everyone *must* have this year. The joy is less from opening the packages under the tree than from watching the faces of those who unwrap them.

Yes, gifts are at the heart of this season. But what gifts? Surely not just those that are wrapped with bows and ribbons.

THE GIFT OF PRESENCE

The first great gift of Christmas is obvious: the gift of God's presence with us. In this season we celebrate Immanuel. This gift—wrapped not in shiny paper but in swaddling cloths—comes in the form of the baby, the child of Bethlehem, and is probably the gift many people associate most readily with Christmas.

It is the gift of incarnation. We rejoice in the Word made flesh, dwelling here in our midst. Because of this gift, we know that we are not alone, that God has entered into our lives and shares them with us.

THE GIFT OF REDEMPTION

But incarnation means more than that God dwells with us. It also means that we dwell with God. Our lives have been changed, made worthwhile because we share them with God. In taking on human nature, Christ has given value to that nature.

In a world so ready to view human life as disposable, this gift is remarkable. It condemns the violence, physical and emotional, that we inflict on one another. It calls us to see the body of Christ, to be the body of Christ, to cherish the body of Christ. By this gift we are made what God intended us to be.

THE GIFT OF PARTNERSHIP

By bringing God into our midst and bringing us into God's presence, the gifts of Christmas work a remarkable change in our existence. Jesus shares in our nature and we in his, which means, in a sense, we share in the divine. We have not, however, become worthy of worship. No, we are not called to sit upon a throne, high and lifted up, adored and praised. Nor does it mean that we are free to do as we please. We may not, like the builders of the Tower of Babel, bring ourselves greatness.

What our divinization means is that we share the work of God in the world. We have been made partners in the task of rebuilding creation. It may seem strange that the greatest gift of Christmas means we have work to do, but such is the case. The joy of this gift is that the work is not drudgery. It is a return to what God always intended for us. It is an invitation to learn again our deepest nature. Could there be a finer gift?

CHRISTMAS

ENVIRONMENT AND ART FOR THE SEASON

Light a match in darkness and you will see a softly burning flame, an electric blue at the base becoming white tinged with gold at its peak. The flame burns quietly, creating light yet consuming the paper, wood, or wick on which it glows. In a way that may be difficult for us to imagine, the ancients were drawn to the dense symbolism of light, to the whiteness—the purified gold—that could be seen in a crackling fire or a brief glance at the sun. In our dark nights, we simply flick a switch and the artificial light of a bulb pops on. In an earlier age, however, people were surrounded and guided by living flames whose color and form sparked the imagination.

In contrast to blue and purple (both cool and retreating colors), white and gold and red are warm and advancing. Like a bride surrounded by black-jacketed groomsmen, white draws the eye. It says, Look at me. It can shimmer like the far-seeing sun, bringing light out of an inscrutable darkness. For the ancients, the rising of the sun's white light at dawn was a lively metaphor of enlightenment: "Those who lived in a land of deep darkness—on them light has shined" (Isa. 9:2, Christmas Eve). But with them, we know the power of the sun's fire cast on earth. While it may appear clear and bright against the sky, a white, racing fire will leave behind a swath of black scars on the land. Scorched earth, we call it. Indeed, we buy "fire" insurance because we know too well that a small white light—innocent and charming on a dinner table—can turn into a mighty conflagration that reduces a house to an empty charred ruin.

In the art and vesture of ancient Rome, when Augustus ruled the known world, white was associated with power. A bride's white garment could display and conceal the promise of her fertility. A senator's legislative toga, while an echo of the empire's humble origins among farmers, signaled a member of the inner ruling circle. On state occasions, the emperor was covered in a robe of pure white lamb's wool. At the winter solstice, he painted his face white in imitation of the returning sun, his heavenly "father." Yes, even Daniel the prophet would see such power in his vision of the Ancient One, "his clothing was white as snow, . . . his throne was fiery flames, . . . its wheels were burning fire" (Dan. 7:9, proper 29).

It is no small wonder that in the deepest darkness of the longest nights and shortest days of the year, Christians keep a festival of light. But here we must be careful, very careful, and we must listen again as if for the first time: the ancient story tells us how to celebrate the paradox of the festival. We name him "Prince of peace" and "Sun of justice" yet he does not come among us today as Daniel's Ancient One, robed in garments of lightening power. He does not descend from some fiery throne in the sky, an ancient emperor impatiently waiting for this world to recognize his rule and give him "glory." Nor does he appear as we would have him: a cute baby wrapped in a fresh, white cloth. In this birth, as in all births, the whiteness of cloth is stained with blood and mess. He comes to our world not as an infant but as a body broken for the hungry, as blood spilled for the thirsty. And so in the celebration of his nativity, the church already keeps the festival of his death when from his pierced side, blood pours forth.

Yes, it is our light, our festival of light in the midst of the world's winter feasting. It is the pouring forth of God's loving presence among the broken ones and little things of this earth in food and drink. Thus, we place bread and wine on white altar cloths to tell and to eat the truth of the story: "This, this is Christ the king, the sweetest wine of heaven" ("What feast of love," WOV 701). So with one hand, Christians hold forth the bright, white light of the festival and with the other hand receive the cup filled with holy drink. Not one without the other. He comes from Bethlehem, "the house of bread," to the many houses of the church. Not as an idea, a spirit, or a memory of the past but as bread to be shared by hungry people. With the winter feasting of the Northern Hemisphere, Christians gladly keep a festival of light. Yet we hold our lights around the center of the feast: this sweet manna come down from heaven.

At this time of the year, if you drive down streets in neighborhoods, poor and middle class alike, you will see homes and yards decorated with lights, evergreens, manger scenes, and a range of other images. As the festival of third importance in the year (after the Three Days and Pentecost), Christians rightfully enrich the house of the church with additional elements for the twelve days of Christmas. While some continuity can be found between home and church (e.g., wreaths, trees, and lights), we notice a marked difference as well. In the church, the centers of congregational life stand out clearly: the baptismal font, the place of the word, and the eucharistic table. At these places, the worshiping assembly encounters Christ, the sacrament of God's forgiveness and mercy. No amount of decoration should ignore or obscure these primary centers. If the doors to the worship space have been adorned with plain evergreen or natural wreaths throughout Advent, these wreaths may need to be refreshed for the twelve days. The use of white ribbon will offer a subtle distinction from the floral industry's predictable employment of velveteen red.

Some congregations now place southwestern luminaria along the walks leading to church buildings for services on Christmas Eve, New Year's Eve, and Epiphany Eve. Local weather and walkway conditions will dictate whether such decoration is possible. Small white paper bags filled with sand and burning votive candles create a welcoming path into the worship space. And their welcoming characteristic is the point; they serve a practical purpose. Lining up luminaria on an external wall misses the point. Let these subtle lights be seen by people as they walk into the space. And by all means, forsake the notion of using electric lights.

If you have employed a large Advent wreath floating above the assembly, keep it in place for the twelve days with these changes. Remove the evergreens and four large candles. Clean the base and then fill it with many fat white candles of various heights that are secured well to the base. In some places, a new garland of greens with white ribbons is added. Before the people arrive for the worship services during the twelve days, lower the wreath and light all the candles. The wheel of time has become a crown of light for the people of God. In some parishes in Sweden on the fourth Sunday in Advent, each household brings a new white candle to be used in the Christmas crown, a communal expansion of the domestic crown worn on St. Lucy's Day. It is one more way in which the congregation participates in the enrichment of its house.

While in many churches it is a common practice to "decorate" the sanctuary (the area in which the altar and perhaps the pulpit are found, what most people in the pew think of as "up front"), a few congregations have taken seriously the insight that the baptized people are the church. This way of thinking means that those who gather to worship—the baptized assembly—are active participants in the liturgy. This insight that, while in worship, the baptized are not passive observers or spectators, clearly contradicts the culture of entertainment in which we live. The artistic corollary to this theological insight is that the space (the nave) in which the people gather is to receive as much artistic attention as font and table. Filling up the sanctuary with trees, flowers, and banners draws one's attention to the leaders of worship. In contrast to this late medieval and truly hierarchical view of the church, some congregations have begun decorating the entire space, pushing some elements out into the larger body of the church. Evergreen garlands may be secured along the walls of the space. Groupings of large candles can be placed safely in window or wall niches. Christmas trees may be placed outside, in the narthex/gathering space, or in other locations throughout the worship space where they will not impede the movement of the worshipers.

Various interpretations have attached themselves to the Christmas tree. Against winter's cold and lifeless landscape, the enduring evergreen is a sign of life. For various cultures, such as certain American Indian tribes of the Pacific Northwest, it is the tree of life. Christians welcome these images of the tree and also see it is a sign of the life-giving cross, the tree of death transformed into the tree of life now filled with brightly burning lights. So pervasive is the presence of the tree in religious art, poetry, and literature that its meaning can never be reduced to one thing. Yet within a Christian context, it may be helpful to make the connection between the Christmas tree and the tree of life. The second verse of "What child is this" (LBW 40) makes the connection clear: the Christmas festival points toward and finds its source and meaning in the Three Days.

From time to time, the newspapers will report disputes over the sponsorship of Christmas trees and manger scenes on city or state properties. If you can imagine it, even John Paul II encountered considerable resistance when he suggested that a manger scene be installed on the main square of St. Peter's Basilica in Rome. Perhaps the resistance was due, in part, to the Italian custom of placing a manger scene within a church. Why inside, not outside? Italian manger scenes are filled to the brim with dozens of characters who represent all aspects of Italian life finding their way to the manger at Bethlehem. Many of the figures are dressed in contemporary clothing, as if to say the incarnation is taking place in our time. So, it is fun to look at all these figures, to pray in the presence of this remarkable and lowly scene, to look for the imaginative ways in which artists have portrayed the many characters of the story (not just Mary, Joseph, and Jesus, but all those who appear in the scriptural stories associated with the entire Christmas cycle). Who wants to stand outside in rain, snow, or cold temperatures to gaze over these many characters? No one! If you will install a Christmas manger scene, then do so indoors in a place where people can gather to look and to pray. In one congregation, the empty stall itself will be set up on the first Sunday in Advent, empty for four weeks until Mary, Joseph, Jesus, the angels, and shepherds appear on Christmas Eve. On the next day, Sunday, December 26, Stephen can be added to the group. On Sunday, January 2, John the Evangelist, the Holy Innocents, and the magi (if there will be no worship on the Epiphany) can find their way to the Christ child.

Even in the coldest climates, flowers and blooming plants are readily available for use in decorating the worship space. Some congregations continue to order red poinsettias year after year and line them up in rows or circles in close proximity to the chancel steps. Perhaps a welcome change would be the use of white poinsettias or other white flowers mixed with a variety of greens. The difficulty with a sustained use of poinsettias is their tendency to begin to droop or lose leaves if they are not tended carefully. Some congregations invite people to take a poinsettia home after the Christmas Day services. But then what visual continuity will obtain through the Epiphany and Baptism of Our Lord liturgies?

Many medieval Christmas carols speak of the newborn Christ as a rose (see "Cold December flies away," LBW 53; "Lo, how a rose is growing," LBW 58). Such songs suggest a selective use of white roses (red ones possess too many other associations in North American culture). But if no roses are available or their purchase is too costly, what other white or perhaps yellow- or gold-tinged flowers are available? While florists will push fat, red "holiday" carnations, why not use whatever is available in your region? Because ordering flowers is relatively simple in most parts of North America, it may seem silly to suggest that a congregation use the natural gifts of its region, especially if flowers or blooming plants are few and far between. But, then, consider this: the Word comes among us where we are and uses whatever we have to proclaim the good news visually.

SUNDAYS & SEASONS

PREACHING WITH THE SEASON

Christmas captures public imagination as no other festival of the liturgical year. The fusion of secular passions with sacred paraphernalia is at once and the same time the most wonderful opportunity and the biggest headache for the Christian preacher. This exotic mixture of the earthly and the heavenly places us squarely at the heart of H. Richard Niebuhr's reflections on "Christ and culture." What stance should the preacher take toward this strange cohabitation of worldly consumerism and the deepest Christian pieties? Should the church do battle with the secular powers that invite the faithful to worship at the high altars of the materialistic? Or does the preacher take advantage of this strange spirituality where Christian hymns blare from shopping mall PA speakers?

In one sense these various tactical strategies are the heart of the feast, for what we come to celebrate in the nativity of our Lord is the incarnation, the "enfleshing" of God in human nature. In Jesus, God took on not only hands and feet and kidneys; God also placed the divine self into a culture. Jesus lived a truly human life in all the networks of human relationships, mediated by human language, using human symbols, and struggling with issues of human value. God comes to us not in some otherworldly gnostic spirituality but squarely into the gritty stuff of human experience, scratchy straw and all. True, the story unfolded two millennia ago, but had it happened today, part of it surely would take place at the shopping mall. Just how would Jesus overturn the tables of the moneychangers today?

In one sense the preacher can delight at the sacred/secular confusions of the season. This festival, like no other, will bring the curious through our doors and into the midst of the community of the faithful. Something here invites even agnostics to peer into the manger and see what is there. If what draws them is nothing more than a hunger for the innocence and wonder of a lost childhood, it is an expression of the Advent darkness that becomes, as Luther called it, the "bed soft, undefiled, within my heart" into which God may come (see "Preaching with the Season: Advent" in this volume).

The negative side of the Christmas challenge is that in many ways our Christmas can be only as good as our Advent. Here secular consumerism threatens to undo the benefits the incarnation offers for the redemption of the culture. The world's "advent" *does* focus on hunger and longing, just as the church does. But these secular hungers are not our truest, deepest hungers. Rather, they are artificially created wants commercially twisted into imaginary needs to make somebody else rich. The secular holiday discipline creates such hungers as can be filled only by purchasing and exchanging gifts. "What we want for Christmas" has nothing to do with our deepest need of God but rather with lesser gods that promise to fill and fulfill us. They don't. They never do. They never will. December 26 and beyond provide no realization of our secular advent hope; we find only a hollow emptiness and the gnawing awareness that somehow the holiday did not meet our deepest needs.

With honest elucidation, the two Christmas stories—Luke's and Matthew's—become an antidote to this betrayal of God's good news. Each in its own way invites us to discover the gospel surprise that undoes us (and our world) and tears open the present to God's future. For all the sentimental tinsel that encrusts our perception of these biblical narratives, the stories themselves are powerful, revolutionary, countercultural declarations that the world as we know it is indeed coming to an end. God is preparing to "tear open the heavens and come down," just as we cried out in hope when Advent began. And when God comes among us, everything and everyone is undone.

Although in both secular and pious imagination the two Christmas stories are conflated—shepherds and magi rubbing shoulders at a manger beneath a star—the two stories are unique both in their content and history. Each has produced a celebration of the incarnation on two different dates. The West focused on Luke's story celebrated in the Christian cult on December 25. The East, on the other hand, celebrated the incarnation from Matthew's story on January 6. East and West borrowed from each other so that today we have both Christmas and Epiphany. But each story of the Savior's birth deserves our exploration. The celebration of this event focuses upon the story itself. Christian preaching for this short season (twelve days) should shy away from talking *about* the event. What is demanded from us is that we tell the story again in such a way that its romanticized familiarity is undone; the sheer shock of God's presence among us should once again ignite over our heads like angelic glory above shepherds' fields, like a supernova exploding in the night and leading us to the revelation.

New Testament scholar Raymond Brown has suggested that each of the two Christmas stories is an expression of late first-century christology (see *The Birth of the Messiah* in the bibliography). The initial "christological moment" for the early church was Jesus' death and resurrection, when the God-forsaken one is shown to be a unique and shocking manifestation of God's presence among us. By the time of the writing of Mark's gospel (circa A.D. 70), we see this christological identity pushed back earlier in the story, to the time of Jesus' baptism by John in the Jordan. Several decades later, Matthew and Luke independently push the moment back even further, to stories that describe Jesus' birth as "the beginning of the good news." The fourth evangelist will push this christological moment back even earlier in his poem, which ties the identity of Jesus of Nazareth to the creative Word that was with God and was God from the beginning.

The issue in the two birth narratives is the genesis of the good news. Where does it start? Brown suggests that for all their radical differences—differences that simply cannot be reconciled to each other as hard as we may try—both Luke's and Matthew's stories bear a remarkable resemblance to each other. This similarity is the major clue to preaching in this season. In each story, only one parent is informed of the approaching birth. The birth itself is mentioned only in passing, as the narrative focus shifts to "outsiders" who receive revelatory announcement of the event and are led by divine guidance to Bethlehem. Their coming to the place of birth is an acknowledgment of what God has accomplished and, in both cases, the outsiders return home to share the news with others. The implication is profound and astounding: Christmas is at its heart a kerygmatic event meant to bring outsiders in! These strangers who wander into our churches Christmas Eve don't just happen to stumble into our building by mistake. They have been invited by God! It is the Christian community's task to welcome them as we welcome Christ and to give them good news they might take with them to tell others.

Now to the particulars: Luke's story is set against a backdrop of world affairs and political events. Although we focus on a remote corner of the Mediterranean, always on the horizon we cannot help but be aware of the vast power of the Empire. In Rome, Caesar Augustus can snap his fingers and people half a world away have to move, even if they are nine months pregnant. The focus quickly shifts to a barn in Bethlehem—the hometown of David, Israel's greatest king—and from there we are led out to the very fields where the child who would one day be king once romped and played with sheep. It is no accident that the birth is announced here, nor that the divine revelation that bursts over the heads of befuddled shepherds should be described as an *army* of God's angels. The angels' message curiously mimics a royal proclamation heralding Caesar Augustus as "savior of the whole world" and the day of his birth as the beginning of a new era of peace. Although Luke's overall project is meant to calm Roman fears about a Christian threat to the Empire, the implication is subtle yet clear: a new king is born in obscurity but backed up by angelic armies. He will prove to be the world's true Savior and guardian of peace. That Luke knew neither about Constantine nor invading barbarian hordes makes this insight even more profound. The only question left to consider is: What became of the Jesus movement, and where is the Roman Empire today?

Although our celebration of Matthew's Christmas story is left to Epiphanytide, it is helpful to consider it here for contrast and comparison to Luke's. If Luke's story aimed at political shock, then Matthew's is targeted for theological commotion. Like Luke, Matthew sets the story within the scandal of an unplanned pregnancy. The potential interpretation of the baby's strange (and, without insider knowledge, "illegitimate") birth, however, is but a prelude to an even more profound surprise: astrologers from the East, practicing what could only be called by biblical standards a "false religion," are led first to Herod and then to the child who is to be king of the Jews and shepherd of the Lord's flock. The magi come to Christ not by studying scripture or by direct angelic revelation but only by being good heretics who know how to ply their trade. Evidently, many roads lead to Bethlehem!

Praise God that we have at least twelve days to unpack and ponder such mysteries. Mary and Joseph, magi and shepherds have plenty to keep in their hearts. And so do you and I! What is celebrated quietly in intimate candlelit darkness on Christmas Eve is scrutinized in the bright light of a low-slung winter sun the next morning. The feasts of the three companions and the first Sunday after Christmas help us deromanticize the story. The second Sunday after Christmas, however, blows the story into cosmic dimensions, which lead us to "second Christmas" on Epiphany. A closer consideration of these days can be found in the pages ahead.

Meanwhile, find a place of quiet. Get in touch once more with the emptiness within. Detour the lesser hungers and get down to the deepest unfulfilled wants, the broken dreams, the unresolved aches—the straw of your life. But it is also the quiet place, undefiled, waiting for your Savior. He is here, even in your own flesh and blood! Even in the face of the stranger! Greet him!

SHAPE OF WORSHIP FOR THE SEASON

BASIC SHAPE OF THE EUCHARISTIC RITE IN CHRISTMAS

- Confession and Forgiveness: see alternate worship text for Christmas in *Sundays and Seasons*

GATHERING

- Greeting: see alternate worship text for Christmas in *Sundays and Seasons*
- Use the Kyrie, particularly for the most festive liturgies during this season
- Use the hymn of praise ("Glory to God")

WORD

- Use the Nicene Creed
- The prayers: see alternate forms and responses for Christmas in *Sundays and Seasons*

MEAL

- Offertory prayer: see alternate worship text for Christmas in *Sundays and Seasons*
- Use the proper preface for Christmas (see *LBW* Ministers edition and *WOV* Leaders edition for each musical setting of the liturgy)
- Eucharistic prayer: in addition to the four main options in *LBW*, see "Eucharistic Prayer B: The Season of Christmas," in *WOV* Leaders edition, p. 66
- Invitation to communion: see alternate worship text for Christmas in *Sundays and Seasons*
- Post-communion prayer: see alternate worship text for Christmas in *Sundays and Seasons*

SENDING

- Benediction: see alternate worship text for Christmas in *Sundays and Seasons*
- Dismissal: see alternate worship text for Christmas in *Sundays and Seasons*

OTHER SEASONAL POSSIBILITIES

PROCLAMATION OF THE BIRTH OF CHRIST

- The services on Christmas Eve may begin with the Proclamation of the Birth of Christ (see text in the section titled "Seasonal Rites"), taken from the ancient martyrology. The proclamation should be understood as the announcement of the incarnation within human history rather than a literal counting of years. The lights may be turned down,

and, following a period of silence, the proclamation is preferably sung or read (the proclamation may be sung on one note). The congregation may face the reader/cantor at the entrance to the church.
- Following the proclamation the lights are turned on as the musician(s) introduce the entrance hymn. "Oh, come, all ye faithful" (LBW 45) is an appropriate hymn following the proclamation. The congregation turns to the front as the cross passes them in procession. "Glory to God in the highest" is the most appropriate hymn of praise for the Christmas season.

CANDLELIGHTING OPTIONS FOR CHRISTMAS EVE
OPTION 1
- The liturgy may begin with a service of light as at evening prayer. The congregation may face the entrance to the church, and handheld candles may be lit. As the procession passes during the Christmas versicles, all turn to face forward.
- Christmas versicles (from "Propers for Daily Prayer," *LBW*, p. 175; these may be sung to the tones given in evening prayer, *LBW*, p. 142)
- Hymn of light (LBW 42, 45, 49, 56, or 65)
- Thanksgiving for light (see *LBW*, p. 144)
- The service may then continue with the greeting, followed by the hymn of praise and the prayer of the day. Electric lights may be turned on gradually as the hymn of praise is begun (though a rather subdued level of lighting may be desired throughout the service, in order not to overwhelm tree lights and candles). Handheld candles may be extinguished at this time.

OPTION 2
- Another option for the lighting of handheld candles is to use them at the reading of the gospel. A hymn, such as "The first Noel" (LBW 56) or "Angels, from the realms of glory" (LBW 50), may be sung as handheld candles are lit. The gospel may be read from the midst of the people. "Silent night, holy night!" (LBW 65) may be sung following the gospel, after which the handheld candles would be extinguished.

OPTION 3
- A final option for the lighting of handheld candles is at the close of the service. Following the distribution of communion (or at a service without communion, following the receipt of the offering and the prayers) handheld candles are lit (instrumental or choral music may accompany the candlelighting).
- Reading from John 1:1-14 (especially fitting if the gospel reading earlier in the service was from Luke 2)
- Hymn: "Silent night, holy night!" (LBW 65; or another hymn of light, as listed in option 1)
- Post-communion prayer (see seasonal alternate text in *Sundays and Seasons*)
- Benediction
- (Sending hymn)
- Dismissal

BLESSING OF A NATIVITY SCENE
- The text for the blessing of a nativity scene, found in the seasonal rites section, may be used after the sermon or after the communion of the people on Christmas Eve.

NEW YEAR'S EVE
- Though gathering for worship on New Year's Eve may not be a common experience for most congregations, those wishing to observe the passing into the year 2000 this year may wish to use the New Year's Eve suggestions in the seasonal rites section.

ASSEMBLY SONG FOR THE SEASON

Christmas music is like that burgeoning platter of Christmas cookies at the holiday party: so many sweets, so little time. One key is to choose and place the right song at the right time to give its message maximum impact.

GATHERING

See "Shape of Worship for the Season," above, for a number of musical options for the gathering rite, especially on Christmas Eve.

WORD

At a time in the church's history when hymn-singing in the liturgy was rare, Christmas was one of the few times when a "sequence hymn" was provided to acclaim the reading of the gospel. In today's church the acclamation of the gospel of the incarnation might be highlighted by surrounding its reading with a hymn, particularly if the book of readings is processed into the midst of the congregation. Such a frame might be created using "From heaven above" (LBW 51; st. 1–4 before the gospel, 5–8 after, then 9–14 at the hymn of the day) or "Holy Child within the manger" (WOV 638; st. 1–2 before, st. 3 after).

MEAL

As an offertory hymn, "What child is this" (LBW 40; use st. 3 alone if only one stanza needed) may be used through Epiphany. Make generous use of the most familiar carols during the communion on Christmas Eve, a time when people are less likely to read from the worship book than simply to sing or hum along.

SENDING

As a seasonal post-communion or sending song, use a paraphrase of Simeon's song such as LBW 339, "O Lord, now let your servant." Or, to highlight the passage of time in this season that straddles a millennial turn, sing the first and last stanzas of "Of the Father's love begotten" (LBW 42).

MUSIC FOR THE SEASON

VERSE AND OFFERTORY

Boehnke, Paul. *Festive Verse Settings for Christmas, Epiphany and Transfiguration.* MSM 80-100. SATB, opt kybd.

Hillert, Richard. *Verses and Offertory Sentences 1: Advent through Christmas.* CPH 97-5501. U.

Wetzler, Robert. *Verses and Offertories: Advent 1 through Baptism of Our Lord.* AFP 11-09541. SATB, kybd.

CHORAL MUSIC FOR THE SEASON

Buxtehude, Dietrich. "The Infant Jesus." CPH 97-6341. SATB, str, org.

Cherwien, David. "Ever Since the Savior Came." CPH 98-3351. U, org, opt fl.

Ferguson, John. "How Far Is It to Bethlehem." AFP 11-10756. SSA, pno.

Hyslop, Scott. "The Christmas Candles Glow." AFP 11-10956. SATB, kybd, fl.

Nanino, Giovanni Barnardino. "Hodie nobis coelerum Rex." (On This Day a King from Heaven). GIA G-4396. SATB.

Neswick, Bruce. "The Blessed Son of God." AFP 11-10787. SATB, org.

Poulenc, Francis. "Hodie Christus natus est." Salabert 15 (EAS 16762). SATB.

Schalk, Carl. "Where Shepherds Laterly Knelt." AFP 11-2456. SATB, org.

Scheidt, Samuel. "Psallite unigenito" (Sing, Rejoice) in *Christmas Magnificat*. CPH 98-2806. SATB, org. Lat/Ger/Eng.

Schulz-Widmar, Russell. "Midnight Clear." AFP 11-10250. SATB, org.

Sedio, Mark. "The Coventry Carol." SEL 405-234. 2 pt, org.

CHILDREN'S CHORAL MUSIC FOR THE SEASON

Beebe, Hank. "Huddle Close." CG CGA798. U/2 pt, kybd.

McRae, Shirley. " 'Twas in the Moon of Wintertime" in *Let Us Praise God*. AFP 11-7208. U, Orff inst, perc.

Page, Anna Laura. "O Little Town of Bethlehem." KIR K159. 2 pt, kybd, opt 2 oct hb.

Pelz, Walter. "Christmas Wonder." CG CGA523. U, flute, 2 oct hb, kybd.

Tucker, Margaret. "Welcome Song for the Baby Jesus." MSM 50-1400. U, kybd.

Wetzler, Robert. "Still, Still, Still." AFP 11-0401. U, org. opt fl.

Young, Philip. "When Christ, the Son of Mary." AFP 11-10779. SA, kybd.

INSTRUMENTAL MUSIC FOR THE SEASON

Burkhardt, Michael. "Three Carols for Oboe and Organ." MSM 20-164. Ob, org.

Callahan, Charles. "Christmas Music for Manuals, set 2." MSM 10-135. Org/kybd.

Marohic, Chuck. "Silent Night, Holy Night" in *Christmas Jazz: 5 Carols for Piano*. MSM 15-808. Pno.

Nelson, Ronald. "Three French Carols." AMSI OR-28. Org.

Osterland, Karl. "There's a Star in the East" in *I Wonder As I Wander: Seasonal Music for Organ*. AFP 11-10858. Org.

Wegner, Richard. "Christmas Meditation on an Old French Melody." MSM 10-138. Org.

HANDBELL MUSIC FOR THE SEASON

Helman, Michael. "The Friendly Beasts and We Wish You a Merry Christmas." AFP 11-10807. 3-5 oct.

Kinyon, Barbara. "Let's All Ring at Christmas." BEC HB 94. 2-3 oct.

Lloyd, Sallie. "Bring a Torch, Jeanette Isabella." BEC HB 27. 3 oct.

McChesney, Kevin./arr. Kastner. "O Holy Night." Jeffers S9139. Solo hb, kybd.

Rogers, Sharon Elery. "A Carol Festival." MSM 30-113. 3-5 oct.

Rogers, Sharon Elery. "The Snow Lay on the Ground." MSM 30-114. 2 oct.

Tucker, Margaret. "A German Christmas." CG CGB134. 3-5 oct, opt inst/SATB.

Wagner, Douglas. "An English Christmas." BEC HB 115. 3-5 oct or 2 oct w/org.

Young, Philip. "Sussex Carol." BEC HB 38. 4-5 oct.

ALTERNATE WORSHIP TEXTS

CONFESSION AND FORGIVENESS
In the name of the Father, and of the ✛ Son,
and of the Holy Spirit.
Amen

Beholding the miracle born in human flesh,
let us approach the God of grace
to confess our human sin and weakness.

Silence for reflection and self-examination.

God of grace,
we confess before you
that we have fled from your presence
to seek the false glory
of other gods around us.
We have often looked for you
in places of power and wealth,
not seeing your presence among
the ordinary dwelling places of our world.
Forgive our wandering ways,
and redirect us to forms of service
that fulfill your desire for us. Amen

In the mercy of God, Jesus Christ was given to die for you,
and for his sake God forgives you all your sins.
Amen

GREETING
A child has been born for us, a son given to us.
He is called Wonderful Counselor, Mighty God,
Everlasting Father, Prince of Peace.
The grace of our Lord Jesus Christ, the love of God,
and the communion of the Holy Spirit be with you all.
And also with you.

PRAYERS
Rejoicing in God's gift of gentle grace, let us pray for the church,
the world, and all on whom the light of Christ shines.

A brief silence.

Each petition ends:
God of grace,
hear our prayer.

Concluding petition
Hear our prayers, gracious God,
and bathe us always in the light of your Word made flesh,
Jesus Christ our Lord.
Amen

OFFERTORY PRAYER
God of time and eternity,
you have given your only Son,
born of Mary, to save and redeem us.
Bless us with all good things,
that the works of our hands
through all the years of our lives
may proclaim the news of your redeeming love
in Jesus Christ our Lord. Amen

INVITATION TO COMMUNION
In this holy sacrament
God makes a home with us.
Let us approach in wonder
at all that God has done.

POST-COMMUNION PRAYER
In this meal, O God,
we have beheld your glory,
and have been renewed in soul and body.
Strengthen us to be true to our calling to serve you,
and to proclaim the news
of your redeeming love
to all who are in need.
We ask this through Christ our Lord.
Amen

BENEDICTION
May you glory in the birth of the Son of God,
and may the blessing of almighty God,
the Father, ✛ Son, and Holy Spirit
be among you today and always.
Amen

DISMISSAL
Go in the peace of God's gift of love.
Thanks be to God.

CHRISTMAS

SEASONAL RITES

PROCLAMATION OF THE BIRTH OF CHRIST
Today, the twenty-fifth day of December,
unknown ages from the time when God created the heavens
and the earth and then formed man
and woman in his own image.

Several thousand years after the flood,
when God made the rainbow shine forth
as a sign of the covenant.
Twenty-one centuries from the time of Abraham and Sarah;
thirteen centuries after Moses led the people of Israel out of Egypt.

Eleven hundred years from the time of Ruth and the Judges;
one thousand years from the anointing of David as king;
in the sixty-fifth week according to the prophecy of Daniel.

In the one hundred and ninety-fourth Olympiad;
the seven hundred and fifty-second year from the foundation
    of the city of Rome.

The forty-second year of the reign of Octavian Augustus;
the whole world being at peace,
Jesus Christ, the eternal God and Son of the eternal Father,
desiring to sanctify the world by his most merciful coming,
being conceived by the Holy Spirit,
and nine months having passed since his conception,
was born in Bethlehem of Judea of the Virgin Mary.

Today is the nativity of our Lord Jesus Christ according to the flesh.

The Proclamation of the Birth of Christ may be reproduced for reader usage only, and should bear the following copyright notice: Text copyright © 1989 United States Catholic Conference, Washington, D.C. All rights reserved. Used by permission.

LESSONS AND CAROLS FOR CHRISTMAS
This service may be used during the twelve days of Christmas.

Stand
ENTRANCE HYMN
LBW 45   Oh, come, all ye faithful
WOV 643   Once in royal David's city

DIALOG
The people who walked in darkness have seen a great light.
The light shines in the darkness,
and the darkness has not overcome it.
Those who dwelt in the land of deep darkness,
on them light has shined.
We have beheld Christ's glory,
glory as of the only Son from the Father.
For to us a child is born, to us a Son is given.
In him was life, and the life was the light of all people.

OPENING PRAYER
The Lord be with you.
And also with you.
Let us pray.
Almighty God, you have filled us with the new light of the Word who became flesh and lived among us. Let the light of our faith shine in all we do; through your Son, Jesus Christ our Lord, who lives and reigns with you and the Holy Spirit, one God, now and forever.
Amen

Sit
LESSONS AND CAROLS
First Reading: Isaiah 9:2-7
LBW 58   Lo, how a rose is growing

Second Reading: Micah 5:2-5a
LBW 41   O little town of Bethlehem

Third Reading: Luke 1:26-35, 38
LBW 40   What child is this
WOV 634   Sing of Mary, pure and lowly

Fourth Reading: Luke 2:1-7
WOV 642   I wonder as I wander
WOV 644   Away in a manger

Fifth Reading: Luke 2:8-16
LBW 44   Infant holy, infant lowly
WOV 636   Before the marvel of this night

Sixth Reading: Luke 2:21-36
LBW 184   In his temple now behold him
May also be sung to REGENT SQUARE, *LBW 50.*

Seventh Reading: Matthew 2:1-11
LBW 56   The first Noel
WOV 646   We three kings of Orient are

Eighth Reading: Matthew 2:13-18
WOV 639   Oh, sleep now, holy baby
or Coventry Carol (*The Hymnal 1982*, 247)

Ninth Reading: John 1:1-14
LBW 42   Of the Father's love begotten
LBW 57   Let our gladness have no end

Stand
RESPONSIVE PRAYER
Glory to God in the highest,
and peace to God's people on earth.
Blessed are you, Prince of peace.
You rule the earth with truth and justice.
Send your gift of peace to all nations of the world.
Blessed are you, Son of Mary. You share our humanity.
Have mercy on the sick, the dying, and all who suffer this day.
Blessed are you, Son of God.
You dwell among us as the Word made flesh.
**Reveal yourself to us in word and sacrament
that we may bear your light to all the world.**

THE LORD'S PRAYER

BLESSING AND DISMISSAL
Let us bless the Lord.
Thanks be to God.
May you be filled with the wonder of Mary, the obedience of Joseph, the joy of the angels, the eagerness of the shepherds, the determination of the magi, and the peace of the Christ child. Almighty God, Father, ✝ Son, and Holy Spirit bless you now and forever.
Amen

SENDING HYMN
LBW 60   Hark! The herald angels sing

SERVICE FOR NEW YEAR'S EVE

During the evening of December 31, which is the eve of the Name of Jesus and also the eve of the civil New Year, the following service may be used.

This order for worship may begin with the service of light, pp. 142–45 in LBW. The prayer of the day for New Year's Eve may replace the prayer of thanksgiving on p. 144 of LBW.

After the service of light, two or more of the following readings are used, each followed by a Psalm, canticle, or hymn, and a prayer. The last reading would normally be from the New Testament.

THE HEBREW YEAR
Exodus 23:9-16, 20-21
Psalm 111 *or* Psalm 119:1-8
Hymn: Of the Father's love begotten (LBW 42)

Let us pray.
Silence
O God our Creator, you have divided our life into days and seasons, and called us to acknowledge your providence year after year. Accept your people who come to offer their praises, and, in your mercy, receive their prayers; through Jesus Christ our Lord.
Amen

THE PROMISED LAND
Deuteronomy 11:8-12, 26-28
Psalm 36:5-10 or Psalm 89:1-18
Hymn: Lift every voice and sing (LBW 562)

Let us pray.
Silence
Almighty God, the source of all life, giver of all blessing, and savior of all who turn to you: Have mercy upon this nation; deliver us from falsehood, malice, and disobedience; turn our feet into your paths; and grant that we may serve you in peace; through Jesus Christ our Lord.
Amen

A SEASON FOR ALL THINGS
Ecclesiastes 3:1-13
Psalm 90 *or* Psalm 8
Hymn: Day by day (WOV 746)

Let us pray.
Silence
In your wisdom, O Lord our God, you have made all things, and have allotted to each of us the days of our life. Grant that we may live in your presence, be guided by your Holy Spirit, and offer all our works to your honor and glory; through Jesus Christ our Lord.
Amen

REMEMBER YOUR CREATOR

Ecclesiastes 12:1-8

Psalm 130

Hymn: O God, our help in ages past (LBW 320)

Let us pray.

Silence

Immortal Lord God, you inhabit eternity, and have brought us your unworthy servants to the close of another year. Pardon, we entreat you, our transgressions of the past, and graciously abide with us all the days of our life; through Jesus Christ our Lord.

Amen

MARKING THE TIMES AND WINTER

Sirach 43:1-22

Psalm 19 *or* Psalm 148

Hymn: 'Twas in the moon of wintertime (LBW 72)

Let us pray.

Silence

Almighty Father, you give the sun for a light by day, and the moon and the stars by night. Graciously receive us, this night and always, into your favor and protection, defending us from all harm and governing us with your Holy Spirit, that every shadow of ignorance, every failure of faith or weakness of heart, every evil or wrong desire may be removed far from us; so that we, being justified in our Lord Jesus Christ, may be sanctified by your Spirit, and glorified by your infinite mercies in the day of the glorious appearing of our Lord and Savior Jesus Christ.

Amen

THE ACCEPTABLE TIME

2 Corinthians 5:17—6:2

Psalm 63:1-8

Hymn: Greet now the swiftly changing year (LBW 181)

Let us pray.

Silence

Most gracious and merciful God, you have reconciled us to yourself through Jesus Christ your Son, and called us to new life in him. Grant that we, who begin this year in his name, may complete it to his honor and glory; who lives and reigns now and forever.

Amen

A THOUSAND YEARS AS ONE DAY

2 Peter 3:8-15a

Psalm 119:89-96

Hymn: The Lord will come and not be slow (LBW 318; *alternate tune*: Carol, LBW 54)

Let us pray.

Silence

O God, through your Son you have taught us to be watchful, and to await the sudden day of judgment. Strengthen us against Satan and his forces of wickedness, the evil powers of this world, and the sinful desires within us; grant that, having served you all the days of our life, we may finally come to the dwelling place your Son has prepared for us; who lives and reigns forever and ever.

Amen

NEW HEAVENS AND NEW EARTH

Revelation 21:1-6a

LBW Canticle 21

Hymn: O Christ the same (WOV 778)

Let us pray.

Silence

Almighty and merciful God, through your well-beloved Son Jesus Christ, the King of kings and Lord of lords, you have willed to make all things new. Grant that we may be renewed by your Holy Spirit, and may come at last to that heavenly country where your people hunger and thirst no more, and the tears are wiped away from every eye; through Jesus Christ our Lord.

Amen

Matthew 25:31-46

A homily, sermon, or instruction may follow the readings.

An affirmation of baptism may follow, using the form provided on pp. 198–201 of LBW. *Begin with #12 on p. 199 and continue to the end of that order.*

The service may conclude in one of the following ways: with the singing of a hymn of praise, followed by the Lord's Prayer, the prayer of the day for the Name of Jesus, and benediction (see LBW, *p. 152); or with communion, beginning with the offering.*

Adapted from *The Book of Occasional Services* © 1994 Church Pension Fund. Used by permission.

DECEMBER 24, 1999

THE NATIVITY OF OUR LORD
CHRISTMAS EVE (I)

INTRODUCTION

At darkest night we gather to celebrate the great light of our salvation. More than the celebration of a birth, Christmas marks the mystery of the incarnation—God sharing our humanity. In this liturgy Christ is present among us—as the word of hope and peace proclaimed to us, and as the word made flesh in communion. With the heavenly host we sing, "Glory to God in the highest heaven," and like the shepherds we return to our homes, workplaces, and communities to tell of the wonders we have seen and heard.

PRAYER OF THE DAY

Almighty God, you made this holy night shine with the brightness of the true Light. Grant that here on earth we may walk in the light of Jesus' presence and in the last day wake to the brightness of his glory; through your only Son, Jesus Christ our Lord, who lives and reigns with you and the Holy Spirit, one God, now and forever.

READINGS

Isaiah 9:2-7

Originally, this poem was written to celebrate either the birth or the coronation of a new Davidic king. After the fall of Jerusalem, this poem came to be viewed as an expression of the hope that eventually God would raise up a new ruler who would possess the qualities described in the text.

Psalm 96

Let the heavens rejoice and the earth be glad. (Ps. 96:11)

Titus 2:11-14

The brief letter to Titus is concerned with matters regarding church leadership. Here the letter cites an early confession of faith as an example of sound Christian doctrine.

Luke 2:1-14 [15-20]

Luke tells the story of Jesus' birth with reference to rulers of the world because this birth has significance for the whole earth, and conveys a divine offer of peace.

COLOR White

THE PRAYERS

Rejoicing in God's gift of gentle grace, let us pray for the church, the world, and all on whom the light of Christ shines.

A BRIEF SILENCE.

Wonderful Counselor, you increase our joy as the church gathers on this holy night to sing of our dear Savior's birth. May the story of salvation live in the hearts of all who sing of its wonders. God of grace,
hear our prayer.

Mighty God, you have broken the yoke of sin's burden through the birth of your Son. Comfort those whose burdens distract them from the deeper peace of this holy night and grant them a restful mind. God of grace,
hear our prayer.

Everlasting Father, uphold all who are in sorrow or need of your divine goodness and mercy (especially . . .). We remember with thanksgiving all who have died and who now rest in your peaceful light. God of grace,
hear our prayer.

Prince of Peace, may your reign be known in all places that know fighting and unrest, and grant resolution to conflicts throughout the world. God of grace,
hear our prayer.

HERE OTHER INTERCESSIONS MAY BE OFFERED.

Hear our prayers, gracious God, and bathe us always in the light of your Word made flesh, Jesus Christ our Lord.
Amen

IMAGES FOR PREACHING

Some things can only be seen in the dark. The flicker of candlelight or a lantern brings out subtle details that would be missed in the bright light of day. People who have walked in a land of deep darkness are ready to see many things, their pupils dilated to take in all of God's revelation. Advent was meant to get our eyes used to the dark. It means the flash of glory may be blinding!

But the real story this night is not the flutter of angel wings nor the brilliance of ground zero over shepherds' fields. No, the one who is center stage is to be found also in the dark. The miracle is the wrapping of the light in that which is opaque—human flesh and blood—and laid within a feeding trough. The sign is not the angel song but something as common as a diaper and a blanket.

As with the packages waiting at our homes, so here in the Christmas story, the full meaning of the gift is both package and what is inside. Sometimes the wrapping is as important as the contents. The wrapping is usually what tells for whom the gift is given and from whom the gift has been received. So it is also with this first and best of all Christmas gifts. "For you" is so profound once we realize it means God is now one of us. The phrase stands beside others: "with you" (Immanuel!), "in you" (eucharistic, but also, as we shall see come Christmas Day, God working divine nature into our very human flesh and blood).

Thus, the grace of God has appeared not merely for our entertainment or our sentimental enjoyment of lost innocence. No! God has appeared among us, giving the divine self for us, that we might be trained and transformed. Jesus' birth is meant to be the beginning of new birth for us. And it begins not in the bright glory of day. It begins in the dark.

WORSHIP MATTERS

The propers for Christmas Eve abound with images of the incarnation as the bursting of God's light within the midst of absolute darkness. These images should be developed fully within the Christmas Eve liturgy, especially when the service is celebrated under the cloak of darkness, preferably at midnight. Although the three traditional Christmas services were all eucharists, many congregations may also celebrate a service of the word or an evening prayer on Christmas Eve. This celebration would commend the use of the service of light (*LBW* Ministers edition, pp. 58–61) with the seasonal propers (p. 93). The themes of light and darkness suggest the abundant use of candles. Artificial light should be kept at a minimum to accentuate the advent of God's light in the midst of human darkness.

LET THE CHILDREN COME

The mystery of the incarnation is what Christmas celebrates. Those who use a crèche might consider placing the Jesus figure near the altar. Children especially appreciate the concrete connection between the shepherds going to the manger to see Jesus and the congregation going to the altar to receive Jesus' body and blood. Here we see and hear this word that has taken place. Here we see and hear Jesus. Children, with the whole congregation, are a living crèche as the living Word is heard and seen in our midst.

MUSIC FOR WORSHIP
SERVICE MUSIC

As offertory music, consider the hymn "Let all mortal flesh keep silence" (LBW 198), the text of which has its origins at this place in the service on this night. With instrumental interludes, it may be long enough to cover both the gathering of the gifts and their presentation at the altar as the assembly stands on stanza 4. The setting by Gustav Holst (Mercury Music) may serve in the same way.

GATHERING

LBW 39   Joy to the world
WOV 643 Once in royal David's city

PSALM 96

Christopherson, Dorothy. "The Lord Is King." AFP 11-10173. U, opt cong, kybd.

Haas, David/Marty Haugen. "Psalm 96: Proclaim to All the Nations" in *Gather Comprehensive*. GIA.

Harbor, Rawn. "Let the Heavens Rejoice and the Earth Be Glad" in *This Far by Faith*.

Hobby, Robert. PW, cycle B.

Hurd, David. "Psalm 96." AFP 11-10107. SATB/U, opt cong.

Jenkins, Stephen. "A Christmas Psalm." MSM 80-102. SATB/U, cong, org.

Ollis, Peter. "Today a Saviour Has Been Born." PS, vol. 1.

HYMN OF THE DAY

WOV 636 Before the marvel of this night
         MARVEL

VOCAL RESOURCES

Schalk, Carl. "Before the Marvel of This Night." AFP 11-2005. Also in *The Augsburg Choirbook*. 11-10817. SATB, org, opt 2 vln, vla, vc, hrn fl/ob. 11-2004. Inst pts.

INSTRUMENTAL RESOURCES

Powell, Robert. "Marvel" in *Thine the Praise, vol. II*. CPH 97-6280. Org.

Young, Jeremy. "Before the Marvel of This Night" in *Pianoforte Christmas: Christmas Carols for Piano Solo*. AFP 11-10716. Kybd.

ALTERNATE HYMN OF THE DAY

LBW 51   From heaven above
LBW 47   Let all together praise our God

COMMUNION

LBW 44   Infant holy, infant lowly
WOV 644   Away in the manger

SENDING

LBW 65   Silent night, holy night!
WOV 641   Peace came to earth

ADDITIONAL HYMNS AND SONGS

LLC 297   Gloria en las alturas/Glory in the highest
TFF 56   Hush, little Jesus boy
PH 47   Still, still, still
W&P   All is ready now

MUSIC FOR THE DAY

CHORAL

Brandvik, Paul. "What Is This Fragrance?" AFP 11-10954. SATB.
Britten, Benjamin. "A Boy Was Born." OXF X92. SATB.
Franck, César/arr. K. Lee Scott. "Nativity Lullaby" in *Rejoice Now, My Spirit; Vocal Solos for the Church Year*. AFP 11-10228 (MH); 11-10229 (ML).
Hurd, David. "A Cradle Song." AFP 11-10460. SATB, org.
Hyslop, Scott. "Hush You, My Baby." AFP 11-10885. SAB, org, ob.
Nelson, Bradley. "Song for Christmas Eve." AFP 11-10894. SATB, pno.
Reger, Max/arr. K. Lee Scott. "The Virgin's Slumber Song" in *Sing a Song of Joy; Vocal Solos for Worship*. AFP 11-8194 (MH); 11-8195 (ML).

Sedio, Mark. "To Thee with Joy I Sing." CPH 98-3443. SATB.
Stultz, Marie. "Quem pastores laudavere" in *Suite on the Nativity*. MSM 70-105. SATB, desc.
Sweelinck, Jan Pieter. "Hodie Christus natus est." Columbo. FC338. SSATB.

CHILDREN'S CHOIRS

Nelson, Betty Lou and Ronald A. "The King of Love" (A Christmas Carol Play). CG CGC30. U/2 pt, cong, kybd.
Wetzler, Robert. "Still, Still, Still." AFP 11-0401. U, org, opt fl.

KEYBOARD/INSTRUMENTAL

Farlee, Robert Buckley. "Past Three O'Clock" in *Carols for Organ and Oboe*. AFP 11-10865. Org, inst.
Langlais, Jean. "La Nativité" in *Poemes Evangeliques*. Philippo distributed by Elkan Vogel. P32.359. Org.

HANDBELL

Afdahl, Lee J. "Three Spanish Carols." AFP 11-10990. 2-3 oct.
Kinyon, Barbara. "Song of the Crib." CPH 97-6669. 2-3 oct hb, 2-3 oct hc.
Tucker, Sondra K. "Sweet Little Jesus Boy." CPH 97-6667. 2-3 oct, fl.

PRAISE ENSEMBLE

Angerman, David and Joseph M. Martin. "Sing! Shout! Jubilate!" FLA A7134. SATB, acc.
Estes, Jerry. "Hark! The Herald Angels Sing." Lavirt Music HT9701. 3 pt mxd, pno.
Gorieb and Hosman. "A King Is Born" in *Hosanna! Music Songbook 8*. INT.
Gruber, Franz/arr. Robinson. "Silent Night." Sparkle SV9830. SATB, acc. Also available in SAB.
Landis, Keith. "Name of All Majesty" in *Renew*. HOP.
Lindh, Jody W. "Come, Let Us Sing." CG CGA-478. U, kybd.
Sterling, Robert. "Away in a Manger." WRD 301095316x. SATB, orch.

DECEMBER 25, 1999

THE NATIVITY OF OUR LORD
CHRISTMAS DAWN (II)

INTRODUCTION

The liturgy proclaims, "To you is born this day a Savior!" The scriptures announce the presence of God among the people of the earth. At the table, we meet the child born of Mary, our crucified and risen Lord. Through baptism we have become children of the true Light. We go forth to proclaim the news of great joy: God is with us.

PRAYER OF THE DAY

Almighty God, you have made yourself known in your Son, Jesus, redeemer of the world. We pray that his birth as a human child will set us free from the old slavery of our sin; through Jesus Christ our Lord, who lives and reigns with you and the Holy Spirit, one God, now and forever.

READINGS

Isaiah 62:6-12
Salvation will come to the holy city of Jerusalem.
Psalm 97
Light has sprung up for the righteous. (Ps. 97:11)
Titus 3:4-7
Because of Jesus' earthly appearance, we know that we are saved by the grace of God.
Luke 2:[1-7] 8-20
A song from angels and news announcing Jesus' birth come first to shepherds living in the fields outside Bethlehem.

COLOR White

THE PRAYERS

Rejoicing in God's gift of gentle grace, let us pray for the church, the world, and all on whom the light of Christ shines.

A BRIEF SILENCE.

Kind and loving God, we bless you for the wondrous appearance of your Son who became human to dwell among us. On this blessed morning that celebrates his birth, may Christ be born in us today. God of grace,
hear our prayer.

Saving God, you proclaim to the ends of the earth the salvation that is for all people. Bless all servants of your church who tell again the story of your wondrous love. God of grace,
hear our prayer.

O Light of the world, you entered the creation to become one with it. Cure the warring madness of the nations, that peace may prevail on the earth you have made. God of grace,
hear our prayer.

Holy and redeeming one, you never forsake us but always seek us out. In the quiet of this Christmas dawn, remind all who suffer of your tender love which guards and guides us until our life's end (especially . . .). God of grace,
hear our prayer.

God of hope and comfort, you promise an eternal dawn to those who love your appearing. Keep us united with those who have died and who now rest in your holy wings. God of grace,
hear our prayer.

HERE OTHER INTERCESSIONS MAY BE OFFERED.

Hear our prayers, gracious God, and bathe us always in the light of your Word made flesh, Jesus Christ our Lord.
Amen

IMAGES FOR PREACHING

The real test of Christmas comes with the daylight. It is easy to wax romantic about a birth in a barn when it happens in the dark. The snorts and bleats of animals feel warm and friendly when the beasts are in the shadow. But what does the scene look like in the light of day? The straw is not so clean! The earthy smells come from various scatological piles scattered everywhere. How does the Christmas gospel play at 7 A.M.?

The real test of Christmas comes with the daylight. How good is this news? Will it hold up after the rest of the gifts are opened, when the broken bows and ripped wrappings lay scattered like Yuletide carcasses? What were Mary's musings on the morning after? Oh yes, even birth in a barn is a wonder when shepherds bring stories of angelic birth announcements. After all, Mary has had visitors of her own! But now it is day, and the full weight of the revelation is about to sink in. What has happened? What has happened to them? What will happen to them now that they hold the flesh of God?

Mary not only ponders; she also treasures. She is an amazing woman! It is what she said from the beginning: "I am the handmaid." She is willing to let her very flesh and blood be entangled with God. It happens to us, too, as the second reading reminds us, through the water of rebirth. As beautiful as angel song at midnight might be, this story is going to be played out in the full light of day—in what will happen at the office or in the classroom or the kitchen come Monday morning. The miracle is only beginning! You see, it is dawn.

WORSHIP MATTERS

Isaiah's description of Zion's sentinels praying as they await the advent of God's salvation is a good description of how the church lives between Christ's incarnation and his second coming. Like Israel, the church conceived of itself as a body continually at prayer. The church should not allow practical concerns to undermine this divinely appointed responsibility. Concerns of insufficient time and cost effectiveness should not be the only factors when determining whether to offer services. When services are eliminated on the basis of such arguments, the people of God are encouraged to think that prayer is an occasional activity. Offer opportunities to gather for prayer frequently, especially during festivals. Encourage the assembly to use the daily prayer services at home. Worship leaders can motivate the use of worship resources in the home and assist the assembly in knowing how to use the daily prayer services at home.

LET THE CHILDREN COME

God is with us in Jesus. We are joined to God by the living Word and the Holy Spirit in baptism (compare Titus 3:5). Some congregations might place the baptismal font front and center, open and containing water, with the crèche nearby. Baptism is our entrance into the saving events depicted in the crèche. When we touch the water and make the sign of the cross, touching our forehead, chest, and shoulders, we remember that Jesus is "true God, begotten of the Father from eternity," and also truly human, "born of the virgin Mary" (Small Catechism, second article of the creed).

MUSIC FOR WORSHIP

SERVICE MUSIC

At a simpler early service on Christmas Day, a congregational setting of the Gloria may be all the music that is needed in the gathering rite, omitting entrance hymn and Kyrie.

GATHERING

LBW 60	Hark! The herald angels sing
LBW 43	Rejoice, rejoice this happy morn

PSALM 97

Beckett, Debbie. "This Day New Light Will Shine" in PS, vol. 1.
Guimont, Michel. "Psalm 97: The Lord Is King" in *Gather Comprehensive*. GIA.
Hobby, Robert. PS, Cycle B.
Hopson, Hal H. "Psalm 97" in *Psalm Refrains and Tones for the Common Lectionary*. HOP 425. U, cong.
Hopson, Hal H. "Psalm 97" in TP.
Marcus, Mary. "The Nativity of Our Lord/Christmas Day" in *Psalm Antiphons-2*. MSM 80-722.

HYMN OF THE DAY

LBW 70	Go tell it on the mountain
	GO TELL IT

VOCAL RESOURCES

Best, Harold. "Go Tell It on the Mountain." HOP HO 1825. SATB, kybd.

INSTRUMENTAL RESOURCES

Albrecht, Timothy. "Go Tell It" in *Grace Notes, vol. I*. AFP 11-9925. Org.
Callahan, Charles. "Go Tell It" in *Spirituals for Keyboard*. MSM 10-890. Kybd.
Ferguson, John. "Go Tell It" in *Hymn Tune Harmonizations, Book III*. LUD 0-10. Org.
Hassell, Michael. "Go Tell It" in *Jazz December*. AFP 11-10796. Pno.

ALTERNATE HYMN OF THE DAY

LBW 55	Good Christian friends, rejoice
WOV 643	Once in royal David's city

CHRISTMAS DEC 25

COMMUNION
LBW 40   What child is this
WOV 701   What feast of love

SENDING
LBW 161   O day full of grace
WOV 645   There's a star in the East

ADDITIONAL HYMNS AND SONGS
DATH 52   For all people Christ was born
H82 91   Break forth, O beauteous heavenly light
H82 106   Christians, awake, salute the happy morn
W&P   Trees of the field

MUSIC FOR THE DAY

CHORAL
Batastini, Robert J. "Gaudete." GIA G-3056. SATB, hb, fc, drm.
Caracciolo, Stephen. "There Is No Rose of Such Virtue." MSM 50-1028. SATB.
Ferguson, John. "Unto Us Is Born God's Son." AFP 11-10449. SATB, org.
Franck, César/arr. K. Lee Scott. "Nativity Lullaby" in *Rejoice Now, My Spirit; Vocal Solos for the Church Year.* AFP 11-10228 (MH); 11-10229 (ML).
Handel, G. F./arr. Hal H. Hopson. "Sing and Be Joyful." AFP 11-10915. SATB, kybd.
Nestor, Leo. "A Child Is Born." ECS 4389. SATB. org.
Praetorius, Michael. "En Natus Est Emmanuel." BEL OCT 02531. SATB, opt brass (OCT 02531A).

CHILDREN'S CHOIRS
Collins, Dori Erwin. "Hasten Now, O Shepherds/Vamos Pastorcitos." AFP 11-10726. U, desc, pno, fl, gtr, perc.
Mozart/arr. Hal H. Hopson. "Prepare the Way of the Lord." CG CGA624. 2/3 pt. mxd, kybd.

KEYBOARD/INSTRUMENTAL
Bach, J. S. "Chorale Prelude on 'In dulci jubilo'" in *The Oxford Book of Christmas Organ Music.* OXF. Org.
Willcocks, David. "Prelude on 'Irby'" in *The Oxford Book of Christmas Organ Music.* OXF. Org.

HANDBELL
Krentz, Michael E. "Angels We Have Heard on High." AFP 11-10715. 3 oct.
Larson, Katherine Jordahl. "When Christmas Morn Is Dawning." AFP 11-10470. 3-5 oct.
Moklebust, Cathy. "Carol of the Bells." CG CGB164. 2 oct.
Morris, Hart. "Feliz Navidad." Red River Music HB0013. 3-5 oct, opt hc, gtr, perc.

PRAISE ENSEMBLE
Carter, John. "Dancing into the Promise." SOM AD2056. 3 pt mxd, pno.
Catherwood, David. "Child in the Manger." ALF 7958. SAB, acc, fl.
Estes, Jerry. "Angels We Have Heard on High." Lavirt Music HT9501. SAB, pno.
Founds, Rick and Batstone. "We Praise You for Your Glory" in *Maranatha! Music Praise Chorus Book, 3rd ed.* WRD/MAR.
Keaggy, Cheri. "There Is Joy in the Lord" in *Maranatha! Music Praise Chorus Book, 3rd ed.* WRD/MAR.
Martin, Gilbert M. "The Jesus Gift." HIN HMC-235. SATB, pno.

DECEMBER 25, 1999

THE NATIVITY OF OUR LORD
CHRISTMAS DAY (III)

INTRODUCTION

Since the beginning of time, the coming of light has been a sign of life and hope. The sun and the stars transform the darkness into an inhabitable space. On the festival of the Lord's nativity, the church gathers to celebrate the light of God's grace present in Christ. In the holy bath of baptism, he enlightens and claims us as brothers and sisters. In the holy word of scripture, he speaks to us of God's love for each human being. In the holy meal of the eucharist, he gives us the bread of eternal life. From this festive liturgy we go forth to be lightbearers in the ordinary rhythms of daily life.

PRAYER OF THE DAY

Almighty God, you wonderfully created and yet more wonderfully restored the dignity of human nature. In your mercy, let us share the divine life of Jesus Christ who came to share our humanity, and who now lives and reigns with you and the Holy Spirit, one God, now and forever.

READINGS

Isaiah 52:7-10

In chapters 40–55, the prophet announces that the Lord will soon end the exile of God's people in Babylon. In today's reading, the prophet again announces this victory. Note that he is so certain this victory will take place that he announces his message in the past tense, as though it has already happened.

Psalm 98

All the ends of the earth have seen the victory of our God. (Ps. 98:4)

Hebrews 1:1-4 [5-12]

The opening words of this stately epistle present Jesus as the ultimate message of God to us, as the one who perfectly reveals God's glory and being.

John 1:1-14

The prologue to the Gospel of John describes Jesus as the creative Word of God made flesh, God's true presence among us, the one whose very existence reveals God as "full of grace and truth."

COLOR White

THE PRAYERS

Rejoicing in God's gift of gentle grace, let us pray for the church, the world, and all on whom the light of Christ shines.

A BRIEF SILENCE.

Let us pray that we, being anointed with the oil of gladness, may celebrate the birth of our Savior with joy and thanksgiving. God of grace,

hear our prayer.

Let us pray for bishops, pastors, and all the people of your church who speak the glories of the Word made flesh, that they may proclaim your reign of love. God of grace,

hear our prayer.

Let us pray for the peoples of all nations, whose eyes are straining to see peace and salvation. May they be governed by good rulers who are led by your wisdom and justice. God of grace,

hear our prayer.

Let us pray for those in need, whose minds and bodies cry out for hope and healing (especially . . .), that they may know your mercy and lovingkindness. God of grace,

hear our prayer.

Let us pray for those who travel during these holy days, that their journeys may be safe and their homecomings full of joy. God of grace,

hear our prayer.

HERE OTHER INTERCESSIONS MAY BE OFFERED.

Let us give thanks for our beloved dead, with whom we remain united in your eternal communion of saints. God of grace,

hear our prayer.

Hear our prayers, gracious God, and bathe us always in the light of your Word made flesh, Jesus Christ our Lord.
Amen

IMAGES FOR PREACHING

The impact of the good news of Christmas is so expansive that it finally must break beyond the Christmas story itself. The explosion of light that takes place above shepherds' fields sends out shock waves and (as we shall discover twelve days from now) even will ignite a star.

In the weeks ahead we will see the christological moment working itself out on many levels in many places in the Jesus story. But here, in these propers for Christmas Day, the story gets projected onto a cosmic screen: *in the beginning . . . from the beginning . . . Creating-Word made flesh!* We will hear these words again toward the end of the feast two Sundays down the road. But here, in the full light of the Christmas sun, we exult in the warmth of that love that announces salvation. And even more, as the prayer of the day proclaims, that love restores the dignity of our human nature by sharing the divine life of Christ with us.

The warmth of this love is working its way inside us—as warm as the eucharistic wine, which we not only taste but feel. God is here! Not only among us, but working the divine self into our own flesh and blood. Thus, we too are born with Christ—not of blood, not of the will of flesh, but of God! It is not only Jesus' Christmas; it is ours!

The gift we have been given this day is nothing less than ourselves. We have been given our very selves, our nature, back to us again. We have been given the gift to be and become what we were meant to be all along. Miracle of miracles! Eden's apple has been unbitten! And so, as Hebrews reminds us, we have left one epoch behind and entered another. These are, indeed, the last days! Something wondrous and incredible is beginning to happen—in us, through us. And one thing is for certain—it is day!

WORSHIP MATTERS

"The Word became flesh and lived among us, and we have seen his glory" (John 1:14). At every eucharist the incarnate Word appears enfleshed before the assembly in the earthy, sacramental substances of bread, water, and wine, and in the expressions of human speech. The reading and preaching of the written word, central acts within the eucharistic celebration, should be conducted so as to demonstrate the respect, awe, and joy the incarnation itself produces. Especially on the festival of the incarnation these two central acts should be highlighted. The lectionary, which on all occasions should be a prominent and visible symbol of the incarnate Word, could be prominently displayed in a procession, held before the assembly for all three readings, and honored with incense. A gospel procession might be considered. Worship leaders might choose more elaborate musical selections for the psalm and gospel acclamation, so as to highlight the reading of the word. Through such heightened emphasis, the assembly rejoices in the presence of the incarnate Word.

LET THE CHILDREN COME

Children learn best through concrete experience. Literal young minds find it hard to grasp "Jesus is in your heart," for they can see neither their heart nor Jesus. Christmas changes things: Jesus is a baby we can see, a rabbi we can hear, a crucified savior visible to all. He is visible in his body, the church; we see, hear, and touch him in baptism, absolution, and communion. Wherever the church is gathered, we see Jesus. Whenever we see Jesus, we see God. Read the gospel from an illustrated text, allowing the children to use multiple senses in "seeing Jesus."

MUSIC FOR WORSHIP

GATHERING

LBW 45	Oh, come, all ye faithful
LBW 55	Good Christian friends, rejoice

PSALM 98

Beall, Mary Kay. "Psalm 98" in *Sing Out! A Children's Psalter*. WLP. U/kybd.

Grotenhuis, Dale. "New Songs of Celebration/Ps 98." SEL 241-098, SATB, org, brass, cong.

Haugen, Marty/arr. David Haas. "All the Ends of the Earth: Psalm 98." GIA G-2703. U/SATB, cant/choir, cong, opt gtr.

Hobby, Robert. PW, Cycle B.

Hurd, David. "Cantate Domino-Psalm 98." AFP 11-10151. SATB.

Johnson, Alan. "All the Ends of the Earth" in PS, vol. 1.

Lau, Robert. "Sing to the Lord a New Song." AFP 11-10086. SATB.

LBW 39   Joy to the world (psalm paraphrase)

Pelz, Walter L. "Psalm 98." AFP 11-10052. SATB, cong, 2 tpt, 2 tbn.

HYMN OF THE DAY

LBW 60	Hark! The herald angels sing
	MENDELSSOHN

VOCAL RESOURCES

Powell, Robert J. "Hark! The Herald Angels Sing." GIA G-2533. SATB, cong, str.

Willcocks, David. "Hark! The Herald Angels Sing" in *One Hundred Carols for Choirs*. OXF 0-19-353227-1.

INSTRUMENTAL RESOURCES

Cherwien, David. "Mendelssohn" in *Interpretations, Book XI*. AMSI SP-108. Org.

Leavitt, John. "Hark! The Herald Angels Sing" in *A Little Nativvity Suite*. AFP 11-10351. Org.

McChesney, Kevin. "Angel Glory." AFP 11-10515. Hb.

Young, Jeremy. "Hark! The Herald Angels Sing" in *Pianoforte Christmas: Christmas Carols for Piano Solo*. AFP 11-10716. Pno/kybd.

ALTERNATE HYMN OF THE DAY

LBW 70	Go tell it on the mountain
LBW 55	Good Christian friends, rejoice

COMMUNION

LBW 42	Of the Father's love begotten
WOV 638	Holy Child within the manger

SENDING

LBW 47	Let all together praise our God
LBW 50	Angels, from the realms of glory

ADDITIONAL HYMNS AND SONGS

PH 27	Gentle Mary laid her child
H82 633	Word of God, come down on earth
TFF 99	How lovely on the mountains
W&P	What have we to offer

MUSIC FOR THE DAY

CHORAL

Christopherson, Dorothy and Tom. "The Virgin Mary Had a Baby Boy." CPH 98-3284. SAB, perc, pno.

Ferguson, John. "Rejoice, Rejoice, This Happy Morn." MSM 50-1053. SATB, vla.

Franck, César/arr. Patrick Liebergren. "O Lord, I Pray to Thee" (Panis angelicus) in *Favorite Sacred Classic for Solo Singers*. ALF 11482 (ML); 11481 (MH).

Hovland, Egil. "The Glory of the Father." WAL W 2973. SATB.

Roberts, Paul. "The Word Became Flesh." AFP 11-10899. SATB, fl.

Spivak, J./arr. Valerie Shields. "Ma navu." MFS 820. SA, vln, pno.

Victoria, T. L. "O Magnum Mysterium." GSCH 10193. SATB.

CHILDREN'S CHOIRS

Marshall, Jane. "Psalm 98." CG CGA427. U antiphonal, kybd.

Mendelssohn/arr. Coggin. "How Lovely Are the Messengers." CG CGA501. SAB, kybd.

KEYBOARD/INSTRUMENTAL

Hopson, Hal. "French Carol Miniatures for Organ and Harpsichord or Piano." SMP FCMC-2. Org/hpd/pno.

Willcocks, David. "Postlude on 'Hark, the Herald Angels Sing'" in *The Oxford Book of Christmas Organ Music*. OXF. Org.

HANDBELL

Krentz, Michael E. "Angels We Have Heard on High." AFP 11-10715. 3 oct.

Larson, Katherine Jordahl. "When Christmas Morn Is Dawning." AFP 11-10470. 3-5 oct.

Moklebust, Cathy. "Carol of the Bells." CG CGB164. 2 oct.

Morris, Hart. "Feliz Navidad." Red River Music HB0013. 3-5 oct, opt hc, gtr, perc.

PRAISE ENSEMBLE

Angerman, David and Joseph M. Martin. "Sing! Shout! Jubilate!" FLA A7134. SATB, acc.

Dearman, Kirk. "Above All Else" in *Songs for Praise and Worship*. WRD.

Smith, Byron J. "Worthy to Be Praised." LAW 52654. SATB, pno.

Smith, Leonard E. "Our God Reigns" in *Songs for Praise and Worship*. WRD.

Ylvisaker, John. "Great Is Our God" in *Borning Cry*. NGP.

Ziegenhals, Harriet. "Oh, Sing to the Lord." CG CGA640. U/2 pt, kybd, perc.

DECEMBER 26, 1999

ST. STEPHEN, DEACON AND MARTYR

INTRODUCTION

The joy of Christmas is juxtaposed with the harsh realities of the world as we commemorate St. Stephen, the first Christian martyr. Having heard the angels sing of peace to God's people on earth at the birth of Christ, we now hear of Stephen being stoned to death. Even as we continue to celebrate the birth of Christ during the twelve days of Christmas, today we mark Stephen's birth into eternal life. Nourished by Christ's body and blood, we pray that we would also forgive our enemies as did Jesus and Stephen, and thus witness to a love that is stronger than death.

PRAYER OF THE DAY

Grant us grace, O Lord, that like Stephen we may learn to love even our enemies and seek forgiveness for those who desire our hurt; through your Son, Jesus Christ our Lord, who lives and reigns with you and the Holy Spirit, one God, now and forever.

READINGS

2 Chronicles 24:17-22

In this reading, a chief's son, Zechariah, is stoned in the temple for testifying that the people had abandoned God. This story serves both as a parallel to the martyrdom of Stephen and as a reminder that actions have consequences, and that God cares how people act.

Psalm 17:1-9, 16 (Psalm 17:1-9, 15 [NRSV])

I call upon you, O God, for you will answer me. (Ps. 17:6)

Acts 6:8—7:2a, 51-60

The Christian community is growing rapidly. Even priests, along with Jews from all sorts of backgrounds, have joined the group of disciples. But as the community grows, so does the opposition, which now becomes violent. Listen as Stephen echoes Jesus' prayer of forgiveness for his opponents.

Matthew 23:34-39

Matthew 23 is a polemic aimed at the religious leaders of Jesus' day. This passage is one of the most radical, accusing the "scribes and Pharisees" (verse 29) of murdering God's messengers. The picture of the Pharisees is one-sided and, therefore misleading, but it shows Matthew's concern that all come to repentance.

COLOR Red

THE PRAYERS

Rejoicing in God's gift of gentle grace, let us pray for the church, the world, and all on whom the light of Christ shines.

A BRIEF SILENCE.

Let us pray for all places of the world, that those facing persecution would be given courage and strength to hold fast to the confession of your name. God of grace,
hear our prayer.

Let us pray for the leaders of nations who sanction religious discrimination, that their hearts would be moved to embrace a governance of openness and tolerance. God of grace,
hear our prayer.

Let us pray for those who suffer from abuse and intolerance, for all who are persecuted for their faith, and for all who look to you for hope and healing (especially . . .). God of grace,
hear our prayer.

Let us pray for our society, which is on the threshold of the third millennium. May justice and peace take possession of our world as we enter by your grace into this new era. God of grace,
hear our prayer.

HERE OTHER INTERCESSIONS MAY BE OFFERED.

Let us remember with thanksgiving those who have gone before us and who, with St. Stephen, now rest from their labors in the company of all your saints in everlasting light. God of grace,
hear our prayer.

Hear our prayers, gracious God, and bathe us always in the light of your Word made flesh, Jesus Christ our Lord.
Amen

IMAGES FOR PREACHING

The three days after Christmas have been reserved for the companions of Christ *(comites Christi)*. St. Stephen (whose day falls this year on a Sunday) is remembered as a martyr in deed as well as in will. St. John is commemorated December 27—a martyr in will, if not in deed. The slaughter of the Holy Innocents—who were martyrs in deed, if not in will—is remembered December 28. In many ways, these three make strange companions for the infant Jesus. (Would you want *your* child to have such playmates?) And that is precisely the point!

The gift of the three companions is to shock us out of nostalgia and romanticism and to startle us into a recognition of the implications of God's coming among us. This child is here not on a state visit or a package tour; this child has come here to die.

Luke has so structured his two-volume story of Jesus that a number of significant details from the passion narrative end up in Acts as incidents in the deaths of the martyrs (see Raymond Brown, *Death of the Messiah*). The lesson is clear: the story of Jesus is unfolding in the lives of disciples. They, too, forgive. And yes they, too, die for their faith. This mixing of life and death is the implication of incarnation: what happens when God gets wrapped up in our human flesh and blood. In one sense it is nothing new; it happened to Zechariah long ago. But something *is* new: those who live and die entangled in Christ seek not vengeance but forgiveness.

How strange that songs of Passion Sunday and words of the Sanctus should drift into our ears mere hours after the birth. But then, this story is all about a startling juxtaposition—not only for Jesus, not only for Stephen, but for us as well, *this generation* of disciples, as Matthew says. This living and dying is all part of what is meant when we sing, "Blessed is the one who comes in the name of the Lord!"

WORSHIP MATTERS

See the first Sunday after Christmas.

LET THE CHILDREN COME

"Deacon" refers to one set apart to serve the poor and widowed, particularly at the Lord's supper (compare Acts 6:1-7). Show children how the altar is set for communion. Explain the importance of setting the table and cleaning up afterward. If you have eucharistic ministers, tell the children that these deacons take the bread and wine and Jesus' word to the people who cannot come to church. When deacons are installed, have children give each one a Bible and containers for the elements. Invite the children to pray with them before they go out. When possible, include children in the visits.

MUSIC FOR WORSHIP

GATHERING

LBW 55	Good Christian friends, rejoice
WOV 642	I wonder as I wander

PSALM 17:1-9, 16

Honoré, Jeffrey. "Psalms Together." CG CGC-18.
Marcello, B. "Oh, Hold Thou Me Up." CPH 98-1046. 2pt.
Pavlechko, Thomas. PW, Cycle C.

HYMN OF THE DAY

LBW 54	It came upon the midnight clear
	CAROL

VOCAL RESOURCES

Burkhardt, Michael. "Carol" in *Accompaniments and Descants for Carols Sung in Harmony*. MSM 10-129.
Frahm, Frederick. "It Came Upon the Midnight Clear." Live Oak House 2231. U/SATB/str, opt C inst, org.
Powell, Robert. "It Came Upon the Midnight Clear." GIA G-2534. SATB, cong, str.

INSTRUMENTAL RESOURCES

Burkhardt, Michael. "Carol" in *'Tis the Season*. MSM 1-0129. Org, inst.
Cherwien, David. "It Came Upon the Midnight Clear" in *Interpretations, Boox IX*. AMSI SP-106. Org.
Corinna, John. "Carol" in *Suite for Christmas, No. III*. ABI APM-666. Org.
Larson, Katherine Jordahl. "It Came Upon the Midnight Clear." AFP 11-10625. Hb.

ALTERNATE HYMN OF THE DAY

LBW 177	By all your saints in warfare (stanza 7)

COMMUNION

LBW 40	What child is this
LBW 74	A stable lamp is lighted

SENDING

LBW 73	All hail to you, O blessed morn!
WOV 638	Holy Child within the manger

ADDITIONAL HYMNS AND SONGS

TFF 213   We shall overcome
W&P   Emmanuel

MUSIC FOR THE DAY

CHORAL

Carter, Andrew. "Christ Is the Morning Star." OXF. SATB/org.

Honoré, Jeffrey. "Song of the Promise." MSM 50-0008. SATB, opt cong, kybd.

Pavone, Michael. "On the Feast of Stephen." GIA G-3713. SATB, 6 hb.

Vaughan Williams, Ralph. "The Souls of the Righteous." OXF 19-353516.

CHILDREN'S CHOIRS

Kosche, Kenneth T. "Keep Me as the Apple of Your Eye." CG CGA800. U/2 pt, kybd.

Marshall, Jane. "Psalm 98" in *Psalms Together*. CG CGC18, U, cong/U antiphonal, kybd.

KEYBOARD/INSTRUMENTAL

Hysop, Scott M. "By All Your Saints in Warfare" in *Six Chorale Fantasias*. AFP 11-10799. Trbl inst, pno.

Langlois, Kristina. "It Came Upon the Midnight Clear" in *Three for Christmas*. MSM 10-134. Org.

PRAISE ENSEMBLE

Green, Keith. "Oh, Lord, You're Beautiful" in *Praise Hymns & Choruses, 4th ed.* MAR.

Ledner, Michael. "You Are My Hiding Place" in *Songs For Praise and Worship*. WRD.

Medema, Ken/arr. Jack Schrader. "Lord, Listen to Your Children." HOP GC850. SATB, acc.

Nelson, Greg. "Purify My Heart" in *Maranatha! Music Praise Chorus Book, 3rd ed.* WRD/MAR.

Paris, Twila/arr. Bruce Greer. "How Beautiful." WRD 3010830165. SATB, orch.

DECEMBER 26, 1999

FIRST SUNDAY AFTER CHRISTMAS

INTRODUCTION

With Simeon and Anna, the church proclaims that salvation has come to the people of God in Christ Jesus. "The splendor of the Lord is over heaven and earth"—Christ is present in the world for all people in all conditions of life. In, with, and through Jesus, the Christian community welcomes all people to the scriptures, the baptismal bath, and the holy supper.

Today the church also celebrates the festival of St. Stephen, considered the first Christian martyr.

PRAYER OF THE DAY

Almighty God, you have made yourself known in your Son, Jesus, redeemer of the world. We pray that his birth as a human child will set us free from the old slavery of our sin; through Jesus Christ our Lord, who lives and reigns with you and the Holy Spirit, one God, now and forever.
or
Almighty God, you wonderfully created and yet more wonderfully restored the dignity of human nature. In your mercy, let us share the divine life of Jesus Christ who came to share our humanity, and who now lives and reigns with you and the Holy Spirit, one God, now and forever.

READINGS

Isaiah 61:10—62:3

The people who returned to Jerusalem and Judah after the exile were greatly disappointed. The prophet's promises about the glories of the renewed Jerusalem and the wonderful life the people would experience were not fulfilled. Nevertheless, the prophet declares with certainty that the Lord's salvation will fully come to pass.

Psalm 148

The splendor of the LORD is over earth and heaven. (Ps. 148:13)

Galatians 4:4-7

Paul proclaims the ultimate significance of the nativity: Jesus was born the Son of God so that, because of him, we all may be God's children.

Luke 2:22-40

Luke's narrative continues with stories that emphasize Jesus' connection to Judaism. His family is devout in its observance of the law, and Jesus himself is recognized as one who will bring glory to Israel.

COLOR   White

THE PRAYERS

Rejoicing in God's gift of gentle grace, let us pray for the church, the world, and all on whom the light of Christ shines.
A BRIEF SILENCE.
O God, you clothe us with the garments of salvation and cover us with the robe of righteousness. Grant unity to your church as we claim the common clothing that is ours through baptism into Christ. God of grace,
hear our prayer.
O God, your glory is seen by the nations, and your wonders shall be known by all people. Rescue all who are trampled by war and violence, and bring an end to bloodshed and hatred in the world you have made. God of grace,
hear our prayer.
O God, in your presence is healing and wholeness. Touch the lives of all who are sick and sorrowful (especially . . .), that they may know the comfort and consolation of your Holy Spirit. God of grace,
hear our prayer.
O God, you are the hope of every generation. We give you thanks for the elderly in our midst who point us to your faithfulness. Remind them of your steadfast and unchanging love. God of grace,
hear our prayer.
O God, in you we grow in strength and wisdom. Deepen the nurturing love of all fathers, mothers, and guardians of children, a love that is rooted in your fatherly goodness and motherly care. God of grace,
hear our prayer.
O God, giver and keeper of all time, the years of our lifetime are safe in your hands. Guide us as we move forward into a new millennium, confident in your great faithfulness that has led us from of old. God of grace,
hear our prayer.
HERE OTHER INTERCESSIONS MAY BE OFFERED.

O God, you are the life of the world to come. With St. Stephen we commend to your eternal care our beloved dead. Keep us united with them always in the communion of saints. God of grace,
hear our prayer.
Hear our prayers, gracious God, and bathe us always in the light of your Word made flesh, Jesus Christ our Lord.
Amen

IMAGES FOR PREACHING

The key to these propers is to be found in the Roman designation of this day from the late nineteenth century on as "Feast of the Holy Family." In cycle B, we see Joseph and Mary coming to Jerusalem to offer the sacrifice for purification. Luke pictures Jesus' parents as pious Jews, performing what the law requires. Their offering is the "low budget" version because the couple seems to be unable to afford the lamb yearling, which is the first choice. They are, thus, part of the pious poor— the *anawim*.

But the focus quickly shifts from their piety to an encounter with another pious Israelite, Simeon. He speaks, first prophetically and eloquently about his own faith journey of waiting for salvation, and then mysteriously and mystically to Mary about the journey that awaits her. The child is to be something of a litmus test, an MRI into the hearts and souls of people. An ominous note hinting at a suffering yet to come insists that Mary's own soul, too, will be pierced.

The day is an antidote to Christmas romanticism that oohs and ahs about the mother and child, the beauty of the quiet stable, the warmth of candlelight and wonder of the shepherds. The sign, once again, is humanity in poverty, and the straw is scratchy. However this is but the beginning of the sufferings to come! It does, though, start right here, at the very beginning.

The incarnation includes families in the formula. Parents also will suffer with the son who goes the way of the cross. And, wonder of wonders, this family is expansive: the child goes the way of suffering to redeem others who might be adopted as children, and that includes us, as Paul insists. We, too, are part of this holy family! It is a precious privilege, but it also points to a present and a future sharing in the sufferings of the child.

WORSHIP MATTERS

In baptism, the people of God have been clothed with the garments of salvation and covered with the robe of righteousness. The baptismal robe placed upon the newly baptized symbolizes that they have been clothed in Christ who took the robe of flesh upon himself. The vesture of all who serve the assembly should call to mind the baptismal garment and reflect the joyous reality of being robed in the incarnate Christ. Where possible, vestments should be made of rich colors and substantial fabrics, perhaps silks. Earthy fabrics might also be used to reflect the shepherds' reception of God's message of righteousness. Acquiring a set of vestments and paraments solely for use during the Christmas season might be considered. (See Peter Mazar, *To Crown the Year: Decorating the Church through the Seasons*, Chicago: Liturgy Training Publications, 1995). The white Christmas vestments should luminously reflect the joy of being robed in Christ.

LET THE CHILDREN COME

The incarnation of God is not just a church or family celebration, but a celebration of cosmic proportions; the impact of Jesus' birth transforms the highest heights, the deepest depths, and the broadest breadths. Consider letting the children lead the congregation in Psalm 148. Because the opening lines are simple to learn, assign them to nine of the youngest children. A good reader or readers could lead verses 5-14 responsively. All together should pray the final "Praise the LORD."

MUSIC FOR WORSHIP

GATHERING

LBW 50	Angels from the realms of glory
LBW 52	Your little ones, dear Lord

PSALM 148

Bell, John L. "Glory to God Above!" in *Psalms of Patience, Protest and Praise*. Iona/GIA G-4047.

Hobby, Robert. PW, cycle B.

Hopson, Hal H. "Psalm 148" in *Psalm Refrains and Tones for the Common Lectionary*. HOP 425. U, cong.

LBW 540   Praise the Lord! O heavens (paraphrase)
LBW 541   Praise the Lord of heaven! (paraphrase)

Marcus, Mary. "First Sunday after Christmas" in *Psalm Antiphons-2*. MSM 80-722.

Ogden, David. "Let All Creation Sing" in PS, vol. 1.

Vaughan Williams, Ralph. "Psalm 148" in UMH.

HYMN OF THE DAY

LBW 62	The bells of Christmas
	DET KIMER NU TIL JULEFEST

INSTRUMENTAL RESOURCES

Bender, Jan. "The Bells of Christmas" in *The Concordia Hymn Prelude Series, vol. 3*. CPH 97-5538. Org.

Cherwien, David. "Det kimer nu til Julefest" in *Hymn Preludes and Free Accompaniments, vol. 21*. AFP 11-9419. Org.

Nelson, Ronald A. "The Happy Christmas Comes Once More" in *Hymntune Sketches*. AMSI OR-23. Org.

ALTERNATE HYMN OF THE DAY

WOV 641	Peace came to earth
LBW 40	What child is this

COMMUNION

LBW 198	Let all mortal flesh keep silence
WOV 642	I wonder as I wander

SENDING

LBW 339	O Lord, now let your servant
WOV 639	Oh, sleep now, holy baby

ADDITIONAL HYMNS AND SONGS

H82 257	O Zion, open wide thy gates
LLC 247	Ahora, Señor/At last, Lord
W&P	Let there be praise

MUSIC FOR THE DAY

CHORAL

Bass, Claude L. "At Bethlehem." AFP 11-10878. SATB, kybd.

Hopson, Hal H. "The Song of Simeon." MSM 50-7032. SATB (div), opt acc.

Marshall, Jane. "Song of Simeon." ECS 4956. SATB, org.

Resch, Richard. "Oh, Sing of Christ." CPH 98-3434. TTBB.

White, Nicholas. "Poor Little Jesus." AFP 11-10955. SATB.

Willcocks, David. "Sussex Carol." OXF X75. SATB, org.

CHILDREN'S CHOIRS

Hruby, Dolores. "Norwegian Dance Carol." AFP 11-2453. U, kybd, tamb.

Powell, Robert. "Praise the Lord from the Heavens." SEL 422-772. U, kybd.

KEYBOARD/INSTRUMENTAL

Daquin, Louis-Claude. "Noel Etranger" in *Noels*. KAL. Org.

Wasson, Laura. "Christmas Glory and Praise" in *A Christmas Season Tapestry*. AFP 11-10861. Pno.

HANDBELL

Kinyon, Barbara. "Go, Tell It on the Mountain." CG CGB143. 2 oct. CGB144. 3-4 oct.

McChesney, Kevin. "O Lord, Now Let Your Servant." AFP 11-10687. 3-5 oct.

McFadden, Jane. "Pastorale on 'Lord, How a Rose E'er Blooming.'" AFP 11-10522. 3-5 oct.

PRAISE ENSEMBLE

Grier, Gene. "Joseph's Song." Exciting Gospel Music Products EMP-0158. SAB acc. EMP-0103. SATB, acc.

Hopson, Hal H. "Glory to God." HOP MA500. SATB, kybd.

Liebergen, Patrick M. "At Christmas Time All Christians Sing." ALF 7895. SATB, kybd, fl.

McHugh, Phill/arr. Mauldin. "God and God Alone." BRM OT-1084. SAB, orch.

Ray, Mel. "Arise and Sing" in *Songs for Praise and Worship*. WRD.

SUNDAY, DECEMBER 26
ST. STEPHEN, DEACON AND MARTYR

Since the thirteenth century the feasts on the three days after Christmas have been called *comites Christi* ("companions of Christ"). In different ways these three observances further illumine the mystery of the incarnation. Stephen is remembered as the first Christian martyr. In his death he closely imitated the death of Christ, praying for his executioners and commending his soul to the hands of God.

Because Stephen was a deacon whose ministry was to care for widows and those in need, this day is appropriate for a congregation to remember those who are hungry or homeless. A gift of money, food, or clothing might be delivered to a charitable organization. Amid the sentimental overtones of Christmas, the day of St. Stephen reminds us of one who offered his very life for Christ, and our baptismal call to follow.

MONDAY, DECEMBER 27
ST. JOHN, APOSTLE AND EVANGELIST

John is traditionally regarded as the author of the fourth gospel, three epistles that bear his name, and the book of Revelation. During the twelve days of Christmas we read the prologue of John's gospel, which speaks of the Word made flesh among us. John is assumed to be the "beloved disciple" to whose care Jesus entrusted his mother at the crucifixion.

According to legend, John's enemies tried to murder him with poisoned wine, hence his symbol is a serpent in a chalice. His great love, it was said, vanquished the poison's power. Some still observe the medieval custom of blessing and drinking a cup of wine today, making a toast with the words: I drink to you the love of John. Remember John in prayer today, and with a toast at dinner. How will your congregation extend the love of the Word made flesh throughout the days of the coming year?

TUESDAY, DECEMBER 28
THE HOLY INNOCENTS, MARTYRS

The Innocents were the children of Bethlehem, two years and under, killed by King Herod in his attempt to destroy the infant Jesus. Because they were killed for the sake of Christ, the church honored these Jewish babies as the "buds of the martyrs," killed by the frost of hate as soon as they appeared. This observance so close to Christmas is a bittersweet reminder of the place of suffering and death in the story of our redemption.

It is appropriate today to remember the innocent victims of all ages killed in the slaughters of recent history. It is also a day to hold up the needs of battered children all over the world, and children who live in poverty.

DECEMBER 31, 1999

NEW YEAR'S EVE

PRAYER OF THE DAY

Eternal Father, you have placed us in a world of space and time, and through the events of our lives you bless us with your love. Grant that in this new year we may know your presence, see your love at work, and live in the light of the event which gives us joy forever—the coming of your Son, Jesus Christ our Lord.

READINGS

Ecclesiastes 3:1-13

Psalm 8

How exalted is your name in all the world. (Ps. 8:1)

Revelation 21:1-6a

Matthew 25:31-46

COLOR White

WORSHIP MATTERS

It nearly goes without saying that this New Year's Eve will be more spectacular than most. In addition to the many celebrations taking place today and for several days surrounding this big event, be sure to acknowledge the new millennium through congregational worship and in providing devotional resources for use at home.

LET THE CHILDREN COME

Worship on this night can be an oasis in the midst of secular revelry. Pattern the prayers after the familiar evening prayer of the catechism (*LBW,* p. 166, prayer 268). Use members of different ages to offer the prayer petitions. Help children to see that the daily prayer of the Christian extends to all time, just as the prayer of all time is for daily use.

MUSIC FOR WORSHIP

GATHERING

LBW 315	Love divine, all loves excelling
WOV 797	O God beyond all praising

PSALM 8

Geary, Patrick. "Your Name is Praised" in PS, vol. 3.

Hassell, Michael. PW, cycle C.

Shute, Linda Cable. PW, cycle A

HYMN OF THE DAY

LBW 320	O God, our help in ages past
	ST. ANNE

VOCAL RESOURCES

Busarow, Donald. "O God, Our Help in Ages Past." CPH 98-2849. SATB, brass.

Hopson, Hal H. "Festival St. Anne." AMSI 498. SATB, opt brass.

INSTRUMENTAL RESOURCES

Albrecht, Mark. "O God, Our Help in Ages Past" in *Timeless Hymns of Faith for Piano.* AFP 11-10863. Pno.

Cherwien, David. "O God, Our Help in Ages Past" in *Postludes on Well-Known Hymns.* AFP 11-10795. Org.

Moklebust, Cathy. "O God, Our Help in Ages Past" in *Hymn Stanzas for Handbells.* AFP 11-10722. 4-5 oct. 11-10869. 2-3 oct.

Ore, Charles. "O God, Our Help in Ages Past." CPH 97-6299. Org.

Wolff, S. Drummond. "Processional on 'O God, Our Help in Ages Past.'" CPH 97-6148. Org, inst.

ALTERNATE HYMN OF THE DAY

LBW 54	It came upon the midnight clear
WOV 736	By gracious powers

COMMUNION

LBW 61	The hills are bare at Bethlehem
WOV 704	Father, we thank you

SENDING

LBW 274	The day you gave us, Lord, has ended
WOV 771	Great is thy faithfulness

ADDITIONAL HYMNS AND SONGS

W&P	Great is the Lord

MUSIC FOR THE DAY

CHORAL

Bach, J. S./arr. John Leavitt. "Jesus Who Didst Ever Guide Me." GIA G-3871. SATB, kybd, opt fl.

Britten, Benjamin. "A New Year Carol" in *100 Carols for Choirs.* OXF 0-10-353227-1. U, kybd.

Fleming, Larry L. "His Voice." AFP 11-10789. SATB div.

Lovelace, Austin C. "Another Year of Grace." MSM 50-1975. 2 pt mxd/opt SATB, kybd.

Rutter, John. "What Sweeter Music." OXF X319. SATB, org.

CHILDREN'S CHOIRS

Hopson, Hal H. "Love One Another." CG CGA741. U/2 pt, kybd.

Leaf, Robert. "A Time to Sing Praise." CG CGA615. U/2 pt, kybd.

KEYBOARD/INSTRUMENTAL

Bach, J. S. "In Thee Is Gladness" in *Orgelbuchlein.* CPH 97-5774. Org.

Hampton, Calvin. "Fanfare for the New Year." Wayne Leupold 700007. Org.

HANDBELL

Matheny, Gary. "A Christmas Medley." AMSI HB-5. 2 oct.

Young, Philip C. "In Thee Is Gladness." AFP 11-10624. 4-5 oct.

PRAISE ENSEMBLE

Ball, Diane. "In His Time" in *Songs for Praise and Worship.* WRD.

Batstone and Kristianson. "Only Your Love" in *Tell the World, Maran- tha! Praise Band 5.* WRD/MAR.

Hanson, Handt. "Psalm 8" in *Spirit Touching Spirit.* CCF.

Makeever, Ray. "Who Are We" in DATH.

Smith, Michael W. and Deborah D. Smith/arr. Lojeski. "Great Is the Lord." HAL 08307232. SAB, pno. Also available SATB, SSA.

Smith, Michael W./arr. Don Marsh. "How Majestic Is Your Name." MEA MTM-105. SATB, pno.

JANUARY 1, 2000

THE NAME OF JESUS

PRAYER OF THE DAY

Eternal Father, you gave your Son the name of Jesus to be a sign of our salvation. Plant in every heart the love of the Savior of the world, Jesus Christ our Lord, who lives and reigns with you and the Holy Spirit, one God, now and forever.

READINGS

Numbers 6:22-27

Psalm 8

How exalted is your name in all the world. (Ps. 8:1)

Galatians 4:4-7

or Philippians 2:5-11

Luke 2:15-21

COLOR   White

WORSHIP MATTERS

This festival marks the naming and circumcision of Jesus eight days after his birth. The observance of the Octave (eighth day) of Christmas goes back to the sixth century, and Lutheran calendars often called it "The Circumcision and the Name of Jesus" until the revision of the calendar in 1973. The festival falls during the twelve days of Christmas and invites continued celebration of Jesus' incarnation.

Amid New Year's Day events, consider holding a brief service in honor of this liturgical day. Baptized into Christ, we begin the new year in the name of Jesus, our Savior, this the year of our Lord, *anno Domini* 2000. Plan to make traditional New Year's Day visits to friends or loved ones. The welcoming spirit of Christ encourages us to practice hospitality with others.

LET THE CHILDREN COME

Connect the name "Jesus" with its Hebrew equivalent, "Joshua." Tell the story of Joshua (Josh. 1:1—5:9) and how God used him to lead the people into the promised land, substituting Jesus' name for Joshua. Jesus' name makes it possible for us to call him Savior and

Lord. Some Christian traditions have the custom of bowing the head whenever Jesus' name is spoken in the liturgy. Pay particular attention to Jesus' name in the "Glory to God in the highest," the creed, the eucharistic prayer, and evening prayer's service of light.

MUSIC FOR WORSHIP

Many of the suggestions for New Year's Eve are also appropriate for the celebration of the Name of Jesus.

GATHERING

LBW 170   Crown him with many crowns
LBW 552   In thee is gladness

PSALM 8

Geary, Patrick. "Your Name Is Praised." in PS, vol. 3.
Hassell, Michael. PW, cycle C.
Shure, Linda Cable. PW, cycle A

HYMN OF THE DAY

LBW 328/9   All hail the power of Jesus' name!
CORONATION/MILES LANE

VOCAL RESOURCES

Powell, Robert J. "All Hail the Power of Jesus' Name." GIA G-3222. SATB, cong, brass.
Wolff, Drummond. "All Hail the Power of Jesus' Name." CPH 98-2576, SATB, kybd, tpts, opt cong.

INSTRUMENTAL RESOURCES

Burkhardt, Michael. "Coronation" in *Easy Hymn Settings—Easter*. MSM 10-415. Org.
Callahan, Charles. "Coronation" in *Great American Hymns*. MSM 10-883. Kybd.
Courtney, Mark. "Coronation." AMSI B-22. Brass, perc, org.
Pelz, Walter L. "Coronation" in *Hymn Settings for Organ and Brass, Set 1*. AFP 11-10184.

ALTERNATE HYMN OF THE DAY

LBW 181   Greet now the swiftly changing year

COMMUNION

LBW 345   How sweet the name of Jesus sounds
WOV 700   I received the living God

SENDING

LBW 559   Oh, for a thousand tongues to sing
LBW 262   Savior, again to your dear name

ADDITIONAL HYMNS AND SONGS

TFF 268   Jesus, name above all names
W&P   How majestic is your name

MUSIC FOR THE DAY

CHORAL

Grotenhuis, Dale. "Jesus! Name of Wondrous Love." MSM 50-9089. SATB, org.
Handl, Jacob. "In Nomine Jesu." GIA G-1860. SATB.
Paulus, Stephen. "Hallelu!" European American EA 511. 2 pt, kybd.
Willcocks, David. "The Infant King" in *100 Carols for Choirs*. OXF ISBN 0-19-353227-1. SATB.

CHILDREN'S CHOIRS

Hopson, Hal H. "God, I Look Up." CG CGA811. U/2 pt, kybd.
Horman, John. "Run to the Stable." CG CGA368. U, kybd.

KEYBOARD/INSTRUMENTAL

Fedak, Alfred V. "A Carol for the New Year" in *A Collection of Hymns*. CLP DM9601. Org.
Powell, Robert J. "All Hail the Power of Jesus' Name" in *Early American Hymn-Tune Preludes, Set I*. CPH 97-6673. Org.

HANDBELL

Afdahl, Lee J. "Savior, Again to Thy Dear Name." NMP HB-436. 2-3 oct.
Kinyon, Barbara. "All Hail the Power of Jesus' Name" (Coronation). AG 1658. 2-3 oct.

PRAISE ENSEMBLE

Funk, Billy. "Lift Him Up" in *Hosanna! Music Songbook* 7. INT.
Hanson, Handt. "Psalm 8" in *Spirit Touching Spirit*. CCF.
Makeever, Ray. "Who Are We" in DATH.
Riches. "Jesus, What a Beautiful Name" in *God Is in the House*. MAR.
Smith, Michael W. and Deborah D. Smith/arr. Lojeski. "Great Is the Lord." HAL. 08307232. SAB, pno. Also available SATB, SSA.
Smith, Michael W./arr. Marsh. "How Majestic Is Your Name." MEA MTM-105. SATB, pno.

JANUARY 2, 2000

SECOND SUNDAY AFTER CHRISTMAS

INTRODUCTION

During the twelve days of Christmas we continue to sing and be radiant over the goodness of God. We celebrate the light that the darkness has not overcome, Jesus Christ our Lord. That light is made known to us in the incarnation, God sharing our humanity in the Word made flesh. In communion, the Word is made flesh in us as well, that we may go forth from worship to share the light of Christ in our daily lives.

Today the church commemorates Johann Konrad Wilhelm Loehe, a German pastor in the nineteenth century whose witness to the light was through his emphasis on the Lutheran confessions, the revival of the diaconate, and foreign missions.

PRAYER OF THE DAY

Almighty God, you have filled us with the new light of the Word who became flesh and lived among us. Let the light of our faith shine in all that we do; through your Son, Jesus Christ our Lord, who lives and reigns with you and the Holy Spirit, one God, now and forever.

READINGS

Jeremiah 31:7-14

Like the prophets who announce homecoming and salvation in the book of Isaiah, Jeremiah announces the wondrous homecoming of God's people from exile. Once again the Lord enters in human history to fulfill the covenantal promise made during the exodus from Egypt so long ago: "I will be your God, and you will be my people."

or Sirach 24:1-12

Psalm 147:13-21 (Psalm 147:12-20 [NRSV])

Worship the LORD, O Jerusalem; praise your God, O Zion. (Ps. 147:13)

or Wisdom of Solomon 10:15-21

Ephesians 1:3-14

The Letter to the Ephesians addresses the church concerning God's plans and purpose for the world. It begins with a prayer thanking God for the blessings that already belong to us in Christ and for the yet more glorious future that awaits us.

John 1:[1-9] 10-18

John's gospel presents Jesus as the full embodiment of God's grace and truth, as the one who reveals God's love for the whole creation.

COLOR   White

THE PRAYERS

Rejoicing in God's gift of gentle grace, let us pray for the church, the world, and all on whom the light of Christ shines.

A BRIEF SILENCE.

Let us pray that in the new millennium, all who have been baptized into Christ Jesus will resolve to testify to his light with renewed zeal. God of grace,

hear our prayer.

Let us pray that in this new century, nation shall not rise up against nation, and that mutual understanding and a spirit of righteousness will prevail over all peoples of the earth. God of grace,

hear our prayer.

Let us pray that in this new year, your saving health and Spirit of comfort will be known among all the children of the earth (especially . . .) so that they may rejoice once again in healing and wholeness. God of grace,

hear our prayer.

Let us pray for all students and young persons, that they may be supported by their families and faith communities as they learn and grow. God of grace,

hear our prayer.

HERE OTHER INTERCESSIONS MAY BE OFFERED.

Let us pray for grace to entrust our faithful departed to your never-failing care, which sustained them in their pilgrimage on earth and which continues to hold them in communion with us and all your saints in light. God of grace,

hear our prayer.

Hear our prayers, gracious God, and bathe us always in the light of your Word made flesh, Jesus Christ our Lord.

Amen

CHRISTMAS JAN 2

IMAGES FOR PREACHING

Even if you used the propers for Christmas Day (III) for the Nativity of Our Lord, coming back to the prologue of John is a far different experience a mere nine days later. On Christmas Day the feast is fresh and new and just beginning, but here the new year is past and the holiday is starting to "wind down." Classes resume and vacations come to a close. Kids home from college will soon be returning to school and leaving the nest suddenly empty once again. If it has not happened already, it soon will: the tree taken down, the ornaments packed away, the decorations and mementos put back into their boxes, stacked again on the shelf to wait out another whole year. And perhaps the post-Yuletide blahs are ready to set in once we realize that the joy is coming to a close, and that quite a few weeks still must pass before spring, and that the hopes we had for a happy holiday did not quite materialize the way we had planned.

What makes John's prologue so welcomed this time around is its pairing with the opening verses of Ephesians. Yes, Jesus is indeed the Word from the beginning—with God, really God—the one through whom all things were made. Nothing new here; we've been singing about it for two weeks now. But the new surprise is the most forceful statement yet of the startling implications of the incarnation: "he chose us in Christ before the foundation of the world." The ramification is astounding! You have been on God's mind a long, long time. Even before the big bang, God knew the universe would be incomplete without you. It is your inheritance, your birth with Christ. And it means we have a future. God's plan for all creation is tangled up with who we are and what we are to become.

Christmas may be coming to a close, but we can be glad to know a box sits on a shelf in our house. Inside that box it will be Christmas for eleven more months until the feast comes round again. But better yet is the place in the Father's house where the perfect Christmas resides eternally, and it is where we are heading.

WORSHIP MATTERS

The Lord's word to Jeremiah depicts the joyous return of the exiled Israelites to Zion, a symbol of the Lord's gathering of the church from the ends of the earth. Every liturgical assembly is also a symbol of the church spread throughout time and place. How might each worshiping assembly give witness to the breadth of the church as it gathers? Does the gathering rite allow people to witness the diverse places from which people come? Gathering spaces, whether inside or outside the building, need to allow ample opportunities for people to see one another gathering. The gathering rite can encourage those assembled to interact with one another. Both the gathering space and rite can together evoke the sense that the church is gathering from many places both within the community and from across the globe. The universality and catholicity of the church are then readily apparent.

LET THE CHILDREN COME

Children learn by repetition. They learn the Ten Commandments, creeds, Lord's Prayer, Bible stories, and the church's hymns and prayers by using them over and over again. A portion of the appointed reading from Jeremiah is the basis for LBW Canticle 14, "Listen! you nations of the world." This canticle is easy for children to learn because of its repeated refrain. Take this opportunity to have the children or children's choir lead the congregation in singing that canticle as a response to the reading of scripture.

MUSIC FOR WORSHIP

GATHERING

LBW 45	Oh, come, all ye faithful
WOV 716	Word of God, come down on earth

PSALM 147

Bell, John L. "Sing to God with Joy" in *Psalms of Patience, Protest and Praise*. Iona/GIA G-4047.

Folkening, John. "Psalm 147" in *Six Psalm Settings with Antiphons*. MSM 80-700. SATB/cong, opt kybd.

Hobby, Robert. PW, Cycle B.

Hopson, Hal H. "Psalm 147" in *Psalm Refrains and Tones for the Common Lectionary*. HOP 425. U, cong.

Marcus, Mary. "Second Sunday after Christmas" in *Psalm Antiphons-2*. MSM 80-722. U, cong, hb/org.

Phillips, J. Gerald. *Psalms for the Cantor, vol. III*. WLP 2504.

Polyblank, Christopher. "Praise the Lord" in PS, vol. 3.

HYMN OF THE DAY

LBW 42	Of the Father's love begotten
	DIVINUM MYSTERIUM

VOCAL RESOURCES

Behnke, John. "Of the Father's Love Begotten." MSM 60-1000. SATB, cong, hb, org.

Grier, Gene/arr. Lowell Everson. "Of the Father's Love Begotten." GIA G-4566. 2pt, acc.

INSTRUMENTAL RESOURCES

Callahan, Charles. "Divinum mysterium" in *Christmas Music for Manuals, set. 2*. MSM 10-135. Kybd.

Cherwien, David. "Divinum mysterium" in *Hymn Preludes and Free Accomapniments, vol. 21*. AFP 11-9419. Org.

Hyslop, Scott. "Divinum mysterium" in *Six Chorale Fantasias for Solo Instrument and Piano*. AFP 11-10799. Pno, inst.

Leavitt, John. "Divinum mysterium" in *Hymn Preludes for the Church Year*. AFP 11-10134. Org.

ALTERNATE HYMN OF THE DAY

WOV 641	Peace came to earth
LBW 57	Let our gladness have no end
LBW 64	From east to west

COMMUNION

| LBW 49 | O Savior of our fallen race (*alternate tune:* PUER NOBIS, LBW 36) |
| WOV 638 | Holy Child within the manger |

SENDING

| LBW 56 | The first Noel |
| LBW 170 | Crown him with many crowns |

ADDITIONAL HYMNS AND SONGS

DATH 103	Between the times
H82 92	On this day earth shall ring
UMH 237	Sing we now of Christmas
W&P	There is a Redeemer
W&P	All is ready now

MUSIC FOR THE DAY

CHORAL

Mendelssohn, Felix. "There Shall a Star Come Out of Jacob." B&H 6333. SATB, org.

Oomen, Antoine. "Song to Light." OCP 10654. SATB, cong, org.

Roberts, Paul. "The Word Became Flesh." AFP 11-10899. SATB, fl.

Sedio, Mark. "The Wexford Carol." AFP 11-10585. SATB, U, org, C inst.

Vivaldi, Antonio. "Domine Fili Unigenite" in *Gloria*. RIC R131415. SATB, org/str, cont. Lat/Eng.

Weber, Michael Ryan. "In the Beginning Was the Word." AFP 11-10032. SATB, kybd.

CHILDREN'S CHOIRS

Bach, J. S./arr. Janet Hill. "Alleluia, O Come and Praise the Lord." CG CGA174. 2 pt, hpd, org/pno, 2 C inst (vln, fl/rec).

Wagner, Douglas S. "A Round of Praise." CG CGA208. U/2 pt, kybd.

KEYBOARD/INSTRUMENTAL

Osterland, Karl. "I Wonder as I Wander" in *I Wonder as I Wander: Seasonal Music for Organ*. AFP 11-10858. Org.

Wasson, Laura. "The First Noel" in *A Christmas Season Tapestry*. AFP 11-10861. Pno.

HANDBELL

Gramann, Fred. "I Wonder as I Wander" GSCH ED-3924. 3-5 oct.

Helman, Michael. "Rise Up, Shepherd: Three for Christmas" (Rise Up, Shepherd; Tempus Adest floridum; Three Kings of Orient). AFP 11-10721. 2-3 oct.

Kinyon, Barbara. "Brightest and Best of the Stars." CPH 97-6709. 2-3 oct, opt hc.

PRAISE ENSEMBLE

Card, Michael. "The Word" in *Find Us Faithful*. Sparrow Corp.

Harrah, Walt. "The Lord Is My Light" in *Maranatha! Music Praise Chorus Book, 3rd ed.* WRD/MAR.

Haugen, Marty. "He Came Down." GIA G-3808. SATB, children, solo, gtr, pno, perc.

Pote, Allen. "A Song of Joy." HOP AP450. SATB, pno.

Tunney, Dick and Melodie/arr. Larson. "Seekers of Your Heart." GS A-6292. SATB, orch.

SUNDAY, JANUARY 2
JOHANN KONRAD WILHELM LOEHE, PASTOR, 1872

During the nineteenth century Loehe was a parish pastor in the small German village of Neuendettelsau. As a young man Loehe studied in Erlangen, there discovering the Lutheran confessions. He founded a foreign mission society and sent pastors to North America, Australia, and Brazil. He labored for a clear confessional basis for the Bavarian church, and was sometimes in conflict with the ecclesiastical bureaucracy. Loehe taught that holy communion was the center of parish life, and that the ministries of evangelism and social ministry flowed from it.

Has your congregation looked at *The Use of the Means of Grace*? How does it help to guide your congregation to be one centered in word and sacrament?

WEDNESDAY, JANUARY 5
KAJ MUNK, MARTYR, 1944

Munk, a Danish Lutheran pastor and playwright, was an outspoken critic of the Nazis who occupied Denmark during the Second World War. His plays frequently highlight the eventual victory of the Christian faith despite the church's weak and ineffective witness. Munk was feared by the Nazis because his patriotic sermons and articles helped to strengthen the Danish resistance movement.

Munk's life and death invite us to ponder the power of the gospel in the midst of social and political conflicts. Offer prayers for those who face persecution, and for those who resist and challenge tyranny. Use drama and all the arts to proclaim the liberating power of the gospel.

ADVENT
CHRISTMAS
EPIPHANY

EPIPHANY

*Epiphany continues to show us more
of the gift than we may have noticed*

IMAGES OF THE SEASON

The Christmas season has ended, and, like children who have opened all of their presents, we are not sure what to do next. Is the excitement over? Do we go back to what we had been doing a few weeks ago? What difference has it all made?

Epiphany has a hard act to follow, but it offers riches to those who seek them.

THE COMING OF THE LIGHT

The major themes and images of the Epiphany season are readily apparent. The first reading for the day of Epiphany clearly marks it as a celebration of light, with the prophet Isaiah singing out: "Arise, shine, for your light has come!" It is a time for rejoicing in the light that shines in our darkness, the light that reveals both our sin and the one who comes to forgive it.

Historically, of course, the Christian festival of Epiphany was shaped by the pagan celebrations of the victory of the sun over the darkness of winter. For Christians it was the perfect time to exult in the light that had come into a dark world by way of a stable in Bethlehem.

A PROBLEMATIC SEASON

The message of triumph over death and of God's revelation to a world hungry for new life remains a vital one for today's world. Epiphany continues to show us more of the gift than we may have noticed as we tore off the wrapping paper. But this season presents difficult issues as well, issues that point to a troubling cultural bias.

Linking Epiphany to the turn of the seasons and the annual lengthening of days can be an effective metaphor. Even in societies or communities that do not draw their sense of time from the cycle of planting and harvesting, the increase of daylight remains a significant change. Science increasingly has identified shorter days with depression and other emotional stresses, so that the coming of light does indeed in some profound way mean the coming of life. Nevertheless, we need to be cautious about linking God's revelation with changing seasons. While most of us may belong to churches in the Northern Hemisphere, for half of the world Epiphany marks the height of summer. Thinking of this season only in terms of more light betrays our rootedness in a northern culture.

A more disturbing aspect of the imagery of this season, however, is its emphasis on light as the symbol of God, breaking into a world of darkness in need of cleansing and renewal. The danger is that, again, a northern cultural bias will determine our theology. Equating God with all things light, and evil with all things dark, confirms and perpetuates a profound stereotyping of which we need to be suspicious.

UNLIKELY SOURCES, UNLIKELY GIFTS

Other aspects of this season are worthy of notice. Gifts often reveal a great deal about the giver provided we take the time to consider how and why they were given, and so it is here. The first remarkable thing we notice is that, in this celebration of light, it may well have been dark-skinned people who first came to worship the Christ child. The identity of the visitors from the East is a mystery, of course, but they certainly were not blond, blue-eyed Nordic types. Nor did they find the one they sought among the powerful or even the comfortable. This one sent to reveal God to the nations comes by way of an oppressed people and is greeted by foreigners. Here is the message of Epiphany: light shines not only in darkness, but God acts through the unlikely to touch the lives of the excluded.

That theme continues throughout this season. God's call comes to those who least expect it: the boy, Samuel, and the tax collector, Levi. Healing is given to those who are not worthy of it, and forgiveness to those who do not even ask for it. And as the Epiphany season comes to an end with the Transfiguration of Our Lord, revelation comes even to those who persistently misunderstand it. "Behold," says God, "I am about to do a new thing" (Isa. 43:19). The celebration begun at Christmas turns out to be a surprise party, and we're all invited!

ENVIRONMENT AND ART FOR THE SEASON

From *green* grows our common word *grass*. It is the color of a fertile field, a bouquet of fragrant herbs, and a young shoot springing from a stump. Throughout the world, a green light means you are free to go, the way is open. Dissatisfied with our usual place, we may indeed move on to greener pastures, our hearts filled with high hopes. A "green" recruit may be inexperienced, perhaps young and unseasoned, yet willing to take a risk. Would you begrudge someone who is "in the green," filled with strength and energy? Consider those who "immediately left their nets and followed Jesus" (Mark 1:18, Epiphany 3).

In photographs taken from satellites and space shuttles, we can now see the range of green that covers the earth's land surface. Is it any wonder that contemporary environmental movements claim green as their color? It is a sign of compassion for the planet's health as well as a warning: green can turn to black. Forests and farm fields give way to asphalt and unchecked housing development. Throughout the world, *green* parties form to protect the universal garden.

For the medievals, the land's green growth was not simply an object to be used by humans. It was honored as the "book of creation" in which the eyes of faith could readily perceive the gracious hand of God. Among those who loved this living book was the eleventh-century mystic, Hildegard of Bingen. With her Benedictine sisters, she established a monastery along the Rhine River in the lush, fertile Nahe Valley of western Germany. Hildegard was a remarkable woman: church musician and composer, herbalist and gardener, poet, preacher, head of her community, scripture scholar, and artist. She created paintings based on the creed, religious hymns and poems, sermons, and a famous account of her heavenly visions. In her writings, music, and art, she manifested a deeply Christ-centered faith. Indeed, one of her more imaginative insights emerged from her contemplation of John 1:1-14. She wrote that Christ, through whom all things are created, is our *viriditas*, the greening power in whom all things find life.

For humans who suffer spiritual dryness and aridity, Christ is the moisture who falls from above, the hidden energy who causes things to grow green with love. One does not need to live in a wintry landscape, longing for spring, to recognize the truth of Hildegard's insight. Most people are drawn to living, growing, green things simply because they are signs of hope. Yet in our appreciation of spring's green growth, we may overlook the great struggle that takes place in the earth, what Jesus referred to as the mystery of the dying seed: unless a grain falls into the ground and dies, it cannot bring forth life. From years of labor in her gardens and vineyards, Hildegard knew that viriditas, the greening power, always bears the seed of self-giving. Life begets life. "The lifegiving greenness of God's hand," she writes, "has planted a vineyard." The green grape grows to ripeness and then is crushed, its juices flowing into the cask where it will become sweet wine.

What are the winter shades of green throughout the land? The dark green of the fir and the holly bush. The aqueous green of the sharp-needled spruce. The noble cedar's yellow-tinged viridian. The faintly iridescent green of the southwestern saguaro. The palm tree's jade and dusty shades. Clearly, there is no one green. Yet they all point to the living greenness of the one who says, "I am about to do a new thing; now it springs forth, do you not perceive it?" (Isa. 43:19, Epiphany 7).

The flow of the incarnation cycle, with its emphasis on the light of God revealed in the person of Jesus, moves from the nativity to the epiphany and baptism, meanders through the early ministry, and then leaps up again on the Transfiguration of Our Lord. This "hop, skip, and a jump" from Nativity, Epiphany, Baptism, to Transfiguration of Our Lord is underscored by the use of white and the appointment of "light" readings for these festivals. What the festival of the Baptism makes clear is that the preceding festivals are not isolated events but the beginning of the church's baptismal mission. Indeed, the Baptism of Our Lord stands with All Saints, Pentecost, and the Easter Vigil as primary days for celebrating baptisms in the church.

From the baptism, the ensuing season is guided by gospel readings that set forth the Lord's purpose: he gathers a community of disciples and enlightens them through his words and deeds. In these green weeks, the contemporary church rightly reflects on three significant dimensions of its baptismal consecration: the social mission to the poor and needy of this world; the ecumenical mission to pray and work for the unity of Christ's body; and the catechetical mission among those who will be preparing for baptism or reception into the church at Easter. The Epiphany of Our Lord, January 6, falls on a Thursday this year. Will you gather on this chief Christian festival to celebrate communion?

If your congregation has used a large hanging wreath, now filled with many candles, let them burn brightly on Epiphany. In some congregations, the Epiphany festival is celebrated with evening prayer that includes a short "concert" of Christmas music following the reading from scripture. This setting is an appropriate and welcome one for the final singing of Christmas carols and music, far better than during Advent. Where an indoor manger scene has been erected, make sure that the magi have now arrived at the stable. If your congregation does not gather on the Epiphany, the manger scene can be dismantled prior to the worship services on the Baptism of Our Lord. The large, hanging wreath can be removed as well.

The logic of the Epiphany season moves from the Lord's baptism to his ministry. Of course, the church celebrates this season as a model of its own life today: in baptism, the people of God are consecrated to the Lord's mission. Consider this charge from the baptismal liturgy: "Through Baptism God has made these new sisters and brothers members of the priesthood we all share in Christ Jesus, that we may proclaim the praise of God and bear his creative and redeeming Word to all the world" (*LBW*, p. 124). The gospel readings for this season are models of the church's baptismal mission. From the font flows the "greening power" of God's life.

Consider, then, these suggestions concerning the font. If your font is moveable, can it be placed where it is accessible to the people as they enter or leave the worship space, yet located within the space so that when baptisms are celebrated, the people can turn and face the baptismal party at the font? The difficulty with placing the font "up front" in the chancel area is that it communicates a "boundary" not to be crossed. While such a placement makes the font prominent visually, it distances the water from the people. How will children and adults be able to feel the waters of Christian birth traced over the foreheads or bodies? Baptism is not simply a great theological idea, but an action that invites renewal.

If the font is at a distance and immovable, one might consider placing an array of tall, brightly burning white candles to one side of the font. This arrangement needs to be handled carefully so that if a baptism is celebrated, the candles do not impede movement. Where the paschal candle is placed close to the font, this other bank of candles should not be higher or obscure its centrality. Light imagery continues to appear in the scriptural readings and many of the hymns written for this festival. But the light points to something: to the gracious action of God.

If no baptisms are to be celebrated on this festival, some congregations will renew their baptismal promises at the Sunday liturgy. After the hymn of the day, the presiding minister may address the assembly, ask the people to reject the forces of evil, and then profess their faith (see *LBW*, p. 199). Following the pattern set in the Vigil of Easter service, the people then may be sprinkled with water from the font in remembrance of their baptism. Or they may be invited to come to the font after the liturgy, dip their fingers in the water, and trace a cross over the forehead. Both actions connect the people with the original baptismal action.

After the festival of baptism, the season's color moves from white to green. Most congregations will see only one shade of green in the following weeks and throughout the lengthy season after Pentecost that begins after Trinity Sunday and continues up to the festival of Christ the King. Consideration could be given to creating or purchasing a green vesture of another shade for use in the season after Epiphany. At a minimum, it would entail new stoles and paraments, if not also a chasuble and perhaps a wall hanging. Let this set of Epiphany raiment "speak" a different and rich texture of green. Consider this sound principle:

The color and form of vestments and their difference from everyday clothing invite an appropriate attention and are part of the . . . festive character of a liturgical celebration. The more these vestments (and other hangings) fulfill their function by their color, design and enveloping form, the less they will need the signs, slogans, and symbols which an unkind history has fastened on them (*The Liturgy Documents*, Liturgy Training Publications, 1991, p. 336).

By all means, avoid the manufactured look of vesture and hangings that have "doo-dads," or little symbols attached to them. The Transfiguration of Our Lord concludes the season after Epiphany and the entire incarnation cycle that began on the first Sunday in Advent. It is a remarkable "hinge" feast: the readings have led the worshiping assembly from the Lord's baptism (light, voice, mission), through glimpses of his ministry, to this turning point on the mountain (again: light, voice, mission).

From the incarnation cycle (the Lord's advent, nativity, epiphany, and ministry), the church turns with him on the road that leads to the paschal cycle (the Lord's ministry, entrance into Jerusalem, supper, passion, death, resurrection, and bestowal of the Spirit). "As they were coming down the mountain, he ordered them to tell no one about what they had seen, until after the Son of Man had risen from the dead" (Mark 9:9, Transfiguration). This festival would be an appropriate day to secure or borrow an icon of the Transfiguration, a biblical feast loved so dearly among the Eastern Orthodox Church. The icon can be placed on a stand approximately four feet high, surrounded on each side by two or more burning processional torches or tall candles. Of course, you will want to write about the icon and its significance in the bulletin. While it would be good to avoid talking about icons during the service (that's been done in the printed bulletin), the more imaginative preacher will be able to weave some of its imagery into the sermon.

The quaint English custom of "bidding farewell to the Alleluia" is practiced in some congregations as a way of acknowledging the absence of this shout of praise during the Lenten season. Caution should be exercised so that this secondary paraliturgical tradition does not assume undue importance in the rite. If congregations find it useful to end the Epiphany season by "saying good-bye" or burying a banner in the backyard, let it be at the end of the liturgy as part of the procession out of the worship space. If an "Alleluia" banner is hanging in the worship space, simply roll it up in a dignified manner after the final blessing and have one of the acolytes carry it outdoors where it can be placed in a box and then buried, or placed in a safe place until Eastertide.

PREACHING WITH THE SEASON

Epiphany is the season out of sorts. To many Christians in the West the feast from which these weeks are named seems something of a misplaced Christmas. Popular piety and more than one Christmas Eve liturgy have placed the magi at the manger beside shepherds. Then what are the Eastern sages doing here twelve days later, arriving at a scene they have already visited? The truth of the matter, however, is that Epiphany developed as the Eastern celebration of the incarnation, a more ancient festival of the beginning of good news. A strong case can be made that the dates for both Christmas and Epiphany came into being through independent calculations of the date of Jesus' resurrection, some thinking it to be March 25 and others April 6. Since Easter is the beginning of a "new birth," the date was also used for the beginning of Mary's pregnancy and thus the birth-feasts would be nine months later—either December 25 (our Christmas) or January 6 (our Epiphany).

Here is a starting question, then, for our understanding of Epiphany: Where does the good news begin? We enter these weeks having just come from an affirmation of the beginning of good news at a manger in Bethlehem. Epiphany reminds us that in other places, other traditions have marked the beginning of good news. Matthew starts the story with a visit from Eastern sages. Mark sees the beginning with John the Baptist encountering the man from Nazareth at the Jordan. Both of these events launch the season of Epiphany. The good news begins here. It is a time to look for revelations, disclosures, flashes of light and glory.

This time of year is especially good for such searching. The energy of the holidays comes to a close. Tinsel and ornaments, confetti and noisemakers all get packed away. It is time to get back to business as usual, which comes with an inevitable letdown, but it gives us a clue to something important about this season. How do we go back to "business as usual" if God has come among us? How do we operate in "ordinary time" (as the weeks of this season are sometimes called) if the heavens above Bethlehem have been shattered by angel song and God has pushed the divine self into the world through a very narrow birth canal? If what Christmas suggests is true, then nothing around us is as it appears.

And yet, the world goes on. How can anyone maintain eschatological fervor for 365 days, let alone two millennia? And how do we reflect on the meaning of God's incarnation when the world, indeed, does seem to be in the same old rut? The problem of evil has not been solved among us, even with God's coming. And so we look for revelations, seek out epiphanies, disclosures of the ultimate that will provide a guiding star by which we might chart our way into a new year, a new decade, a new century, a new millennium. Each level of strategic planning has its own particular parameters. You cannot plan for a millennium the way you might plan for one year. But each level of our chronological revolution deserves some reflection. We do not have the luxury of wandering. The results of our exponential growth curves, together with the technologies we have in our own hands, demand that we chart a course into the future. Now is the time to do it, to implement our New Year's resolutions.

The lessons and liturgies of Epiphany give the preacher something important to talk about during these weeks. The major feature of the Christian epiphany is that it provides us with an affirmation that whatever disclosures of the ultimate might come among us, they most likely will be ambiguous. That ambiguity, however, does not mean that the revelation is any less certain. Not at all! Rather, the very essence of God's disclosure in and through Jesus lays bare both the complexity of our own existence and the wonder of God's being.

This theme is announced in the very first day of the season, as astrologers find their way to the Christ child simply by being good astrologers. Evidently, the people of God do not have a corner on the revelation market! The "for you" of the angelic Christmas gospel becomes astounding when the "you" includes the *whole* world that God loves. An obvious mission thrust is heard here, and a not-so-obvious implication for plotting mission strategy. The feast suggests that although the revelation can be found in the book, it may not be limited to the book, and God's people will continue to find strange and exotic collaborators with whom they will work to watch the story unfold.

As we enter a new era in these weeks after the millennial rollover, it will be especially instructive to focus on Mark's gospel. Mark also inaugurated a new era when he put the Jesus story into writing. This gospel manifests remarkable skill in ambiguous storytelling. As we remembered in Advent, Mark begins his book by telling his readers exactly who Jesus of Nazareth is: the Christ, the Son of God. However, Mark's narrative space describes how disciples and Pharisees, allies and enemies alike try to figure out just who this Jesus might be. Even though Jesus finds out at his baptism, the vision and audition are private to him alone. However, one group of characters in Mark's story, from the very first chapter on, consistently gets the riddle right and "spill the beans." They are the demons that Jesus confronts in the bodies of the possessed. Clear christological confession in Mark does not wait until the centurion's affirmation near the end of the book. The powers of evil and darkness know from the beginning who this Jesus is. They get it right, and not only that—they obey him!

Mark thus weaves ambiguity throughout his tale from beginning to end, without becoming much clearer along the way. This evangelist will suggest that the ending of the story, which is the climax of Jesus' ministry, is his death on a cross and the undoing of his status as God's special agent. Even the fact that this dark event seems to be reversed on Easter morning gets eclipsed by the women scared senseless at the tomb, running away in confusion, and determined they will not tell a soul. Epiphanies abound throughout, and their hallmark is ambiguity and paradox. Even nearly two millennia after its writing, Mark's story still possesses the remarkable ability to surprise and shock preacher and parishioner alike.

Second readings after Epiphany will take us into the early Christian congregation at Corinth. This community majored in revelations and exotic "spiritualities." Their hybrid hyper-faith apparently can be expressed in some kind of "ascetic libertinism." They also fight. How they fight! And throughout these weeks we will watch their former pastor trying to help them make sense of who they are. He never writes them off. Instead, he calls them at times to greater moderation and at other times to intensify the complex ambiguity of their lives. The ultimate revelation of God's absolute love is disclosed in the subtle paradoxes that twist through their lives: slave and free, sinner and saint, human and divine.

The first readings for this season introduce us to characters from the Hebrew scriptures to whom God has been revealed: Samuel, Jonah, Moses, Naaman, Hosea, and exiles in Babylon. Like us, they lived out their lives in the warp and woof of the ordinary and the extraordinary. The weaving makes the pattern. The ultimate is both *hidden* and *revealed* in the everyday. The ambiguity never leaves us, and yet it is accompanied by motion and growth and increasing insight. It mirrors the light of day in the Northern Hemisphere during these weeks: it begins with the dim light of the morning star, but moves toward the approaching spring, the rebirth of life and hope. Epiphany ends with the glory-burst of transfiguration, but only as prelude to the plunge into Lent and a death and resurrection. Even in its circular patterning the story never ceases to amaze us. The gospel springs out always from the direction in which we were not looking—to surprise us, shock us, slay us, and raise us—to claim us and make us people of good news, people of the light. An epiphany!

SHAPE OF WORSHIP FOR THE SEASON

BASIC SHAPE OF THE EUCHARISTIC RITE IN EPIPHANY

- Confession and Forgiveness: see alternate worship text for Epiphany in *Sundays and Seasons*

GATHERING

- Greeting: see alternate worship text for Epiphany in *Sundays and Seasons*
- Consider omitting the Kyrie on Sundays after Epiphany; but use the Kyrie on the festivals of Epiphany of Our Lord, Baptism of Our Lord, and Transfiguration of Our Lord
- Use the hymn of praise throughout Epiphany ("Glory to God")

WORD

- Use the Nicene Creed for festival days and Sundays in this season; use the Apostles' Creed for the Sundays after Epiphany
- The prayers: see alternate forms and responses for Epiphany in *Sundays and Seasons*

BAPTISM

- Consider having a baptismal festival on the Baptism of Our Lord (January 9)

MEAL

- Offertory prayer: see alternate worship text for Epiphany in *Sundays and Seasons*
- Use the proper preface for Epiphany (see *LBW* Ministers edition, and *WOV* Leaders edition for each musical setting of the liturgy)
- Eucharistic prayer: in addition to the four main options in *LBW*, see "Eucharistic Prayer C: The Season of Epiphany," *WOV* Leaders edition, p. 67
- Invitation to communion: see alternate worship

text for Epiphany in *Sundays and Seasons*
- Post-communion prayer: see alternate worship text for Epiphany in *Sundays and Seasons*

SENDING
- Benediction: see alternate worship text for Epiphany in *Sundays and Seasons*
- Dismissal: see alternate worship text for Epiphany in *Sundays and Seasons*

OTHER SEASONAL POSSIBILITIES
- Celebrate the Epiphany of Our Lord (January 6) with evening prayer or with communion. It is a fitting occasion to use incense. *Worship Wordbook* (pp. 103–4) or *Manual on the Liturgy* (pp. 279–82) are two possible resources to consult for instructions on using incense.

ECUMENICAL SERVICES DURING THE WEEK OF PRAYER FOR CHRISTIAN UNITY (JANUARY 18–25)
- One way to observe this week is by using the service in the seasonal rites section for Epiphany in *Sundays and Seasons*. For Lutherans celebrating with one or more congregations of the Reformed family, "Guidelines and Worship Resources for the Celebration of Full Communion," available from Augsburg Fortress (AFP 69-4519), may be consulted. Similar resources for interim sharing of the eucharist are available from denominational offices for Lutheran and Episcopal congregations worshiping together.

LECTIONARY OPPORTUNITIES FOR HEALING SERVICES
- Fourth and fifth Sundays after Epiphany (gospel); sixth Sunday after Epiphany (first reading, gospel)

BLESSING OF HOMES
- The blessing of homes is customary to the season after Epiphany. See "Blessing of a Dwelling," *Occasional Services*, pp. 186–91.

ASSEMBLY SONG FOR THE SEASON

GATHERING
The season that includes and follows Epiphany may be the only extended time in the year when "Glory to God" is used consistently. Because of its length, musical settings of this canticle tend to be more complex. This is the time to cement the assembly's familiarity with a Gloria setting in its repertoire, or to introduce a new one.

WORD
Create a simple seasonal gospel acclamation for Epiphany. All sing "alleluia" twice to the melody of the last phrase of "O Morning Star, how fair and bright!" (LBW 76). A cantor sings the proper verse to LBW tone 3. All repeat the alleluias.

BAPTISM
Introduce the practice of a sung musical response in the liturgy of baptism. "You have put on Christ" (WOV 694) or "Springs of water, bless the Lord" (from *Welcome to Christ: Lutheran Rite for the Catechumenate*, Augsburg Fortress, 1997) are adaptable to a variety of contexts.

MEAL
Use "Now the silence" (LBW 215) as the offertory hymn during this season. "Now, Lord, let your servant go in peace" (WOV 624) is a fitting choice for the post-communion song throughout Epiphany.

EPIPHANY

MUSIC FOR THE SEASON

VERSE AND OFFERTORY

Boehnke, Paul B. *Festive Verse Settings for Christmas, Epiphany, and Transfiguration.* MSM 80-100. SATB, opt kybd.

Cherwien, David. *Verses for the Epiphany Season.* MSM 80-200. U/hb, org.

Johnson, David N. *Verses and Offertories for Epiphany 2 through Transfiguration.* AFP 11-9544. U, kybd.

Shephard, Richard. "The Baptism of the Lord" in *Gospel Acclamations.* Kevin Mayhew 1400050. U/org.

Verses and Offertory Sentences, Part II: Epiphany through Transfiguration. CPH 97-5502.

Werning, Daniel J. *Verse Settings for Festival Days.* CPH 97-5787. SATB.

CHORAL MUSIC FOR THE SEASON

Amner, John. "Blessed Be the Lord God." GIA G-3986. SATB.

Christiansen, F. Melius. "Beautiful Savior." AFP 11-0051. Revised by O. C. Christiansen in *The Augsburg Choirbook.* 11-10817. SATB div.

Erickson, Richard. "I Want to Walk as a Child of the Light." AFP 11-10957. SATB, org.

Hirten, John Karl. "For Glory Dawns Upon You." AFP 11-10650. 2 pt mxd, kybd.

Neswick, Bruce. "Epiphany Carol. Sing of God Made Manifest." AFP 10511. Also in *The Augsburg Choirbook.* 11-10817. U, org.

Proulx, Richard. "Alleluia, Song of Gladness." GIA G-3984. U, hb, perc.

Sowerby, Leo. "Now There Lightens Upon Us" HWG GCMR 1307. SATB, org.

Telemann, G. P./arr. Joan Conlon. "Jesus, Joyous Treasure" AFP 11-9242. SATB, str, cont. Eng/Ger.

Victoria, T. L. "Accende Lumen Sensibus" (Light Now a Light) in *Eleven Motets for Treble Voices.* GIA 2143. SSA. Lat/Eng.

Zgodava, Richard. "Out of the Orient Crystal Skies." AFP 11-2300. SATB.

CHILDREN'S CHORAL MUSIC FOR THE SEASON

Davis, Katherine K. "Who Was the Man." CG CGA110. U, kybd.

Kemp, Helen. "Set the Sun Dancing!" CG CGA780. U, kybd, opt 3-4 oct hb.

Kemp, Helen. "Three Wise Men" in *Let's Sing.* AFP 11-7210. U, kybd.

Neswick, Bruce. "Epiphany Carol." AFP 11-10511. Also in *The Augsburg Choirbook.* 11-10817. U, org.

Rotermund, Donald. "The Only Son from Heaven." CPH 98-2820. Concertato for U choir, cong, trbl inst, org.

INSTRUMENTAL MUSIC FOR THE SEASON

Burkhardt, Michael. "Carol Miniature on 'See the Eastern Star' " in *The Balboa Park Organ Suite.* MSM 10-710. Org.

Burkhardt, Michael. "I Want to Walk as a Child of the Light" in *Eight Improvisations on 20th Century Hymn Tunes.* MSM 10-707. Org.

Cox, Michael. "Nowell for Two Violins and Piano." MSM 15-809. Kybd, vln.

Keesecker, Thomas. "Rise Up, Shepherd" in *Together Again: Piano Music.* AFP 11-10717. Kybd.

Litaize, Gaston. "Epiphanie." Editions Europart; available through Schola Cantorum, Paris. Org.

HANDBELL MUSIC FOR THE SEASON

Haydn/arr. Hollis. "The Heavens Are Telling." BEC HB60. 4-5 oct.

Kinyon, Barbara. "A Star O'er Bethlehem Shining." CG CGB 174. 3 oct.

Larson, Katherine Jordahl. "Beautiful Savior." AFP 11-10516. 3-4 oct.

McChesney, Kevin. "The First Noel." CG CGB 199. 2-3 oct.

Rogers, Sharon Elery. "The Star Medley." MSM 30-115. 2-3 oct.

White, Gary C. "Epiphany Carol." BEC HB59. 3 oct.

SUNDAYS & SEASONS

ALTERNATE WORSHIP TEXTS

CONFESSION AND FORGIVENESS
In the name of the Father, and of the ✢ Son,
and of the Holy Spirit.
Amen

As God's beloved daughters and sons,
let us call to mind our sin
and our need for reconciliation with God and one another.
Silence for reflection and self-examination.

God of the nations,
**in baptism you anoint us
to be your holy people in the world,
yet we have not been faithful to you.
We have not loved and accepted one another.
We have not reached out
to those who are poor, hungry, or lost.
Forgive us, and fill us with your light,
that we may delight in your goodness
and serve you with joy,
through Jesus Christ our Lord. Amen**

In Christ the grace and mercy of God
are revealed among us.
In Christ your sins are forgiven.
Let us then walk as children of the light.
Amen

GREETING
Blessed be the Lord God of Israel,
who alone does wondrous deeds!
Blessed be God's glorious name forever!
The grace of our Lord Jesus Christ, the love of God,
and the communion of the Holy Spirit be with you all.
And also with you.

PRAYERS
Let us pray that the radiance of Christ will illumine the church,
the nations, and all who seek the light.

A brief silence.

Each petition ends:
Lord, in your mercy,
hear our prayer.

Concluding petition
Hear our spoken and silent prayers, O God of light, and reveal
yourself to us, through your Son, Jesus Christ our Lord.
Amen

OFFERTORY PRAYER
Merciful God,
**as the magi offered gifts to the Christ child,
receive the treasures of ourselves,
our time, and our possessions.
Through this meal unite us as your body,
that we may be a light to all nations;
for the sake of him who gave himself for us,
Jesus Christ our Lord. Amen**

INVITATION TO COMMUNION
The gifts of God for the people of God.
Thanks be to God.

POST-COMMUNION PRAYER
God of glory,
in this sacrament you unite us in the body of your Son.
May we who have been guests at this table
grow in love for one another,
that through us your light may shine in all the world,
through Jesus Christ our Lord.
Amen

BENEDICTION
May God, who led the magi to Christ
by the shining of a star,
accompany you on your journey this day and always.
The Lord bless you and keep you.
The Lord's face shine on you with grace and mercy.
The Lord look upon you with favor and ✢ give you peace.
Amen

DISMISSAL
Go in peace to spread the light of Christ.
Thanks be to God.

Permission is granted for congregations to reproduce the Alternate Worship Texts, provided copies are for local use only and the following copyright notice appears: From *Sundays & Seasons*, copyright © 1999 Augsburg Fortress. May be reproduced by permission for use only between November 28, 1999 and December 2, 2000.

EPIPHANY

SEASONAL RITES

LESSONS AND CAROLS FOR EPIPHANY

Stand

ENTRANCE HYMN
LBW 55   Good Christian friends, rejoice
LBW 56   The first Noel

DIALOG
The people who walked in darkness have seen a great light.
The light shines in the darkness,
and the darkness has not overcome it.
Those who dwelt in the land of deep darkness,
on them light has shined.
We have beheld Christ's glory,
glory as of the only Son from the Father.
For to us a child is born, to us a Son is given.
In him was life, and the life was the light of all people.

OPENING PRAYER
See prayer of the day for Epiphany (LBW, p. 15 or WOV *Leaders edition*, p. 78).

Sit

LESSONS AND CAROLS
First Reading: John 1:1-14
LBW 42   Of the Father's love begotten
LBW 45   Oh, come, all ye faithful
LBW 57   Let our gladness have no end

Second Reading: John 1:18-25
LBW 44   Infant holy, infant lowly
LBW 67   Away in a manger
WOV 644 Away in a manger

Third Reading: Matthew 2:1-12
LBW 75   Bright and glorious is the sky
WOV 645 There's a star in the East
WOV 646 We three kings of Orient are

Fourth Reading: Matthew 2:13-23
LBW 177 By all your saints in warfare (st. 9)
WOV 639 Oh, sleep now, holy baby
         or Coventry Carol (H82 247)

Fifth Reading: Luke 2:41-51
LBW 417 In a lowly manger born
WOV 634 Sing of Mary, pure and lowly
WOV 643 Once in royal David's city

Sixth Reading: Matthew 3:13-17
LBW 85   When Christ's appearing was made known
LBW 88   Oh, love, how deep
WOV 647 When Jesus came to Jordan

Seventh Reading: John 2:1-11
LBW 205 Now the silence
WOV 648 Jesus, come! for we invite you

Stand

RESPONSIVE PRAYER
Glory to God in the highest,
and peace to God's people on earth.
Blessed are you, Prince of Peace.
You rule the earth with truth and justice.
Send your gift of peace to all nations of the world.
Blessed are you, Son of Mary. You share our humanity.
Have mercy on those who are sick, dying,
and all who suffer this day.
Blessed are you, Son of God.
You dwell among us as the Word made flesh.
Reveal yourself to us in word and sacrament,
that we may bear your light to all the world.

THE LORD'S PRAYER

BLESSING AND DISMISSAL
Let us bless the Lord.
Thanks be to God.
May you be filled with the wonder of Mary, the obedience of Joseph, the joy of the angels, the eagerness of the shepherds, the determination of the magi, and the peace of the Christ child. Almighty God, Father, ☩ Son, and Holy Spirit bless you now and forever.
Amen

SENDING HYMN
LBW 90   Songs of thankfulness and praise

ECUMENICAL SERVICE DURING THE WEEK OF PRAYER FOR CHRISTIAN UNITY

CONFESSION AND FORGIVENESS
We gather as the people of God
to offer our repentance and praise,
to pray for the unity of the church
and the renewal of our common life.
Trusting in God's mercy and compassion,
let us ask for the forgiveness of our sins.

Silence for reflection and self-examination.

Lord Jesus, you came to reconcile us
to one another and to the Father.
Lord, have mercy on us.
Lord, have mercy on us.
Lord Jesus, you heal the wounds
of pride and intolerance.
Christ, have mercy on us.
Christ, have mercy on us.
Lord Jesus, you pardon the sinner
and welcome the repentant.
Lord, have mercy on us.
Lord, have mercy on us.
May almighty God grant us pardon and peace,
strengthen us in faith,
and make us witnesses to Christ's love.
Amen

HYMN OF PRAISE

PRAYER OF THE DAY
For unity, LBW, p. 39.

THE WORD OF GOD
Isaiah 2:2-4
Psalm 133
Ephesians 4:1-6
John 17:15-23

SERMON

HYMN OF THE DAY

THANKSGIVING FOR BAPTISM
The people remain standing after the hymn as the minister(s) gather at the font. After the prayer, the people may be sprinkled with water from the font; or at the conclusion of the service, they may be invited to dip their hands in the font and trace the sign of the cross over themselves.

The Lord be with you.
And also with you.
Let us give thanks to the Lord our God.
It is right to give our thanks and praise.
Holy God and mighty Lord, we give you thanks
for you nourish and sustain us and all living things
with the gift of water.
In the beginning your Spirit moved over the waters
and you created heaven and earth.
By the waters of the flood you saved Noah and his family.
You led Israel through the sea out of slavery
into the promised land.
In the waters of the Jordan
your Son was baptized by John and anointed with the Spirit.
By the baptism of his death and resurrection
your Son set us free from sin and death
and opened the way to everlasting life.

We give you thanks, O God,
that you have given us new life in the water of baptism.
Buried with Christ in his death,
you raise us to share in his resurrection
by the power of the Holy Spirit.
May all who have passed through the water of baptism
continue in the risen life of our Savior.
To you be all honor and glory, now and forever.
Amen

APOSTLES' CREED

THE PRAYERS
After the conclusion of the prayers, the people are invited to pray the Lord's Prayer.

GREETING OF PEACE
The Lord Jesus prayed for the unity of his disciples.
We look for the day when the church will shine forth
in unity at his holy supper.
The peace of the Lord be with you always.
And also with you.

The people exchange a sign of Christ's peace.

BLESSING AND DISMISSAL

SENDING HYMN

JANUARY 6, 2000

THE EPIPHANY OF OUR LORD

INTRODUCTION

In the East three great epiphanies are celebrated on this day: the magi's adoration of the Christ Child, Jesus' baptism in the Jordan River, and his first miracle in which he changes water into wine. Epiphany celebrates Christ being made known, or made "manifest," to all nations.

The sacraments are for us the great epiphany of God's grace in which we behold the mystery of God among us. The magi offered gifts of gold, frankincense, and myrrh. Having seen the light of Christ, we offer the gift of ourselves, our time, and our possessions—that others may also know the epiphany of God's mercy and love.

PRAYER OF THE DAY

Lord God, on this day you revealed your Son to the nations by the leading of a star. Lead us now by faith to know your presence in our lives, and bring us at last to the full vision of your glory, through your Son, Jesus Christ our Lord, who lives and reigns with you and the Holy Spirit, one God, now and forever.

READINGS

Isaiah 60:1-6

Isaiah promises that God's salvation, light, and glory will shine out to all nations, and people shall come bearing gifts to the place of that light, the restored Jerusalem.

Psalm 72:1-7, 10-14

All kings shall bow down before him. (Ps. 72:11)

Ephesians 3:1-12

Paul understands the secret purpose of Christ: In the "rich variety" of God's wisdom, the "boundless riches" of Christ are given to Jews and Gentiles alike.

Matthew 2:1-12

The spiritual quest of all human beings is mirrored in the journey of the three magi. They find and adore the Christ Child, the fulfillment of their hope, the epiphany and glory of God.

COLOR White

THE PRAYERS

Let us pray that the radiance of Christ will illumine the church, the nations, and all who seek the light.

A BRIEF SILENCE.

God of light, break through the thick layers of darkness that cover our hearts from receiving the full radiance of your life-giving word and sacraments. Lord, in your mercy,

hear our prayer.

Shine on your holy church, that it may behold your glory and radiantly proclaim your praise. Lord, in your mercy,

hear our prayer.

Lead the nations to your light, and reveal to their leaders the new dawn of your justice and truth, that violence and war may give way to peace and goodwill. Lord, in your mercy,

hear our prayer.

Illumine those who struggle in sickness and in sorrow (especially . . .), that the warmth of your healing presence will remind them that they are not alone. Lord, in your mercy,

hear our prayer.

Enlighten all who seek your face and yearn to be led into the light of your truth and wisdom. Lord, in your mercy,

hear our prayer.

HERE OTHER INTERCESSIONS MAY BE OFFERED.

Remind us always that we are surrounded by a great cloud of witnesses—all your saints in light. Keep us united with those who have gone before us, and bring us with them to your light. Lord, in your mercy,

hear our prayer.

Hear our spoken and silent prayers, O God of light, and reveal yourself to us, through your Son, Jesus Christ our Lord.

Amen

IMAGES FOR PREACHING

Arising from their daily tasks, the magi were sent to look for the child. Guided by a star, their search brought them to the place of birth. Kneeling, they offered gifts befitting royalty.

Light lifts up toward the heavens. Light carries the spirit in expectation of a clearer and more distinct vision. Light offers clarity in the midst of confusion brought on by darkness. The magi were moved by the light, and when they finally reached their destination they fell on their knees. Brought low by the surprise of this birth, they extended gifts of honor and praise. Reaching toward the child, they were unknowingly reaching toward the culmination of all creation and the light of God present in a human being. By placing life in their midst, God met them in the midst of their journey, and sent them off toward home in a new direction.

Sometimes, the shining Epiphany light helps people to see in a new way. Sometimes the Epiphany light redirects vision, and sometimes the Epiphany light provides the *only* light and simply calls one to dwell in its presence. The light, however, does not diminish, or disappear, or overpower. The light of grace shines on everyone. The light from heaven bestows wisdom on all who come in contact with it. The light of promise rests over the newborn hope of life for all people.

WORSHIP MATTERS

The magi lavished gifts upon the infant Jesus, greeting the king of heaven in his humble throne room. When the people of God celebrate the liturgy they enter the throne room of God. They bring gifts during the offering for use in the kingdom of God. Some, like incense, may be brought for use within the liturgical celebration itself. Incense has a symbolic richness. As Psalm 141 of evening prayer indicates, incense is a symbol of the sweet aroma of prayer billowing up toward the face of God. It reminds the assembly that their prayer is pleasing to God. Incense is also a symbol of purification. It could be used on Epiphany for the censing of the altar, eucharistic vessels, worship leaders, and the worshipers. This action would indicate that both the assembly and the various furnishings and vessels are set apart, or *purified*, for the praise and worship of God.

LET THE CHILDREN COME

Older children may grasp the irony that the star did not lead the magi to Jesus. Let this remind them of the catechism on the third article of the creed. The hymn "Bright and glorious is the sky" (LBW 75) puts it well:

"As a star, God's holy Word leads us to our King and Lord." As the scriptures are read for this festival, consider using torches at the lectern, or a gospel procession in which the reading of the word is brought into the midst of the people. The procession could later lead the people to the altar, the manger of our Lord.

MUSIC FOR WORSHIP

GATHERING

| LBW 75 | Bright and glorious is the sky |
| LBW 646 | We three kings of Orient are |

PSALM 72

Hobby, Robert. PW, cycle B.

Hughes, Howard. "Psalm 72" in TP.

Joncas, Michael. "Psalm 72: Every Nation on Earth" in *Gather*. GIA.

Marcus, Mary. "The Epiphany of Our Lord" in *Psalm Antiphons-3*. MSM 80-723. U, cong, hb/org.

Ogden, David. "In His Days" in PS, vol. 1.

| LBW 87 | Hail to the Lord's anointed (paraphrase) |
| LBW 530 | Jesus shall reign (paraphrase) |

HYMN OF THE DAY

| LBW 84 | Brightest and best of the stars of the morning |
| | MORNING STAR |

INSTRUMENTAL RESOURCES

Callahan, Charles. "An Epiphany Prelude for Flute and Organ." MSM 20-260. Org, fl.

Leavitt, John. "Morning Star" in *A Little Nativity Suite*." AFP 11-10351. Org.

Meyer, Edward. "Morning Star" in *Easy Hymn Accompaniments for Organ or Piano*." CPH 97-6608. Org/kybd.

ALTERNATE HYMN OF THE DAY

| WOV 649 | I want to walk as a child of the light |
| LBW 76 | O Morning Star, how fair and bright! |

COMMUNION

| LBW 518 | Beautiful Savior |
| LBW 226 | Draw near and take the body of the Lord |

SENDING

| LBW 50 | Angels, from the realms of glory |
| LBW 530 | Jesus shall reign |

ADDITIONAL HYMNS AND SONGS

H82 125/6   The people who in darkness walked
H82 124   What star is this
TFF 60   Sister Mary
W&P   All hail King Jesus!

MUSIC FOR THE DAY

CHORAL

Cornelius, Peter. "The Kings" in *Rejoice Now My Spirit*.
   AFP 11-10228 (MH); 11-10229 (ML).
Jennings, Kenneth. "Arise Shine" in *The Augsburg Choirbook*.
   AFP 11-10817. SATB.
Nanino, Giovanni Maria. "Difussa est gratia" (Grace Is Poured Out).
   GIA G-4150. SATB.
Shute, Linda. "The Magi Who to Bethlehem Did Go."
   AFP 11-10960. SATB, pno, opt perc.
Willan, Healey. "The Three Kings." OXF OCS 718. SATB.

CHILDREN'S CHOIRS

Christopherson, Dorothy. "The Night of the Star." AFP 11-10890.
   U, opt desc, pno, fl. perc.
Harris, Patricia Lou. "Led By a Brilliant Light." CG CGA785. U/2 pt,
   kybd, HD/tamb, opt fl/C inst.
Kemp, Helen. "See the Glowing Star!" CG CGA629. U, kybd, perc.

KEYBOARD/INSTRUMENTAL

Lachenauer, George. "De Tierra Lejana Venimos" in *Three Hispanic Carols*. GIA G-4494. Org.
Manz, Paul. "I Want to Walk as a Child of the Light." MSM 10-520. Org.
Pinkham, Daniel. "Pastorale on 'The Morning Star'" in *A Galaxy of Hymn Tune Preludes for Organ*. GAL GMC 2353. Org.

HANDBELL

Kinyon, Barbara. "O Morning Star, How Fair and Bright." AG 1690.
   2-3 oct, opt hc.
Larson, Katherine Jordahl. "Celestia" (Bright and Glorious Is the Sky). AFP 11-10622. 3-4 oct.

PRAISE ENSEMBLE

Damazio, Sharon. "We Are Your Church" in *Hosanna! Music Songbook* vol. 7. INT HMSB07.
Goreib and Riso. "The Light of Life" in *God Is Able*. INT.
Jolly, Todd. "Rise and Shine." PVN P1025. SAB, kybd.
Kendrick, Graham. "Shine, Jesus, Shine" in *Shine Jesus Shine Songbook*. Alleluia Community Ministries, Inc. 00957. SATB, kybd.
O'Brien, Chris and Margaret Davis. "Arise, Shine" in *The Maranatha! Singers I: See the Lord*. WRD/MAR.

JANUARY 9, 2000

THE BAPTISM OF OUR LORD
FIRST SUNDAY AFTER THE EPIPHANY

INTRODUCTION

In the waters of baptism, we have been joined to the Son in whom the Father is well pleased. The font is our Jordan where the Holy Spirit comes to us, strengthening and enlightening us for service in the world. On this great baptismal day, the church prays that all who are reborn as daughters and sons of God will continue to grow in faith, hope, and love.

PRAYER OF THE DAY

Father in heaven, at the baptism of Jesus in the River Jordan you proclaimed him your beloved Son and anointed him with the Holy Spirit. Make all who are baptized into Christ faithful in their calling to be your children and inheritors with him of everlasting life; through your Son, Jesus Christ our Lord, who lives and reigns with you and the Holy Spirit, one God, now and forever.

READINGS

Genesis 1:1-5

To a people experiencing the chaos of defeat, devastation, and exile, these familiar words bring great comfort. Out of chaos, God brings order. Creation by command demonstrates God's absolute sovereignty, which is not shared with any other gods. Notice the sequence of "evening" and "morning"—the Jewish day begins with sunset.

Psalm 29

The voice of the LORD is upon the waters. (Ps. 29:3)

Acts 19:1-7

Just as the Holy Spirit came upon Jesus at his baptism, so

early Christians recognized that the Holy Spirit would come to them when they were baptized in Jesus' name.
Mark 1:4-11
Mark's gospel reports the story of Jesus' baptism with some irony: the one on whom the Spirit descends is himself the one who will baptize others with the Holy Spirit.

COLOR   White

THE PRAYERS

Let us pray that the radiance of Christ will illumine the church, the nations, and all who seek the light.
A BRIEF SILENCE.
Holy God, strengthen and unite your one holy church in its common baptismal life, that your Holy Spirit may empower all the baptized to be light-filled witnesses of the gospel. Lord, in your mercy,
hear our prayer.
Lord of the nations, protect all who live in regions where the darkness of war and bloodshed threatens to overpower the light of reconciliation. Lord, in your mercy,
hear our prayer.
God of mercy, make us sensitive to your Spirit, which calls us to welcome all into community. Hold the sick among us in your healing hand (especially . . .), that they might be restored to wholeness. Lord, in your mercy,
hear our prayer.
Spirit of God, descend upon those who are baptized this day and make them powerful proclaimers of your love. Bless those who are inquiring into the faith, that they too may come closer to your light. Lord, in your mercy,
hear our prayer.
HERE OTHER INTERCESSIONS MAY BE OFFERED.
Holy God, your radiance unites us and our beloved dead. Keep us united with them until that day when we all stand before your unveiled glory. Lord, in your mercy,
hear our prayer.
Hear our spoken and silent prayers, O God of light, and reveal yourself to us, through your Son, Jesus Christ our Lord.
Amen

IMAGES FOR PREACHING

Baptism is both a beginning and an ending, or fulfillment. It is the place where Mark begins his gospel. It is the place where, for Jesus, the heavens are torn open and an identity is conferred. And in that sense, it is the fulfillment of our Advent wish: "Oh, that you would tear open the heavens and come down." The prayer was answered at Christmas, when God came among us, as one of us. But this prayer is also answered at the baptism of our Lord.

It is something of a subtle apocalypse. Only Jesus sees it, a kind of *private* revelation. A voice comes from heaven but it is addressed to Jesus alone. Later gospel writers would make of the event a public pronouncement of who this Jesus of Nazareth really is. Some would raise the issue of why Jesus—if he is who the voice says he is—should need a baptism of repentance anyway! For Mark there is no explanation, just the mystery.

But is it not that way with us as well? After all, baptism is a pretty subtle epiphany! A sprinkle of water, and words spoken by an all-too-human pastor. No torn sky. No booming voice. No dove.

Some disciples in Ephesus know such a baptism. They got it from John, just as Jesus did. Like his, theirs was also a baptism of repentance. It is the point of Acts that this baptism needs the name of Jesus to be complete, to be a baptism with Spirit as well as water, just as John himself declared. But with the name of Jesus, and even without bird or torn sky, the voice in proclaiming the name is the Word from the beginning: the booming, cosmic voice that echoes from the big bang down the canyons of time. No bird. No torn sky. But new creation!

WORSHIP MATTERS

Ideally, every eucharistic celebration is a return to holy baptism, filled with images that remind the assembly of baptism. Baptism occurs within the heart of the eucharistic celebration and can be celebrated on any Sunday. Yet, rather than baptizing individuals on random Sundays, consideration might be given to observing specific baptismal festivals. Such days provide opportune moments to accentuate this sacrament. Celebrating baptismal festivals a few times each year at such festivals as the Easter Vigil, Pentecost, the Baptism of Our Lord, and All Saints Day intertwines baptism with significant markers from salvation history. The multiplicity of baptisms at a festival highlights baptism's role as the initiatory sacrament, the means by which the church grows. Finally, a baptismal festival demands that the liturgy be planned in such a way that baptism pervades the entire service, from the hymns to the sermon to the eucharistic meal.

LET THE CHILDREN COME

The voice of the Lord is certainly loud and mighty as a thunderstorm, but incomprehensible. At his baptism, Jesus was revealed as God's intelligible voice among us. Here's one way to demonstrate this difference. Play an instrumental piece, then ask the children to tell you what God said to them in the music. Then have someone say to the children, "The Lord says to you, 'I call you by your name' " (Isa. 45:4b). Again ask the children to tell you what God said to them. Which "voice" was clearer? God calls us by name in baptism; therefore we listen carefully to God's word.

MUSIC FOR WORSHIP

GATHERING

| LBW 189 | We know that Christ is raised |
| WOV 799 | When long before time |

PSALM 29

Busarow, Donald. "It Is a Good Thing to Give Thanks." CPH 98-3126. SATB, cong, hb.

Hobby, Robert. PW, cycle B.

Hopson, Hal H. "Psalm 29" in TP.

Marshall, Jane. "Psalm 29" in *Psalms Together II*. CG CGC-21. U.

Smith, Geoffrey Boulton. "Give Strength to Your People, Lord" in PS, vol. 1.

HYMN OF THE DAY

| LBW 83 | From God the Father, virgin-born |
| | DEUS TUORUM MILITUM |

VOCAL RESOURCES

Kosche, Kenneth. "From God the Father, Virgin-Born." GIA G-3645. SATB, cong, opt brass.

INSTRUMENTAL RESOURCES

Heschke, Richard. "Deus tuorum militum" in *Twenty-Two Hymn Settings*. CPH 97-6063. Org.

Johnson, David N. "Deus tuorum militum" in *Free Hymn Accompaniments for Manuals, Book 2*. AFP 11-9186. Org/kybd.

Rotermund, Don. "Deus tuorum militum" in *Seven Hymn Preludes, Set 3*. CPH 97-6243. Org.

ALTERNATE HYMN OF THE DAY

| LBW 88 | Oh, love, how deep |
| WOV 647 | When Jesus came to Jordan |

COMMUNION

| LBW 486 | Spirit of God, descend upon my heart |
| WOV 693 | Baptized in water |

SENDING

| LBW 557 | Let all things now living |
| WOV 721 | Go, my children, with my blessing |

ADDITIONAL HYMNS AND SONGS

H82 121	Christ, when for us you were baptized
NCH 326	Crashing waters at creation
TFF 114	Wade in the water
W&P	Waterlife

MUSIC FOR THE DAY

CHORAL

Bach, J. S. "Christ unser Herr zum Jordan kam" chorus from *Cantata BWV 7*. Hanssler 31 007/03. SATB, kybd/str, ob d'amore, cont. Ger/Eng.

Neswick, Bruce. "Jesus Came from Nazareth." AFP 11-10643. 2 pt, org.

Ore, Charles W. "This Is My Son." CPH 98-3288. SATB, opt cong, trpt, org.

Uhl, Dan. "This Is My Beloved Son" in *The Augsburg Choirbook*. AFP 11-10817. SATB, org.

Wyton, Alec. "When Jesus Went to Jordan's Stream." PAR PPM08606. SATB, fl, hb, org.

CHILDREN'S CHOIRS

Callahan, Charles. "The Baptism of Our Lord." MSM 50-2003. U, opt desc, org.

Fleming, Tomas J. "I Believe in God." MSM 50-9403. U, opt desc, kybd.

KEYBOARD/INSTRUMENTAL

Albrecht, Timothy. "When Jesus Came to Jordan" in *Grace Notes VI*. AFP 11-10825. Org.

Manz, Paul. "O Morning Star, How Fair and Bright" in *A New Liturgical Year*. AFP 11-10810.

HANDBELL

Tucker, Sandra. "Wade in the Water." HOP 2074. 3-5 oct.

PRAISE ENSEMBLE

Leck, Henry H. "Siyahamba" in *South African Suite*. PLY HL-400. SAB.

Makeever, Ray. "In the Water" in DATH.

Park, Andy. "The River Is Here" in *Hosanna! Music Songbook 11*. INT.

Runyan, William M./arr. Nelhybel. "Great Is Thy Faithfulness." HOP VN109. SATB, kybd.

Wimber, John. "Spirit Song" in *Songs for Praise and Worship*. WRD.

THURSDAY, JANUARY 13
GEORGE FOX, RENEWER OF SOCIETY, 1691

George Fox is remembered as the founder of the Society of Friends, also known as the Quakers. Fox severed his ties of family and friendship in search of enlightenment. Finding no comfort in the traditional church he became a wandering preacher, teaching the inner light of God as the real source of authority and comfort. His preaching led to the establishment of preaching bands of women and men known as the "Publishers of the Truth."

The Quakers are known for the long periods of silence in their meetings. Use this day to consider how your community uses silence in worship. In addition to words and music, are there periods of corporate silence? Consider growing into this practice, allowing silence after the readings, the sermon, during communion, and before the benediction. How are both words and silence part of our spiritual life?

FRIDAY, JANUARY 14
EIVIND JOSEF BERGGRAV, BISHOP OF OSLO, 1959

In 1937, Berggrav was elected bishop of Oslo and primate of Norway. In 1940, he was asked to negotiate with the Nazi regime in order to ascertain its intentions regarding the social and religious life of the Norwegian people. Rejecting any compromise with the occupation forces, he left the negotiations and demanded that the Nazis recognize the rights of the Jews and the autonomy of the church. Deprived of his episcopal title in 1942, he was placed under arrest, only to escape and remain in hiding in Oslo until the end of the war.

During the season of Epiphany the life of Berggrav is another witness to the light of Christ. Are we willing to risk title, power, and prestige to speak for the oppressed and seek truth in the midst of the issues that face us in the world today?

SATURDAY, JANUARY 15
MARTIN LUTHER KING JR., RENEWER OF SOCIETY, MARTYR, 1968

Martin Luther King Jr. is remembered as a man who encouraged nonviolent resistance to racism in the United States. We commemorate him as a pastor whose faith empowered his yearning for justice. Preaching nonviolence, he demanded that love be returned for hate. He was awarded the Nobel Peace Prize in 1964, and was killed by an assassin on April 4, 1968. His birthday is a U.S. holiday, observed on the third Monday of January.

Congregations may choose to remember King tomorrow by naming him in the prayers and by singing "We shall overcome" (TFF 213) or "Holy God, you raise up prophets" (TFF 298).

JANUARY 16, 2000

SECOND SUNDAY AFTER THE EPIPHANY

INTRODUCTION

In the weeks of Epiphany, the church focuses on its mission in the world. Like Samuel we seek to hear God's voice as we pray: "Speak, your servant is listening." In baptism God calls us to be servants who go forth with a simple mission: invite others to come and see. Having seen God's great epiphany in Christ Jesus, we now graciously invite others to see Christ who is with us in the word, the waters of rebirth, and the holy supper.

The Week of Prayer for Christian Unity begins Tuesday (January 18).

PRAYER OF THE DAY

Lord God, you showed your glory and led many to faith by the works of your Son. As he brought gladness and healing to his people, grant us these same gifts and lead us also to perfect faith in him, Jesus Christ our Lord.

READINGS

1 Samuel 3:1-10 [11-20]
  Today's reading recounts the transition from the leadership of Eli the priest to Samuel. At a time when visions and auditions were rare and unexpected, the Lord comes to Samuel and calls him to speak the divine word.

Psalm 139:1-5, 12-17 (Psalm 139:1-6, 13-18 [NRSV])
  You have searched me out and known me. (Ps. 139:1)

1 Corinthians 6:12-20
  Some recent converts in the Corinthian church believed that God was interested only in what was spiritual so that what they did with their bodies did not matter. Paul's response affirms God's concern for the entire person.

John 1:43-51
  In John's gospel, Jesus' ministry begins with the call of disciples, who then bring others to Jesus. Philip's friend Nathanael moves from skepticism to faith when he accepts the invitation to "Come and see."

COLOR Green

THE PRAYERS

Let us pray that the radiance of Christ will illumine the church, the nations, and all who seek the light.

A BRIEF SILENCE.

Let us pray for the church, that it might have a sense of urgency in its proclamation, and that the world may know of God's love for the whole creation. Lord, in your mercy,

hear our prayer.

Let us pray for all bishops, pastors, associates in ministry, and diaconal ministers, that they might hear the word of God and have courage for their tasks of proclamation and service. Lord, in your mercy,

hear our prayer.

Let us pray for all who seek to find the common ground between peoples of the world who are divided by nation, race, religion, economics, gender, age, and ability. Lord, in your mercy,

hear our prayer.

Let us pray for all in need, those who are facing illness, those who are grieving losses, those who are unemployed, those to whom death draws near (especially . . .). Lord, in your mercy,

hear our prayer.

Let us pray for all who are teachers of young people in our parish and community, that they might responsibly lead and nurture them in ways of wisdom, knowledge, and the fear of the Lord. Lord, in your mercy,

hear our prayer.

HERE OTHER INTERCESSIONS MAY BE OFFERED.

Let us pray in thanksgiving for the lives of all who have died, for Martin Luther King Jr., and especially those most dear to us, that we will be kept united with them while we live and when we die. Lord, in your mercy,

hear our prayer.

Hear our spoken and silent prayers, O God of light, and reveal yourself to us, through your Son, Jesus Christ our Lord.

Amen

IMAGES FOR PREACHING

A rare word and an infrequent vision—the description is about the days of Samuel, but could it not describe our own time as well? With all the babble of cyberspace and the sensory pollution that assaults us from every direction, we barely are able to hear or see anything. Like Samuel, we lie in our bed at night not sure what we are hearing. Like Eli, our sight has grown dim.

The issue, as Nathanael discovers, is not merely to see but to be seen. A prophet from Nazareth? Nathanael cannot see it—no way! But Nathanael *is seen* by the one who sees in Nathanael an Israelite without deceit, a son of Jacob who will not trick or be tricked. Jesus perhaps sees in Nathanael more than Nathanael sees in himself. Jesus looks at Nathanael with eyes of a love that wins him over.

That love claims us. It does strange things to us. It makes us so that we are no longer our own: we belong to someone else. We belong to Love. Not even our appetites can we now call our own; neither our stomachs nor any other parts of our bodies are simply there for our pleasure or use. We belong to another. And because we have been claimed and ultimately alienated from our old selves we now find ourselves to be gifts of love given to others. In this realization is the beginning of that gladness and healing of which the prayer of the day speaks. The voice in the dark knows us, calls us, sees in us more than we see in ourselves, and calls us to new life that is the beginning of our epiphany!

WORSHIP MATTERS

Freedom within liturgical planning does not imply that worship planners have license to do anything they desire with the liturgy. Liturgical planning is best done within a freedom that determines what is most helpful for the assembly's life. The Lutheran confessions, when discussing church practice (see *Apology of the Augsburg Confession*, article 15, and *Formula of Concord*, article 10), provide some questions for determining whether a liturgical practice is beneficial: Does it encourage order within worship? Does it inspire discipline within the life of the Christian? Does it provide a context in which the gospel can be heard? Does it teach the truth that is revealed in Jesus Christ? When these questions are answered positively then the practice will prove helpful to the church's life.

LET THE CHILDREN COME

For God, revelation is not only a matter of the eyes, but the ears as well. God uses names to be revealed to us, and God uses names to call us as children. When we are baptized, God calls our given name and baptizes us in the triune name. Encourage the use of names among members, and remember to include the children, by name, in the sharing of Christ's peace and at the Lord's table, where it is precisely the Lord who speaks to us.

MUSIC FOR WORSHIP

GATHERING

LBW 393	Rise, shine, you people!
WOV 718	Here in this place

PSALM 139:1-5, 12-17

Farrell, Bernadette. "O God, You Search Me" in PS, vol. 3.

Hopson, Hal H. PW, cycle B.

Lisicky, Paul. "Psalm 139: Filling Me With Joy" in *Gather Comprehensive*. GIA.

Mahnke, Allan. "Psalm 139" in *17 Psalms for Cantor and Congregation*. CPH 97-6093. Cong, cant.

Marshall, Jane. "Psalm of Praise." AFP 11-04673. SATB.

LBW 311   Wondrous are your ways, O God (paraphrase)

HYMN OF THE DAY

LBW 503   O Jesus, I have promised
   MUNICH

INSTRUMENTAL RESOURCES

Elmshaeuser, Dale. "O Word of God Incarnate." Live Oak House 445-1137. SET. Brass.

Gawthrop, Daniel. "Munich" in *Sacred Suite for Organ*. AMSI SP-101. Org.

Tryggestad, David. "Munich" in *Deo Gracias*. AFP 11-10471. Org.

Wellman, Samuel. "O Jesus, I Have Promised" in *Keyboard Hymn Favorites*. AFP 11-10820. Pno.

Wolff, S. Drummond. "Munich" in *Hymn Descants, Set IV*. CPH 97-6275. Org, inst.

ALTERNATE HYMN OF THE DAY

WOV 752	I, the Lord of sea and sky
LBW 434	The Son of God, our Christ

COMMUNION

LBW 506	Dear Lord and Father of mankind
WOV 707	This is my body

SENDING

LBW 536   O God of God, O Light of light
WOV 650   We are marching in the light of God

ADDITIONAL HYMNS AND SONGS

H82 541   Come, labor on
UMH 582   Whom shall I send?
TFF 146   I can hear my Savior calling
W&P   Come to the mountain

MUSIC FOR THE DAY

CHORAL

Byrd, William/arr. Austin Lovelace. "Lord, Make Me to Know Thy Ways." CPH 98-2935. SATB.

Keesecker, Thomas. "The Silent Stars Shine Down on Us." AFP 11-10958. 2 pt mxd, pno, fc.

Manuel, Ralph. "Jesus Calls Us." MSM 50-8822. SATB, kybd.

Moore, Undine Smith. "I Believe This Is Jesus." AFP 11-559. Also in *The Augsburg Choirbook*. 11-10817. SATB.

Schutte, Dan/Ovid Young. "Here I Am, Lord." AFP 11-10747. SATB, pno.

Sedio, Mark. "Take My Life That It May Be. AFP 11-10967. SAB, kybd.

CHILDREN'S CHOIRS

Page, Sue Ellen. "Body, Mind, Spirit, Voice." CG CGA391. U, org, fl, opt tri and fc.

Pote, Allen. "Psalm 139." CG CGA610. SATB, piano.

KEYBOARD/INSTRUMENTAL

Chauvet/arr. Gordon Schuster. "Organ Noels for the Time of Christmas." CPH 97-6301. Org.

Hassell, Michael. "Here I Am, Lord" in *More Folkways*. AFP 11-10866. Trbl. inst., pno.

Honoré, Jeffrey. "Shine, Jesus, Shine." CPH 97-6698. Pno.

HANDBELL

Afdahl, Lee J. "Dear Lord and Father of Mankind." AFP 11-10770. 3-5 oct.

PRAISE ENSEMBLE

Butler, Terry. "Cry of My Heart" in *Maranatha! Music Praise Chorus Book, 3rd ed.* WRD/MAR.

Knapp, Phoebe P./Whaley and Clevenger. "Blessed Assurance." PLY SHS9705. SATB, pno.

LeBlanc, Lenny. "Come and See" in *Maranatha! Music Praise Chorus Book, 3rd ed.* WRD/MAR.

Makeever, Ray. "When You Call" in DATH.

Pote, Allen. "Psalm 139." CG CGA610. SATB, pno.

Schutte, Dan/arr. Mark Hayes. "Here I Am, Lord." GS A7101. SATB, orch.

TUESDAY, JANUARY 18
THE CONFESSION OF ST. PETER
WEEK OF PRAYER FOR CHRISTIAN UNITY BEGINS

The Week of Prayer for Christian Unity is framed by festivals centered in the two great apostles of the Christian faith—Peter and Paul. Both are jointly commemorated on June 29, but these two days give us an opportunity to focus on two key events from each of their lives. The Confession of St. Peter invites us to declare with him that Jesus is "the Christ, the Son of the living God." This common confession unites us with other Christians.

This coming week is the most natural occasion for an ecumenical service. The ELCA's full communion agreement with the Reformed churches provides a special opportunity this week. What other ecumenical ministries can evolve from the celebrations? Remember to include petitions for Christian unity in congregational prayers.

WEDNESDAY, JANUARY 19
HENRY, BISHOP OF UPPSALA, MISSIONARY TO FINLAND, MARTYR, 1156

Henry became bishop of Uppsala (Sweden) in 1152 and went with the king of Sweden to Finland. After the king returned home, Henry remained in Finland to organize the church. Murdered there in 1156, his burial place became a center of pilgrimage, and he became a popular saint in Sweden and Finland.

Today is an appropriate day to celebrate the Finnish presence in the Lutheran church. Consider singing "Lost in the night" (LBW 394), which uses a Finnish folk tune. During Epiphany we celebrate the light of Christ revealed to the nations. How does Henry inspire us to carry the light to all the world? How can Christian unity be a witness in our missionary efforts?

JANUARY 23, 2000
THIRD SUNDAY AFTER THE EPIPHANY

INTRODUCTION

In today's gospel reading, Jesus uses the common experience of fishing and turns it upside down. Each baptized Christian, born in God's gracious sea, is called to fish for people. We are given the net of God's mercy and the gift of the Holy Spirit's presence as we go forth and invite others to join us in our communal journey of discipleship.

The Week of Prayer for Christian Unity continues through Tuesday.

PRAYER OF THE DAY

Almighty God, you sent your Son to proclaim your kingdom and to teach with authority. Anoint us with the power of your Spirit, that we, too, may bring good news to the afflicted, bind up the brokenhearted, and proclaim liberty to the captive; through your Son, Jesus Christ our Lord.

READINGS

Jonah 3:1-5, 10

Unlike other prophetic books that focus on the prophet's message, this book focuses on the prophet himself. The book of Jonah is really a comedy starring a reluctant prophet who is given a one-sentence message: Nineveh will be destroyed in forty days. The point of the story is to get the reader to wrestle with the question: "On whom should God have mercy?"

Psalm 62:6-14 (Psalm 62:5-12 [NRSV])

In God is my safety and my honor. (Ps. 62:8)

1 Corinthians 7:29-31

In his letters to the Corinthians, Paul addresses many problems experienced by those who want faith to shape daily life. Here he insists that our future hope in Christ ought to affect the way we conduct ourselves in the present.

Mark 1:14-20

Before Jesus calls his first disciples, he proclaims a message that becomes known as the gospel or good news from God. God is ready to rule our lives. Those who recognize this good news will respond with repentance and faith.

COLOR   Green

THE PRAYERS

Let us pray that the radiance of Christ will illumine the church, the nations, and all who seek the light.

A BRIEF SILENCE.

Unite all Christians of the world, that petty differences and profound divisions alike would be reconciled as we strengthen our baptismal bonds. Lord, in your mercy,
hear our prayer.

Even as Jesus taught his disciples to fish for people, may we who follow in your way always strive to care for all people without reserve. Lord, in your mercy,
hear our prayer.

Bless the cities of our world with honest leaders and responsible citizens. Give urban dwellers patience as they live and work among many people. Lord, in your mercy,
hear our prayer.

Help all who experience economic stress because of lack of work, that they might find employment in which they can produce a good livelihood for themselves and their loved ones. Gently watch over those who are ill (especially . . .). Lord, in your mercy,
hear our prayer.

Energize the ministries of outreach in this congregation so that many will hear your message of hope and forgiveness. Raise up new workers to help us tend to our tasks of service and proclamation. Lord, in your mercy,
hear our prayer.

HERE OTHER INTERCESSIONS MAY BE OFFERED.

Give us a sense of continuity and community with those who have died and now rest from their labors. Comfort all those who are mourning the loss of a loved one. Lord, in your mercy,
hear our prayer.

Hear our spoken and silent prayers, O God of light, and reveal yourself to us, through your Son, Jesus Christ our Lord.
Amen

IMAGES FOR PREACHING

So early in the year it may seem strange to think about time running out. We've only just begun! But after

John's arrest, Jesus picks up the baptizer's message: "The time is fulfilled; repent!" Of course, it is more than time running out. No, this time is "fulfilled." The Greek verb could just as easily mean "filled full," a "fullness of time," a *kairos*.

James and John sense the immediacy. They drop everything and follow Jesus. Zebedee is left with the family business and nets needing mending and no sons to help him. Does he think of this message as "good news"? The gospel is disruptive to the status quo. This disruption too is part of what it means to repent, to have "the new mind."

Paul speaks about it also to the Corinthians. Time grows short. When the form of the world is passing away, behaviors and even basic relationships must be reconfigured. It is no time for "business as usual"!

The deadline is strongest in the first reading; forty days is all the Ninevites have. It's like a modern disaster movie: the comet hurling toward earth. What are we going to do? The readings hold a mirror to our lives and make us realize that we think we have forever, especially at the beginning of a new year, especially when the world clock has just rolled over four digits. But the immediacy of grace asks for resolution now. We dare not be lulled into thinking that grace means we can wait around for a better day. Jesus says "Follow me" and then moves on his way. The decision is now or never. But when the decision is made, the time is filled full. The present moment transformed by grace becomes a doorway to eternity. When the present order of things passes away, what lies before us is an infinity of love, and what we gain by grabbing hold of grace is *now* and *forever*.

WORSHIP MATTERS

In this Sunday's gospel reading, Jesus invites four disciples to follow him and fish for people. The image of fishing for people evokes a multitude of biblical images associated with water, among them, Noah's ark and Jonah in the whale's belly. These symbols provide powerful ways to speak to children who can relate to water's role in daily life. How might these symbols be employed to communicate with children? How might the children make use of these images in the worship space? For instance, if children are invited to gather around the baptismal font for a baptism, perhaps one of them could present a baptismal shell to the presiding minister. What are other tangible ways to involve the children with the water-laden symbols of salvation?

LET THE CHILDREN COME

Many children know the story of God saving Jonah, but fewer will be as familiar with God saving the people of Nineveh through Jonah's preaching. Retell the story from Nineveh's standpoint. God delivered Jonah from the fish for the sake of all the people of Nineveh. In the same way, God delivered Jesus from death so that all might be saved through him. So it is that we hear "To those who believe in Jesus Christ he gives the power to become the children of God." Children of God live with God forever.

MUSIC FOR WORSHIP

GATHERING

| LBW 400 | God, whose almighty word |
| WOV 800 | Each morning brings us |

PSALM 62:6-14

Haas, David/arr. Jeanne Cotter. "In God Alone" in PCY, vol III.
Hopson, Hal H. PW, cycle B.
Marcus, Mary. "Third Sunday after the Epiphany" in *Psalm Antiphons-3*. MSM 80-723. U, opt hb.

HYMN OF THE DAY

| LBW 380 | O Christ, our light, O Radiance true |
| | O JESU CHRISTE, WAHRES LICHT |

VOCAL RESOURCES

Hobby, Robert. "O Christ, Our Light, O Radiance True." CPH 98-2891. 2pt, ob, kybd.

INSTRUMENTAL RESOURCES

Diemer, Emma Lou. "O Jesu Christe, wahres Licht" in *Hymn Preludes and Free Accompaniments, vol. 2*. AFP 11-9398. Org.
Herl, Joseph. "O Jesu Christe, wahres Licht" in *Six Hymn Inventions for Organ*. CPH 97-6654. Org.
Manz, Paul. "O Jesu Christe, wahres Licht" in *Improvisations on General Hymns*. MSM 10-830. Org.

ALTERNATE HYMN OF THE DAY

| LBW 449 | They cast their nets |
| WOV 784 | You have come down to the lakeshore |

COMMUNION
- LBW 494   Jesus calls us: o'er the tumult
- WOV 761   Now we offer

SENDING
- LBW 200   For the bread which you have broken
- WOV 754   Let us talents and tongues emloy

ADDITIONAL HYMNS AND SONGS
- DATH 30   This bread that we break
- NCH 504   You walk along the shoreline
- TFF 65   This little light of mine
- W&P   Go, make disciples

MUSIC FOR THE DAY

CHORAL

Bach, J. S./arr. Patrick Liebergren. "Dedication Prayer" (Bist du bei mir) in *Favorite Sacred Classic for Solo Singers.* ALF 11482 (ML); 11481; (MH).

Christiansen, F. Melius. "O Day Full of Grace." AFP 11-0206. SSATTBB.

Graham, John. "Jesu dulcis memoria" (Jesus, the very thought of thee). ION CH 1022. 2 pt, opt 4 pt.

Hassell, Michael. "This Little Light of Mine." AFP 11-10889. SATB, kybd.

Helman, Michael. "Come, Great God of All the Ages." AFP 11-10881. SATB, kybd.

Olson, Howard. "When Jesus Worked Here on Earth" in *Set Free, Set Free.* AFP 3-420. SATB.

Wood, Dale. "Rise, Shine!" AFP 11-642. Also in *The Augsburg Choirbook.* 11-10817. SATB, org.

CHILDREN'S CHOIRS

Pote, Allen. "Sing a Song of Praise." CG CGA182. U, org, opt fl.

Sleeth, Natalie. "God Is Like a Rock." CG CGA395. U, kybd.

KEYBOARD/INSTRUMENTAL

Callahan, Charles. "They Cast Their Nets in Galilee" in *Gift of Finest Wheat.* CPH 97-6268. Org.

Rippen, Piet. "O Jezus Christus, licht ze bij" in *Drie partita's voor orgel.* PRE 513-00749. Org.

HANDBELL

Afdahl, Lee J. "Lead On, O King Eternal." AFP 11-10770. 3-5 oct.

Afdahl, Lee J. "You Have Come Down to the Lakeshore" in *Two Spanish Tunes for Handbells.* AFP 11-10874. 3-5 oct, opt perc.

PRAISE ENSEMBLE

Althouse, Jay. "Come Follow Me." ALF 4255. SAB, acc. Also available 4254, SATB; 4256, 2 pt.

Barbour and Barbour. "I Will Follow" in *Maranatha! Music Praise Chorus Book, 3rd ed.* WRD/MAR.

Chapman, Steven Curtis/arr. Hamby. "For the Sake of the Call." in *Men of God Arise!* BRM SPBK4006. SATB, children, acc.

Kendrick, Graham. "Shine, Jesus, Shine" in *Shine Jesus Shine Songbook.* Alleluia Community Ministries, Inc. 00957. SATB, acc.

Kendrick, Graham. "We Declare That the Kingdom of God Is Here" in *Come & Worship.* INT.

Makeever, Ray. "Rest in God Alone" in DATH.

TUESDAY, JANUARY 25
THE CONVERSION OF ST. PAUL
WEEK OF PRAYER FOR CHRISTIAN UNITY ENDS

The commemoration of Paul's conversion was first celebrated among the Christians of Gaul. It is inspired by narratives describing this event in the Acts of the Apostles, Galatians, and 1 Corinthians. The risen Christ appeared to Paul on the road to Damascus and called him to proclaim the gospel of Christ.

As the Week of Prayer for Christian Unity ends, use this occasion to reflect on the meaning of our oneness in Christ. How can your congregation, along with other churches, more faithfully witness to the light of Christ?

WEDNESDAY, JANUARY 26
TIMOTHY, TITUS, AND SILAS

Following the festival of the Conversion of St. Paul, we remember three of his companions. Timothy accompanied Paul on his second missionary journey and became the first bishop of Ephesus. Titus joined Paul on the journey to the apostolic council at Jerusalem and became the first bishop of Crete. Silas was a companion of Paul on his first visit to Macedonia and Corinth.

As you commemorate these three early Christian leaders, consider the pastors, teachers, and lay leaders who were influential in your Christian formation. In a committee meeting or small group allow each person to name a significant person who was an Epiphany light for them.

EPIPHANY JAN 30

THURSDAY, JANUARY 27
LYDIA, DORCAS, AND PHOEBE

Today we remember three women in the early church. Lydia and her household were baptized by Paul, who with his companions stayed for a time at her house. Dorcas was known for her charitable works and her skill and generosity in making clothing. Her name was used in the later Dorcas societies of church women devoted to good works. Phoebe was a deaconess or helper of the church at Cenchreae. Paul praises her as one who looked after a great many people.

Today provides an opportunity to give thanks for women who have served faithfully in the church as pastors, teachers, deaconesses, and lay leaders. How has the ordination of women as pastors provided the church with new gifts and resources for ministry and mission? Tell stories of women who have been influential in your life of faith.

JANUARY 30, 2000

FOURTH SUNDAY AFTER THE EPIPHANY

INTRODUCTION

In the scriptures the word is announced through prophets who speak for God, and later through Jesus who teaches with authority. The church continues to proclaim the gospel of God's great love for humankind. We gather around Christ, the Word made flesh, to hear that God is gracious and full of compassion. It is the authority of the gospel that enables us to announce a prophetic word of judgment and mercy to the world in which we live.

PRAYER OF THE DAY

O God, you know that we cannot withstand the dangers which surround us. Strengthen us in body and spirit so that, with your help, we may be able to overcome the weakness that our sin has brought upon us; through Jesus Christ, your Son our Lord.

READINGS

Deuteronomy 18:15-20

Today's reading, part of a longer discussion of prophecy in Deuteronomy 18, stands within a still broader context: an updating of the law for the Israelite community as the people wait to enter the promised land. Here Moses assures the people that God will continue to guide them through prophets who will proclaim the divine word.

Psalm 111

The fear of the LORD is the beginning of wisdom. (Ps. 111:10)

1 Corinthians 8:1-13

God's people are set free by Jesus' death and resurrection. Customary restrictions no longer apply. Notice, though, that those for whom Christ died find this freedom has limits. The gospel compels us to care about each other.

Mark 1:21-28

The story has barely begun, and already the battle is joined. Jesus sides with humanity against every force that would bring death and disease. These forces recognize Jesus and know what his power means for them. This battle, however, is only the first fight. The war will go on much longer.

COLOR   Green

THE PRAYERS

Let us pray that the radiance of Christ will illumine the church, the nations, and all who seek the light.
A BRIEF SILENCE.

For the church of Christ, that God will raise up prophetic voices to proclaim God's living word without reserve. Lord, in your mercy,
hear our prayer.

For the natural resources of creation, the environment, and all living creatures, that all would be preserved from abuse and neglect. Lord, in your mercy,
hear our prayer.

For those who have no voice in our society, for immigrants and refugees, for those in exile or being held

captive, and for all others who are stifled in speech and expression. Lord, in your mercy,
hear our prayer.
For those in this congregation who struggle in relationships, and for those whose spirits contend with forces that wish them harm. For those whose bodies are weak and in need of God's healing strength (especially . . .). Lord, in your mercy,
hear our prayer.

HERE OTHER INTERCESSIONS MAY BE OFFERED.

For those who have died, that with them we may at length find rest in your gracious and eternal presence where there will be no more sorrow or pain. Lord, in your mercy,
hear our prayer.
Hear our spoken and silent prayers, O God of light, and reveal yourself to us, through your Son, Jesus Christ our Lord.
Amen

IMAGES FOR PREACHING

Prophets, idols, and demons move through the readings appointed for this day. Although each character type is different from the others, they all bear a common mark of a reality touched by the supernatural. Moses is the benchmark for every prophet to follow. It was an agreement made in Israel's infancy, when the people cried to God to be protected from that divine voice and fire they knew could slay them. As the prayer of the day suggests, we are surrounded by dangers we cannot withstand, and one of them could be God! There is a divine power that does not appreciate tinkering. The prophet is meant to protect people from that power.

Idols are make-believe. They are false gods who have no power. But C. S. Lewis, in the concluding volume of the Chronicles of Narnia, *The Last Battle,* does a masterful job of showing how we can be controlled by our idols, imaginary or not. Paul knows the same thing. The issue is not whether an idol is real but rather what it can do to us. The consequence goes beyond offending weak sisters and brothers. The deeper issue is whether we can be controlled even by things we believe to be unreal. We can. We are.

What unclean spirits lurk within us? Where do we need exorcism? We believe ourselves immune from such superstitious apprehension. But even though Tash may be of our own making, it is still a danger we cannot withstand. Good Lord, deliver us! From all the idols and demons, protect us, especially those of our own making.

A prophet like Moses moves among us, one whom the demons recognize and obey. The touch of the man from Nazareth offers hope and healing for all, and his story still has power to amaze us.

WORSHIP MATTERS

As displayed by his teaching in the Capernaum synagogue in this Sunday's gospel reading, Jesus' authority was recognized in his teaching ministry. Although Jesus' authority did reside within his own person as the Son of God, he did not flaunt it, but allowed it to come to expression through his ministry of service. How should the assembly's ministers approach the authority given them in liturgical service? Their authority does not reside in their own person, but is a gift given them by Christ and his body, the church. It is an authority that should be used in service to the assembly's worship and life. This authority is a service that seeks what is best for the assembly's life: proclaiming the gospel, teaching the Word that is Christ, and forming disciplined attitudes within the lives of those assembled together. Any authority that derives from the person or perceived status of the liturgical minister ceases to be an authority that comes from Christ.

LET THE CHILDREN COME

Teach children the psalm antiphon. Children understand fear. Human beings fear what we do not understand and cannot control. To fear God is to recognize that God is bigger than we are and bigger than we ever will be, no matter how much we discover and engineer. Wisdom is knowing that God is with us in Jesus and that no matter how afraid, perplexed, or troubled we may be, we can cry to God for help. Ask children to help make a list of things people fear and include them in one of the prayer petitions.

MUSIC FOR WORSHIP
GATHERING
LBW 550	From all that dwell below the skies
WOV 802	When in our music God is glorified

PSALM 111

Cherwien, David. "I Will Give Thanks to the Lord." CPH 98-2930. U, desc.

Hopson, Hal H. "Psalm 111" in *Psalm Refrains and Tones for the Common Lectionary*. HOP 425. U, cong, kybd.

Hopson, Hal H. PW, cycle B.

Marshall, Jane. "Psalm 111" in UMH.

Nelson, Ronald. "I Will Give Thanks." AFP 11-04678. SATB, U.

HYMN OF THE DAY

LBW 393   Rise, shine, you people!
            WOJTKIEWIECZ

VOCAL RESOURCES

Wood, Dale. "Rise, Shine!" AFP 11-10737. Also in *The Augsburg Choirbook*. 11-10817. SATB, org, opt cong.

INSTRUMENTAL RESOURCES

Cherwien, David. "Rise, Shine You People: Toccata and Fugue for Organ." AFP 11-10523. Org.

Cook, Larry D. "Earth and All Stars and Rise, Shine, You People!" AFP 11-10712. Org, brass, cong, opt perc.

Dahl, David P. "Wojtkiewiecz" in *The Concordia Hymn Prelude Series, vol. 42*. CPH 97-5860. Org.

Linker, Janet and Jane McFadden. "Rise, Shine, You People!" AFP 11-10628. Hb, org, opt tpt.

ALTERNATE HYMN OF THE DAY

WOV 737   There is a balm in Gilead
LBW 90   Songs of thankfulness and praise

COMMUNION

LBW 439   What a friend we have in Jesus
WOV 738   Healer of our every ill

OTHER SUGGESTIONS

DATH 26   Christ, have mercy on us all

SENDING

LBW 559   Oh, for a thousand tongues to sing
WOV 796   My Lord of light

ADDITIONAL HYMNS AND SONGS

GS2 22   The right hand of God
H82 584   God, you have given us power
TFF 207   Satan, we're going to tear your kingdom down
W&P   I will delight

MUSIC FOR THE DAY

CHORAL

Gerike, Henry V. "In You, Lord, I Have Put My Trust." CPH 98-3353. SSA/SSB/TTB, cont.

Hobby, Robert A. "Open Your Ears, O Faithful People." AFP 11-10752. U, opt desc, hb, fl, perc.

Poston, Elizabeth. "The Apple Tree." Eboracum 141. SATB.

Schulz-Widmar, Russell. "God Remembers." AFP 11-10882. SATB, kybd.

Titcomb, Evertt. "O Love, How Deep." HWG 2226. SATB, org.

CHILDREN'S CHOIRS

Handel/arr. Hal H. Hopson. "Blest Are They Whose Spirits Long." CG CGA183. 2 pt mxd, kybd.

Ziegenhals, Harriet. "Oh, Sing to the Lord" (Cantad al Señor) CG CGA640. U/2 pt, kybd, opt maracas.

KEYBOARD/INSTRUMENTAL

Leavitt, John. "Epiphany" in *Simple Gifts*. CLP EL9510. Pno.

Mitchell-Wallace, Sue and John Head. "March of the Three Kings" in *Christmas Majesty*. HOP 313. Org, tpt.

HANDBELL

Linker, Janet/arr. Jane McFadden. "Rise, Shine, You People!" AFP 11-10628. Full score; AFP 11-10629. Hb.

PRAISE ENSEMBLE

Davis, Greg and Greg Fisher/arr. John Innes. "Honor the Lord." HOP WT1522. SATB, kybd.

Haugen, Marty. "He Came Down." GIA G-3808. SATB, children, solo, gtr, pno, perc.

Hendricks, J. "The Mighty One of Israel" in *Come & Worship*. INT.

Owens and Collins. "The Battle Belongs to the Lord" in *Songs for Praise and Worship*. WRD.

Pethel, Stan. "He Is Exalted" (with "O For a Thousand Tongues to Sing") in *The Sunday Celebration Choir Kit*. WAR 08741317. 2 pt mxd, kybd.

WEDNESDAY, FEBRUARY 2
THE PRESENTATION OF OUR LORD

Forty days after the birth of Christ we celebrate his presentation in the temple by his parents. Two aged saints, Anna and Simeon, recognize him as the promised messiah. Simeon speaks the words of the beloved Nunc dimittis in which he calls Jesus a "light for the nations."

This day is also called Candlemas, a traditional time to bless candles for the coming year. We are midway between winter and spring, and the custom of the groundhog looking for his shadow symbolizes our hope for the coming light and warmth of spring. Whenever congregational groups gather today, let them light candles and read the account of the presentation from Luke. Consider a festive evening prayer service with the church illumined by candlelight. Make sure to sing a setting of the Song of Simeon (such as LBW 339 or 349). Children's groups might tell the stories of Jesus as a child or play games from other areas of the world.

THURSDAY, FEBRUARY 3
ANSGAR, ARCHBISHOP OF HAMBURG,
MISSIONARY TO DENMARK AND SWEDEN, 865

Ansgar was a missionary who brought the Epiphany light of Christ to the peoples of Scandinavia. A monk of the ninth century, Ansgar was committed to preaching and care for the poor. So deep was his love for the poor that he would wash their feet and serve them at table with food provided by the parish. Ansgar preached in Denmark and then in Sweden where he built the first church. He was named archbishop of Hamburg in 831, and from there he sent missions to the north. At his death missionary work to these lands stopped for 300 years.

Ansgar is honored by Scandinavian Lutherans today, especially the Danes. Numerous churches, societies, and educational institutions are named for him. The commemoration of Ansgar allows another opportunity for a parish to reflect on its mission. How do we witness to Christ's light through preaching, education, and social outreach? How do we prepare the next generation to share the story of faith?

SATURDAY, FEBRUARY 5
THE MARTYRS OF JAPAN, 1597

This day commemorates the crucifixion of three Japanese Jesuits, six Franciscans, one Korean, and sixteen Japanese laypersons in the city of Nagasaki in 1597. Fifty years after Francis Xavier brought the Christian faith to Japan, these twenty-six Christians became the first martyrs of the Far East. Persecutions extended over the next century in an effort to prohibit the celebration of the eucharist. When Christian missionaries returned to Japan more than 200 years later, they discovered—to their utter surprise—thousands of Christians in the Nagasaki region who gathered to worship in secret.

This commemoration challenges us to consider the cost of discipleship, and to pray for boldness in our witness to Christ. How can the martyrs of Japan inspire the church today to be faithful to its calling to walk in the way of the cross?

FEBRUARY 6, 2000

FIFTH SUNDAY AFTER THE EPIPHANY

INTRODUCTION

In today's gospel Jesus cures the sick, proclaims the gospel, and casts out demons. His ministry reveals God's compassionate heart in which the lowly are lifted up and the brokenhearted are healed. As we gather around Christ present in word and meal, we are given strength to wait for the Lord in the midst of our suffering. Living as the body of Christ, our very lives are signs of God's gracious intent for humankind.

PRAYER OF THE DAY

Almighty God, you sent your only Son as the Word of life for our eyes to see and our ears to hear. Help us to believe with joy what the Scriptures proclaim, through Jesus Christ our Lord.

READINGS

Isaiah 40:21-31

The Judeans in exile have a reason to be hopeful: the One who will bring them to freedom is the God who created the world and gives strength to those who are weary.

Psalm 147:1-12, 21c (Psalm 147:1-11, 20c [NRSV])

The LORD heals the brokenhearted. (Ps. 147:3)

1 Corinthians 9:16-23

Paul continues his careful argument about the freedom of God's people. In Christ we are free, he says, not to injure one another, but to help. Using his own work as an example, Paul argues that we are not so much free from each other as free for each other.

Mark 1:29-39

Everywhere Jesus goes, many people expect him to set them free from oppression. Everywhere he goes, he heals them, and sets them free. Disease, devils, and death are running for their lives. The forces that diminish human life are rendered powerless by Jesus.

COLOR Green

THE PRAYERS

Let us pray that the radiance of Christ will illumine the church, the nations, and all who seek the light.

A BRIEF SILENCE.

O God of the weary and faint, grant strength to your people that the church would radiate the healing wholeness that is the birthright of all creation. Lord, in your mercy,

hear our prayer.

O God of all, you bring rulers and those in authority to justice in your light. Show your wise and all-loving face to the leaders of the nations, that they may govern fairly and rule wisely. Lord, in your mercy,

hear our prayer.

O God of healing, guide medical researchers who search for cures to illnesses that are chronic or fatal. Comfort and cure those among us who are sick with various diseases (especially . . .). Lord, in your mercy,

hear our prayer.

O God of the weak and the strong, bless the ministries of all parish nurses, hospitals, and homes for the elderly with a spirit of compassion and mercy. Lord, in your mercy,

hear our prayer.

HERE OTHER INTERCESSIONS MAY BE OFFERED.

O God of life and death, knowing that the faithful departed are in your hands, we commend ourselves to those same hands of steadfast faithfulness and love. Lord, in your mercy,

hear our prayer.

Hear our spoken and silent prayers, O God of light, and reveal yourself to us, through your Son, Jesus Christ our Lord.

Amen

IMAGES FOR PREACHING

What do you know? Have you not heard? Have you not seen? Reality can escape us, especially when we know it already, or when it seems commonplace. But as the prayer of the day suggests, God sent a word of life for eyes to see and ears to hear. So that it does not blend into the background of what we already perceive, the epiphany is meant to surprise us.

Paul has a strange contract, a commission from God. He has to be all things to all people, a task as impossible as it is thankless, like the pastor who is supposed to have the energy and idealism of a seminary graduate and the experience and wisdom of a preacher nearing retirement. But even more astounding is the wage: it is zero, grace given free of charge. These are strange economics! Perhaps your congregation has recently passed its budget. How could the economics of grace infect us and shape our corporate life? The preacher giving up a salary is not the only way. Perhaps we must be freed from the fevers that infect us!

Last Sunday's readings invited us to reflect on our demons and idols. They infect us all. The fever of panic, of not having enough, of fearing for the future—all this can flow from pastor to people or people to pastor. We spread the disease in the very air we breathe when we are together.

We are rich! Have you not known? Have you not heard? The wonder of creation is trumped by the treasuries of grace and unconditional love. With wings of eagles we can soar into the skies of God's love. We can run and not be weary. We can offer our very selves, modeling that new life but even more, becoming the channel through which it flows into others. *What do you know!*

WORSHIP MATTERS

The service of all ministers, both lay and ordained, is to proclaim the gospel, both in the liturgical assembly and in the local community. This obligation requires all ministers of the gospel to tailor their proclamation of the gospel message for the particular people among whom they are ministering. It requires flexibility and a willingness to identify with the needs and weaknesses of the people to whom the gospel is proclaimed.

The weaknesses of the community and points of resistance to the gospel message must first be identified and overcome. What are the points of resistance within your community? Poverty? Wealth? Prejudice? Racial discrimination? Moral laxity? Crime? How can the church's worship serve as a means to address these points of resistance? Worship leaders, in their teaching and preaching, should draw from the liturgy the means by which the assembly can overcome resistance to the gospel within the community.

LET THE CHILDREN COME

The Isaiah reading vividly sets the stage for hearing the gospel. Use children and youth in a visual and audible presentation of this text. The repeated "Have you not known? Have you not heard?" could be taught to younger children. Verses 22-23 are easily mimed (let the children decide how) while a reader speaks the text, including verse 24. Verse 25 is an "I don't know" gesture and verse 26 is portrayed by shading the eyes looking up and counting the stars while the lector reads verses 25-27. The two questions are repeated and the acclamation is spoken by all youth in unison, or by individuals reading one line at a time through verse 31.

MUSIC FOR WORSHIP

GATHERING

LBW 265	Christ, whose glory fills the skies
WOV 652	Arise, your light has come!

PSALM 147:1-12, 21

Hopson, Hal H. PW, cycle B.

Polyblank, Christopher. "Praise the Lord" in PS, vol. 3.

HYMN OF THE DAY

LBW 493	Hope of the world
	DONNE SECOURS

VOCAL RESOURCES

Lovelace, Austin. "Hope of the World." CPH 98-2434. SATB/2 pt mxd, kybd.

INSTRUMENTAL RESOURCES

Diemer, Emma Lou. "Donne secours" in *Hymn Preludes and Free Accompaniments*, vol. 2. AFP 11-9398. Org.

Rotermund, Don. "Donne secours" in *Seven Hymn Preludes, set 4*. CPH 97-6573. Org.

ALTERNATE HYMN OF THE DAY

WOV 779	You who dwell in the shelter of the Lord
LBW 543	Praise to the Lord, the Almighty

COMMUNION

LBW 481	Savior, like a shepherd lead us
WOV 702	I am the Bread of life

SENDING

LBW 390	I love to tell the story
WOV 790	Praise to you, O God of mercy

ADDITIONAL HYMNS AND SONGS

H82	476	Can we by searching find out God
NCH	176	Silence! Frenzied, unclean spirit
TFF	190	God has smiled on me
W&P		Beauty for brokenness

MUSIC FOR THE DAY

CHORAL

Busarow, Donald. "Jesus Has Come and Brings Pleasure." CPH 98-3160. Full Score 97-6400. SATB, bar solo, hrn, org.

Hopson, Hal H. "When We Are Living" (Pues Si Vivimos). AFP 11-10966. SATB, kybd.

Nystedt, Knut. "Get You Up." HIN HMC-439. SATB div.

Powell, Robert J. "The Great Creator of the Worlds." AFP 11-10883. SATB, org.

Tcimpidis, David. "Hail to the Lord's Anointed." GIA G-3182. SATB, org.

Telfer, Nancy. "Sun of the World." Beaudoin SAC 4. SATB, org/hp.

CHILDREN'S CHOIRS

Hinnant, Henry. "Wait on the Lord." CG CGA661. U/2 pt, kybd.

Sleeth, Natalie. "Make Music for the Lord." CG CGA469. 2 pt, kybd.

KEYBOARD/INSTRUMENTAL

Kihlken, Henry. "March of the Kings" in *Glory to the Newborn King*. FLA HF5209. Org.

Organ, Anne Krentz. "On Eagle's Wings" in *On Eagle's Wings*. AFP 11-10711. Pno.

HANDBELL

Honore, Jeffrey. "On Eagle's Wings." CPH 97-6429. 3-5 oct.

Joncas, Michael/arr. John A. Behnke "I Want to Walk as a Child of the Light." CPH 97-6611. 3-5 oct.

PRAISE ENSEMBLE

Allen, Tricia and Martin J. Nystrom. "We Will Wait" in *Hosanna Music Songbook, vol. 7*. INT. HMSB07.

Fragar, Russell. "All the Power You Need" in *Hosanna! Music Songbook 11*. INT.

Joncas, Michael/arr. Mark Hayes. "On Eagle's Wings." ALF 16104. SATB. acc.

Manzo, Laura. "They Shall Soar Like Eagles." Fred Bock Music Co. BG2109. SATB, kybd, fl. Also available BG2023, 2 pt; BG2078, SAB.

Pote, Allen. "A Song of Joy." HOP AP450. SATB, pno.

FEBRUARY 13, 2000

SIXTH SUNDAY AFTER THE EPIPHANY
PROPER 1

INTRODUCTION

Today's readings include two stories of lepers cleansed of their disease. Naaman washes in the Jordan River, and Jesus stretches out his hand and touches a leper. In the waters of baptism we are cleansed of our sin, and throughout our lives we continue to be nourished by the healing power of the eucharistic meal. With our words and deeds we touch others with God's compassion and love.

PRAYER OF THE DAY

Lord God, mercifully receive the prayers of your people. Help us to see and understand the things we ought to do, and give us grace and power to do them; through your Son, Jesus Christ our Lord.

READINGS

2 Kings 5:1-14

Elisha tells Naaman, a Syrian general, to immerse himself in the Jordan River where he is cleansed of his leprosy, revealing not the magic of certain water but the power of Israel's God.

Psalm 30

My God, I cried out to you, and you restored me to health. (Ps. 30:2)

1 Corinthians 9:24-27

Paul uses two athletic images—the runner and the boxer—to call us to a life of discipline in which self-control is for the sake of a higher good, in this case the good of all God's people.

Mark 1:40-45

Jesus cures a leper and asks him to tell no one but a priest, in accordance with Levitical law. Though Jesus performs miracles, his identity as Messiah will not be understood until the cross.

COLOR Green

THE PRAYERS

Let us pray that the radiance of Christ will illumine the church, the nations, and all who seek the light.

A BRIEF SILENCE.

That the preaching and teaching of the church would be done so freely that many will be awakened to faith and become fervent proclaimers of your word of unfailing love. Lord, in your mercy,
hear our prayer.

That the work of world health organizations would extend to all areas of the world where your children are steeped in disease and disability. Lord, in your mercy,
hear our prayer.

That those who are living with terminal illness and other diseases will find compassionate care from loving persons whom you call to vocations of healing service (especially . . .). Lord, in your mercy,
hear our prayer.

That those who are candidates for baptism might be nurtured by faithful mentors and supportive faith communities. Lord, in your mercy,
hear our prayer.

HERE OTHER INTERCESSIONS MAY BE OFFERED.

That those who have died will surround us in the great cloud of witnesses as we continue on our earthly pilgrimage. Lord, in your mercy,
hear our prayer.

Hear our spoken and silent prayers, O God of light, and reveal yourself to us, through your Son, Jesus Christ our Lord.
Amen

IMAGES FOR PREACHING

In a race, you cannot think your way across the finish line. Your legs have to move, and if you want to win, they have to move faster than anyone else's. What do we need to be able to run the race? The prayer of the day suggests two pairs of ingredients for success: we need to *see and understand* and we also need *grace and power* to do so. These two sides of the same reality are well demonstrated in the readings.

Naaman, the commander-turned-leper, knows what he wants—it is health—and his young slave girl captured in the Aramean raids knows where he can get it. She sees and understands. Naaman does, too, but somehow the regimen Elisha prescribes seems way too simple. *How can water do such great things?* The ways of grace are tricky. "Doing nothing" seems a strange way to win a race or find a cure! But in his eventual turning around at his servants' insistence, Naaman is transformed. He lets go of his own power and begins to acknowledge the power of the God who can save him.

"If you choose, you can make me clean," the leper says to Jesus. To get to that point, you have to see and understand: we cannot do it alone. All the king's horses and chariots standing at Elisha's gate have next to nothing to do with the power that can heal Naaman, that can give him true life. When we see and understand that life comes from grace, we also gain the "power to do," to implement that force in our life and move us toward the finish line. Water *can* do great things, especially when connected to God's word. It is a power that becomes unstoppable with a force as relentless as the currents of the Jordan, the Abana, the Pharpar, and all the rivers of Damascus combined.

WORSHIP MATTERS

Given the silence that echoes from many congregations following the Sunday eucharist, one might think that nothing of much significance occurs in church. Yet what happens in the eucharist is no less profound than Jesus' healing of the leper in this Sunday's gospel reading. The leper freely proclaimed what had happened to him, apparently to all who could hear him. What in our worship can move the assembly to such proclamation following the eucharist? The assembly must sense in the eucharist that they have been touched by the divine. They should also sense the joy that comes through the divine touch, especially in the eucharistic communion itself. However, the assembly often does not know what words they are to speak outside of the worship setting. How can the liturgy provide them with the words that convey their joy to the world in which they live?

LET THE CHILDREN COME

Sickness always separates us from others and from the worship of God's people. That Jesus heals the sick means that he also draws them back into communion with him. Jesus' healing by the forgiveness of sin makes it possible for us to shake hands and share his peace. Teach the children to say "Peace be with you" and remind them (and adults) that when we share the peace, it is not a friendly hello or a time for being newsy. Jesus has given us a precious treasure that we are to share by repeating his word "Peace be with you," until all have gotten it. That treasure is the peace of Jesus' forgiveness.

MUSIC FOR WORSHIP

GATHERING
LBW 465	Evening and morning	
WOV 800	Each morning brings us	

PSALM 30
Hopson, Hal H. PW, cycle B.
Inwood, Paul. "I Will Praise You, Lord" in *RitualSong*. GIA.
Smith, Alan. "I Will Praise You" in PS, vol. 2.

HYMN OF THE DAY
LBW 90	Songs of thankfulness and praise
	SALZBURG

VOCAL RESOURCES
Powell, Robert J. "Songs of Thankfulness and Praise." GIA G-2456. SATB, cong, brass, timp.

INSTRUMENTAL RESOURCES
Bisbee, B. Wayne. "Salzburg" in *From the Serene to the Whimsical*. AFP 11-10561. Org.
Callahan, Charles. "Salzburg" in *Easter Music for Manuals*. MSM 10-408. Kybd.
Cherwien, David. "Songs of Thankfulness and Praise" in *Interpretations, Book IX*. AMSI SP-106. Org.
Wold, Wayne L. "Songs of Thankfulness and Praise, Set I." MSM 10-711. Org.

ALTERNATE HYMN OF THE DAY
WOV 737	There is a balm in Gilead
LBW 360	O Christ, the healer, we have come

COMMUNION
LBW 309	Lord Jesus, think on me
WOV 741	Thy holy wings

SENDING
LBW 480	Oh, that the Lord would guide my ways
WOV 722	Hallelujah! We sing your praises

ADDITIONAL HYMNS AND SONGS
UMH 709	Come, let us join our friends above
H82 443	From God Christ's deity came forth
TFF 111	I've just come from the fountain
W&P	Create in me a clean heart

MUSIC FOR THE DAY

CHORAL
Mendelssohn, Felix. "All Ye That Cried Unto the Lord" in *Hymn of Praise*. NMP NPM-102. SATB, org.
Pinkham, Daniel. "Wash Yourself in the Jordan" in *Alleluia for the Waters*. ECS 4971. SATB, org. 4970. TTBB, org.
Roberts, William Bradley. "In All These You Welcomed Me." AFP 11-10661. U, opt ob/C-B-flat inst.
Shepperd, Mark. "Balm in Gilead." AFP 11-10923. SATB, kybd.
Wienhorst, Richard. "Lord, Whose Love In Humble Service." MSM 50-9059. SATB, kybd.

CHILDREN'S CHOIRS
Handel, G. F./arr. Robert J. Powell. "Then Will I Jehovah's Praise." CG CGA220. U, kybd.
Page, Sue Ellen. "Jesus' Hands Were Kind Hands." CG CGA485. U, fl, kybd.

KEYBOARD/INSTRUMENTAL
Billingham, Richard. "There Is a Balm in Gilead" in *Seven Reflections on African American Spirituals*. AFP 11-10762. Org.
Cherwien, David. "Healer of Our Every Ill" in *Six Organ Preludes*. GIA G-4291. Org.

HANDBELL
Afdahl, Lee J. "If Thou But Suffer God to Guide Thee." AFP 11-10574. 3-4 oct.
Rogers, Sharon Elery. "The Star Medley." MSM 30-115. 2-3 oct.

PRAISE ENSEMBLE
Elliott, John G. "Mourning Into Dancing" in *I Call You to Praise*. SP 80030/1762-79434-7. SATB, orch.
Espinosa, Eddie. "Change My Heart, O God." *The Celebration Hymnal*. MAR.
Founds, Rick. "I Will Not Be Shaken" in *Praise Hymns & Choruses, 4th ed.* MAR.
Pethel, Stan. "He Is Exalted" (with "O For a Thousand Tongues to Sing") in *The Sunday Celebration Choir Kit*. WAR 08741317. 2 pt mxd, acc.

MONDAY, FEBRUARY 14
CYRIL, MONK, 869; METHODIUS, BISHOP, 885; MISSIONARIES TO THE SLAVS

These two brothers are known as the apostles to the southern Slavs. They were sent by the emperor to preach the gospel in Moravia during the ninth century. There they translated the scriptures and the liturgy into Slavonic, the vernacular language. The Czechs, Slovaks, Croats, Serbs, and Bulgars honor Cyril and Methodius as founders of their alphabet, translators of the liturgy, and builders of the foundation of Slavonic literature.

As the Epiphany season concludes, these two missionaries are another example of the light of Christ proclaimed to the nations. A congregation could remember them in the prayers, and the preacher could mention them in the sermon. Just as the voice from the cloud bid the disciples to listen to Jesus, Cyril and Methodius allowed the Slavic people to hear the gospel in their own language.

FRIDAY, FEBRUARY 18
MARTIN LUTHER, RENEWER OF THE CHURCH, 1546

Luther taught biblical exegesis at Wittenberg from 1511 until his death on this day in 1546. He posted his Ninety-five Theses concerning indulgences in 1517. He is honored by the church as a biblical scholar, a translator of the Bible, a reformer of the liturgy, a theologian and educator, and the father of German vernacular literature. His great love of scripture and music, and his profound sense of pastoral care for ordinary people remain prominent aspects of a distinctively Lutheran spirituality.

A Lenten study group might study Luther's Large Catechism. Use the season of Lent to teach the congregation to dip their hands in the baptismal font, make the sign of the cross, and repeat Luther's famous words: I am baptized!

FEBRUARY 20, 2000

SEVENTH SUNDAY AFTER THE EPIPHANY
PROPER 2

INTRODUCTION

Though we often proclaim God's faithfulness in ages past, God continues to do new things in our midst. In baptism God provides water in the wilderness, and in the Lord's supper God gives us food and drink for sustenance. The cross placed on our brow in baptism is the seal of the Spirit's presence in our lives, and by the authority of Christ each pastor proclaims that we are forgiven. Healed and restored, we pray that God's healing and forgiveness would be made known in our daily lives.

Today the church commemorates Rasmus Jensen, the first Lutheran pastor in North America.

PRAYER OF THE DAY

God of compassion, keep before us the love you have revealed in your Son, who prayed even for his enemies; in our words and deeds help us to be like him through whom we pray, Jesus Christ our Lord.
or
Lord God, we ask you to keep your family, the Church, always faithful to you, that all who lean on the hope of your promises may gain strength from the power of your love; through your Son, Jesus Christ our Lord.

READINGS

Isaiah 43:18-25

Addressing the Jewish exiles in Babylon, the prophet announces that God is sending refreshing water. God will remove their transgressions and forget their sins.

Psalm 41

Heal me, for I have sinned against you. (Ps. 41:4)

2 Corinthians 1:18-22

When some in the Corinthian community perceive Paul as someone unreliable, he defends himself by affirming the "yes" of God's promises and the Spirit as the seal of that pledge.

Mark 2:1-12

Jesus' power over sin and disease is revealed in his healing of a paralytic. Behind the story is a controversy over whether the Messiah has the authority to forgive sin.

COLOR Green

THE PRAYERS

Let us pray that the radiance of Christ will illumine the church, the nations, and all who seek the light.
A BRIEF SILENCE.

God of guidance, lead all who endure challenging times in their lives, that in the midst of wearisome ways they might know your assurance. Lord, in your mercy,
hear our prayer.

God of creation, give faith in your continual work to your whole church, that we might trust you for the new things you long to give us. Lord, in your mercy,
hear our prayer.

God of forgiveness, give to the leaders of the nations a strong sense of your merciful justice, that they may govern your people wisely. Lord, in your mercy,
hear our prayer.

God of healing, show yourself to those who are suffering, grant comfort to those who are sick (especially . . .), and may all find hope in your never-failing promises. Lord, in your mercy,
hear our prayer.

God of love, bless those who contemplate life-long commitments of friendship, marriage, and parenthood. May they learn ways of trust and forgiveness as they look to you. Lord, in your mercy,
hear our prayer.

HERE OTHER INTERCESSIONS MAY BE OFFERED.

O God, you lead all saints to their home in your eternal light. Reunite us with Rasmus Jensen and all who have served you, when you shall finally call us all to be in your presence. Lord, in your mercy,
hear our prayer.

Hear our spoken and silent prayers, O God of light, and reveal yourself to us, through your Son, Jesus Christ our Lord.
Amen

IMAGES FOR PREACHING

"Yes" and "No" are mutually exclusive. Our yes can be only as good as our no. The prophet in today's first reading accuses Israel of trying to live the yes and no together—of accepting their status as people of God and accepting the miracle of a new exodus from their exile in Babylon—yet continuing to burden God with sins and iniquities. But God's solution to this dilemma is astounding! God does not raise the bar higher or threaten them with eternal damnation if they do not shape up. No! God emphatically announces, "I am the one who blots out your transgression for my own sake, and I will not remember your sins." God's unconditional yes trumps our no and, at the same time, opens up the possibility of our leaving behind the old ways of no to grab hold of God's new yes.

The paralytic in Capernaum knows the no and yes of his own life. His no are legs that won't work; his yes would be the power to walk again, power he believes can come from Jesus. He is right. But Jesus ups the ante by giving a deeper diagnosis. "Son, your sins are forgiven." Those words of forgiveness also up the ante in the conflict between Jesus and his opponents and raises the charge of blasphemy, which will eventually send Jesus to the cross.

We may think we know the yes and no of our lives. We may think we have discerned the old things we must release and the new things we must grasp in order to pull us into the future. Jesus invites us to plumb the moral dimensions of our illnesses and problems. The yes of God in the forgiveness of sins is the one power in the universe that can dissolve the past and open the future—rivers in the desert and drink for thirsty people. God says yes to sinners seeking new life! Always.

WORSHIP MATTERS

The church, like its God, is tradition-bound. Yet, like its God as well, the church is always introducing new things into its worship, reflecting the church's journey through different times and cultures. The church's tradition provides the foundation upon which new things can be introduced into worship, but careful preparation is necessary when new things are introduced. Connections must be made with the tradition of the church, so that the new things may be seen as in continuity with that tradition. What are the best ways to prepare the people of God to receive new hymns, new musical settings of the eucharist, and new ritual practices within worship? How can the people be prepared so that the gospel is heard and experienced in that new element? At minimum, it requires planning, a sense of purpose, and an evangelical attitude on the part of worship leaders. What new things might you introduce into your worship this church year?

LET THE CHILDREN COME

Today's scriptures point to boldness of faith in coming to God with our sinful frailty. We pray "Our Father in heaven" "in order that we may approach [God] boldly and confidently in prayer, even as beloved children approach their dear father" (Small Catechism, Lord's Prayer Introduction). Have the children write or suggest prayer petitions that ask God for forgiveness, healing, and mercy. During the hymn of the day, have the children bring the petitions forward and hand them to the assisting minister who will lead the prayers.

MUSIC FOR WORSHIP

GATHERING

| LBW 546 | When morning gilds the skies |
| WOV 717 | Come, all you people |

PSALM 41

Carroll, J. Robert. "Lord, Heal My Soul" in *RitualSong*. GIA.
Hopson, Hal H. PW, cycle B.

HYMN OF THE DAY

WOV 737   There is a balm in Gilead
                 BALM IN GILEAD

VOCAL RESOURCES

Dawson, William. "There Is a Balm." KJO T105. SATB.
Shepperd, Mark. "Balm in Gilead." AFP 11-10923. SATB, kybd.

INSTRUMENTAL RESOURCES

Billingham, Richard. "There Is a Balm in Gilead" in *Seven Reflections on African American Hymns*. AFP 11-10762. Org.
Nicholson, Paul. "There Is a Balm in Gilead." AFP 11-10760. Org, inst.
Powell, Robert J. "Balm in Gilead" in *Sing a New Song*. AFP 11-10766. Org.
Young, Philip M. "There Is a Balm in Gilead." AFP 11-10469. 3-5 oct.

ALTERNATE HYMN OF THE DAY

| LBW 519 | My soul, now praise your maker! |
| LBW 549 | Praise, my soul, the King of heaven |

COMMUNION

| LBW 305 | I lay my sins on Jesus |
| WOV 733 | Our Father, we have wandered |

SENDING

| LBW 333 | Lord, take my hand and lead me |
| WOV 721 | Go, my children, with my blessing |

ADDITIONAL HYMNS AND SONGS

UMH 355	Depth of mercy
H82 634	I call on thee, Lord Jesus Christ
TFF 70	Lead me, guide me
W&P	Lead me, guide me

MUSIC FOR THE DAY

CHORAL

Hurford, Peter. "Litany to the Holy Spirit." OXF E164. U, org.
Powell, Robert J. "The Great Creator of the Worlds." AFP 11-10883. SATB, org.
Schalk, Carl. "Who Is the One We Love the Most." CPH 98-3404. SATB, org.

CHILDREN'S CHOIRS

McRae, Shirley W. "Your Trusting Child." CG CGA614. U, kybd, opt fl, opt sop glock, opt fc.
Shepherd, John. "A Living Faith." CG CGA580. U/2 pt, kybd.

KEYBOARD/INSTRUMENTAL

Lovelace, Austin. "Star in the East." RME EO-139. Org.
Rendler, Elaine. "Spiritual Offerings" in *Keyboard Praise, vol. 2*. OCP 9081GC. Kybd.

HANDBELL

Kinyon, Barbara. "Daystar." HOP 1930. 2-3 oct.
Muschick, John H. "Variations on Noel." BEC HB71. 4 oct.

PRAISE ENSEMBLE

Bullock, Geoff. "Jesus, Jesus" in *Hosanna! Music Songbook 11*. INT.
Burkhardt, Michael. "Go, My Children, with My Blessing." MSM 50-9416. U, 2-3 pt, pno.
Honoré, Jeffrey. "How Can I Keep from Singing." CG CGA-567. SATB, pno.
Sutton "Your Mercy Flows" in *Songs for Praise and Worship*. WRD.
Ylvisaker, John. "Blest in the Land" in *Borning Cry*. NGP.

SUNDAY, FEBRUARY 20
RASMUS JENSEN, THE FIRST LUTHERAN PASTOR IN NORTH AMERICA, 1620

Jensen was the first Lutheran pastor in North America. He came in 1619 with an expedition sent by King Christian IV of Denmark. The expedition took possession of the Hudson Bay Area, naming it Nova Dania. Within a few months of their arrival, most of the members of the expedition died, including Jensen.

Use this occasion to remember the founders of your congregation. Of what synods or districts has it been a part during its history? What has its presence been in the community over the years? Get out the pictures. Update the congregation's archives.

WEDNESDAY, FEBRUARY 23
POLYCARP, BISHOP OF SMYRNA, MARTYR, 156

Polycarp is an important link between the apostolic age and the great Christian writers who flourished at the end of the second century. He was burned at the stake for his refusal to renounce the Christian faith. His name means "many fruits," and he has been cherished among Christians as one of the first "saplings" of the church to die for Christ. After the first martyrs mentioned in the New Testament (Stephen, Peter, Paul), Polycarp is considered one of the earliest martyrs for the faith. How do Polycarp and other martyrs inspire us to remain steadfast in our calling to follow Christ?

BARTHOLOMAEUS ZIEGENBALG, MISSIONARY TO INDIA, 1719

As a missionary among the Tamil people of India, Ziegenbalg endured imprisonment, illness, and the suspicions of other Christian missionaries. Believed to be the first Protestant missionary, he established mission schools, a seminary for native preachers, and built a church called New Jerusalem, which is still in use. Ziegenbalg learned the Tamil language and translated Luther's Small Catechism, the New Testament, parts of the Old Testament, and compiled a grammar text.

Ziegenbalg is an example of one who was able to proclaim the gospel in the context of another culture. How can we effectively share the good news in our own communities today? How does your congregation help to spread the good news to people of other cultures?

THURSDAY, FEBRUARY 24
ST. MATTHIAS, APOSTLE

Matthias was chosen to fill the vacancy among the twelve disciples following the death of Judas. Although he is not mentioned elsewhere in the New Testament, the account of his election in Acts 1:15-26 implies that he was a follower of Jesus from the beginning of his ministry. Both Ethiopian and Greek Christians claim him as a missionary in their communities.

Matthias can be raised up as a faithful disciple whose call came in a rather unusual way, by the casting of lots. Consider the unique ways God calls us to follow Christ in the way of the cross and resurrection.

FRIDAY, FEBRUARY 25
ELIZABETH FEDDE, DEACONESS, 1921

Fedde was trained as a deaconess and in 1882 was asked to come to New York to minister to the poor and to Norwegian seamen. Her influence was wide ranging, and she established the Deaconess House in Brooklyn, and the Deaconess House and Hospital of the Lutheran Free Church in Minneapolis.

Fedde is an example of selfless service to those in need. How does your congregation reach out to those who are sick, in need, or forgotten?

FEBRUARY 27, 2000

EIGHTH SUNDAY AFTER THE EPIPHANY
PROPER 3

INTRODUCTION

Eating is one of the most intimate things that we do. Our divisions have often kept us apart from one another at the Lord's table, and disagreement regarding who is welcome to share the church's meal still festers among denominations. Jesus was criticized for eating with tax collectors and sinners, the outsiders of his day. We who follow Christ are called to invite all people to share the riches of God's faithful love. We share the new wine of the kingdom, that our lives will proclaim the justice and righteousness of God's ways.

PRAYER OF THE DAY

Almighty and everlasting God, ruler of heaven and earth: Hear our prayer and give us your peace now and forever; through your Son, Jesus Christ our Lord.

READINGS

Hosea 2:14-20

The northern kingdom abandoned the worship of God to worship the god Baal. The prophet Hosea uses marital imagery to describe the covenant relationship between Yahweh and Israel.

Psalm 103:1-13, 22

The LORD is full of compassion and mercy. (Ps. 103:8)

2 Corinthians 3:1-6

Paul defends himself against those who discount his authority as an apostle of Christ. One claim by false prophets was that he brought no letter of recommendation with him from other churches.

Mark 2:13-22

This passage reveals controversy regarding table fellowship. First, Jesus is accused of eating with "sinners," a label for those excluded from the synagogue for moral or ritual reasons. Also, the occasions when Jesus and his followers fast give rise to misunderstandings.

COLOR   Green

THE PRAYERS

Let us pray that the radiance of Christ will illumine the church, the nations, and all who seek the light.

A BRIEF SILENCE.

Let us pray for the bride of Christ, the church, that it may be a faithful partner, proclaiming the word and celebrating the sacraments of God's household. Lord, in your mercy,

hear our prayer.

Let us pray for all Christians who strive to heed God's gracious call to serve among people most in need of a word of freedom. Lord, in your mercy,

hear our prayer.

Let us pray for the nations of the world undergoing great change, that stability and freedom would be in abundance as new forms of government come into being. Lord, in your mercy,

hear our prayer.

Let us pray for all who are experiencing human need in any way (especially . . .), that they would see the grace of God revealed to them in new ways. Lord, in your mercy,

hear our prayer.

HERE OTHER INTERCESSIONS MAY BE OFFERED.

Let us pray for our loved ones who have died, that we might carry them in our hearts even as they have been carried by the everlasting arms of Christ. Lord, in your mercy,

hear our prayer.

Hear our spoken and silent prayers, O God of light, and reveal yourself to us, through your Son, Jesus Christ our Lord.

Amen

IMAGES FOR PREACHING

The preacher will look hard and long to find the clever thread that ties these readings together. We seem to wander through the word this day, and perhaps that is the best place to begin.

We may wander, but in reality we are led. It began weeks ago with a star, and we marveled how magi could use their astrology to find their way to the Christ child. But through the weeks after Epiphany, it turns out, *we* are the ones who must make the journey: from darkness to light, from unknowing to revelation, from simplicity to complexity and back to simplicity again.

Sometimes you have to go back to where you once were. Israel is called back into the desert again. It was the place of their honeymoon, the strange geography where Yahweh and his people were wedded, where promises were made. Does it seem strange to take a honeymoon in the wilderness? Sometimes it is in facing a hardship together that people are most deeply bonded.

Levi reminds us that disciples are called to follow. Here it is Jesus who wanders into the wilderness, a moral wilderness where he fraternizes with the wrong kinds of people. He is the bridegroom of the soul, as well as the physician. His love is meant to restore us to wholeness and health, but it begins by accepting us as we are, where we are.

It is indeed strange that Paul should call the Corinthian Christians his "letter of recommendation." He has not been on the best terms with them. They are a cantankerous lot! But he sees beneath the surface, sees what they might become, sees what they are in the sight of God. They are epistles under construction, and God is doing the writing.

WORSHIP MATTERS

Jesus welcomed and ate with tax collectors and sinners—the ostracized within first-century Palestinian society—on their own turf. It is easy for Christian assemblies to embrace only those of like mind, social status, or racial and ethnic background. How might liturgical assemblies learn to embrace all kinds of people within worship? How might assemblies reach out to the forlorn and despised within their communities?

Avenues for the assembly's service among those in need should be pursued. Active service to the places in which others live opens doors to the opportunity to welcome them into the liturgical assembly. Perhaps the ministry that flows from worship might include service at the community homeless shelter, food and clothing outreach, or ministry to a local prison. Worship leaders should challenge the assembly to let all others know that they are invited by encountering all types of people within their own environments.

LET THE CHILDREN COME

During this Epiphany season, the spotlight has been on Jesus and his deeds of power as God's kingdom breaking in upon our world. During worship, sit with children in such a way that they, too, are able to see the liturgical action and not simply the backs of people's heads. Help children to develop the habit of closing the worship book after the offertory prayer and focusing their eyes and ears on the mighty deeds of God taking place at the altar and in the prayers.

MUSIC FOR WORSHIP

GATHERING

| LBW 369 | The Church's one foundation |
| WOV 747 | Christ is made the sure foundation |

PSALM 103:1-13, 22

Berthier, Jacques. "Bless the Lord, My Soul" in PS, vol. 2.
Weiland, Brent. PW, cycle B.

LBW 519	My soul, now praise your maker! (paraphrase)
LBW 543	Praise to the Lord, the Almighty (paraphrase)
LBW 549	Praise, my soul, the King of heaven (paraphrase)
WOV 798	Bless the Lord, O my soul (Ps. 103:1)

HYMN OF THE DAY

| LBW 298 | One there is, above all others |
| | AMEN SJUNGE HVARJE TUNGA |

INSTRUMENTAL RESOURCES

Schultz, Ralph C. "One There Is, above All Others" in *The Concordia Hymn Prelude Series, Vol. 19.* CPH 97-5710. Org.

ALTERNATE HYMN OF THE DAY

| WOV 790 | Praise to you, O God of mercy |
| LBW 542 | Sing praise to God, the highest good |

COMMUNION

| LBW 215 | O Lord, we praise you |
| WOV 764 | Blest are they |

SENDING

| LBW 424 | Lord of glory, you have bought us |
| WOV 780 | What a fellowship, what a joy divine |

ADDITIONAL HYMNS AND SONGS

H82 681	Our God, to whom we turn
H82 600/1	O day of God, draw nigh
W&P	By grace we have been saved
W&P	Come and taste

MUSIC FOR THE DAY

CHORAL

Bach, J. S. "Chorale settings in 'Jesus, Priceless Treasure' " (Jesu Meine Freude). Oliver Ditson 332-14424. SATB. Eng.

Busarow, Donald. "Day by Day." MSM 50-6004. SATB.

Hurd, David. "Love Bade Me Welcome." SEL 418-610. SATB.

Wagner, Douglas E. "Joy in the Morning Shall Be Mine." GIA G-2278. SATB, hb.

CHILDREN'S CHOIRS

Cherubini/arr. Lovelace. "Like as a Father." CG CGA156. SAB or combined U/2 pt mxd.

Kosche, Kenneth T. "Bless God's Holy Name." CG CGA766. 2 pt, kybd, opt 6 hb.

KEYBOARD/INSTRUMENTAL

Leavitt, John. "Gloria" in *Simple Gifts*. CLP EL9510. Pno.

Manz, Paul. "Evening and Morning" in *Three Hymns for Flute, Oboe, and Organ*. MSM 20-87. Fl, ob, org.

HANDBELL

Hopson, Hal H. "Simple Gifts." HOP 1736. 3-5 oct.

McFadden, Jane. "The Londonderry Air: O Christ the Same." AFP 11-10769. 2-3 oct, opt C/B-flat inst, opt hc.

PRAISE ENSEMBLE

Baloche, Paul and Ed Kerr/arr. Burgess. "All His Benefits." INT 4602OC. SATB, orch.

Crouch, Andraé. "Bless His Holy Name" in *Sing and Rejoice*. BRM BK-3041.

Founds, Rick. "Jesus, Draw Me Close" and "Turn Your Eyes Upon Jesus" in *Maranatha! Music Praise Chorus Book, 3rd ed.* WRD/MAR.

Grondin, Alan and Jeff Hamlin. "By Your Blood" in *Hosanna! Music Songbook, vol. 6*. INT HMSB06.

Harris, Ron and Martin Nystrom. "Times of Refreshing" in *Hosanna! Music Songbook 8*. INT.

Kosche, Kenneth T. "Bless God's Holy Name." CG CGA766. 2 pt, kybd, hb.

WEDNESDAY, MARCH 1
GEORGE HERBERT, PRIEST, 1633

Herbert, a priest of the Church of England, is remembered for his poetry and other writings. His poems breathe a gentle freshness and grace with a profound love of virtue, and some of his hymns are still sung today. His famous work, *A Priest to the Temple* or *The Country Parson*, describes the clergyman as well-read, temperate, given to prayer, and devoted to his flock.

Perhaps Herbert's most popular hymn text is "Come, my way, my truth, my life" (LBW 513). How does this poem shed hope and light on the path of our journey in faith? How do poets help to express the mystery of our faith, putting into words a truth beyond words?

THURSDAY, MARCH 2
JOHN WESLEY, 1791; CHARLES WESLEY, 1788; RENEWERS OF THE CHURCH

John and Charles were brothers and priests of the Church of England, although their ministry moved them to itinerant preaching, hymn writing, and social outreach on the edges of the established church. Their spiritual discipline or method—frequent communion, fasting, and advocacy of social justice—won them the disparaging title "methodists." Following an experience of religious conversion, John was perhaps the greatest single force in the eighteenth-century revival.

Charles wrote more than 600 hymns, twelve of which are in *LBW* (see p. 945). Look up some of his better and lesser known hymns, and sing one or more of them today.

MARCH 5, 2000

THE TRANSFIGURATION OF OUR LORD
LAST SUNDAY AFTER THE EPIPHANY

INTRODUCTION

This Epiphany festival concludes the cycle of the year that is suffused with the image of light. In Advent, the church prays for the light of God's justice in the world. At Christmas, we celebrate this light in Christ, and throughout the weeks of Epiphany, we welcome this gracious light in the diverse cultures of the world. From the mountain of transfiguring light, Christ goes forth to Jerusalem and leads us to the passover from death to life. Here we find the meaning of his birth and baptism: he was born to die, so that in our death, we might be born to eternal life.

PRAYER OF THE DAY

Almighty God, on the mountain you showed your glory in the transfiguration of your Son. Give us the vision to see beyond the turmoil of our world and to behold the king in all his glory; through your Son, Jesus Christ our Lord, who lives and reigns with you and the Holy Spirit, one God, now and forever.

or

O God, in the transfiguration of your Son you confirmed the mysteries of the faith by the witness of Moses and Elijah, and in the voice from the bright cloud you foreshadowed our adoption as your children. Make us with the king heirs of your glory, and bring us to enjoy its fullness, through Jesus Christ our Lord, who lives and reigns with you and the Holy Spirit, one God, now and forever.

READINGS

2 Kings 2:1-12

Today's reading centers on the transfer of power and authority from the prophet Elijah to Elisha. Their travels, which retrace the path of Joshua back to Moab (the place where Moses died), and the parting of the waters demonstrate that Elisha and Elijah are legitimate successors of the great lawgiver Moses.

Psalm 50:1-6

Out of Zion, perfect in beauty, God shines forth in glory. (Ps. 50:2)

2 Corinthians 4:3-6

The epiphany, or revelation of God, at Jesus' transfiguration is renewed in every believer's life when the light of Christ shines in the heart to reveal God's glory.

Mark 9:2-9

Mark's gospel presents the transfiguration as a preview of what would become apparent to Jesus' followers after he rose from the dead. Confused disciples are given a vision of God's glory manifest in the beloved Son.

COLOR White

THE PRAYERS

Let us pray that the radiance of Christ will illumine the church, the nations, and all who seek the light.
A BRIEF SILENCE.
God of grace, your people long to see a glimpse of your face and to hear your voice speak plainly. Bless your church with faithful bishops, pastors, and other leaders who will direct people to your saving glory. Lord, in your mercy,
hear our prayer.
God of awe and mystery, show yourself plainly to all who seek spiritual direction, that their search would be complete as they behold the wonders of your love. Lord, in your mercy,
hear our prayer.
God of all nations, manifest your glory in providing relief and assistance to people suffering from natural disasters and major crises. Lord, in your mercy,
hear our prayer.
God of wellness and health, people you have created suffer from illness and infirmity, from depression and grief (especially . . .). Show them the light of your face. Lord, in your mercy,
hear our prayer.
HERE OTHER INTERCESSIONS MAY BE OFFERED.
God of continuity, teach us to value our days, and keep us in communion with all those we love whose earthly lives have come to an end. Lord, in your mercy,
hear our prayer.

Hear our spoken and silent prayers, O God of light, and reveal yourself to us, through your Son, Jesus Christ our Lord.
Amen

IMAGES FOR PREACHING

This day is undoubtedly one of the most difficult days for preaching. Whatever we say, it seems to come out as babbling. But that is precisely the point of the festival and the center of the story. With Peter we find ourselves dumb struck. But then what are you supposed to say when your friend is glowing like an arc lamp?

We find ourselves here at the halfway point between the Baptism and the Resurrection of Our Lord. What was spoken to Jesus in private at the Jordan is now proclaimed and attested on the mountain in the presence of Moses and Elijah as well as Peter, James, and John. Yes, the three disciples are sworn to silence, but then what would they say anyway? The best they seem to be able to do is turn a revelation into a camping trip.

Sometimes it is difficult to understand. Elisha has a hard time figuring out why his mentor must leave him. Forty days through Lent and forty days through Eastertide we, too, will stand again in wordless awe as our Lord is taken up into heaven. Maybe Paul gets closest to the heart of the matter: Yes, we have seen the light that shines out of darkness. Yes, we have witnessed spectacular love, miracles abounding. But the light that shattered the darkness of a Judean night above shepherds and ignited a star to lead astrologers to a new manifestation of the truth is the light that shines in our hearts. The epiphany, and even a part of the transfiguration, is within us. "If I cannot have you here beside me, then please let me inherit a double share of your spirit." Jesus will answer that request, completing what was begun in incarnation by blowing resurrection life into our bodies with pentecostal breath.

WORSHIP MATTERS

Worship leaders are servants of Christ, the assembly, and the eucharistic liturgy. They do not, as the second reading indicates, proclaim themselves and their talents in worship. In a sense, liturgical ministry is a transparent enterprise. The assembly should see only the service performed, not the person performing it. How might we conduct worship so as to make it transparent? Liturgical vestments are intended to evoke transparency, to cloak the person so that the light of Christ might be seen. The liturgy should be conducted smoothly so that the ministers' performance might not be an obstacle to the rest of the assembly. Mistakes within the liturgy should be handled with ease, appearing to be as natural a part of the liturgy as possible. Anything that merely draws attention to the worship leaders, whether in the sermon or the liturgy itself, should be avoided.

LET THE CHILDREN COME

Jesus' mantle, the gospel reports, was dazzling white, brighter than anyone could bleach it. The liturgical color for today is also white, a color we will not see again until the church celebrates the Lord's resurrection at Easter, or perhaps on Maundy Thursday—the foretaste of the feast to come. Call the children's attention to the changing colors, and identify white as a special color used in the church for Jesus and for those belonging to his kingdom, the saints.

MUSIC FOR WORSHIP
SERVICE MUSIC

As the gospel acclamation on this day, use "Jesus on the mountain peak" (WOV 653, st. 1–3 before the gospel, st. 4 after) or the refrain to "Shine, Jesus, shine" (WOV 651).

GATHERING

LBW 526	Immortal, invisible, God only wise
WOV 649	I want to walk as a child of the light

PSALM 50:1-6

Bell, John L. "Let the Giving of Thanks" in *Psalms of Patience, Protest and Praise.* Iona/GIA G-4047.

Dean, Stephen. "I Will Show God's Salvation" in PS, vol. 3.

Folkening, John. "Six Psalm Settings with Antiphons." MSM 80-700. SATB, cong, opt. kybd.

Hobby, Robert. PW, cycle B.

Hopson, Hal H. "Psalm 50" in TP.

HYMN OF THE DAY

LBW 80	Oh, wondrous type! Oh, vision fair
	DEO GRACIAS

VOCAL RESOURCES

Crosier, Carl. "O Wondrous Type! Oh, Vision Fair!" GIA G-2836. SATB, cong, hb.

Schalk, Carl. "Oh, Wondrous Type, Oh, Vision Fair." CPH 98-1524. SATB, kybd.

Wetzler, Robert. "Deo gracias." AMSI B-19. Cong, brass, org.

INSTRUMENTAL RESOURCES

Langlois, Kristina. "Deo gracias" in *Three for Christmas*. MSM 10-134. Org.

Sedio, Mark. "Deo gracias" in *Seven Hymn Reflections for Organ*. AMSI OR-20. Org.

Tryggestad, David. "Deo gracias." AFP 11-10471. Org.

ALTERNATE HYMN OF THE DAY

| LBW 518 | Beautiful Savior |
| WOV 653 | Jesus on the mountain peak |

COMMUNION

| LBW 222 | O Bread of life from heaven |
| WOV 801 | Thine the amen, thine the praise |

SENDING

| LBW 552 | In thee is gladness |
| WOV 651 | Shine, Jesus, shine |

ADDITIONAL HYMNS AND SONGS

H82 465/6	Eternal light shine in my heart
PH 73	Swiftly pass the clouds of glory
TFF 61	The Lord is my light
W&P	Suddenly, upon the mountain

MUSIC FOR THE DAY

CHORAL

Bouman, Paul. "Christ upon the Mountain Peak." CPH 98-2856. SATB, org.

Helman, Michael. "Go Up to the Mountain of God." AFP 11-10961. SATB, kybd, fl.

Praetorius, Michael. "How Brightly Shines the Morning Star." B&H OC286419. 2 pt trbl.

Schalk, Carl. "Jesus, Take Us to the Mountain." MSM 50-2601. SATB, opt cong, org.

Willan, Healey. "Grant Us Thy Light" CPH 98-1014. SATB.

CHILDREN'S CHOIRS

Bridges, David. "O Splendor of God's Glory Bright." CPH 98-2956. U, 2 oct hb, kybd.

Crutchfield, Jonathan. "Fairest Lord Jesus." CG CGA743. U, vocal/inst desc, kybd.

KEYBOARD/INSTRUMENTAL

Wasson, Laura E. "Beautiful Savior" in *A Piano Tapestry*. AFP 11-10821. Pno.

Wood, Dale. "Processional for a Joyful Day" in *Festive Processionals for Organ*. SMP 70/1175. Org.

Woodman, James. "Fairest Lord Jesus." PRE 493-00066.

HANDBELL

Dobrinski, Cynthia. "Glorious Triumph." HOP 1899. 3-5 oct.

Keller, Michael R. "Transfiguration." AGEHR AG57002. 5-7 oct.

Moklebust, Cathy. "Meditation on 'Beautiful Savior.'" CG CGB175. 3-5 oct.

PRAISE ENSEMBLE

Baloche. "Guiding Light" in *Hosanna! Music Songbook* 7. INT.

Fettke, Tom. "Beautiful Savior." WRD 3010638167. SATB, pno.

Smith, M. "Shine on Us" in *My Utmost for His Highest*. WRD.

Starke, Stephen P. "Greet the Rising Sun" in *Hymnal Supplement 98*. CPH.

TUESDAY, MARCH 7

PERPETUA AND HER COMPANIONS,
MARTYRS AT CARTHAGE, 202

Perpetua, her servants, and other African catechumens were arrested for their enrollment and participation in the catechumenate. The Roman emperor Severus forbade conversions to Christianity, and Perpetua and her companions were condemned to execution in the arena at Carthage. According to the contemporary account of the martyrdom, Perpetua and Felicity survived the wild beasts and were killed by the sword, having first exchanged the kiss of peace. These catechumens were baptized in their own blood. Action-filled stories of martyrs and early Christians are powerful witnesses and guaranteed to capture the attention of after-school youth groups.

THOMAS AQUINAS, TEACHER, 1274

Thomas Aquinas was a brilliant and creative theologian and philosopher. He was first and foremost a student of the Bible and profoundly concerned with the theological formation of the church's ordained ministers. As a member of the Order of Preachers (Dominicans), he labored to correlate scripture with the cultural questions and philosophical controversies of his day in order to improve preaching.

Several eucharistic hymns have generally been ascribed to Aquinas. Consider using "Thee we adore, O hidden Savior" (LBW 199) as a communion hymn this week.

LENT

THE THREE DAYS

EASTER

LENT

Lent is a time for taking care of the soul

IMAGES OF THE SEASON

Lent is a hard season to sell. It has a bad reputation, and it doesn't fit with what modern people want from religion. In a time when *entertainment* and *worship* are used in the same sentence, it's difficult to know what Lent has to offer.

THE DISMAL SEASON

The most common images or moods associated with Lent are probably those of darkness, mourning, sorrow, and distress. Perhaps Lutherans are even more given to this attitude than are other Christians. In Luther's phrase, our cry tends to be "cross, cross, suffer, suffer," and Lent certainly lends itself to that mood.

Indeed, suffering and sorrow are largely the themes of Ash Wednesday, with its picture of the looming day of the Lord and its call to turn and repent. The difficulty arises when that lugubrious note is stretched out from the initial day of the Lenten observance, and the somber tones of Good Friday are dragged backward until the two meet to create an entire season of lamenting and wailing. This Lent is the Lent many of us grew up knowing: the despair of sin and the agony of the cross presented in painful detail for seven weeks. Even the traditional hymnody of the season sets the tone: "O Lamb of God most holy! Who on the cross didst suffer. . . ." "By the cross, the nail, the thorn, Piercing spear, the torturing scorn. . . ." "Deep were his wounds, and red . . ."

If this predisposition to despair is what Lent is about, it is hardly surprising to hear of churches renaming this season "pre-Easter," a sort of "Lent Lite" that is more palatable to the modern taste. Even for those already convicted of their sinful nature, the danger of overburdening the soul with a message of unrelieved mourning is ever present. It is like offering a bandage for a mortal wound.

THE POSITIVE SIDE

But in fact this woe of the cross is not the entirety of Lent. To focus on the cross as the only image of this season is to blind ourselves to the fullness of God's activity. The reality is that Christians do not live out the liturgical year as if the events it marks were happening for the first time. We already know how the story ends. Therefore, even our most somber of observances contain the seeds of celebration. While the cross is an appropriate focus for our reflections, we always see it not simply as an instrument of torture but as the vehicle of salvation.

The tone of the Lenten season, even in the midst of its call to turn, repent, and be cleansed of sin, is one of optimism. The first reading on the first Sunday in Lent sounds this note. The rainbow is placed in the heavens, a sign of God's presence and promise, and life goes on with that assurance. Sunday after Sunday, the same theme is presented. A promise is made to Abraham, even though he is too old for it to be kept. Fiery serpents bring death, but God sends healing. Those who lose their lives actually save them. God sends the Son not to condemn the world but to rescue it. Over and over, impossible difficulties contain the seeds of God's saving action.

Lent is not a time for wallowing in sin. It is a time for taking care of the soul. The image for Lent is not punishment but bodybuilding. The church has always known it, even when we have lost sight of it in our focus on wailing and gnashing of teeth. It is why Lent has traditionally been of significance to those preparing for baptism. It is the season for preparing for salvation, for learning what being forgiven and made whole means. Repentance may tear down what is weak and twisted, but it also builds up that which is of God.

This focus sheds a new light on the traditional disciplines of Lent. Prayer, fasting, and acts of love are not punishments. They are exercises, bodybuilding techniques. They are not mortification, just as the cross is not just an instrument of torture. They are the power of God at work in us to make us ready for the joy of Easter!

ENVIRONMENT AND ART FOR THE SEASON

When a touch of red is added to blue, the eye sees violet, a blue purple called *violaceus*. But if fairly equal amounts of red and blue are blended together, a reddish purple, *purpureus*, appears. We see deep purple in the skin of a shiny eggplant and lighter shades in a cluster of grapes hanging on the vine. While many people living in the United States may claim red and blue as their favorite colors, studies suggest that they are secretly intrigued by purple, the dark and exotic child born of the marriage between democracy's red and blue. Many people do not wear purple (though a trend toward richer colors is growing), but they will honor those who have been wounded in battle with a "purple heart." A "purple" heart? Perhaps red and blue are not adequate to the task of giving thanks for those who have shed their blood.

Before the invention of artificial dyes, purple was not an easy color to come by. For most of history, the dye was extracted from the *murex brandaris* and the *murex trunculus*, two forms of seawater mollusk (mussel). A truly labor-intensive process, it would take more than 12,000 harvested mussels, exposed to the sun and then crushed by hand, to produce a mere 1.5 grams of pure purple dye. Only the wealthy could afford purple cloth, and the wealthiest of the world tended to be monarchs—thus the phrase, "born to the purple." At one time kings and emperors, eager to display their political authority (gained largely through military conquest, subversion, or murder), would reserve to themselves the sole right to wear purple. Arrive at the emperor's ball with a purple blouse or scarf and you'd likely be suspected of fomenting political intrigue. The emperor's *cappa purpura*, his purple robe or cape, came to symbolize a frequently capricious and brutal exercise of power.

Is it not amazing that a single color could provoke such feelings as awe, fear, and dread in people's hearts? One could not only be "born to the purple" (England's William and Harry come to mind), but also "take the purple" from a ruler. Indeed, much of Western history reveals the sometimes peaceful but mostly violent changing of the purple. Self-serving ambition, character assassination, and palace coups are not unknown in the contemporary world, although we now tend to associate such behavior with a "power" suit of blue or gray.

Many Christian bishops (and some pastors) wear purple shirts these days, colorful backdrops to a cross worn over the heart. One might wonder, Why purple? It can't be that these people possess imperial pretensions, can it? Or, to use the medieval view of purple, is it a sign of lifelong repentance, a life given over to fasting, prayer, and compassionate care of the poor? Is that what bishops and pastors are communicating with purple shirts?

Oscar Romero was a Salvadoran bishop who wore purple, that is until the moment when he recognized that purple was the color of privilege in his country, and any sign of privilege associated with the ministry of Jesus was a countersign to the gospel. He then wore a plain black suit or cassock and worked among his impoverished people, defending them against government terrorists trained in the United States. While wearing a simple white alb, he was assassinated in the midst of the liturgy, his blood soaking the cloth a purplish red. He was buried in a clean, white alb, the garment of his baptized flock, a poor people rich in grace. Isn't it remarkable that this man's profound conversion of heart could be traced in the movement from purple to white?

Lent bears within its grace this movement from purple to white. Yet many Christians experience the season as if they lived in the late Middle Ages: "Lent is about my sin, the forgiveness of my sin, and the price Jesus paid on the cross to gain my forgiveness." Inspired by this understanding, many Lenten hymns focus on the cross or the Savior's suffering. From this viewpoint, worship spaces might reflect a certain schizophrenia: some worshiping assemblies will find any and every image of the cross or crucified Lord veiled in purple or unbleached linen; others will encounter a large, rough wood cross in the space, have nails handed to them by greeters, or gaze on "cross" banners. Six weeks at the foot of the cross, veiled or unveiled.

Late medieval practices might continue to find a welcome in some congregations. After all, one of Luther's greatest gifts to the ecumenical church is his theology of the cross. Indeed, Lutheran preaching is to be filled with the wisdom of the cross, "foolishness to those who are perishing but the power of God to save" (1 Cor. 1:18, Lent 3). But isn't the wisdom of the cross to be alive in the churches at all times, not just Lent? And isn't that "wisdom" to be proclaimed throughout the entire year, on every Sunday and festival, in baptism, preaching, and the supper?

In the past thirty years, Christian theologians and historians have uncovered an understanding of Lent that will come as no surprise to those who understand Luther's profound baptismal theology, an understanding inspired by the Bible and early Christian practice. Lent is, first of all, about God baptizing us into a life of faithful discipleship or, to use Luther's lovely phrase, "creeping back to the font." That is, "we await the healing waters of our Savior's victory." ("As the sun with longer journey," WOV 655). Lent prepares us and leads us to the baptismal font and the Lord's table as we are reminded of our baptism into the Lord's death and resurrection (celebrated especially in the Three Days).

With the Hebrews in the wilderness and with the disciples going up to Jerusalem, together we turn to God (the meaning of "repentance") and ask this of our Creator: "Refresh within us the grace of baptism so that we might serve you faithfully in this world marked by so much suffering." This grace-meets-repentance is the purpose of Ash Wednesday: to enact the baptismal gesture of tracing the cross of ash on our foreheads while speaking a double truth: you are mortal yet embraced for all eternity by the immortal one. The "cross" is always present during Lent, but it is the baptismal cross by which we are marked as the Lord's disciples. Even though we are conscious of our sin—personal and communal—we rejoice all the more in the forgiveness that is ours through baptism, confession and absolution, and the Lord's supper. Perhaps this juxtaposition of suffering and rejoicing is why one preface says, "Ever-living God, each year you give us this joyful season when we prepare to celebrate the paschal mystery," our passover with the Lord from death to resurrection.

Let this time be fulfilled with a practical focus for two things. First, plan a thorough cleaning of every item used in worship (e.g., vestments, vessels, altar and baptismal cloths, windows, any carpet or rugs, ceilings, windows, and walls). Spring cleaning is a worthwhile activity. Include cupboards and storage spaces; let ardent "throwers" and zealous "keepers" work together. But be sure to plan a party at the end of a hard day of work! Second, prepare a comprehensive plan for the entire cycle, from Ash Wednesday to Pentecost Sunday. Again, avoid any sudden and alarming "switch" from Lent to the Three Days to the Easter season. The community should experience a modulating movement from one season to the other. This subtlety means that some elements, while remaining throughout the ninety days, will change with each season.

You may also want to consider the fact that the retail industry, eager to make a profit in winter and thus willing to expend much effort and money, has not laid hold of Lent or Easter. Churches experience less cultural pressure at this time, yet Easter or the paschal cycle is the primary cycle of the entire year. Lent gives a congregation the opportunity to signal to passersby that business as usual has been set aside: "We are entering into a forty-day baptismal retreat." Purple or gray weatherproofed cloth hangings or bunting communicate that something different within is happening.

Imagine that worship begins as people drive or walk by and enter the parking lot. How will the use of color lead people into the worship space? Would a gradual alteration in the use of color outdoors help in creating an evident rhythm toward the Three Days? At the same time, consider the hangings that might be placed outdoors during the Easter season. If you jump immediately to the thought of white banners or bunting, consider how the color white will fare in your region. If outdoor hangings are weatherproofed, you will avoid the unfortunate sight of dreary or dirty-looking cloths. As people enter the worship space, everything should announce that a new season has begun. Perhaps the most effective way to do this is by stripping the space. Follow this simple principle: prepare an environment that signals a new season yet does not detract from the central elements of worship: gathering, proclamation of the word and prayers, thanksgiving meal, and sending forth.

Whether or not your congregation used a large, overhanging wreath during Advent and Christmas, Lent is another appropriate time to employ a wreath through the entire cycle. Again, such a wreath will measure between three to six feet in diameter, hanging over a central aisle, a great wheel floating over the worshipers. Instead of evergreen branches and candles, secure plain branches to the base. Perhaps the branches will extend outward a bit so that they can be seen. By the fourth or fifth Sunday in Lent, a few green leaves might begin to appear. On Passion Sunday, a few more leaves or ferns will be in evidence. At the Easter Vigil or Easter Sunday, flower blossoms will be noticed by worshipers for the first time. Throughout the weeks of Easter, more blossoms will be added until Pentecost Sunday, when the wreath will appear as a full and beflowered crown of bursting life hanging over the people. Each week, then, something small but noticeable will change that marks the movement of the seasons yet does not detract from the liturgy. And by all means, do not say anything about the wreath. Let the worshiping assembly notice what is happening.

Here is an instance where the "logic" of the lectionary and the church year guides pastoral practice: with the exception of emergencies, many churches will reserve the celebration of baptism for the Easter season; that is, the Easter Vigil, Easter Sunday, or one of the Sundays of Easter. Consider emptying, cleaning, and marking the baptismal font with a cross of neatly tailored purple cloth. Likewise, remove the old paschal candle—except for funerals—and be sure that you have ordered a new one for the "new year" that begins at the Easter Vigil.

In many congregations, a processional cross will lead the people into the worship space on the first Sunday in Lent and Passion Sunday (if not throughout the entire year). In some African and South American congregations, the cross is adorned with a simple wreath or gathering of local branches or leaves as the seasons change. On Passion Sunday, a garland of palm branches might be placed around the processional cross. If there is no processional cross, a palm garland might adorn a stationary or hanging cross. This practice is worthy of imitation, if not through the entire year, at least during the seasons of the paschal cycle. By all means, avoid the temptation to transform Lent into a six-week Passiontide. The focus on the Lord's suffering appears on Passion Sunday and the three weekday readings that lead to the Three Days. Filling the space with additional crosses or images of the crucified Lord contradicts the essentially baptismal focus of the season. If the vesture or hangings are filled with "instruments of the passion," replace them with a plain set of visual simplicity. The color of Passion Sunday is scarlet, not red. Avoid using vesture reserved for Pentecost, a brighter orange red.

PREACHING WITH THE SEASON

We mark the start of Lent with the ashes of Ash Wednesday, and from that moment we are reminded that the church and the world are pursuing very different agendas. In a culture where "image is everything," we deliberately and ritually disfigure ourselves, bearing on our foreheads the sign of the cross smudged in the dark grit of ashes. The symbolism goes even deeper when we understand that the grit is the residue of the palms from Passion Sunday, ashes of the tokens of worldly success that had been raised in triumph as Jesus entered Jerusalem for the last time.

Nonetheless, it is possible to overlook the call to humility that comes with the ashes. After all, having survived the excesses of the day known (in many parts of the country) inelegantly but accurately as Fat Tuesday, it is hard not to feel a little self satisfied at making the effort to come to worship on Wednesday. It is not such an easy thing to fit another event into our weekday schedules, but here we are. What more could God want from us?

The question echoes throughout the forty days, but the answer comes early, in the alternate first reading from Isaiah. God wants a great deal more from us than just our presence in worship, and the prophet calls us to account when we have failed to do it. Lent is an invitation to a fast, but the kind of fast God wants us to observe is not merely an abstention from gluttony, but a deliberate, dedicated campaign aimed at achieving justice for all God's children. It was the challenge Isaiah offered his listeners; it is the challenge that remains for us today.

Isaiah told the people then (and those now who wear the ashes like a merit badge) that they missed the point by concentrating on their dramatic portrayal of repentant suffering. The focus should be on what is really important: those who are poor, oppressed, hungry, and homeless. It was (and is) a profoundly countercultural indictment of things the way they were, and of the way the people had allowed them to become. To observe the fast Isaiah spoke of meant you could not simply hang your head in self-absorbed pity, but that you needed to look around, to become aware of and do something to help remedy the suffering around you.

We know the same temptation to self-absorption, and we have reached the point in our society where observing Lent is a radical idea, too. Lent is a season of limits, observed in the midst of a culture that does not do well with limits. Part of our identity and temperament seems to push us on until we can go no further, until all our energy and resources are spent in pursuit of our own goals.

Lent reminds us of our call to Christian servanthood, and leads us to acknowledge that, no matter how hard we try, we cannot save ourselves. "Remember that you are dust, and to dust you will return." The words are not meant to be an ironic admission of human futility, but a recognition that we are not God, not even "gods" with a lowercase g. Lent comes with the power to throw us on our knees, to remind us we can do nothing without God's tender mercies.

Lent is a season of discipline that takes place within a culture increasingly unsure about what discipline means, and suspicious about it when it is seen or heard. Each of us is her own judge; each of us sets his own standards of behavior that cannot be challenged by another. We lift up freedom as the chief of all virtues, but are ever more reluctant to supply appropriate guidelines wherein we can exercise that freedom. We are willing to give things up, but mostly to lose weight or save money or demonstrate the power of our own will to do without. Those behaviors miss the point.

The real discipline of Lent is intended to clear away what is extra so that we might focus on what is essential: our relationship with God. Lent invites us to fast because we do not live by bread alone. Lent calls us to give alms in memory of what God gives us in Christ. Lent reminds us to pray, not to get something from God, but because God is God, and worthy of our prayers and thanks and praise.

Lent is the season in the church year we begin by explicitly (and in great detail) confessing that not only do we not have all the answers, but that we are, in fact, part of the problem. We do things that are wrong. We do things that are hurtful. We do things that are sinful, and still we confess that we are unable to stop ourselves from doing them. The world does not respond well to that kind of candor.

Those who bear the cross of ashes can claim to know the truth of that candor. It is a truth we must not forget even as so much of the world, so many of our colleagues and friends, so many members of our own families and those we love are swept along by the tide of the world's glib assurances that I'm OK and you're OK—in fact, we're both just fine. We would even be better if they would only leave us alone for a while and stop bugging us with the news of hungry people living in every community, of homeless people, not only in the big cities, but in our towns as well, of people in need all around us who are oppressed, and ill, frightened and despairing.

Isaiah knew the temptation to ignore the truth, and it is hardly news to us who will mark the start of Lent with ashes. But it is hard to resist that temptation, and hard to do God's will, and hard to work for justice. Those challenges are not news, either, but they are the truth, and Lent should be a time for telling the truth.

"Remember that you are dust, and to dust you will return." The words are not spoken in mockery, derision, or despair. They are not meant to absolve us from the guilt of what we have done, nor to make us feel bad for doing it. For even as they are spoken to us we are marked with the sign of the cross, marked with the sign of him who died for each and every one of us, to save us from our sins. It is a promise—a promise that though we are separated from God, we are not disowned. It is an understanding—an understanding that though we are exiles, one day we will be called home. It is a confession—a confession that we have sinned, but that we trust we will be forgiven. It is an acknowledgment—an acknowledgment that we are hungry, and at God's table we will be welcomed and fed. Remember that you are dust, yes. And remember the cross and the promise. Remember the Lenten fast.

SHAPE OF WORSHIP FOR THE SEASON

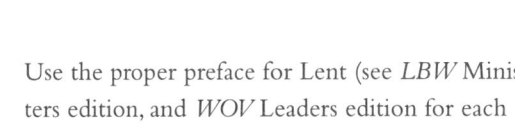

BASIC SHAPE OF THE EUCHARISTIC RITE IN LENT

- Confession and Forgiveness: see alternate worship text for Lent in *Sundays and Seasons*

GATHERING

- Greeting: see alternate worship text for Lent in *Sundays and Seasons*
- Use the Kyrie during Lent
- Omit the hymn of praise during Lent

WORD

- Use the Nicene Creed
- The prayers: see alternate forms and responses for Lent in *Sundays and Seasons*

MEAL

- Offertory prayer: see alternate worship text for Lent in *Sundays and Seasons*
- Use the proper preface for Lent (see *LBW* Ministers edition, and *WOV* Leaders edition for each musical setting of the liturgy)
- Use of the proper preface for Passion would begin with Passion Sunday
- Eucharistic prayer: in addition to four main options in *LBW*, see "Eucharistic Prayer D: The Season of Lent" in *WOV* Leaders edition, p. 68
- Invitation to communion: see alternate worship text for Lent in *Sundays and Seasons*
- Post-communion prayer: see alternate worship text for Lent in *Sundays and Seasons*

SENDING

- Benediction: see alternate worship text for Lent in *Sundays and Seasons*
- Dismissal: see alternate worship text for Lent in *Sundays and Seasons*

OTHER SEASONAL POSSIBILITIES

- Ash Wednesday liturgy: see *LBW* Ministers edition, pp. 129–31; and congregational leaflets available from Augsburg Fortress (AFP 3-5325)
- Enrollment of Candidates for Baptism (for first Sunday in Lent): see *Welcome to Christ: Lutheran Rites for the Catechumenate*, pp. 18–21
- Midweek Lenten Worship: see order for evening prayer services in seasonal rites section
- Blessing of Candidates for Baptism (for third, fourth, and fifth Sundays in Lent): see *Welcome to Christ: Lutheran Rites for the Catechumenate*, pp. 22–34
- Procession with Palms liturgy for Passion Sunday: see *LBW* Ministers edition, pp. 134–35; and congregational leaflets available from Augsburg Fortress (AFP 3-5326)
- Blessing of oil: for synodical gatherings (and other groupings of congregations wishing to celebrate this order), see "Dedication of Worship Furnishings" in *Occasional Services*, pp. 176–77

LECTIONARY OPPORTUNITY FOR HEALING SERVICES

- Wednesday in Holy Week (second reading)

ASSEMBLY SONG FOR THE SEASON

The traditional disciplines of Lent include repentance, fasting, prayer, and works of love. How might these bodybuilding exercises be encouraged by and incorporated within the music of the assembly during this season?

An obvious answer is to choose hymns and other music with these themes. But these principles can be at work in other ways. Musical *fasting* need not mean a diet of dullness, but rather a deliberate choice of marking limits. Set aside for these weeks the more festive extremes of the instrumental palette, bright reeds and bells and cymbals, and dwell in the rich simplicity of the human voice. Let the time gained by a worship pattern focused on the central elements be expended in a more generous use of silence. Look for additional ways to use forms of sung *prayer* during this season: evening and morning prayer on weekdays; music during communion that uses prayer texts and/or ostinato refrains; hymn texts that address God.

GATHERING

Highlight the confession and forgiveness used during this season with a more generous than usual opportunity for silence. After the rite, have the assembly seated for a deliberate minute or two of silence before introducing the gathering hymn.

WORD

Since the gospel acclamation does not include the alleluia, various options may be considered in addition to "Return to the Lord." Proper verses may be sung by the choir, or the congregation may sing a brief hymn such as "On my heart imprint your image" (LBW 102). At the prayers, use "O Christ, our king, creator, Lord" (LBW 101) as a frame: sing stanza 1 as the introduction, have the intercessor sing the petitions on a single tone E, and let the people's response be "Lord, hear our prayer" to the first four notes of the hymn, concluding the prayers with stanza 5.

MEAL

Lent is the season in which it makes the most sense to recover "Create in me" as an offertory song. Several recent settings are available in *Libro de Liturgia y Cántico* (442, with English text) and *This Far by Faith*.

SENDING

Choose a single post-communion song for the season, such as "Lord, now you let your servant" (various settings), "Praise and thanks and adoration" (LBW 470), or "I want Jesus to walk with me" (WOV 660), and forgo yet another sending song. Use a simple chorale setting for a postlude.

MUSIC FOR THE SEASON

VERSE AND OFFERTORY

Busarow, Donald. *Verses and Offertories, Part III-Ash Wednesday through Maundy Thursday*. CPH 97-5503. SATB, org.

Cherwien, David. *Verses for the Sundays in Lent*. MSM 80-300. U/2 pt, org.

Farlee, Robert Buckley. *Verses and Offertories for Lent*. AFP 11-10065. U/SATB.

Norris, Kevin. *Verses and Offertories* (Lent). AFP 11-9545. U, kybd.

Schalk, Carl. "Return to the Lord, Your God." MSM 80-3033. SATB, opt kybd.

Schramm, Charles. *Verses for the Lenten Season*. MSM 80-301.

CHORAL MUSIC FOR THE SEASON

Burkhardt, Michael. "What Wondrous Love Is This." MSM 60-3002. SA/ST-AB/SATB, cong, org, opt trbl inst, 10 hb.

Cherwien, David. "By the Babylonian Rivers." GIA G-4290. SA, pno, opt vc.

Elgar, Edward. "Ave Verum." B&H B6332. SATB, org.

Ferguson, John. "Lord in All Love." AFP 11-19788. SATB, org, opt cong.

Fleming, Larry L. "Embellishments for Choir" (Lent and Easter). AFP 11-10658. SATB.

Scarlatti, Alessandro/arr. Peek. "Kyrie Eleison." CPH 98-3068.

Schalk, Carl. "Show Me Your Ways, O Lord." CPH 98-3207. SATB, opt kybd.

Schütz, Heinrich. "Glory Be to Christ" in *St. Matthew Passion*. GSCH 12058. SATB.

Unruh, Eric. "Kyrie eleison." AFP 11-10847. SAB, pno.

CHILDREN'S CHORAL MUSIC FOR THE SEASON

Hopson, Hal. "I Want Jesus to Walk with Me." CG CGA701. 2 pt trbl/mxd, kybd.

Jennings, Carolyn. "Ah, Holy Jesus." AFP 11-0302. SA, cont, vc.

McIver, Robert. "Pie Jesu." CG CGA814. 2 pt, pno, fl, ob/vc, opt str. CGA815. Str pts.

Pergolesi/arr. Burkhardt. "Agnus Dei." MSM 50-3752. U, C inst, cont.

INSTRUMENTAL MUSIC FOR THE SEASON

Billingham, Richard. "Calvary" in *Seven Reflections on African American Spirituals*. AFP 11-10762. Org.

Jones, Mark C. *Three Lenten Hymn Meditations*. MSM 10-323. Org.

Jordan, Alice. "Aria." MSM 20-972. Ob/fl, org.

Lasky, David. "Meditation on 'St. Agnes.'" WAR BHS9804. Org.

Linker, Janet. "Hymns of the Cross." BEC OC3. Org.

Nixon, Robin. "When Jesus Wept." SEL 830-322. Pno.

Rodriguez, Penny. *Portraits of the Cross*. BEC PC3. Pno.

HANDBELL MUSIC FOR THE SEASON

Anderson, C./arr. Page. "Be Still My Soul." HOP 1983. Solo.

Bizet/arr. Wagner. "Agnus Dei." HOP 1452. 3 oct.

Dobrinski, Cynthia. "Lead Me to Calvary." HOP 1685. 3-5 oct.

Dobrinski, Cynthia. "Processional on 'All Glory, Laud and Honor.'" HOP 1902. 3-5 oct, opt cong.

Kinyon, Barbara. "My Faith Looks Up to Thee." CG CGB 167. 2-3 oct, opt ch.

Linker/arr. McFadden. "When I Survey the Wondrous Cross." BEC HB121. 3-5 oct, org.

Satie, E./arr. Wright. "Gymnopedie #1." HOP CP 6015. 2 oct, qrt.

Sherman, Arnold. "O Sacred Head, Now Wounded." HOP 1732. 3-5 oct.

ALTERNATE WORSHIP TEXTS

CONFESSION AND FORGIVENESS
In the name of the Father, and of the ☩ Son,
and of the Holy Spirit.
Amen

Trusting in the promise of God's covenant with us,
let us confess our rebellious ways to God.

Silence for reflection and self-examination.

Most faithful God,
**we confess our inability
to be faithful in our promises to you
and to walk in the way of Christ.
We have neglected to serve others,
and we have sought our own well-being
rather than good for all creation.
We look to you for mercy and healing.
Strengthen our faith, increase our hope,
and guide us in the path of humble service. Amen**

God does not desire the death of sinners,
but rather that they may turn from their wickedness and live.
Therefore we ask God to give us true repentance
and the gift of the Holy Spirit,
that those things we do on this day may please God,
and that at the last we may come to eternal joy;
through Jesus Christ our Lord.
Amen

GREETING
Blessed be the God of grace,
who bears our burdens and saves us from sin.
The grace of our Lord Jesus Christ, the love of God,
and the communion of the Holy Spirit be with you all.
And also with you.

PRAYERS
As we journey through the wilderness of Lent,
let us return to God who gives us the joy of Easter's promise.

A brief silence.

Each petition ends:
Hear us, O God;
your mercy is great.

Concluding petition
Merciful God, hear our cry when we call to you,
and renew and uphold us with your Spirit,
through Jesus Christ our Lord.
Amen

OFFERTORY PRAYER
Compassionate God,
**we offer you these gifts
as signs of our time and labor.
Receive the offering of our lives,
and feed us with your grace,
that, even in the midst of death,
all creation might feast on your unending life
in Jesus Christ our Lord. Amen**

INVITATION TO COMMUNION
Behold the Lamb of God who takes away the sin of the world.
Happy are those who are called to his supper.
**Lord, I am not worthy to receive you,
but only say the word and I shall be healed.**

POST-COMMUNION PRAYER
God of our pilgrimage,
in this meal you nourish us
with the gifts of faith and hope.
Sustain us on our journey,
that refreshed by your grace,
we may reach the promised land,
the Easter feast of victory
in Jesus Christ our Lord.
Amen

BENEDICTION
May God give you strength to raise up the ancient ruins,
wisdom to follow in the cross of Christ,
and the guidance of the Spirit in the desert places of our world.
Amen

DISMISSAL
Go in peace. Proclaim God's eternal joy.
Thanks be to God.

SEASONAL RITES

MIDWEEK EVENING PRAYER FOR LENT

This flexible order of evening prayer may be celebrated as the midweek service. It is an adaptable form of vespers with readings and music that highlight the Lenten journey from ashes to the baptismal font of Easter.

OVERVIEW
Midweek baptismal themes from the Sunday readings for Lent, cycle B.

Week of 1 Lent
Saved in the waters of the flood
Week of 2 Lent
Baptized into the way of the cross
Week of 3 Lent:
Marked with the cross of Christ
Week of 4 Lent
Blessed with grace and created for good works
Week of 5 Lent
Buried with Christ like seed in the earth

SERVICE OF LIGHT
A lit vesper candle may be processed during the versicles and placed in its stand near the altar.

LENTEN VERSICLES
From LBW, p. 176; these versicles may be sung to the tones given in evening prayer, LBW, p. 142.

Behold, now is the acceptable time;
now is the day of our salvation.
Turn us again, O God of our salvation,
that the light of your face may shine on us.
May your justice shine like the sun;
and may the poor be lifted up.

HYMN OF LIGHT
LBW 248   Dearest Jesus, at your word
WOV 728   O Light whose splendor thrills
WOV 729   Christ, mighty Savior

THANKSGIVING FOR LIGHT
This is set to music in LBW, p. 144.

The Lord be with you.
And also with you.
Let us give thanks to the Lord our God.
It is right to give our thanks and praise.
Blessed are you, O Lord our God, king of the universe,
who led your people Israel by a pillar of cloud by day
and a pillar of fire by night:
Enlighten our darkness by the light of your Christ;
may his Word be a lamp to our feet and a light to our path;
for you are merciful, and you love your whole creation,
and we, your creatures, glorify you, Father, Son, and Holy Spirit.
Amen

PSALMODY
The first psalm may be Psalm 141, as printed in LBW, pp. 145–46, or another setting of this psalm may be used.

An additional psalm may be used for each of the weeks during the Lenten season:

1 Lent   Ps. 46
2 Lent   Ps. 13
3 Lent   Ps. 29
4 Lent   Ps. 84
5 Lent   Ps. 42

HYMN
Possibilities for hymns related to the readings for each of the weeks of Lent follow:

1 LENT
WOV 741   Thy holy wings

2 LENT
LBW 195   This is the Spirit's entry now

3 LENT
WOV 693   Baptized in water

4 LENT
WOV 697   Wash, O God, our sons and daughters

5 LENT
WOV 659   O Sun of justice

Other hymn options include:
WOV 698   We were baptized in Christ Jesus
WOV 695   O blessed spring
LBW 194   All who believe and are baptized

READINGS
Readings for each of the weeks of Lent are given:

1 Lent   Gen. 9:8-17 and 1 Peter 3:18-22
2 Lent   Mark 8:31-38
3 Lent   1 Cor. 1:18-25
4 Lent   Eph. 2:1-10
5 Lent   John 12:20-33

A homily or meditation may be given at this time.

Silence is kept by all.

RESPONSE
In many and various ways God spoke to his people of old
by the prophets.
But now in these last days he has spoken to us by his Son.

GOSPEL CANTICLE
LBW 180   My soul now magnifies the Lord
or
WOV 730   My soul proclaims your greatness

LITANY
For a musical form of the litany, see LBW, p. 148.

In peace, let us pray to the Lord.
Lord, have mercy.
For the peace from above, let us pray to the Lord.
Lord, have mercy.
For the peace of the whole world,
for the well-being of the Church of God, and for the unity of all,
let us pray to the Lord.
Lord, have mercy.
For those who are preparing for the Easter sacraments,
let us pray to the Lord.
Lord, have mercy.
For the baptized people of God
and for their varied ministries within the church,
let us pray to the Lord.
Lord, have mercy.
For those who are poor, hungry, homeless, or sick,
let us pray to the Lord.
Lord, have mercy.
Help, save, comfort, and defend us, gracious Lord.

Silence is kept by all.

Rejoicing in the fellowship of all the saints, let us commend
ourselves, one another, and our whole life to Christ, our Lord.
To you, O Lord.

PRAYER OF THE DAY
From the previous Sunday if a service is held during the week.

THE LORD'S PRAYER

BLESSING
For a musical setting, see LBW, p. 152.

Let us bless the Lord.
Thanks be to God.

The almighty and merciful Lord, the Father, the Son,
and the Holy Spirit, bless and preserve us.
Amen

SERVICE OF THE WORD FOR HEALING IN LENT

An order for Service of the Word for Healing is presented in the seasonal materials for Autumn. It may also be adapted for use during Lent in the following ways:

DIALOG
Behold, now is the acceptable time;
now is the day of salvation.
Return to the Lord, your God,
who is gracious and merciful, slow to anger,
and abounding in steadfast love.
God forgives you all your sins,
and heals all your infirmities.
God redeems your life from the grave,
and crowns you with mercy and lovingkindness.
God satisfies you with good things,
and your youth is renewed like an eagle's.
Bless the Lord, O my soul,
and all that is within me bless God's holy name.

FIRST READING: Isaiah 53:3-5
PSALM: Psalm 138
GOSPEL: Matthew 8:1-3, 5-8, 13-17

THE PRAYERS

HYMNS
Either of these hymns may be used when the Service of the Word for Healing occurs during Lent:
LBW 93   Jesus, refuge of the weary
LBW 104   In the cross of Christ I glory

MARCH 8, 2000

ASH WEDNESDAY

INTRODUCTION

Christians gather on Ash Wednesday to mark the beginning of Lent's baptismal preparation for Easter. On this day, the people of God receive an ashen cross on the forehead (a gesture rooted in baptism), hear the solemn proclamation to keep a fast in preparation for Easter's feast, and contemplate anew the ongoing meaning of baptismal initiation into the Lord's death and resurrection. While marked with the ashes of human mortality, the church hears God's promise of forgiveness and tastes God's mercy in the bread of life and the cup of salvation. From this solemn liturgy, the church goes forth on its journey to the great baptismal feast of Easter.

PRAYER OF THE DAY

Almighty and ever-living God, you hate nothing you have made and you forgive the sins of all who are penitent. Create in us new and honest hearts, so that, truly repenting of our sins, we may obtain from you, the God of all mercy, full pardon and forgiveness; through your Son, Jesus Christ our Lord, who lives and reigns with you and the Holy Spirit, one God, now and forever.

READINGS

Joel 2:1-2, 12-17

The context of this reading is a liturgy of communal lamentation. The prophet has called the temple community to mourn a devastating plague of the past and to announce a day of darkness, the day of the Lord. The community is called to repent, to return to God who is gracious and merciful.

or Isaiah 58:1-12

Psalm 51:1-18 (Psalm 51:1-17 [NRSV])

Have mercy on me, O God, according to your lovingkindness. (Ps. 51:1)

2 Corinthians 5:20b—6:10

Out of love for humankind, the sinless one experienced sin and suffering so that the redemptive power of God could penetrate the darkest, most forbidding, and tragic depths of human experience. No aspect of human life is ignored by the presence of God's grace. With faith in this redemption, Paul announces that this day is a day of God's grace, an acceptable time to turn toward God's mercy.

Matthew 6:1-6, 16-21

In this passage Matthew sets forth a vision of genuine righteousness illustrated by three basic acts of Jewish devotion: almsgiving, prayer, and fasting. Jesus does not denounce the acts—in the New Testament they are signs of singular devotion to God—rather, he criticizes those who perform them in order to have a sense of self-satisfaction or to gain public approval. Care for those who are poor, intense prayer, and fasting with a joyous countenance are signs of loving dedication to God.

COLOR   Black *or* Purple

THE PRAYERS

As we journey through the wilderness of Lent, let us return to God who gives us the joy of Easter's promise.
A BRIEF SILENCE.

O God, you call your people to turn from sin and to live in the joy and freedom of forgiveness. Give endurance to all the baptized who seek to practice the disciplines of Lent. Hear us, O God;
your mercy is great.

O God, you call all people to work together for the common good. Assist the leaders of the nations to remove all obstacles that would deter the reconciling efforts of peacemakers. Hear us, O God;
your mercy is great.

O God, grant compassion to all who minister in the healing arts: medical professionals, healing practitioners, and all caregivers. Show your mercy to those who are ill (especially . . .) and bring them peace of mind and heart. Hear us, O God;
your mercy is great.

O God, you call your people to turn from sin to live for you alone. Guide all who are preparing for baptism, that the forty days of Lent would bring them to the waters of life. Hear us, O God;
your mercy is great.

HERE OTHER INTERCESSIONS MAY BE OFFERED.

O God, you call your people to be with you in endless light. Bless the memory of our faithful departed, and keep us ever one with them in the communion of saints. Hear us, O God;
your mercy is great.
Merciful God, hear our cry when we call to you, renew and uphold us with your Spirit, through Jesus Christ our Lord.
Amen

IMAGES FOR PREACHING

Matthew's gospel, repeated every Ash Wednesday, is a reminder that the object of our worship is never to impress others with our piety or devotion, but that we worship in order to be in relationship with God. The irony, of course, is that the prohibition not to disfigure our faces is usually spoken to a sanctuary filled with worshipers who bear on their foreheads a gritty black cross. This tension between expectation and reality runs throughout the forty days of Lent.

Matthew's text acknowledges that tension. It suggests that the Christian's life of faith is a balance between public and private. It argues that each of us possess some worship needs that can only be met in community, and others that are a matter for private devotion. Admitting that "where your treasure is, there your heart will be also," Matthew is a clear-eyed observer who calls individuals and the community to consider carefully the nature of their "treasure," and to make good and godly choices about its disposal.

On this occasion it may be helpful to preach about the imposition of ashes. Making the mark and the symbol of the cross are enormously powerful, not only in themselves but as they bear the echoes of the anointing that comes with baptism. Just as in that sacrament, the ashen cross reminds us that we are dealing with issues of life and death. The bitterness and grit of the ashes are redeemed in and through the sign of the cross. Remember also that the cross of ashes is superimposed on the cross of oil given at baptism. The oil makes it possible for us to bear the ashes in hope, and makes the ashes into a promise of redemption and rebirth.

WORSHIP MATTERS

As ashes are marked on our foreheads, we confront the ash of our existence: those moments, circumstances, and relationships in which we truly remember that we are dust, and to dust we shall return. At these times, when pain, powerlessness, loneliness, limitation, shame, sickness, despair, and death overwhelm us, the sign of Christ's cross—the cross marked on our foreheads in baptism, and again today in ash—provides a most powerful prayer. This prayer is always available to us so that, when we are too afraid, ashamed, or angry to turn to God, when we cannot put our thoughts together, let alone find the words, we make the sign of Christ's cross and remember who we are: children of God and inheritors of eternal life. We remember how very much God loves us and that, on Christ's cross, the ashes of our existence become invitations to new life.

LET THE CHILDREN COME

Almsgiving, prayer, and fasting are the three traditional expressions of Christian devotion. Encourage children to develop these habits by providing opportunity for them throughout Lent. Place three baskets in the narthex or other gathering place. One basket is for offerings (alms) designated for those who are poor. Another basket is for prayers—either prayers they write or concerns they pray about. The third basket is to encourage fasting. Offer a choice: ask children and adults to (a) do without an unessential food and to place here the money that would have been spent, or (b) bring in nonperishable food for local food banks.

MUSIC FOR WORSHIP
SERVICE MUSIC

Even as the visual environment speaks the contrast between festive Transfiguration and this day of penitence, let the aural environment do the same. Unadorned accompaniments to hymns and service music may be all the instrumental music needed on this day, with the possible addition of simple chorale settings as prelude or postlude.

GATHERING

LBW 99	O Lord, throughout these forty days
LBW 657	The glory of these forty days

PSALM 51

Cooney, Rory. "Psalm 51: Create Me Again." GIA G-3975. U/2 pt, cong, opt inst.

Hopson, Hal H. "Psalm 51" in *Ten Psalms*. HOP HH 3930. SATB, cong.
Hurd, Bob. "Create in Me" in STP, vol. 1.
Marshall, Jane. "Psalm 51" in *Psalms Together II*. CGC-21. U.
Rees, Elizabeth. "O Lord, You Love Sincerity of Heart" in PS, vol. 2.
Schwarz, May. PW, cycle B.
Wellicome, Paul. "I Will Leave This Place" in PS, vol. 2.

HYMN OF THE DAY

LBW 91   Savior, when in dust to you
ABERYSTWYTH

VOCAL RESOURCES

Busarow, Donald. "Aberystwyth" in *All Praise to You Eternal God*. AFP 11-9076. Choir/cong, org.

INSTRUMENTAL RESOURCES

Held, Wilbur. "Aberystwyth" in *Those Wonderful Welsh, set 2*. MSM 10-842. Org.

Manz, Paul. "Aberystwyth" in *Improvisations for the Lenten Season, set 1*. MSM 10-300. Org.

Organ, Anne Krentz. "Savior, When in Dust to You" in *Christ, Mighty Savior: Reflections on Four Hymntunes*. AFP 11-10819. Pno.

Wellman, Samuel. "Aberystwyth" in *Keyboard Hymn Favorites*. AFP 11-10820. Pno.

ALTERNATE HYMN OF THE DAY

LBW 295   Out of the depths I cry to you
WOV 659   O Sun of justice

COMMUNION

LBW 296   Just as I am, without one plea
WOV 732   Create in me a clean heart

SENDING

LBW 263   Abide with us, our Savior
WOV 729   Christ, mighty Savior
WOV 743   Stay with us

ADDITIONAL HYMNS AND SONGS

H82 140/1   Wilt thou forgive
H82 666   Out of the depths I call
TFF 69   What can wash away my sin?
W&P   Out in the wilderness

MUSIC FOR THE DAY

CHORAL

Chepponis, James J. "Lenten Proclamation." GIA G-2761. 3 equal vcs/mxd, opt hb.

Farrant, Richard and John Hilton/Edward Klammer. "Lord for Thy Tender Mercies Sake." GIA G-3049. SATB.

Hallock, Peter. "Wash Me Through and Through." ION CH-1014. SATB, opt U, opt hb.

Schalk, Carl. "Have Mercy on Me, O God." AFP 11-10937. SATB.

Scott, K. Lee. "Out of the Depths I Cry to Thee" in *Rejoice Now My Spirit, Vocal Solos for the Church Year*. AFP 11-10228 (MH); 11-10229 (ML).

Tallis, Thomas. "Purge Me, O Lord." OXF TCM67. SATB.

CHILDREN'S CHOIRS

Marshall, Jane. "Create in Me, O God." CG CGA750. U antiphonal, kybd.

Handel/arr. Hopson. "Lord, I Lift My Soul to You." CG CGA440. 2 pt mxd, kybd.

KEYBOARD/INSTRUMENTAL

Albrecht, Mark. "Communion Meditation on Three Tunes" in *Three for Piano and Sax*. AFP 11-10929. Pno, inst.

Bach, J. S. "O God Be Merciful to Me" (Psalm 51) in *Music for Lent and Easter*. HWG.

HANDBELL

Moklebust, Cathy. "Kyrie." AFP 11-7182. 2 oct.

Wiltse, Carl. "The Beautiful Treasures of Heaven." SGM 3882.

PRAISE ENSEMBLE

Camp and Licciarello. "Revive Us, Oh Lord" in *Songs For Praise and Worship*. WRD.

Espinosa, Eddie and Bob Kilpatrick/arr. Wilson. "Change My Heart/Lord, Be Glorified." HOP GC992. SATB, kybd.

Makeever, Ray. "Be Merciful, O God" in DATH.

Nelson, Jeff. "Purify My Heart" in *Raise the Standard Worship Team Book*. MAR 3010124368. 3pt.

Paris, Twila. "Lamb of God" in *Songs for Praise and Worship*. WRD.

MARCH 12, 2000

FIRST SUNDAY IN LENT

INTRODUCTION

Jesus joins the church in the wilderness for forty days as we contemplate the meaning of our baptism into his death and resurrection. We are with Noah in the ark, Israel in the desert, and Elijah on rocky Mount Horeb for a time of prayer, fasting, and preparation. We do this together as a people who have been brought into existence by God's mercy. We hear this covenant proclaimed in the word of God and share this promise in the body and blood of Christ.

Today the church commemorates Gregory the Great, bishop of Rome, who died on this date in 604, and is remembered for leading the church during a time of upheaval and change.

PRAYER OF THE DAY

Lord God, you led your ancient people through the wilderness and brought them to the promised land. Guide now the people of your Church, that, following our Savior, we may walk through the wilderness of this world toward the glory of the world to come; through your Son, Jesus Christ our Lord, who lives and reigns with you and the Holy Spirit, one God, now and forever.

or

Lord God, our strength, the battle of good and evil rages within and around us, and our ancient foe tempts us with his deceits and empty promises. Keep us steadfast in your Word and, when we fall, raise us again and restore us through your Son, Jesus Christ our Lord, who lives and reigns with you and the Holy Spirit, one God, now and forever.

READINGS

Genesis 9:8-17

Today's reading centers on the conclusion to the flood story. The Lord destroys the earth by flood, except for Noah, his family, and the animals on the ark. Yet, divine destruction, because of human sinfulness, gives way to divine commitment. As in the first creation (Genesis 1), God blesses the human community and establishes a covenant with all creatures.

Psalm 25:1-9 (Psalm 25:1-10 [NRSV])

Your paths are love and faithfulness to those who keep your covenant. (Ps. 25:9)

1 Peter 3:18-22

In this reading, the author emphasizes God's saving action on behalf of Noah, his family, and the creatures. This saving presence continues to be manifested through Christ in the act of baptism.

Mark 1:9-15

The Spirit that comes upon Jesus at his baptism sustains him when he is tested by Satan so that he might proclaim the gospel of God's reign.

COLOR   Purple

THE PRAYERS

As we journey through the wilderness of Lent, let us return to God who gives us the joy of Easter's promise.
A BRIEF SILENCE.

O God of promise, strengthen all the baptized in the sacred relationship you have made with us in baptism, and empower us to speak your promises in the wilderness of this world. Hear us, O God;
your mercy is great.

O God of voice and word, speak tenderly to the world that you have made, that the nations may know your loving presence, and their leaders your guiding wisdom. Hear us, O God;
your mercy is great.

O God of patience and kindness, remember those who approach death, and strengthen those who keep watch with them. Heal the sick (especially . . .) and assure them of your abiding presence. Hear us, O God;
your mercy is great.

O God of our relationships, bless those preparing for baptism. Give holy guidance to those who mentor them and to congregations who will receive them. Hear us, O God;
your mercy is great.

HERE OTHER INTERCESSIONS MAY BE OFFERED.

O God of all eternity, keep our blessed dead in your eternal embrace until, with Gregory the Great and all

your saints, we are reunited with them by your grace. Hear us, O God;
your mercy is great.
Merciful God, hear our cry when we call to you, renew and uphold us with your Spirit, through Jesus Christ our Lord.
Amen

IMAGES FOR PREACHING

Immediately after his baptism (and just where one might have expected some kind of celebration of that event), Jesus is driven out into the wilderness. Despite the tearing of the heavens, despite the descent of the Spirit, despite the voice from heaven with the blessing and commendation, Jesus takes no time to bask in the glory of the moment. Instead he heeds an urgency, and submits to a period of rigorous preparation for the tasks that lie just beyond the horizon.

Jesus' wilderness experience is not, however, one of isolation and solitude. Not only is he tempted by Satan, but he is described as being with the wild beasts, with angels to wait on him. Jesus' struggle over the forty days was certainly difficult, but it was not one he undertook alone. He found companionship with the beasts, and comfort from the angels.

It is possible to understand this episode not only as a time of preparation, but also as a period of redemption that prefigures Jesus' final victory. In taking his place between the wild beasts and the angels, Jesus reorders and reclaims creation; offering a vision of an unspoiled Eden, redeemed through his presence. This understanding may lead us to recast Lent, not just as a time of discipline and asceticism, but as an opportunity to reclaim our own "proper" place in the orders of creation.

WORSHIP MATTERS

Lent is a season of repentance, of turning toward God and away from self-centeredness, hate, negligence, waste, and all that separates us from love of God and neighbor. Confession is an opportunity for repentance, but it is not the only opportunity we have to turn toward God when we worship. When we say the creed, we embrace faith in God and reject all other belief systems. When we join our lives in prayer, we turn toward a vision of God's kingdom and away from the ways of the world. When we share the peace, we choose reconciliation and commit to work toward that for which we have just prayed. And when we come to the Lord's table, we witness to a community where all are welcome, connected, and one. "Return to the Lord your God!" the season calls. It is a time and a place to begin the journey of repentance.

LET THE CHILDREN COME

Today, open the font with water. Ask the children to imagine the water in the font being so deep, they cannot swim in it. Then imagine turning the church upside-down so that the roof is in the water like a boat and the people are safe inside. Just as God saved Noah, so in baptism Jesus reaches into the water to pull us safely into the boat of his church. Older children will enjoy learning that the portion of the church where the people sit is traditionally called the *nave*, from the Latin for ship.

MUSIC FOR WORSHIP
SERVICE MUSIC

The premier placement for the Great Litany (*LBW*, p. 168) is the gathering rite on the first Sunday in Lent, when it may be sung in a slow extended procession, replacing confession/forgiveness, entrance hymn, and Kyrie. Establishing a flowing and insistent cadence is key to the effective use of this ancient sung prayer. Another possibility is a similar procession to the spiritual "I want Jesus to walk with me" (WOV 660); intersperse the stanzas with spoken prayers to a piano accompaniment using the harmonic progressions of the spiritual; end with a repeat of stanza 1.

GATHERING

LBW 343	Guide me ever, great Redeemer
WOV 660	I want Jesus to walk with me

PSALM 25

Brugh, Lorraine. PW, cycle B.

Haas, David/arr. Jeanne Cotter. "Remember Your Mercies" or "Teach Me Your Ways" in PCY.

Hallock, Peter/arr. Carl Crosier. "Psalm 25" in *The Ionian Psalter*. ION.

Hurd, Bob. "To You, O God, I Lift Up My Soul" in STP, vol. 2.

Mahnke, Allan. "Psalm 25" in *Seventeen Psalms for Cantor and Congregation*. CPH 97-6093.

Ogden, David. "Here I Am" in PS, vol. 3.

Wellicome, Paul. "Remember Your Mercy, Lord" in PS, vol. 1.

HYMN OF THE DAY

WOV 741   Thy holy wings
               BRED DINA VIDA VINGAR

VOCAL RESOURCES

Burkhardt, Michael. "Thy Holy Wings." MSM 50-5552. U/2 pt, pno, opt ob, cl, vc.

Erickson, Karle. "Thy Holy Wings." AFP 11-0594. SATB, 2 fl.

INSTRUMENTAL RESOURCES

Cherwien, David. "Thy Holy Wings" in *Rejoice in God's Saints*. AFP 11-10713. Org.

McFadden, Jane. "Two More Swedish Melodies." AFP 11-10806. Hb.

Sedio, Mark. "Thy Holy Wings" in *Dancing in the Light of God*. AFP 11-10793. Pno.

ALTERNATE HYMN OF THE DAY

LBW 366   Lord of our life
LBW 230   Lord, keep us steadfast in your Word

COMMUNION

LBW 226   Draw near and take the body of the Lord
WOV 707   This is my body

SENDING

LBW 341   Jesus, still lead on
WOV 724   Shalom

ADDITIONAL HYMNS AND SONGS

GS2 20   Sarantañani
H82 152   Kind Maker of the world
NCH 167   Mark how the Lamb of God's self-offering
TFF 195   Yield not to temptation
W&P   Amazing love

MUSIC FOR THE DAY

CHORAL

Farrant, Richard. "Call to Remembrance." ECS 1639. SATB.

Parker, Alice. "Take Me to the Water." GIA G-4238. SAATB.

Scott, K. Lee. "Redeeming Grace" in *Sing a Song of Joy, Vocal Solos for Worship*. AFP 11-8194 (MH); 11-8195 (ML).

Trinkley, Bruce. "I Want Jesus to Walk with Me." AFP 11-10846. SATB, pno.

Young, Jeremy. "Passion Chorale: Lenten Processional." GIA G-4354. SA(B), kybd, perc.

CHILDREN'S CHOIRS

Hobby, Robert. "Thy Holy Wings/I Lift My Soul." MSM 50-9453. U, fl, pno.

Powell, Robert. "A Lenten Prayer." CG CGA159. U, fl, org.

KEYBOARD/INSTRUMENTAL

Langlais, Jean. "Prelude" in *Suite Medievale*. Editions Salabert. Org.

Martinson, Joel. "Aria on a Chaconne." CPH 97-6271. Org.

HANDBELL

Kastner and McChesney. "Jesus Walked This Lonesome Valley." JEF JHS9189. 2-3 oct, hb solo/duet.

Waldrop, Tammy. "Noah and the Ark" in *Ring Out!* 910100611. 2 oct, narr.

PRAISE ENSEMBLE

Haugen, Marty. "Tree of Life" (Lenten verses) in *Gather*. GIA.

Honoré, Jeffrey. "How Can I Keep from Singing." CG CGA-567. SATB, pno.

Joncas, Michael/arr. Mark Hayes. "On Eagle's Wings." ALF 16104. SATB, acc.

Lowry, Nancy. "Wellspring" in *Maranatha! Music Praise Chorus Book, 3rd Ed.* WRD/MAR.

Makeever, Ray. "In the Water" in DATH.

SUNDAY, MARCH 12
GREGORY THE GREAT, BISHOP OF ROME, 604

Gregory the Great was an important and wealthy figure until he decided to sell his vast property, give the proceeds to the poor, and enter one of the seven monasteries he had founded. He accepted election to the papacy only after great inner struggle, and was a tower of strength to the church in a time of famine, flood, pestilence, invasion, and political struggle. He effected important changes in the liturgy and described his role of pope as "servant of the servants of Christ."

Use Gregory's life to reflect on connections between liturgy and social justice. How does the eucharist form us to be the body of Christ in the world, serving those who are in need? Does our Lenten journey of conversion lead us not only inward, but also outward to struggle against the poverty and injustice in society?

FRIDAY, MARCH 17
PATRICK, BISHOP, MISSIONARY TO IRELAND, 461

At sixteen, Patrick was captured and taken to Ireland to serve as a herdsman. After his escape, he became a missionary monk, eager to preach the faith to the Irish in their native language. In time he was consecrated bishop, established churches and religious communities, and organized Christian communities he found in the north, bringing Ireland much closer to the Western church. He used the three-leafed shamrock to teach catechumens about the Holy Trinity.

Use Patrick's famous hymn, "I bind unto myself today" (LBW 188), as basis for meditation on Lent's call to return to our baptism.

MARCH 19, 2000
SECOND SUNDAY IN LENT

INTRODUCTION

The readiness of Abraham and Sarah, and the eagerness of Jesus to do God's will are models for contemporary disciples in the church. Baptized into Christ's death and resurrection, we are called to live a distinctive style of life shaped by faith in God's mercy. As followers of Christ, we take up our cross and stand with all those who suffer in our midst. Our Lenten journey always takes us to the cross, the heart of God's love for the world.

Today we commemorate Joseph, guardian of our Lord, portrayed in the scriptures as a devout and honest man.

PRAYER OF THE DAY

Eternal God, it is your glory always to have mercy. Bring back all who have erred and strayed from your ways; lead them again to embrace in faith the truth of your Word and to hold it fast; through Jesus Christ your Son our Lord, who lives and reigns with you and the Holy Spirit, one God, now and forever.

READINGS

Genesis 17:1-7, 15-16

In today's reading, the writer connects the covenant made with Abraham and Sarah to the "everlasting" covenant made with Noah. The relationship between God and Abraham's descendants is as sure as the relationship between God and the seasons and times of the year. The name changes further emphasize the firmness of God's promise.

Psalm 22:22-30 (Psalm 22:23-31 [NRSV])

All the ends of the earth shall remember and turn to the LORD. (Ps. 22:26)

Romans 4:13-25

Paul is trying to persuade the Roman Christians that people are made right with God through faith rather than by works of the law. Abraham became the ancestor of God's chosen people not by keeping the law but by trusting God to keep his promises.

Mark 8:31-38

After Peter confesses his belief that Jesus is the Messiah, Jesus tells his disciples for the first time what is to come. Peter's response indicates that he does not yet understand the way of the cross that Jesus will travel.

COLOR   Purple

THE PRAYERS

As we journey through the wilderness of Lent, let us return to God who gives us the joy of Easter's promise.
A BRIEF SILENCE.

God Almighty, the promises you give to us rest on your grace, not on our faith. Like Abraham and Sarah, help us always to trust in your word and believe in your faithfulness. Hear us, O God;
your mercy is great.

O God, you are the author of a multitude of nations. Guide their leaders with peacemaking hearts and lead them always in honesty and justice. Hear us, O God;
your mercy is great.

Bless all who serve those who are unemployed or homeless. Strengthen those who care for the sick (especially . . .), that they might see your work in their lives. Hear us, O God;
your mercy is great.
Guide all who lead in the worship of this congregation—musicians and artists, lectors and ushers, assisting ministers and altar guilds—that by their ministry we will be enabled to set our minds on holy things. Hear us, O God;
your mercy is great.

HERE OTHER INTERCESSIONS MAY BE OFFERED.

Challenge us, O God, to see beyond ourselves and to know that we are surrounded always by a great cloud of witnesses, including Joseph and all our dearly departed. Hear us, O God;
your mercy is great.
Merciful God, hear our cry when we call to you, renew and uphold us with your Spirit, through Jesus Christ our Lord.
Amen

IMAGES FOR PREACHING

As Mark tells the story, Jesus speaks openly about what is going to happen to him once they reach Jerusalem. Shocked by what he has heard, Peter pulls Jesus to one side and begins to rebuke him. We can only imagine what the disciple said.

"How can you say that? Why would you say that? Do you think that anybody wants to hear that sort of thing from you? I thought it would be a march toward victory—you're saying it's a funeral procession? Who else will follow you, now that you've told them the truth?"

Notice, however, that in order to say those things (or whatever else he did say), Peter took Jesus aside. That is, Peter literally took Jesus out of the place he had been standing and pulled him to the edge, away from the middle, out of his position at the center and off to the side where he could deal more easily with him.

Jesus' response is to put Peter back in his place and to call the crowd with the disciples gathering around him once more. The lesson? No disciple can put anything in Jesus' place—not even their love for him or for his safety. No follower—not even Peter—can successfully drag Jesus out of the center. Our place may change, nearer or farther, as our faith grows and develops. Jesus remains central and offers this instruction to help us remember. Take up your cross and follow him.

WORSHIP MATTERS

"If any want to become my followers, let them deny themselves and take up their cross and follow me" (Mark 8:34). When many Christians visualize "their cross," it is the one they see in church. The cross in our worship space reminds us of what it means to follow Jesus. A crucifix, wood with a corpus, teaches that God meets us in our suffering, and that we meet others in their suffering. An empty cross, gold and glistening, instructs that death is the gate to new life. A beautiful cross, jeweled and handcrafted, leads us to contemplate the paradox that Christ's humiliation and defeat are, in fact, his hour of glory and that the greatest in God's kingdom is the servant of all. "If any want to become my followers, let them . . . take up their cross . . ." (Mark 8:34). As we take up "our cross" with our eyes, we rediscover what it means to follow Jesus.

LET THE CHILDREN COME

By means of parents and a child, God created his chosen people, a great nation. The elders passed down the faith to the children, from generation to generation. At baptism, parents and sponsors promise to bring children to worship and teach them the Ten Commandments, the creed, and the Lord's Prayer, all of which hand down the faith. Children can honor the elders of the community of faith by sitting with them in worship, asking them to be mentors, visiting the homebound, making phone calls to the lonely, or sending a note of thanks for their example and encouragement.

MUSIC FOR WORSHIP

GATHERING

LBW 544	The God of Abraham praise
WOV 733	Our Father, we have wandered

PSALM 22

Brugh, Lorraine. PW, cycle B.

Haugen, Marty. "Psalm 22: My God, My God" in *Gather Comprehensive*. GIA.

Harbor, Rawn. "My God, My God" in *This Far by Faith*.

Hopson, Hal H. "Psalm 22" in *Eighteen Psalms for the Church Year*. HOP HH3941. U/SATB.

Manion, Tim. "My God, My God" in STP, vol. 1.
Sarum plainsong/arr. Christopher L. Webber. "Lord, Why Have You Forsaken Me" in PH.
Schiavone, John. "My God, My God" in STP, vol. 3.
Smith, Alan. "My God, My God" in PS, vol. 2.

HYMN OF THE DAY

LBW 325   Lord, thee I love with all my heart
           HERZLICH LIEB

VOCAL RESOURCES

Ferguson, John. "Lord, in All Love." AFP 11-10788. SATB, org, opt cong.

INSTRUMENTAL RESOURCES

Krapf, Gerhard. "Chorale-Partita on Lord, You I Love with All My Heart." MSM 10-870. Org.
Manz, Paul. "Herzlich lieb" in *Nine Hymn Improvisations*. MSM 10-875. Org.
Weber, S. "Herzlich lieb" in *Four Hymn Preludes*. CPH 97-6089. Org.

ALTERNATE HYMN OF THE DAY

WOV 660   I want Jesus to walk with me
LBW 496   Around you, O Lord Jesus

COMMUNION

LBW 406   Take my life, that I may be
WOV 655   As the sun with longer journey

SENDING

LBW 504   O God, my faithful God
WOV 785   Weary of all trumpeting

ADDITIONAL HYMNS AND SONGS

GS2 40   Bread for the Journey
H82 476   Can we by searching find out God
TFF 235   All to Jesus I surrender
W&P   Father, I adore you

MUSIC FOR THE DAY

CHORAL

Beck, John Ness/arr. Craig Courtney. "Assurance" in *Hymn Settings of John Ness Beck*. BEC VC4. M voice, kybd.
Busarow, Donald. "Come, Ye Sinners, Poor and Needy" in *A Sacred Harp Quartet*. MSM 50-9840. SATB div.
Hopson, Hal. "Take Up Your Cross." AFP 11-10570. 2 pt mxd, kybd.
Martinson, Joel. "God So Loved the World." CPH 98-3098. SA, org.

Neswick, Bruce. "Hearken to My Voice, O Lord, When I Call." AFP 11-10901. Also in *The Augsburg Choirbook*. 11-10817. 2 pt, kybd.
Reger, Max. "I Stand Fast with Jesus Christ" (Meinen Jesum lass ich nicht). Carus-Verlag 50.406/01 (score). 50.406/05 (choir). S, SATB, vln, vla, org. Ger/Eng.

CHILDREN'S CHOIRS

Horman, John. "God So Loved the World." CG CGA477. U, vln/fl.
Riehle, Kevin. "Song for Beginnings." CG CGA493. U/2 pt, kybd, opt cong, opt C inst.

KEYBOARD/INSTRUMENTAL

Bach, J. S. "O God, My Faithful God." Various ed. Org.
Peeters, Flor. "Adagio" in *Modale Suite*. LEM. Org.
Uehlein, Christopher. "Martyrdom Cross" in *Blue Cloud Abbey Organ Book*. AFP 11-10394. Org.

HANDBELL

Beck/arr. John Muschick. "Offertory." BEC HB166. 4-5 oct.
McFadden, Jane. "Day by Day" in *Two More Swedish Melodies*. AFP 11-10871. 3-4 oct, opt 2-4 oct, hc.

PRAISE ENSEMBLE

Boltz, Ray. "Take Up Your Cross" in *The Ray Boltz Anthology*. Diadem Music.
Goebel-Komala, Felix. "Psalm of Hope." GIA G-4403. SATB, cant, cong, kybd, gtr, timp.
Paris, Twila/arr. Torrans. "We Bow Down." Songpower ZJP7006. SAB, kybd.
Rodgers and Wyse. "Wonderful, Merciful Savior" in *Songs for Praise and Worship*. WRD.

SUNDAY, MARCH 19
JOSEPH, GUARDIAN OF OUR LORD

Joseph, husband of Mary, was a carpenter who is portrayed in the scriptures as a devout and honest man, showing care for his wife and the child Jesus. The infancy narratives in the book of Matthew portray Joseph as a faithful man who responds to God's leading in visionary dreams. Because Joseph is not mentioned during Jesus' adult life, it is assumed he died by that time.

As you commemorate Joseph, consider the importance of parents, especially fathers, in sharing religious faith with children. How do parents model both devotion to God, as well as just and honorable living? Invite fathers to a breakfast today.

WEDNESDAY, MARCH 22
JONATHAN EDWARDS, TEACHER,
MISSIONARY TO THE AMERICAN INDIANS, 1758

Edwards was a Congregational minister of Connecticut who preached and promoted spiritual revival with a special emphasis on original sin. He became well known for his refusal to commune those he believed were not fully "converted" to the faith. After dismissal from his parish, Edwards ministered among the Housatonic Indians and then became the president of what would become Princeton University.

Edward's keen intellect and contributions to theology in America and Britain are a reminder of both the mind's contributions and limits in understanding the mystery of God. In light of various spiritual disciplines, reflect on the ways you experience God's presence through intellectual inquiry, meditation, and corporate worship.

FRIDAY, MARCH 24
OSCAR ROMERO, BISHOP OF EL SALVADOR, 1980

Romero is remembered for his advocacy on behalf of the poor in El Salvador. After being appointed bishop he preached against the political repression in his country. He and other priests and church workers were considered traitors for their bold stands for justice, especially defending the rights of the poor. After several years of threats to his life, Romero was assassinated while presiding at the eucharist. During the 1980s thousands died in El Salvador during the political unrest.

Romero is remembered as a martyr who gave his life in behalf of the powerless in his country. Our Lenten journey of conversion calls us to be bold in our witness to Christ. Who are the powerless in our society? How can we be their voice in advocating justice and equality for all people created in the image of God?

SATURDAY, MARCH 25
THE ANNUNCIATION OF OUR LORD

Exactly nine months before Christmas we celebrate the annunciation in which the angel Gabriel announced to Mary that she would give birth to the Son of God. Ancient scholars believed that March 25 was also the day on which creation began, and the date of Jesus' death on the cross. Thus, from the sixth to eighteenth centuries, March 25 was observed as New Year's Day in much of Christian Europe.

Set within Lent, Mary's openness to the mysterious will of God is an example of faithful discipleship. Observe this important day in the church year by singing "The angel Gabriel" (WOV 632), or a setting of the Magnificat, such as the paraphrase "My soul proclaims your greatness" (WOV 730).

MARCH 26, 2000

THIRD SUNDAY IN LENT

INTRODUCTION

In our society, even churches can become like marketplaces, and congregations can be characterized chiefly as consumers. The drive to satisfy every taste and opinion can distract the church from its center: Jesus Christ among us in the regular celebration of word and sacrament. In the word of God and the eucharistic meal, the temple of Christ's body is strengthened for its witness in daily life.

PRAYER OF THE DAY

Eternal Lord, your kingdom has broken into our troubled world through the life, death, and resurrection of your Son. Help us to hear your Word and obey it, so that we become instruments of your redeeming love; through your Son, Jesus Christ our Lord, who lives and reigns with you and the Holy Spirit, one God, now and forever.

READINGS

Exodus 20:1-17

This covenant is the third one the church hears in this cycle of readings. After escaping from slavery, the Israelites come to Mount Sinai where God instructs them how to live together in community. The Ten Commandments recognize that God is the creator of all things. Flowing from God, the life of the community flourishes when marked by the basic building blocks recounted in today's reading: honesty, trust, fidelity, and respect for life, family, and property.

Psalm 19

The commandment of the LORD gives light to the eyes. (Ps. 19:8)

1 Corinthians 1:18-25

Paul's preaching about the salvation God offers through the cross was met with suspicion. How can victory come out of death? Some thought this message was nonsense. But Paul announces that God's wisdom overturns common expectations about who God is and where God intends to be.

John 2:13-22

Jesus attacks the commercialization of religion by driving merchants out of the temple. When challenged, he responds mysteriously, with the first prediction of his own death and resurrection. In the midst of a seemingly stable religious center, Jesus suggests that the center itself has changed.

COLOR Purple

THE PRAYERS

As we journey through the wilderness of Lent, let us return to God who gives us the joy of Easter's promise.

A BRIEF SILENCE.

Let us pray that the whole church on earth would be united in its love for the commands of God and in its embrace of the whole creation. Hear us, O God;
your mercy is great.

Let us pray that the wisdom of the world will be overtaken by God's foolishness, and that human strength will be overshadowed by God's weakness. Hear us, O God;
your mercy is great.

Let us pray for those suffering from addictions and all who are ill (especially . . .), that destructive life patterns and disease will be driven out by the healing presence of Christ. Hear us, O God;
your mercy is great.

Let us pray for all who are entering the community of faith through baptism, that their journey will bring them to the font of forgiveness and to the table of truth. Hear us, O God;
your mercy is great.

HERE OTHER INTERCESSIONS MAY BE OFFERED.

Let us pray in thanksgiving for the faithful departed, that their lives continue to bear witness to the light of Christ in which they now abide eternally. Hear us, O God;
your mercy is great.

Merciful God, hear our cry when we call to you, renew and uphold us with your Spirit, through Jesus Christ our Lord.
Amen

IMAGES FOR PREACHING

From practically the time that we are old enough to crawl around on our own, we discover that other people place limitations on us, and if we don't obey them, we will be punished. A three-year-old hears her mother say that she shouldn't play in the street, otherwise she could get run over by a car. But to the three-year-old, the even bigger threat may be that if she does play in the street, her mommy won't like it and she'll get a spanking.

That model of loving our parents can mirror the way it works between us and God. Some of us who have read the Ten Commandments may have grown up only learning to fear God. But when we mature in our faith, we fear, love, and respect God because we want to, not simply because we must.

We could simplify the whole matter and separate religion into two categories. One kind is that of a person trying to achieve a satisfactory relationship with God by doing something to win God's favor, such as being good, believing in the right doctrine, and expecting rewards for good behavior. This category is the religion of righteousness by the law.

But another kind of religion does not begin with us at all. It begins with God. God was in Christ reconciling the world, and God has forgiven us all our sins. We respond in gratitude to God's love. We obey God's law because God has loved us first.

WORSHIP MATTERS

"Stop making my Father's house a marketplace!" (John 2:16). Remember when this verse from today's gospel was the response to any suggestion of congregational fund-raising? Today financial realities lead many congregations to undertake all sorts of moneymaking activities. We are caught in the tension between our offerings and the bottom line, between stewardship and paying the bills. The key to living in this tension is recognizing what the real "bottom line" is. Our offering is our way of thanking God for all the blessings God gives us and committing our lives to the work of God's kingdom. Sometimes fund-raising is necessary to make ends meet. But when fund-raising lessens our gratitude to God and commitment to God's kingdom, when it becomes the major focus of a congregation, when money becomes an end in itself and not a means to carrying out Christ's mission, we turn our Father's house into a marketplace.

LET THE CHILDREN COME

The Ten Commandments are fundamental to the Christian faith, but are not used as often in public worship as the Apostles' Creed and Lord's Prayer. Consider using one of Luther's adaptations of the commandments either for a confession of sin or the prayers. In this way, children see how the commandments are used in the church's worship and how the faith of the church is exercised in the home and in daily life. Encourage them to commit the commandments to memory, including Exodus 19:2 and 19:5b-6 that pertain to all commandments, as the catechism rightly teaches.

MUSIC FOR WORSHIP

GATHERING

LBW 320   O God, our help in ages past
WOV 750   Oh, praise the gracious power

PSALM 19

Bell, John L. "May the words of my mouth" in *Psalms of Patience, Protest and Praise.* Iona/GIA G-4047. U.

Brugh, Lorraine. PW, cycle B.

Dohms, Ann Celeen. *Sing Out! A Children's Psalter.* WLP/S. Paluch Co. U/kybd.

Hruby, Dolores. *Seasonal Psalms for Children.* WLP 7102.

Inwood, Paul. "You, Lord, Have the Message" in STP, vol. 2.

Joncas, Michael. "Lord, You Have the Words" in STP, vol. 1.

Ogden, David. "You, Lord, Have the Message of Eternal Life" in PS, vol. 2.

HYMN OF THE DAY

LBW 104   In the cross of Christ I glory
           RATHBUN

INSTRUMENTAL RESOURCES

Albrecht, Timothy. "Rathbun" in *Grace Notes V.* AFP 11-10764. Org.

Burkhardt, Michael. "Rathbun" in *Easy Hymn Settings—Lent.* MSM 10-315. Org.

Cherwien, David. "Toccata on 'In the Cross of Christ I Glory.' " MSM 10-303. Org.

ALTERNATE HYMN OF THE DAY

LBW 415   God of grace and God of glory
WOV 782   All my hope on God is founded

COMMUNION

LBW 199   Thee we adore, O hidden Savior
WOV 706   Eat this bread, drink this cup

SENDING

LBW 368   I love your kingdom, Lord
WOV 796   My Lord of light

ADDITIONAL HYMNS AND SONGS

H82 584   God, you have given us power
NCH 509   How deep the silence of the soul
TFF 73   Jesus, keep me near the cross
W&P   Come and taste

MUSIC FOR THE DAY

CHORAL

Bruckner, Anton. "Christus factus est." AMC AE 157. SATB.

Keesecker, Thomas. "Jesus, Keep Me Near the Cross." AFP 11-10744. SATB, pno.

Mozart, W. A. "De profundis clamavi" K 93 (From the Depths Have I Called Unto Thee) in *A First Motet Book.* CPH 97-5230. SATB, org. Lat/Eng.

Weitzel, Thomas. "Teach Me the Way." GIA G-3887. SATB, opt cong.

CHILDREN'S CHOIRS

Bach/arr. Burkhardt. "The Heavens Declare Thy Glory." MSM 50-7503. U, 2 trbl inst, kybd, opt bass inst.

Erickson, John. "We Come with Joy." CG CGA554. U, org.

KEYBOARD/INSTRUMENTAL

Hopson, Hal. "Variations on 'Cwm Rhondda.' " HWG GSTC 9520. Org.

Young, Jeremy. "Stabat Mater" in *At the Foot of the Cross.* AFP 11-10688. Pno.

HANDBELL

Colvin, Parrish. "Surely the Lord Is in This Place."
WRD 3014057312. SATB, 4-5 oct.

Tucker, Margaret K. "Northern Lights" (Lacquiparle). AMSI HB-7.
3-5 oct.

PRAISE ENSEMBLE

Altrogge, Mark. "You Are My God" in *Hosanna! Music Songbook 7.*
INT.

Harris, Ron. "On Our Side" in *Hosanna! Music Songbook 7.* INT.

Klein, Laurie/arr. Jack Schrader. "I Love You, Lord." HOP GC936.
SATB, pno.

Kreutz, Robert E./arr. John Ferguson. "Gift of Finest Wheat."
GIA G-3089. SATB, cong, org.

Starke, Stephen P. "Greet the Rising Sun" in *Hymnal Supplement 98.*
CPH.

WEDNESDAY, MARCH 29
HANS NIELSEN HAUGE, RENEWER OF THE CHURCH, 1824

After a mystical experience Hauge began preaching, first to his own parish, and then throughout Norway. Itinerant preaching was against the law, and he was frequently arrested. His writings emphasized a person's vocation as service to God, warned against separatism, and urged his followers to remain faithful to the national church. He influenced Norwegians who emigrated to North America by his emphasis on private prayer, devotional reading, Bible study, singing, and preaching.

Some might remember Hauge by singing the Norwegian hymn "My heart is longing" (LBW 326), with its devotional response to the death of Christ.

FRIDAY, MARCH 31
JOHN DONNE, PRIEST, 1631

This seventeenth-century priest of the Church of England is commemorated for his poetry and spiritual writings. Donne was named dean of St. Paul's Cathedral and became the most celebrated preacher of his day. In his poetry, he mixed sensual passion, intellectual austerity, and fervent devotion.

Find his poem "Good Friday, 1613. Riding westward." In it Donne speaks of Jesus' death on the cross: "Who sees God's face, that is self life, must die; What a death were it then to see God die?"

APRIL 2, 2000

FOURTH SUNDAY IN LENT

INTRODUCTION

In today's gospel reading, Jesus compares himself to the serpent in the wilderness. He is lifted up on the cross so that all who hold to him will be healed. God sent the Son, not to condemn, but to save the world. We who have heard the words of love and mercy in today's scriptures go forth to speak with forgiveness rather than condemnation. Our baptism calls us to a life of good works, not to point to ourselves but to the immeasurable riches of God's grace made known to all the world in Christ our Lord.

PRAYER OF THE DAY

God of all mercy, by your power to heal and to forgive, graciously cleanse us from all sin and make us strong; through your Son, Jesus Christ our Lord, who lives and reigns with you and the Holy Spirit, one God, now and forever.

READINGS

Numbers 21:4-9

Throughout the Hebrew scriptures, the time of Israel's wandering in the desert is seen as a period of testing. Though God delivers the people from slavery and provides for all their needs on the journey, they whine and grumble. They fail to see the gift of salvation in the exodus. Yet God's anger is not the final word. God continues to lead the people toward the land promised to their ancestors.

Psalm 107:1-3, 17-22

The LORD delivered them from their distress. (Ps. 107:19)

Ephesians 2:1-10

God raised us up to new life while we yet belonged to powers of evil. If such was our past, we now live with Christ and will spend eternity discovering the breadth of God's goodness.

John 3:14-21

To explain the salvation of God to the religious leader, Nicodemus, Jesus refers to the scripture passage quoted in today's first reading. Just as those who looked upon the bronze serpent were healed, so people will be saved when they behold Christ lifted up on the cross.

COLOR Purple

THE PRAYERS

As we journey through the wilderness of Lent, let us return to God who gives us the joy of Easter's promise.
A BRIEF SILENCE.

Let us pray for patience on our journey through these Lenten forty days. Give strength to all servants of the church who lead people on the way of the cross. Hear us, O God;
your mercy is great.

Let us pray for a way of life centered in works of justice and peace for people of all races and nationalities. Hear us, O God;
your mercy is great.

Let us pray for farmers and all who prepare the soil for planting, that the seeds they sow will be reaped in a bountiful harvest. Hear us, O God;
your mercy is great.

Let us pray for those who are sick, for those who have suffered natural disasters, and for all who cry out to you (especially . . .). Hear us, O God;
your mercy is great.

Let us pray for all preparing to affirm their faith, for those preparing for first communion, and for all who seek to deepen their spiritual knowledge, that their faith would be deepened in this season. Hear us, O God;
your mercy is great.

HERE OTHER INTERCESSIONS MAY BE OFFERED.

Let us pray in thanksgiving for the members of this congregation who have died, and all the blessed dead, who now live in the light of your eternal love. Hear us, O God;
your mercy is great.

Merciful God, hear our cry when we call to you, renew and uphold us with your Spirit, through Jesus Christ our Lord.
Amen

IMAGES FOR PREACHING

In the second chapter of Ephesians, we read words that have been central to the Reformation heritage for five centuries: "by grace you have been saved through faith, and this is not your own doing; it is the gift of God." The words from our gospel are probably even more familiar to hearers today: "For God so loved the world that he gave his only Son, so that everyone who believes in him may not perish but have eternal life."

Our thoughts as preachers on this day may be, "Haven't we heard all this before? Isn't that old news? Haven't I preached about God's love and forgiveness enough already?"

But then we may think of people who have always had to prove themselves to their families or coworkers. Think of all the folks trying to improve their lives by reading self-help books and attending time management seminars. We are all in need of hearing these bedrock texts about God's love again.

This message may seem like old news. It may seem strange to us that we should have to repeat the basic message that God loves us. But let us not be so dulled by this news. Many people in our world need to hear it. Like spouses or children who daily need to hear the words "I love you," we need to preach the news of God's love again as well.

We, the people of God, are also called to be a sign of God's love. It might seem amazing to us, but many people would never expect to find love in a church. Many people aren't aware of a loving God. Some people only think of Christians as stern and judgmental. They would be afraid even to enter our buildings. Let there be no misunderstanding today: Tell the story of God's love.

WORSHIP MATTERS

Does your congregation use a processional cross? A cross carried into our worship reminds us it is Jesus who gathers us: "So must the Son of Man be lifted up, that whoever believes in him may have eternal life" (John 3:14). At the conclusion of worship we follow the cross into the world (see the hymn "Lift high the cross," LBW 377). In worship, the processional cross points to where the "action" is, moving from baptismal space, to the place of the word, to the table. As a symbol of the Christian life, the processional cross assures us that our God accompanies us everywhere: from death, when the cross is traced on our foreheads in baptism; to resurrection, when the sign of the cross is made on our coffins; and all the places in between.

LET THE CHILDREN COME

If a crucifer-led procession is used, instruct the people to face the procession as it begins and to bow as the cross passes them. Not only does this show reverence for Christ as our Lord, but in light of today's readings, it also clearly helps us to orient our body to him as our savior and redeemer. Ask parents to make a habit of seating children where they can see a cross during worship, and be sure that the cross is not obscured.

MUSIC FOR WORSHIP
GATHERING

| LBW 377 | Lift high the cross |
| WOV 658 | The Word of God is source and seed |

PSALM 107

Brugh, Lorraine. PW, cycle B.
Hopson, Hal H. TP.
Stewart, Roy James. "Give Thanks to the Lord" in *Choral Refrains from Psalms for the Church Year, vol. 5.* GIA G-3746-A.

HYMN OF THE DAY

| LBW 448 | Amazing grace, how sweet the sound |

VOCAL RESOURCES
Bertalot, John. "Amazing Grace." AFP 11-10020. Also in *The Augsburg Choirbook.* 11-10817. SATB, org.
Schrader, Jack. "Amazing Grace." HOP GC 1006. SATB, kybd.

INSTRUMENTAL RESOURCES
Albrecht, Mark. "Amazing Grace" in *Timeless Hymns of Faith for Piano.* AFP 11-10863. Pno.
Callahan, Charles. "Fantasy-Prelude on Amazing Grace." MSM 10-720. Org.

Frahm, Frederick. "Variations on 'New Britain.'" Live Oak House 245-0124. SET. Ww.
Kosnik, James. "New Britain" in *Laudate! vol. 4.* CPH 97-6665. Org.

ALTERNATE HYMN OF THE DAY

| WOV 668 | There in God's garden |
| LBW 385 | What wondrous love |

COMMUNION

| LBW 513 | Come, my way, my truth, my life |
| WOV 705 | As the grains of wheat |

SENDING

| LBW 524 | My God, how wonderful thou art |
| WOV 781 | My life flows on in endless song |

ADDITIONAL HYMNS AND SONGS

UMH 372	How can we sinners know
H82 700	O love that casts out fear
TFF 68	That priceless grace
W&P	There is a Redeemer

MUSIC FOR THE DAY
CHORAL
Beck, John Ness. "Amazing Grace" in *Hymn Settings of John Ness Beck.* BEC VC4. M voice, kybd.
Busarow, Donald. "A Nobler Life." MSM 50-3031. SATB.
Christiansen, Paul. "What Wondrous Love." AFP 11-1140. SATB.
Martinson, Joel. "God So Loved the World." CPH 98-3098. SA, org.
Schulz-Widmar, Russell. "We Are Not Our Own." AFP 11-10913. SATB, kybd.
Schütz, Heinrich. "God So Loved the World." CPH 98-1472. SATT(Bar)B. Eng/Ger.

CHILDREN'S CHOIRS
Cherwien, David. "Maria Walks Amid the Thorn." CG CGA597. U.
Johnson, Ralph. "As Moses Lifted Up." CG CGA550. U, fl, org.

KEYBOARD/INSTRUMENTAL
Cherwien, David. "There in God's Garden" in *O God Beyond All Praising.* AFP 11-10860. Org.
Shearing, George. "Amazing Grace, How Sweet the Sound" in *Sacred Sounds from George Shearing for Piano.* SMP SSG-SP-32. Pno.

HANDBELL
Handel, G. F./arr. John F. Wilson. "Thanks Be to Thee." AG 1396. 2-4 oct, opt C inst.
Nelson, Susan T. "Lenten Prayer." CPH 97-6616. 3 oct, opt fl/hb solo, pno.

PRAISE ENSEMBLE

Altrogge, Mark. "How Great is Your Love" in *Hosanna! Music Book 7.* INT.

Lloyd, Kit. "John 3:16" in *Praise Chorus Book.* MAR 3100002377.

Lojeski, Ed. "Amazing Grace." HAL 08300531. SATB, pno, gtr, perc.

Mohr, Jon & Randall Dennis. "More Than Anything" in *Point of Grace Songbook.* WRD. 3010294492. 3 pt, kybd.

TUESDAY, APRIL 4
BENEDICT THE AFRICAN, 1589

Born a slave on the island of Sicily, Benedict joined a community of hermits when he was freed. After serving as superior he returned to his former position of cook, and his fame as a confessor brought many visitors to visit the humble and holy cook. Also known as Benedict the Moor, African Americans in the United States remember him for his patience and understanding when confronted with racial prejudice.

Benedict the African is a witness to the gospel that sets us free from sin, death, and all forms of oppression. In his honor, sing the African American spiritual "I want Jesus to walk with me" (WOV 660).

THURSDAY, APRIL 6
ALBRECHT DÜRER, PAINTER, 1528
MICHELANGELO BUONARROTI, ARTIST, 1564

Today we commemorate two great artists who revealed, through their work, the mystery of salvation and the wonder of creation. Dürer was a painter and engraver whose work is a close examination of the splendor of creation—the human body, animals, grasses, and flowers. He was Catholic yet sympathetic with the Reformation. Michelangelo, the most famous late Renaissance artist, earned fame as a painter, sculptor, architect, and poet. His art embodies a new concept of human dignity, projecting the human body on a new scale of grandeur. Michelangelo's contemporaries believed him to be divinely inspired, and he saw in sculpture an allegory of divine creativity and human salvation.

Turn to the famous works of Dürer and Michelangelo today. How do they give witness to the paschal mystery? How have you planned to use the arts in the coming days of celebration?

APRIL 9, 2000

FIFTH SUNDAY IN LENT

INTRODUCTION

In today's gospel reading, Jesus speaks of grain dying in the earth as an image of his death and resurrection. Christ is the seed fallen to earth that yields the harvest of life, health, and salvation. Christ is the one who accompanies us in our baptismal death and raises us to life with him. Christ is the grain of wheat that we share in the breaking of the bread. Christ's Spirit strengthens us in lives of fruitful service to those who hunger and thirst for life.

Today the church commemorates Dietrich Bonhoeffer, a pastor and teacher, who was killed for his opposition to the Nazi regime on this date in 1945.

PRAYER OF THE DAY

Almighty God, our redeemer, in our weakness we have failed to be your messengers of forgiveness and hope in the world. Renew us by your Holy Spirit, that we may follow your commands and proclaim your reign of love; through your Son, Jesus Christ our Lord, who lives and reigns with you and the Holy Spirit, one God, now and forever.

READINGS

Jeremiah 31:31-34

The Judeans in Babylon blamed their exile on their ancestors who had broken the covenant established at Sinai. Here the prophet looks to a day when the people can no longer make such a complaint. There will be no need to teach the law because God will write the holy law in their hearts.

Psalm 51:1-13 (Psalm 51:1-12 [NRSV])

Create in me a clean heart, O God. (Ps. 51:11)

or Psalm 119:9-16

I treasure your promise in my heart. (Ps. 119:11)

Hebrews 5:5-10

The Bible often speaks of Jesus as the "lamb of God" who takes away the sin of the world. This reading from Hebrews expands upon this image with another: Jesus is also the high priest whose suffering became the gracious gift of salvation.

John 12:20-33

Jesus entered Jerusalem for the last time to celebrate the Passover festival. Here Jesus' words about seeds planted in the ground turn the disaster of his death into the promise of a harvest in which everyone will be gathered.

COLOR Purple

THE PRAYERS

As we journey through the wilderness of Lent, let us return to God who gives us the joy of Easter's promise.

A BRIEF SILENCE.

God of all seeing and knowing, help us to see and know your presence in the waters of baptism and in the bread and wine of your holy supper. Hear us, O God;
your mercy is great.

God of eternal beckoning, may the world and all its inhabitants be brought into your open arms of grace and to abundant life. Hear us, O God;
your mercy is great.

God of healing, may those who are sick and distressed be given a glimpse of your mercy (especially . . .), that they may find you in the midst of their pain and hardship. Hear us, O God;
your mercy is great.

God of gathering, you promise to be with us wherever two or three come together. Watch over the ministry of this congregation as we seek to be faithful in this community. Hear us, O God;
your mercy is great.

HERE OTHER INTERCESSIONS MAY BE OFFERED.

God of all time, you hold your servant Dietrich Bonhoeffer, together with all our departed brothers and sisters, in your eternal safekeeping. Grant that we may all one day awaken to see you face-to-face. Hear us, O God;
your mercy is great.

Merciful God, hear our cry when we call to you, renew and uphold us with your Spirit, through Jesus Christ our Lord.
Amen

IMAGES FOR PREACHING

"Unless a grain of wheat falls into the earth and dies, it remains just a single grain; but if it dies, it bears much fruit."

Jesus frequently put things in the language of farmers and gardeners, because many people in his day had a direct relationship with the land. People understood how seeds had to be buried in the ground before there could be a harvest.

Reading the passage in today's gospel, it is easy for us to understand that the wheat in this passage refers to Jesus' death and burial, which will be followed shortly by the resurrection. So that all might be saved from their sins and have eternal life, it was necessary for the Son of Man to die.

In carrying the analogy one step further, we may also get the message that in order to be fruitful, we are to be like grains of wheat—in a sense dying—so as to have life. Along with the grains of wheat and the grapes that have given up life for our benefit, we offer ourselves to God's service. We dedicate our lives to the proclamation of the gospel, in a world that is broken and literally dying to hear it. We are crucified with Christ. We become food for others.

Of course it doesn't stop there. We also believe that the seeds that have been sown will be raised—and that all people will become a part of the Lord's rich and plentiful harvest when he returns in glory.

WORSHIP MATTERS

"Sir, we wish to see Jesus" (John 12:21). These words from today's gospel reading, carved into many pulpits, remind us that the heart of Christian preaching is not how-to, pop psychology, social commentary, or even scriptural exegesis. Christian preaching at its core is the activity of Jesus Christ himself calling Christians to flee to God's grace and trust in God's promise. Luther understood the preaching of the gospel as Christ's continued "advent," the means by which Jesus comes to every generation in order to establish fellowship with his own and offer the righteousness that he obtained by his death on the cross. As Paul says, "We proclaim Christ crucified" (1 Cor. 1:23), and both church and world "see Jesus."

LET THE CHILDREN COME

The secular culture surrounding Easter and the church's observance of Holy Week collide. Children are caught in the middle of this collision. Help them to focus on the church's faith in Jesus. Invite the children to be part of the congregation's ministry to those who are homebound. Have them memorize a Bible verse or a brief prayer to share with those they visit. Examples might be John 3:16, Mark 10:45, or a psalm verse. Teach them this prayer: "Jesus teach us so to live, that we believe you do forgive. Amen."

MUSIC FOR WORSHIP

GATHERING

LBW 104	In the cross of Christ I glory
WOV 662	Restore in us, O God

PSALM 119

Brugh, Lorraine. PW, cycle B.
Grant, Amy/arr. Michael Smith. "Thy Word" in W&P.
Hallock, Peter/arr. Carl Crosier. "Psalm 119" in *The Ionian Psalter*. ION.
Walker, Christopher. "Teach Me, O God" in PS, vol. 3.

CHILDREN'S PSALM SUGGESTIONS

Cooney, Rory. "Psalm 119: Happy Are Those Who Follow" in *Gather Comprehensive*. GIA. U.

HYMN OF THE DAY

LBW 101	O Christ, our king, creator, Lord
	OAKLEY

INSTRUMENTAL RESOURCES

Sensmeier, Randall. "O Christ, Our King, Creator, Lord" in *The Concordia Hymn Prelude Series, vol. 8*. CPH 97-5615. Org.

ALTERNATE HYMN OF THE DAY

LBW 479	My faith looks up to thee
WOV 658	The Word of God is source and seed

COMMUNION

LBW 199	Thee we adore, O hidden Savior
WOV 769	Mothering God, you gave me birth

SENDING

LBW 344	We sing the praise of him who died
WOV 778	O Christ the same

ADDITIONAL HYMNS AND SONGS

GS2 26	I shall walk in the presence of God
OBS 108	Rich in promise
H82 559	Lead us, heavenly Father
TFF 227	How to reach the masses
W&P	Create in me a clean heart

MUSIC FOR THE DAY

CHORAL

Beethoven, Ludwig van. "A Contrite Heart" in *Sing a Song of Joy, Vocal Solos for Worship*. AFP 11-8194 (MH); 11-8195 (ML).
Brahms, Johannes. "Create in Me a Clean Heart" (Schaffe in mir, Gott, ein rein Herz). GSCH 43227c. SATBB. Eng/Ger.
Collins, Dori. "Mothering God." AFP 11-10914. SATB. kybd, fl.
Foley, John. "May We Praise You." OCP 9934. SATB, pno, gtr, cong.
Kreutz, Robert E. "The Word Became in Jesus." GIA G-4299. SATB, org.
Monteverdi, Claudio/arr. Ehert. "Christe, Adoramus Te." NOV 19653. SATB, cont. Lat/Eng.
Schalk, Carl. "Have Mercy on Me, O God." AFP 11-10937. SATB.
Sedio, Mark. "Rich in Promise." AFP 11-10924. 2 pt mxd, kybd.

CHILDREN'S CHOIRS

Lovelace, Austin. "God of Beauty." CG CGA172. U, kybd.
Marshall, Jane. "Dear Lord, Lead Me Day by Day." CG CGA637. U, kybd, opt fl.

KEYBOARD/INSTRUMENTAL

Davies, Walford. "Solemn Melody." NOV 01 0066. Org.
Jones, Mark C. "My Faith Looks Up to Thee" in *Three Lenten Hymn Meditations*. MSM 10-323. Org.

HANDBELL

Dobrinski, Cynthia. "Canticle of Hope." AG 1150. 3 oct. AG 1167. 5 oct.
Faure/arr. FitzSimons Mathis. "Pie Jesu" in *Requiem*. Flagstaff Publications F0703. 3-5 oct.

PRAISE ENSEMBLE

Altrogge, Mark. "Thank You for the Cross" in *Hosanna! Music Book*. INT.
Espinosa, Eddie and Bob Kilpatrick/arr. John Wilson. "Change My Heart/Lord, Be Glorified." HOP GC992. SATB, kybd.
Harlan, Benjamin. "Open Thou Mine Eyes." GS A-6722. SATB, kybd.
Merkel. "More of You" in *Let Your Glory, Fall Choral Collection*. INT.
Nelson, Jeff. "Purify My Heart" in *Raise the Standard Worship Team Book*. MAR 3010124368. 3pt, kybd.

SUNDAY, APRIL 9
DIETRICH BONHOEFFER, TEACHER, 1945

Bonhoeffer was a German theologian who resisted the Nazis and was linked to a failed attempt to assassinate Hitler. He was arrested in 1943 for his antiwar activities and was taken to a concentration camp and then to a prison. After conducting a service on April 8, 1945, Bonhoeffer was taken away to be hanged the next day. An English prisoner told of his last words as he was led away: "This is the end, but for me the beginning of life."

Bonhoeffer's courageous life and death is a bold witness to the paschal mystery of Christ's dying and rising. Commemorating him might include reading a passage from his famous work *The Cost of Discipleship*.

MONDAY, APRIL 10
MIKAEL AGRICOLA, BISHOP OF TURKU, 1557

Agricola was a Finnish archbishop who carried out a thoroughgoing evangelical reformation in Finland. He worked diligently to translate the prayerbook, the mass, and the New Testament into Finnish, and he devised an orthography that is the basis for modern Finnish spelling. He is remembered as a learned man, moderate and conciliatory, concerned for the well-being of his people.

Remember the Church of Finland in prayers today, and give thanks for the Finnish presence in the former Suomi Synod, one of the Lutheran ethnic groups in this country that merged with others during the past half-century. Sing "Your kingdom come, O Father" (LBW 384), which uses a Finnish folk tune as its melody.

APRIL 16, 2000

SUNDAY OF THE PASSION
PALM SUNDAY

INTRODUCTION

On this day the church continues its procession with our crucified and risen Lord. He is in our midst as we hear of his life-giving death and as we share his body and blood. At the beginning of this great week, the passion gospel sets forth the central mystery of the Christian faith: Christ emptied himself in death so that we might know God's mercy and love for all creation.

READINGS FOR PROCESSION WITH PALMS

Mark 11:1-11
or John 12:12-16
Psalm 118:1-2, 19-29

Blessed is he who comes in the name of the Lord. (Ps. 118:26)

PRAYER OF THE DAY

Almighty God, you sent your Son, our Savior Jesus Christ, to take our flesh upon him and to suffer death on the cross. Grant that we may share in his obedience to your will and in the glorious victory of his resurrection; through your Son, Jesus Christ our Lord, who lives and reigns with you and the Holy Spirit, one God, now and forever.

READINGS FOR LITURGY OF THE PASSION

Isaiah 50:4-9a

The image of the servant of the Lord is one of the notable motifs in the third servant song of Isaiah. Today's reading is a description of the mission of the servant. When early Christians read this text they heard in this servant of God the voice of Jesus. Thus, the reading was associated with the Lord's passion. The servant does not strike back at his detractors but trusts in God's steadfast love.

Psalm 31:9-16

Into your hands, O LORD, I commend my spirit. (Ps. 31:5)

Philippians 2:5-11

Paul quotes from an early Christian hymn that describes Jesus' death on the cross as the primary model for Christians of obedience and unselfishness.

Mark 14:1—15:47

The passion story in Mark's gospel presents Jesus as one who

dies abandoned by all. He shows himself to be the true Son of God by giving his life for those who have forsaken him.
or Mark 15:1-39 [40-47]

COLOR   Scarlet *or* Purple

THE PRAYERS

As we journey through the wilderness of Lent, let us return to God who gives us the joy of Easter's promise.
A BRIEF SILENCE.

O God, your Son endured triumphs and terrors in his return to Jerusalem. Give endurance to all your people in this holy week, and give us courage to enter fully into its life and mystery. Hear us, O God;
your mercy is great.

O God, may the gentle rule of Jesus as the prince of peace be a reality in every nation of the earth. Hear us, O God;
your mercy is great.

O God, may your grace sustain all who face religious persecution, abuse, or discrimination of any kind. Bless those who are sick and sorrowing with your comforting presence (especially . . .). Hear us, O God;
your mercy is great.

O God, guide those who are preparing to receive the grace of baptism at the conclusion of this week, that they may be prepared to enter fully into the Christian faith. Hear us, O God;
your mercy is great.
HERE OTHER INTERCESSIONS MAY BE OFFERED.

O God, your days are without number and your love is without limit. Keep us in communion with those who have entered into your endless joy, and bring us with them into the fullness of light. Hear us, O God;
your mercy is great.

Merciful God, hear our cry when we call to you, renew and uphold us with your Spirit, through Jesus Christ our Lord.
Amen

IMAGES FOR PREACHING

Mark's report of the crucifixion shows us the righteous suffering servant of God, the innocent one who was executed in a way that was reserved for the worst of criminals. And yet, Mark's gospel also depicts the agonizing conflict between the powers of light and darkness, the Jesus whose loud cry is an announcement of triumph over the power of death.

As we enter into Mark's story, we also see and come to know so many other characters: Simon the leper, Simon of Cyrene, the scribes and chief priests, the servant girls, Peter, Barabbas, the twelve disciples, the crowd, a woman, a young man, rebels and elders, two insurgents and a rooster. The story unfolds with several supporting roles as well as heroes, heroines, and major stars. All the characters add something essential; their involvement helps to shape our experience of the passion account.

Finally, we are drawn to the climactic moment of the whole gospel, when the secular Roman centurion breaks out of the blindness surrounding the truth about Jesus' death. Simply watching what God was doing built faith and revealed the inner meaning of this event. "Truly," the centurion cried, "this man was the Son of God."

Where do we see ourselves in the annual retelling of this story? Are we somehow lost in the crowd, indistinguishable? Or do we have an active part in this experience? How do we share in the passion, death, and resurrection of our Lord? Are we willing to be vulnerable enough to stay with him and live through this suffering, passion, and death?

The event of Jesus' death on the cross was originally recorded in the hearts of people who believed and then shared that story with others. Even without all the high-tech video equipment we have today, that story has lasted for two thousand years.

If others depended upon our version of the story, what would they learn about the passion, death, and resurrection of Jesus? Let us, in the words of Philippians, proclaim a God who emptied himself in the form of a servant. Let us share the profound belief that light has triumphed over darkness. Let us enter into the passion of our Lord Jesus Christ.

WORSHIP MATTERS

"Hosanna! Blessed is he who comes in the name of the Lord!" We sing "All glory, laud and honor" (LBW 108) and process with palms not in an attempt to reenact what Jesus did, but in order that we may, as the liturgy for the day says, "enter with joy upon the contemplation of those mighty acts whereby you [God] have given us life everlasting" (*LBW* Ministers edition, p. 135). Participating in God's work of salvation involves more than thinking it through and intellectually agreeing. Faith involves our whole self, our whole life. The liturgies for the coming days include movements (darkness to light, silence to song, austerity to festivity), actions (kneeling, laying on of hands, washing, adoration, eating and drinking), and objects (basin, cross, candle, bread and cup) intended to draw us completely into God's continuing drama of salvation—the drama of Calvary that extends to us and beyond in time—so that we may "ever hail Jesus as our Lord and King and follow him with confidence" (*LBW* Ministers edition, p. 135).

LET THE CHILDREN COME

Ask the children to listen for Jesus' name in today's liturgy. Remind them of last week's story of the seeds. Jesus is the seed that died and was buried so that we might be the fruit of his new life. Each time we hear God's word, it is a seed planted in us. Invite children to worship during this Holy Week and receive more "seeds" of God's word to share.

MUSIC FOR WORSHIP
SERVICE MUSIC

Music for the procession with palms needs careful planning in light of space and movement factors. An assembly in a winding single file procession will not be able to sing together easily. The refrain to "All glory, laud, and honor" (LBW 108) might be sung by all, with stanzas sung by strategically placed cantors. Or use brass instruments to lead the singing. Be flexible, but walk through the logistics with the key players.

GATHERING

| LBW 121 | Ride on, ride on in majesty |
| WOV 631 | Lift up your heads, O gates |

PSALM 31

Bell, John L. "In You, O Lord, I Found Refuge" in *Psalms of Patience, Protest and Praise*. GIA G-4047. U/choir.

Cooney, Rory. "I Place My Life" in *Choral Refrains from Psalms for the Church Year, vol. 4*. GIA G-3612-A. U/SATB.

DeBruyn, Randall. "Father, I Put My Life in Your Hands" in STP, vol. 4.

Farlee, Robert Buckley. PW, cycle B.

Haas, David. "I Put My Life in Your Hands/Pongo Mi Vida." GIA G-3949. U/SATB, cong, inst.

Plainchant, arr. G. Boulton Smith. "Father, into Your Hands" in PS, vol. 2.

Schiavone, John. "Father, I Put My Life in Your Hands" in STP, vol. 1.

HYMN OF THE DAY

LBW 94	My song is love unknown
WOV 661	My song is love unknown
	RHOSYMEDRE/LOVE UNKNOWN

VOCAL RESOURCES

Cherwien, David. "My Song Is Love Unknown." AFP 11-10708. SAB, org, fl, opt. cong.

Leavitt, John. "My Song Is Love Unknown." AFP 11-10114. SATB/SA, org, inst.

INSTRUMENTAL RESOURCES

Burkhardt, Michael. "Love Unknown" in *Five Lenten Hymn Improvisations*. MSM 10-309. Org.

Held, Wilbur. "Rhosymedre" in *Those Wonderful Welsh, set 1*. MSM 10-841. Org.

Leavitt, John. "My Song Is Love Unknown: A Suite for Organ and Instrument." AFP 11-9292. Org, inst.

Vaughan Williams, Ralph. "Rhosymedre" in *Three Preludes*. GAL. Org.

ALTERNATE HYMN OF THE DAY

| LBW 116/7 | O sacred head, now wounded |
| LBW 123 | Ah, holy Jesus |

COMMUNION

| LBW 93 | Jesus, refuge of the weary |
| WOV 740 | Jesus, remember me |

SENDING

| LBW 107 | Beneath the cross of Jesus |
| WOV 668 | There in God's garden |

ADDITIONAL HYMNS AND SONGS

DATH 59	Hosanna! Come and deliver
LW 116	Stricken, smitten, and afflicted
TFF 85	Calvary
W&P	Lift up your heads

MUSIC FOR THE DAY
CHORAL

Adams, Stephen. "The Holy City" in *Sing Solo Sacred*. OXF 0-19-345785-7. ML, kybd.

Albrecht, Mark. "Lamb of God." AFP 11-10670. SATB, pno.

Distler, Hugo. "A Lamb Goes Uncomplaining Forth" in *In Truth He Took Up Our Own Sickness*. CPH 67-5892. SATB.

Gesius, Bartholomew. "Sing Hosanna to the Son of David." PRE 312-41450. SATB. Eng/Ger.

Shepperd, Mark.. "Ride On, Ride On in Majesty." CPH 98-3390. SATB, org.

CHILDREN'S CHOIRS

McRae, Shirley. "Hail the King Who Comes A-Riding" in *Let Us Praise God*. AFP 11-7203. U, Orff inst, sop rec.

Tucker, Margaret R. "Shout Hosanna Today." MSM 50-3925. U/2 pt, kybd, opt 3 oct hb.

Yarrington, John. "O Thou, Eternal Christ, Ride On." AFP 12-477620. 2 pt mx, org, hb, snare drm.

KEYBOARD/INSTRUMENTAL

Hobby, Robert A. "Ride On, Ride On in Majesty" in *Three Lenten Hymn Settings*. MSM 10-311. Org.

Langlais, Jean. "Les Rameaux" (The Palms) in *Poemes Evangeliques*. Philippo distributed by Elkan Vogel.

HANDBELL

Dobrinski, Cynthia. "Lift High the Cross." HOP 1491. 3-5 oct.

Gramann, Fred. "Fantasy on 'King's Weston.'" AG 1671. 3-6 oct.

Moklebust, Cathy and David. "Lift High the Cross." CG CGB192. Full score; CGB193. Hb score; CGB194. Brass score.

Stephenson, Valerie W. "Lift Up Your Heads." AGEHR AG35081. Full score: org, brass, timp, opt cong. AG35080. 3-5 oct.

PRAISE ENSEMBLE

Choplin, Pepper. "Jazz Hosanna." Fred Bock Music Co. BG2303. SATB, acc, tamb.

Jabusch, Willard. "The King of Glory" in *The Other Song Book*. Fellowship Publications.

Kendrick, Graham. "Welcome the King" in *Hosanna Music Songbook, vol 12*. INT. 12906.

Dempsey, Larry. "Glory to the King" in *Renew*. HOP.

Pote, Allen. "Hosanna." CG CGA596. SATB, kybd, gtr.

Smith, Michael W. and Deborah D. Smith/arr. Wolaver. "Hosanna." WRD 3010268165. SATB, kybd.

MONDAY, APRIL 17
MONDAY IN HOLY WEEK

Monday, Tuesday, and Wednesday in Holy Week focus on the events of the last week of Jesus' earthly life. Rather than trying to "walk where Jesus walked," the church uses these days to view Christ more particularly in our lives today. Jesus comes to us in our day through the reading of scripture, through preaching, through the water of baptism, through the bread and wine of communion, and through the prayers.

Be open to the surprising ways in which Christ is made known to you this week. Also look for opportunities to share the gift of his life with others.

This week concludes with the Three Days: Maundy Thursday, Good Friday, and the Resurrection of Our Lord.

TUESDAY, APRIL 18
TUESDAY IN HOLY WEEK

WEDNESDAY, APRIL 19
WEDNESDAY IN HOLY WEEK
OLAVUS PETRI, PRIEST, 1552; LAURENTIUS PETRI, ARCHBISHOP OF UPPSALA, 1573; RENEWERS OF THE CHURCH

These two brothers are commemorated for their introduction of the Lutheran reformation to Sweden. Under the patronage of King Gustavus Vasa (the liberator of Sweden from Danish rule), Olavus was appointed pastor of the city church, and Laurentius became the royal chancellor. From these influential positions, the two brothers worked carefully to establish an intellectual and liturgical foundation for the Lutheran Church of Sweden, including the retention of the historic episcopate.

Remember the Church of Sweden in prayers today, and give thanks for the Swedish presence in the former Augustana synod, one of the Lutheran ethnic synods in this country, which merged with others during the past fifty years. Sing "Thy holy wings" (WOV 741), which uses a Swedish folk tune, and whose text includes baptismal imagery appropriate for Lent and Holy Week.

LENT
THE THREE DAYS
EASTER

THE THREE DAYS

These days are about the entire sweep of history

IMAGES OF THE SEASON

The greatest problem in thinking about images for the Three Days is simply the overabundance of them. They give meaning to the phrase "an embarrassment of riches." While some may speak more clearly or forcefully to us than others, and some may be more helpful in one setting than in another, they offer a plethora of pictures in our minds.

Each of these days brings with it its own set of images. Maundy Thursday moves in several directions at once. We hear the story of the Passover, and we give thanks for the Lamb of God, the unspotted one offered to bring freedom to the prisoners. The table is spread, and we remember our ancestors in Egypt as well as our ancestors in the upper room. The cup of blessing is shared, and we await the promised feast of victory. The new commandment is spoken, and we feel ourselves called to a life of discipleship.

The obvious image for Good Friday is the cross, but many stories cluster around it. Frightened disciples flee, while three watch the agony unfold. A centurion recognizes what others cannot see.

The Three Days culminate in the Easter Vigil. Here is paradox at its most complete. We meet in the dark night to praise Christ as the light. We praise the flame of a single candle as if it is brilliantly illuminating the entire room. We baptize infants as if they were adults, by asking them questions of lifelong commitment, and we baptize adults as if they were infants, by washing them again in the womb of the font. We conclude with the eucharistic meal eaten in the middle of the night. One paradox follows another.

THE JOURNEY OF SALVATION

Two difficulties accompany this wealth of images. The first is simply that it is overwhelming. Where shall we begin? How shall we choose? The second is that it can lead to a disjointed observance of what should be the most cohesive of times in the church. Perhaps then we would fare better in looking for an organizing principle or a guiding image for the Three Days.

One approach derives from the understanding of these days as being the conclusion of Holy Week, a re-creation and reexperiencing of the events of Jesus' last days. Viewed from this perspective, the overarching image is that of a journey, following in the footsteps of our Lord. Like most trips, it begins with enthusiasm as we enter Jerusalem on Passion Sunday. Along the way is need for direction, "I give you a new commandment" (John 13:34), as well as for nourishment, "Take and eat . . . take and drink." Toward the end, the way is uphill and hard. Some travelers turn aside and even mock those who persist, but others stay the course, supporting one another. Then comes a time when it seems that we can go no further. We stop, exhausted and near to despair. But when we discover that we have indeed arrived, our destination is even more glorious than we expected. True, this sort of journey requires that we pretend we do not already know every step of the way. Nevertheless, it continues to provide new insights as well as a deep sense of participation in the events of the week.

A second way of experiencing this time recognizes the integrity of the Three Days themselves. A flow courses from Maundy Thursday through Good Friday into the Resurrection of Our Lord on Saturday and Sunday, rather than separating Thursday from Friday, with a break on Holy Saturday, and then finally the real celebration on Easter Day. This sense of continuity grows out of, rather than just coming at the end of, Lent. In recent years the church has recovered an understanding of the triduum as the fulfillment of the Lenten season, not just a re-creation of a series of historical happenings.

The image at work in this view of the Three Days is no small one; these days are about the entire sweep of history. The God of the Three Days is a surprising, paradoxical God, a God who lived on earth, rather than safely in heaven; a God who knelt before the faithful people to serve them, rather than the other way around; a God who chose the cross as a throne; a God who overcame death by dying and by enlivening the Christian community.

ENVIRONMENT AND ART FOR THE SEASON

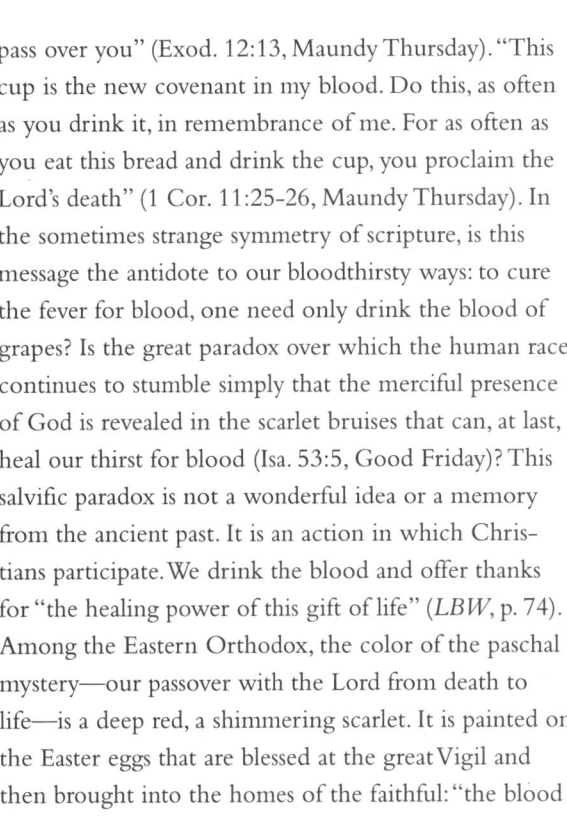

Our world knows much of blood. We analyze its properties in test tubes and under microscopes. We know that a blood donation gives life to another human being and so we respond to the Red Cross appeal. "Blood is life" (Deut. 12:23). It is that simple: if you shed blood, you strike at life itself. But we also know that blood is feared. One of the first lessons every healthcare professional learns is this: Do not ever touch blood without wearing protective gloves. Oh yes, we know that deathly viruses course through the bloodstream.

Gift of life or the end of life? Much ambiguity surrounds our sense of blood. We know this fact as well: like a distorting and heated fever, a thirst for blood—spilled blood—can overtake the human spirit. Blood-thirst we call it (Ps. 5:6). Angry Cain kills his brother Abel (Gen. 4:8-11); David's lusty loins drive him to betray Uriah in battle (2 Sam. 11:2-27); a fearful and furious Herod orders the death of boy children (Matt. 2:16-18). Little wonder that the psalmist cries out in a fit of remorse, "Deliver me from bloodshed, O God" (Ps. 51:14). The ancients knew this fever that causes the human race to spill innocent blood. They also knew its color: "Your hands are full of blood," shouts the prophet, "Wash yourselves; . . . remove the evil of your doings . . . though your sins are like scarlet, they shall be like snow; though they are red like crimson, they shall become like wool" (Isa. 1:15-16, 18). While blood runs through the veins, unseen to the eye, it remains a deep blue. But when the skin is cut and bleeds, oxygen transforms blood into a deep red, tinged with hints of purple.

The ancient Israelites recognized a similar process in the vineyard. When the skin of a ripe, deep-red grape is cut, the juices flow dark and freely over the hand. In his great hymn to God the rock, Moses recounts the mercies of God toward the Hebrew people: "Together with the choicest wheat—you drank fine wine from the blood of grapes . . . [from] the God who gave you birth" (Deut. 32:14, 18). To drink the blood of the grape is to taste the mercy of God, but also "the blood shall be a sign for you . . . when I see the blood, I will pass over you" (Exod. 12:13, Maundy Thursday). "This cup is the new covenant in my blood. Do this, as often as you drink it, in remembrance of me. For as often as you eat this bread and drink the cup, you proclaim the Lord's death" (1 Cor. 11:25-26, Maundy Thursday). In the sometimes strange symmetry of scripture, is this message the antidote to our bloodthirsty ways: to cure the fever for blood, one need only drink the blood of grapes? Is the great paradox over which the human race continues to stumble simply that the merciful presence of God is revealed in the scarlet bruises that can, at last, heal our thirst for blood (Isa. 53:5, Good Friday)? This salvific paradox is not a wonderful idea or a memory from the ancient past. It is an action in which Christians participate. We drink the blood and offer thanks for "the healing power of this gift of life" (*LBW*, p. 74). Among the Eastern Orthodox, the color of the paschal mystery—our passover with the Lord from death to life—is a deep red, a shimmering scarlet. It is painted on the Easter eggs that are blessed at the great Vigil and then brought into the homes of the faithful: "the blood will be a sign for you." When cracked open, gold and white flow forth.

One look at the revised calendar of this book should make it clear that our understanding of this "season" has changed. The late medieval practice (still maintained in parts of this country) kept the penitential character of Lent until the end of Good Friday. "Holy Week" became an intense preparation for Easter Sunday. A more ancient sensibility now marks the ecumenical calendar: Lent comes to an end on Maundy Thursday as the evening liturgy begins. It marks the beginning of the Three Days, the triduum. The Three Days follow the Jewish pattern of reckoning time from sunset to sunset, so that the first day extends from Thursday evening to Friday evening, the second day from Friday evening to Saturday evening, the third day from Saturday evening to Sunday evening (closing with Easter Sunday vespers).

But why this shift? To underscore the theological unity of these final and central events in the Lord's life. It is this one reality—the Lord's passover from death to life—celebrated in three distinct but inseparable moments: the giving of himself in the supper, the giving of himself on the cross, the giving of himself as our light, word, font, and meal.

What are the central environmental and artistic concerns of these days? The central actions of the liturgies! No amount of decoration can serve as a substitute for the careful planning and rehearsal of these services that constitute the center of the entire year. Why such an emphasis on the central actions? At the heart of its life, the church celebrates God's gracious presence among us today through grace. Where do we find the Lord Jesus? Not in the past, but in the present through his word, community, washing, and meal. Thus, the worship of the Three Days is not a journey back into Bible times, pretending that we are at the last supper or at Golgotha or at a tomb. The worship of these days is the celebration of our entrance into the life of Christ through the proclamation of the word, the washing of baptism, and the sharing of his risen life in the supper.

What requires special attention? A spotlessly clean church devoid of clutter in the gathering and worship spaces. Greeters and ushers who have been trained not only to welcome people but to care for visitors and those who might require special attention (such as those with limited mobility, parents with young children). Well-organized service bulletins that not only give clear instructions but offer the occasional comment on the significance of a particular action. A detailed list of what needs to be prepared for each service, who will do this work, and when it will be done. The preparation and rehearsal of all readers, assisting ministers, musicians, acolytes, and any other assistants. The cleaning of all vestments, vessels, and additional linens.

How will worshipers be welcomed into the worship space? The Easter Vigil takes place in the evening after sunset. Luminaria can mark a large open circle in which the new fire will burn before the procession into the darkened church. In some congregations, the entire congregation will assemble outside or in a hall and then process into the church, an image of our Hebrew ancestors moving forward in the night. Assisting ministers (altar guild members?) might carry baskets of fragrant flowers (but not lilies, which are to be saved for later) at the head of a procession into the empty worship space.

On Maundy Thursday, particular attention can be given to these actions: preparation of scarlet vesture and hangings; preparation of water pitchers, bowls, and thick white towels for the foot washing and facilities for the ministers who need to wash their hands before the eucharistic liturgy; baking of adequate amounts of fresh bread; rehearsal of congregational members (of diverse ages) who will remove vessels, furniture, and hangings at the end of the service as Psalm 22 is sung.

On Good Friday, these central actions invite particular care: the silent gathering of the people in a clean and empty worship space; rehearsal of readers who will proclaim the gospel reading; the printed invitation to keep silence when appropriate throughout the liturgy; preparation of a large wooden cross to be carried into the church at the appropriate time of the liturgy or set up in front of the altar prior to the service; placement of cushions or kneelers to the side of the cross for those who will stay to pray. No color is designated for this day; since paraments have been removed, other colored vestments are also unnecessary.

At the Vigil of Easter—the culmination of the Three Days and the beginning of the Easter season—keep in mind these central elements: the preparation of a large bonfire outdoors (if weather prevents an outdoor fire, then light the paschal candle at the church entrance); a new, tall paschal candle with the year properly inscribed and a stable candleholder placed next to the pulpit/reading stand in the church; white vesture for the ministers (the old maxim, however, holds here: use your best vestments whether they be white, gold, or scarlet); handheld candles for the assembly; rehearsal of the Easter proclamation (Exsultet) by the assisting minister; rehearsal of readers (careful preparation of the text allows the lector to proclaim rather than simply "read" the text); ringing of bells during the hymn of praise and procession of flowers into the space (the use of a repeating refrain sung by the people can extend the hymn of praise if needed to accompany the action); preparation of the font (with warm water, oil, candles, and white albs for the newly baptized) and evergreen branches for the sprinkling of the people during the renewal of the baptismal covenant; clothing the altar with its white cloth and linens immediately before the great thanksgiving, the candles being lit from the paschal candle; the presentation of baked bread and flagons of wine. Many congregations will hold a grand and festive party after the vigil to extend the hospitality of the eucharist, to welcome the newly baptized or newly received members, and to greet each other again with the peace of the risen Christ.

What is the central sign of the risen Christ? It is not a wooden cross placed outdoors, draped with a wispy white sheet and gold streamers. Nor is it a picture or painting of the risen Lord. Rather, it is this baptized assembly among whom "the Gospel is preached in its purity and the holy sacraments are administered according to the Gospel" (Augsburg Confession, VII). Or as the hymn suggests, "Thine the amen thine the praise alleluias angels raise/thine the everlasting head thine the breaking of the bread/thine the glory thine the story thine the harvest then the cup/thine the vineyard then the cup is lifted up lifted up" (WOV 801). Here we pour the wine, lift the cup, and drink the blood. Here is no fear, only healing and thanksgiving.

PREACHING WITH THE SEASON

Many of us were raised with a medieval style Holy Week, a ritual pattern that developed after the fourth century when Christians visited the Holy Land to try to trace the steps of Jesus' last days.

On Passion Sunday, we watched as Jesus entered Jerusalem. On Thursday he ate with his disciples, and on Friday he died. On Saturday we waited, and on Sunday morning we accompanied the women to the empty tomb. On Easter morning, men dress with colorful ties, women wear fancy outfits, the sunshine brightens the banks of spring flowers, the trumpeters are wide awake, and it is easy to believe that life conquers death.

But in recent decades many Christian churches have revived a more ancient Christian observance of these days. The pattern of the first centuries was a much more paradoxical ritual. On Maundy Thursday the church gathers to eat with Christ. The food itself is Christ. Christ, the master, kneels before us to wash our feet, and we, now the body of Christ in the world, kneel before one another to wash each other's feet. On Good Friday we read an ancient poem about a man killed as though he was a lamb slaughtered. We read not Matthew, Mark, or Luke in which Jesus' sufferings are clearly described, but John, in which Christ strides into his passion calling out to the arresting soldiers. We then reverence the cross, and call it Good.

The Three Days culminate in the Easter Vigil. Here is paradox at its most complete. We meet in the dark night to praise Christ as the light. We praise the flame of a single candle as if it is brilliantly illuminating the entire room. We read four or seven or twelve stories that tell in paradoxical language the resurrection story: God created the world from chaos; God saved Noah and the animals from the flood; God rescued Isaac from death; God freed the people of Israel from slavery; God serves up a feast for all peoples on the mountain; God rules the world with wisdom and justice; God puts flesh on dry bones; God stands with the three young people in the fiery furnace. After these readings, with the announcement of the resurrection, we baptize infants as if they were adults, by asking them questions of life-long commitment, and we baptize adults as if they were infants, by washing them again in the womb of the font. We conclude with the eucharistic meal eaten in the middle of the night. One paradox follows another.

The Three Days go on without much help from either nature or the secular culture. Thursday and Friday are regular workdays. Our culture does not halt to eat with Christ, to wash feet, to reverence the cross. True, the malls are filled with pink bunnies and decorated eggs. But these symbols of springtime have more to do with family get-togethers on Sunday afternoon than with the church's gathering in the middle of Saturday night. Despite meeting in the dark, we affirm our faith in the light. Despite dressing warmly for our walk outside, we sing ancient hymns about the birth of spring. Keeping the Great Vigil reminds us that Easter is more than the age-old expectation that chickens will continue to lay eggs and rabbits will keep having litters. Our faith in the resurrection of the body of Christ is more paradoxical than surface images.

The Three Days give Christians their most concentrated practice of enacting the life of faith. We assemble, perhaps in small numbers, to affirm our faith that in spite of death, we trust in God's life. Most of us need this practice, for we all live through times of mysterious paradox. We all know of times when a pregnancy is met with dread; when death would be a blessing; when our precious children break our hearts; when we must forgive a bitter betrayal; when our choices are despised by others; when we are supposed to sing an Easter hymn at the grave of our beloved. These painful ironies remind us life is not easy.

But the God of the Three Days is a surprising, paradoxical God, a God who lived on earth, rather than safely in heaven; a God who knelt before the faithful people to serve them, rather than the other way around; a God who chose the cross as a throne; a God who overcame death by dying and by enlivening the Christian community.

Together the Three Days are the Christian Passover, or *Pasch*, from the Greek. They developed organically in the sense that the nucleus was the vigil on Saturday night in which the church awaited the resurrection of Christ. This vigil was observed by a fast for Christ, which was broken on the third day with the eucharist. Evidence of this vigil can be found already by the year 100. The Good Friday liturgy was the next element to be developed. We see it in the writings of a pilgrim, Egeria, about the year 385. It is a fully articulated liturgy at this time, a liturgy whose development is attributed to the Jerusalem church. Maundy Thursday was the last liturgy to receive a liturgical form. Like Good Friday, its already developed liturgical structure is found in Egeria.

MAUNDY THURSDAY

One of the ancient names for this day was "Thursday of the Old Passover," a profoundly important title because it helps situate the "new" Passover. When we focus on the Lord's supper we are subject to a tendency to misunderstand it as the Passover. The readings don't help because they are from Exodus 12:1-4, 11-14, which is the prescription for the Passover. But we must remember the early title, "Thursday of the Old Passover." The second reading from 1 Corinthians 11:23-26 is the narrative of the tradition: on the night before he died Jesus took bread and blessed it. The meal is to be interpreted as a memorial of the death. Finally, the gospel—John 13:1-17—is the foot washing and the great mandate to be foot washers, a baptismal allusion. This gospel has long been associated with Thursday's liturgy. We must see the gospel more widely than Jesus' last meal; it is equally about relationships within the body of Christ.

When we focus on the Lord's supper itself we need to distinguish between its liturgical development and the theology with which the scriptures portray it. Theologically, Maundy Thursday is filled with thematic material. At its earliest description (1 Cor. 11:17 and following), this observation comes with an already imposed datum from the resurrection. It is called the "Lord's supper." The title "Lord" is primarily a post-resurrection appellation. Jesus' last meal is described as a Passover in the synoptics (but not in John). There is a kingdom image, references to the sacrifice of Isaac, a final messianic banquet. Each of these thematic elements creates a rich pool from which to draw theology.

The history of the day's liturgical development is more strongly connected with Lent. Traditionally it was the day to reconcile sinners (adulterers, apostates, murderers) and to prepare candidates for initiation: two of the major foci of Lent. In the fourth century, Egeria records three celebrations of the Eucharist on the day and even more importantly, an all-night vigil on the Mount of Olives, which is broken only by a procession to Golgotha on Friday. The liturgies of Jerusalem weave Thursday night into Friday.

How can we observe the day? Like Good Friday, Maundy Thursday is fundamentally joined to the Christian Passover/Vigil on Saturday. It is classically the beginning of the paschal fast and the inauguration of the Paschal Vigil. Maundy Thursday stands at the gate between Lent and the full celebration of the triduum. It is the beginning of the great feast. In this way of thinking, Maundy Thursday is not the day to celebrate a separate feast, nor to focus exclusively on the Lord's supper. The central eucharist these days is at the end of the Easter Vigil on Saturday/early Sunday when we recognize the Lord in the breaking of the bread.

GOOD FRIDAY

Egeria describes each of the days of the Great Week beginning with a service of readings at about 3:00 P.M. and followed by a lamp lighting. Good Friday differed from the pattern by a reverence of the relic of the cross that was placed on Golgotha. That veneration began in the morning and continued until noon, when a series of readings and psalms were proclaimed including the four accounts of the passion. At 3:00, the community moved from the outer court of the cross to the Martyrium and Anastasis containing the traditional location of the tomb where the passage from John (19:38-42) describing the burial was read. In its fully developed liturgical form, Good Friday is a focus on the passion. It was observed by a fast and a vigil that consisted of readings and psalms. It was also stational; that is, moving from one place to the next.

Several challenges face current pastoral practice when it comes to Good Friday. Good Friday is not a celebration of a separate historical event; it is part of the wider liturgy that includes Holy Saturday's vigil and Easter Sunday. This insight is frequently contradicted in preaching and hymn selection. Therefore, our prayer needs an intentional continuity, focusing on connections to the next gathering of the church. The readings focus on the fourth servant song from Isaiah (52:13—53:12). It is a life given as atonement in which the servant bears the faults of many. The selection from Hebrews (10:16-25) portrays Jesus as the supreme priest, who makes covenant in his dying. The passion according to John has been reserved for Friday since the earliest lectionaries. It presents not the slaughter of an innocent victim but the offering of a ruler who willfully gives his life for others. This narrative is filled with dignity and serenity. We don't need to feel sorry for "poor dead Jesus," but we do need to reckon with the image of the powerful one giving up power, out of love, for the good of others. Here is the challenge: the simplicity of the ritual must be allowed to shake us out of the history of the event into its mystery in our present day.

HOLY SATURDAY: THE VIGIL OF EASTER

The church has revised its Holy Week liturgies in the last forty years. Even though lectionary changes and minor alterations have been made since then, the basic pattern remains. That change was not so much in the order of prayer as in the time frame for the liturgy moving the vigil from Saturday morning to Saturday night. Today the addition of baptism and first communion of adult candidates and the renewal of baptismal promises has further completed the liturgical pattern. Many communities do not observe the vigil at all. Yet this liturgy is the earliest that developed from Sunday and laid the foundation of an annual cycle of festival and seasonal celebrations. The historical descriptions date to 100, the same time we have more descriptive accounts of Sunday eucharist in Justin (about 110).

The vigil is essentially the assembled community's faith-filled waiting for Christ. It is the Christian observance of Christ's passover from death to life set in the darkness of night, in expectation of the dawn. The earliest observances marked the passion of Christ and later his passage from death. This understanding quickly shifted to the Christian passage with Christ in baptism.

How was the vigil observed? The early church observed the vigil through fasting and a reading cycle that the Jewish community used for the Passover. That reading cycle was focused on four nights: the separation of darkness and light at creation's edge, the night God promised Abraham the heritage under the stars (including the sacrifice of Isaac), the night of Passover when the angel of death swept over the Hebrew encampment, and the final Messianic night (thus, the significance of these four readings in the Easter Vigil). These nights were a Jewish proleptic of salvation that Christians came to understand as their own. Marking the nights was a memorial of salvation history, covenant renewal, and expectation of fulfillment. Like Advent, it marked past, present, and future.

The structure of the liturgy developed around the vigil by adding a lucernarium/light service with the Gallican spring fire and Easter candle. It was augmented by baptism, which focused on Exodus 14 and the theology of passage, rather than Exodus 12 and the slaughter of the lambs. Likewise Romans 6:1-11 became the Christian focus on baptism with its theology of immersion into Christ's death. The focus on the passion and passage of the Christian into the paschal mystery has remained a central element of the festival from the time of Tertullian, and it is deeply part of how the Western church understands the paschal festival. The eucharistic meal concludes the feast. Egeria mentioned that the eucharist commenced when the newly baptized were led back into the church for the anointing. This meal brings together all the pieces of the Three Days because it proclaims that Christ has conquered. "He has put death to death and opened the graves of all who believe in him."

The name we assign the feast—Easter—comes from Eastre, the Teutonic goddess of spring. It is curious that the central Christian feast still retains the name of a pagan deity. Perhaps greater emphasis can be placed on the term *paschal* to describe the cycle, the season, the Three Days, the vigil, and the sacraments.

SHAPE OF WORSHIP FOR THE SEASON

BASIC SHAPE OF THE EUCHARISTIC RITE FOR MAUNDY THURSDAY

- See Maundy Thursday Liturgy in *LBW* Ministers edition, pp. 137–38; also available as a congregational leaflet from Augsburg Fortress (AFP 3-5327).

GATHERING

- The sermon may begin the liturgy
- The order for corporate confession and forgiveness may be used (*LBW*, pp. 193–95)
- The peace follows the order for confession and forgiveness

WORD

- The washing of feet may follow the reading of the gospel
- No creed is used on Maundy Thursday
- The prayers: see alternate worship text for the Three Days in *Sundays and Seasons*

MEAL

- Offertory prayer: see alternate worship text for the Three Days in *Sundays and Seasons*
- Use the proper preface for Passion: (see *LBW* Ministers edition, and *WOV* Leaders edition for each musical setting of the liturgy)
- Eucharistic prayer: in addition to the four main options in *LBW*, see "Eucharistic Prayer D: The Season of Lent" in *WOV* Leaders edition, p. 65
- Invitation to communion: see alternate worship text for the Three Days in *Sundays and Seasons*
- Post-communion prayer: see alternate worship text for the Three Days in *Sundays and Seasons*
- No post-communion canticle
- Stripping of the altar follows post-communion prayer
- No benediction on Maundy Thursday
- No dismissal on Maundy Thursday

BASIC SHAPE FOR THE GOOD FRIDAY LITURGY

- See Good Friday Liturgy in *LBW* Ministers edition, pp. 139–43; also available as a congregational leaflet from Augsburg Fortress (AFP 3-5328)

WORD

- The Passion according to St. John is read
- The bidding prayer for Good Friday may be used (*LBW* Ministers edition, pp. 139–42)
- Adoration of the Crucified (*LBW* Ministers edition, p. 142)
- No communion for Good Friday
- No benediction for Good Friday
- No dismissal for Good Friday
- See additional options for Good Friday in the seasonal rites section

BASIC SHAPE OF THE EUCHARISTIC RITE FOR THE EASTER VIGIL

- See Vigil of Easter in *LBW* Ministers edition, pp. 143–53; *WOV* Leaders edition, pp. 88–89; *Vigil of Easter* Music edition (AFP 3-5330); *Welcome to Christ: Lutheran Rites for the Catechumenate*, pp. 36–57; also see congregational leaflet from Augsburg Fortress (AFP 3-5329)

LIGHT

- The service of light may begin outside at the lighting of a new fire
- The congregation processes into the darkened nave following the lit paschal candle
- The Easter proclamation (Exsultet) is sung by a cantor

WORD

- Twelve readings appointed for the Easter Vigil (each of which may be followed by a sung response and a prayer) are listed in *WOV* Leaders edition, pp. 88–89.
- Canticle of the Sun (a version is printed in the autumn seasonal rites) may conclude the service of readings

BAPTISM

- If no candidates will be baptized, a congregational renewal of baptism may be used; notes for this portion of the liturgy are printed in *LBW* Ministers edition, p. 152

MEAL

- Hymn of praise (traditionally "Glory to God")
- During the hymn of praise, lights may be turned on, accompanied by the ringing of bells
- Prayers: see alternate worship text for the Three Days in *Sundays and Seasons*
- Offertory prayer: see alternate worship text for the Three Days in *Sundays and Seasons*
- Eucharistic prayer: in addition to four main options in *LBW*, see "Eucharistic Prayer E: The Season of Easter," in *WOV* Leaders edition, p. 69
- Invitation to communion: see alternate worship text for the Three Days in *Sundays and Seasons*
- Post-communion prayer: see alternate worship text for the Three Days in *Sundays and Seasons*
- Benediction: see alternate worship text for the Three Days in *Sundays and Seasons*
- Dismissal: see alternate worship text for the Three Days in *Sundays and Seasons*

BASIC SHAPE OF THE EUCHARISTIC RITE FOR EASTER DAY

- Confession and Forgiveness: see alternate worship text for Easter in *Sundays and Seasons*

GATHERING

- Greeting: see alternate worship text for Easter in *Sundays and Seasons*
- Use the Kyrie
- Use the hymn of praise ("This is the feast")

WORD

- Use Nicene Creed
- The prayers: see alternate forms and responses for Easter in *Sundays and Seasons*

MEAL

- Offertory prayer: see alternate worship text for Easter in *Sundays and Seasons*
- Use the proper preface for Easter (see *LBW* Ministers edition, and *WOV* Leaders edition for each musical setting of the liturgy)
- Eucharistic prayer: prayer II in *LBW* is especially appropriate; also, see "Eucharistic Prayer E: The Season of Easter" in *WOV* Leaders edition, p. 69
- Invitation to communion: see alternate worship text for Easter in *Sundays and Seasons*
- Post-communion prayer: see alternate worship text for Easter in *Sundays and Seasons*

SENDING

- Benediction: see alternate worship text for Easter in *Sundays and Seasons*
- Dismissal: see alternate worship text for Easter in *Sundays and Seasons*

OTHER SEASONAL POSSIBILITIES
PASCHAL VESPERS

- If you are fortunate to be able to gather for worship on Easter Sunday evening, a festival form of evening prayer may be desired. Consider appending the paschal blessing to evening prayer (*LBW*, pp. 138–41) anytime in the Easter season, even though it is printed as a part of morning prayer. See notes for this order in *LBW* Ministers edition, p. 16; and *Manual on the Liturgy*, pp. 294–95. A hymn, such as "We know that Christ is raised" (LBW 189), "I bind unto myself today" (LBW 188), or "O blessed spring" (WOV 695), may replace the canticle "Te Deum," which is customarily associated with morning prayer.

LECTIONARY OPPORTUNITY FOR HEALING SERVICES

- Easter Day (first reading)

ASSEMBLY SONG FOR THE SEASON

The Three Days are a passage, a journey. They require music for people on the move: kneeling for absolution, washing, stripping the altar, processing with the cross, walking in darkness, washing at the font, eating and drinking with joy.

Such music is sensible about human limits when singing is combined with action and inadequate light: easily memorable, richly repetitive, satisfyingly predictable. Such music is also "sensible" by employing vivid language that engages all the senses, if only through imagination.

MAUNDY THURSDAY

In addition to the liturgy's customary places for movement, up to three additional distinctive places characterize this rite (absolution, footwashing, stripping of the altar). What are the sensible songs that facilitate movement and best suit the character of these places? When can music get out of the way of natural sensory experience—the cadence of forgiving words, the splash of water, the clank of a vessel, the smell of candles extinguished, the plaintive single voice (suggesting Christ's own) singing Psalm 22?

GOOD FRIDAY

In the sea of endless prattle in which moderns are immersed, Good Friday offers a welcome island of silence and measured, time-trued words. Even as those who console the grieving are learning that presence is more important than a stream of well-meaning words, this liturgy is economical in the face of death, letting the community staying and watching in the presence of the cross be its own profound expression. Assembly song can mirror this leanness: unaccompanied, led by a strong voice or the choir; singing texts and melodies that link to the church deep and wide in time and place; willing to sound lament and sorrow alongside firm confidence in the triumph of the cross. It is not a time for casual experimentation with the new, but for well-planned and incremental additions to the day's repertoire: hymns such as "There in God's garden" (WOV 668), "Calvary" (TFF 85), "They crucified my Lord" (TFF 80); a setting of Psalm 22 with congregational refrain (see TFF 2); a single voice or choir chanting "The royal banners forward go" (LBW 126, stanzas interspersed with the sung or spoken versicles) as the cross moves slowly forward in procession.

VIGIL OF EASTER

Traditionally, the response at the opening procession ("The light of Christ." "Thanks be to God.") is sung three times, at successively higher pitches. The same theme of heightening intensity applies to the music of this rite. It may move from simpler responses at the time of the readings to musical climaxes at the baptisms and at the acclamations of the eucharist. Two resources offer convenient collections of music for this night. *Psalter for Worship, Cycle C* (Augsburg Fortress, 1997) includes easily learned psalm and canticle responses (in unison or harmony) for each of the twelve Vigil readings. *Welcome to Christ: Lutheran Rites for the Catechumenate* (Augsburg Fortress, 1997) offers a number of short responses that may accompany the liturgy of baptism, as well as "Springs of water, bless the Lord" and a litany of thanksgiving for the saints, which are especially suited to this service. Both resources include congregational pages that are reproducible for local use in service folders.

MUSIC FOR THE SEASON

VERSE AND OFFERTORY

Cherwien, David. *Verses for the Sundays of Easter.* MSM 80-400. U, org.

Pelz, Walter L. *Verses and Offertories: Easter–The Holy Trinity.* AFP 11-9546. SATB, org.

CHORAL MUSIC FOR THE SEASON

Buxtehude, Dietrich. "Behold, He Bore All Our Infirmities" KAL 6129. S, B, SSATB, str, cont. Ger/Eng.

Cherwien, David M. "All You Works of the Lord, Bless the Lord." CPH 98-3330. SATB, opt cant(s), cong, opt hb.

Haas, David. "Song of the Lord's Command." GIA G-4682. U, desc, cant, cong, gtr/kybd, C inst(s).

Poulenc, Francis. "Timor et Tremor." Salabert 16767. SATB.

Proulx, Richard. "Were You There." AFP 11-10571. Also in *The Augsburg Choirbook.* 11-10817. SATB.

Proulx, Richard. "You, Lord, We Praise." CPH 98-3448. 2 pt mxd, 5 hb.

Roger-Ducasse, Jean-Jules Aimable. "Crux Fidelis." DUR 312-41396. S, SATB, org. Lat/Eng.

Schweizer, Mark. "Let All the Rivers Clap Their Hands." CPH 98-3427. SATB, kybd.

Yarrington, John. "O Savior of the World." AFP 12-484750. SATB, org.

CHILDREN'S CHORAL MUSIC FOR THE SEASON

Anderson, Norma. "The Walk to Calvary." CG CGA739. U, kybd.

Pooler, Marie. "Lamb of God" in *Unison and Two-Part Anthems.* AFP 11-9517. U/2 pt, kybd.

Pooler, Marie. "Wondrous Love" in *Unison and Two-Part Anthems.* AFP 11-9517. U/2 pt, kybd.

Schram, Ruth Elaine. "Roses and Thorns." CG CGA737. 2 pt, kybd, opt gtr, opt 3 oct hb.

INSTRUMENTAL MUSIC FOR THE SEASON

Carter, John. *Reflections on Holy Week.* HOP 1939. Pno.

Henkelmann, Brian. *A Lenten Collection for Treble Instrument and Organ.* CPH 97-6471.

Nicholson, Paul. "Were You There." AFP 11-10528. Org, fl.

Owens, Sam Batt. *Three Meditations on Spirituals.* MSM 10-895. Org.

Weaver, Georgeann. "Meditation for Cello, Horn or Sax and Keyboard." AFP 11-10695.

Young, Jeremy. *At the Foot of the Cross: Piano for the Lenten Journey.* AFP 11-10688. Kybd.

HANDBELL MUSIC FOR THE SEASON

Dobrinski, Cynthia. "What Wondrous Love Is This?" HOP 1848. 3-5 oct, opt ch/inst.

McChesney, Kevin. "Were You There." HOP CP 6048. Qrt.

Nelson, Susan T. "Elegy." AFP 11-10554. 2 oct, opt inst.

Rogers, Sharon Elery. "The Road to Calvary." MSM 30-114. 2 oct.

Sherman, Arnold. "He Never Said a Mumbalin' Word." HOP 1844. 3-5 oct.

ALTERNATE WORSHIP TEXTS

PRAYERS (MAUNDY THURSDAY)

As we enter into the mystery of our salvation during these great three days, let us pray for new life in the church, and new hope for the world and all who are in need.

A brief silence.

Each petition ends:
Lord, in your mercy,
hear our prayer.

Concluding petition
We offer you these prayers, O God, in the shadow of the cross, in the hope of the paschal feast to come, and in the name of Jesus Christ who endured the cross and grave.
Amen

PRAYERS (THE RESURRECTION OF OUR LORD)

As we celebrate the joy of the resurrection, let us pray for new life in the church, and new hope for the world and all who are in need.
A brief silence.

Each petition ends:
Lord, in your mercy,
hear our prayer.

Concluding petition
Gracious God, hear our prayers and receive them for the sake of the crucified and risen one, our Savior Jesus Christ.
Amen

OFFERTORY PRAYER

God of glory,
**receive these gifts and the offering of our lives.
As Jesus was lifted up from earth,
draw us to your heart in the midst of this world,
that all creation may be brought from bondage to freedom,
from darkness to light,
and from death to life;
through Jesus Christ our Lord. Amen**

INVITATION TO COMMUNION (MAUNDY THURSDAY)

Come to the banquet God has prepared.
Happy are those who are called to the supper of the Lamb.

INVITATION TO COMMUNION (EASTER VIGIL)

Alleluia! Christ our Passover is sacrificed for us.
Therefore, let us keep the feast. Alleluia!

POST-COMMUNION PRAYER (MAUNDY THURSDAY)

Lord God, in a wonderful sacrament
you have left us a memorial of your suffering and death.
May this sacrament of your body and blood
so work in us that the way we live
will proclaim the redemption you have brought;
for you live and reign with the Father and the Holy Spirit,
one God, now and forever.
Amen

POST-COMMUNION PRAYER (EASTER VIGIL)

Eternal God,
through our baptism into the death and resurrection of Christ
you give us the water of life
and nourish us at this table
with the food and drink of the promised land.
Send us forth into the world,
that we may be witnesses to your glory
made known to us in Jesus Christ, our risen Lord.
Amen

BENEDICTION (EASTER VIGIL)

May God, by whose glory Christ was raised from the dead,
strengthen you to walk in newness of life.
Almighty God, Father, ✛ Son, and Holy Spirit
bless you now and forever.
Amen

DISMISSAL (EASTER VIGIL)

Alleluia! Christ is risen!
Christ is risen indeed! Alleluia!
Go in peace. Serve the risen Lord.
Thanks be to God.

SEASONAL RITES

THE THREE DAYS

GOOD FRIDAY

SERVICE OF LIGHT AND DARKNESS

This service is designed for those parishes that celebrate Tenebrae, yet would like to move toward the revised Good Friday liturgy included in LBW Ministers edition (pp. 23–24) as well as in the current Episcopal, Roman Catholic, Methodist, and Presbyterian worship books.

Tenebrae (Latin for "darkness") was the name given to the medieval predawn morning prayer celebrated by monks during the last three days in Holy Week. In recent centuries, this monastic liturgy—despite its early morning light imagery—was transferred to Wednesday evening in Holy Week. In the monastic practice, it was a service of prayers and readings from scripture. As the light began to dawn, the candles used for reading were gradually extinguished, so that at the end of the service, the rising sun provided the necessary light for reading and singing. This element has been retained in the contemporary practice but with the curious addition of the removal and return of a single candle, variously interpreted as the presence of the risen Christ.

In the service printed here, these elements have been placed within the reading of the Passion according to John, the ancient gospel narrative for the day. With this form, seven or fourteen candles are used, with a larger candle representing Christ. Following each section, one or two candles are extinguished until the eighth reading, at which time the "Christ" candle (not the paschal/Easter candle) is removed without being returned.

The Johannine passion account is appointed for Good Friday because the synoptic passion accounts are read in successive years on the Sunday of the Passion. John's passion account sees Jesus' death as his glorification. Rather than "mourning" the dying or dead Jesus on Good Friday, the cross is acclaimed as the sign of the world's redemption. The procession of the cross and adoration of the crucified Christ become the primary symbolic action of this day. We offer honor and reverence to the one, who lifted up from the earth, draws all people to himself. This service does not end in darkness and sadness, as if the assembly were reenacting the death of Christ. Rather, the liturgy ends with Christ exalted on the cross, an image from John's gospel.

Pastoral preaching and teaching will help to place this liturgy appropriately within the Three Days. The procession of the cross has an important connection to the procession of the paschal candle in the Easter Vigil. More importantly, all three days celebrate the mystery of Jesus' dying and rising. We do not wait until Easter Sunday to see what will happen. Already on Good Friday, the church celebrates the Lord's death and resurrection as the central event of our salvation.

GATHERING

The liturgy begins in silence after all have been seated. The ministers process into the worship space in silence.

PRAYER OF THE DAY

READINGS
Isaiah 52:13—53:12

PSALM OR HYMN

The Passion According to John
John 18:1-11
First candle(s) may be extinguished.
Hymn: Christ, the life of all the living (LBW 97, st. 1)

John 18:12-27
Second candle(s) may be extinguished.
Hymn: Ah, holy Jesus (LBW 123, st. 2)

John 18:28-40
Third candle(s) may be extinguished.
Hymn: On my heart imprint your image (LBW 102)

John 19:1-7
Fourth candle(s) may be extinguished.
Hymn: O sacred head, now wounded (LBW 117, st. 1)

John 19:8-16a
Fifth candle(s) may be extinguished.
Hymn: Were you there (LBW 92, st. 1)

John 19:16b-22
Sixth candle(s) may be extinguished.
Hymn: O sacred head, now wounded (LBW 117, st. 2)

John 19:23-25a
Seventh candle(s) may be extinguished.
Hymn: O sacred head, now wounded (LBW 117, st. 3)

John 19:25b-30
The large "Christ" candle may be removed.
John 19:31-42
Hymn: Were you there (LBW 93, st. 3)

HOMILY OR MEDITATION

Silence is kept by all.

THE PRAYERS

Bidding Prayer: See LBW *Ministers edition, pp. 139–42. For an alternate version, see* Book of Common Worship *(Louisville, KY: Westminster/John Knox Press, 1993), pp. 283–86.*

PROCESSION AND VENERATION OF THE CROSS

A large, rough-hewn cross is carried in and placed in the chancel. The following response is sung or said three times: as the procession begins, halfway to the altar, and as the procession ends at the altar.

Behold, the life-giving cross on which was hung
the salvation of the whole world.
Oh, come, let us worship him.

A period of silence is kept. Those who desire may come forward to offer a sign of reverence, such as touching the cross, kneeling briefly, or bowing. Hymns may be sung during this period, or the Solemn Reproaches may be said or sung (see Book of Common Worship, *pp. 288–91).*

HYMNS
LBW 118   Sing, my tongue (may be sung to Picardy)
LBW 123   Ah, holy Jesus
LBW 124   The royal banners forward go
LBW 482   When I survey the wondrous cross
WOV 668   There in God's garden

We adore you, O Christ, and we bless you.
By your holy cross you have redeemed the world.

The congregation departs in silence. The service continues with the Vigil of Easter.

VIGIL OF EASTER

LITANY OF THE SAINTS
Lord, have mercy.
Lord, have mercy.
Christ, have mercy.
Christ, have mercy.
Lord, have mercy.
Lord, have mercy.

Be gracious to us.
Hear us, O God.
Deliver your people.
Hear us, O God.
You loved us before the world was made:
Hear us, O God.
You rescued the people of your promise:
Hear us, O God.
You spoke through your prophets:
Hear us, O God.
You gave your only Son for the life of the world:
Hear us, O God.

For us and for our salvation he came down from heaven:
Great is your love.
And was born of the virgin Mary:
Great is your love.
Who by his cross and suffering has redeemed the world:
Great is your love.
And has washed us from our sins:
Great is your love.
Who on the third day rose from the dead:
Great is your love.
And has given us the victory:
Great is your love.
Who ascended on high:
Great is your love.
And intercedes for us at the right hand of God:
Great is your love.

For the gift of the Holy Spirit:
Thanks be to God.
For the one, holy, catholic, and apostolic church:
Thanks be to God.
For the great cloud of witnesses into which we are baptized:
Thanks be to God.

For Sarah and Abraham, Isaac and Rebekah:
Thanks be to God.
For Gideon and Deborah, David and Esther:
Thanks be to God.
For Moses and Isaiah, Jeremiah and Daniel:
Thanks be to God.
For Miriam and Rahab, Abigail and Ruth:
Thanks be to God.
For Mary, mother of our Lord:
Thanks be to God.
For John, who baptized in the Jordan:
Thanks be to God.
For Mary Magdalene and Joanna, Mary and Martha:
Thanks be to God.
For James and John, Peter and Andrew:
Thanks be to God.
For Paul and Apollos, Stephen and Phoebe:
Thanks be to God.

Other names may be added

For all holy men and women, our mothers and fathers in faith:
Thanks be to God.
For the noble band of the prophets:
Thanks be to God.
For the glorious company of the apostles:
Thanks be to God.
For the white-robed army of martyrs:
Thanks be to God.
For the cherubim and seraphim, Michael and the holy angels:
Thanks be to God.

Be gracious to us:
Hear us, O God.
Deliver your people:
Hear us, O God.

Give new life to these chosen ones by the grace of baptism:
Hear us, O God.
Strengthen all who bear the sign of the cross:
Hear us, O God.
Clothe us in compassion and love:
Hear us, O God.
Bring us with all your saints to the river of life:
Hear us, O God.

Lord, have mercy.
Lord, have mercy.
Christ, have mercy.
Christ, have mercy.
Lord, have mercy.
Lord, have mercy.

See Welcome to Christ: Lutheran Rites for the Catechumenate, *pages 70–71 for musical setting.*

SUNDAYS & SEASONS

APRIL 20, 2000

MAUNDY THURSDAY

INTRODUCTION

On this day the Christian community gathers to share in the holy supper Christ gave the church to reveal his unfailing love for the human family. In the actions of this liturgy, Christ demonstrates this love by speaking his faithful word, washing our feet, and giving us his body and blood. From this gathering we are sent to continue these actions in daily life: to serve those in need, to offer mercy, to feed those who are hungry.

This first liturgy of the Three Days has no ending; it continues with the worship of Good Friday and concludes with the Vigil of Easter. Together the Three Days proclaim the mystery of our faith: Christ has died. Christ is risen. Christ will come again.

PRAYER OF THE DAY

Holy God, source of all love, on the night of his betrayal, Jesus gave his disciples a new commandment: To love one another as he had loved them. By your Holy Spirit write this commandment in our hearts; through your Son, Jesus Christ our Lord, who lives and reigns with you and the Holy Spirit, one God, now and forever.

or

Lord God, in a wonderful Sacrament you have left us a memorial of your suffering and death. May this Sacrament of your body and blood so work in us that the way we live will proclaim the redemption you have brought; for you live and reign with the Father and the Holy Spirit, one God, now and forever.

READINGS

Exodus 12:1-4 [5-10] 11-14

Israel remembered its deliverance from slavery in Egypt by celebrating the festival of Passover. This festival featured the slaughter, preparation, and consumption of the Passover lamb, whose blood was used to protect God's people from the threat of death. The early church described the Lord's supper using imagery from the Passover, especially in portraying Jesus as the lamb who delivers God's people from sin and death.

Psalm 116:1, 10-17 (Psalm 116:1-2, 12-19 [NRSV])

I will take the cup of salvation and call on the name of the LORD. *(Ps. 116:11)*

1 Corinthians 11:23-26

The only story from the life of Jesus that Paul recounts in detail is this report of the last supper. His words to the Christians at Corinth are reflected today in the liturgies of churches throughout the world.

John 13:1-17, 31b-35

The story of the last supper in John's gospel recalls a remarkable event not mentioned elsewhere. Jesus performs the duty of a slave, washing the feet of his disciples and urging them to do the same for each other.

COLOR   Scarlet *or* White

THE PRAYERS

As we enter into the mystery of our salvation during these great three days, let us pray for new life in the church, and new hope for the world and all who are in need.

A BRIEF SILENCE.

For the church, that it would proclaim the love of Christ by demonstrating in word and deed its love for one another and its care for the earth. Lord, in your mercy,

hear our prayer.

For the world, that its strife and tensions would be alleviated by leaders blessed with your wisdom's counsel. Lord, in your mercy,

hear our prayer.

For all who are in need, that the followers of Christ would serve those who are suffering, learning from Christ's example as a servant of all. Lord, in your mercy,

hear our prayer.

For all members of this congregational community, and especially those preparing for baptism, that these three days might be a living experience of the body of Christ who promises to meet us always in the bread and wine of the holy supper. Lord, in your mercy,

hear our prayer.

HERE OTHER INTERCESSIONS MAY BE OFFERED.

For the faithful departed, with whom we are united in a holy communion, that our voices may join with theirs in the unending hymn of heaven. Lord, in your mercy,

hear our prayer.

We offer you these prayers, O God, in the shadow of the cross, in the hope of the paschal feast to come, and in the name of Jesus Christ who endured the cross and grave.

Amen

IMAGES FOR PREACHING

F. Pratt Green, in his hymn, "The Church of Christ, in ev'ry age," writes:

> Then let the servant Church arise,
> A caring Church that longs to be
> A partner in Christ's sacrifice,
> And clothed in Christ's humanity.

This contemporary hymn summarizes the various dimensions of Maundy Thursday.

The story of Jesus insisting upon washing the feet of the disciples is one of the more shocking stories told by the fourth evangelist. It is such an abrupt turnaround. "Are you to wash *my* feet?" Peter asks. "Surely I should be washing yours." And yet this paradigm informs our ministry too. This humbling task is what it means to be a servant church.

We can't even begin to grasp the oddity of Jesus washing the disciples' feet. In a day when one either walked or rode a horse for transportation, cleaning feet was a necessary but unpleasant job. It was unthinkable that God's anointed one should bend over to serve in such an unassuming way.

But what Christ teaches us during this holiest of weeks is that our mission is for the likes of the criminals who were crucified on either side of him, or to those whose feet and whole bodies are dirty. So the true servant church stoops down to do whatever work needs to be done.

Do we have the genuine commitment to get involved in Christ's mission to all who are in need? It is for the sake of this mission, and our failures to respond adequately to it, that we begin our worship this evening in humble confession to God.

WORSHIP MATTERS

The eucharist is rooted in the Passover observance. Passover remembers the angel of death passing over houses marked with the lamb's blood, sparing the lives of Hebrew firstborn. Primarily Passover celebrates the exodus, when Israel was liberated from slavery in Egypt and made a free people by God's own hand. Passover also anticipates the day when all people will be free. God's mighty acts are proclaimed not just as past events, but as ways that God is still at work.

When Jesus shared the bread and cup with his disciples, he proclaimed and gave thanks to God for God's liberating work. Jesus' words interpreting the bread and cup do not recall God's work of freedom in the exodus. They remember and celebrate God's new work of liberation for all people in and through Jesus. Jesus' giving himself over to death accomplished a new freedom—forgiveness of sin and new life. Thus, the supper fulfills the Passover.

LET THE CHILDREN COME

The Lord's supper is the focal point of tonight's liturgy. Be sure the children know that when Jesus says, "This is my body, given for you" and "This is my blood shed for you for the forgiveness of sin" he means for them; it is their baptismal birthright to hear these words and share this gift of the Lord. Children can help set the table by bringing the bread and wine forward with the offering. They can help strip the altar also, each carrying one item at a time. Remind them it is a time for silence and reverence.

MUSIC FOR WORSHIP

GATHERING

LBW 215   O Lord, we praise you
WOV 666   Great God, your love has called us

PSALM 116

Brown, Teresa. "The Blessing Cup" in PS, vol. 2.

Daigle, Gary/arr. Rory Cooney. "I Will Walk in the Presence of God" in *Choral Refrains from Psalms for the Church Year, vol. 4.* GIA G-3612-A. U.

Farlee, Robert Buckley. PW, cycle B.

Glynn, John. "Lord, How Can I Repay" in PS, vol. 2.

LBW, pp. 67, 87, 108, "What Shall I Render to the Lord"

Mahnke, Allan. *Seventeen Psalms for Cantor and Congregation.* CPH 97-6093. U/SATB, cong.

Roberts, Leon C. "I Will Call upon the Name of the Lord" in *This Far by Faith*.

Schalk, Carl. "Now I Will Walk at Your Side" in *Sing Out! A Children's Psalter*. WLP 7191. 1-2 pt.

HYMN OF THE DAY

LBW 199   Thee we adore, O hidden Savior
                ADORO TE DEVOTE

INSTRUMENTAL RESOURCES

Callahan, Charles. "Adoro te devote" in *Chant Based Hymns for Manuals*. MSM 10-849. Kybd.

Cherwien, David. "Adoro te devote" in *Interpretations based on Hymn Tunes, Book III*. AMSI OR-6. Org.

Organ, Anne Krentz. "Adoro te devote" in *Christ, Mighty Savior: Reflections on Four Hymntunes*. AFP 11-10819. Pno.

Willan, Healey. "Adoro te devote" in *Organ Works of Healey Willan*. CPH 97-6676. Org.

ALTERNATE HYMN OF THE DAY

WOV 663   When twilight comes
LBW 126   Where charity and love prevail

COMMUNION

LBW 206   Lord, who the night you were betrayed
WOV 665   Ubi caritas et amor

ADDITIONAL HYMNS AND SONGS

PH 94   An upper room did our Lord prepare
PH 515   Now to your table spread
TFF 126   Taste and see
W&P   Now in this banquet

MUSIC FOR THE DAY

CHORAL

Durufle, Maurice. "Ubi Caritas." DUR 312-41253. SATB.

Farlee, Robert Buckley. "Mandatum." AFP 11-10535. SATB.

Heim, Bret. "Lord of Lords Adored by Angels." CPH 98-3309. SATB, org.

Hopson, Hal H. "Canticle of Love." AFP 11-10911. SATB, org.

Tallis, Thomas. "O Sacrum Convivium." OXF TCM74. SAATB.

CHILDREN'S CHOIRS

Kemp, Helen. "A Lenten Love Song." CG CGA486. U, kybd.

Nelson, Ronald A. "If You Love One Another." SEL 422-841. U/2 pt, kybd.

Pote, Allen. "The Last Supper." CG CGA532. SATB, narr, kybd, opt gtr, opt bass.

KEYBOARD/INSTRUMENTAL

Near, Gerald. "Adoro te devote" in *Saint Augustine's Organbook*. AUR 86. Org.

Sedio, Mark. "Jesu, Jesu, Fill Us with Your Love" in *Dancing in the Light of God*. AFP 11-10793. Pno.

HANDBELL

Adcock, Albert V. "Let Us Break Bread Together." AGEHR AG4042. 4 oct.

Afdahl, Lee J. "Gethsemane." AFP 11-10485. 3-5 oct.

Semmann, Barbara. "Processionals for the Time of Lent" (Gethsemane, Aberystwyth, Fortunatus New). CPH 97-6524. 5 oct.

PRAISE ENSEMBLE

Foley, John B./arr. Schrader "One Bread, One Body." HOP A709. 3 pt mxd, pno.

Makeever, Ray. "Take Off Your Shoes" in DATH.

Martin, Joseph. "He Loved Them to the End." GS A-6768. SATB, acc.

Paris, Twila/arr. Rhodes. "Lamb of God." WRD 301092416x. SATB, orch.

Webb, Richard. "In Remembrance of Me" (The Lord's Prayer). Faith Inkubators.

APRIL 21, 2000

GOOD FRIDAY

INTRODUCTION

On this day the church gathers to hear the proclamation of the passion, to pray for the life of the world, and to meditate on the life-giving cross. The ancient title for this day—the triumph of the cross—reminds us that the church gathers to offer thanksgiving for the wood of the tree on which hung our salvation.

PRAYER OF THE DAY

Almighty God, we ask you to look with mercy on your family, for whom our Lord Jesus Christ was willing to be betrayed and to be given over to the hands of sinners and to suffer death on the cross; who now lives and reigns with you and the Holy Spirit, one God, forever and ever.

or

Lord Jesus, you carried our sins in your own body on the tree so that we might have life. May we and all who remember this day find new life in you now and in the world to come, where you live and reign with the Father and the Holy Spirit, now and forever.

READINGS

Isaiah 52:13—53:12

Today's reading reinterprets the common idea that suffering is God's punishment for sin: "It's God's will." What is new is the idea that the innocent sufferer brings benefits for the community. The suffering and death of the servant serve God's purposes: the redemption of God's people.

Psalm 22

My God, my God, why have you forsaken me? (Ps. 22:1)

Hebrews 10:16-25

The writer to the Hebrews uses the Hebrew scriptures to understand the meaning of Christ's death on the cross. Like a great priest, Jesus offered his own blood as a sacrifice for our sins so that now we can worship God with confidence and hope.

or Hebrews 4:14-16; 5:7-9

John 18:1—19:42

On Good Friday, the story of Jesus' passion—from his arrest to his burial—is read in its entirety from the Gospel of John.

BIDDING PRAYER

See *LBW* Ministers edition, pages 139–42; or *Book of Common Worship*, pages 283–86.

IMAGES FOR PREACHING

The crossing of two lines holds a deep symbolic force in the western mind. It signifies the meeting of the cardinal points of N-S-E-W, the four seasons, and the unity of the fundamental elements of earth-water-air-fire. It symbolizes human life "rooted" in the earth yet "reaching" outward and upward toward the infinite heavens.

In the Christian scriptures, the cross incorporates and reinterprets this mythic symbolism through the death and resurrection of Christ. The cross symbolizes unjust suffering in every age, the union of heaven and earth in Christ, the meeting of human death and divine life, the healing of our frailty with divine mercy. The cross symbolizes the universal and tragic experience of losing the beloved. Yet we believe that no life is lost on the tree of divine grace: the cross is the profound sign of Christ whose death transformed the tree of death into the tree of eternal life. On this day, the church celebrates the triumph of the holy cross and the one whose death has brought us life.

WORSHIP MATTERS

On Good Friday our desire to thank and praise our Lord for his suffering and death on the cross can tempt us to be inventive in order to make worship special, and so we add processions, choral anthems and special music, darkness and ritual acts aimed at producing drama, and preaching designed to be powerful and profound. The danger is that our efforts to make Good Friday worship special may serve only to clutter up the service and block our view of the cross. On this day, more than any other, worship leaders do best to get out of the way and trust the liturgy to reveal the mystery of Christ's death and our salvation. Through the disciplined reading of our Lord's passion according to John, deliberate praying of the bidding prayer, and discovery of what it is to participate in the adoration of the cross, we see Christ alone.

LET THE CHILDREN COME

Let the stark bareness of the chancel leave its impression on the children today. As our Lord fasted and forsook riches, so we too take no sacramental food on this day and remove from our eyes all claims to wealth and splendor. The altar is stripped bare. The ornamentation of flowers, banners, and other decorative items has been removed. In some places, ornate crosses have been veiled. A crude, rough-hewn cross, as two tree trunks lashed together, stands before us a reminder that the Lord's death was neither pretty nor rich, and yet gives life to all.

MUSIC FOR WORSHIP

GATHERING

The liturgy begins in silence on Good Friday.

PSALM 22

Farlee, Robert Buckley. PW, cycle B.

Harbor, Rawn. "My God, My God" in *This Far By Faith*.

HYMN OF THE DAY

| LBW 92 | Were you there |
| | WERE YOU THERE |

ALTERNATE HYMN OF THE DAY

| LBW 118 | Sing, my tongue |
| WOV 668 | There in God's garden |

ADDITIONAL HYMNS AND SONGS

DATH 61	Strange King
PH 86	When we are tempted to deny your Son
TFF 80	They crucified my Lord
W&P	Amazing love

MUSIC FOR THE DAY

CHORAL

Casals, Pablo. "O Vos Omnes." Tetra AB 128. SATB. Lat/Eng.

Fleming, Larry L. "Sing and Ponder." AFP 11-10451. SATB.

Niedmann, Peter. "The Earth Did Tremble." AFP 11-10922. SATB. org.

Schulz-Widmar, Russell. "Good Friday Anthems." GIA G-4390. SATB, vc.

Schütz, Heinrich. *Passion according to St. John*. Chantry. T, SATB.

CHILDREN'S CHOIRS

Christopherson, Dorothy. "There Was a Man." AFP 11-10843. U, pno, ob.

Jennings, Carolyn. "Ah, Holy Jesus." AFP 11-302. SA, vc.

KEYBOARD/INSTRUMENTAL

Brahms, Johannes. "Prelude and Fugue on 'O Darkest Woe' " in *Werke für Orgel*. G. Henle Verlag. Org.

Reger, Max. "Passion." BRE 4160. Org.

HANDBELL

Larson, Katherine Jordahl. "Were You There?" AFP 11-10353. 3 oct.

Sherman, Arnold. "When I Survey the Wondrous Cross." Red River Music HB0010A. 2-3 oct. HB0010B. 4-5 oct.

PRAISE ENSEMBLE

Barbour and Skidmore "The Holy Heart" in *Maranatha! Music Praise Chorus Book, 3rd ed*. WRD/MAR.

Goebel-Komala, Felix. "Psalm of Hope." GIA G-4403. SATB, cant, cong, gtr, kybd, timp.

Paris, Twila. "Lamb of God" in *Songs for Praise and Worship*. WRD.

Rouse, Jay/arr. Kirkland and Rouse. "Behold Calvary's Lamb." Sparrow AO8189. SATB, orch.

Schram, Ruth Elaine. "Not My Will but Thine." FLA. A6603. SATB, acc, ob.

FRIDAY, APRIL 21
ANSELM, ARCHBISHOP OF CANTERBURY, 1109

This eleventh-century Benedictine monk, theologian, and bishop is best known for his theological explanation of the atonement, referred to as the "satisfaction" theory. Anselm is believed to be the greatest theologian between Augustine and Thomas Aquinas, and he understood the pursuit of theology as prayer. He is also counted among the medieval mystics who emphasized the maternal aspects of God. He addressed Christ as our "mother who tasted death in longing to bring forth children to life."

A commemoration of Anselm might include a discussion of ways we use feminine images to speak of the divine. Look at two hymns in *With One Voice* (688 and 769), which are based on texts by two other medieval mystics, Hildegard of Bingen and Julian of Norwich.

APRIL 22, 2000

THE RESURRECTION OF OUR LORD
VIGIL OF EASTER

INTRODUCTION

This liturgy's Easter proclamation announces, "This is the night in which all who believe in Christ are rescued from evil and the gloom of sin, are renewed in grace, and are restored to holiness." It is the very foundation of our Christian faith, and it is what makes this vigil celebration the crowning moment of the church's year. This night the church celebrates the presence of the risen Lord as he brings us to new life in baptism, gives us his body and blood, speaks his word of promise, and comes to us in the Christian community.

PRAYER OF THE DAY

O God, who made this most holy night to shine with the glory of the Lord's resurrection: Stir up in your Church that Spirit of adoption which is given to us in Baptism, that we, being renewed both in body and mind, may worship you in sincerity and truth; through Jesus Christ our Lord, who lives and reigns with you, in the unity of the Holy Spirit, one God, now and forever.

READINGS

Creation: Genesis 1:1—2:4a
Response: Psalm 136:1-9, 23-36
   God's mercy endures forever. (Ps. 136:1b)
The Flood: Genesis 7:1-5, 11-18; 8:6-18; 9:8-13
Response: Psalm 46
   The LORD of hosts is with us; the God of Jacob is our stronghold. (Ps. 46:4)
The Testing of Abraham: Genesis 22:1-18
Response: Psalm 16
   You will show me the path of life. (Ps. 16:11)
Israel's Deliverance at the Red Sea: Exodus 14:10-31; 15:20-21
Response: Exodus 15:1b-13, 17-18
   I will sing to the LORD who has triumphed gloriously. (Exod. 15:1)
Salvation Freely Offered to All: Isaiah 55:1-11
Response: Isaiah 12:2-6
   With joy you will draw water from the wells of salvation. (Isa. 12:3)

The Wisdom of God: Proverbs 8:1-8, 19-21; 9:4b-6
or Baruch 3:9-15, 32—4:4
Response: Psalm 19
   The statutes of the LORD are just and rejoice the heart. (Ps. 19:8)
A New Heart and a New Spirit: Ezekiel 36:24-28
Response: Psalm 42 and Psalm 43
   My soul is athirst for the living God. (Ps. 42:2)
The Valley of the Dry Bones: Ezekiel 37:1-14
Response: Psalm 143
   Revive me, O LORD, for your name's sake. (Ps. 143:11)
The Gathering of God's People: Zephaniah 3:14-20
Response: Psalm 98
   Lift up your voice, rejoice and sing. (Ps. 98:5)
The Call of Jonah: Jonah 3:1-10
Response: Jonah 2:1-3 [4-6] 7-9
   Deliverance belongs to the LORD. (Jonah 2:9)
The Song of Moses: Deuteronomy 31:19-30
Response: Deuteronomy 32:1-4, 7, 36a, 43a
   The LORD will give his people justice. (Deut. 32:36)
The Fiery Furnace: Daniel 3:1-29
Response: Song of the Three Young Men 35-65
   Sing praise to the Lord and highly exalt him forever. (Song of the Three Young Men 35b)

NEW TESTAMENT READING

Romans 6:3-11
Response: Psalm 114
   Tremble, O earth, at the presence of the LORD. (Ps. 114:7)

GOSPEL

Mark 16:1-8

COLOR   White *or* Gold

THE PRAYERS

As we celebrate the joy of the resurrection, let us pray for new life in the church, and new hope for the world and all who are in need.
   A BRIEF SILENCE.

On this holy night, let us pray for the church, that it would be strengthened to proclaim the message of freedom and new life in the resurrection of Jesus Christ from death. Lord, in your mercy,

hear our prayer.

On this holy night, let us pray for the world, that the redeeming word of the crucified and risen Christ will reach its farthest corners and every inhabitant. Lord, in your mercy,

hear our prayer.

On this holy night, let us pray for all who are in the darkness of despair or depression, for all who are suffering from chronic pain, and for all who await your healing and life-giving touch upon their lives (especially . . .). Lord, in your mercy,

hear our prayer.

On this holy night, let us pray for the newly baptized and for all who have renewed their baptism, that the power of Christ's resurrection will send them out to proclaim the gospel of their salvation. Lord, in your mercy,

hear our prayer.

HERE OTHER INTERCESSIONS MAY BE OFFERED.

On this holy night, let us pray for those who have been standing in sorrow at the graves of loved ones, that they might be comforted with the blessed hope of an Easter people. Lord, in your mercy,

hear our prayer.

Gracious God, hear our prayers and receive them for the sake of the crucified and risen one, our Savior Jesus Christ.

Amen

IMAGES FOR PREACHING

We gather in the darkness of this night to orient ourselves to those things of central importance for the Christian faith. We do things on this night that Christians have done for hundreds of years. And rehearsing these ancient things helps us to know our faith, whether we've just become members of the church tonight, or whether we have been in it for more than ninety years.

In the singing of the Easter proclamation (Exsultet) we praise the awe-inspiring power of this night through words that are quite possibly more than 1,500 years old. Think of the generations of Christians that have sung the praises of this night, while bathed in the light of similar pillars of fire!

In the recital of several long Old Testament readings, we link ourselves up with Jewish stories of creation and Passover that are thousands of years old. We give thanks for the waters of creation, the waters of Noah, the waters of the Red Sea, the water of the Jordan, and the water in our congregation's baptismal font. We hear tell of what happened on that first Easter morn when the women went carrying spices to the tomb.

We retrace many steps of our own faith. And now we come to this Easter. Here we celebrate something as old as the foundations of the earth and as new as the fire of these candles and the oil-drenched crosses on our newly-baptized members.

We come here this night to ask the God of all that has ever been to brighten our path in the many dark nights to come and to lead us home whenever we've forgotten the road. We stop for a time to orient ourselves in order to know we can go no place where God will not be. God who hung the stars is with us if we move into another state, or if we travel 100,000 light years away. No matter where we go or what we do, God who redeemed Israel and raised Christ from the grave will be with us too.

WORSHIP MATTERS

Though the rubrics for the Easter Vigil do not require a sermon, the readings having proclaimed the biblical narrative of salvation, people appreciate a word that helps them understand all that they have seen and heard in the last three days and throughout the Lenten season, and how what has gone before connects to the Easter celebration at hand. Tonight's homily, therefore, is to draw the hearers into the mysteries, moving them to enter spiritually and thoughtfully into what they have previously not fully understood. Preaching is to have a persuasive, enlightening, deepening effect on the hearers' understanding of the church's rites that leads them to live in the different, new dimension that is the resurrection life. One way to reach hearers is to select a single image—water, light, word—and allow it to weave together the many rites and actions of this holy time.

LET THE CHILDREN COME

The drama of this liturgy invites the participation of children. Those who read well can be lectors. The sermon could be a play, with children presenting a brief dramatic portrayal of one of the narratives. Invite children to gather near the font for the baptism or baptism renewal, where they can see the action, hear the word, and feel the water. Similarly, they should be a part of the eucharist: assisting with the lighting of the candles and the setting of the table, being where they can focus on the word and action, and gathering at the table.

MUSIC FOR WORSHIP
SERVICE MUSIC
AROUND THE GREAT FIRE

    Berthier, Jacques. "Within Our Darkest Night" in *Songs and Prayers from Taizé*. GIA.

    Biery, James. "Easter Sequence." MSM 80-404. U/brass qrt or org.

    Schutte, Dan. "Holy Darkness." OCP 9906CC. Cong, kybd, gtr, vl, vla, vc, hrn.

AROUND THE LIGHT OF CHRIST

    Batastini, Robert. "Exsultet" (Easter Proclamation). GIA G-2351. U chant.

    "Rejoice Now, All Heavenly Choirs" in *Music for the Vigil of Easter*. AFP 3-5330. Cant, cong.

    Tamblyn. "Lumen Christi." OCP 7235CC. Presider, cant, SATB, org, perc.

    "The Exsultet" in TP.

AROUND THE READINGS

    Reponses to all readings in PW, Cycle C.

    Trapp, Lynn. "Responses for the Triduum." MSM 80-305. Cant/cong/kybd, opt solo/C inst.

First Reading

    Carmona. "A Canticle of Creation." OCP 9973. U/cant, desc, org, tr.

    Hopson, Hal. "O Praise the Lord Who Made All Beauty." CG CGA 143. U, kybd.

    Smith, Alan. "God's Love Is Forever!" in PS, vol. 2.

Second Reading

    Cherwien, David. "God Is Our Refuge and Strength." MSM 80-800. U, org.

    Harbor, Rawn. "The Lord of Hosts Is with Us" in *This Far by Faith*.

Third Reading

    Inwood, Paul. "Centre of My Life" in PS, vol. 2.

Fourth Reading

    Barker, Michael. "Miriam's Song." CG CGA 740. U, kybd, opt tamb.

    Cherwien, David. "Go Down, Moses." Evangel/AMSI. U, kybd.

    Daw, Carl, Jr. "Metrical Canticles 25 and 26" in *To Sing God's Praise*. HOP 921. Cong, kybd.

    Gibbons, John. "Canticle of Moses" in PS, vol. 2.

Fifth Reading

    DeLong, Richard. "Seek Ye the Lord" in *Five Sacred Songs*. ECS 4759. Solo, kybd.

    Lindh, Jody. "Behold, God Is My Salvation." CPH 98-3193. U/2 pt, org.

    Rusbridge, Barbara. "Sing a Song to the Lord" in PS, vol. 1.

    WOV 635   Surely it is God who saves me

    W&P   First Song of Isaiah

Sixth Reading

    Cox, Joe. "Psalm 19" in *Psalms for the People of God*. SMP 45/1037S. Cant, choir, cong, kybd.

    Ogden, David. "You, Lord, Have the Message of Eternal Life" in PS, vol. 2.

Seventh Reading

    Howells, Herbert. "Like as the Hart." OXF 42.066. SATB, org.

    Hurd, Bob. "As the Deer Longs" in PS, vol. 2.

    LBW 452   As pants the hart for cooling streams

    W&P   As the deer

Ninth Reading

    Johnson, Alan. "All the Ends of the Earth" in PS, vol. 1.

    Jothen, Michael. "O Sing Ye!" BEC BP1128. U, kybd.

    Martinson, Joel. "Psalm 98." CPH 98-3225. SATB, cong, tr, org.

Tenth Reading

    WOV 752   I, the Lord of sea and sky

Twelfth Reading

    Daw Jr., Carl. "Metrical Canticles 13 and 14" in *To Sing God's Praise*. HOP 921. Cong, kybd.

    Proulx, Richard. "Song of the Three Children." GIA G-1863. U, opt 2 pt, cant, cong, perc, org.

AROUND THE FONT

    "A Litany of the Saints" and "Springs of water, bless the Lord" in *Welcome to Christ: Lutheran Rites for the Catechumanate*. AFP 3-142.

    Cherwien, David and Susan. "Life Tree." CPH 98-3190. SAB, org, opt fl.

    Cooney, Rory/arr. Gary Daigle. "Glory to God/Sprinkling Rite." GIA G-4020. Choir, cong, gtr, kybd, fl.

    Farlee, Robert Buckley. "O Blessed Spring." AFP 11-10544. SATB, ob, org, opt cong.

    Keesecker, Thomas. "Washed Anew." AFP 11-10676. SAB/SATB, opt 2 oct hb, opt cong.

    Palmer, Nicholas. "Cleanse Us, O Lord: Sprinkling Rite." GIA G-4064. Cant, SATB, cong, gtr, org, opt inst.

    Taylor-Howell, Susan. "You Have Put on Christ." CG CGA 325. U/3 pt, opt orff.

    Trapp, Lynn. "Music for the Rite of Sprinkling." MSM 80-901. SATB, org.

    WOV 694   You have put on Christ

PSALM 114

Farlee, Robert Buckley. PW, cycle C.
Hopson, Hal H. *Psalm Refrains and Tones.* HOP 425.
The Psalter-Psalms and Canticles for Singing. WJK.

HYMN OF THE DAY

LBW 135   The strife is o'er, the battle done
                 VICTORY

VOCAL RESOURCES

Gerike, H. "The Strife Is O'er, the Battle Done." CPH 98-2446. SATB, kybd, tpt, cong.

INSTRUMENTAL RESOURCES

Callahan, Charles. "Victory" in *Funeral Music for Manuals.* MSM 10-857. Kybd.
Fedak, Alfred V. "Improvisation-Toccata: 'The Strife Is O'er'" in *A Lenten/Easter Suite.* SEL 160-123. Org.
Shoemaker-Lohmeyer, Lisa. "The Strife Is O'er." MSM 10-418. Org.
Sherman, Arnold. "The Strife Is O'er." HOP 1847. 3-5 oct hb.
Webster, Richard R. "A Paschal Suite for Organ and Trumpet." AFP 11-10831. Org, tpt/fl.

ALTERNATE HYMN OF THE DAY

WOV 679   Our Paschal Lamb, that sets us free
LBW 189   We know that Christ is raised

COMMUNION

LBW 214   Come, let us eat
WOV 702   I am the bread of life

SENDING

LBW 135   The strife is o'er, the battle done
WOV 793   Shout for joy loud and long

ADDITIONAL HYMNS AND SONGS

DATH 63   Awake, O sleeper!
H82 455/6   O Love of God, how strong
TFF 100   We praise thee, O God
W&P   Come and see

MUSIC FOR THE DAY

CHORAL

Amner, John. "I Will Sing unto the Lord." NOV 29 0640. SAATB.
Erickson, Richard. "Come Away to the Skies." AFP 11-10816. Also in *The Augsburg Choirbook.* 11-10817. SATB, fl, fc.
Jennings, Kenneth. "All You Works of the Lord." AFP 11-0581. SATB, org.
Leavitt, John. "Rejoice!" AFP 11-10832. SATB, org/pno, opt brass, perc, hb.
Schein, Johann H. "Christ Lay in Death's Dark Tomb." Broude. SAB, cont. Ger/Eng.

CHILDREN'S CHOIRS

Kemp, Helen. "God's Great Lights." CPH 98-3072. U antiphonal, kybd, opt cong, opt windchimes.
Shute, Linda Cable. "Creation Song" (La canción de la creatión). AFP 11-10588. U/2 pt, pno.

KEYBOARD/INSTRUMENTAL

Leavitt, John. "Come Away to the Skies" in *A Little Easter Suite.* CPH 97-6646. Org.
Powell, Robert. "At the Lamb's High Feast We Sing" in *Ten Seasonal Hymntune Preludes for the Church Year.* GIA G-3829. Org.

HANDBELL

Afdahl, Lee J. "For as the Rain Comes Down." AFP 11-10981. 3-5 oct, rainstick, fc.
Boersma. "Dry Bones." NMP169. 3-5 oct.
White, Jack Noble. "The First Song of Isaiah." HWG CMR3347. SATB, cong, hb, opt gtr, perc, dance.

PRAISE ENSEMBLE

Klein, Laurie/arr. Schrader. "I Love You, Lord." HOP GC936. SATB, pno.
Nystrom, Martin/arr. Christopher. "As the Deer." WAR 08740834. SATB, acc, fl.
Paris, Twila. "We Bow Down" in *Songs For Praise and Worship.* WRD.
Smith, Byron J. "Worthy to Be Praised." LAW 52654. SATB, pno.
Ylvisaker, John. "Great Is Our God." in *Borning Cry.* NGP.
Ziegenhals, Harriet. "Oh, Sing to the Lord." CG CGA640. U/2 pt, kybd, perc.

SATURDAY, APRIL 22
DAY OF THE CREATION

APRIL 23, 2000

THE RESURRECTION OF OUR LORD
EASTER DAY

INTRODUCTION

The story of Mary Magdalene is the church's story. We hear the voice of the risen Lord in the scriptures. We receive his body and blood in the holy supper. We encounter him in our brothers and sisters and in all those in need who look for salvation. We are charged to go forth in daily life and proclaim with our words and deeds that we have seen the Lord. It is the day of resurrection, the day the Lord has made. Let us be glad and rejoice.

On this day the church commemorates Toyohiko Kagawa, a renewer of society who died in 1960.

PRAYER OF THE DAY

O God, you gave your only Son to suffer death on the cross for our redemption, and by his glorious resurrection you delivered us from the power of death. Make us die every day to sin, so that we may live with him forever in the joy of the resurrection; through Jesus Christ our Lord, who lives and reigns with you and the Holy Spirit, one God, now and forever.

or

Almighty God, through your only Son you overcame death and opened for us the gate of everlasting life. Give us your continual help; put good desires into our minds and bring them to full effect; through Jesus Christ our Lord, who lives and reigns with you and the Holy Spirit, one God, now and forever.

READINGS

Acts 10:34-43

Peter's sermon, delivered at the home of Cornelius, a Roman army officer, is a summary of the essential message of Christianity: Everyone who believes in Jesus, whose life, death, and resurrection fulfilled the words of the prophets, receives forgiveness of sins through his name.

or Isaiah 25:6-9

Psalm 118:1-2, 14-24

On this day the LORD has acted; we will rejoice and be glad in it. (Ps. 118:24)

1 Corinthians 15:1-11

Paul discusses many things in his letters to the Corinthians, but in these verses he tells them what he thinks is most important of all: the good news that Jesus has been raised from the dead.

or Acts 10:34-43

John 20:1-18

This morning began with confusion: the stone was moved and the tomb was empty. Disciples arrive, then angels, and finally Jesus himself. Out of the confusion, hope emerges, and a weeping woman becomes the first to confess her faith in the risen Lord.

or Mark 16:1-8

COLOR White *or* Gold

THE PRAYERS

As we celebrate the joy of the resurrection, let us pray for new life in the church, and new hope for the world and all who are in need.

A BRIEF SILENCE.

O God, as the church celebrates Jesus' glorious resurrection from the dead, may we be made bold in the witness of Christ's resurrection through all that we say and do. Lord, in your mercy,

hear our prayer.

We praise you, O God, for destroying the shroud of sin cast over all peoples, and for saving the world by the resurrection of your Son. Lord, in your mercy,

hear our prayer.

Gracious God, in the midst of her weeping Mary Magdalene was met at the tomb by the risen Christ. Meet all who weep this day with the comfort of your care, and touch the sick with your joy and peace (especially . . .). Lord, in your mercy,

hear our prayer.

Merciful God, we are your forgiven people graced with the gift of new life in Christ. Empower the newly baptized to emerge from the font as faithful disciples and bold proclaimers of the gospel. Lord, in your mercy,

hear our prayer.

HERE OTHER INTERCESSIONS MAY BE OFFERED.

Even as you raised your Son from the dead on the third day, we pray that you will hold our beloved dead, with your servant Toyohiko Kagawa, in your eternal rest until the day when you raise us all to share the marriage feast of the Lamb with you forever. Lord, in your mercy,
hear our prayer.
Gracious God, hear our prayers and receive them for the sake of the crucified and risen one, our Savior Jesus Christ.
Amen

IMAGES FOR PREACHING

Where do we begin? It is superfluous to speak about the significance of Easter Day in a volume such as this one. Neither do we need to add any weight to the burden of responsibility that comes with standing in the pulpit on Easter morning. Still, the preacher needs to be clear that none of our faith makes sense without the Easter gospel, while at the same time recognizing that occasional members and numerous visitors present at worship this morning may be woefully ignorant of that truth.

Easter offers a unique opportunity to speak a word about the mystery of the resurrection, the conquest of sin, the great victory of life over death, and to explain more fully what we mean in the funeral prayers about Jesus' own passage through "the grave and gate of death."

Today "He is risen!" can be heard through every one of our senses. Indeed all of the special elements of Easter worship may also tend to obscure the stark simplicity of Mark's gospel. These eight verses are a kind of litany of exchanges, an inventory of one thing replaced by another, and each replacement becomes more astonishing as the story unfolds. The Passover celebration is over, and in its stead is the women's sad procession to the tomb. The stone that sealed the entrance and marked the end of Jesus' ministry is rolled back, leaving an opening and a new possibility. Instead of a silent corpse in grave clothes, an informative young man/angel stands dressed in a white robe. In the place of death is resurrection and the promise of new life.

Finally, and perhaps what our people need to hear again, the despair of death is replaced—not by immediate triumph, but by terror and amazement. The nearness of God, even when it ought to be expected, is as frightening for them as for the witness of any act of God's power. The power of God could open the tomb, but fear of what they had seen was enough to seal shut the women's mouths. To testify to the one God raised from the dead—especially as they did not know what that truth would mean for them and for their lives—took courage and faith. That much has not changed.

WORSHIP MATTERS

What is the tone of your Easter worship? Is it safe, traditional, predictable? Easter is not. Mark tells us that the women left the tomb in stunned silence: they were afraid. Peter helps us to understand why: "God shows no partiality." *Anyone* who fears God and does what is right is acceptable to God—young and old, rich and poor, black and white, male and female, gay and straight, the faithful Christian and the nominal Easter crowd. God's partiality is for love, life, forgiveness, and reconciliation for all people.

On this tradition-laden festival, how can we move people to stunned silence over the amazing thing God has done? How can we proclaim the news that, because of Christ's resurrection, everything is different, all are acceptable to God? Can we be as daring as God was in raising Christ Jesus from the dead?

LET THE CHILDREN COME

The resurrection simply happened to the unprepared disciples. This approach is the best with children. Avoid domesticating the event with images of bunnies and butterflies, for Jesus' resurrection is not like anything else. Draw children into the joy as the great resurrection hymns with their abundant alleluias are jubilantly sung; the procession of cross, banners, torches, choir, and ministers is made with grandeur; and the Lord's supper is celebrated reverently. Children grasp with all their senses the contrast between the austerity of Lent and Holy Week and today's lavish abundance of joy and adornment of space, time, and language.

MUSIC FOR WORSHIP
SERVICE MUSIC

All too often the great musical acclamations of the liturgy (the hymn of praise, gospel acclamation, Sanctus) seem anticlimactic amidst all the musical hoopla given to Easter hymns on this day. Strive for balance; consider one of the following embellished versions of the *LBW* liturgies:

Cherwien, David. *Alternatives Within*. AFP 11-10611. Org, opt inst.

Ferguson, John. *Festival Setting of the Communion Liturgy* (*LBW*, setting 2). Full score CPH 6127. Choir 98-2994. Org, SATB, opt brass.

Hillert, Richard. *Festival Setting of the Communion Liturgy* (*LBW*, setting 1). Full score CPH 97-5939. Choral desc 97-2755; hb 97-5958. U with desc, org, brass, ob, timp, 3 oct hb.

GATHERING

| LBW 128 | Christ the Lord is risen today |
| WOV 674 | Alleluia! Jesus is risen! |

PSALM 118

Chepponis, James J. "Eastertime Psalm." GIA G-3907. Cant, cong, opt choir, opt tpts/hb.

Farlee, Robert Buckley. PW, cycle B.

Gieseke, Thomas. "Psalm 118." CPH 98-2754. U.

Roberts, Leon C. "The Lord Is My Strength" in *This Far by Faith*.

Trapp, Lynn. "This Is the Day." MSM 80-403. SATB, cong, cant, opt tpt, org.

CHILDREN'S PSALM SUGGESTIONS

Hommerding, Alan J. "This Is the Day" in *Sing Out! A Children's Psalter*. WLP 7191. U.

Hruby, Dolores M. "Psalm 118" in *Seasonal Psalms for Children*. WLP 7102. U, opt Orff.

HYMN OF THE DAY

LBW 210   At the Lamb's high feast we sing
                 SONNE DER GERECHTIGKEIT

INSTRUMENTAL RESOURCES

Ferguson, John. "Partita on 'At the Lamb's High Feast.'" MSM 10-400. Org.

Organ, Anne Krentz. "Partita on 'At the Lamb's High Feast'" in *Reflections on Hymn Tunes for Holy Communion*. AFP 11-10621. Pno.

Rose, Richard. "Sonne der Gerechtigkeit" in *Hymnal Companion for Woodwinds, Brass and Percussion, Series 1*. CPH 97-6714.

Travis, Albert. "Sonne der Gerechtigkeit" in *Three Folk Hymn Improvisations for Organ*. MSM 10-886. Org.

ALTERNATE HYMN OF THE DAY

| WOV 678 | Christ has arisen, alleluia |
| LBW 134 | Christ Jesus lay in death's strong bands |

COMMUNION

| LBW 352 | I know that my Redeemer lives! |
| WOV 671 | Alleluia, alleluia, give thanks |

SENDING

| LBW 144 | Good Christian friends, rejoice and sing! |
| WOV 672 | Christ is risen! Shout hosanna! |

ADDITIONAL HYMNS AND SONGS

CW 159	Morning breaks upon the tomb
H82 201	On earth has dawned this day of days
TFF 90	They crucified my Savior
W&P	The trumpets sound, the angels sing

MUSIC FOR THE DAY

CHORAL

Arguello, Kiko/arr. Lorraine Florindez. "Resuscito, Resuscito." CPH 98-3278. SA, kybd, opt 2 tpt, opt gtr.

Byrd, William. "Sing Praise to God This Holy Day." CPH 98-2091. SSATB.

Handel, G. F./arr. Hal H. Hopson. "Sing and Be Joyful." AFP 11-10915. SATB, kybd.

Mathias, William. "Alleluia! Christ Is Risen!" OXF A347. SATB, org/brass, timp, org.

Proulx, Richard. "Our Paschal Lamb, That Sets Us Free." AFP 12-106. SATB, org.

CHILDREN'S CHOIRS

Arguello/arr. Florindez. "¡Resucitó, Resucitó¡" CPH 98-3278. SA, kybd, opt 2 tpt, opt gtr.

Cáceres, Abe. "This Is the Day." AFP 11-10682. U or SAB, cong, kybd.

Nelson, Ronald A. "He Rose." SEL 422-401. U, opt desc, kybd.

KEYBOARD/INSTRUMENTAL

Langlais, Jean. "Acclamations" in *Suite Medievale*. Editions Salabert. Org.

Powell, Robert J. "Easter Sonata for Flute and Organ." CPH 97-6472. Fl, org.

HANDBELL

Behnke, John A. "The Head That Once Was Crowned with Thorns." CPH 97-6121. 2 oct; 97-6120. Full score; 98-2977. Choir score.

Semmann, Barbara. "Processionals for the Time of Easter." CPH 97-6523. 3-4 oct.

Sherman, Arnold. "Laudation." SHW HP5306. 3-5 oct.

Zabel, Albert. "The Strife Is O'er." AFP 11-10989. 3-5 oct.

PRAISE ENSEMBLE

Batstone. "Glory to the Lamb" in *Maranatha! Music Praise Chorus Book, 3rd ed*. WRD/MAR.

Garrett, Les. "This Is the Day" in *All God's People Sing*. CPH.

Herring, Anne/arr. Wilson. "Easter Song." HOP. F958. SATB, pno, hb.

Rouse, Jay/arr. Kirkland and Rouse. "No Cross, No Crown." Sparrow AO8215. SATB, orch.

Schrader, Jack. "Easter Anthem." HOP A609. SATB, kybd.

APRIL 23, 2000

THE RESURRECTION OF OUR LORD
EASTER EVENING

PRAYER OF THE DAY

Almighty God, you give us the joy of celebrating our Lord's resurrection. Give us also the joys of life in your service, and bring us at last to the full joy of life eternal; through your Son, Jesus Christ our Lord, who lives and reigns with you and the Holy Spirit, one God, now and forever.

READINGS

Isaiah 25:6-9
Psalm 114
  Hallelujah. (Ps. 114:1)
1 Corinthians 5:6b-8
Luke 24:13-49

COLOR White

LET THE CHILDREN COME

Children learn by repetition. Have them listen carefully to the gospel for words they've heard before. The reader of Luke 24 should be sure the words "he took bread, blessed and broke it and gave it to them" are set apart and spoken clearly. From now on, every Sunday is a "little Easter," and every eucharist is a glimpse of God's kingdom as Jesus reveals himself to us in the breaking of the bread. Teach children the prayer for use before communion (*LBW,* p. 47, prayer 207), and use it as a congregational prayer before the supper.

MUSIC FOR WORSHIP
SUGGESTED HYMNS

LBW 132	Come, you faithful, raise the strain
LBW 154	That Easter day with joy was bright
LBW 263	Abide with us, our Savior
WOV 743	Stay with us

ADDITIONAL HYMNS AND SONGS

LLC 362	As I walked home to Emmaus
UMH 613	O Thou who this mysterious bread
TFF 98	Open our eyes, Lord
W&P	We will glorify

SUNDAY, APRIL 23
TOYOHIKO KAGAWA, RENEWER OF SOCIETY, 1960

Kagawa was disinherited by his wealthy Japanese family when be became a Christian. From his seminary studies he became aware of Christian responsibility in the face of social evils, and he worked on behalf of slum dwellers, labor unions, government relief agencies, and church-sponsored social welfare organizations. He was arrested for his efforts to reconcile Japan and China after the Japanese attack of 1940.

In celebration of his witness, recognize those people in your parish who work tirelessly on behalf of the poor and oppressed in your city or county.

LENT
THE THREE DAYS
EASTER

EASTER

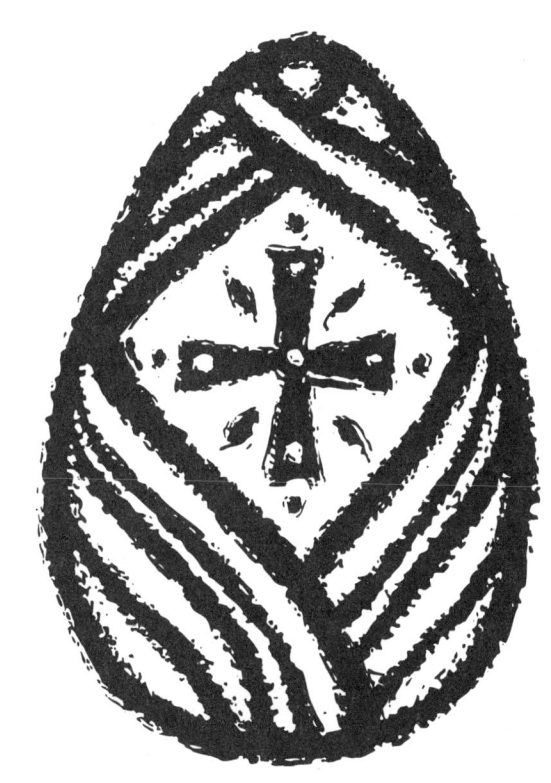

*Human life has become infinitely valuable
because the Lord is risen*

IMAGES OF THE SEASON

An informal survey of preachers shows that the sermon for Easter Day is widely regarded as the year's most difficult to prepare. Why is that? In part, no doubt, it has to do with the awareness that for many in the congregation it will be one of the two times they'll hear the gospel message all year. That awareness puts a great deal of weight on a few minutes of communication. But more likely it comes from the sense that the message of Easter is simply more than we know how to say.

TOO MUCH TO BEAR

An old story reports that an actor once commented to a preacher that the difference between them was that actors speak of things that are not real as if they were, and preachers speak of things that are real as if they were not. That is probably an unfair assessment, but it does point to the difficulty not only of preaching but of speaking our faith in general, perhaps especially at Easter. The message of the resurrection, however firmly we may believe it, however real it may be to us, is extremely hard to communicate. It's a lesson preachers learn early in their homiletical careers. It's easy to find illustrations of sin and images of sorrow. It's even fairly simple to paint pictures of repentance and forgiveness. But resurrection and new life—those don't come so easily.

The problem, of course, is that resurrection is quite simply outside of our human experience. It is impossible, illogical, and thus, virtually inexpressible. How then do we speak of it? What images can convey resurrection in a way that does justice to its reality?

THE FACT OF THE RESURRECTION

Arguments—both scholarly and popular—over the nature of Jesus' resurrection revolve around the exact nature of the actual event. Some contend that a bodily raising—what one Anglican bishop called "tricks with bones"—is an insult to faith. Others have put their emphasis on the reality of the faith of the disciples. It doesn't matter exactly what happened, so says this approach, it's sufficient that it was something so radical as to change lives and produce faith.

While both of those views get around the intellectual difficulties in speaking of resurrection, they tend to prove the actor's contention: we are speaking of reality as if it didn't happen. The scriptural accounts of the events of Easter never try to explain anything. They simply state what happened: "that he was buried, and that he was raised on the third day in accordance with the scriptures" (1 Cor. 15:4). They offer no explanation, no apologetic use of experience. It is simply fact. And this is foundation on which the faith of the apostles was built: on fact.

This fact, however, is of a remarkable sort. The risen Jesus appears within history, on ordinary days, in ordinary rooms where the disciples gathered to eat and to talk. Into this setting comes one who is human but is not limited by the normal conditions of time and space. He eats fish for breakfast but also enters rooms where doors are locked. He is just as always, but also completely different.

EASTER FOR US

Can we speak of that which is and make it real? Only in a limited way. But limitations are the point of this season: our human inadequacies cannot limit the glory of God. The risen Christ did not abandon his human body but rather glorified it. Any image we may use to speak of the resurrection will fail to do it justice. It is simply too great for us to communicate fully. But the paradox of the season is that even our poorest attempts can give some hint of the message of resurrection.

The crowning image of Easter is found there in the joining of human and divine, the promise that "this mortal body puts on immortality" (1 Cor. 15:54). It is an image that looks to its fulfillment at the end of time but is also made real here and now. It says that human life has become infinitely valuable, because the fact is that the Lord is risen!

EASTER

ENVIRONMENT AND ART FOR THE SEASON

For more than fifteen hundred years Christians employed a dizzying array of colors in their worship: black, blue, violet, purple, green, red, scarlet, rose, brown, orange, yellow, and gold. These colors and more were used regularly at different festivals and seasons throughout the year. While the English favored green and deep blue, the Italians thrilled at the sight of scarlet or yellow. Yet this riot of color, as any smart child will tell you, proceeds prism-like from active and intense white.

Although many colors are mentioned in the Bible—black, blue, gold, green, purple, red, and scarlet come to mind—plain white overshadowed them all. Perhaps this focus is so because white was the color of Christ's transfigured clothing (Mark 9:2b-3), of the angels' garments (Matt. 28:3), of that numberless throng mentioned in the vision of John (Rev. 19:7-8). Or perhaps it was so because white held an egalitarian attraction to the early Christians while colors separated ancient people by class and rank.

Clement, an early Christian teacher at Alexandria, wrote that "a white alb is suitable attire for all Christians." Of course he was thinking about the women, men, and children who had been baptized and then clothed in white at the Easter Vigil. Each Sunday of the Easter season, the newly baptized would wear their white robes to the liturgy and lead the assembly to the altar for the eucharistic meal, a striking and enduring sign of baptism's prominence in the early Christian community. In one of his Easter sermons, Cyril of Jerusalem said to the newly baptized, "Now that you have taken off your old garments [in order to be baptized naked] and been clad in white garments, you must also in spirit remain clothed in white. I do not mean that you must always wear white garments," he continues, "but that you should know you are covered with those that are truly white and shining. Then you may say with Isaiah, 'God has covered me with a vestment of joy.'"

In the early church, the practice was not uncommon to bury the dead in a white garment. After all, the funeral liturgy looked much like the baptismal liturgy: the dressing of the dead in white, the presence of the burning paschal candle next to the body, the sprinkling of the deceased and the people with water from the font in remembrance of baptism, and the proclamation of biblical readings that set forth images of a new life flowing from the waters of the font. It would not be difficult to grasp the symmetry between an earthly life begun and ended in a garment of white, a "vestment of joy." One could rightly conclude that this baptized assembly—washed, anointed, clothed, enlightened, welcomed, and fed—clearly was the church.

When baptism was celebrated in the midst of the people, celebrated particularly throughout the Easter season, and celebrated with the fullness of its rich symbolic actions, such celebration left little doubt that one entered into the mystery of the Lord's passover from death to life through baptism. In time, however, baptism was celebrated privately, apart from the assembly, quickly and with minimal activity, a snippet of scripture read, a dab of water placed on the forehead. The great enveloping garment of the baptismal liturgy unraveled into strands.

The white alb—once the garment of all the baptized—was worn now only by the clergy. Did such a practice communicate this meaning: that "the church" was composed essentially of its leaders? Clearly, this mistaken assumption—that the baptized are second-class citizens in the church—troubled Luther. Thus, the great work of promoting the baptismal liturgy and its theology was a recovery of the ancient Christian notion that the church is an active and participatory assembly, fully and consciously attentive to the movement of the Holy Spirit. Who, then, would not want to wear the white alb, "[since you] who were baptized into Christ, have clothed yourselves with Christ" (Gal. 3:27)?

If Lent was the opportunity to signal to passersby that business as usual had been set aside, the fifty days of

Easter present the chance to suggest visually that another season is being kept by this congregation. White or gold weatherproofed cloth hangings or bunting communicate that something different is happening. Keep in mind the concern mentioned earlier, that outdoor hangings—once bright and appealing—can turn dingy and tattered, an unfortunate visual sign. Although we associate wreaths with Advent and Christmas, their use during the Easter season is probably even more appropriate. That is, the wreath is a crown, a victory crown. Use laurel and boxwood in the fashioning of wreaths to be hung on the doors to the church. Some artists will weave thin strands of white or gold ribbon throughout the leaves, the color attracting the eye at some distance.

Some congregations will plant flowers in gray or terra-cotta pots and place these at the entrance doors to the church. If you do this, keep in mind that someone will need to tend to these little gardens on a regular basis. If your congregation has used a large, overhanging wreath during Lent and the Three Days, the Easter season is the time to add more blossoms each week until Pentecost Sunday. In the small and low vases that have been secured to the base of the wreath, add the brighter colored flowers of red or a mixture of red, gold, and white flowers that members have brought from their gardens. You will have a full crown of radiant and variegated color hanging over the people on the final day of the Easter season.

Have you banked the chancel with Easter lilies for the Easter Sunday services? Have they been taken home by parishioners who donated them? If many or a few remain, who will care for them or replace them? What a dreary sight that can be on the third or fourth Sunday of Easter: a few lonely and wilting lilies with leaves turning yellow. As many ancient and contemporary commentators note, one Easter celebration extends throughout the fifty days.

The candle and font should be prominent in the Easter Vigil worship space. By all means, use a new candle each year with the new date properly inscribed. And be sure to use a candle that is proportionate to the size of your space: a large space needs a large candle and a stand of proportionate size and stability. The paschal candle will have a place of prominence either next to the ambo or another location in the chancel throughout the Easter season. After Pentecost the candle will be placed next to the baptismal font.

If the font has a lid, it should be opened or removed for each Sunday of the season and filled with fresh water each week before the people arrive. Here again, consider the old maxim: "out of sight, out of mind." If the font is removed from sight, its central symbolic significance in the Easter season and the baptismal life of the church will be diminished. If the font is at a distance from the people and can be moved, place it where it is accessible to the worshiping assembly, perhaps at a crossing or at the entrance to the worship space. Do you surround the font with lilies and green plants? Be careful not to restrict access, especially for children—you want people to come close and touch the water.

Where a processional cross is used to lead the people or worship leaders into the space, consider the creation of a simple wreath to adorn the cross. If laurel or boxwood is used for outdoor wreaths, use the same for the cross. Another possibility is the creation of a wreath that incorporates small white flowers. Whether or not you use flowers, be attentive to the size of the wreath. It should adorn the cross, rather than dominate. Too many large flowers will draw the eye to the flowers, not the cross.

Try using white or gold hangings in the worship space that are devoid of words. ("Alleluia!" "He is risen!") The principle is rather simple: words properly belong on the lips of worshipers, not on banners. A beautifully textured white, gold, or white and gold hanging will complement the white albs of the worship leaders and white vestments worn by the presiding minister, and therefore be sufficient. On the other hand, white paraments, white vesture, and white flowers would be sufficient to signal that it is a *white* season. Perhaps no other hangings are needed. And speaking of white: pay particular attention to the "shades" of white now sold by vestment-makers and fabric stores. A jarring clash of shades can be distracting.

EASTER

PREACHING with the SEASON

According to one of the creation stories in Genesis, the original home for human beings was a garden. But after the fall, God expelled Adam and Eve from the garden so that they could not eat the fruit of the tree of life and live forever. Throughout the history of the faithful people, there remained a longing for the garden. The prophets anticipated a time coming in the future when the desert all around them would flourish like a blossoming garden. The erotic poem Song of Songs places the lovers in a garden, and Christians during the Middle Ages in particular found this poem a metaphor of what life with God will be like. The book of Revelation, with its visions of the end time, describes a garden inside a city, as if both God's nature and human culture participate in what heaven will be.

With these biblical gardens in mind, we discover that John's gospel describes both Gethsemane, the place of Jesus' betrayal, and the location of Jesus' tomb as gardens. Of course John would do that: see the place of Jesus' death as the site of vibrant life. Thus John's Easter narrative takes place in a garden, with Mary of Magdala even mistaking Jesus as the gardener. It is this garden that we enjoy for the fifty days, leaving finally on Pentecost Sunday to go out preaching to all the ends of the earth.

The readings for the fifty days include both the stories of Jesus' appearances to the disciples and selections from the Johannine discourses. These discourses are particularly intriguing to read during Easter, because the writer of John, although meaning these speeches to be read by the Easter community, puts the words in Jesus' mouth before his death. Thus we recall that the garden we enjoy during these discourses is always also the garden of Jesus' agony. The place of our life is the place of Jesus' death. For the first reading, many Christians read sections from the book of Acts. Here the early Christians, especially Peter and Paul, are able to live extraordinary lives of power and mission because the Spirit of the risen Christ is in them. It is as if for Luke the accounts of the early church are an extended resurrection narrative, Christ alive again in the world doing wonders.

While we are in the garden, we sing hymns penned throughout the Christian centuries. With Fortunatus from the sixth century we sing of "all the fair beauty of the earth." With John of Damascus from the eighth century, we laud this "queen of seasons." In an eleventh-century chant, we recall Mary in the garden with Christ. With Martin Luther we praise Christ as "the sun that warms and lights us." Charles Wesley in the eighteenth century reminds us that "the sun's eclipse is o'er." The twentieth-century hymn "Now the green blade rises" addresses honestly those times when "our hearts are wintry, grieving or in pain." These songs help us to celebrate the springtime of the resurrection.

We want to plan out the fifty days so that Easter keeps on going. Perhaps it means less of a blowout on the first day of Easter so that there are some trumpets and flowers left over to accompany us all seven weeks. Singing "Jesus Christ is risen today" halfway through the season is a happy reminder that Easter is not a single event long ago recalled once a year. Rather, Easter is a fifty-day celebration; it is also the weekly celebration of meeting Christ in the breaking of the bread; it is also the daily "dying and rising" of each baptized Christian. The season concludes with Pentecost and the story of the tongues of fire, Luke's way to say what John said of Easter evening: that Christ gives to the community of believers the Spirit of his resurrected body. Christ is now alive in us.

While the church is enjoying the garden, so is the natural world. During these seven weeks the Northern Hemisphere has been adorned with forsythia, crocuses, daffodils, tulips, azaleas, dogwood, flowering fruit trees, and, finally, roses. The spring processes by us in one bunch of flowers after another. Days are warming, days are lengthening. People are beginning to move outside, to plan their own gardens, to tend their yards, to eat out on the patio, to pack away winter clothes. Rushing the season as always, the stores are displaying swimsuits. It is as if the natural and secular worlds are celebrating God's garden without realizing it.

But the fifty days do not ensure seven weeks of bliss for all the faithful. Sorrow will come, disappointment arrives. No security guard is posted at the garden gates to keep death out. Herein lies yet another reason that we want Easter to last fifty days. Most folk can get all excited one to two days each year, don new clothes, and enjoy the music. But we can't keep up such glee for fifty days. John's gospel knows it, and helps us by placing both Jesus' agony and his resurrection in a garden. Many Christians will have some of these fifty days that are not at all a "Good Morning!" But the hope is that each of the fifty days will be marked by "The Lord be with you," the risen Christ in each of us and within the community. In spite of every sin and sorrow, we practice the joy of the resurrection. Even in the midst of the woods, we recognize the garden, and we practice pointing out to each other the tree of life.

The fifty days are, in Greek, the *pentekost* (*pentecost* means "fifty"). In the Jewish tradition, the period extended from the beginning of the barley harvest, which marked the Passover, until the final harvesting was complete. Celebrating this same period from a Christian perspective happened early. We have evidence in the Acts of Paul (an early Christian text from about the year 100) that the fifty days were marked by no weeping, no kneeling, and no penitential acts. Irenaeus and Tertullian refer to the time as a time of rejoicing. Tertullian compares Sunday to the meaning of the fifty days. By the year 300 the fiftieth day begins to take on special importance and to separate itself from the other fifty days (Council of Elvira). The fiftieth day had two meanings: it represented the ascension and the gift of the Spirit, and it also represented the gift of the Spirit alone. By the 380s the latter was the focus of the fiftieth day.

The church today considers the entire time as a single celebration of Easter. They are the Sundays *of* Easter, not the Sundays after Easter. Each Sunday celebrates the resurrection, the appearances, acknowledgment of Jesus' lordship, the community's experience of the risen Lord, Christ's mission to the disciples, and the promise of the Spirit. Like Epiphany, Easter is revelation and appropriation at the same time. Jesus initiates these things, but we as the community are called to acknowledge them by faith and worship.

In the early church, preachers spoke on the meaning of the baptism and eucharist (celebrated at the Easter Vigil) on the Sundays and weekday liturgies during the fifty days. This purposely focused preaching, on the sacraments or—as they were called among Greek Christians—the mysteries of Christ, so as to reveal Christ in these actions for the worshiping assembly.

THE LECTIONARY FOR THE FIFTY DAYS

An ancient tradition replaces the Hebrew scriptures for Easter with readings from the Acts of the Apostles. Recent lectionary revisions have also included large sections of John's gospel. The sections selected from Acts have two themes: the early preaching and the mission beyond Judaism and Palestine. On the second Sunday we are told that the entire community is united in its testimony to the resurrection (Acts 4:32-35). The third Sunday represents the earliest preaching, a stylized presentation of Jesus' death, resurrection, and the invitation to faith (Acts 3:12-19). It is found in numerous places in Acts and seems to be the community's common memory, which is not totally free of anger at Jesus' dying: The God of Abraham has glorified his servant whom you handed over. You put to death the Author of life.

God raised him from the dead. We are witnesses of this saving action. Therefore reform your lives. Turn to God that your sins may be wiped away.

This early preaching, or kerygma, is extended on the fourth Sunday (Acts 4:5-12). On the fifth, sixth, and seventh Sundays, Acts shows us that the Spirit chooses people beyond Judaism: Philip of Ethiopia (Acts 8:26-40), Cornelius (Acts 10:44-48), and the choice of Matthias (Acts 1:15-17, 21-26).

The readings immerse us in our relationships with one another. That relationship is based in love and is familial: we are brothers and sisters to one another. In any other context these sentiments seem reasonable, but in the context of the resurrection more is being said about the destiny of the new humanity. The baptism at Easter constitutes a new humanity in which all the old divisions no longer hold true. The community of believers are one. It means more than simply being nice to one another. The risen body of Christ manifest in the community is the first gift of the resurrection and the beginning of the new age. So we must hear these texts with resurrection ears.

The reading on the second Sunday presents life made visible and God's visitation as light in which we are called to walk. It is like the dawning of a new day at creation's pure edge. On the third Sunday we are called children of God (1 John 3:1-7). On the fourth Sunday one's life is given in love for our brother/sister (1 John 3:16-24). This same basis in love is continued on the following Sunday (1 John 4:7-21) and summarized by becoming God's children on the sixth Sunday (1 John 5:1-6). All in all, we need to take stock, not merely of our relationships, but of the new humanity that Easter presents to us.

The gospel passages for the Easter season are about Jesus' risen life and relationship with the community. On the second and third Sundays the greeting, "Peace be with you," is given. This greeting is used almost exclusively in the scriptures for a post-resurrectional greeting on the lips of Jesus. Peace in this context is more than a lack of conflict; it represents the wholeness achieved in spite of conflict. Jesus identifies himself and the risen life with peace.

The greeting of peace occurs within an appearance before the assembled disciples. That appearance is part of a tradition of appearances structured with similar content. We should note the form and content. The resurrection appearance is always at Jesus' initiative. He wills it, not the disciples. It is met by both confusion and recognition. Recognition often comes through familiar signs such as the breaking of the bread or eating. Recognition is accompanied by acknowledgment of Jesus' lordship and often an act of worship such as bowing low. That appearance also includes a mission given by Jesus, the promise of the Spirit, and a pledge of remaining with the community. Taken together, the appearances represent Jesus' post-resurrection life, and they constitute belief that extends to us, since we too live in the post-resurrectional era.

The fourth, fifth, sixth, and seventh Sundays come from John and present images of Jesus as the good shepherd, the true vine, the giver of the commandment of love. The fifty days end with John 17:6-19, Jesus' prayer for the continued faith of the disciples.

Taken together the Sundays of Easter present us with not only a manifestation of Jesus, the risen one, but a vocation of the disciples to remain in love. What more could we ask in the festive time?

The fiftieth day, Pentecost, uses the traditional reading of Acts 2:1-21 about the citizens gathered in Jerusalem to hear Peter in their own tongue. It is a marvelous vision of the breadth of the good news and of its fruitfulness. The Romans passage (8:22-27) speaks about creation's groaning until redemption is complete. It is one of the few scripture passages that extends redemption beyond humanity. All creation is restored by Christ's death and resurrection. The Spirit is a witness of this restoration. The gospel (John 15:26-27) proclaims an Advocate who will be Christ's witness, and we too must take up the same vocation.

SHAPE OF WORSHIP FOR THE SEASON

BASIC SHAPE OF THE EUCHARISTIC RITE IN EASTER

- Confession and Forgiveness: see alternate worship text for Easter in *Sundays and Seasons*

GATHERING

- Greeting: see alternate worship text for Easter in *Sundays and Seasons*
- Use the Kyrie throughout Easter
- Use the hymn of praise throughout Easter ("Worthy is Christ")

WORD

- Use the Nicene Creed
- The prayers: see alternate forms and responses for Easter in *Sundays and Seasons*

BAPTISM

- Consider observing Pentecost Day (June 11) as a baptismal festival

MEAL

- Offertory prayer: see alternate worship text for Easter in *Sundays and Seasons*
- Use the proper preface for Easter (see *LBW* Ministers edition and *WOV* Leaders edition for each musical setting of the liturgy); use proper preface for Pentecost on Pentecost Day
- Eucharistic Prayer: *LBW* prayer II is especially fitting during the fifty days; see also "Eucharistic Prayer E: The Season of Easter" in *WOV* Leaders edition, p. 69; and "Eucharistic Prayer F: The Day of Pentecost" in *WOV* Leaders edition, p. 70
- Invitation to communion: see alternate worship text for Easter in *Sundays and Seasons*
- Post-communion prayer: see alternate worship text for Easter in *Sundays and Seasons*

SENDING

- Benediction: see alternate worship text for Easter in *Sundays and Seasons*
- Dismissal: see alternate worship text for Easter in *Sundays and Seasons*

OTHER SEASONAL POSSIBILITIES

BLESSING OF FIELDS AND GARDENS

- See seasonal rites section. May be used to conclude worship on the sixth Sunday of Easter, or at another time when such a blessing is appropriate.

VIGIL OF PENTECOST

- A celebration for this evening could be modeled on the Easter Vigil, but using these elements:
  - Service of Light (from *LBW*, pp. 142–44)
  - Service of Word (from the prayer of the day through the hymn of the day)
  - Service of Baptismal Affirmation (from *LBW*, pp. 199–201, with the congregation gathering around the font, space permitting; water may be sprinkled from the font during the recitation of the creed)
  - Service of Communion (from the offering through the dismissal)
- Consider using the Affirmation of the Vocation of the Baptized in the World on Pentecost Day, from *Welcome to Christ: Lutheran Rites for the Catechumenate*

EASTER

ASSEMBLY SONG FOR THE SEASON

As trees and flowers unfold their beauty during this time, so the fifty days are a time for unfolding the packed richness of the resurrection event. Likewise, it takes a week of weeks to let the song of Easter truly flower.

GATHERING

Choose service music that lends itself best in your context to festive elaboration, and adorn it in various ways across the seven weeks through Pentecost. If the congregation is looking for a new challenge, several new settings of "This is the feast of victory" are available in *This Far by Faith* and *Worship & Praise*. If the context calls for a briefer gathering rite, a more extended setting of this canticle (such as *LBW* setting 1) may be sufficient for the entrance, followed by greeting and prayer of the day. A hymn that sounds the same Revelation themes (such as "Blessing and honor," LBW 525) can work in the same way. Another way to elevate the service music is to chant the greeting, salutation, prayer of the day, and benediction.

WORD

One or two alleluias at the gospel acclamation seem stingy during Eastertide. At least for these weeks, find an alternative to the standard "Lord, to whom shall we go?"—one with more chances to sing this glorious Easter word. Among the options: the Caribbean "Halle, halle, hallelujah" (WOV 612); the alleluias connected to "The strife is o'er" (LBW 135) or "Good Christian friends, rejoice and sing" (LBW 144); two dancelike settings of "¡Aleluya!" (LLC 204, 205—you *can* sing this word in Spanish!). For further elaboration, the proper verse for each week may be inserted between two singings of the alleluias.

MEAL

Don't let the gospel be the only occasion for singing alleluia. The acclamations listed above and others like them can be used effectively as travelling music during the movement of people in communion procession. What better time for people to approach the table with a little spring in their step, and hands free to clap! Or, sing an Easter hymn that works with a random peal of bells—and send each ringer down the aisle to communion with a bell in hand, to infuse the assembly with the sound.

SENDING

This may be the one season to double up an exuberant and brief "Thank the Lord/Thankful hearts" postcommunion song with another sending hymn just prior to the dismissal (or after the dismissal if the people sing while walking out).

MUSIC FOR THE SEASON

VERSE AND OFFERTORY

Cherwien, David. *Verses for Ascension, Pentecost, and Trinity.*
MSM 80-540. U, org.

Pelz, Walter L. *Verses and Offertories, Easter–The Holy Trinity.*
AFP 11-9546.

Verses and Offertory Sentences, Part V: Vigil of Pentecost thru Pentecost 9.
CPH 97-5505. U/2 pt. 97-5510. Acc ed.

CHORAL MUSIC FOR THE SEASON

Bach, J. S. "Alleluia" in *Motet, No. 6.* "Lobet den herrn."
Broude AB 1054. SATB.

Fleming, Larry L. "Lord of the Dance." AFP 11-10705. SATB.

Hallock, Peter. "Phoenix." ION CH-1001. SATB, hp, vc, org.

Kaplan, Abraham. "Halleluya." Hansen House C811. SATB, marimba, xyl orch bells, drm set, temple blocks, DB.

Kimberling, Clark. "This Easter Morn." GIA G-4374. SATB, org.

Kosche, Kenneth T. "Ignite My Heart O Holy Flame." GIA G-4077. SATB, org.

Larkin, Michael. "O Sons and Daughters." MSM 50-4034. SA(T)B, kybd.

Leavitt, John. "Easter." AFP 11-4513; choral, pno. 11-4514; complete. 11-4515; inst pts.

Schutte, Daniel L. "Sing a New Song." HOP A-718. SATB, kybd.

Shute, Linda. "This Joyful Eastertide." AFP 11-10750. 2 pt mxd, desc, 5 oct hb, perc, kybd.

CHILDREN'S CHORAL MUSIC FOR THE SEASON

Proulx, Richard. "Easter Carol." GIA G-4465. U/2 pt, fl, kybd.

Running, Joseph. "An Easter Carol." MSM 50-4751. U, kybd.

McRae, Shirley W. "Now the Green Blade Rises." CG CGA795. 2 pt, fl, 2 oct hb, kybd.

Schulz-Widmar, Russell. "The Royal Banners of Our King." GIA G-4366. U, org.

Telemann/arr. Conlon. "Come, Enjoy God's Festive Springtime." AFP 11-2443. U, vln, kybd.

Christopherson, Dorothy. "Nature Sings in Celebration." AFP 11-10547. 2 pt trbl, kybd, rec/fl.

INSTRUMENTAL MUSIC FOR THE SEASON

Haan, Raymond. "Upp, Min Tunga" in *Four Hymns of Rejoicing.* MSM 10-518. Org.

Handel, G. F. "The Rejoicing/La Rejouissance" in *Music for a Celebration, Set I.* MSM 10-940. Org.

Hannahs, Roger C. "Carillon on 'He Is Risen.'" HWG GSTC9814. Org.

McCabe, Michael. "Fanfares and Flourishes." AMSI OR-4. Org.

Meyer, Lawrence J. "Processional of Joy." AFP 11-10797. Pno or org.

Powell, Robert J. "Easter Sonata for Flute and Organ." CPH 97-6472. Org, fl.

Waters, Kevin. "Fantasy on 'Jesus Christ Is Risen Today.'" MSM 10-417. Org.

Wetzler, Robert. "Death to Life." AMSI B-5. Brass, org.

Willcocks, David. "Variations on 'Breslau'" (We Sing the Praise of Him Who Died). OXF. Org.

HANDBELL MUSIC FOR THE SEASON

Campra, A./arr. Martha L. Thompson. "Rigaudon." HOP 1234. 3-5 oct.

Dobrinski, Cynthia. "Exuberant Praise." CG CGB66. 3 oct.

Larson/Various. *Easter Resonance.* CPH 97-6624. 2-3 oct.

Semann, Barbara. *Processionals for the Time of Easter.* CPH 97-6523. 3 oct.

Sleeth, Natalie/arr. Martha L. Thompson. "Joy in the Morning." HOP 1973. 3-5 oct, opt ch.

Thompson, M. L. "The Morning Trumpet." HOP 1937. 3-5 oct.

Tucker, Sondra. "Halle, Halle, Halle." HOP 1985. 3-5 oct, perc.

EASTER

ALTERNATE WORSHIP TEXTS

CONFESSION AND FORGIVENESS
In the name of the Father, and of the ✠ Son,
and of the Holy Spirit.
Amen

By our baptism into the death and resurrection of Christ,
God has raised us to new life.
Let us confess to God our sins
and all that waits for resurrection in our lives.
Silence for reflection and self-examination.

God of love,
in our failure to keep your commandments
we have clung to the old life of sin within us.
We have not loved you with all our heart,
nor have we loved our neighbors as ourselves.
Free us from the power of sin,
guide us by your Spirit,
and help us in our weakness,
that we may live as your children,
restored to new life. Amen

By God's grace you are forgiven and born anew.
May you be strengthened daily with the power
to walk in God's light and love.
Amen

GREETING
Alleluia! Christ is risen.
Christ is risen indeed. Alleluia!
The grace of our Lord Jesus Christ, the love of God,
and the communion of the Holy Spirit be with you all.
And also with you.

PRAYERS
Standing in the glorious light of the resurrection, let us pray for Christ's church, the world, and all who wait for the Spirit's revealing power.

A brief silence.

Each petition ends:
We pray to the Lord:
Lord, hear our prayer.

For Pentecost, each petition ends:
We pray:
Come, Holy Spirit.

Concluding petition
Gracious God, hear our prayers and receive them for the sake of the crucified and risen one, our Savior Jesus Christ.
Amen

OFFERTORY PRAYER
Living God,
**in Christ's resurrection you have raised up
new life for the world.
Receive what we offer,
that others might have life
through the gifts you have entrusted to us
to use and share. Amen**

INVITATION TO COMMUNION
This is the bread
that comes down from heaven
and gives life to the world.
Whoever eats this bread will live forever.

POST-COMMUNION PRAYER
O God of love,
you bind us to yourself in this sacrament,
and strengthen us through this meal
for service to the world.
Guide us by your Spirit
that we may forever witness to the name
of Jesus Christ, Lord of life.
Amen

BENEDICTION
May almighty God, who has raised Christ from death to life,
bring forth in you the fruits of the Holy Spirit.
Amen

DISMISSAL
Alleluia! Go and tell the news that Christ is risen.
Christ is risen indeed. Alleluia!

Permission is granted for congregations to reproduce the Alternate Worship Texts, provided copies are for local use only and the following copyright notice appears: From *Sundays & Seasons*, copyright © 1999 Augsburg Fortress. May be reproduced by permission for use only between November 28, 1999 and December 2, 2000.

SEASONAL RITES

EASTER HYMN FESTIVAL

PRELUDE
Reading from Exodus 15:1-11
Hymn: Come, you faithful, raise the strain (LBW 132)
Stanzas: 1-all; 2-women; 3-all; 4-men; 5-all

GREETING

READINGS
Reading from Leo the Great ("But it is not only the martyrs who share in his passion"), from "The Liturgy of the Hours," as printed in *An Easter Sourcebook: The Fifty Days*, Chicago: Liturgy Training Publications, 1988, p. 38
Hymn: I'll Praise My Maker (H82 429; text and tune line may be reproduced from this source)
Stanzas: 1-all; 2-women, men join at "whose truth forever..."; 3-men, women join at "he helps the stranger..."; 4-all
Hymn: Praise the Almighty (LBW 539)
Stanzas: 1-all; 2-women; 3-men; 4-all

Reading from the Orthodox Liturgy for Easter Sunday, as printed in *A Triduum Sourcebook*, Chicago: Liturgy Training Publications, 1983, p. 157
Hymn: The day of resurrection! (LBW 141)
Stanzas: 1-all; 2-men; 3-women; 4-all

Reading from Jonah 2:1-10
Hymn: Shout for joy loud and long (WOV 793)
Stanzas: 1-all; 2-women; 3-men; 4-all

Reading from Balthasar Fischer, "It Is an Unusual Word" from *Signs, Words, and Gestures*, as printed in *An Easter Sourcebook*, pp. 17–18.
Hymn: Good Christian friends, rejoice and sing! (LBW 144)
Stanzas: 1-all; 2-men; 3-women; 4-all

Reading from Brian Wren, "Lord God, Your Love" as printed in *An Easter Sourcebook*, p. 48
Hymn: My life flows on in endless song (WOV 781)
Stanzas: 1-all; 2-women; 3-men; 4-all

Reading from Richard Baxter, "Ye Holy Angels Bright", hymn 409 in *Service Book and Hymnal*
Hymn: The God of Abraham praise (LBW 544)
Stanzas: 1-all; 3-women; 9-all; 10-men; 11-all

Reading from 1 Corinthians 15:50-57
Hymn: With high delight let us unite (LBW 140)
Stanzas: 1-all; 2-women; 3-all

OFFERING

Hymn: Christ has arisen, alleluia (WOV 678)
Stanzas: Refrain-all; 1-all; 2-men; 3-women; 4-all; 5-all

PRAYERS

BLESSING
Hymn: Now all the vault of heaven resounds (LBW 143)
Stanzas: 1-all; 2-men; 3-women; 4-all

BLESSING OF FIELDS AND GARDENS

Let us bless God, the creator of all things. God has given us the earth to cultivate, so that we might receive the bounty of its fruits. Just as the rain falls from heaven and waters the earth, bringing forth vegetation, so God's Word will flourish and will not return empty.

READING
Genesis 1:1, 11-12, 29-31

PRAYER
Almighty God, we thank you for making the earth fruitful,
so that it might produce what is needed for life.
Bless those who work in the fields;
give us seasonable weather;
and grant that we may all share the fruits of the earth,
rejoicing in your goodness;
through Jesus Christ our Lord.
Amen

HYMN
LBW 409   Praise and thanksgiving
LBW 563   For the fruit of all creation
WOV 760   For the fruit of all creation

TUESDAY, APRIL 25
ST. MARK, EVANGELIST

Mark, though not an apostle, was likely a member of one of the early Christian communities. The gospel attributed to Mark is brief and direct, and is considered by many to be the first gospel. Because of its emphasis on the suffering of Christ, it is sometimes called a "passion narrative with a long introduction." The Gospel of Mark also challenges the reader to share in Jesus' sufferings. Mark was martyred in Alexandria. His symbol is the winged lion.

As you reflect upon the reading of the passion according to Mark on Passion (Palm) Sunday, consider the possibility that the whole gospel may have been originally organized around a Holy Week observance, and that its structure comes from that celebration.

SATURDAY, APRIL 29
CATHERINE OF SIENA, TEACHER, 1380

Catherine is honored for her service to the church as a political negotiator, a mystic, a reformer, and a minister to the imprisoned and the poor. Though known for her visions of Jesus and for mystical ecstasy, Catherine was also considered a down-to-earth woman. Her most famous writing is *The Dialogue*, a series of conversations between Catherine and the Holy Trinity in which she uses vivid imagery to interpret the life of the Christian, the church, and the ministry. Among Roman Catholics, she is recognized as the first woman to receive the title "Doctor of the Church."

Catherine experienced deep union with Christ and had a significant impact on the public life of her day. Name others who lived a contemplative life while making important contributions to society.

APRIL 30, 2000
SECOND SUNDAY OF EASTER

INTRODUCTION

In the waters of baptism, God raises us up in Jesus and gives us life that endures. Though we do not see him in the flesh, he continues to reveal himself to us in the breaking of the bread, our foretaste of the feast to come. Day by day, we pray that God would strengthen our faith, so that we who have not seen Christ Jesus may truly confess him as our Lord and God.

PRAYER OF THE DAY

Almighty God, with joy we celebrate the festival of our Lord's resurrection. Graciously help us to show the power of the resurrection in all that we say and do; through your Son, Jesus Christ our Lord, who lives and reigns with you and the Holy Spirit, one God, now and forever.

READINGS

Acts 4:32-35

In today's reading, the church glimpses the life of the first Christian community. Here the author of Acts describes the social dimension of Christian life. Animated by the Spirit of the risen Lord, the body of Christ cares for those in need and holds all things in common.

Psalm 133

How good and pleasant it is to live together in unity. (Ps. 133:1)

1 John 1:1—2:2

This letter of John begins with poetic testimony to Jesus as the word of life. Through him we have firsthand experience of God and know for certain that God loves us and forgives us our sin.

John 20:19-31

The story of Easter continues as the risen Lord appears to his disciples. His words to Thomas offer a blessing to all who entrust themselves in faith to the risen Lord.

COLOR White

THE PRAYERS

Standing in the glorious light of the resurrection, let us pray for Christ's church, the world, and all who wait for the Spirit's revealing power.
SILENCE IS KEPT.
Let us pray that God's gifts of word and sacraments would bring deeper unity among those who celebrate Christ's Easter victory. We pray to the Lord:
Lord, hear our prayer.
Let us pray that the joy of the resurrection would create a world in which those in need will not be forsaken and the resources of all people will be distributed fairly and honestly. We pray to the Lord:
Lord, hear our prayer.
Let us pray that the joy of the resurrection would bestow grace upon all who, like Thomas, are full of doubts and questions, that they might be given a trusting and believing heart. We pray to the Lord:
Lord, hear our prayer.
Let us pray that the joy of the resurrection would bring complete healing to those who struggle with illness (especially . . .). May all who are in pain be touched with the peace from God. We pray to the Lord:
Lord, hear our prayer.
Let us pray that the joy of the resurrection would sustain all who have been newly baptized and those who have renewed their baptism. May inquirers continue to be drawn to the joy of this faith community. We pray to the Lord:
Lord, hear our prayer.
HERE OTHER INTERCESSIONS MAY BE OFFERED.
Let us pray that the joy of the resurrection would cross the boundaries of time and eternity, so that all who are in grief may know the hope of the new creation. We pray to the Lord:
Lord, hear our prayer.
Gracious God, hear our prayers and receive them for the sake of the crucified and risen one, our Savior Jesus Christ.
Amen

IMAGES FOR PREACHING

The Easter theme of replacement—a kind of "now you see it, now you don't" that permeates Mark's account of the resurrection—is continued in the traditional gospel for the second Sunday of Easter. The setting sounds as though it might have been borrowed from a murder mystery: ten men in a locked room; once they had numbered thirteen, but now two were dead and one was missing. Darkness falls. It seems only a matter of time before the rest of them will meet with similar fates. But the power of Easter is also present. The story does not go on as they expect.

Despite the locks, despite the darkness, despite the fear, Jesus takes his place once more there among them. He speaks his peace upon them, casting out their fear. He shows the wounds that killed him, even as he stands in their presence and breathes new life and the Holy Spirit upon them. He tells them they will be sent in his place.

During this encounter, Thomas was missing. (He was, literally, out of place.) For him, no certainty exists outside his own experience, but a week later he too encounters the risen Christ. The disciples' fellowship that had been broken by death is restored. In the house where the disciples had been staying, the doors that had been locked are now merely shut. Jesus' appearance transforms what was a prison into a sanctuary and a shelter, the inhabitants are changed from fugitives to evangelists. Starting with a handful of people, the world is about to change.

WORSHIP MATTERS

Acts 4 records that property was distributed to all who had need. In the early church, Christians brought food to the altar as their offering, some of which was used for the Lord's supper. The rest was distributed among those in need. Today a portion of our tithes and offerings is designated as benevolence that goes to ministries that help those who are hungry and in need in our community, nation, and world.

Use this opportunity to hold up benevolent ministries that are particularly significant to your congregation. Show how your congregation's offerings help those in need and feed those who are hungry, bringing new life to those most in need today.

LET THE CHILDREN COME

The gesture of the presiding minister for sharing the peace extends the hands and arms to show the wounds of the Crucified. Remind the children that what we are doing is sharing Jesus' peace with others. Discourage extraneous conversation during the sharing of the peace so that they can hear and be heard as they say, "Peace be with you."

MUSIC FOR WORSHIP
GATHERING

LBW 189	We know that Christ is raised
WOV 672	Christ is risen! Shout hosanna!

PSALM 133

Hopson, Hal H. "Psalm 133" in TP.
Young, Jeremy. PW, cycle B.

GS2 21	Miren qué bueno/Behold, how pleasant
LLC 475	Mirad cuán bueno/Behold, how good and delightful

HYMN OF THE DAY

LBW 139	O sons and daughters of the King
	O FILII ET FILIAE

VOCAL RESOURCES

Wolff, Drummond. "O Sons and Daughters of the King." CPH 98-2583. SATB, kybd, tpts, cong.

INSTRUMENTAL RESOURCES

Burkhardt, Michael. "O Sons and Daughters of the King" in *Five Easter Season Hymn Improvisations, set 2*. MSM 10-412. Org.

Callahan, Charles. "O filii et filiae" in *Easter Music for Manuals*. MSM 10-408. Kybd.

Schalk, Carl. "O filii et filiae" in *Festival Hymn Settings for the Small Parish*. CPH 97-5828. Org, inst.

Uhl, Dan. "O filii et filiae" in *Easter Suite for Trumpet, Organ and Optional Timpani*. AFP 11-10692. Org, tpt, opt perc.

ALTERNATE HYMN OF THE DAY

WOV 649	I want to walk as a child of the light
LBW 132	Come, you faithful, raise the strain

COMMUNION

LBW 215	O Lord, we praise you
WOV 703	Draw us in the Spirit's tether

SENDING

LBW 145	Thine is the glory
WOV 774	Dona nobis pacem

ADDITIONAL HYMNS AND SONGS

OBS 54	Day of arising
H82 465/6	Eternal light, shine in my heart
NCH 54	These things did Thomas count as real
TFF 63	We are marching in the light of God
W&P	Come and see

MUSIC FOR THE DAY
CHORAL

Billings, William. "The Lord Is Risen Indeed." CPH 98-3273. SATB.

Cherwien, David. "Blessing Be and Glory to the Living One." AFP 11-10918. U/2 pt, org, 2 C inst.

Handl, Jakob, "Stetit Iesus" (There Came Jesus). GIA G-2460. SATB.

Marenzio, Luca. "Quia Vidisti Me, Thoma" (Because You Have Seen Me, Thomas). CPH 98-2617. SATB. Lat/Eng.

Proulx, Richard. "Easter Carol." GIA G-4465. 2 pt, fl, kybd. G-4465INST. Fl pt.

CHILDREN'S CHOIRS

Cox, Joe and Jody Lindh. "Jesus, Son of God Most High." CG CGA377. U, opt desc, pno, fl, gtr, bass.

Reilly, Dadee. "Resurrection." AFP 11-2370. 2 pt, kybd, opt rhythm bells.

KEYBOARD/INSTRUMENTAL

Bedard, Denis. "Meditation sur 'O filii et filiae.'" Editions Cheldar. Org.

Fedak, Alfred V. "O Sons and Daughters" in *A Collection of Hymns*. CLP DM9601. Org.

Hopson, Hal H. "Processional in C." HOP 345. Org, opt tpt.

HANDBELL

Lange, Kinley. "Peaceful Reverie." Ring Out! 920201703. 3 oct.

PRAISE ENSEMBLE

Grant, Amy and Wes King. "Salt and Light" in *Songs from the Loft*. WRD.

Harris, Margaret J. "I Will Praise Him" in *Hosanna! Music Songbook vol. 6*. INT HMSB06.

Pote, Allen. "Many Gifts, One Spirit." Coral Key Music 392-41417. SAB, kybd. Also available: 392-41388, SATB; 392-41466, SSA.

Smith, Gary Alan. "Peace I Leave with You." ABI 02742-X. SATB, pno.

Zschech, Darlene. "Walking in the Light" in *God Is in the House*. MAR.

MONDAY, MAY 1
ST. PHILIP AND ST. JAMES, APOSTLES

Philip was one of the first disciples of Jesus, who after following Jesus invited Nathaniel to "come and see." According to tradition, he preached in Asia Minor and died as a martyr in Phrygia. James, the son of Alphaeus, is called "the less" to distinguish him from another apostle named James, commemorated on July 25.

Their invitation to "come and see" is at the heart of the catechumenate. How has your community invited others to come and see? Are you using the principles of the catechumenate? (See the set of resources titled *Welcome to Christ*.)

TUESDAY, MAY 2
ATHANASIUS, BISHOP OF ALEXANDRIA, 373

Athanasius attended the Council of Nicaea in 325, where as a deacon he defended the divinity of Christ. From that time on he was a defender of Christian orthodoxy against the heresy of Arianism. He was Bishop of Alexandria for forty-five years, and because his enemies accused him of a variety of crimes, he lived in constant danger of death.

Though Athanasius did not write the Athanasian Creed, it was named for him and incorporates his ideas. Because it is one of the three great ecumenical creeds, today would be an appropriate day to recite the Athanasian Creed (*LBW*, p. 54).

THURSDAY, MAY 4
MONICA, MOTHER OF AUGUSTINE, 387

Monica is remembered as the mother of Augustine who prayed fervently for his conversion. Monica was a disciple of Ambrose, and eventually Augustine came under his influence, turning from his wayward life and becoming baptized. In his Confessions, Augustine writes tenderly of his mother and her dying wish to be remembered at the altar of the Lord. He speaks of her "truly pious way of life, her zeal in good works, and her faithfulness in worship."

Any parent would do well to ponder these qualities. We sometimes hear today, "I'll let my children decide if they want to be Christians on their own." Is it faithful to assume children will find their own way to God when they are old enough, without the guiding example of others?

MAY 7, 2000

THIRD SUNDAY OF EASTER

INTRODUCTION

The church gathers in the power of the risen Lord. Here in this assembly made holy by its consecration in baptism, Christ opens the scriptures and reveals himself to us. Gathered at his table as the bread is broken, we see that his life has been broken for us, so that our broken lives might be healed. From the table of the word and the table of the eucharist, Christ feeds us with his love and abundant mercy.

PRAYER OF THE DAY

O God, by the humiliation of your Son you lifted up this fallen world, rescuing us from the hopelessness of death. Grant your faithful people a share in the joys that are eternal; through your Son, Jesus Christ our Lord, who lives and reigns with you and the Holy Spirit, one God, now and forever.

READINGS

Acts 3:12-19

Peter testifies to the Easter faith, proclaiming that Christ's resurrection fulfills the promises of God and brings blessing even to those who killed him.

Psalm 4

The LORD does wonders for the faithful. (Ps. 4:3)

1 John 3:1-7

The First Letter of John encourages Christians to abide in Christ so that God's love will be found in them. The baptized are children of God in Christ. To be a child of God is to have a mission: to offer God's love in a world of conflict.

Luke 24:36b-48

In this account of an appearance after his resurrection, Jesus opens the minds of the disciples to understand him as Messiah. Jesus convinces the disciples that he has been raised, and sends them on a mission to proclaim the message of repentance and forgiveness.

COLOR White

THE PRAYERS

Standing in the glorious light of the resurrection, let us pray for Christ's church, the world, and all who wait for the Spirit's revealing power.

SILENCE IS KEPT.

God of peace, your presence calms our fears and terrors. Give all the baptized such a boldness in faith and proclamation that many will have their minds opened to understand and experience your love. We pray to the Lord:

Lord, hear our prayer.

God of life, grant your wisdom to all who are in positions of power and authority across the world as they guide the peoples of all nations. We pray to the Lord:

Lord, hear our prayer.

God of compassion, grant to all who are facing surgery or medical treatments a generous measure of peace in mind and heart. Touch the sick with your tenderness (especially . . .), that they may be reassured of your love. We pray to the Lord:

Lord, hear our prayer.

God of strength, empower the youth ministry of this congregation and of the whole church, that young people will hear and be kept firmly in the joy and freedom of the gospel. We pray to the Lord:

Lord, hear our prayer.

HERE OTHER INTERCESSIONS MAY BE OFFERED.

God of comfort, you promise that one day we shall see you as you are. Until that day, keep us united in the communion of saints with all who have died and who rest peacefully in you. We pray to the Lord:

Lord, hear our prayer.

Gracious God, hear our prayers and receive them for the sake of the crucified and risen one, our Savior Jesus Christ.

Amen

IMAGES FOR PREACHING

In this year of Mark, we borrow from Luke's account for this Sunday's gospel. In it is a repetition of the feelings of the disciples' fear and uncertainty, which is useful for all those who never hear the gospel for the second Sunday of Easter. Once again Jesus shows his wounds and shares a meal with his disciples. Peace is shared among them as well, and something more.

For the first time, Jesus opens their minds to understand the scriptures. For the first time, the disciples' confusion with the law, the prophets, and the psalms is replaced by a clarity that comes only through the light of the Messiah's suffering, death, and resurrection. Indeed, what Jesus tells them is that his followers can understand scripture properly *only* with the knowledge of Easter and the events leading to it. It must have been a word of grace to a group so frequently confused or mistaken about his meaning. Easter changes everything. Former things, past mistakes, wrongs, and hurts are forgiven.

For this reason, the gospel for the day is nothing less than an invitation to a new world order. The disciples (and we) are invited, called, and welcomed into a new creation, and it will be their (and our) task to share this invitation with the rest of the world, beginning always with the Easter story.

WORSHIP MATTERS

"Peace be with you." When we exchange the peace, we share the gift of Christ's resurrection, just as Jesus shared the gift of his peace with the disciples, restoring them to life. In the word of peace and the touch that accompanies it, we too receive the resurrected Christ and we are at peace. We touch and are touched by Christ, celebrating the victory of his resurrection in our very own flesh. When we receive the peace, we who know ourselves to be frightened, flawed, failing followers are touched by Christ in the flesh of one another, and in the words "Peace be with you," we are assured of Christ's life, love, presence, power, and promise. When we say "Peace be with you" and offer our hand or hug or kiss, Christ is in our flesh as we bestow and proclaim the resurrection to another.

LET THE CHILDREN COME

Christian children are doubly blessed: they are children of the world by birth and inherit the world's goods, and they are children of God by baptism and inherit heaven's goods. Children not only inherit, but they are also given the opportunity to serve. If your congregation takes Easter flowers to the homebound, or does some other service project, give children a chance to share that joy.

MUSIC FOR WORSHIP

GATHERING

LBW 149	This joyful Eastertide
WOV 676	This joyful Eastertide
WOV 674	Alleluia! Jesus is risen!

PSALM 4

Haugen, Marty. "Psalm 4: Let Your Face Shine upon Us" in *Gather Comprehensive*. GIA.

Schütz, Heinrich. "Psalm 4: Oh, Hear When I Cry to Thee" in *Ten More Psalms from the "Becker Psalter."* CPH 97-4880.

Young, Jeremy. PW, cycle B.

HYMN OF THE DAY

| LBW 140 | With high delight let us unite |
| | MIT FREUDEN ZART |

VOCAL RESOURCES

Beck, Theodore. "With High Delight." MSM 60-4003. SATB, cong, brass, org.

INSTRUMENTAL RESOURCES

Bobb, Barry/ed. James Kosnik. "Mit Freuden zart" in *Laudate! vol. 1.* CPH 97-6487. Org.

Ferguson, John. "Mit Freuden zart" in *Three Psalm Preludes.* AFP 11-10823. Org.

Leavitt, John. "With High Delight Let Us Unite" in *A Little Easter Suite.* CPH 97-6646. Org.

Sedio, Mark. "Mit Freuden zart" in *Music for the Paschal Season.* AFP 11-10763. Org.

Wolniakowski, Michael. "Partita on 'With High Delight Let Us Unite.'" MSM 10-416. Org.

ALTERNATE HYMN OF THE DAY

| LBW 135 | The strife is o'er, the battle done |
| WOV 675 | We walk by faith and not by sight |

COMMUNION

| LBW 214 | Come, let us eat |
| WOV 710 | One bread, one body |

OTHER SUGGESTIONS

| DATH 31 | Now the body broken |

SENDING

| LBW 143 | Now all the vault of heaven resounds |
| WOV 671 | Alleluia, alleluia, give thanks |

ADDITIONAL HYMNS AND SONGS

OBS 50	Blessing be and glory
H82 546	Awake, my soul
W3 627	Forth in the peace of Christ we go
TFF 218	Behold, what manner of love
W&P	Come and taste

MUSIC FOR THE DAY

CHORAL

Benson, Robert. "Let the Peoples Praise You." AFP 11-10921. SATB, org.

Bertalot, John. "Come, Risen Lord." AFP 11-10927. Also in *The Augsburg Choirbook*. 11-10817. SATB, org.

Cruger, Johann/ed. Wm. Tortolano. "Awake, My Heart with Gladness." GIA G-3559. SATB, 2 trbl inst, opt kybd.

DiLasso, Orlando. "Christ Has Arisen" (Christ ist erstanden). Schott AP 520. SATB. Ger/Eng.

Mendelssohn, Felix. "See What Love Hath the Father" in *St. Paul*. AFP 11-1281. SATB, org.

Meyer, Daniel C. "At the Lamb's High Feast." GIA G-4145. SAB, pno, fl, rec/vln.

Sedio, Mark. "Each New Day" (Al despuntar en la loma el dia). AFP 11-10968. SATB, kybd, 2 C inst.

CHILDREN'S CHOIRS

Jothen, Michael. "We Are Children of Our God." CG CGA731. U/2 pt, kybd, opt fl, opt 3-4 oct hb, opt cong.

Schalk, Carl. "The Whole Bright World Rejoices Now." CG CGA560. U, org, opt fl, 1 oct hb.

Wetzler, Robert. "Tell the News: Victory!" AMSI 557. 2pt.

KEYBOARD/INSTRUMENTAL

Callahan, Charles. "Easter Victory." CPH 97-6159. Org.

Lovinfosse, Dennis/ed. John Ferguson. "Victory" in *A New Liturgical Year*. AFP 11-10810. Org.

HANDBELL

Afdahl, Lee J. "Savior, Again to Thy Dear Name." NMP HB 436. 2-3 oct.

PRAISE ENSEMBLE

Althouse, Jay. "Someone Is There." GS A-6306. SATB, acc.

Butler. "At the Cross" in *Fifteen Best Loved Worship Classics from Vineyard Music, Change My Heart, O God, vol 2*. Vineyard Publications.

Espinosa. "Change My Heart, O God" in *Songs for Praise and Worship*. WRD.

Hanson, Handt. "Come Touch" in *Spirit Touching Spirit*. CCF.

Lowery, Robert/arr. Schreiner. "Here Is Love" in *Favorite Hymns of Promise Keepers*. MAR 3010133367. 3pt, kybd.

Smith, Gary Alan. "Peace I Leave with You." ABI. 02742-X. SATB, pno.

MAY 14, 2000

FOURTH SUNDAY OF EASTER

INTRODUCTION

Like our Good Shepherd who holds all people in love, the church is called to lead those who thirst to living waters. At the banquet table set before us, the shepherd who lays down his life for the lost gives himself to us. Here is a great promise: Christ leads us through the shadows and valleys of life. He will neither abandon nor forget us. He is with us, now and forever.

PRAYER OF THE DAY

God of all power, you called from death our Lord Jesus, the great shepherd of the sheep. Send us as shepherds to rescue the lost, to heal the injured, and to feed one another with knowledge and understanding; through your Son, Jesus Christ our Lord, who lives and reigns with you and the Holy Spirit, one God, now and forever.

or

Almighty God, you show the light of your truth to those in darkness, to lead them into the way of righteousness. Give strength to all who are joined in the family of the Church, so that they will resolutely reject what erodes their faith and firmly follow what faith requires; through your Son, Jesus Christ our Lord, who lives and reigns with you and the Holy Spirit, one God, now and forever.

READINGS

Acts 4:5-12

Peter and John are arrested when the healing of a lame man becomes an occasion for preaching in public about Jesus. When questioned by religious leaders, Peter attributes the healing to the power of the risen Christ.

Psalm 23

The Lord is my shepherd; I shall not be in want. (Ps. 23:1)

1 John 3:16-24

The First Letter of John speaks of the great gift of God's love bestowed on all people in Christ. Here John notes that love is a social gift, something to be shared.

John 10:11-18

In language that recalls the twenty-third psalm, Jesus describes himself as the shepherd who cares for his sheep. He is willing to die for them, and he is able to overcome death for them.

COLOR White

THE PRAYERS

Standing in the glorious light of the resurrection, let us pray for Christ's church, the world, and all who wait for the Spirit's revealing power.

SILENCE IS KEPT.

Watchful God, give to your church faithful bishops and pastors who will shepherd their synods and congregations with vision and compassion. We pray to the Lord:

Lord, hear our prayer.

Abundant God, help the people of the world to find ways to share their resources and thus to care for one another in their need. We pray to the Lord:

Lord, hear our prayer.

Knowing God, assure all who are sick that you will not forsake them (especially . . .), and that you are present with them in their pain and discomfort. We pray to the Lord:

Lord, hear our prayer.

Saving God, bless all mothers who honor you by making your love known to the families in their care. We pray to the Lord:

Lord, hear our prayer.

HERE OTHER INTERCESSIONS MAY BE OFFERED.

Abiding God, sustain the dying and those who watch with them, comfort those who grieve (especially . . .), and keep us united with all our brothers and sisters who have died in your arms. We pray to the Lord:

Lord, hear our prayer.

Gracious God, hear our prayers and receive them for the sake of the crucified and risen one, our Savior Jesus Christ.

Amen

IMAGES FOR PREACHING

This text from John, one of Jesus' "I am" statements, offers a series of images that may help us to understand in human terms something of the nature of the second person of the Trinity. It is also, of course, an echo of the answer the Lord gave when Moses pressed to discover the name of the one who would send him to free the children of Israel from bondage. Beyond that, the image of Christ the good shepherd is one of the most beloved in all scripture. So it's easy to lose focus when planning for "Sheep Sunday."

John and Mark may be the most dissimilar of the gospels, but here as in Mark, the theme of replacement is evident. Not only is Jesus the good shepherd, but a good shepherd willing to exchange his life for the lives of the sheep. This willingness to become a sacrifice is what distinguishes the shepherd from the hired hand who neither owns nor cares for the sheep, and runs at the first sight of danger.

It may also be worth noting that the good shepherd has sheep "that do not belong to this fold." In those words we are given the promise of a final reconciliation: "there will be one flock, one shepherd."

The links between the gospel text and the first reading, Acts 4:5-12, are strong. At their trial before the high priest, Peter and John act the role of good shepherds, standing fast in the face of great personal danger. The man who denied Jesus three times is filled with the Holy Spirit and speaks boldly, charging the authorities with rejecting the "stone" that has become the "cornerstone" of God's new plan for salvation. It is Jesus, and Jesus alone, who is able to free all the children of God from their bondage to sin, and who has done so by laying down his life.

WORSHIP MATTERS

"So there will be one flock, one shepherd" (John 10:16). How does your congregation witness to our one Lord? Does your congregation see itself as an independent kingdom or as part of the one holy catholic and apostolic church? Does your worship help participants understand that they belong to a flock that extends over two thousand years and all the way around the world? Do you practice "open" communion? Have you discovered ways to join with congregations of other denominations in order to provide greater witness to your community?

LET THE CHILDREN COME

If you are singing one of the hymn paraphrases for Psalm 23 elsewhere in the liturgy today, consider speaking the psalm in unison at its normal place, using the antiphon before verse 1 and after every two verses. Remember to speak slowly so that early readers can join in.

MUSIC FOR WORSHIP
GATHERING

LBW 144	Good Christian friends, rejoice and sing!
WOV 789	Now the feast and celebration

PSALM 23

Cherwien, David. "Psalm 23: The Lord Is My Shepherd." MSM 80-840. U, cong, org.

Christopherson, Dorothy. "The Lord Is My Shepherd." AFP 11-4691. U, hb, kybd, opt sign language.

Glynn, John. "My Shepherd Is the Lord" in PS, vol. 2.

Haugen, Marty. "Shepherd Me, O God." GIA G-2950. SATB, cong, kybd, C inst, opt glock, str.

Niedmann, Peter. "My Shepherd Will Supply My Need." SEL 410-822, U, kybd, opt desc.

Ollis, Peter. "The Lord Is My Shepherd" in PS, vol. 2.

Roberts, Leon C. "The Lord Is My Shepherd" in *This Far by Faith*.

Smith, T. R. "The Lord Is My Shepherd" in STP, vol. 4.

Young, Jeremy. PW, cycle B.

LBW 451	The Lord's my shepherd (paraphrase)
LBW 456	The King of love my shepherd is (paraphrase)

HYMN OF THE DAY

LBW 206	Lord, who the night you were betrayed
	Song 1

INSTRUMENTAL RESOURCES

Farlee, Robert Buckley. "Song 1" in *Gaudeamus!* AFP 11-10693. Org.

Ferguson, John. "Song 1" in *Hymn Preludes and Free Accompaniments*, vol. 17. AFP 11-9413. Org.

Wolff, S. Drummond. "Song 1" in *Hymn Descants, set IV*. CPH 97-6275. Org, inst.

ALTERNATE HYMN OF THE DAY

LBW 476	Have no fear, little flock
LBW 451	The Lord's my shepherd

COMMUNION

LBW 345	How sweet the name of Jesus sounds
WOV 711	You satisfy the hungry heart

SENDING

LBW 352	I know that my Redeemer lives!
WOV 371	With God as our friend

ADDITIONAL HYMNS AND SONGS

DATH 63	Awake, O sleeper!
H82 191	Alleluia, alleluia! Hearts and voices
H82 478	Jesus, our mighty Lord
TFF 254	Savior, like a shepherd lead us
W&P	Step by step

MUSIC FOR THE DAY
CHORAL

Ellingboe, Bradley. "Jesus, Good Shepherd." AFP 11-10969. SATB, pno/hp.

Pickard, John. "The King of Love." AFP 11-10910. U with desc, kybd.

Schalk, Carl. "The God of Love My Shepherd Is." MSM 50-8812. SATB, 2 vln, org.

Schubert, Franz. "The Lord Is My Shepherd." GSCH 5302. SSAA. 50304810. SATB.

Thompson, Randall, "The Lord Is My Shepherd." ECS 2688. SATB, org, pn/hp.

CHILDREN'S CHOIRS

Lindh, Jody W. "Lord, Make Me an Instrument of Thy Peace." CG CGA612. SAB, kybd.

Lord, Suzanne. "Do You Know Your Shepherd's Voice?" CG CGA673. 2 pt, kybd.

Roberts, William Bradley. "Savior, Like a Shepherd Lead Us." AFP 11-2558. U, kybd, opt fl.

Seivewright, Andrew. "Loving Shepherd." GIA G-4467. 2 pt trbl/mxd, org.

KEYBOARD/INSTRUMENTAL

Diemer, Emma Lou. "Psalm 23" in *Psalms for Organ*. SMP 70/1003.

Schaffner, John. "Three Variations and Fughetta on 'Song 1'" in *Organ Music for the Seasons*. AFP 11-10859. Org.

HANDBELL

Behnke, John A. "The Lord's My Shepherd." CPH 98-3400. SATB. 97-6694. 3 oct, cant, cong, pno.

Kerr, J. Wayne. "The Shepherd's Psalm." CG CGB116. 3-5 oct, fl, narr.

Wagner, Douglas. "Fanfare Prelude on 'Aurelia.'" AGEHR AG35074. 3-5 oct. AG35075. Org score. PP361. Brass, timp score.

PRAISE ENSEMBLE

Barbour and Barbour. "Greater Love" in *Maranatha! Music Praise Chorus Book, 3rd ed.* WRD/MAR.

Bradbury, William. "Savior Like a Shepherd Lead Us." in *Praise Worship Songbook, vol 3.* INT.

Kingsley, Gershon/arr. Knight. "Shepherd Me, Lord." BRN 115735. SAB, gtr, pno, perc. Also available: SA/TB, SSA, SATB.

Nystrom. "Shepherd of My Soul" in *Maranatha! Music Praise Chorus Book, 3rd ed.* WRD/MAR.

Pote, Allen. "The Lord Is My Shepherd." CG CGA-551. SATB, pno.

SUNDAY, MAY 14
PACHOMIUS, ABBOT, 348

Pachomius was the founder of cenobitic monasticism, and his rule was later instrumental in formulating the Rule of St. Benedict. He also extended women the opportunity to live in Christian communities in Egypt, establishing the first nunneries in Africa. Give thanks for the African Egyptian (Coptic) presence in the church today, and find ways to incorporate African spirituality in your congregation's worship and musical life. How can monastic traditions inform our community life?

THURSDAY, MAY 18
ERIK, KING OF SWEDEN, MARTYR, 1160

Erik, long considered the patron saint of Sweden, is honored for his crusades to spread the Christian faith in Scandinavia. As king of Sweden, he was a man noted for his goodness and his concern for those who were poor and sick. On an expedition to Finland he was accompanied by Henry of Uppsala who founded the church in Finland. Erik was murdered by a Danish pagan prince assisted by rebels.

This commemoration could provide a fruitful discussion of the relationship between church and state. Why do some assume that free exercise of religion implies that the church is not to be involved in the affairs of the nation?

FRIDAY, MAY 19
DUNSTAN, ARCHBISHOP OF CANTERBURY, 988

Dunstan is remembered for his role in the revival of monasticism in England. As a monk at Glastonbury he later became abbot, founding new monasteries and developing new rules for their good order. He was made Archbishop of Canterbury, and carried out a reform of church and state. Dunstan corrected abuses by the clergy, encouraged laity in their devotional life, and was committed to concerns of justice. He was also known as a musician, illuminator, and metalworker.

Consider a retreat to a monastery or abbey in your area. Pray for those communities and for this gift to the whole church.

MAY 21, 2000

FIFTH SUNDAY OF EASTER

INTRODUCTION

Like vines that grow from a single strong root, we are grafted into Christ at baptism and nourished on his life with the eucharist. Christ feeds our hunger and satisfies our thirst with his word and sacraments and encourages us so that we might become fruitful in service to others. Today Christ calls the church to remember the source of our faith, hope, and love.

Today the church commemorates John Eliot, a seventeenth-century missionary among American Indians.

PRAYER OF THE DAY

O God, form the minds of your faithful people into a single will. Make us love what you command and desire what you promise, that, amid all the changes of this world, our hearts may be fixed where true joy is found; through your Son, Jesus Christ our Lord, who lives and reigns with you and the Holy Spirit, one God, now and forever.

READINGS

Acts 8:26-40

Philip and Stephen were among the first deacons chosen for service in the early church. After Stephen was martyred, Philip and the rest were scattered but continued to preach. In this encounter, reflection on scripture leads to baptism into the body of Christ.

Psalm 22:24-30 (Psalm 22:25-31 [NRSV])

All the ends of the earth shall remember and turn to the LORD. *(Ps. 22:26)*

1 John 4:7-21

This letter is a commentary on Jesus' command to "love one another." Love is the mark of God's abiding presence, because God is love. Love gives itself away in service to those in need.

John 15:1-8

On the night of his arrest, Jesus taught his disciples about the relationship they would have with him. Those who abide in his word and love would bear fruit, for apart from him, they could do nothing.

COLOR   White

THE PRAYERS

Standing in the glorious light of the resurrection, let us pray for Christ's church, the world, and all who wait for the Spirit's revealing power.

SILENCE IS KEPT.

Let us pray for the church, that its ministries of education and learning would be deepened by teachers who are impassioned by God's word and eager to impart its joys and promises to their students. We pray to the Lord:

Lord, hear our prayer.

Let us pray for the world God has created, that where war paralyzes people with fear, peace and unity will be restored. We pray to the Lord:

Lord, hear our prayer.

Let us pray for those who wait patiently for cures and for medications yet undeveloped. May strength be given to all who live in chronic pain or sickness that they will never be forsaken (especially . . .). We pray to the Lord:

Lord, hear our prayer.

Let us pray for vibrant and fruitful congregational life rooted in the word of God and the sacraments of God's love. May we make disciples who will join us in bearing fruit for the reign of God. We pray to the Lord:

Lord, hear our prayer.

HERE OTHER INTERCESSIONS MAY BE OFFERED.

Let us pray with thanksgiving for John Eliot and all who rest in the sure and certain hope of the resurrection. We pray to the Lord:

Lord, hear our prayer.

Gracious God, hear our prayers and receive them for the sake of the crucified and risen one, our Savior Jesus Christ.

Amen

IMAGES FOR PREACHING

Once more, the text is from John. "I am the true vine," Jesus says, "and my Father is the vinegrower." Another "I am" statement, yet one that paints a far different kind of relationship between Jesus and his followers than the good shepherd metaphor we heard last week. In it we hear an invitation to a deepening connection with Jesus, one in which those who belong to the Lord are both nourished by him and become part of his greater life in the world.

To become a branch on the vine is to enter into a relationship of stability. "Abiding" is the word John uses, a word that perhaps no longer means so much in our culture of transient populations and often disconnected families. But notice also that the stability of abiding comes not from resisting all change, but from willingly undergoing pruning, a constant series of transformative changes that lead to more fruit on the branch.

The process can hardly be enjoyable for the branch, and the preparation for change must almost certainly mean the pain of loss as the old is cut away to make way for the new. And yet, in just this manner both the vine and the branches are strengthened and renewed. Such renewal leads to great harvests, and glory to the Father.

It might be possible to link this text with the first reading, the story of the Ethiopian eunuch from the eighth chapter of Acts. By virtue of his sudden baptism, the eunuch is grafted onto a new vine. Such a connection would have been impossible under the law, where his origin and his injury would have prevented him from entering the temple. Through grace, however, and with a new baptismal identity, he is able to start a new life and proceed on his way rejoicing.

WORSHIP MATTERS

How does your congregation minister with adults inquiring for baptism? The account of the Ethiopian eunuch (Acts 8:26-40) reminds us that baptism is a journey and not an isolated event. It all began with a personal encounter initiated by the Christian: the Ethiopian was searching for meaning, and Philip was led to reach out to him. Next followed a period of instruction in which the good news of Jesus is proclaimed and explained from the scriptures. The man then expresses his desire to be baptized. The two go down into the water, where the Ethiopian is baptized and then rejoices over what God has done. With care and attention, our baptismal process can likewise lead to joy in new life. Congregations seeking to grow in their ministry of leading others to baptism may be interested in the *Welcome to Christ* series of resources.

LET THE CHILDREN COME

Today's use of the image of the vine and branches focuses our attention on Jesus as the source of our life. Eternal life is not something we produce on our own, but rather it is something we receive from Jesus. Jesus connects us to himself by speaking to us directly: *I am the vine, you are the branches*. Let there be an abundance of such speech today, so that children hear Jesus alive speaking to them.

MUSIC FOR WORSHIP

GATHERING

| LBW 551 | Joyful, joyful we adore thee |
| WOV 802 | When in our music |

PSALM 22

Brugh, Lorraine. PW, cycle B.

Harbor, Rawn. "My God, My God" in *This Far by Faith*.

Young, Jeremy. PW, cycle B.

HYMN OF THE DAY

WOV 674   Alleluia! Jesus is risen!
                 EARTH AND ALL STARS

INSTRUMENTAL RESOURCES

Burkhardt, Michael. "Earth and All Stars." MSM 60-7010. Org, choir, brass.

Cherwien, David. "Earth and All Stars" in *Interpretations, Book III*. AMSI OR-6. Org.

Cook, Larry. "Earth and All Stars/Rise, Shine, You People." AFP 11-10712. Org, brass, timp, cong.

Powell, Robert J. "Earth and All Stars" in *Sing a New Song: Folk, Spiritual, and Hymn Preludes for Organ*. AFP 11-10766. Org.

ALTERNATE HYMN OF THE DAY

| LBW 378 | Amid the world's bleak wilderness |
| WOV 695 | O blessed spring |

COMMUNION

| LBW 209 | Come, risen Lord |
| WOV 765 | Jesu, Jesu, fill us with your love |

SENDING

| LBW 260 | On our way rejoicing |
| WOV 722 | Hallelujah! We sing your praises |

ADDITIONAL HYMNS AND SONGS

GS2 10	We will go with God
PH 418	God, bless your church with strength!
TFF 111	I've just come from the fountain
W&P	We bring the sacrifice of praise

MUSIC FOR THE DAY

CHORAL

Boyce, William/arr. Richard Proulx. "Alleluia Round." GIA G-2494. 3 pt canon, org, fl, 2 hrn/tbn, bass.

Distler, Hugo. "Dear Christians, One and All Rejoice." CPH 98-1901. SATB.

Farlee, Robert Buckley. "O Blessed Spring." AFP 11-10544. Also in *The Augsburg Choirbook.* 11-10817. SATB, ob, opt cong.

Haan, Raymond. "I Am the Vine." HWG GCMR 3473. SATB, org.

Hopson, Hal H. "Canticle of Love." AFP 11-10911. SATB, org

CHILDREN'S CHOIRS

Hopson, Hal H. "Love One Another." CG CGA741. U/2 pt, kybd.

Jothen, Michael. "You Are the Branches." CG CGA755. U, 2-3 pt trbl/mxd, kybd, opt cong, opt inst (gtr, bass gtr, hb, perc).

KEYBOARD/INSTRUMENTAL

Lau, Robert C. "Variations on 'Noel Nouvelet.'" FLA HH-5048. Org.

Powell, Robert. "Variations on 'Earth and All Stars'" in *Sing a New Song.* AFP 11-10766. Org.

HANDBELL

Hopson, Hal H. "The Gift of Love." HOP 1419. 3-5 oct, opt vcs.

Jothen, Michael. "You Are the Branches." CG CGA755. U, 2-3 pt trbl/mxd vcs, kybd, opt cong, gtr, bass gtr, 3 oct hb, perc.

PRAISE ENSEMBLE

Beall, Mary Kay. "Come to the Feast." PP PP151. 2 pt mxd, kybd.

Dearman and Dearman. "Instruments of Your Peace" in *Hosanna! Music Songbook 11,* INT.

Jothen, Michael. "You Are the Branches." CG CGA755. U, 2-3 pt, kybd, gtr, hb, perc.

Rouse, Jay. "I Will Abide." Sparrow AO8200. SATB, orch.

Walker, Tommy. "No Greater Love" in *The Maranatha! Singers, I See the Lord, vol. 1.* WRD/MAR.

SUNDAY, MAY 21
JOHN ELIOT,
MISSIONARY TO THE AMERICAN INDIANS, 1690

As a seventeenth-century missionary among the Algonkian Indians, Eliot learned their language and customs. His Algonkian translation of the scriptures was the first complete Bible printed in the colonies. In addition, Eliot trained those he ministered among to be missionaries to their own people.

As we pray for a greater respect and justice for American Indians/Alaska Natives, use this opportunity to learn of various tribal spiritualities and traditions. The response "Heleluyan" (WOV 609) is from the Muscogee (Creek) Indians and can be used as an acclamation before the reading of the gospel.

TUESDAY, MAY 23
LUDWIG NOMMENSEN, MISSIONARY TO SUMATRA, 1918

The apostle to the Bataks was a man of deep faith, courage, and prophetic vision. In 1861 he left for Sumatra where he worked among the Bataks, a people then untouched by either Islam or Christianity. The developing church had a thoroughly Batak flavor—a translation of the Bible, acceptance of features of customary law, and the training of Batak Christians as evangelists, pastors, and teachers.

WEDNESDAY, MAY 24
NICOLAUS COPERNICUS, 1543; LEONHARD EULER, 1783; TEACHERS

Scientists such as Copernicus and Euler invite us to ponder the mysteries of the universe and the grandeur of God. Copernicus's thirst for knowledge led him to put forth the revolutionary idea that the earth was not the center of the solar system, but that the earth revolved around the sun. Euler is regarded as one of the founders of the science of pure mathematics, and made important contributions to mechanics, hydrodynamics, astronomy, optics, and acoustics.

Some people see a conflict between science and religion. How can the church honor the contributions of science to our understandings of the world and universe? What does our Christian faith offer to these understandings?

SATURDAY, MAY 27
JOHN CALVIN, RENEWER OF THE CHURCH, 1564

Calvin, the French reformer and theologian, experienced a conversion in which he embraced the views of the Protestant reformation. He left the Roman Catholic Church and formulated his theological ideas in the *Institutes of the Christian Religion*. He organized the reform in Geneva with a rigid, theocratic discipline.

Calvin is considered the father of the Reformed churches. ELCA congregations are invited to find creative ways to learn more about Presbyterians, members of the United Church of Christ, and the Reformed Church in America, and to express in concrete ministries the full communion we now share.

MAY 28, 2000

SIXTH SUNDAY OF EASTER

INTRODUCTION

The church is called to be an apostolic community that dwells in the new commandment of Christ. The challenge of the gospel is not to love others as others love us, but to love others as Jesus Christ loves us. He sees our failings and fears with utter clarity, yet offers us the gentle gifts of forgiveness and healing. Here we find ground for hope: we have been made friends of God in baptism.

PRAYER OF THE DAY

O God, from whom all good things come: Lead us by the inspiration of your Spirit to think those things which are right, and by your goodness help us to do them; through your Son, Jesus Christ our Lord, who lives and reigns with you and the Holy Spirit, one God, now and forever.

READINGS

Acts 10:44-48

Jesus is raised from the dead as Lord of all creation. The risen Christ comes to all persons regardless of their condition in life. In today's reading, a Roman army officer welcomes Peter's witness to Christ. The Holy Spirit descends on these Roman "outsiders," causing amazement among the witnesses.

Psalm 98

*Shout with joy to the L*ORD*, all you lands. (Ps. 98:5)*

1 John 5:1-6

John calls upon Christians to love God and to love one another.
Toward the end of this text, John says exactly what this faithfulness means: we love God when we obey God's commandments.

John 15:9-17

On the night of his arrest, Jesus delivers a final testimony to his disciples to help them in the days ahead. Here, he repeats the most important of all his commands, that they love one another.

COLOR White

THE PRAYERS

Standing in the glorious light of the resurrection, let us pray for Christ's church, the world, and all who wait for the Spirit's revealing power.

SILENCE IS KEPT.

Gracious God, nurture your church in its ministries of pastoral care and leadership. Challenge us to be concerned for the needs of others. We pray to the Lord:
Lord, hear our prayer.

Gracious God, in the risen Christ you have befriended the world. Bless all communities with safety and a deep desire to serve the common good. We pray to the Lord:
Lord, hear our prayer.

Gracious God, help us to hear your call to come to the aid of people who are alone and despairing, forgotten and lonely, sick and low in spirit (especially . . .). We pray to the Lord:
Lord, hear our prayer.

Gracious God, bless the efforts of this congregation to help people discover places where lasting spiritual friendships are formed. We pray to the Lord:
Lord, hear our prayer.

HERE OTHER INTERCESSIONS MAY BE OFFERED.

Gracious God, bless the memory of all who have died for the cause of peace, and bring us with them to that world where our joy will be complete and you will be our all in all. We pray to the Lord:
Lord, hear our prayer.

Gracious God, hear our prayers and receive them for the sake of the crucified and risen one, our Savior Jesus Christ.
Amen

IMAGES FOR PREACHING

The three verses (9-11) at the beginning of the reading are as near to poetry as anything Jesus says in John. Once again Jesus' followers are invited to "abide" in his love, and Jesus draws an explicit (and very Jewish) connection between keeping the commandments and the profound joy that comes from righteousness with God.

Beyond this link to the fifth Sunday of Easter, however, these verses present a remarkable reiteration of the theme of replacement, which has been present throughout these texts. Even as Jesus makes preparation to leave them (the Ascension is, after all, the next event in the Easter cycle), still another profound shift takes place. The disciples and all of Jesus' followers are transformed; "servants," are replaced by "friends." This transformation is a direct result of a growth in understanding, because "a servant does not know what the master is doing." With his friends, however, Jesus has been able to share everything he has heard from the Father. Trust replaces ignorance.

The issue of Jesus' commandment, "That you love one another as I have loved you," might be best understood in this context not as a replacement of the Ten Commandments, but as an amplification of Jesus' own commentary on them. It would be possible (perhaps!) to satisfy the law by loving your neighbor as yourself, but Jesus' followers are expected to go further, modeling their love for each other upon the example of Jesus' sacrificial love.

These words, and the promise of complete joy that accompany them, are first spoken against the stark background of Good Friday. Jesus must leave them, but offers in his place a new law of love that will serve both to strengthen and unite the followers he leaves behind.

WORSHIP MATTERS

Loving God and obeying the commandments are one and the same. Worship leads to Christian service. The readings and sermon instruct us how to love God and keep the commandments. In the prayers we lift up the needs of our neighbors and set the agenda for the assembly's Christian service. The peace is a sign that marks our commitment to work for that for which we have prayed. In the offering we commit ourselves to God's service and dedicate our lives to the care and redemption of all that God has made. When we come to the Lord's table, our sins are forgiven and we are strengthened for God's service. Then we are sent in peace to serve the Lord. Worship and service cannot be separated. In what ways does your congregation's worship strengthen this connection?

LET THE CHILDREN COME

Are the alleluias still ringing out? Children need to learn that events such as Easter and Christmas are not mere one-day events, but seasons of some length. Using hymns such as "Jesus Christ is risen today" (LBW 151) throughout the season reinforces this understanding and serves to remind us all that each Sunday is a celebration of the resurrection of our Lord.

MUSIC FOR WORSHIP

GATHERING

LBW 315	Love divine, all loves excelling
WOV 750	Oh, praise the gracious power

PSALM 98

Haas/arr. Haugen. "Psalm 98: All the Ends of the Earth." GIA G-2703. U/SATB, cong.

Hopson, Hal H. "Psalm 98" in *Ten Psalms*. HOP HH 3930. U/SATB, cong.

Johnson, Alan. "All the Ends of the Earth" in PS, vol. 1.

Smith, T. R. "The Lord Has Revealed" in STP, vol. 4.

Young, Jeremy. PW, cycle B.

CHILDREN'S PSALM SUGGESTIONS

Beall, Mary Kay. *Sing Out! A Children's Psalter*. WLP. U, kybd.

HYMN OF THE DAY

LBW 189 We know that Christ is raised
ENGELBERG

VOCAL RESOURCES

Wolff, Drummond. "We Know That Christ Is Raised." CPH 98-2609. SATB, kybd, tpts.

INSTRUMENTAL RESOURCES

Cherwien, David. "When in Our Music God Is Glorified: Suite for Organ." AFP 11-10765. Org.

Langlois, Kristina. "Engelberg" in *Five Hymns of Praise*. MSM 10-722. Org.

Moklebust, Cathy. "Engelberg" in *Hymn Stanzas for Handbells*. AFP 11-10869. 2-3 oct hb. 11-10722. 4-5 oct hb.

Sedio, Mark. "Engelberg" in *How Blessed This Place: Hymn Preludes for Organ*. AFP 11-10934. Org.

ALTERNATE HYMN OF THE DAY

WOV 789 Now the feast and celebration
LBW 143 Now all the vault of heaven resounds

COMMUNION

LBW 200 For the bread which you have broken
WOV 665 Ubi caritas et amor

SENDING

LBW 397 O Zion, haste
WOV 723 The Spirit sends us forth to serve

ADDITIONAL HYMNS AND SONGS

DATH 95 With all your heart
H82 704 O thou who camest from above
TFF 97 I heard an old, old story
W&P As the deer

MUSIC FOR THE DAY

CHORAL

Fedak, Alfred V. "Go and Bear Fruit." MSM 50-8823. SATB, org.

Pachelbel, Johann/arr. Donald Rotermund. "Sing to the Lord a New Song." CPH 98-3329. 2 SATB choirs.

Rorem, Ned. "Sing My Soul, His Wondrous Love." PET 6386. SATB.

Tallis, Thomas. "If Ye Love Me." OXF TCM69. SATB.

CHILDREN'S CHOIRS

Bedford, Michael. "Cantate Domino." CG CGA689. U/2 pt, kybd.

Owens, Sam Batt. "Sing to the Lord." GIA G-4717. U, cong, opt cant, hb, vocal/inst, desc.

KEYBOARD/INSTRUMENTAL

Kolander, Keith. "Vruechten" in *All Things Are Thine*. AFP 11-10931. Org.

Leavitt, John. "Joyous Day." HWG GSTC01112. Org.

HANDBELL

McChesney, Kevin. "Cantad al Señor: Oh, Sing to the Lord." AFP 11-10690. 2-3 oct.

PRAISE ENSEMBLE

Angerman, David and Joseph M. Martin. "Sing! Shout! Jubilate!" FLA A7134. SATB, acc.

Kallman, Daniel. "What a Friend We Have in Jesus." MSM 50-9065. SATB, pno.

Smith, Byron. J. "Worthy to Be Praised." LAW 52654. SATB, pno.

Ylvisaker, John. "Great Is Our God" in *Borning Cry*. NGP.

Ziegenhals, Harriet. "Oh, Sing to the Lord." CG CGA640. U/2pt, kybd, perc.

MONDAY, MAY 29
JIRI TRANOVSKY, HYMNWRITER, 1637

Tranovský is considered the "Luther of the Slavs" and the father of Slovak hymnody. Trained at the University of Wittenberg in the early seventeenth century, Tranovský eventually became a pastor in Slovakia where he issued a translation of the Augsburg Confession and published his hymn collection *Cithara Sanctorum* (Lyre of the Saints), the foundation of Slovak Lutheran hymnody.

Use this commemoration to pray for the Slovak church and to give thanks for the gifts of church musicians. Sing one of Tranovský's hymns, such as "Your Heart, O God, Is Grieved" (LBW 96) or "Make songs of joy" (LBW 150).

WEDNESDAY, MAY 31
THE VISITATION

The Visitation marks the occasion of Mary visiting her cousin Elizabeth. After Elizabeth calls her "blessed among women," Mary sings the famous song called the Magnificat.

The Visitation celebrates the incarnation of Christ and the witness of John, but it also raises up the hopes and expectations of pregnancy. Even if we have never given birth to a baby, how are we pregnant with the Word, bearers of Christ to others, and faithful to God's call?

JUNE 1, 2000

THE ASCENSION OF OUR LORD

INTRODUCTION

The risen Lord enters the invisible presence of God in order to be present in all times and places to the church and to the world. Where shall we find the risen and ascended Lord today? In his word and his bread, in his people and his washing with water and the Spirit, and in all who cry out for mercy.

Today the church commemorates Justin, a martyr at Rome, c. 165.

PRAYER OF THE DAY

Almighty God, your only Son was taken up into heaven and in power intercedes for us. May we also come into your presence and live forever in your glory; through your Son, Jesus Christ our Lord, who lives and reigns with you and the Holy Spirit, one God, now and forever.

READINGS

Acts 1:1-11

Before he is lifted into heaven, Jesus promises that the missionary work of the disciples will spread out from Jerusalem to all the world. His words provide an outline for the book of Acts.

Psalm 47

God has gone up with a shout. (Ps. 47:5)

or Psalm 93

Ever since the world began, your throne has been established. (Ps. 93:3)

Ephesians 1:15-23

After giving thanks for the faith of the Ephesians, Paul prays that they might also see the power of God, who in the ascension has now enthroned Christ as head of the church, his body.

Luke 24:44-53

At the time of his ascension, Jesus leaves the disciples with the promise of the Holy Spirit and an instruction that they should await the Spirit's descent.

COLOR White

THE PRAYERS

Standing in the glorious light of the resurrection, let us pray for Christ's church, the world, and all who wait for the Spirit's revealing power.

SILENCE IS KEPT.

Let us pray for eyes to see and ears to hear, that by baptism into Christ our minds would be open to understand God's word and recognize God's activity in our midst. Lord, in your mercy,

hear our prayer.

Let us pray for love toward all the saints and toward all the world, that a spirit of wisdom and revelation will be given to all authorities and those in power. Lord, in your mercy,

hear our prayer.

Let us pray for hearts of compassion that are moved to action toward those who are troubled, lonely, fearful, and in need of your healing touch (especially . . .). Lord, in your mercy,

hear our prayer.

Let us pray for those preparing to make public affirmation of their baptism, that they would be ready to renew the covenant God has already made with them. Lord, in your mercy,

hear our prayer.

Let us pray for all who like Justin have given a faithful witness to the gospel and have been faithful servants unto death. Lord, in your mercy,

hear our prayer.

HERE OTHER INTERCESSIONS MAY BE OFFERED.

Let us pray for the grieving, that we may be signs of God's presence with them in their loss, and that the hope of the resurrection will keep them united with their beloved departed. Lord, in your mercy,

hear our prayer.

Gracious God, hear our prayers and receive them for the sake of the crucified and risen one, our Savior Jesus Christ.

Amen

IMAGES FOR PREACHING

Ascension marks the fortieth day of Easter, and Luke's text offers us a vision of Jesus' final good-bye, a good-bye we heard all the way back on the third Sunday of Easter. As much as the Easter season is a time of victory, it is also the time when we hear Jesus preparing his disciples for the day when he would finally leave them. Ascension is this day.

His last words to them are an echo of "the Word" spoken at the very beginning. The Law, the Prophets, the Psalms, and the minds of the disciples are opened up with new understanding, one that can encompass both the events of Holy Week and the evangelism that must follow as a result of the great commission. Jerusalem, which was the goal of Jesus' pilgrimage during his earthly ministry, will now become the starting point of the new age of repentance and forgiveness that will be for all the nations.

And what will be sent in Jesus' place? The Holy Spirit is expected shortly, which will clothe them with power from on high. They must relinquish Jesus' physical, bodily presence among them in order to experience this new relationship. For the moment, at least, their task is to wait upon the movement of the Spirit. The disciples find that they are done "doing" for a while, now they must learn what it means to be entrusted with Jesus' ministry, empowered by the Spirit rather than directed by him. It is a profound transition, both of life and understanding.

They make one last journey together, this one just as far as Bethany, and then he leaves them, carried away to heaven. But what a difference from the last time he had been carried away! The disciples scattered at Jesus' arrest, seeking their own safety. Now they return to Jerusalem as a group, with an identity, and rather than treating the temple as the stronghold of the enemy, they are there constantly, blessing God and God's faithfulness.

WORSHIP MATTERS

Ascension services have fallen into neglect partly because humanity journeyed to the heavens and did not find Jesus sitting at God's right hand. A key to revitalizing this festival may be understanding the ascension not in terms of space but fulfillment. The risen Christ ascends to that "place" or "time" in which the kingdom of God is fulfilled. From there Jesus sends the Holy Spirit and intercedes for us in order to bring us along so that where he is we may be also. Viewed this way, Jesus' ascension becomes the occasion for celebrating our hope-filled future.

LET THE CHILDREN COME

At key places in the liturgy, such as immediately before the declaration of grace, before each scripture reading, before the sermon, before the words of institution, and before the benediction, say boldly, "Look up!" Draw the hearers' attention to the presence of Christ in his word. Before the dismissal, however, say instead, "Look around!" We are sent to serve the Lord in the world and to proclaim him to all who will hear.

MUSIC FOR WORSHIP

GATHERING

| LBW 156 | Look, the sight is glorious |
| WOV 669 | Come away to the skies |

PSALM 47

Beckstrand, William. PW, cycle B.

Bell, John L. "Psalm 47: Clap your hands all you nations" in *Psalms of Patience, Protest and Praise*. GIA G-4047. U/SATB.

Chepponis, James J. "Eastertime Psalm: Psalms for Easter, Ascension, and Pentecost." GIA G-3907. Cant, cong, opt choir, opt tpts, hb.

Brown, Teresa. "God Goes Up" in PS, vol. 2.

Hughes, Howard. "Psalm 47: God Mounts His Throne and God Is King." GIA G-2029. Cant, cong, acc.

Inwood, Paul. "A Blare of Trumpets" in PS, vol. 2.

Sterk, Valerie Stegink. "Psalm for Ascension." SEL 241-047. SATB, org, children, cong, tamb.

HYMN OF THE DAY

| LBW 159 | Up through endless ranks of angels |
| | ASCENDED TRIUMPH |

VOCAL RESOURCES

Gerike, Henry. "Up through Endless Ranks of Angels." CPH 98-2709. SAB, kybd, tpt, cong.

INSTRUMENTAL RESOURCES

Eggert, John. "Ascended Triumph" in *Six Hymn Preludes, set I*. CPH 97-5893. Org.

Herald, Terry. "Ascended Triumph" in *Hymn Accompaniments for Instrumental Ensembles*. CPH 97-6263. Kybd, inst.

Hobby, Robert. "Partita on 'Ascended Triumph.'" CPH 97-5987. Org.

ALTERNATE HYMN OF THE DAY

| WOV 756 | Lord, you give the great commission |
| LBW 157 | A hymn of glory let us sing! |

COMMUNION
    LBW 518   Beautiful Savior
    WOV 709   Eat this bread

SENDING
    LBW 158   Alleluia! Sing to Jesus
    LBW 171   Rejoice, the Lord is King!

ADDITIONAL HYMNS AND SONGS
    LW 150   On Christ's ascension I now build
    TFF 99   How lovely on the mountains
    W&P   Majesty

MUSIC FOR THE DAY
CHORAL
    Billings, William. "Rejoice Ye Shining Worlds on High."
        CPH 98-3281. SATB.
    Haydn, Joseph. "Achieved Is the Glorious Work" in *Creation*.
        WAL W6001. SATB, org.
    Sweelinck, Jan P./arr. Robert S. Hines. "Men of Galilee."
        AFP 11-10283. SSATB.
    Spiritual/arr. K. Lee Scott. "Jesus, My All, to Heaven Is Gone" in
        Rejoice Now My Spirit, Vocal Solos for the Church Year.
        AFP 11-10228. MH. 11-10229. ML.

CHILDREN'S CHOIRS
    Bach/arr. Scott. "Come with Hearts and Voices Sounding."
        MSM 50-9402. 2 pt trbl, kybd.
    Helman, Michael. "Jesus, We Want to Meet." AFP 11-10734.
        U, 3 oct hb, perc.

KEYBOARD/INSTRUMENTAL
    Messiaen, Olivier. "Priere du Christ montant vers son Pere" in
        L'Ascension. LED AL 18,826. Org.
    Reger, Max. "On Christ's Ascension I Now Build" in *Chorale Preludes
        for the Church Year, Op. 67*. CFP N4892. Org.

HANDBELL
    Kosche, Kenneth T. "Look, Oh, Look, the Sight Is Glorious."
        CPH 98-3186. SATB. 97-6476. 3 oct. 97-6461. Full score: opt
        brass qrt, org.

PRAISE ENSEMBLE
    Barrett, Michael. "Truly God Is Good" in *Two S.A.B. Praise Anthems*.
        GS D-5450. SAB, acc.
    Davis, Greg and Greg Fischer/arr. Innes. "Honor the Lord."
        HOP WT1522. SATB, pno.
    Liles, Dwight. "Clap Your Hands" in *Spirit Touching Spirit*. CCF.
    Smith, Tim. "Our God Is Lifted Up" in *Songs for Praise and Worship*.
        WRD.

THURSDAY, JUNE 1
JUSTIN, MARTYR AT ROME, C. 165

Born of pagan parents, Justin became a Christian and taught at Ephesus and Rome. Justin was one of the first Christian thinkers to attempt to reconcile the claims of truth and reason. He and some of his students were denounced as Christians, and upon their refusal to make a pagan sacrifice, were scourged and beheaded. The record of their martyrdom, based on an official court, survives.

Justin's description of early Christian worship is an important document for understanding the beginnings of our liturgy. Read Justin's description of second-century worship (*WOV*, p. 6). How is it similar to the pattern of our Holy Communion service today?

SATURDAY, JUNE 3
JOHN XXIII, BISHOP OF ROME, 1963

At age seventy-seven, Angelo Roncalli was elected pope. He was expected to be a transitional pope, but he astonished many with his energy and reforming spirit. In 1962 John XXIII convened the Second Vatican Council, the major achievement of his papacy, to "let in the fresh air of the modern world." The reforms of Vatican II brought about changes in Roman Catholic thought and practice, and opened up a spirit of ecumenism among Christians. John was a remarkably humble man, and his death was mourned by the whole world.

Discuss how Lutherans and Roman Catholics have become closer to each other in the past three decades. Has your parish studied the Lutheran–Roman Catholic declaration on justification by faith? Have you shared in prayer, service, or Bible studies with a neighboring Roman Catholic parish?

JUNE 4, 2000

SEVENTH SUNDAY OF EASTER

INTRODUCTION

This past Thursday the church celebrated the Ascension of Our Lord. Today's gospel includes the words of Jesus' high priestly prayer the night before his death. Though he is absent from us, Christ has given the church his word and sacraments so that we may be one in him, and united in his service to all who seek God. Even as Jesus' followers waited for the promised Holy Spirit, we pray during these days before Pentecost that the Spirit would renew the lives of all who profess faith in Christ.

PRAYER OF THE DAY

Almighty and eternal God, your Son our Savior is with you in eternal glory. Give us faith to see that, true to his promise, he is among us still, and will be with us to the end of time; who lives and reigns with you and the Holy Spirit, one God, now and forever.

or

God, our creator and redeemer, your Son Jesus prayed that his followers might be one. Make all Christians one with him as he is one with you, so that in peace and concord we may carry to the world the message of your love; through Jesus Christ our Lord, who lives and reigns with you and the Holy Spirit, one God, now and forever.

READINGS

Acts 1:15-17, 21-26

The image of Israel's twelve tribes is mirrored in the twelve apostles of Jesus. They signify the Lord's mission to his people, to all others who welcome him, and to the new community of the church, a light to the nations. In this reading, the early church selects Matthias to fill the vacancy among the twelve caused by the death of Judas Iscariot.

Psalm 1

The LORD knows the way of the righteous. (Ps. 1:6)

1 John 5:9-13

On this Sunday of the Easter season, the second reading offers a final witness to the risen Christ. John points to the continuing presence of God's Son in the lives of those who believe.

John 17:6-19

In this reading the church hears Jesus' words on the night before his death. This gospel reports the words of Jesus' prayer, a prayer for his disciples and for all who would believe in him through their words.

COLOR White

THE PRAYERS

Standing in the glorious light of the resurrection, let us pray for Christ's church, the world, and all who wait for the Spirit's revealing power.

SILENCE IS KEPT.

God of truth, sanctify your church in the truth, and bless our seminaries and theological schools with instructors who are faithful to your word. Lord, in your mercy,
hear our prayer.

Holy One, protect people in every land who face imminent danger and violence. Send peacemakers and mediators to assist the leaders of nations at war. Lord, in your mercy,
hear our prayer.

Living God, you know the hearts of all your children. Touch those who are in need of healing (especially . . .), that they may sense your nearness. Lord, in your mercy,
hear our prayer.

Merciful One, watch over the children of our congregational community, and grant parents and guardians wisdom as they oversee the growth of their children. Lord, in your mercy,
hear our prayer.

HERE OTHER INTERCESSIONS MAY BE OFFERED.

Kind and compassionate God, bless the dying and those who keep watch with them. Keep us united with those who have gone before us in the communion of saints. Lord, in your mercy,
hear our prayer.

Gracious God, hear our prayers and receive them for the sake of the crucified and risen one, our Savior Jesus Christ.
Amen

IMAGES FOR PREACHING

The gospel text from John is Jesus' high priestly prayer. Throughout this prayer we can see the theme of replacement and relocation worked through in almost every aspect of the life and mission of Jesus' followers in the world, starting (once more) with the word that comes from God and has been given in turn to the disciples.

This shift also takes place with the disciples themselves: they had been from the world, belonged to the Father, who then entrusted them to the Son. As a part of his legacy, both to them and to the Father, Jesus once more puts them under the Father's care and protection, careful at the same time to point out that the only one he had lost was the one destined to be so. "All mine are yours, and yours are mine," is Jesus' word to and about his followers, knowing the world is about to see the truth that "we [Jesus and the Father] are one."

Finally, having asked for their safety, and even as he makes it clear that he intends to remove himself physically from the world, Jesus prepares to send out the disciples in his place. Protected by the Father and supported by the Spirit, it will be the disciples' task to be salt and light and truth to a world in desperate need of all three.

The first reading reflects this theme of replacement also, though on a more prosaic level: Matthias is chosen by lot to fill the spot left open by Judas's defection. Compare this process with Jesus' words from last Sunday: "You did not choose me, but I chose you. . . ."

WORSHIP MATTERS

Christians do not identify completely with the world. In worship we rehearse how to live in the world but according to the ways of God's kingdom. Whereas the world often responds to confessions of faults and failings with ridicule or retribution, in worship we announce forgiveness and new life. Though the world teaches us to look out for ourselves, in prayer we make the needs of others our priority. And the Lord's table is the place where everyone is welcome, where everyone has a place, where all receive their share and no one goes away hungry. By teaching us kingdom values, worship equips us to live as God's people in the world.

LET THE CHILDREN COME

The church continues to bask in the glow of the resurrection, still singing the alleluias and the hymns that proclaim that Christ was raised to die no more. But basking is not that for which we were created or baptized: We need to live and we need to learn to ask the giver of life for the gift of life—the Holy Spirit. Invite children and the whole congregation to use next week's response to the prayers (Come, Holy Spirit) as a one-sentence prayer throughout this coming week.

MUSIC FOR WORSHIP

GATHERING

LBW 245	All people that on earth do dwell
WOV 793	Shout for joy loud and long

PSALM 1

Bell, John L. "Psalm 1: Happy is the one" in *Psalms of Patience, Protest and Praise*. GIA G-4047. U/SATB.

Hallock, Peter/arr. Carl Crosier. *The Ionian Psalter*. ION.

Harbor, Rawn. "Happy Are They" in *This Far by Faith*.

Schenbachler, Tim. "Happy Are They" in STP, vol. 2.

Young, Jeremy. PW, cycle B.

CHILDREN'S PSALM SUGGESTIONS

Howard, Julie. *Sing for Joy: Psalm Settings for God's Children*. Liturgical Press 8146-2078-7.

HYMN OF THE DAY

LBW 88	Oh, love, how deep
	DEO GRACIAS

VOCAL RESOURCES

Schalk, Carl. "O, Love, How Deep, How Broad, How High." CPH 98-1524. SATB.

INSTRUMENTAL RESOURCES

Burkhardt, Michael. "Partita on Deo Gracias." MSM 10-844. Org.

McIntyre, John. "Deo Gracias" in *Three English Hymns*. Live Oak House 344-0131 SET. Brass.

Pelz, Walter. "Oh, Love, How Deep." CPH 97-5675. Org.

Willan, Healey. "O Love, How Deep" in *Ten Hymn Preludes, set II*. CFP 6012. Org.

ALTERNATE HYMN OF THE DAY

LBW 367	Christ is made the sure foundation
WOV 747	Christ is made the sure foundation
LBW 158	Alleluia! Sing to Jesus

COMMUNION

LBW 492	O Master, let me walk with you
WOV 705	As the grains of wheat

SENDING

LBW 262	Savior, again to your dear name
WOV 704	Father, we thank you

ADDITIONAL HYMNS AND SONGS

CW 448	In you, O Lord, I put my trust
H82 538	God of mercy, God of grace
TFF 234	Lord, I want to be a Christian
W&P	Blessing, honor and glory

MUSIC FOR THE DAY

CHORAL

Nelson, Ron. "I Will Not Leave You Comfortless" in *Four Anthems for Young Choirs*. B&H 5576. U, org.

O'Brien, Francis Patrick. "Your Wonderful Love." GIA G-4520. SAB, cant, cong, gtr, kybd.

Pelz, Walter. "Peace I Leave With You." AFP 11-1364. SATB.

Proulx, Richard. "Though We Are Many, In Christ We Are One." MSM 80-834. SATB, cant, opt cong, org.

CHILDREN'S CHOIRS

Ferguson, John. "Jesus, My Lord and God." AFP 11-2246. U, org.

Sleeth, Natalie. "Go into the World." CG CGA209. 2-3 pt trbl/mxd, kybd.

KEYBOARD/INSTRUMENTAL

Baker, Richard C. "A Fancy on 'Westminster Abbey.'" RME. Org.

Fedak, Alfred V. "Toccata on 'Gelobt sei Gott'" in *A Collection of Hymns*. BEL DM 9601. Org.

HANDBELL

Moklebust, Cathy. "Lord, You Give the Great Commission" in *Hymns Stanzas for Handbells*. AFP 11-10722. 4-5 oct.

PRAISE ENSEMBLE

Gardner. "My Life Is in You" in *Songs for Praise and Worship*. WRD.

Haugen, Marty. "Gather Us In." GIA G-2651. SATB, pno, gtr, ww.

Kendrick, Graham. "Shine, Jesus, Shine" in *Maranatha! Music Praise Chorus Book*. WRD/MAR.

Ylvisaker, John. "We Shall Not Be Moved" in *Borning Cry*. NGP.

MONDAY, JUNE 5
BONIFACE, ARCHBISHOP OF MAINZ, MISSIONARY TO GERMANY, MARTYR, 754

An English Benedictine, Boniface was called to missionary work among the Vandals, a warring tribe that lived in Germany. It became clear that many superstitious and violent practices endured despite the first efforts to plant the gospel. Boniface sent for large numbers of Benedictine monks and nuns who established churches, schools, and seminaries where the faith could be taught and the liturgy celebrated. Much of the christianization of the Germanic peoples began with Boniface.

Pray for the German people, and recall some of the great German theologians and musicians who have shaped our Christian faith.

WEDNESDAY, JUNE 7
SEATTLE, CHIEF OF THE DUWAMISH CONFEDERACY, 1866

Seattle was chief of the Suquamish tribe and became chief of the allied tribes, the Duwamish Confederacy. Unlike many of his day, he rejected war and chose the path of peace. After he became a Roman Catholic, he lived in such a way that he had the respect of both his own people and white people. On the centennial of his birth, the city of Seattle—named for him against his wishes—erected a monument over his grave.

Chief Seattle initiated the practice of holding morning and evening prayer in his tribe. When small groups from your congregation gather for meetings and other special events, consider beginning or ending with morning or evening prayer.

FRIDAY, JUNE 9
COLUMBA, 597; AIDAN, 651; BEDE, 735; CONFESSORS

Today we commemorate three monks from the British Isles who kept alive the light of learning and devotion during the early Middle Ages. Columba was an abbot and missionary who established a community on the island of Iona, and evangelized the mainland and established monasteries on the islands nearby. Aidan, a monk of Iona, was sent to revive missionary work in England. He was admired for both his asceticism and his gentleness. Bede, called the Venerable, was a biblical scholar and the father of English history. He devoted himself to study, teaching, and writing.

How do we keep alive the light of learning and devotion today? What role do church-related colleges have in this regard? Do our congregations see Christian study as a lifelong process of enlightenment, rather than one that ends with confirmation?

JUNE 10, 2000

VIGIL OF PENTECOST

INTRODUCTION

Pentecost is one of the principal festivals of the liturgical year. Several of the festivals have the tradition of night vigils preceding them. In this night of extended prayer and silence, we anticipate being filled with the power of the Spirit, perhaps as the believers were in the second chapter of Acts (an alternate first reading this night). The Spirit gathers the church together. It is the same Spirit that enlightens us by the word, calls us in baptism, and sanctifies us with the bread of life and the cup of salvation. Come, Holy Spirit!

PRAYER OF THE DAY

Almighty and ever-living God, you fulfilled the promise of Easter by sending your Holy Spirit to unite the races and nations on earth and thus to proclaim your glory. Look upon your people gathered in prayer, open to receive the Spirit's flame. May it come to rest in our hearts and heal the divisions of word and tongue, that with one voice and one song we may praise your name in joy and thanksgiving; through your Son, Jesus Christ our Lord, who lives and reigns with you and the Holy Spirit, one God, now and forever.

READINGS

Exodus 19:1-9
  God establishes the covenant with Israel at Mt. Sinai.
or Acts 2:1-11
Psalm 33:12-22
  The LORD is our help and our shield. (Ps. 33:20)
or Psalm 130
  There is forgiveness with you. (Ps. 130:3)
Romans 8:14-17, 22-27
  The Spirit prays for us.
John 7:37-39
  Jesus nourishes believers with the living water and leads them to the Spirit of God.

COLOR Red

THE PRAYERS

Standing in the glorious light of the resurrection, let us pray for Christ's church, the world, and all who wait for the Spirit's revealing power.
SILENCE IS KEPT.
Spirit of God, descend upon our hearts so that from them may flow rivers of living water. Empower your church to share this water with all who thirst for you. We pray:
Come, Holy Spirit.
Spirit of God, descend upon our hearts so that your people might be a holy nation and a priestly kingdom to serve you across this whole earth. We pray:
Come, Holy Spirit.
Spirit of God, descend upon our hearts with the fire of your compassion for all in need. Come to the aid of those who are weak with illness (especially . . .). We pray:
Come, Holy Spirit.
Spirit of God, descend upon our hearts so that this congregation will boldly and courageously speak about your mighty deeds of power in our lives. We pray:
Come, Holy Spirit.
HERE OTHER INTERCESSIONS MAY BE OFFERED.
Spirit of God, descend upon the hearts of all who are bowed down with grief (especially . . .). Through your eternal Spirit, may we be kept in union with all the beloved who have died. We pray:
Come, Holy Spirit.
Gracious God, hear our prayers and receive them for the sake of the crucified and risen one, our Savior Jesus Christ.
Amen

IMAGES FOR PREACHING

The gospel is the story of Jesus' celebration of the Festival of Booths, a festival he then invests with a different meaning, transforming the old into something new.

The scene from John is set on the last day of the festival, the day he describes as "the great day," the culmination and pinnacle of the people's rejoicing. And it is then, on that most holy day, and standing on the very steps of the temple (the most holy place) that Jesus offers a new invitation: "Let anyone who is thirsty come to me, and let the one who believes in me drink."

With Jesus' words comes a lesson, and a most visible sign of the new dispensation: the old feasts will no longer satisfy the ones who are thirsty for God's mercy and justice. The temple is no longer to be seen as the place of refuge and sanctuary for those who seek it, but instead it is Jesus himself who is the ultimate source of rest and refreshment.

Paul echoes this theme of the exchange of old for new with his assertion that by the Spirit we have received not a spirit of slavery, but one of adoption. Our cries of fear are replaced by cries of "Abba!" as we lay claim to this new relationship with God the Father, the grace of our brother Jesus Christ.

WORSHIP MATTERS

"We do not know how to pray as we ought" (Rom. 8:26). What a wonderful gift prayer is! Not only is God always ready to hear and answer our prayers, God also gives us the Holy Spirit who helps us to pray when we cannot. When we feel too angry, ashamed, or unworthy to come before God, when we cannot understand our thoughts and needs, let alone find the words to express them, the Spirit intercedes for us, and God hears our prayers. Thus, some of our most fervent praying occurs during the silence in which we struggle with our God, and in the sighs, tears, and joy that transcend thoughts and words.

LET THE CHILDREN COME

As then, so now the church is gathered together in one place (Acts 2:1), calling out to God for that divine life that has no end. As children call, "Daddy!" so the church prays, "Abba. Our Father in heaven." Use repetition in the prayers: Begin, "Abba, Father, pour out your Holy Spirit upon us." Use the Lord's Prayer that begins "Our Father in heaven"; its short phrases are easier for children to learn and say. Pray with hands outstretched as a bodily way of showing eagerness to receive God's gift of the Holy Spirit.

MUSIC FOR WORSHIP

GATHERING

LBW 161   O day full of grace
WOV 686   Veni Sancte Spiritus

PSALM 33

Farlee, Robert Buckley. PW, cycle C.
Inwood, Paul. "The Lord Fills the Earth with His Love" in STP, vol. 3.

HYMN OF THE DAY

LBW 472/3   Come, Holy Ghost, our souls inspire
VENI, CREATOR SPIRITUS/
KOMM, GOTT SCHÖPFER

VOCAL RESOURCES

Fleming, Larry. "Embellishments for Choir" (Pentecost). AFP 11-10657. SATB.
Schalk, Carl. "Creator Spirit, Heavenly Dove." CPH 98-2582. SATB, kybd, brass, cong.

INSTRUMENTAL RESOURCES

Callahan, Charles. "Komm, Gott Schöpfer" in *Pentecost Music for Manuals*. MSM 10-540. Kybd.
Larsen, Libby. "Veni, Creator Spiritus" in *A New Liturgical Year*, ed. John Ferguson. AFP 11-10810. Org.
Leavitt, John. "Komm, Gott Schöpfer" in *Hymn Preludes for the Church Year*. AFP 11-10134. Org.
Manz, Paul. "Komm, Gott Schöpfer" in *Improvisations for Pentecost and Trinity Sunday*. MSM 10-500. Org.
Powell, Robert J. "Pentecost Fanfare" in *Two Spring Fanfares*. Live Oak House 345-0123.SET. Brass, org, opt timp.

ALTERNATE HYMN OF THE DAY

WOV 684   Spirit, Spirit of gentleness
LBW 508   Come down, O Love divine

COMMUNION

LBW 486   Spirit of God descend upon my heart
WOV 685   Like the murmur of the dove's song

OTHER SUGGESTIONS

OBS 107   O sacred river

SENDING

LBW 282   Now rest beneath night's shadow
WOV 729   Christ, mighty Savior

ADDITIONAL HYMNS AND SONGS

H82 515   Holy Ghost, dispel our sadness
H82 465/6   Eternal light, shine in my heart
TFF 107   Holy Spirit, descend
W&P   Spirit song

MUSIC FOR THE DAY

CHORAL

Biery, James. "The Waters of Life." AFP 11-10902. Also in *The Augsburg Choirbook*. 11-10817. SATB, org.

Hassell, Michael. "Spirit, Spirit of Gentleness." AFP 11-10850. SATB, pno, sax/cl.

Hogan, Charles. "Veni Sancte Spiritus." AFP 11-10855. SATB, fl, perc.

Rorem, Ned. "Breathe on Me, Breath of God" B&H OCTB6543. SATB.

Tallis, Thomas. "O Lord, Give Thy Holy Spirit" CPH 98-2249. SATB.

CHILDREN'S CHOIRS

Callahan, Charles. "Creator Spirit, By Whose Aid." MSM 50-5400. U, opt desc, org.

White, David Ashley. "Like the Murmur of the Dove's Song." CG CGA352. U/2 pt, kybd.

Wilkinson, Sandy. "Spirit Trilogy." CG CGA769. SAB, kybd.

KEYBOARD/INSTRUMENTAL

Burkhardt, Michael. "Like the Murmur of the Dove's Song" in *Eight Improvisations on 20th Century Hymn Tunes*. MSM 10-707. Org.

Duruflé, Maurice. "Choral varié sur le theme du 'Veni creator'" in *Prelude, Adagio et Choral varié*. DUR. Org.

PRAISE ENSEMBLE

Fragar. "I Believe the Presence" in *Hosanna! Music Songbook 11*. INT.

Talbat, John Michael. "Send Us Out" in *Renew*. HOP.

JUNE 11, 2000

THE DAY OF PENTECOST

INTRODUCTION

On Pentecost, the fiftieth day of Easter, the church prays that God would send forth the flame of the Holy Spirit and fill the church with an abundance of gifts needed to carry out its baptismal mission. We pray that the Holy Spirit would lend fire to our words and strength to our witness. We ask that God would send us forth to proclaim with boldness the wondrous work of raising Christ, who is our life and our hope.

PRAYER OF THE DAY

God, the Father of our Lord Jesus Christ, as you sent upon the disciples the promised gift of the Holy Spirit, look upon your Church and open our hearts to the power of the Spirit. Kindle in us the fire of your love, and strengthen our lives for service in your kingdom; through your Son, Jesus Christ our Lord, who lives and reigns with you in the unity of the Holy Spirit, one God, now and forever.

READINGS

Acts 2:1-21

Pentecost was a Jewish harvest festival that marked the fiftieth day after Passover. In time, the festival came to celebrate the covenant made at Mount Sinai. Still later, Luke associated the outpouring of the Holy Spirit with Pentecost as the fiftieth day after the resurrection, a new covenant sealed in the body and blood of Christ.

or Ezekiel 37:1-14

Psalm 104:25-35, 37 (Psalm 104:24-34, 35b [NRSV])

Alleluia or *Send forth your Spirit and renew the face of the earth. (Ps. 104:31)*

Romans 8:22-27

In this text, Paul speaks of the Spirit's presence in the cosmos. The entire creation groans in hope and testifies to what each Christian knows: the Spirit is the principle of new life gathering all into the harvest of hope.

or Acts 2:1-21

John 15:26-27; 16:4b-15

When speaking to his disciples before his death, Jesus referred to the Holy Spirit as "the Helper" and described the difference the Spirit would make in their lives and in the world.

COLOR Red

THE PRAYERS

Standing in the glorious light of the resurrection, let us pray for Christ's church, the world, and all who wait for

the Spirit's revealing power.
SILENCE IS KEPT.

Come to your church and inflame the hearts of your people to convey your love faithfully and boldly to the world. We pray:
Come, Holy Spirit.

Come from the four winds, O Breath of God, and breathe your peace into the hearts of every nation, that violence and war may cease in all the world. We pray:
Come, Holy Spirit.

Come and let your healing wind surround the sick (especially . . .), that they may be given new breath and new health. We pray:
Come, Holy Spirit.

Come and let the new wine of your presence give us vision as we gather at your table of mercy, there to be strengthened and sent into the world empowered with your good news. We pray:
Come, Holy Spirit.

HERE OTHER INTERCESSIONS MAY BE OFFERED.

Come and intercede for those who groan in grief, that together with all your blessed saints, they might be united by your Spirit with those for whom they mourn. We pray:
Come, Holy Spirit.

Gracious God, hear our prayers and receive them for the sake of the crucified and risen one, our Savior Jesus Christ.
Amen

IMAGES FOR PREACHING

The Day of Pentecost brings the theme of relocation to a marvelous crescendo. The seventh Sunday of Easter lays out the new place of the disciples, sent out into the world to carry on Jesus' earthly ministry. The Vigil of Pentecost lifts up Jesus instead of the old festivals and the old places. Finally, the Day of Pentecost is about the place of the Spirit, God's breaking into the world in a new and different way.

Until now, Jesus has led the disciples. Until now, Jesus has taught the disciples. From this day forward, the Spirit will assume these responsibilities, acting as the Advocate sent from the Father to lead them into all the truth.

Even as Jesus describes this exchange, he is aware that the disciples will feel a sense of loss, perhaps even a sense of abandonment. What, after all, is the "Spirit" when compared to the comfort and reliability of Jesus' physical presence? After all this time, it would seem that the disciples have finally come to trust their eyes and ears, and to know that Jesus' presence with them is evidence of God's presence; and that to walk with Jesus is to walk (quite literally) in the way of the Lord.

What Pentecost asks of the disciples and those who come afterwards, is to accept that the Advocate, sent by Jesus from the Father, is also a Spirit of truth that will abide always. It is the Advocate—acting through and by and with the disciples—who will prove the world wrong, and offer a chance of correction and repentance to those who could not see the truth of Jesus Christ. Indeed, Jesus tells his listeners that it is to their advantage that the Advocate comes in his place, for the Advocate will not have to leave them, but will remain in the world to empower them for ministry and witness to the entire world.

WORSHIP MATTERS

Every community is multilingual. Even in those that are not multinational, the languages of the young, the streets, business, and religion are spoken. Pentecost reminds us that it is not enough to speak the good news of God. People must hear this good news proclaimed in their own languages. A first step is for Christians to break through barriers of theological language and church talk: what *do* we mean by "justified by grace through faith"? A second step is for congregations to listen to the members of their communities in order to learn to speak their languages. A third step is for congregations to understand occasions when the community comes together as opportunities to speak and to listen. Most importantly, be attentive to the movements of the Spirit, who opens ears and loosens tongues.

LET THE CHILDREN COME

On this day baptism and/or confirmation are often celebrated. In places where there are no candidates, adapt the order for Affirmation of Baptism (*LBW*, p. 198) for use as a congregational renewal of baptismal vows. Open the font and have water in it so that people might dip their fingers in it and make the sign of the cross. Consider going from worship out into the community—perhaps making a witness in the neighborhood by delivering scripture cards or congregational brochures door-to-door or providing a meal for those in need. Be sure to include the children!

MUSIC FOR WORSHIP

GATHERING

LBW 508	Come down, O Love divine
WOV 687	Gracious Spirit, heed our pleading

PSALM 104

Busarow, Donald. "Psalm for Pentecost." AFP 11-04618. SATB, brass, cong.

Chepponis, James J. "Eastertime Psalm: Psalms for Easter, Ascension, and Pentecost." GIA G-3907. Cant, cong, opt choir, opt tpts, hb.

Farlee, Robert Buckley. PW, cycle B.

Hopson, Hal H. "Psalm 104" in *Ten Psalms*. HOP HH 3930. U, cong.

Kreutz, Robert E. "Lord, Send Out Your Spirit." OCP 9457. SATB, cong, gtr, org, solo inst.

Proulx, Richard. "Psalm 104" in TP.

Saliers, Don. "Psalm 104." OXF 94.234. Cant, cong, SATB, org, hb.

Schoenbachler, Tim. "Send Out Your Spirit" in STP, vol. 2.

Wright, Andrew. "Send Forth Your Spirit, O Lord" in PS, vol. 2.

HYMN OF THE DAY

LBW 161	O day full of grace
	DEN SIGNEDE DAG

VOCAL RESOURCES

Schalk, Carl. "O Day Full of Grace." AFP 11-1946. SATB, opt cong, org, 2 tpt, 2 tbn. Inst pts code 11-1947.

INSTRUMENTAL RESOURCES

Burkhardt, Michael. "Den signede Dag" in *Five Pentecost Hymn Improvisations, set 1*. MSM 10-501. Org.

Pelz, Walter L. "Den signede Dag" in *Hymn Settings for Organ and Brass, Set 4*. AFP 11-10435. Full score. 11-10436. Brass score.

Pelz, Walter. "Pentecost Suite." CPH 97-6712. Org, inst.

Wold, Wayne L. "Suite on O Day Full of Grace." AFP 11-10827. Org.

ALTERNATE HYMN OF THE DAY

LBW 163	Come, Holy Ghost, God and Lord
WOV 685	Like the murmur of the dove's song

COMMUNION

LBW 488	Breathe on me, breath of God
WOV 680	O Spirit of life

SENDING

LBW 387	Spirit of God, unleashed on earth
WOV 688	O Holy Spirit, root of life

ADDITIONAL HYMNS AND SONGS

DATH 71	Fill us with your spirit
PH 129	Come, O Spirit, dwell among us
H82 223/4	Hail this joyful day's return
TFF 101	Spirit of the living God
W&P	Wind of the spirit

MUSIC FOR THE DAY

CHORAL

Burkhardt, Michael. "Come, Holy Ghost, Our Souls Inspire." MSM 50-5551. 2 pt, hb.

Carter, Andrew. "Come, Holy Ghost, Our Souls Inspire." OXF A427. SATB, org.

Handl, Jakob. "Repleti sunt omnes" (And They All Were Filled). CPH 98-2394. SATB/SATB or SATB/brass. Lat/Eng.

Proulx, Richard. "Christ Sends the Spirit" in *The Augsburg Choirbook*. AFP 11-10817. SAB, org, fl.

Schwarz, May. "Come, Holy Spirit, Blow across the Waters." AFP 11-10920. SATB. org, opt br, cong.

CHILDREN'S CHOIRS

Boyce, William/arr. Jane McFadden and Janet Linker. "Psalm of Joy." CG CGA760. 2 pt, kybd, opt 2 oct hb.

Cherwien, David. "Every Time I Feel the Spirit." AMSI 3020. U.

Graham, Robert. "Song of the Spirit." AMSI 519. 2 pt.

KEYBOARD/INSTRUMENTAL

Albrecht, Timothy. "Come, Oh Come, Thou Quickening Spirit" in *Grace Notes VII*. AFP 11-10856. Org.

Fedak, Albert V. "Improvisation on Veni Creator Spiritus." SEL 160-513. Org.

HANDBELL

Afdahl, Lee J. "Spirit in the Wind." AFP 11-10698. 3-5 oct, windchimes or chimetree.

Moklebust, Cathy. "Come, Holy Spirit." AMSI HB-21. 3-5 oct.

Semmann, Barbara. "Processionals for the Day of Pentecost." CPH 97-6525. 5 oct.

PRAISE ENSEMBLE

Baloche, Richard. "Revival Fire Fall" in *Hosanna! Music Songbook 11*. INT.

Carter, John. "A Pentecost Meditation." ALF 4266. SAB/2 pt mxd.

Chisum. "Let Your Spirit Come" in *Hosanna! Music Songbook 7*. INT.

Joncas, Michael. "Send Forth Your Spirit." GIA G-3436. SATB, cant, cong, org, synth.

Medema, Ken/arr. Schrader and Scholz. "Lord, Listen to Your Children." MFS YS500. SSA, kybd.

Snowden, Judith. "Come into the Presence." CIM CIM1000. SATB, pno, fl.

MONDAY, JUNE 12
ST. BARNABAS, APOSTLE (TRANSFERRED)

In the Eastern church Barnabas is commemorated as one of the seventy commissioned by Jesus, and his observance dates from the fifth century. Barnabas was not actually one of the twelve apostles, but the book of Acts gives him the title of apostle. Barnabas was originally called Joseph, and with Paul he organized the first missionary journey, but he was soon overshadowed by Paul.

At the Council of Jerusalem, Barnabas defended the claims of Gentile Christians in relation to the Mosaic law. Knowing that conflict and disagreement is a given in the church, what kind of wisdom do we seek today in dealing with such situations?

WEDNESDAY, JUNE 14
BASIL THE GREAT, BISHOP OF CAESAREA, 379;
GREGORY OF NAZIANZUS,
BISHOP OF CONSTANTINOPLE, C. 389;
GREGORY, BISHOP OF NYSSA, C. 385

This day commemorates three Cappadocian fathers from the East. Basil was a defender of orthodoxy and was known for his eloquence, learning, and great personal holiness. He is considered the father of Eastern communal monasticism. Gregory of Nazianzus, called the Theologian in the East, restored the Nicene faith at Constantinople where he was appointed bishop. Gregory of Nyssa, a younger brother to Basil, was also a defender of the Nicene faith, and was a thinker and theologian of great originality and learning.

As a reflection of these fathers' exploration of the mystery of the Holy Trinity, discuss some contemporary understandings of trinitarian faith. Identify stumbling blocks to trinitarian understanding in today's church members.

SUMMER

AUTUMN

NOVEMBER

SUMMER

Summertime is about living

IMAGES OF THE SEASON

Summertime. Perhaps you can hardly say the word without hearing, somewhere in the back of your mind, an earthy soprano voice singing the words from George Gershwin's opera, *Porgy and Bess*, "Summertime, and the livin' is easy." That's what summer is about—taking it easy. Schools close down, factories slow production, offices work with skeleton staffs. It's time for vacation, time to relax, ease up, sleep in, chill out. It is vacation time, whatever that may mean. For some it's travel—mountains or shore, down the road or over the sea. For some it's a hammock in the backyard. It may be catching up with the weeds in the garden or the novels you've been meaning to read. It may be swimming lessons or soccer camp or hot dogs on the grill or just sitting in the sun.

Most of all, summertime is about living. It's about having time, time for yourself, time to do what's important. Vacation doesn't require travel or equipment or expense. It only requires a sense of priorities. What's important to you? What makes you who you are? The answers to those questions will tell you how to make yourself new, how to renew yourself. And another word for that is re-creation—recreation. Vacation is about renewal, whatever that means for you.

For the church summer often means vacation, too, in the traditional sense. It can be a time of low attendance, low activity, low energy. Often it means that summer is when nothing much happens. It is simply a holding pattern, waiting until September when the real business of living will resume. But if vacation is indeed about living, then the same should be true for the church. Summer is for re-creation here, too.

Summer worship should provide an opportunity for renewal, but that does not necessarily mean that it should be easy-going or unchallenging. Our theological understanding of Sunday is that it is not only a day of rest but also, and indeed primarily, a day of worship. During the summer as throughout the year we come to church not to escape from the world but to enter into relationship with it more fully. Our worship should be asking the same questions about priorities that shape what we do with our vacation time. What matters most to us as Christians? What makes us who we are? How do we live in a way that gives us joy and fulfillment?

All of us need re-creation. Summer worship is a chance to discover what that means. Traditionally the readings for the Sundays after Pentecost have focused on the nature of faith and the Christian life. While that might seem demanding for a summer Sunday, it is in fact exactly what summer is about: living.

Social scientists and economists tell us that the pattern of vacationing for U.S. workers has changed in recent years. The customary two weeks away in midsummer is less and less common, replaced by more frequent but briefer breaks spread throughout the year. But whether we are on vacation or not, the longer days and warmer weather continue to make summer a season that is slower and more relaxed. The images of renewal and recreation remain appropriate for worship in these summer months, but those images also point to the need to carry them into the other seasons as well. One of the tasks of the church, carried out in worship and in learning, is to equip the saints for ministry. Just as vacation sends us back to our daily tasks reenergized, so worship sends us out to feed the hungry, clothe the naked, visit the prisoner, and speak God's word of love.

Summertime. It's about relaxing, growing, believing, serving. Mostly, it's about living.

ENVIRONMENT AND ART FOR THE SEASON

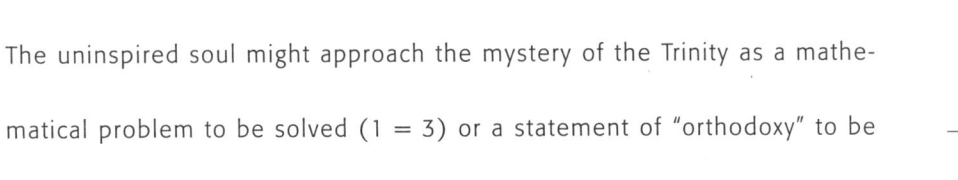

The uninspired soul might approach the mystery of the Trinity as a mathematical problem to be solved (1 = 3) or a statement of "orthodoxy" to be explained ("begotten, not made, of one being with the Father"). Alas, the Trinity has not fared well in the preaching and theology of Western churches. Living with a paradox can be a pain, and thinking in metaphors can be mystifying. While Western Christians find it easy to assert oneness ("only Jesus"), we have found it difficult to enjoy the rich and diverse possibilities of threeness. Even our religious art betrays our perplexity: the sacred three are reduced to overlapping circles, triangles, or the occasional painting of an old man holding a crucified body as a dove hovers above their heads.

In the Eastern churches, however, the Trinity has had better luck, probably because the Orthodox have understood that God first reveals God's remarkable life as a diverse and living reality, a sacramental reality to be welcomed and received with gratitude. Andre Rublev, the medieval Russian monk and painter, knew that this holy presence is the source of all existence (what a twentieth-century theologian would call the very "ground" of our being). But he knew something more as well: every loving mother who gives birth to a child will feed her offspring, even if it means giving her own food, her own blood, for the sake of that child's life. Rublev saw God as the origin of all creation and as the sustainer of life. So he searched through the Bible for images of the Holy Trinity—the source of all creation—feeding our hungry world.

The story he favored is found in Genesis 18, God's visit as three men to Abraham and Sarah. But did he make a mistake? At first it appears to be the wrong story, for here it is Abraham and Sarah who are the hosts, the ones who feed the three visitors. Read a little more carefully, however, and something else becomes apparent. The simple meal becomes the occasion in which the Lord gives life to Abraham and Sarah where they thought it impossible. This old woman gives birth to a son. Is that where the story ends? Not in Rublev's mind. In these three, he recognized the Trinity as the one who gives birth to the whole world and feeds this world with the bread and wine of the church's meal (see "Mothering God, you gave me birth," WOV 769).

And so Rublev painted one of the greatest visions of the Trinity in the history of the church. Three angels sit around a four-square table, their gaze directed at the viewer who is welcomed at the fourth seat. In the center of the table is a large cup filled with wine to which one of the angels points with outstretched finger. You are welcome here, the painting says. You are invited into this communion of the Trinity. Please, take your seat at table and drink from this cup. Taste and see that the Lord is good.

For two thousand years, Christians have gathered on Sunday to celebrate the eucharist, the Lord's giving of himself in the bread of life and the cup of blessing. Throughout most of these twenty centuries, they have eaten ordinary bread baked to a shade of deep gold and sipped the fruit of the vine, red, and sometimes, white wine. Perhaps deep gold and dark red are the colors of God's self-giving (see "Grains of wheat," WOV 708).

The first Christians ate round barley or wheat loaves and shared a common cup. For the next thousand years, both leavened and unleavened breads were used while the entire assembly drank from one or two large cups, many of them made of gold, silver, or glass. In the sixteenth century, Martin Luther critiqued the late medieval practice of withdrawing the cup from the people and serving small flavorless wafers as bread. With uncanny sensitivity to the ordinary things of life, Luther called for the restoration of weekly eucharist celebrated in the language of the people, with scripture-based preaching, and the reception of bread and wine by all the baptized. This return to a common meal and sharing of the word was intended to deepen the early Christian sense that the marvelous diversity of human life (its "threeness") possesses, at its very center, a gracious and abiding unity (its "oneness"), a unity in diversity, a communion in the Trinity (see 1 Cor 10:16-17; "One bread, one body," WOV 710).

In the Northern Hemisphere, the weeks of summer witness the growth of grains that will become ripe and ready for harvest. In the vineyards of our land, the sun is warming the grapes as they grow fat with the juices that will become sweet and dry wines. In the gospels, we frequently see Jesus at table sharing bread and cup with people who were hungry, poor, and outside the circles of social or political influence. His presence among them was a tangible sign of God's gracious presence. In a world of hungry people, is it any wonder, then, that God would come among us as bread to be shared, as wine to be sipped from a common cup? The land of summer is filled with green-growing sheaves and vines. Yet in the midst of green's overwhelming presence, the church holds forth the golden bread and scarlet wine, the one bread and the one cup, our communion in the life of the sacred three, the blessing of the Trinity.

As readers of this book will know, the Sundays after Pentecost are divided into the three "seasons" of summer, autumn, and November. This year Pentecost will be celebrated quite late in the spring (June 11), the festival of the Holy Trinity following on June 18. The next five Sundays (propers 7–11) focus on Christ calming the sea, healing, sending the Twelve, the death of John the Baptist, and Christ healing the multitudes. The following five Sundays (propers 12–16) focus on Christ feeding the multitudes and the bread of life discourse from John, an ideal time for pastors to preach on the visible word of the eucharistic meal and to gather interested members for a weekly meal and discussion of the ELCA statement, *The Use of the Means of Grace* (AFP 3-3500). On September 3 (proper 17) and September 10 (proper 18), the lectionary returns to Mark: Jesus' teaching on authentic "religion" followed by two healing stories. The gospel reading for the following Sunday, September 17 (proper 19), marks a significant movement in Mark's narrative (8:27-38). Likewise, this Sunday can be a turning point from summer to autumn. Here Jesus speaks of the anointed servant who will suffer and the call to discipleship under the sign of the cross. The lectionary thus sets forth a logical time to mark the resumption of "ordinary" activities in the congregation: the trajectory of the Sunday gospel readings will move now toward Jesus' embrace of the cross (proper 29).

Those who care for the environment and art of the worship space can follow a pattern for summer from June 18 (Holy Trinity, Pentecost 1), to and including September 10 (Pentecost 13, proper 18). Blessed is the congregation with two sets of green vestments, paraments, and other hangings. If a darker green set was used during the season after Epiphany, begin this longer season after Pentecost with the lighter green shades and then shift to the darker ones in autumn. Keep in mind that the entire space, not just the *front*, is the focus of artistic concern.

Remember that green cloth hangings with no words or appliqued symbols can be hung in different ways: flat with rods at top or bottom against a wall or away from a wall; as a great green canopy over the altar or over the central space where the people sit; as neatly tailored strips fastened to poles carried in a procession; gathered around pillars and draped as bunting from one pillar to another; in long strips hanging in arcs over the people; as a sheer fabric that is hung close to windows in order to catch the light. Is it really enough to say that we use green to symbolize our growth as disciples of the Lord (or some similar sentiment)? If you are interested in speaking about green, consider the comments on color in the Epiphany section of this book. Green will always mean more than one thing to the people who gather for worship. Where does green appear in the Bible and the hymns of the church? What does green mean in these different settings?

Since this season begins with the Holy Trinity, why not find a large reproduction of Rublev's icon of the Holy Trinity (sometimes called "The Hospitality of Abraham") or another Trinity icon, place it on a handsome stand, and add burning candles or torches to each side? If space allows, it could be placed to one side of the altar or at a crossing or at the entrance to the worship space as a sign of hospitality to all who gather for worship.

One is tempted to use flowers in the same traditional manner: people sign up to pay for arrangements that are ordered from a florist who delivers them on Saturday. The flowers, usually in a tight, symmetrical design, are placed on two stands, one to each side of the altar. That's it. Why not try something different, at least during the weeks of summer? Invite members to bring flowers from their gardens to the church on Saturday. Spend some time together arranging the flowers in simple glass vases. These can be placed in clusters throughout the worship space: at the font, by the reading desk, close to (but never on) the altar.

Remember that the plant life of your region can be used throughout the weeks of summer and early autumn. Another option is to follow the common European practice of attaching small bouquets of flowers to the end of pews (maybe not every pew, but at least every other one). Sounds like "wedding" decorations? Guess where the wedding practice came from.

PREACHING WITH THE SEASON

While the Sundays of summer bear the name of Pentecost, they can feel disconnected, removed from the power and activity of Pentecost itself, more ambling and pedestrian than whirling and rushing. And yet it is the activity of Pentecost that provides the lens through which we observe, interpret, and carry out the gospel message given to us throughout the summer season.

Let us take a moment to remember the Pentecost event: a rush of violent wind fills the house where the disciples are gathered; as divided tongues of fire rest on each one, they are filled with the Holy Spirit and begin speaking in a number of languages. A crowd gathers around the house when they hear many languages being spoken, including their own. In response to hearing the disciples tell of God's great deeds of power, some are amazed and perplexed, asking, "What does this mean?" Others sneer and say, "They are filled with new wine." Peter speaks, citing the words of Joel that the spirit of God will rest on "all flesh" and all shall be prophets of the word of God. The climax are the words, "Everyone who calls on the name of the Lord shall be saved."

This Pentecost dynamic plays out throughout the Sundays after Pentecost. God's transforming power comes into our midst, inviting all to a new relationship with God. Some are amazed and perplexed; some sneer. Proclamation of Jesus' power, mirroring the power of God who stills the storm and hushes the waves (Ps. 107), meets amazing acts of belief. The hemorrhaging woman reaches out and touches Jesus; Jairus insists that Jesus can heal his daughter. But also we hear startling responses of unbelief: the hometown crowd dismisses Jesus' teaching in the synagogue, and Herod has John the Baptist beheaded.

The promise proclaimed by our readings in the summer season is that, regardless of our response, God never stops inviting. God invites through the challenging words of prophets such as Isaiah, Ezekiel, Amos, and Jeremiah, to a people who hear and do not hear; through repeated invitations to live in ways that reflect new life in Christ to people who are struggling with their identity; and through Jesus Christ, who embodies the love of God in a world living in darkness. Jesus proclaims, "I am the bread of life," inviting hearers again and again to a new relationship with God.

The movement of these texts provides a frame for understanding our activities throughout the summer months. God comes into our midst in the promise proclaimed and the sacraments offered, and we respond, sometimes in belief, other times in unbelief. Through it all, God continues to engage and invite us. Two aspects of this movement are worth highlighting. First, God comes to us on hillsides, on the water, in small towns, wherever God finds us throughout the summer months.

The invitation to a relationship with God—to believe—is not an otherworldly encounter. It takes place in the green grass, the dirty water, and the dust of the towns where we live. As we roll in the grass, walk on hot pavement, play in the water, sit behind desks, and open the windows of our homes, the embodied love of God comes where we live and play. God's invitation to a new relationship comes not as an escape from life, but as a meeting in everyday activities and concerns.

Second, God's embodied love does not come into a fantasy world where everything is wonderful and bright, and where all people who see God at work and hear the invitation stand up and say, "Oh, yes, Lord, I believe." God comes into a world that is real, that is complex, where belief and unbelief dance together daily. Beauty and ugliness, great compassion and deep hatreds, astounding abundance and mind-blowing want. Even summer months, though often wrapped in idyllic images of vacationing families, romps on beaches, and picnics in parks, are the witness to other images of families disrupted by violence, faces behind bars, bloated bellies, and skeletal limbs. Summer is not a "time-out" from the complexities, ambiguities, opportunities, and limits of this life. People's lives continue, full of the best, the worst, and the mundane middle at full tilt. God's invitation enters these complexities, and works through these realities so that they become places of transformation and sites of new possibilities in our relationship with God and with others.

These realities can be a challenge for preachers. At a time when people often long for a break from the complexities of their lives, we are proclaiming a message that invites and requires hearers to enter into life's complexities, albeit in a new way. We might be tempted to go light with the message in the summer and to coast into our own summer routine. Here is where the Pentecost lens is particularly helpful. The power of the Holy Spirit itself rests on us and emboldens us to proclaim God's great deeds of power in language that will speak to and be understood by the hearers.

If God's invitation meets people wherever they are, another challenge for preachers might be to carry the message to people wherever they are through the summer months. Where might we be found as preachers if we carry the message to people rather than assume that they will come to us? What might the worshiping community look like? What shape would our preaching take? Whatever the site, however many are gathered, in these summer months we are blessed to proclaim again and again the great deeds of God who so loved the world as to give the only Son of God to save the world and not condemn it.

SHAPE OF WORSHIP FOR THE SEASON

BASIC SHAPE OF THE EUCHARISTIC RITE IN SUMMER

- Confession and Forgiveness: see alternate worship text for summer in *Sundays and Seasons*

GATHERING

- Greeting: see alternate worship text for summer in *Sundays and Seasons*
- Omit the Kyrie during the summer (except on the festival of the Holy Trinity)
- Omit or use the hymn of praise during the summer (use for the festival of the Holy Trinity)

WORD

- Nicene Creed for Holy Trinity (though favored by some congregations, the Athanasian Creed is a difficult text for communal reading); Apostles' Creed for remaining Sundays in this season
- Prayers: see alternate forms and responses for summer in *Sundays and Seasons*

MEAL
- Offertory prayer: see alternate worship text for summer in *Sundays and Seasons*
- Use the proper preface for Holy Trinity on the festival of the Holy Trinity; use the proper preface for Sundays after Pentecost for the remainder of the season (see *LBW* Ministers edition and *WOV* Leaders edition for each musical setting of the liturgy)
- Eucharistic prayer: in addition to four main options in *LBW*, see "Eucharistic Prayer G: Summer" in *WOV* Leaders edition, p. 71
- Invitation to communion: see alternate worship text for summer in *Sundays and Seasons*
- Post-communion prayer: see alternate worship text for summer in *Sundays and Seasons*

SENDING
- Benediction: see alternate worship text for summer in *Sundays and Seasons*
- Dismissal: see alternate worship text for summer in *Sundays and Seasons*

OTHER SEASONAL POSSIBILITIES
BLESSING FOR TRAVELERS
- See seasonal rites. Use before the benediction whenever groups from the congregation set out to travel.

FAREWELL AND GODSPEED
- See *Occasional Services*, pp. 151–52, for a rite to use whenever people are leaving the congregation. It may be used either after the prayers or following the post-communion prayer.

LECTIONARY OPPORTUNITIES FOR HEALING SERVICES
- Proper 8 on July 2 (gospel), and proper 9 on July 9 (gospel)

ASSEMBLY SONG FOR THE SEASON

Bread figures prominently in this season's gospels. When it comes to music for worship, the *people's song* is daily bread, the essential staple especially in these weeks when other ensembles may not be rehearsing. How will it stay fresh?

GATHERING
Seven-grain, dense liturgical music may not be as fitting during these weeks of bright daylight as music that is more sprightly in style. This may be an ideal time for building the service music around hymns and hymn paraphrases (see *WOV* setting 6, *All Times and Places;* the hymn mass in *Sundays and Seasons 1999*, p. 26). If the music of the gathering rite is streamlined to a single hymn (no Kyrie or hymn of praise), let it be familiar and strong. Consider also a time of informal singing as people gather in place of an instrumental prelude.

WORD
Relieve the sameness of having the congregation sing every verse of every psalm and hymn by exploring several dialogical possibilities. Use responsorial psalms (several examples are listed under each day) in which a cantor sings the verses and the assembly sings only the refrain. Position the cantor to be seen by the assembly, ensure that he or she knows the psalm well, employ a simple refrain that can be sung without noses buried in service folders, and the result will be a livelier interplay of persons and voices. With choir members now often in the pews, the hymn of the day offers an opportunity for singing stanzas in alternation (high voices, low voices; left, right; call and response). Have the people

face each other across the aisle and sing to one another.

MEAL

Carefully plan the singing for the "bread of life" sequence. What are the nuances of each week's gospel that can be reflected in particular songs? What new seasonal bread of life song will be learned and sung (and, given the fact of summer travel, by the end of five weeks many people will have sung only once or twice)?

SENDING

A season focused on mission may benefit by the inclusion each week of a strong and substantial sending hymn with themes of mission and service. In this case the post-communion canticle may perhaps be omitted and the clearing of the altar accomplished at the conclusion of the communion of the people.

MUSIC FOR THE SEASON

VERSE AND OFFERTORY

Cherwien, David. *Verses for Ascension, Pentecost and Trinity.*
MSM 80-540. U/SATB, org.

Cherwien, David. *Verses for the Season of Pentecost, Set 1.*
MSM 80-541. U, kybd.

Pelz, Walter L. *Verses and Offertories* (Easter–Holy Trinity).
AFP 11-09546. SATB, kybd.

Verses and Offertory Sentences, Part V. CPH 97-5505. U/SATB, kybd.

CHORAL MUSIC FOR THE SEASON

Bisbee, B. Wayne. "Teach Me Your Way, O Lord." AFP 11-10603.
2 pt mxd, kybd.

Carter, Andrew. "God Be in My Head." OXF E159. SATB, org.

Croce, William. "O sacrum convivium." FLA A-6448. SATB.

Di Lasso, Orlando. "Alleluia" in *Eleven Motets for Treble Voices.*
GIA 2143. SSAA.

Hassell, Michael. "Jesus Loves Me." AFP 11-10790. SATB, pno, sax.

Leavitt, John. "My Father's Gifts." CPH 98-3431. 2 pt vcs, pno.

Proulx, Richard. "My Heart Is Full Today" (Psalm 111).
CPH 98-3361. 2 pt, tamb, 4 hb/glock, kybd.

Scott, K. Lee. "King of Glory, King of Peace" in *Rejoice Now My Spirit: Vocal Solos for the Church Year.* AFP 11-10228. Sop solo.

CHILDREN'S CHORAL MUSIC FOR THE SEASON

Kosche, Kenneth. "Lord Jesus, Be My Song." CG CGA678. U, kybd.

Oliver, Curt. "Come, Holy Spirit, Calm My Mind." MSM 50-9206.
SA, org.

Powell, Robert J. "Treasures of the Heart." AFP 11-10605. 2 pt, kybd, fl.

Rutter, John. "All Things Bright and Beautiful." HIN HMC-663.
2 pt, kybd.

INSTRUMENTAL MUSIC FOR THE SEASON

Bach, J. S. "Pastorale." Various ed. Org.

Callahan, Charles. "Canticle for English Horn and Organ."
CPH 97-6115.

Diemer, Emma Lou. *Eight Hymn Preludes.* AFP 11-10349. Org.

Henry, Raymond/arr. Henry Sexton. "The Lord Will Make a Way" in
I'll Fly Away. AFP 11-10458, Org.

Vivaldi, Antonio. "Vivaldi for Instrument and Keyboard."
CPH 97-6283. Kybd, inst.

Wold, Wayne L. "Suite on O Day Full of Grace." AFP 11-10827. Org.

HANDBELL MUSIC FOR THE SEASON

Anderson, Christine. "Holy, Holy, Holy." HOP 1834. Solo, pno, opt ch.

Anderson, Christine/arr. Kramlich. *Classic Baroque Solos.* HOP 1618.
Solo hb.

Herbek, Raymond H. *Three Unaccompanied Handbell Duets.*
High Meadow.

Mears, D. *Three Early American Hymn Tunes.* JEF S8914. Qrt/ensemble.

Mendelssohn/McChesney. "Lift Thine Eyes." HOP CP 6064. 2 oct qrt.

Wagner, Douglas. *Five by Five, II.* HOP 1476. Qnt.

Wagner, Douglas. *Five Hymn Tune Duets.* HOP 1692. Duet, kybd.

SUMMER

ALTERNATE WORSHIP TEXTS

CONFESSION AND FORGIVENESS
In the name of the Father, and of the ☩ Son,
and of the Holy Spirit.
Amen

Let us confess our sin in the presence of God
and of one another.
Silence for reflection and self-examination.

Reconciling God,
**you seek peace and unity among us,
but we have chosen walls of isolation.
Break down the barriers we have created,
that we might see your love for us more clearly
and trust more deeply your promise of eternal life.**

We who once were far off
have been brought near to God
through the cross of Jesus Christ.
May almighty God grant you grace
to forgive one another
as God in Christ has forgiven you.
Amen

GREETING
The steadfast love of God never ceases.
God's mercies never come to an end.
The grace of our Lord Jesus, the love of God, and the communion of the Holy Spirit be with you all.
And also with you.

PRAYERS
Growing in the soil of the Spirit, let us pray for the church, the world, and all who seek the richness of life in God.
A brief silence.

Each petition ends:
Gracious God,
hear our prayer.

Concluding petition
Hear us as we pray, living God, and nourish us always at your table of grace, for the sake of Jesus Christ, our Lord and Savior.
Amen

OFFERTORY PRAYER
Gracious God,
**as grains of wheat are gathered for bread,
and grapes together are poured out as wine,
so may we be united in your presence
through this sacrament of grace. Amen**

INVITATION TO COMMUNION
Come and eat the living bread of God.
Lord, give us this bread always.

POST-COMMUNION PRAYER
O God,
we thank you for the living bread
that rains down from heaven.
From this feast of love
may we carry your eternal life
as daily food for the well-being of the world;
through Jesus Christ, our Lord.
Amen

BENEDICTION
May you be strengthened with the power of God,
the love of Christ,
and the help of the Holy Spirit.
Amen

DISMISSAL
Go in peace to bear Christ's love to the world.
Thanks be to God.

SEASONAL RITES

BLESSING FOR TRAVELERS
Use this prayer before leaving on a journey

O God,
our beginning and our end,
you kept Abraham and Sarah in safety
throughout the days of their pilgrimage,
you led the children of Israel through the midst of the sea,
and by a star you led the magi to the infant Jesus.
Protect and guide us now as we [or substitute the names
of travelers] set out to travel.
Make our ways safe and our homecomings joyful,
and bring us at last to our heavenly home,
where you dwell in glory with our Lord Jesus Christ
and the life-giving Holy Spirit,
one God, now and forever.
Amen

Adapted from *Lutheran Book of Worship*, prayer 269.

JUNE 18, 2000

THE HOLY TRINITY
FIRST SUNDAY AFTER PENTECOST

INTRODUCTION

The festival of the Holy Trinity celebrates the mystery of God, both transcendent and immanent. Though the nature of God is beyond our rational explanation, we ascribe glory to the one who is holy, whose glory fills the whole earth. Christians are born of water and the Spirit, and when we make the sign of the cross, we remember our baptism in the name of the triune God. Born anew in baptism, and nourished at the Lord's table, we now live as witnesses to God's love for us and all the world.

PRAYER OF THE DAY

Almighty God our Father, dwelling in majesty and mystery, renewing and fulfilling creation by your eternal Spirit, and revealing your glory through our Lord, Jesus Christ: Cleanse us from doubt and fear, and enable us to worship you, with your Son and the Holy Spirit, one God, living and reigning, now and forever.

or

Almighty and ever-living God, you have given us grace, by the confession of the true faith, to acknowledge the glory of the eternal Trinity and, in the power of your divine majesty, to worship the unity. Keep us steadfast in this faith and worship, and bring us at last to see you in your eternal glory, one God, now and forever.

READINGS

Isaiah 6:1-8

This first reading narrates the prophet's vision of the Lord surrounded by the angelic company. They sing "Holy, holy, holy," a song the church sings at the beginning of the great thanksgiving. In the liturgy, this text invites the church and all creation to sing in praise of God's glory. This glory is God's mercy toward sinners.

Psalm 29

Worship the LORD in the beauty of holiness. (Ps. 29:2)

Romans 8:12-17

In describing the new life of faith, Paul refers to all three persons of the Trinity: the Spirit leads us to recognize that we are children of God the Father and sisters and brothers with Christ the Son.

John 3:1-17

Jesus' miracles prompt Nicodemus to visit him in secrecy. Jesus tells him about being born of the Spirit and about the Son who has been sent by God to save.

COLOR White

THE PRAYERS

Growing in the soil of the Spirit, let us pray for the church, the world, and all who seek the richness of life in God.

A BRIEF SILENCE.

Triune God, the fullness of your identity is a mystery, and yet you reveal to the church your awesome presence. Teach us to worship you in the beauty of your holiness. Gracious God,

hear our prayer.

Be with all who care for the environment and make us sensitive to the ways in which we can preserve our natural resources for the good of all. Gracious God,

hear our prayer.

Draw near to those whose bodies know pain and illness (especially . . .). Assure them of your living presence with them, and grant them healing. Gracious God,

hear our prayer.

Help fathers to provide for the families in their care, that their service might be a sign of your fatherly love for us all. Gracious God,

hear our prayer.

Guide the work of parish worship and music leaders, and the ministry of all among us who point to your beauty and assist us as we gather in your presence. Gracious God,

hear our prayer.

HERE OTHER INTERCESSIONS MAY BE OFFERED.

Holy are you, O God; you have made us your holy people. Keep us united with the faithful who have gone before us, and who now make their home with you. Gracious God,

hear our prayer.

Hear us as we pray, living God, and nourish us always at your table of grace, for the sake of Jesus Christ, our Lord and Savior.
Amen

IMAGES FOR PREACHING

Trinity Sunday provides an opportunity to explore the depths of God's love for humanity, a love so deep that it comes to us in three ways. While we know our ability to convey the reality of God is limited, we can be bold in inviting hearers to an encounter with a God who goes to such great lengths to be in relationship with us.

Who is this God we proclaim? Just as a woman heralds the birth of her child with great shouts that shake the world around her, God, whose voice "shakes the wilderness, causes oaks to whirl, strips forests bare" (Ps. 29), brings us to life. God nourishes and nurtures us, preparing us to grow into life and relationships with God and the world around us.

Just as a steadfast friend is present in times of deep suffering and pain, weeping in shared grief and offering words of healing and life in the face of sickness and death, Jesus comes to us in our brokenness, intent on making us whole.

Just as an interpreter listens intently and translates what is heard, the Holy Spirit creates understanding where none has been, even creating the possibility for relationship where none was before. The Holy Spirit translates God's love and steadfastness, and whispers God's invitation to life in our ears.

WORSHIP MATTERS

In the first reading, Isaiah has a vision of God, full of glory, before whom the sinful human cannot survive. Although images of God's transcendence were typical among ancient people, much of worship today has lost that sense of awe in God's presence. Modern church architecture, which emphasizes community and intimacy among the people and with the presiding minister, has sometimes contributed to the loss of transcendence in worship. Cultural values of casualness and informality have made their way into worship, eroding further that sense of mystery and awe before God.

While informality in worship style and emphasis on community and intimacy through ritual space may express an incarnational theology, it is important to maintain a healthy tension between a transcendent and an incarnate God.

LET THE CHILDREN COME

Let the ancient language of the Holy Trinity ring out in abundance today. Be deliberate in using the name of the Trinity at invocation and benediction. Speak carefully the prayers addressed to God the Father, through his Son, Jesus Christ, who lives and reigns with the Father and the Holy Spirit, one God, now and forever. Sing hymns that proclaim the mystery of the Trinity. Resist the urge to "explain" the Trinity. Just as we do not generally explain our names, but use them to address and identify one another, so the church does with the blessed name of the Holy Trinity.

MUSIC FOR WORSHIP
GATHERING

LBW 544	The God of Abraham praise
WOV 717	Come, all you people

PSALM 29

Busarow, Donald. "It Is a Good Thing to Give Thanks." CPH 98-3126. SATB, cong, hb.

Christiansen, David. PW, cycle B.

Guimont, Michel. "Psalm 29: The Lord Will Bless His People" in *Gather Comprehensive*. GIA.

Smith, Geoffrey Boulton. "Give Strength to Your People, Lord" in PS, vol. 1.

CHILDREN'S PSALM SUGGESTIONS

Hopson, Hal H. TP.

Hughes/Hopson. *Psalm Refrains and Tones for the Common Lectionary*. HOP. U, cong, kybd.

Marshall, Jane. *Psalms Together II*. CG CGC-21. U.

HYMN OF THE DAY

LBW 166	All glory be to God on high
	ALLEIN GOTT IN DER HÖH

VOCAL RESOURCES

Decius/arr. Schroeder. "All Glory Be to God on High." CPH 98-3114. SATB, kybd.

INSTRUMENTAL RESOURCES

Albrecht, Timothy. "All Glory Be to God on High" in *Grace Notes, vol. 1*. AFP 11-9925. Org.

Burkhardt, Michael. "All Glory Be to God on High" in *Five Hymn Accompaniments for Brass Quartet and Organ*. MSM 20-842. Org, brass.

Held, Wilbur. "All Glory Be to God on High." MSM-10-706. Org.
Johns, Donald. "Allein Gott in der Höh." NPH Mc27N0011. Org/kybd.
Ore, Charles. "Allein Gott in der Höh" in *Eleven Compositions for Organ, Set 1*. CPH 97-5019. Org.

ALTERNATE HYMN OF THE DAY

WOV 769	Mothering God, you gave me birth
LBW 165	Holy, holy, holy

COMMUNION

LBW 528	Isaiah in a vision did of old
WOV 787	Glory to God, we give you thanks

SENDING

LBW 517	Praise to the Father
WOV 721	Go, my children, with my blessing

ADDITIONAL HYMNS AND SONGS

H82 367	Round the Lord in glory seated
OBS 107	O sacred river
TFF 143	The Lord is in his holy temple
W&P	Holy ground

MUSIC FOR THE DAY

CHORAL

Bernstein, Leonard. "Sanctus" in *Mass*. GSCH 11973. SA, SATB, pno.
Collins, Dori Erwin. "Mothering God." AFP 10914. SATB, kybd, fl.
Hassell, Michael. "Spirit, Spirit of Gentleness." AFP 11-10850. SATB, sax/cl, pno.
Helman, Michael. "Come, Great God of All the Ages." AFP 11-10881. SATB, kybd.
Mendelssohn, Felix. "I Will Sing of Thy Great Mercies" in *Sing a Song of Joy, Vocal Solos for Worship*. AFP 11-8194 (MH); 11-8195 (ML).
Praetorius, Michael/arr. Story. "All Glory Be to God on High." MFS 296. SATB, rec, fc, hb.

CHILDREN'S CHOIRS

Burkhardt, Michael. "From All That Dwell Below the Skies." MSM 50-9415. U, kybd.
Glover, Rob. "Praise to the Trinity." CG CGA668. U, kybd, opt gtr.

KEYBOARD/INSTRUMENTAL

Cherwien, David. "Mothering God, You Gave Me Birth" in *O God Beyond All Praising*. AFP 11-10860. Org.
Schaffner, John Hebden. "Prelude and Gigue on 'St. Patrick's Breastplate'" in *Organ Music for the Seasons*. AFP 11-10859. Org.

HANDBELL

Dobrinski, Cynthia. "Holy, Holy, Holy." AG 1905. 3-5 oct, opt narr.

Moklebust, Cathy. "Festival Sanctus." AFP 11-10659. 4-5 oct.
Sherman, Arnold. "Immortal, Invisible." Red River Music HB0008. 3-4 oct.

PRAISE ENSEMBLE

Altrogge, Mark. "I Stand in Awe" in *Come & Worship*. INT.
Chisum and Moen. "I See the Lord" in *Come & Worship*. INT.
Clydesdale, David T. "Holy Is He" (Holy, Holy, Holy). David C. Cook Church Ministries 3100506162. SATB, orch.
Cull, Bob. "Open Our Eyes" in *Praise and Worship*. MAR BK06008.
Martin, Joseph M. "Bethlehem Wind." ALF 16440. SATB, acc.
Mohr, Jon and Randall Dennis. "More Than Anything" in *Point of Grace Songbook*. WRD 3010294492. 3 pt, kybd.
Schutte, Dan/arr. Mark Hayes. "Here I Am, Lord." GS A7101. SATB, orch.

WEDNESDAY, JUNE 21
ONESIMOS NESIB, TRANSLATOR, EVANGELIST, 1931

Nesib was captured by slave traders and taken from his Galla homeland in Ethiopia to Eritrea where he was bought and freed by Swedish missionaries. He became an evangelist, translated the Bible into Galla, and returned to preach the gospel in his homeland. His tombstone includes a verse from Jeremiah 22:29, "O land, land, land, hear the word of the LORD!"

Does your congregation support mission work through synod or churchwide offerings, or do you have a specific missionary whom you support? How do you inform your members that their gifts go to support missions as well as the needs of the local congregation?

SATURDAY, JUNE 24
THE NATIVITY OF ST. JOHN THE BAPTIST

The birth of St. John the Baptist is celebrated exactly six months before Christmas Eve. John said that he must decrease as Jesus increases, and from now until Christmas the hours of daylight will become shorter. The church uses the cycle of the sun to teach about John's and Jesus' relationship.

The Nativity of St. John the Baptist is a wonderful day for parishes to have a summertime festival tied to the unfolding of the liturgical year. Consider a church picnic, and creatively use John's traditional symbols of fire and water in decorations and games. It is also a popular day around the world for bonfires.

JUNE 25, 2000

SECOND SUNDAY AFTER PENTECOST
PROPER 7

INTRODUCTION

Life is sometimes like a storm that causes our hearts to fear. In today's gospel the disciples encounter a storm on the waters while Jesus is asleep. Upon waking, Jesus bids the wind to cease, and he speaks words of peace to his troubled disciples. We gather amid life's obstacles and hardships to hear words of comfort and promise, to greet one another with peace, and to celebrate Jesus' enduring presence among us at the Lord's table and in the community of faith.

On this day in 1530 the Augsburg Confession was read to Emperor Charles V of the Holy Roman Empire. Philipp Melanchthon, drafter of this primary Lutheran confessional document, is also commemorated today.

PRAYER OF THE DAY

O God our defender, storms rage about us and cause us to be afraid. Rescue your people from despair, deliver your sons and daughters from fear, and preserve us all from unbelief; through your Son, Jesus Christ our Lord.

READINGS

Job 38:1-11

Confronted with great suffering, Job attempts to prove his innocence to God. God speaks from the whirlwind, and speaks of the power of the sea and its waves. A series of ironical questions shows that Job, as a finite human, is incapable of judging the Creator.

Psalm 107:1-3, 23-32

God stilled the storm and quieted the waves of the sea. (Ps. 107:29)

2 Corinthians 6:1-13

Paul writes of the great hardships and calamities that he has faced, yet he is able to rejoice because what appears to be loss is great gain.

Mark 4:35-41

Jesus' calming of the storm on the sea reveals his power over evil, because the sea represents evil and chaos. The boat on the sea is a symbol of the church, and invites us to trust God amid life's turbulence.

ALTERNATE FIRST READING/PSALM

1 Samuel 17:[1a, 4-11, 19-23] 32-49

In this passage, the description of the soldier Goliath vividly depicts the superiority of Philistine military might. In contrast, David is armed by the name of the Lord.

or 1 Samuel 17:57—18:5, 10-16

Psalm 9:9-20

The LORD will be a refuge in time of trouble. (Ps. 9:9)

or Psalm 133

How good and pleasant it is to live together in unity. (Ps. 133:1)

COLOR Green

THE PRAYERS

Growing in the soil of the Spirit, let us pray for the church, the world, and all who seek the richness of life in God.

A BRIEF SILENCE.

Let us pray for hearts wide open to receive the affection of God for all people, that the church might be a community of love for one another and the world. Gracious God,
hear our prayer.

Let us pray for the land, planted and bringing forth growth, that those who till the soil and watch over the fields will be given strength for their labor. Gracious God,
hear our prayer.

Let us pray for all who are anxious or depressed, sick or suffering (especially . . .), that they may hear the gentle stillness of Christ amid the storms of life. Gracious God,
hear our prayer.

Let us pray for those who practice a ministry of hospitality in this parish: ushers, greeters, hosts, and all who serve in the name of the Spirit who welcomes and embraces all. Gracious God,
hear our prayer.

Let us pray for the unity of the church, that all who commemorate the presentation of the Augsburg Confession today would continue to strive for a deeper knowledge of Christ and his benefits. Gracious God,
hear our prayer.

HERE OTHER INTERCESSIONS MAY BE OFFERED.

Let us pray in thanksgiving for all who have died and who are now at rest in Jesus, whose Spirit keeps us united with our beloved departed. Gracious God,
hear our prayer.
Hear us as we pray, living God, and nourish us always at your table of grace, for the sake of Jesus Christ, our Lord and Savior.
Amen

IMAGES FOR PREACHING

Summer storms come up quickly. In just a moment, trees sway, grasses shimmer, birds break into a fevered pitch. Gray clouds sweep in, casting dark shadows across pavement and around buildings. Just moments before there had been sunshine, gentle breezes, languid heat radiating from pavement and off porches. We are lulled into a feeling of easy routine. Then the winds turn, and just that quickly, the energy of the day shifts and a storm sweeps in, catching us in sun-drenched surprise.

The activities of our summer lives shift some, but they quickly become routines. Getting the kids to their summer programs and activities, getting ourselves off to work, getting to the grocery store, working around the house. Our lives take on a summer rhythm that moves us along, helps us feel protected. Then a storm sweeps in, catches us by surprise. A loved one is diagnosed with a life-threatening illness; a marriage comes to a startling end; fulfilling work comes to an end. Our routine is upended; we're shocked and scared out of our summer rhythm.

Today's gospel reading cannot guarantee that sudden storms won't sweep into our lives, even in the sunny days of summer. Summer storms can be explosive and disruptive. Lives can be left reeling. What the gospel does affirm is the presence of someone greater than any storm that rocks our lives, someone who is with us in the storm, and who has the power to quiet its threatening gales, bringing us to safety.

WORSHIP MATTERS

People in congregations often are so fearful of changes in the world that they seek security by keeping things at church exactly the same as they have always been. Jesus' words to the disciples in today's gospel link the fear of change with a lack of faith. How can we be led to see that Christ is with us, even as we fear change (just as he was with the disciples in the boat)?

We come to the eucharistic meal, confident of Christ's unchanging presence with us there and pray that God "would strengthen us, through this gift, in faith toward you and in fervent love toward one another" (*LBW*, p. 74). Change is inevitable when we grow in love toward others; and Christ goes with us into change, even as our faith is made firm through participation with Christ in the eucharistic bread.

LET THE CHILDREN COME

Print in the bulletin Psalm 145:15-16, recommended in Luther's Small Catechism as a table grace. Encourage the people to use this prayer at home so that children can learn it. Consider also printing the portion of the Small Catechism pertaining to the petition of the Lord's Prayer, "Give us today our daily bread," in which we also pray that God would "satisfy the needs of every living creature." (See also next Sunday for another idea.)

MUSIC FOR WORSHIP

GATHERING

LBW 520	Give to our God immortal praise!
WOV 731	Precious Lord, take my hand

PSALM 107

Christiansen, David. PW, cycle B.
Haas, David. "Psalm 107" in PCY, vol. 8.
Hopson, Hal H. TP.
Proulx, Richard. "Give Thanks to God" in UMH.
Stewart, Roy James. "Give Thanks to the Lord" in *Choral Refrains from Psalms for the Church Year, vol. 5*. GIA G-3746-A.

HYMN OF THE DAY

LBW 334   Jesus, Savior, pilot me
         Pilot

INSTRUMENTAL RESOURCES

Beck, Theodore. "Pilot" in *Basic Hymn Accompaniments, vol. 4*. CPH 97-6636. Org.
Bisbee, B. Wayne. "Pilot" in *From the Serene to the Whimsical*. AFP 11-10561.
Elmshaeuser, Dale. "Jesus, Savior, Pilot Me." Live Oak House 444-0152.SET.Ww.
Lau, Robert. "Jesus, Savior, Pilot Me" in *Quiet Preludes: Seven Favorite Hymns for Organ*. FLA HG-5191. Org.

ALTERNATE HYMN OF THE DAY

LBW 465 Evening and morning
WOV 781 My life flows on in endless song

COMMUNION

LBW 204 Cup of blessing that we share
WOV 746 Day by day

SENDING

LBW 503 O Jesus, I have promised
WOV 781 My life flows on in endless song

ADDITIONAL HYMNS AND SONGS

H82 689 I sought the Lord
DATH 92 We will serve God
TFF 198 When the storms of life are raging
W&P Give thanks

MUSIC FOR THE DAY

CHORAL

Bach, Anna Magdalena/arr. Patrick Liebergen. "Dedication Prayer" in *Favorite Sacred Classics for Solo Singers.* ALF 11482 (ML); 11481 (MH).

Busarow, Donald. "How Firm a Foundation" in *A Sacred Harp Quartet.* MSM 50-9840. SATB div.

Ellingboe, Bradley. "How Can I Keep from Singing." KJO 8884. SATB, pno, ob.

Gibbons, Orlando. "Almighty and Everlasting God." MFS MF 2032. SATB.

Leavitt, John. "In the Shadow of Your Wings." GIA G-4302. SAB, pno, opt ob/c inst.

Walker, Gwyneth. "Sounding Joy." ECS 4318. SATB.

Young, Jeremy. "God, Here Is My Life and Will." AFP 11-10786. SATB, kybd, opt cong.

CHILDREN'S CHOIRS

Honoré, Jeffrey. "How Can I Keep from Singing?" CG CGA567. SATB, pno.

Leaf, Robert. "Let the Whole Creation Cry." AFP 11-1618. SA, kybd.

KEYBOARD/INSTRUMENTAL

Manz, Paul. "Evening and Morning" in *Three Hymns for Flute, Oboe, and Organ.* MSM 20-871. Fl, ob, org.

White, David Ashley. "Aria." SEL 160-680. Org.

HANDBELL

Behnke, John. "Children of the Heavenly Father." CPH 97-6530. 3-5 oct.

Page, Anna Laura. "The River." ALF 8655. 3-5 oct.

PRAISE ENSEMBLE

Althouse, Jay. "Joyful, Joyful, Sing Praise." ALF 16085. SATB, pno, brass, perc.

Dorsey, Thomas A./arr. Artman. "Precious Lord, Take My Hand." HAL 08708841. SATB, pno, hb, fl. Also available for 2 pt.

Gorieb and Hosman. "Peace" in *Hosanna! Music Songbook 8.* INT.

Honoré, Jeffrey. "How Can I Keep from Singing." CG CGA-567. SATB, pno.

Noblitt. "Be Still My Soul" in *Let Your Glory Fall Choral Collection.* INT.

SUNDAY, JUNE 25
PRESENTATION OF THE AUGSBURG CONFESSION, 1530; PHILIPP MELANCHTHON, RENEWER OF THE CHURCH, 1560

On this day the Augsburg Confession, drafted by Philipp Melanchthon and endorsed by Luther, was read to Emperor Charles of the Holy Roman Empire. In 1580, when the *Book of Concord* was compiled, the unaltered Augsburg Confession was included as the principal Lutheran confession. In addition to teaching Greek, Melanchthon taught theology and scripture at Wittenberg. He was a popular teacher, and with Luther's presence there also, Wittenberg was one of the leading European universities of the sixteenth century.

What are the gifts of the Augsburg Confession for our day? Do pastors occasionally refer to it, so that congregations are familiar with this important document? How is our heritage of the gospel a gift for the ecumenical movement today?

WEDNESDAY, JUNE 28
IRENAEUS, BISHOP OF LYONS, C. 202

Irenaeus believed that the way to remain steadfast to the truth was to hold fast to the faith handed down from the apostles. Irenaeus was a strong opponent of Gnosticism, dualistic thinking that separated the mind or soul from the body, and he also wrote on the restoration of human nature in Christ.

What does it mean that the church is apostolic? What are ways that the apostolic faith is preserved and passed down through the generations?

THURSDAY, JUNE 29
ST. PETER AND ST. PAUL, APOSTLES

This date commemorating the two great apostles has been observed since at least 258. Peter and Paul were two of the most important leaders in the early church. Both apostles died in Rome, said to have been founded by the twins Romulus and Remus. Among the early Christians of this city, Peter and Paul were considered the twin founders of the new Rome, a city to be transformed by the love of Christ and the blood of the martyrs. An early tradition places their martyrdom at Rome in the same year.

As you observe this festival, reflect on the unique ways that Peter and Paul shared complementary gifts and witnessed to the Christian faith in the first century—a witness that continues for future generations. How do we share the gospel of Christ today? Look at the readings assigned for St. Peter and St. Paul for some insights into these questions.

FRIDAY, JUNE 30
JOHAN OLOF WALLIN, ARCHBISHOP OF UPPSALA, HYMNWRITER, 1839

Wallin was consecrated archbishop of Uppsala and primate of the Church of Sweden, and was considered the leading churchman of his day in Sweden. Yet his lasting fame rests upon his poetry and his hymns. Of the 500 hymns in the Swedish hymnbook of 1819, 130 were written by Wallin, and approximately 200 were revised or translated by him. For more than a century the Church of Sweden made no change in the 1819 hymnbook.

Take a look at the three of Wallin's hymns that are in *LBW*: "All hail to you, O blessed morn!" (73), "We worship you, O God of might" (432), and "Christians, while on earth abiding" (440).

SATURDAY, JULY 1
CATHERINE WINKWORTH, 1878;
JOHN MASON NEALE, 1866; HYMNWRITERS

Neale was an English priest associated with the movement for church renewal at Cambridge, and Winkworth lived most of her life in Manchester, supporting the rights of women among other things. These two hymnwriters translated many hymn texts into English. Catherine Winkworth devoted herself to the translation of German hymns, and John Mason Neale specialized in ancient Latin and Greek hymns. Winkworth has thirty hymns in *LBW*, and Neale has twenty-one. In addition, two texts by Neale are in *WOV*. Use the indexes at the back of both books and research some of their most familiar translations. Sing some of your favorites at congregational events during this week. This week provides a good opportunity for a midsummer hymn festival or lunch-hour mini organ concerts.

JULY 2, 2000

THIRD SUNDAY AFTER PENTECOST
PROPER 8

INTRODUCTION

The Christian assembly gathers each Lord's day to praise God's faithfulness and steadfast love. With faith we come to hear the word and share the meal, and to know the healing that sets us free from sin and the ailments of body, mind, and soul. We go in peace to tell others of God's power to bring life from death.

PRAYER OF THE DAY

O God, you have prepared for those who love you joys beyond understanding. Pour into our hearts such love for you that, loving you above all things, we may obtain your promises, which exceed all that we can desire; through your Son, Jesus Christ our Lord.

READINGS

Lamentations 3:22-33

The book of Lamentations is one of our most important sources of information about the terrible conditions in Jerusalem after the Babylonian siege in 587 B.C. Though the people admit that God's judgment was just, today's reading declares a fervent trust that God will not leave them forever.

or Wisdom of Solomon 1:13-15; 2:23-24

Psalm 30

I will exalt you, O Lord, because you have lifted me up. (Ps. 30:1)

2 Corinthians 8:7-15

In a world where compassion burns out and people may limit their concerns to problems in their own backyards, Paul urges the Corinthian church to support the Macedonians.

Mark 5:21-43

Jairus, a respected leader, begs Jesus to heal his daughter. A woman with a hemorrhage is ritually unclean, treated as an outcast in Jewish society. Both Jairus and the unnamed woman come to Jesus in faith, believing in his power to heal and bring life out of death.

ALTERNATE FIRST READING/PSALM

2 Samuel 1:1, 17-27

This reading is a lament by David over the death of Saul. The fate of Saul illustrates the nature of power; David will also err when he turns the power he has gained toward personal ends.

Psalm 130

Out of the depths have I called to you, O Lord. (Ps. 130:1)

COLOR Green

THE PRAYERS

Growing in the soil of the Spirit, let us pray for the church, the world, and all who seek the richness of life in God.

A BRIEF SILENCE.

O God, your steadfast love never ceases and your mercies never come to an end. Give to your church leaders whose lives will reflect the abundance of your compassionate love in their ministry. Gracious God,

hear our prayer.

O God, you bring healing to the nations and peace to all peoples. Guide our elected leaders, and all the people of our country, that we would be moved to help those who seek freedom and justice. Gracious God,

hear our prayer.

O God, you are the strength of all who seek you and the rest of all whose souls wait quietly for you. Comfort all who suffer with chronic pain and illness (especially . . .), that they would know the tender touch of your healing hand. Gracious God,

hear our prayer.

O God, you are the giver of every good and perfect gift. Help the members of this congregation to share from their abundance of resources, so that the needs of our community will be met equitably. Gracious God,

hear our prayer.

HERE OTHER INTERCESSIONS MAY BE OFFERED.

O God, your children cry no cry that you do not hear and shed no tear that you do not see. Touch the lives of those who grieve losses (especially . . .), and keep us in communion with all the saints in your eternal embrace. Gracious God,

hear our prayer.

Hear us as we pray, living God, and nourish us always at your table of grace, for the sake of Jesus Christ, our Lord and Savior.

Amen

IMAGES FOR PREACHING

We are, on the whole, reasonable people. We know what it takes to live day to day. We know what life is about, its ins and outs. We know what is possible and what is not, and we live accordingly.

And yet, Jesus does not operate in the realm of what is reasonable, but in the realm of the unreasonable. Jesus does not participate in those events that seem doable, Jesus walks right into the desperate and the life-threatening. Jesus chooses a life of poverty and service so that we can be rich (2 Cor. 8:9); that is, have a full, healed relationship with God. Jesus heals a woman with a long-time hemorrhage. He raises Jairus's daughter from the dead. Such unreasonable activities fall outside the way we know things work.

But Jesus is not contained by our limited expectations, our reasonable ideas of what is possible. He doesn't leave us to die under the weight of our limited expectations. Jesus reaches out to us, invites us, heals us, stirs us up, wraps us up in the life-giving activity of God. Jesus is so passionate, so unreasonable, about a relationship with each one of us that in the end, he will give his life so we can have a new life with God.

WORSHIP MATTERS

To encourage the congregation at Corinth to complete its collection for the poor, Paul reminds it of "the generous act of our Lord Jesus Christ, that though he was rich, yet for your sakes he became poor, so that by his poverty you might become rich" (2 Cor. 8:9).

To identify with those who are poor, congregations can name specific needs or ministries in their community or region in the prayer of the church. Instead of taking a vacation from food pantry collecting, congregations can highlight such service during the summer, when many food pantries run short of supplies.

LET THE CHILDREN COME

The gospel stories in early Pentecost tell that where Jesus is, there is life and salvation. Make a display in the narthex or other gathering space to engage children in the stories. A boat on water with a Jesus figure and other human figures would serve for last week's story from Mark 4. Today, figures of Jesus, a woman, a man, and a girl on a bed are used. Have the texts of the stories laminated and easily accessible for reading, perhaps in a loose-leaf binder. Consider using the simpler text of the CEV or TEV translations of the Bible.

MUSIC FOR WORSHIP

GATHERING

LBW 352	I know that my Redeemer lives!
WOV 794	Many and great, O God, are your works

PSALM 30

Christiansen, David. PW, cycle B.
Cooney, Rory/arr. Daigle. "I Will Praise You, Lord" in PCY, vol. IV.
Haas, David/arr. Jeanne Cotter. "I Will Praise You, Lord" in PCY, vol. III.
Hopson, Hal H./arr. William Byrd. TP.
Smith, Alan. "I Will Praise You" in PS, vol. 2.

HYMN OF THE DAY

LBW 453	If you but trust in God to guide you
	WER NUR DEN LIEBEN GOTT

INSTRUMENTAL RESOURCES

Afdahl, Lee J. "If Thou But Suffer God to Guide Thee." AFP 11-10574. Hb.
Powell, Robert. "If You But Trust in God to Guide You." MSM 10-873. Org.
Reger, Max. "If You But Trust in God to Guide You" in *Chorale-Preludes for the Church Year, Op. 67*. CFI 04665. Org.
Sedio, Mark. "Wer nur den lieben Gott" in *Let Us Talents and Tongues Employ*. AFP 11-10718. Org.

ALTERNATE HYMN OF THE DAY

WOV 771	Great is thy faithfulness
LBW 360	O Christ, the healer, we have come

COMMUNION

LBW 406	Take my life, that I may be
WOV 738	Healer of our every ill

SENDING

LBW 263	Abide with us, our Savior
WOV 778	O Christ the same

ADDITIONAL HYMNS AND SONGS

GS2 14	Come, the banquet hall is ready
PH 261	God of compassion
DATH 97	Tell what God has done for us
TFF 191	I'm so glad Jesus lifted me
W&P	We praise you for your glory

MUSIC FOR THE DAY

CHORAL

Beethoven, Ludwig van. "Prayer" in *Rejoice Now My Spirit, Vocal Solos for the Church Year*. AFP 11-10228 (MH); 11-10229 (ML).
Hassell, Michael. "I'm So Glad." MSM 50-8834. Sop solo, SATB, kybd.
Meyer, Daniel C. "You Will I Love." GIA G-4146. SAB, pno.
Palestrina, G.P. "Jesu! Rex Admirabilis" (Jesus, Thou Wondrous King) in *Eleven Motets for Treble Voices*. GIA G-2143. SSA. Lat/Eng.
Schütz, Heinrich. "Lord, My Hope Is in Thee." SWV 312 (Herr, ich hoffe darauf). MCF DMC 8093 (Carus-Velag 20.312). 2 pt cont. Eng/Ger.
Weber, Paul. "I Will Sing the Story of Your Love." AFP 11-10839. SATB, org, opt cong.

CHILDREN'S CHOIRS

Handel/arr. Robert J. Powell. "Then Will I Jehovah's Praise." CG CGA220. U, kybd.
Manz, Paul. "Let Us Ever Walk with Jesus." MSM 50-9405. U, org.

KEYBOARD/INSTRUMENTAL

Barr, John G. "Arabesque on 'Great Is Thy Faithfulness.'" HWG GSTC 01059. Org.
Carter, John. "Like the Murmur of the Dove's Song" in *Today's Hymns and Songs for Piano*. HOP 224. Kybd.

HANDBELL

Honoré, Jeffrey. "Jesus in the Morning and Somebody's Knockin' at Your Door." AFP 11-10626. 2 oct.

PRAISE ENSEMBLE

Dorsey, Thomas A./arr. Artmen. "Precious Lord, Take My Hand." HAL 08708841. SATB, pno, hb, fl. Also available for 2 pt.

Elliott, John G. "Mourning Into Dancing" in *I Call You To Praise*. SP 80030/1762-79434-7. SATB, orch.

Owens, Carol. "Freely, Freely" in *The Other Songbook*. Fellowship Publications.

Runyon, William M./arr. Nelhybel. "Great Is Thy Faithfulness." HOP VN109. SATB, org, brass.

Underwood, Scott. "New Every Morning" in *Hosanna! Music Songbook 11*. INT.

THURSDAY, JULY 6
JAN HUS, MARTYR, 1415

Hus was a Bohemian priest who spoke against abuses in the church of his day. He believed that the Bible and the liturgy should be in the language of the people rather than Latin, and he sought to allow laity to receive both the bread and wine in communion. As he became more outspoken, Hus was excommunicated from the church and was eventually burned at the stake on this day in 1415. Hus's followers continued as the Czech Brethren and eventually as the Moravian church of today. Use this day to find out more about the Moravian church and its similarities with Lutheranism, especially as our ecumenical dialogues with this church continue.

JULY 9, 2000

FOURTH SUNDAY AFTER PENTECOST
PROPER 9

INTRODUCTION

The prophets of God speak with both conviction and compassion. Because prophetic words can threaten the security of even the most devout people, prophets are seldom popular in the church or in society as a whole. Yet in baptism, each Christian has been made a prophet, one who speaks on behalf of God in this time and place. Finding strength in God's grace, we are able to offer our merciful words and actions on behalf of all those who suffer in our world.

PRAYER OF THE DAY

God of glory and love, peace comes from you alone. Send us as peacemakers and witnesses to your kingdom, and fill our hearts with joy in your promises of salvation; through your Son, Jesus Christ our Lord.

READINGS

Ezekiel 2:1-5

In 597 B.C., the priest Ezekiel was removed into exile in Babylon. While there, he received a vision of God appearing majestically on a chariot throne. Today's reading recounts God's commissioning of Ezekiel during this vision. The prophet is to speak God's word to a people unwilling to hear.

Psalm 123

Our eyes look to you, O God, until you show us your mercy. (Ps. 123:3)

2 Corinthians 12:2-10

Paul uses experiences from his own life to relate his faith to the glory and pain of human existence. Visions of paradise and a mysterious "thorn in the flesh" keep him aware of the power and grace that keep him strong.

Mark 6:1-13

At home and abroad, Jesus and his disciples encounter resistance as they seek to proclaim God's word and relieve affliction.

ALTERNATE FIRST READING/PSALM

2 Samuel 5:1-5, 9-10

The rule of David over the united kingdom (northern and southern tribes) begins with these verses. Jerusalem was chosen as a political and religious center for the new combined territory.

Psalm 48

God shall be our guide forevermore. (Ps. 48:13)

COLOR   Green

THE PRAYERS

Growing in the soil of the Spirit, let us pray for the church, the world, and all who seek the richness of life in God.

A BRIEF SILENCE.

O Holy One, we thank you for your message of salvation, and pray that you would continue to raise up faithful leaders who will proclaim its joy to all the world. Gracious God,
hear our prayer.

Give strength to those who work for international relief organizations, that regions of the world faced with destruction would receive compassionate assistance. Gracious God,
hear our prayer.

Come to the help of all who are in need, touching those who are weak with sickness (especially . . .), that they might sense your nearness. Gracious God,
hear our prayer.

Bless this congregation's ministries of service and outreach into the local community. May our neighborhood experience your love as we serve and welcome all people without reserve. Gracious God,
hear our prayer.

HERE OTHER INTERCESSIONS MAY BE OFFERED.

Anoint those who grieve with the healing balm of your Spirit. Keep them and all of us united with all who have died, kindling in us the hope of the resurrection. Gracious God,
hear our prayer.

Hear us as we pray, living God, and nourish us always at your table of grace, for the sake of Jesus Christ, our Lord and Savior.
Amen

IMAGES FOR PREACHING

Believers are often portrayed as folks who are naive about the ways of the "real" world, focusing instead on the love of God and the goodness of humanity. Today's readings give strong evidence otherwise. Ezekiel is called by God to speak to the people of Israel, who are impudent and stubborn and who have rebelled against God. God is fully aware that this difficult situation will finally have no easy response.

In 2 Corinthians, Paul, the great witness to the gospel, does not have a pain-free life because he is a believer. He struggles with a "thorn in the flesh," praying repeatedly to God for relief from his torment. The relief he asks for does not come. God gives Paul a different answer than he desires. "My grace is sufficient for you, for power is made perfect in weakness" (2 Cor. 12:9).

When Jesus sends his disciples out to teach and to heal, he knows better than to send them out alone. Such activity is not without risk. After all, people from his own town, those who knew him from childhood, took offense at his teaching (Mark 6:3). So Jesus wisely sends his disciples out in pairs, surely companionship for the journey, but just as importantly, for safety in numbers. Believers see the world as it is, a place sorely in need of the transforming love of God, and go wherever that love is needed.

WORSHIP MATTERS

In the gospel for the day, Jesus sends out the disciples in mission. Their journeys are to be marked by simplicity and directness, proclaiming the message they themselves had heard Jesus preach.

The baptism and affirmation of baptism liturgies reflect many of the same themes. Simple water joined to the word of God transforms us into "members of the priesthood we all share in Christ Jesus, that we may proclaim the praise of God and bear his creative and redeeming Word to all the world" (*LBW*, pp. 121, 124). Anointed with the Spirit in baptism, the people of God, as they affirm their priesthood during their journey of faith, pledge "to proclaim the good news of God in Christ through word and deed" (*LBW*, p. 201).

LET THE CHILDREN COME

If you are using the story table (see last week), today you'll want to have twelve apostle figures, Jesus, Mary, Joseph, and Jesus' brothers and sisters, a synagogue, and some other people who are sick. An oil stock or dish with cotton soaked in scented olive oil will give the children an opportunity to feel and smell. Any opportunity for children to pick things up and use their senses will help them to learn.

MUSIC FOR WORSHIP

GATHERING

LBW 270	God of our life, all-glorious Lord
WOV 756	Lord, you give the great commission

PSALM 123

Christiansen, David. PW, cycle B.

Duffy, Philip. "Our Eyes Are on the Lord" in PS, vol. 3.

Guimont, Michel. "Psalm 123: Our Eyes Are Fixed on the Lord" in *Gather Comprehensive*. GIA.

Haas, David. "Ps 123" in PCY, vol. 8.

The Psalter-Psalms & Canticles for Singing. WJK. U, cong, cant.

HYMN OF THE DAY

LBW 396   O God, O Lord of heaven and earth
                WITTENBERG NEW

VOCAL RESOURCES

Bender, Jan. "O God, O Lord of Heaven and Earth." AFP 11-10481. SATB, org, opt tpt, cong.

INSTRUMENTAL RESOURCES

Bender, Jan. "Wittenberg New" in *Twenty-One Hymn Introductions, vol. IV, Op. 56*. CPH 97-5553. Org.

Manz, Paul. "Wittenberg New" in *Improvisations on Reformation Hymns*. MSM 10-803. Org.

Manz, Paul. "Wittenberg New" in *Improvisations on General Hymns*. MSM 10-830. Org.

ALTERNATE HYMN OF THE DAY

WOV 715   Open your ears, O faithful people
LBW 380   O Christ, our light, O Radiance true

COMMUNION

LBW 439   What a friend we have in Jesus
WOV 710   One bread, one body

SENDING

LBW 422   O God, empower us
WOV 754   Let us talents and tongues employ

ADDITIONAL HYMNS AND SONGS

H82 534   God is working his purpose out
TFF 225   I believe I'll testify
W&P   Go, make disciples

MUSIC FOR THE DAY

CHORAL

Bell, John L. "Will You Come and Follow Me." GIA G-4384. SATB, solo, opt kybd, cong.

Bouman, Paul. "I Lift Up My Eyes to the Hills." B&H OCTB6550. SA, org.

Hassell, Michael. "What a Friend We Have in Jesus." AFP 11-10919. SATB, kybd.

Marcello, Benedetto. "Oh, Hold Thou Me Up" in *The Morning Star Choir Book*. CPH 97-6287. SA, org.

Sensmeier, Randall. "Lord, Help Us Walk Your Servant Way." GIA G-4368. SATB, kybd.

CHILDREN'S CHOIRS

Brazzeal, David. "Now Paul, He Was a Servant." CG CGA782. U/2 pt, kybd.

Tucker, Margaret R. "Upon Mount Zion Sits Our God." MSM 50-9550. U/2 pt, kybd, opt fc, tamb, alto xyl.

KEYBOARD/INSTRUMENTAL

Hassell, Michael. "Yisrael V'Oraita" in *Folkways*. AFP 11-10829. Trbl inst, pno.

Staplin, Carl. "3 Sketches for Flute and Organ." MSM 20-963. Fl, org.

HANDBELL

Honore, Jeffrey. "Canon of Peace" (Dona nobis pacem). CPH 97-6657. 3-5 oct, opt C inst.

PRAISE ENSEMBLE

Graves, Denise. "Send Me" in *Break Down the Walls*. MAR 3010133367. 3pt, kybd.

Jernigan, Dennis. "You're My All in All" in *Songs for Praise and Worship*. WRD.

Nystrom, Martin J. "Your Grace Is Sufficient" in *Hosanna Music Songbook, vol 6*. INT HMSB06.

Skidmore. "Tell the World" in *Tell the World, Maranatha! Praise Band 5*. WRD/MAR.

TUESDAY, JULY 11

BENEDICT OF NURSIA, ABBOT OF MONTE CASSINO, C. 540

Benedict, the founder of western monasticism, was educated at Rome where the licentiousness of society led him to retire to a cave to live as a hermit. A community gradually gathered around him, and Benedict wrote his famous Rule, which is a guide to monastic life, dividing the day into periods of prayer, study, work, and rest. He encouraged a generous spirit of hospitality, and even today visitors at Benedictine communities are to be treated as Christ himself.

A small group may choose to read and discuss Joan Chittester's book *Wisdom Distilled from the Daily: Living the Rule of St. Benedict Today* (HarperCollins, 1990). Chittester uses the Rule of St. Benedict as a living guide for all people, suggesting that it affirms the spiritual, psychological, and social values of work, leisure, hospitality, community, listening, humility, stability, obedience, service, and care for the earth.

WEDNESDAY, JULY 12
NATHAN SODERBLÖM, ARCHBISHOP OF UPPSALA, 1931

In 1930, this Swedish theologian, ecumenist, and social activist received the Nobel prize for peace. As the primate of the Church of Sweden, Soderblöm worked for ecumenical convergence and greater understanding among the churches. He advocated practical cooperation among Christians on social questions and encouraged the liturgical movement.

As you commemorate Soderblöm, discuss the ecumenical situation in the church as we have begun the new millennium. What are some achievements of the past century, and what are some hopes for the future?

SATURDAY, JULY 15
VLADIMIR, FIRST CHRISTIAN RULER OF RUSSIA, 1015; OLGA, CONFESSOR, 969

Olga, princess of Kiev, became a Christian and was one of the first persons in that area to be baptized. Her son continued as a Viking and resisted Christianity, but Olga's grandson Vladimir adopted the faith of his grandmother. Vladimir's life had been brutal, bloodthirsty, and ruthless, but he took his new religion seriously, and he sent missionaries into remote areas. Over time Vladimir became a humble and devout person. He was known for his kindness toward criminals and his generosity toward the poor. Olga and Vladimir are honored as the first Christian rulers of Russia.

Use this occasion to learn more about the history of the Russian church. Discuss the different ways religion has been practiced in Russia during this century.

JULY 16, 2000

FIFTH SUNDAY AFTER PENTECOST
PROPER 10

INTRODUCTION

In today's gospel reading, we recognize the danger of being a prophetic voice in the world. John the Baptist denounced the intrigues of the Herodian court and eventually lost his head. Jesus criticized religious leaders who twisted life-giving practices into heavy burdens. He pointed to a justice suffused with love for all people of the earth. Jesus was put to death, as if the grave would silence him. Our worship leads us to believe just the opposite: he is alive among us, still challenging us with the vision of God's justice for this world and inspiring us to be ministers of peace.

PRAYER OF THE DAY

Almighty God, we thank you for planting in us the seed of your word. By your Holy Spirit help us to receive it with joy, live according to it, and grow in faith and hope and love; through your Son, Jesus Christ our Lord.

READINGS

Amos 7:7-15

Amos was not the kind of prophet attached to temples or royal courts. Rather, he was an ordinary farmer from Judah called by God to speak to Israel. God's word of judgment through Amos conflicted with the king's court prophet Amaziah, whom Amos encountered at Bethel.

Psalm 85:8-13

I will listen to what the LORD God is saying. (Ps. 85:8)

Ephesians 1:3-14

Like most of Paul's letters, the epistle to the Ephesians begins with thanksgiving and praise to God. Above all, God is blessed for the glorious grace bestowed on us in Christ.

Mark 6:14-29

As Jesus and his disciples begin to attract attention, Mark recalls the story of John the Baptist's martyrdom. Like John, Jesus and his disciples will also suffer at the hands of those opposed to the gospel of salvation.

ALTERNATE FIRST READING/PSALM

2 Samuel 6:1-5, 12b-19

The ark, long a symbol of God's presence with the people, enters Jerusalem. David seems comfortable with the ark only insofar as it serves his needs.

Psalm 24

Lift up your heads, O gates, and the King of glory shall come in. (Ps. 24:7)

COLOR Green

THE PRAYERS

Growing in the soil of the Spirit, let us pray for the church, the world, and all who seek the richness of life in God.
A BRIEF SILENCE.

Let us pray for the church, that it would be fearless in proclaiming the word of God and faithful in celebrating the supper of the Lord. Gracious God,
hear our prayer.

Let us pray for the leaders of the nations, that they would govern the people with equity and be led in the ways of truth, justice, and peace. Gracious God,
hear our prayer.

Let us pray for the distressed and persecuted, for those living with despair and depression, and for the sick (especially . . .), that they would not be without hope. Gracious God,
hear our prayer.

Let us pray for the vacationing members of this congregation, that they would be granted safe travels, refreshing days away, and a blessed homecoming. Gracious God,
hear our prayer.

HERE OTHER INTERCESSIONS MAY BE OFFERED.

Let us pray in thanksgiving for those who have died (especially . . .), that you would keep them in communion with us until your great and glorious day to come. Gracious God,
hear our prayer.

Hear us as we pray, living God, and nourish us always at your table of grace, for the sake of Jesus Christ, our Lord and Savior.
Amen

IMAGES FOR PREACHING

The advertisement reads, "Wanted: Women and men to work with God Almighty. Must be able to endure pain, suffering, and death. No other qualifications required." It's hard to imagine people standing in line, winding down the street and around the corner, anxiously waiting to be interviewed for such a position. Yet, the New Testament gives us pictures of people at the front of the line: Mary sings yes to God in a hymn of thanksgiving and praise, aligning her life with the divine plan for the world. She raises a son, only to end up standing at the foot of a cross, watching that beloved one die a painful death. John the Baptist shouts yes to God as he strides across the wilderness, thundering repentance to all who will hear. His life ends brutally, beheaded because of the anger and whimsy of others. Jesus embodies yes to God in the movement of his life and ministry, inviting, teaching, healing people in a relationship with God. He is beaten, dragged through the streets, and hung on a cross where he dies.

How do they do it? What enables them, and even us, to contemplate such a commitment, such an unsettled, even dangerous way of life, and to say "yes"? Ephesians 1 gives us a clue. It affirms that we are "marked with the seal of the promised Holy Spirit" (Eph. 1:13). To be sealed is to be kept securely. We might say it is to be wrapped so securely by the Holy Spirit that it infuses our whole being with the knowledge that we are God's. It creates a desire within us to align our lives with the divine plan, and supports us, gives us courage so that we are able to respond to the ad, even in the face of difficult, life-threatening events.

WORSHIP MATTERS

Weekly worship is an opportunity to reset our lives, rather like a watch might be set to a standard time or like a plumb line serves as a mark in today's first reading. The confession of sins at the beginning of the service acts as that plumb line, indicating areas of our lives that have not measured straight. But more important to the resetting of our lives are the central foci of Sunday worship: word and table. Encountering the risen Christ in word and sacrament is the standard to which people need to be in tune. When our lives are reset according to God's gracious activity, our response—living as witnesses of what God has done for us—will also be reset.

LET THE CHILDREN COME

When we think about children in worship, we need to think action: children like to do. Some are able to read;

others are strong enough to carry the cross; some are coordinated enough to light candles; others are able to carry offering plates or bread and wine; some are able to say the dismissal; some can ring the church bell; others can sing and chant the liturgy. These and other acts of worship empower children to be full participants in the household of faith.

MUSIC FOR WORSHIP
GATHERING
LBW 549	Praise, my soul, the King of heaven
WOV 797	O God beyond all praising

PSALM 85
Berthier, Jacques. TP.

Harbor, Rawn. "O Lord, Let Us See Your Kindness" in *This Far by Faith*.

Hopson, Hal H. *Psalm Refrains and Tones for the Common Lectionary*. HOP 425. U, cong.

Makeever, Ray. PW, cycle B.

Marcus, Mary. "Second Sunday in Advent" in *Psalm Antiphons-1*. MSM 80-721. U, hb.

Smith, Alan. "Let Us See, O Lord, Your Mercy" in PS, vol. 1.

CHILDREN'S PSALM SUGGESTIONS
Christopherson, Dorothy. "The Lord Is My Salvation." AFP 11-10254. U, fl, opt fc, movement.

Hruby, Dolores. *Seasonal Psalms for Children*. WLP 7102.

HYMN OF THE DAY
WOV 763	Let justice flow like streams
	St. Thomas

INSTRUMENTAL RESOURCES
Burkhardt, Michael. "St. Thomas" in *Easy Hymn Settings, set 1*. MSM 10-815. Org.

Callahan, Charles. "St. Thomas" in *Advent Music for Manuals*. MSM 10-001. Kybd.

Haan, Raymond. "St. Thomas" in *Three Hymn Partitas, set 2*. CPH 97-6282. Org.

Johnson, David N. "St. Thomas" in *Deck Thyself, My Soul with Gladness, vol. 2*. AFP 11-9101. Org.

Willan, Healey. "St. Thomas" in *Organ Works of Healey Willan*. CPH 97-6676. Org.

ALTERNATE HYMN OF THE DAY
LBW 183	The Son of God goes forth to war
LBW 495	Lead on, O King eternal

COMMUNION
LBW 201	O God of life's great mystery
WOV 766	We come to the hungry feast

SENDING
LBW 260	On our way rejoicing
WOV 790	Praise to you, O God of mercy

ADDITIONAL HYMNS AND SONGS
H82 689	I sought the Lord
OBS 76	Rise, O church, like Christ arisen
TFF 209	We've come a long way, Lord
W&P	There is a Redeemer

MUSIC FOR THE DAY
CHORAL
Bouman, Paul. "Blest Are They." SEL 410-113. SAB.

Buxtehude, Dietrich. "My Jesus Is My Lasting Joy." HWG GCMR 02727. U, org.

Ferguson, John. "Jesus, My Lord and God." AFP 11-2246. U, kybd.

Hampton, Calvin. "Fairest Lord Jesus." GIA G-2766. U, org.

Sedio, Mark. "The Thirsty Fields Drink in the Rain." AFP 11-10845. SATB, org.

CHILDREN'S CHOIRS
Gieseke, Richard W. "Lift Up Your Heads." CPH 98-2959. U/2 pt, kybd.

Scott, K. Lee. "When the Morning Stars Together." CG CGA707. Combined U and SATB org, opt tpt, opt 2-3 oct hb, opt cong.

KEYBOARD/INSTRUMENTAL
Diemer, Emma Lou. "Aria and Scherzo." SMP 70/1200 S. Trbl inst, pno/org.

Weston, Matthew. "Christians, We Have Met to Worship" in *Visions, set I*. MSM 15-814. Pno.

HANDBELL
Behnke, John A. "O Waly, Waly." AFP 11-10876. 2-3 oct, opt fl.

Tucker, Sondra K. "Meditation on 'Hyfrydol.'" CG CGB182. 3 oct.

PRAISE ENSEMBLE
Cooney, Rory. "Psalm 85: Your Mercy Like Rain." GIA G-3971. SATB, cant, cong, gtr, pno, fl, sax.

Green, Keith. "O Lord, You're Beautiful" in SPW.

Liles, Dwight. "We Are an Offering" in SPW.

Makeever, Ray. "Dancing at the Harvest" in DATH.

Tunney, Dick and Melodie/arr. Larson. "Seekers of Your Heart." GS A-6292. SATB, orch.

MONDAY, JULY 17
BARTOLOMÉ DE LAS CASAS, MISSIONARY TO THE INDIES, 1566

Las Casas was among the first missionaries in the Western Hemisphere to expose and vigorously oppose the brutal treatment of the indigenous Indian populations by the Spanish explorers. Throughout the Caribbean islands and Central America, he worked energetically to stop the enslavement of the native people, to halt the brutal treatment of women by the military forces, and to promote laws that humanized the process of colonization. Even after retirement he continued to champion these causes in his writings. Consider his strong words: "The Indians are our brothers, and Christ has given his life for them. Why, then, do we persecute them with such inhuman savagery when they do not deserve such treatment?" How does the gospel bid us to work for the human rights of all people?

SATURDAY, JULY 22
ST. MARY MAGDALENE

Mary is one of the primary witnesses to the resurrection, and she is sometimes called "the apostle to the apostles." Healed by Jesus, Mary of Magdala became a disciple of the Lord, and walked with him on his journeys. Her intense devotion to Christ was confirmed as she stood at the foot of the cross, his other disciples having abandoned him.

This commemoration invites a taste of Easter amid summertime. Sing an Easter hymn, share a festive breakfast with eggs and rich breads, and delight in the goodness of creation!

JULY 23, 2000

SIXTH SUNDAY AFTER PENTECOST
PROPER 11

INTRODUCTION

Built on the living foundation of the apostles and prophets, the local congregation is called to be an agent of reconciliation in a world filled with division and violence. For Christians, the ministry of peace begins and ends with Christ the shepherd, who gathers the scattered children of the world. He is the source of our life together and the center of the church's mission. To those who seek nourishment for daily life, we point to Christ who guides and feeds us in our journey.

Today the church commemorates Birgitta of Sweden, who reached out to the poor and criticized some of the injustices of her native Sweden during the fourteenth century.

PRAYER OF THE DAY

O Lord, pour out upon us the spirit to think and do what is right, that we, who cannot even exist without you, may have the strength to live according to your will; through your Son, Jesus Christ our Lord.

READINGS

Jeremiah 23:1-6

Jeremiah was a priest at Anathoth in Judah. He began his prophetic ministry well prior to the fall of Jerusalem (587 B.C.) and died in Egypt sometime after 587. Using the common metaphor of shepherd to describe the king, the prophet proclaims God's word of judgment and salvation.

Psalm 23

The Lord is my shepherd; I shall not be in want. (Ps. 23:1)

Ephesians 2:11-22

The Ephesians are urged to become an inclusive community, open to those who are near and far. They may begin by remembering that, as Gentiles, they themselves were once the outsiders.

Mark 6:30-34, 53-56

When Jesus sent his disciples out to teach and heal, they ministered among large numbers of people. Their work was motivated by Christ's desire to be among those in need.

ALTERNATE FIRST READING/PSALM

2 Samuel 7:1-14a

Instead of David building a house (temple) for the Lord, the Lord promises to establish David's house (dynasty) forever. Centuries later, after the Babylonian exile, no king sat on the throne. Even then, however, the people of Israel remembered this promise and continued to hope for a king, the messiah, the Lord's anointed.

Psalm 89:20-37

Your love, O LORD, forever will I sing. (Ps. 89:1)

COLOR   Green

THE PRAYERS

Growing in the soil of the Spirit, let us pray for the church, the world, and all who seek the richness of life in God.

A BRIEF SILENCE.

Shepherd your people, O God, with faithful pastors and teachers who listen to your voice and proclaim your word with truth and integrity. Gracious God,

hear our prayer.

Break down the walls of hostility between the nations, O God, and bring peaceful resolution to war-torn regions of the world. Gracious God,

hear our prayer.

Gather those who are homeless and destitute, sick and powerless into your embrace of mercy, O God (especially . . .), that they may be restored to wholeness. Gracious God,

hear our prayer.

Enable the members of this parish to hear your inviting call to rest in this summer season. Give us times of refreshment in the midst of the rigorous demands of schedules and responsibilities. Gracious God,

hear our prayer.

HERE OTHER INTERCESSIONS MAY BE OFFERED.

Enfold those who are dying in your eternal arms of mercy, and comfort those who mourn with the vision of Birgitta and all your saints, forever joined in our heavenly home. Gracious God,

hear our prayer.

Hear us as we pray, living God, and nourish us always at your table of grace, for the sake of Jesus Christ, our Lord and Savior.

Amen

IMAGES FOR PREACHING

Just picture it: men and women running helter-skelter in all directions; bumping into each other; tripping over each other in their rush to get to family, friends, and neighbors who are ill; lifting children in their arms; carefully guiding those who are filled with demons; juggling mats as two or more hoist up those who are unable to walk; speaking in half-finished sentences, "Watch out . . ." "Let me through . . ." " Help me." Twisted limbs, unseeing eyes, seeping wounds, crazed minds, and unfinished words are all brought to Jesus in a flurry of activity. People are laid or dropped, or fall at Jesus' feet, and reach out to touch his cloak. Here is no bashfulness, no reticence—just bursting anticipation that Jesus will heal them.

It is quite interesting that in this passage from Mark, the emphasis and the descriptive power are on this wild collection of souls who rush to Jesus. After telling us of those who come to be healed, we are not told how Jesus reacts to this great rush of activity. We are not given a picture of how he reaches out to the children. We don't hear the words he whispers or shouts to those who are demented. We are only told that all who touched his cloak were healed.

Perhaps the writer of Mark doesn't say much about Jesus here because he wants our eyes to remain on this wild, exuberant, broken crowd of people. They show us, through their great abandon in coming to Jesus, what the life of faith looks like. They invite us to wrap our arms around each other, lift each other up, and come to Jesus for healing.

WORSHIP MATTERS

Our Western, capitalistic culture stresses continual improvement in outcomes: higher grain yields in agriculture, greater productivity in business and manufacturing, better customer satisfaction in the service industry. This ideal serves to promote excellence, and it is an aspect of our culture that the church may often borrow and even emulate. It can be good to test church activities based on productivity and outcome.

But in the midst of all the programs and activities of the church, is time ever offered just to "rest a while," as Jesus did with his apostles? Are opportunities for worship, retreats, picnics, and fellowship events that don't have to produce anything a part of your congregation's community life?

LET THE CHILDREN COME

Jesus showed hospitality in feeding the thousands. Many congregations have a change in summer worship attendance: for some, it decreases due to vacation; for others, the number of visitors increases due to seasonal tourism. How do we show hospitality? Familiar liturgy, the common language of faith, availability of the Lord's supper, and authentic sharing of Christ's peace are all treasures that truly bind us together as one family in Christ. Have children available to be guides to visiting families. A simple checklist or script is helpful in establishing expectations.

MUSIC FOR WORSHIP

GATHERING

| LBW 245 | All people that on earth do dwell |
| WOV 747 | Christ is made the sure foundation |

PSALM 23

Wold, Wayne. PW, cycle B.
See the fourth Sunday of Easter.

HYMN OF THE DAY

LBW 313   A multitude comes from east and west
          DER MANGE SKAL KOMME

INSTRUMENTAL RESOURCES

Peeters, Flor. "Der mange skal komme" in *Hymn Preludes for the Liturgical Year, vol. XVI*. CFP 6416. Org.

Wente, Steven. "A Multitude Comes" in *The Concordia Hymn Prelude Series, vol. 22*. CPH 97-5737. Org.

ALTERNATE HYMN OF THE DAY

| LBW 459 | O Holy Spirit, enter in |
| WOV 750 | Oh, praise the gracious power |

COMMUNION

| LBW 212 | Let us break bread together |
| WOV 710 | One bread, one body |

SENDING

| LBW 429 | Where cross the crowded ways of life |
| WOV 704 | Father, we thank you |

ADDITIONAL HYMNS AND SONGS

DATH 19	Come, bring them to the table
H82 664	My Shepherd will supply my need
TFF 156	Come to Jesus
W&P	Make me a servant

MUSIC FOR THE DAY

CHORAL

Haydn, Joseph. "Lo, My Shepherd Is Divine" in *Mass in G, No. 7*. ECS 1715. SATB, org.

Liddle, Samuel. "The Lord Is My Shepherd" in *Sing Solo Sacred*. OXF 0-19-345785-7.

Marcello, Benedetto. "Teach Me Now, O Lord." MSM 50-9418. 2 pt, kybd.

Pickard, John. "The King of Love My Shepherd Is." AFP 11-10910. U, kybd.

Schoenfeld, William. "I Could Not Live without You, Lord." GIA G-4160. U, kybd, fl.

Thompson, Virgil. "My Shepherd Will Supply My Need." HWG 2571. SAB, org. Also available in SA, SSA, SSAA, SATB, TTBB.

CHILDREN'S CHOIRS

Dobry, Wallace. "The Lord Is My Shepherd." MSM 80-843. Cant/choir, cong/choir, org.

Lutz, Deborah. "Loving Jesus, Gentle Lamb." MSM 50-9500. 2 pt trbl, kybd.

KEYBOARD/INSTRUMENTAL

Kloppers, Jacobus. "Pastorale on the 23rd Psalm." CPH 97-5734. Org.

Widor, Ch. M. "Andante sostenuto" in *Symphonie gothique*. SCH. Org.

HANDBELL

Edwards, Dan R. "The Gentle Shepherd." CG CGB151. 3 oct.

Lichlyter, Mary. "My Shepherd Will Supply My Need." CG CGB 191. 3 oct, opt 2 oct hb.

PRAISE ENSEMBLE

Batstone, Barbour and Barbour. "Let the Walls Fall Down" in *Maranatha! Music Praise Chorus Book, 3rd ed.* WRD/MAR.

Bradbury, William. "Savior, Like a Shepherd Lead Us" in *Praise Worship, vol 3*. INT HMSB03.

Funk, Billy. "By Your Blood" in *Hosanna! Music Songbook 6*. INT.

Kingsley, Gershon/arr. Knight. "Shepherd Me Lord." BRN 115735. SAB, pno, gtr, perc. Also available in SATB, SSA, SA/TB.

Lojeski, Ed. "Amazing Grace." HAL 08300531. SATB, pno, gtr, perc.

Pote, Allen. "The Lord Is My Shepherd." CG CGA-551. SATB, pno.

SUNDAY, JULY 23
BIRGITTA OF SWEDEN, 1373

Birgitta was a wealthy woman with a happy marriage and eight children, but she also reached out to the poor, establishing a hospice on her estate. After her husband's death, Birgitta gave all she owned to the poor and entered a monastery. Her life of intense prayer led her to see many of the injustices that flourished in her native Sweden.

Many religious orders today continue to blend a life of prayer with service in Christ's name. Invite members of a religious community to address a group from your congregation about their vocation and the intersection of their particular ministry with their spiritual life.

TUESDAY, JULY 25
ST. JAMES THE ELDER, APOSTLE

James, son of Zebedee and brother of John, is the only apostle whose martyrdom is recorded in scripture. James is often pictured with a shell, a reminder that he was a fisherman and that he later baptized new Christians. Of the two men named James who became apostles, this James is called the elder, or the greater, because we know more about him. The other James is commemorated with Philip on May 1.

In celebration, have fish for dinner tonight and tell stories of the baptisms in your family.

FRIDAY, JULY 28
JOHANN SEBASTIAN BACH, 1750; HEINRICH SCHÜTZ, 1672; GEORGE FREDERICK HANDEL, 1759; MUSICIANS

These musicians used the gift of composition to enrich the worship and devotional lives of Christians from their day until today. The year 2000 marks the 250th anniversary of Bach's death. In Leipzig he wrote choral cantatas for each Sunday and festival of the church year. Schütz's choral settings of biblical texts show a mastery never surpassed. Handel's music is not church music in the strictest sense, but his oratorios have been cherished proclamations of the scriptures.

Commemorate these three great musicians by playing selections of their great works, or by singing a hymn by each one, such as Bach's arrangement of "Come with us, O blessed Jesus" (LBW 219) or "O Spirit of life" (WOV 680), Handel's famous tune used with "Thine is the glory" (LBW 145), and Schütz's tune used with a paraphrase of the Magnificat (LBW 180).

In this year of Bach, consider programming his music throughout your worship services by utilizing the new choral collection from Augsburg Fortress: *Bach through the Church Year* (AFP 3-5854). The volume includes choral movements from cantatas and oratorios that encompass the liturgical year, and features newly reconstructed keyboard parts along with new English translations.

SATURDAY, JULY 29
MARY, MARTHA, AND LAZARUS OF BETHANY

Mary, Martha, and Lazarus of Bethany are remembered for the hospitality and refreshment they offered Jesus in their home. Mary is identified in the fourth gospel as the one who anointed Jesus before his passion. Following the characterization drawn by Luke, Martha represents the active life, and Mary the contemplative. In the gospel of John, Lazarus is raised from the dead by Jesus as a sign of the eternal life offered to all believers. Congregations might commemorate these three by reflecting on the role of hospitality in both home and church and the blessing of friendship.

OLAF, KING OF NORWAY, MARTYR, 1030

Olaf is considered the patron saint of Norway. A year after arriving there he declared himself king of his country, and from then on Christianity was the dominant religion of the realm. In addition, he revised the laws of the nation and enforced them with strict impartiality, alienating some of the aristocracy. After being driven from the country, he died in battle, trying to regain his kingdom. Tell stories of the giants in the history of your congregation today. Give thanks for the Church of Norway.

JULY 30, 2000

SEVENTH SUNDAY AFTER PENTECOST
PROPER 12

INTRODUCTION

The psalms speak of God as the one who feeds humanity: You open wide your hand, O God, and give us food in every season. The psalmist implies that humans have physical and spiritual hungers, hungers that will be satisfied only by God. In Christ, God satisfies our thirst with living waters and feeds us with living bread. These images speak of our desire for communion with the one who is greater than our frailty and fears. They are biblical images of Christ's presence among us in the waters of baptism and the bread and cup of the eucharist.

PRAYER OF THE DAY

O God, your ears are open always to the prayers of your servants. Open our hearts and minds to you, that we may live in harmony with your will and receive the gifts of your Spirit; through your Son, Jesus Christ our Lord.

READINGS

2 Kings 4:42-44

Today's reading is part of a larger section (2 Kings 4:1—8:6) that presents the miracles of Elisha. Here the prophet asks that food be given to a hungry crowd. He trusts God, who says there shall be enough and even more.

Psalm 145:10-19 (Psalm 145:10-18 [NRSV])

You open wide your hand and satisfy the needs of every living creature. (Ps. 145:17)

Ephesians 3:14-21

Paul prays for the Christians to whom he writes, asking that God will grant them inner strength and spiritual power as they continue to grow in their understanding of the love of Christ.

John 6:1-21

In John's gospel, the miracles of Jesus are called "signs," because they reveal the true character of God. As such, they remain within the mystery of God and cannot be brought under human control.

ALTERNATE FIRST READING/PSALM

2 Samuel 11:1-15

The story of David's adulterous and ultimately murderous actions in regard to Bathsheba and her husband Uriah is one of the most infamous of the Old Testament.

Psalm 14

God is in the company of the righteous. (Ps. 14:5)

COLOR Green

THE PRAYERS

Growing in the soil of the Spirit, let us pray for the church, the world, and all who seek the richness of life in God.

A BRIEF SILENCE.

God of plenty, provide the church with faithful and generous stewards who will share of their resources to carry out your mission in the world. Gracious God,
hear our prayer.

God of fullness, help us to provide food and clothing, shelter and security for all the people of the world who live in places of famine and scarcity, that they may have enough of all they need for this life. Gracious God,
hear our prayer.

God of abundance, look with compassion on children who are living in poverty, and provide for them from the richness of your mercy, that they may be strengthened to play and grow. Gracious God,
hear our prayer.

God of good gifts, may we see your presence as we gather around tables of fellowship to enjoy friendship and the food that we eat together. Gracious God,
hear our prayer.

HERE OTHER INTERCESSIONS MAY BE OFFERED.

God of life, the riches of your glory are beyond our imagination. Hold the sick in your care (especially . . .). Grant peace to the dying and comfort to the grieving, and all for your love's sake. Gracious God,
hear our prayer.

Hear us as we pray, living God, and nourish us always at your table of grace, for the sake of Jesus Christ, our Lord and Savior.
Amen

IMAGES FOR PREACHING

One attribute of servants of God is that they are able to look around them and see abundance where others see scarcity. A man comes to Elisha, bearing first fruits that include twenty loaves of barley and fresh ears of grain. When Elisha commands him to give it to the people to eat, the man sees scarcity, "How can I set this before a hundred people?" He has done a quick calculation: twenty loaves, some fresh ears, one hundred people. No way on earth will this small amount of food feed so many people.

A large crowd gathers around Jesus on a hill by the Sea of Galilee. Because Passover is approaching, Jesus asks where they are to buy bread for the crowd to eat. The disciples see scarcity. First, Philip responds, "Six months' wages would not buy enough." Andrew chimes in, "There is a boy with five barley loaves and two fish. But what are they among so many?" They too can calculate easily enough. This time five thousand are present and hungry. Certainly there is not enough food to go around.

It's not that Elisha and Jesus don't see the numbers of hungry people needing to be fed. It is that they see more. They also see the power of God at work in and through the food that is available. The power of God is the abundance these servants see. It is the abundance that feeds all who are hungry, with plenty left over.

WORSHIP MATTERS

What do you do with the fragments of bread and wine that are left over after the liturgy? Justin Martyr, writing circa A.D. 150 on the practice of the church at Rome, records that "they [the remaining eucharistic elements] are sent through the deacons to those who are not present" (*First Apology*, 67.1).

The custom of carrying the bread and wine used in the Sunday assembly holds rich symbolism of the eucharist as a sacrament of unity; those who are absent from the assembly are still connected with the Christian community by their participation in the one bread and one cup. *The Use of the Means of Grace*, principle 48, states that "[c]ongregations provide for communion of the sick, homebound, and imprisoned." The order for the Distribution of Communion to Those in Special Circumstances provided in *Occasional Services* (pp. 76–81) encourages the careful selection and training of persons to carry out this ministry.

LET THE CHILDREN COME

As we begin a five-week series of John 6, consider a summertime discussion group to study the relation of nourishment in Jesus, the bread of life, and the problem of world hunger. Plan a project for the next few weeks to benefit a local effort to assist those who are hungry or the ELCA World Hunger Appeal. Perhaps children could bake bread or muffins for a soup kitchen, runaway shelter, or prison.

MUSIC FOR WORSHIP

GATHERING

LBW 539	Praise the Almighty
WOV 766	We come to the hungry feast

PSALM 145

Bengtson, Bruce. PW, cycle B.
Haas, David. "I Will Praise Your Name" in PS, vol. 2.
Haugen, Marty/arr. David Haas. PCY.
Stewart, Roy James. "The Hand of the Lord" in PCY, vol. V.

CHILDREN'S PSALM SUGGESTIONS

Hruby, Dolores M. *Seasonal Psalms for Children*. WLP 7102. U.

HYMN OF THE DAY

LBW 235	Break now the bread of life
	BREAD OF LIFE

INSTRUMENTAL RESOURCES

Johnson, David. "Bread of Life" in *Deck Thyself, My Soul with Gladness*, vol. 1. AFP 11-9157. Org.
Jordan, Alice. "Break Thou the Bread of Life" in *Hymns of Grateful Praise*. BRD. Org.

ALTERNATE HYMN OF THE DAY

WOV 704	Father, we thank you
LBW 457/8	Jesus, priceless treasure

COMMUNION

LBW 197	O living Bread from heaven
WOV 711	You satisfy the hungry heart

SENDING

LBW 453	If you but trust in God to guide you
WOV 790	Praise to you, O God of mercy

ADDITIONAL HYMNS AND SONGS

H82 323	Bread of heaven, on thee we feed
DATH 29	Just as Jesus told us
TFF 120	Lord, I hear of showers of blessings
W&P	Here is bread

MUSIC FOR THE DAY

CHORAL

Busarow, Donald. "O Lord, You Are My God and King." AFP 11-10892. SAB, org, trp, hb, opt cong.

Kosche, Kenneth T. "Ignite My Heart O Holy Flame." GIA G-4077. SATB, org.

Praetorius, Michael. "Jubilate Deo." B&H OCTB6350. Canon in 2, 3, or 4 pt.

Proulx, Richard. "The Eyes of All." AFP 12-109. U, org.

Thompson, J. Michael. "Taste and See the Lord Is Good." AFP 11-10842. SATB, org, ob.

CHILDREN'S CHOIRS

Hobby, Robert. "Offertory for Pentecost 7." MSM 80-575. U, org, opt trbl inst.

Proulx, Richard. "The Eyes of All." AFP 12-109. U, org.

KEYBOARD/INSTRUMENTAL

Cotter, Jeanne. "Eat This Bread" in *After the Rain*. GIA G-3390. Pno.

Oliver, Curt. "Father, We Thank You" in *Four Communion Hymn Settings*. MSM 15-825. Pno.

HANDBELL

Afdahl, Lee J. "Here Would I Feed Upon the Bread of God." AFP 11-10874. 3-5 oct.

Sherman, Arnold. "The Journey" (I Want Jesus to Walk with Me). AG 1897. 3-5 oct.

PRAISE ENSEMBLE

Altrogge, Mark. "How Great Is Your Love" in *Hosanna! Music Songbook, vol 7*. INT HMSB07.

Lovelace, Austin C. "Let Us Talents and Tongues Employ." CG CGA619. 2pt mxd, pno.

Paris, Twila/arr. Torrans. "We Bow Down." Songpower ZJP7006. SAB, kybd.

Ross. "You Who Are Thirsty" in *Songs for Praise and Worship*. WRD.

Wimber, John. "Spirit Song" in *Praise Hymns and Choruses, 4th ed.* MAR.

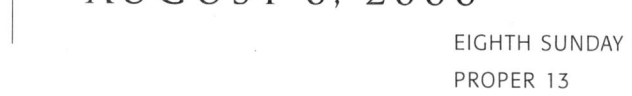

AUGUST 6, 2000

EIGHTH SUNDAY AFTER PENTECOST
PROPER 13

INTRODUCTION

Even when they grumbled and complained, God provided food for the Israelites. In today's gospel, when the disciples ask Jesus for an impressive sign, he offers them himself, the bread of life to all who truly hunger. This gift enables all believers to grow in Christ and to become one with his mission in the world. Though our hunger will always return, Christ is present to nourish us with his very life.

PRAYER OF THE DAY

Gracious Father, your blessed Son came down from heaven to be the true bread which gives life to the world. Give us this bread, that he may live in us and we in him, Jesus Christ our Lord.

READINGS

Exodus 16:2-4, 9-15

Exodus 16 recounts the second of three tests for Israel in the wilderness (see also 15:22-27 and 17:1-7). In this reading, a food crisis becomes a faith crisis. The hunger of the wandering Israelites moves the people to deny God's saving work in the exodus. At least they had food when they were in Egypt! Nevertheless, God meets their need day by day.

Psalm 78:23-29

The Lord rained down manna upon them to eat. (Ps. 78:24)

Ephesians 4:1-16

In the first three chapters of Ephesians, Paul declares that, through grace, Christ has reconciled all people to God and to each other. Now, he traces the specific consequences of this reconciliation for Christian communities that are diverse in their unity.

John 6:24-35

Many of the five thousand people Jesus fed in the wilderness continued to follow him throughout the countryside. Jesus challenges them to consider the real nature of their quest.

ALTERNATE FIRST READING/PSALM

2 Samuel 11:26—12:13a

God sends the prophet Nathan to rebuke David the king for his abuse of power in deceiving and killing Uriah and taking Uriah's wife.

Psalm 51:1-12

Have mercy on me, O God, according to your lovingkindness. (Ps. 51:1)

COLOR Green

THE PRAYERS

Growing in the soil of the Spirit, let us pray for the church, the world, and all who seek the richness of life in God.

A BRIEF SILENCE.

Let us pray for the church, that God would lead many to eat the bread of heaven and drink the cup of salvation, never to hunger and thirst again. Gracious God,
hear our prayer.
Let us pray for the world, that where people know scarcity of food and water they would also know a united effort to help them in their need. Gracious God,
hear our prayer.
Let us pray for those in our communities who are poor, that they would meet with compassionate assistance and opportunities for rewarding employment. Gracious God,
hear our prayer.
Let us pray for all who are hospitalized, all who are in chronic pain, and for all whose health is a concern (especially . . .). Gracious God,
hear our prayer.
Let us pray for the members of this congregation who volunteer with community food shelves, reading programs, and other forms of assistance, that they would be strengthened for service to all they reach. Gracious God,
hear our prayer.

HERE OTHER INTERCESSIONS MAY BE OFFERED.

Let us pray for all who have died (especially . . .), that their memory may be blessed among us, and that their loved ones would be comforted in the hope of the resurrection. Gracious God,
hear our prayer.
Hear us as we pray, living God, and nourish us always at your table of grace, for the sake of Jesus Christ, our Lord and Savior.
Amen

IMAGES FOR PREACHING

Many of us are raised with the admonishment "don't complain." Complaining suggests that we are ungrateful for what we have, that we expect more. No one says, "Oh please, let the complainer be part of my group." We tune such people out, dismiss them, and become angry or annoyed.

The people of Israel are quite accomplished complainers. They eventually complain and murmur their way across the wilderness into the promised land. One can imagine that Moses and Aaron aren't particularly thrilled by it; they're barely out of the land of Egypt when the grumbling begins. This grumbling is going to make for one long journey. Interestingly enough, God does not appear to be put off by such behavior.

God simply listens to their complaints, hearing the fear and anxiety behind them. God hears the fear of the hunger that rumbles through their bellies, and the fear of the wilderness that clings to their limbs and their clothing. Then God provides what they need, manna from heaven that strengthens their bodies for the journey and assures their souls of God's presence. God provides the bread of life—Jesus—so our hungry bodies might be filled and our frightened souls assured of God's presence throughout our wilderness journey.

WORSHIP MATTERS

The second reading celebrates a variety of gifts "for building up the body of Christ" (Eph. 4:12). The gifts of some are more visible to the whole body than others, yet each has its unique purpose. How are various gifts of people in your congregation acknowledged? One resource for publicly identifying Christ's gifts of grace among his people is the service Recognition of Ministries in the Congregation in *Occasional Services* (pp. 143–46).

LET THE CHILDREN COME

Bread is as important to us as it was to our ancestors. Consider its role in our diet of pizza, crackers, cereal, pretzels, pasta, tortillas, croissants, and bagels. What would it be like for us to go without all of these? What might it be like for those who regularly do go without? We are nourished with the bread of life by means of God's word and sacraments. What effect would it have on the health of our faith if we could not feast upon it? What might it be like for those who are starving for this heavenly bread?

MUSIC FOR WORSHIP

GATHERING

LBW 191	Praise and thanksgiving be to God
WOV 760	For the fruit of all creation

PSALM 78

Bengtson, Bruce. PW, cycle B.

Haas, David. "Ps 78" in PCY, vol. 8.

Hallock, Peter/arr. Carl Crosier. *The Ionian Psalter*. ION. SATB/U, org.

Stewart, Roy James. "The Lord Gave Them Bread" in PCY, vol. 5.

CHILDREN'S PSALM SUGGESTIONS

Guimont, Michel. "Psalm 78: The Lord Gave Them Bread" in *Gather Comprehensive*. GIA.

HYMN OF THE DAY

LBW 172	Lord, enthroned in heavenly splendor
	BRYN CALFARIA

VOCAL RESOURCES

Wolff, Drummond. "Lord, Enthroned in Heavenly Splendor." CPH 98-2611. SATB, kybd.

INSTRUMENTAL RESOURCES

Burkhardt, Michael. "Bryn Calfaria" in *Easy Hymn Settings*. MSM 10-415. Org.

Burkhardt, Michael. "Bryn Calfaria" in *Five Easter Season Hymn Improvisations*. MSM 10-403. Org.

Haller, William. "Bryn Calfaria" in *Back to Life Again*. AFP 11-10319. Org.

Langlois, Kristina. "Bryn Calfaria" in *Eight Miniatures for the Seasons of Lent, Easter and Pentecost*. MSM 10-345. Org.

ALTERNATE HYMN OF THE DAY

WOV 700	I received the living God
LBW 358	Glories of your name are spoken

COMMUNION

LBW 211	Here, O my Lord, I see thee
WOV 702	I am the Bread of life

SENDING

LBW 370	Blest be the tie that binds
WOV 699	Blessed assurance

ADDITIONAL HYMNS AND SONGS

DATH 30	This bread that we break
UMH 561	Jesus, united by thy grace
TFF 263	I'm a-going to eat at the welcome table
W&P	Broken in love

MUSIC FOR THE DAY

CHORAL

Byrd, William. "Ego sum panis vivus." J.W. Chester 8747. SATB.

Fay, Peter. "O Sacred and Blessed Feast." AFP 11-10841. Also in *The Augsburg Choirbook*. 11-10817. SATB.

Handel, G. F. "Jesu, Thou Art Watching Ever" in *Sing a Song of Joy, Vocal Solos for Worship*. AFP 11-8194 (MH); 11-8195 (ML).

Issac/arr. Mark Bighley. "O Bread of Life from Heaven." AFP 12-800003. SATB.

Keesecker, Thomas. "I Am the Living Bread." AFP 11-10684. SATB, kybd, opt cong, opt sax/C inst.

Loli, Simon. "I am the Bread of Life." GIA G-4473. SATB, kybd.

CHILDREN'S CHOIRS

Pethel, Stan. "Bless This Gift." CG CGA761. 2 pt mxd, kybd.

Powell, Robert. "A Song of Promise." CG CGA479. U, fl, kybd, opt adult choir.

KEYBOARD/INSTRUMENTAL

Langlais, Jean. "Prelude modal" in *Twenty-four Pieces, bk. I*. Masters Music Pub., Inc.

Williams, R. Vaughan. "Bryn Calfaria" in *Three Preludes on Welsh Hymn Tunes*. GAL 3901. Org.

HANDBELL

Hall, Jefferey A. "I Am the Bread of Life." CPH 97-6659. 3-5 oct, opt. 1-3 oct hc.

Moklebust, Cathy. "Christ Is Made the Sure Foundation" in *Stanzas for Handbells*. AFP 11-10722. 4-5 oct.

Wagner, Douglas. "Fanfare Prelude on 'Aurelia.'" AGEHR AG35075. Full score. AG35074. 3-5 oct hb score. PP361. Brass, timp.

PRAISE ENSEMBLE

Baloche, Paul and Claire Cloninger. "As Bread That Is Broken" in *Hosanna! Music Songbook, vol 10*. INT 08667.

Dearman. "We Remember You" in *Songs for Praise and Worship*. WRD.

Fitts, Bob. "One God" in *Maranatha! Music Praise Chorus Book, 3rd ed.* WRD/MAR.

Knapp, Phoebe P./arr. Whaley and Clevenger. "Blessed Assurance." PLY SHS9705. SATB, kybd.

Pote, Allen. "Many Gifts, One Spirit." Coral Key Music 391-41417. SAB, kybd. Also available in SATB, SSA.

TUESDAY, AUGUST 8
DOMINIC, PRIEST, 1221

Dominic founded an order of itinerant preachers, known today as the Dominicans. He was a man of study and of prayer, and taught his followers to "bring to others what you contemplate." The Order of Preachers, as it was called, was to use kindness and gentle argument, rather than harsh judgment, when bringing unorthodox Christians back to the fold. Dominic was opposed to the practice of burning heretics at the stake simply because of their unorthodox faith.

THURSDAY, AUGUST 10
LAWRENCE, DEACON, MARTYR, 258

Lawrence lived during the time of persecution under the Roman emperor Valerian. According to tradition, when Lawrence learned that he would follow the pope and other deacons to his death as a martyr, he gathered people in need and brought them to a Roman official saying: "Here is the treasure of the Church." Lawrence's martyrdom was one of the first to be observed by the church.

Amid our concerns for the institutional church, reflect on what we consider the treasures of the church today. Are we rooted in the gifts of word and sacrament? Is our response to the needs of the most vulnerable in our society one of obligation, or one that treasures what we can also receive from them?

AUGUST 13, 2000

NINTH SUNDAY AFTER PENTECOST
PROPER 14

INTRODUCTION

Christ has given his flesh for the life of the world. He sustains the pilgrim people of God with the word of life and the bread of heaven. Through the holy supper, Christ comes to us so that we might find the source of our unity and follow him in the way of sacrificial love. Though we will experience frustration or despair, we know that God is ever eager to nourish us back to life. We need only come to the table and receive the gift of life.

Today the church commemorates Florence Nightingale (1910) and Clara Maass (1901), women who used their vocation of nursing to forge new paths of service in their day.

PRAYER OF THE DAY

Almighty and everlasting God, you are always more ready to hear than we are to pray, and to give more than we either desire or deserve. Pour upon us the abundance of your mercy, forgiving us those things of which our conscience is afraid, and giving us those good things for which we are not worthy to ask, except through the merit of your Son, Jesus Christ our Lord.

READINGS

1 Kings 19:4-8

Chapter 18 portrays the contest between Elijah and the prophets of Baal in which God withholds and sends the fire. After the contest, Elijah orders the killing of the prophets of Baal. Angered by the deaths of her prophets, Queen Jezebel threatens to take Elijah's life. This reading finds the prophet fleeing, fatigued, and in utter despair.

Psalm 34:1-8

Taste and see that the LORD is good. (Ps. 34:8)

Ephesians 4:25—5:2

The letter to the Ephesians declares that people are reconciled with God through God's grace, not by doing good works. As these verses indicate, those who experience God's forgiveness are called upon to live as the transformed people they have become.

John 6:35, 41-51

After feeding more than five thousand people in the wilderness, Jesus teaches them regarding the true significance of this remarkable sign.

ALTERNATE FIRST READING/PSALM

2 Samuel 18:5-9, 15, 31-33

This reading begins with a report about the conflict between Absalom and his father. Even though outnumbered, David's forces secured a complete victory, scattering and killing Absalom's force.

Psalm 130

Out of the depths have I cried to you, O Lord. (Ps. 130:1)

COLOR Green

THE PRAYERS

Growing in the soil of the Spirit, let us pray for the church, the world, and all who seek the richness of life in God.

A BRIEF SILENCE.

O living Bread from heaven, nourish your church with the supper of the Lord and give it boldness to invite all people to your table. Gracious God,
hear our prayer.

O God, you gave your Son to be bread for the life of the world. Watch over the fields of the earth now ripening, that many will be fed with the fruits of the harvest. Gracious God,
hear our prayer.

O Bread of life, you satisfy our every hunger. Be with all in need, and draw near to those who are sick and hunger for health (especially . . .). Gracious God,
hear our prayer.

O Healer of all, you raise up servants like Florence Nightingale and Clara Maass to minister to physical illnesses. Help all nurses and caregivers to see your blessing in their work. Gracious God,
hear our prayer.

O God, you call us to imitate you as your beloved children. Bless the fruits of this congregation's ministries, that many may be drawn to you for nourishment. Gracious God,
hear our prayer.

HERE OTHER INTERCESSIONS MAY BE OFFERED.

Bread of heaven, bring us all at length to your banquet table where, in the company of all the saints, we will dine with you for all eternity. Gracious God,
hear our prayer.

Hear us as we pray, living God, and nourish us always at your table of grace, for the sake of Jesus Christ, our Lord and Savior.
Amen

IMAGES FOR PREACHING

At times, life seems more than we can bear. We have high expectations of ourselves and others that come crashing down around our ears. We have deeply hurt one another; we have been the recipients of life-shaking betrayals. We have experienced blinding loss and grief. Struck down, brought to our knees, we feel we don't have the strength to go on. Sometimes we are only a step away from asking God to let us die. Sometimes we cry out to God for final relief from our suffering.

Elijah is at just such a point. Unable to compel the court of Ahab to leave behind worship of the Baals and return to the Lord, he is in deep despair. Jezebel has made a vow to murder him, and he is on the run, fearful for his life. Sitting under a broom tree, awash in failure and fear, he cries out to the Lord, "Take away my life." Depleted, he falls asleep.

The Lord hears the cries of Elijah and responds—not with what Elijah has asked for, but with what Elijah needs. Instead of death, the Lord provides nourishment for life. In the form of a cake and water, Elijah receives what he needs to continue his journey.

The Lord hears our cries and responds—not always with what we ask for, but with what we need. Instead of death, the Lord provides nourishment for our lives. In the form of Jesus, the living bread that comes down from heaven, we receive what we need for this life's journey, and we receive a promise that we will be sustained in our journey beyond the grave.

WORSHIP MATTERS

Do congregational groups and committees follow an intention to put away falsehood, speak the truth, and not let the sun go down on our anger? Community life cannot survive in integrity without the forgiveness God has given through Christ.

Sometimes our ordinary human speech cannot easily verbalize how others have caused us hurt, or how we desire forgiveness for hurts we have caused others. Ritual language, set in the context of a liturgical service, can fill this void. *Lutheran Book of Worship* includes a service for Corporate Confession and Forgiveness (pp. 193–95). Consider using it before a congregational meeting that will be contemplating an issue that has already caused inner conflict.

LET THE CHILDREN COME

God is a cornucopia, and biblical images of abundance of life's necessities abound. Jesus cares for our physical needs as well as our eternal needs. As branches connected to the vine, we need to draw sustenance from the source of all life. Consider the catechism on the first article of the creed or on the fourth petition of the Lord's Prayer and develop prayer petitions along those lines. Children could assist with the prayers.

MUSIC FOR WORSHIP

GATHERING

| LBW 540 | Praise the Lord! O heavens |
| WOV 718 | Here in this place |

PSALM 34

Bengtson, Bruce. PW, cycle B.

Glynn, John. "Look Towards the Lord" in *PS*, vol. 2.

Harbor, Rawn. "Taste and See the Goodness of the Lord" in *This Far by Faith*.

Hobby, Robert. "I Will Bless the Lord." MSM 80-707. U, cong, org.

Moore, James. "Taste and See." GIA G-2784. Cong, cant, acc, gtr.

Walker, Christopher. "Taste and See" in *PS*, vol. 3.

Young, Jeremy. "Taste and See." AFP 11-10895. U, kybd, opt 2 pt, opt cong.

WOV 706 Eat this bread, drink this cup (psalm paraphrase)

CHILDREN'S PSALM SUGGESTIONS

Howard, Julie. *Sing for Joy: Psalm Settings for God's Children*. Liturgical Press 8146-2078-7.

Hruby, Dolores. "I Will Bless the Lord at All Times." CG CGA452. U, cong, perc.

HYMN OF THE DAY

LBW 343 Guide me ever, great Redeemer
CWM RHONDDA

VOCAL RESOURCES

Schroeder, Jack. "Guide Me, O Thou Great Jehovah." HOP CH 671. SATB, kybd.

INSTRUMENTAL RESOURCES

Barr, John G. "Prelude on Cwm Rhondda" in *Three Preludes on Hymn Tunes*. HWG GSTC 0 1079. Org.

Behnke, John. "Cwm Rhondda" in *Variations for Seven Familiar Hymns*. AFP 11-10702. Org.

Dobrinski, Cynthia. "Guide Me, O Thou Great Jehovah." HOP 1911. Hb.

Held, Wilbur. "Cwm Rhondda" in *Those Wonderful Welsh, set 2*. MSM 10-842. Org.

Moklebust, Cathy. "Cwm Rhondda" in *Hymn Stanzas for Handbells*. AFP 11-10722. 4-5 oct hb. 11-10869. 2-3 oct hb.

ALTERNATE HYMN OF THE DAY

| WOV 709 | Eat this bread |
| LBW 224 | Soul, adorn yourself with gladness |

COMMUNION

| LBW 199 | Thee we adore, O hidden Savior |
| WOV 702 | I am the Bread of life |

SENDING

| LBW 352 | I know that my Redeemer lives! |
| WOV 801 | Thine the amen, thine the praise |

ADDITIONAL HYMNS AND SONGS

H82 308/9	O Food to pilgrims given
TFF 145	Jesus, we want to meet
W&P	Seed, scattered and sown

MUSIC FOR THE DAY

CHORAL

Glover, Rob. "Come and Eat This Living Bread." GIA G-4586. Choir, cong, org/pno, opt gtr, b-flat inst, ob, vln, vc, hb, Orff.

Jacobson, Borghild, and Joanna Lange/arr. Bret Heim. "Manna Sweet, Refresh Your Flock. CPH 98-3046. SATB, org.

Keesecker, Thomas. "I Am the Living Bread." AFP 11-10684. SATB, kybd, opt cong, opt sax/C inst.

Pinkham, Daniel. "This Is the Bread." ECS 4447. 2 pt, org.

Vaughan Williams, Ralph. "O Taste and See." OXF A349. SATB.

CHILDREN'S CHOIRS

Mozart/arr. Hopson. "I Feel the Love of God." CG CGA778. U, kybd.

Telemann/arr. David Cherwien. "I Want to Praise the Lord All of My Life." CPH 98-3350. 2-3 pt, kybd, opt inst.

KEYBOARD/INSTRUMENTAL

Diemer, Emma Lou. "Suite Sunday." SMP 70/1144 S. Org, pno/hpd/synth.

Meyer, Lawrence. "Processional of Joy." AFP 11-10797. Org/kybd.

HANDBELL

Helman, Michael. "Gift of Finest Wheat." AFP 11-10872. 3-5 oct, opt hc.

McFadden, Jane. "All Things Bright and Beautiful." BEC HB164. 3-5 oct.

PRAISE ENSEMBLE

Baloche, Paul and Claire Cloninger. "As Bread That Is Broken" in *Hosanna! Music Songbook, vol 10.* INT 08667

Berthier, Jacques/ed. Brother Robert. "Eat This Bread." GIA G-2840. Cant, response.

"Lord, I Want to Be a Christian in My Heart" in *The Worshipping Church.* HOP.

Owens, Jimmy and Carol Owens. "Make Me Like You" in *The Other Songbook.* Fellowship Publications.

Tunney, Dick and Melodie/arr. Ed Lojeski. "O Magnify the Lord." HAL 08346681. SATB, pno. Also available in SAB.

Ylvisaker, John. "I'll Bless the Lord Forevermore" in *Borning Cry.* NGP.

SUNDAY, AUGUST 13
FLORENCE NIGHTINGALE, 1910; CLARA MAASS, 1901; RENEWERS OF SOCIETY

Florence Nightingale and Clara Maass are examples of women who used their vocation of nursing to forge new paths of service in their day. Among other things, Florence established the first school of nursing in England, and Clara researched and nursed victims of yellow fever. They serve as role models of women who used their gifts and calling to make significant contributions to the times in which they lived.

Give thanks for nurses and other healthcare professionals in your congregation. Do you have a parish nurse on your staff? A parish nurse helps keep issues of health and wholeness before the congregation through newsletter articles, classes, and other educational events.

TUESDAY, AUGUST 15
MARY, MOTHER OF OUR LORD

Today we join the church around the world in honoring Mary as the bearer of the Word. In a long line of spiritual writers, Luther refers to Mary as the Mother of God, the God-bearer, *theotokos*. Mary is often seen as a model of devoted motherhood, but her life also reveals God's presence among the humble and poor. The Song of Mary (sometimes called the Magnificat) speaks of the reversals in the reign of God: the mighty are cast down and the lowly lifted up, the hungry are fed and the rich are sent away empty-handed.

Hymns today might include "Sing of Mary, pure and holy" (WOV 634) and a paraphrase of the Magnificat, such as "My soul proclaims your greatness" (WOV 730). When considering Mary's importance to our lives of faith, read together some of Luther's writings on the Magnificat.

AUGUST 20, 2000

TENTH SUNDAY AFTER PENTECOST
PROPER 15

INTRODUCTION

Wisdom sets a table and invites all to taste the wine and bread. Jesus Christ, our Wisdom, gives his life for all, inviting everyone to drink and eat. Wisdom nourishes us with the word of life and the bread from heaven. In all this, we experience the abundant grace of God. How can this congregation be gracious and hospitable to any and all who seek the Lord?

Today we remember Bernard of Clairvaux, an abbot in the twelfth century known for his mystical writings and his influence beyond the monastery.

PRAYER OF THE DAY

Almighty and ever-living God, you have given great and precious promises to those who believe. Grant us the perfect faith which overcomes all doubts, through your Son, Jesus Christ our Lord.

READINGS

Proverbs 9:1-6

Wisdom is portrayed as a woman who invites people to partake of her banquet. Just as ordinary food is necessary for physical life, Wisdom's food—insight and understanding—is necessary for fullness of life with God. Partaking of Wisdom's banquet is the way to life.

Psalm 34:9-14

Those who seek the LORD lack nothing that is good. (Ps. 34:10)

Ephesians 5:15-20

Fully aware of this world's evil, Paul still finds much for which he is grateful. Here he describes the alternative quality of life available to those who have been reconciled with God and one another.

John 6:51-58

In John's gospel, the feeding of the five thousand leads to extended teaching in which Jesus identifies himself as the true "bread of life." Finally, in these verses, he makes a connection that would not be understood until after his death, in light of the church's celebration of the eucharist.

ALTERNATE FIRST READING/PSALM

1 Kings 2:10-12; 3:3-14

This reading deals with the story of the succession of David's throne to Solomon, with the Lord's authorization of Solomon as king.

Psalm 111

The fear of the LORD is the beginning of wisdom. (Ps. 111:10)

COLOR Green

THE PRAYERS

Growing in the soil of the Spirit, let us pray for the church, the world, and all who seek the richness of life in God.

A BRIEF SILENCE.

Let us pray for the church, the community of God's love on the earth, that it may freely offer the bread of heaven and cup of salvation to all who gather at the table of the Lord. Gracious God,

hear our prayer.

Let us pray for the world, that its leaders would seek wisdom from God as they govern the nations entrusted to them, and as they lead their people in ways of justice and truth. Gracious God,

hear our prayer.

Let us pray for those in need, especially those dealing with addictions and all in recovery, that they would be given courage and patience to be made whole. Gracious God,

hear our prayer.

Let us pray for those among us who are sick (especially . . .), that they would be fed with the healing manna of life. Gracious God,

hear our prayer.

Let us pray for those who lead music in this congregation, that all will be inspired to sing psalms, hymns, and spiritual songs with joy and confidence. Gracious God,

hear our prayer.

HERE OTHER INTERCESSIONS MAY BE OFFERED.

Let us pray for those grieving losses among us (especially . . .), that they would be held in communion with

Bernard and all your blessed saints who are at rest in you. Gracious God,
hear our prayer.
Hear us as we pray, living God, and nourish us always at your table of grace, for the sake of Jesus Christ, our Lord and Savior.
Amen

IMAGES FOR PREACHING

It takes courage to grow up. The work of childhood is long hours of play, activities with no benefit other than the sheer delight and pleasure they bring. Adults seem to exist to watch out for you, to be attentive to your needs, to love and care for you.

Growing up inherently comes with disillusionment. Our vision broadens and we can see that there are other angles to what we saw before. Some of the shimmer goes out of the world around us. We learn that the natural world poses threats, that people are hurtful, that adult work is not always as delightful as play. While some doors open, others firmly close.

It takes courage to grow up. It is a struggle to step into the more complex world that maturing eyes uncover. The world of promises made and broken, arms extended in invitation and with the intent to harm, lives beginning and others ending. The world of loves and hates, possibilities and limitations, life and death.

On our own, we might by default settle into a prolonged childhood, sheltered from the magnificent, baffling, often painful mix of it all. Growing up, maturing, is not child's play. How well Jesus knows this when he says that we must eat his body and drink his blood in order to have any life in us. Jesus builds us up with his body and blood so we can mature, see life as it is, and step fully into it.

WORSHIP MATTERS

"Come, eat of my bread and drink of the wine I have mixed," announces Wisdom in today's first reading (Prov. 9:5). How do we announce that God's gifts to us are for all to share? Orders of worship may include an invitation just prior to the distribution, which announces the benefits of the meal and invites the assembly to the table.

In the Large Catechism, Luther echoes the invitation of Wisdom: "when [Christ] says, 'Given *for you*' and 'poured out *for you*,' as if he said 'This is why I give it and bid you eat and drink, that you may take it as your own and enjoy it.' Whoever lets these words be addressed to him and believes that they are true has what the words declare" (*Book of Concord*, 450:34-35).

LET THE CHILDREN COME

Are our children learning the hymns of the faith? When planning liturgy, we should remember this principle: People will remember what they sing, and they'll believe what they remember. Children are often at a disadvantage with hymn-singing because they have difficulty reading both the text and the music. When we teach them by rote, however, they learn even complicated melodies very well. Could a portion of our Sunday school time or our choir rehearsals teach children the hymns that are used in worship? When they know a refrain or a verse, they gladly join in.

MUSIC FOR WORSHIP
GATHERING

LBW 545/6	When morning gilds the skies
WOV 802	When in our music God is glorified

PSALM 34

Bengtson, Bruce, PW, cycle B.

Brown, Teresa. "The Lord Is Close to the Broken Hearted" in PS, vol. 1.

Busarow, Donald. "Proclaim with Me." CPH 98-3127. SATB, cong, opt tpt.

Harbor, Rawn. "Taste and See the Goodness of the Lord" in *This Far by Faith*.

Schalk, Carl. "Be Known to Us, Lord Jesus." CPH 98-3202. SATB, cong, children.

HYMN OF THE DAY

LBW 214	Come, let us eat
	A VA DE

VOCAL RESOURCES

Rhein. "Come, Let Us Eat." CPH 98-3092. 2 pt trbl.mxd, kybd.

INSTRUMENTAL RESOURCES

Busarow, Donald. "A va de" in *Thirty More Hymn Accompaniments for Hymns in Canon*. AFP 11-10163. Inst/voc canon.

Fields, Tim. "Partita on 'Come, Let Us Eat.'" MSM 10-824. Org.

Organ, Anne Krentz. "A va de" in *Global Piano Reflections*. AFP 11-10932. Pno.

ALTERNATE HYMN OF THE DAY
- LBW 409   Praise and thanksgiving
- WOV 702   I am the Bread of life

COMMUNION
- LBW 205   Now the silence
- WOV 707   This is my body

SENDING
- LBW 557   Let all things now living
- WOV 721   Go, my children, with my blessing

ADDITIONAL HYMNS AND SONGS
- NCH 509   How deep the silence of the soul
- H82 321   My God, thy table now is spread
- TFF 126   Taste and see
- W&P   Give thanks

MUSIC FOR THE DAY

CHORAL

Bairstow, Edward. "I Sat Down Under His Shadow." OXF 43.002.

Burkhardt, Michael. "Filled with the Spirit." MSM 50-7402. 3 pt canon, opt hb/kybd.

Faure, Gabriel. "Benedictus" in *Messe Basse*. Heugel&Cie/PRE 312-40598. SA, org.

Johengen, Carl. "I Am the Living Bread." GIA G-4353. Cant, cong, org, opt SATB, ob.

CHILDREN'S CHOIRS

Burkhardt, Michael. "Filled with the Spirit." MSM 50-7402. 3 pt canon, opt 2 oct hb/kybd.

Pethel, Stan. "Bless This Gift." CG CGA761. 2 pt mxd, kybd.

Wright, Vicki Hancock. "I Will Praise God." CG CGA822. U, kybd, opt hc/resonator bells.

KEYBOARD/INSTRUMENTAL

Bock, Fred. "Morning Has Broken" in *Keyboard Duets for Organ and Piano*. HOP 201.

Callahan, Charles. "A Gaelic Improvisation" (Bunessan) in *Thanksgiving Suite*. MSM 10-600. Org.

Ziebell, Carl. "I Come, O Savior, to Your Table." NPH MC27N0018. Org.

HANDBELL

Semmann, Barbara. "Psalms for All Seasons II." AG 1383. 3-4 oct.

Wood, Dale. "Rejoice, Give Thanks, and Sing!" SMP 10/1255S. SATB, org, opt brass qnt, timp, cong, hb.

PRAISE ENSEMBLE

Berthier, Jacques/ed. Brother Robert. "Eat This Bread." GIA G-2840. Cant, response.

Cloninger, Claire and Martin J. Nystrom. "Come to the Table" in *Hosanna Music Songbook, vol 6*. INT HMSB06.

Dearman, Kirk. "We Remember You" in *Songs for Praise and Worship*. WRD.

Leech, Bryan Jeffrey/arr. Tabell. "Come Share the Lord." Fred Bock Music Co. BG2053. SAB, kybd. Also available, BG0502 SATB.

Pote, Allen. "Come to the Table." Coral Key Music 392-41678. SATB, kybd.

SUNDAY, AUGUST 20
BERNARD, ABBOT OF CLAIRVAUX, 1153

Bernard was a Cistercian monk and later an abbot of great spiritual depth. He was a mystical writer who was deeply devoted to the humanity of Christ and, consequently, to the affective dimensions of medieval spirituality. Bernard also had a great impact on the world beyond the monastery: secular leaders came to him because of his peacemaking skills, and he spoke out against excesses of the clergy and the persecution of Jews.

Does your congregation find ways to nurture a balance in the relationship between contemplation and action? Do your Bible studies connect with service in the world? Are your service projects rooted in spiritual convictions? Does your celebration of the eucharist nurture your members to serve God in their various callings?

THURSDAY, AUGUST 24
ST. BARTHOLOMEW, APOSTLE

Bartholomew is mentioned as one of Jesus' apostles in Matthew, Mark, and Luke. The list of apostles in John does not include him, but rather Nathanael, and they are often assumed to be the same person. Beyond his role as a disciple of Jesus, little is known of his life, though various traditions tell of his missionary work following Jesus' resurrection. He is symbolically shown holding a knife, since some believe he was beheaded.

How do we, like Bartholomew, respond to Christ's invitation to follow? What are the various ways we live out our baptismal call in daily life? Do you look at this call as your vocation?

AUGUST 27, 2000

ELEVENTH SUNDAY AFTER PENTECOST
PROPER 16

INTRODUCTION

In the midst of life's challenges and uncertainties we seek to understand God's words of truth and life for us. Like Joshua we make a commitment not to worship the passing gods of the day, but to serve the Lord alone. Today's reading from John includes words many of us sing before the gospel is proclaimed: "Lord, to whom shall we go? You have the words of eternal life." Our hearts yearn for the good news that sets us free and strengthens us for service.

PRAYER OF THE DAY

God of all creation, you reach out to call people of all nations to your kingdom. As you gather disciples from near and far, count us also among those who boldly confess your Son Jesus Christ as Lord.

READINGS

Joshua 24:1-2a, 14-18

In the Near East covenant *means "agreement" or "alliance." It describes relationships and is the primary word used to characterize the relationship between God and Israel. By delivering Israel, God has already begun the relationship. Joshua calls upon the people to respond.*

Psalm 34:15-22

The eyes of the LORD are upon the righteous. (Ps. 34:15)

Ephesians 6:10-20

The military language in this passage calls to mind the power of the Roman Empire in the first century. Followers of Christ are to put on the armor of God and remain strong in the face of cosmic evil forces.

John 6:56-69

The "hard saying" that offends Jesus' disciples is his claim that his followers must eat his flesh and drink his blood. The followers who return to their old lives know something about how odd this sounds. Simon Peter asks the most important question: "To whom shall we go?"

ALTERNATE FIRST READING/PSALM

1 Kings 8:[1,6,10-11] 22-30, 41-43

The dedication of the temple has concluded with the transfer of the sacred utensils and the elaborate gifts deriving from David's conquests. Now Solomon has the ark of the covenant itself brought into the temple.

Psalm 84

How dear to me is your dwelling, O LORD. (Ps. 84:1)

COLOR Green

THE PRAYERS

Growing in the soil of the Spirit, let us pray for the church, the world, and all who seek the richness of life in God.

A BRIEF SILENCE.

O life-giving Spirit of God, you have given your words of eternal life to the church. Give us bold preachers and teachers of this word, so that many may come to believe. Gracious God,

hear our prayer.

Give to the nations of the world your light and your peace. Grant their leaders wisdom and courage, that they may lead with compassion for all people. Gracious God,

hear our prayer.

Heal those among us who are struggling with sickness of any kind (especially . . .), that being touched by you, their sickness may be turned to health. Gracious God,

hear our prayer.

Bless those entrusted with the ministry of prayer in this congregation. Keep them alert to the needs of this community, that they may support all we do with their intercessions. Gracious God,

hear our prayer.

HERE OTHER INTERCESSIONS MAY BE OFFERED.

We remember before you those who have died (especially . . .) and ask that you would keep us in communion with them and all your saints who surround us in the great cloud of witnesses. Gracious God,

hear our prayer.

Hear us as we pray, living God, and nourish us always at your table of grace, for the sake of Jesus Christ, our Lord and Savior.

Amen

IMAGES FOR PREACHING

Wonderful, complex Simon Peter. Confessions seem to spring from him as readily as do doubt and denial. We might appropriately label him inconsistent, unreliable. If we were drowning in a creek, how would we know from one time to the next whether he would throw the rope in to save our life? Whether he'd be driven to act by bravery or shrink back in fear? On the whole, we would much rather associate with people who are a little more stable, perhaps less colorful, but altogether more trustworthy.

Simon Peter's weaknesses seem of less importance to Jesus than his capacity for faith. It's not that his weaknesses are of no account. But somehow, Jesus is not put off by these rather colossal signs of weakness. Jesus is drawn to Peter's equally robust capacity for faith, his repeated openness to Jesus: Peter who responds to Jesus' call to "follow me"; Peter who, despite his doubt, throws out his nets one more time because Jesus commands him; Peter who confesses, "you are the Christ," and "we have come to believe and know that you are the Holy One of God."

Jesus is not particularly interested in consistency, or even flawless, stable faith. What a surprise to us who find such attributes of great importance. What seems of importance to Jesus, what seems to delight him, is faith that is open, again and again, despite the failures and denials, to the call of Jesus.

WORSHIP MATTERS

Paul urges the Ephesians to "persevere in supplications for all the saints" (6:18). How can we as a gathered community persevere in our prayers, and thus in our material support for all in need throughout the world?

In our hectic world, it is impracticable to expect Christians to gather every day to participate in corporate services of prayer, yet when groups gather for other purposes (church meetings, service projects, social events), they often begin or end with a brief devotion. Why not use the services of Morning and Evening Prayer (*LBW*, pp. 131–53) for such gatherings? A simplified, adapted version could emphasize intercessions for parish needs, the immediate community, and the world. Consistently lifting the needs of others before God invites the praying community to action on behalf of those for whom they intercede.

LET THE CHILDREN COME

Today marks the end of the series of gospel readings from John 6. If you have had a summer food project, be sure to acknowledge the fruits of that labor and the efforts of all who participated. Remind children of any upcoming changes in Sunday school and worship schedules, and encourage them to invite friends to worship and learn with them. Thank children for coming to worship and bringing friends. Praise honestly given is a great motivator and helps to build strong relationships.

MUSIC FOR WORSHIP

GATHERING

LBW 561	For the beauty of the earth
WOV 768	He comes to us as one unknown

PSALM 34

Bengtson, Bruce. PW, cycle B.

Brown, Teresa. "The Lord Is Close to the Broken Hearted" in PS, vol. 1.

Harbor, Rawn. "Taste and See the Goodness of the Lord" in *This Far by Faith*.

HYMN OF THE DAY

WOV 706	Eat this bread, drink this cup
	STONERIDGE

VOCAL RESOURCES

Young, Jeremy. "Eat This Bread, Drink This Cup." AFP 11-10651. U, opt. cong, kybd.

INSTRUMENTAL RESOURCES

Hassell, Michael. "Medley: 'The Thirsty Fields Drink in the Rain' and 'Eat This Bread, Drink This Cup' " in *More Folkways*. AFP 11-10866. Trbl inst, pno.

ALTERNATE HYMN OF THE DAY

LBW 493	Hope of the world
LBW 373	Eternal Ruler of the ceaseless round

COMMUNION

LBW 200	For the bread which you have broken
WOV 706	Eat this bread, drink this cup

SENDING

LBW 389	Stand up, stand up for Jesus
WOV 780	What a fellowship, what a joy divine

ADDITIONAL HYMNS AND SONGS

H82 678/9	Surely it is God who saves me
TFF 266	Victory is mine
W&P	Be bold, be strong
W&P	The trumpets sound, the angels sing

MUSIC FOR THE DAY

CHORAL

Howells, Herbert. "My Eyes for Beauty Pine" OXF A14. U, opt SATB, org.

Olson, Howard. "Come, O God, Abide among Us" in *Set Free, Set Free*. AFP 3-420. U.

Peter, Johann. "Adorn Yourself, My Soul." HIN HMC-1123. SATB, org.

Porter, Thomas J. "Let Us Be Bread." GIA G-3355. 2 pt, opt cong, gtr, kybd.

CHILDREN'S CHOIRS

Handel, G. F./arr. Hal H. Hopson. "I Will at All Times Praise the Lord." CG CGA243. U, kybd.

Sleeth, Natalie. "Everywhere I Go." CG CGA171. U/2 pt, kybd, opt C inst.

KEYBOARD/INSTRUMENTAL

Lang, C. S. "Tuba Tune in D Major." B&H. Org.

HANDBELL

McChesney, Kevin. "When We Are Living: Somos del Señor." AFP 11-10631. 3-5 oct, opt hc.

PRAISE ENSEMBLE

Chapman, Gary. "As for Me and My House" (The Family Prayer Song) in *Promise Keepers: Raise the Standard, pt 1 & 2*. WRD/MAR.

Gillard, Richard. "The Servant Song" in *Maranatha! Music Praise Chorus Book, 3rd ed.* WRD/MAR.

Gordon, Nancy and Jamie Harvill. "Because We Believe" in *Hosanna! Music Songbook, vol 12*. INT 12906.

Medema, Ken. "Like a River That Overflows." HOP GC995. SATB, pno.

Oliver, Gary. "You Are the Holy One" in *Hosanna! Music Songbook, vol 6*. INT HMSB06.

Schram, Ruth Elaine. "We Come to Your Table Lord." ALF 16101. SATB, acc.

Ylvisaker, John. "I Believe, I Do Believe" in *Borning Cry*. NGP.

MONDAY, AUGUST 28
AUGUSTINE, BISHOP OF HIPPO, 430

Augustine's conversion to Christianity is described in *Confessions*, his autobiographical work, which includes these famous words: "Our hearts are restless until they rest in thee." Augustine was baptized by Ambrose at the Easter Vigil in 387, and became one of the greatest theologians and defenders of the faith. He established a monastic rule, and more than a millennium later Martin Luther became a monk of the Augustinian order.

Use Augustine's conversion to pose this question: If we were baptized as infants, do we ever undergo conversion? Or is baptism a call to lifelong conversion? Look at the questions in the Affirmation of Baptism service (*LBW*, p. 201) and discuss our baptismal vocation. Conclude by actually participating in the Affirmation of Baptism liturgy around the font.

MOSES THE BLACK, DESERT MONK, C. 400

A man of great strength and rough character, Moses the Black was converted to the Christian faith toward the close of the fourth century. The change in his heart and life became legendary throughout his native Ethiopia. Like Augustine, Moses' life was changed because of the gospel. How do we experience that life-changing power in our lives of faith?

THURSDAY, AUGUST 31
JOHN BUNYAN, TEACHER, 1688

John Bunyan was one of the most remarkable figures in seventeenth-century literature. His spiritual pilgrimage is revealed in his works, most notably *The Pilgrim's Progress*, which some consider to be the most successful allegory in English literature.

Just as Bunyan believed that God worked through all aspects of his life, it is good for us to be aware of the spiritual movements in our own lives. Consider ways to nurture the gifts of writing among your members. Why not encourage them to keep a journal of their spiritual insights, to prepare a series of devotions based on the church year, or to write an occasional column or brief meditation for your church newsletter.

SUMMER
AUTUMN
NOVEMBER

AUTUMN

*Autumn fills us with enthusiasm for new beginnings
even while it points us to endings*

IMAGES of the SEASON

It probably doesn't matter how long it's been since you last went to school, or sent your children off on the school bus, or thought that September was synonymous with homework. I suspect that for all of us it still seems that the year begins in the fall. The civil calendar says it starts in January. The church sees Advent as the beginning. Poets and farmers point to the stirrings of new life in the spring. But at some level most of us still move in the rhythm of the academic year. We slow down in the summer months, and we start up again in September.

Folks we haven't seen much of during the vacation season begin to return to worship. Rally day brings the energy of children back to our buildings. Program plans are made for the months ahead. A feeling of energy, excitement, and enthusiasm is clearly present. It's time to start!

In a sense, autumn is a continuation, even a fulfillment, of summer. If the focus of our worship during the summer months has been living the life of faith, autumn is the time to deepen that message. Now is when seeds planted in the previous months reach maturity. Now is when the harvest approaches.

Worship in September and October points us toward both being faithful Christians in our own lives and planting the seeds of faith in others. We return from vacations, renewed and reenergized, welcoming one another back to our work in Christ's name. We also experience that renewal as an opening to those who may not have been in our midst before. A new program year brings new opportunities for witness and for welcome to the visitor, the seeker, or the wanderer.

But even as this season is a beginning, it contains the seeds of endings as well. The signs of the changing season are clear. Throughout the Northern Hemisphere, the days are already noticeably shorter by September. Different birds appear in our neighborhoods, passing through on their way to their winter homes. October brings a different feel to the air. Streets no longer seem softened by the heat as we cross them. While we welcome all of these indications of the coming of autumn, we also recognize them as harbingers of winter. Harvest home celebrations rejoice in the bounty of our blessings, but they also remind us that now fields are barren and growth has ended.

Autumn is a season of great ambivalence. It fills us with enthusiasm for new beginnings even while it points us to endings. Crops are gathered in, giving stores of food but leaving bare brown fields. City air becomes fresher but hints at the icy winds to come. Leaves blaze with vibrant colors but then shrivel and fall. We welcome autumn for itself even while we may regret the ending of summer and dread the coming of winter.

The true message of this season is that of change. The watchword is, "This too shall pass." At times, that simple notion is good news, when we cling to the assurance that no trial or burden lasts forever. At other times it seems discouraging, when we consider the transitory nature of life and the lack of stability.

For our worship in this ambivalent season, the image of change acknowledges those varied sides to our lives. We gather to rejoice in newness, in harvest, in return, even while we prepare ourselves for passing, for rest, for inactivity. But for Christians change is never chaotic. It never casts us completely adrift. We are able not just to note change but to celebrate it because we retain a stable foundation. The hymnwriter put it well: "Change and decay in all around I see; O thou who changest not, abide with me" (LBW 272). The certainty of God's presence enables change to be accepted, even welcomed, as we rest on the promise of unchanging love.

AUTUMN

ENVIRONMENT AND ART FOR THE SEASON

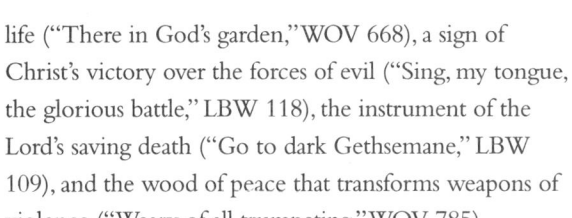

The world of early Christian art is filled with fish, lambs, birds, trees of life, olive branches, palm branches, grapevines, shepherds, and anchors. One must search diligently to find even the hint of a cross before the fourth century. While the image of the cross is present in the ancient world (we find it in Egyptian and Roman temples, tombs, and paintings), we are surprised to find that this central sign of the Christian faith does not appear until the mid-fourth century (a tomb cover discovered in excavations of Vatican Hill). Only in the fifth century do we find an image of the Lord's crucifixion: a carving amid many other carvings on the doors of the Church of Santa Sabina in Rome.

Why did early Christians enjoy white lambs and blue fish and green palm branches? What did these images signify for a community held in suspicion if not persecuted by its neighbors? Perhaps they evoked God's victory over the forces of adversity and evil (the slain lamb who lives), the new life of the resurrection (fish swimming freely and without fear in the sea), and the garden of heaven (blossoming flowers and trees of life filled with luscious fruits). When the cross appears in fourth- and fifth-century Christian churches, it also participates in this vision of a world transformed by the power of the resurrection. We see the "eschatological" cross, the cross of Christ's cosmic presence: colored purple or scarlet or gold, outlined in deep blue or silver, set in a star-studded light blue sky, surrounded by a circle of red or white lines. Imagine, then, walking toward this remarkable cross hanging above the eucharistic table. How would such a "cosmic" image shape one's experience of receiving the Lord's body and blood? Would you think, "I am being drawn into something very personal yet far greater than myself"?

In the cross of Christ, Christians have seen the convergence of the four cardinal points of the compass, the center of the universe, the union of heaven and earth, and the four primal elements of earth, air, fire, and water. The cross is the branch of Jesse and the key to heaven ("Oh, come, oh, come, Emmanuel," LBW 34), the great tree of life ("There in God's garden," WOV 668), a sign of Christ's victory over the forces of evil ("Sing, my tongue, the glorious battle," LBW 118), the instrument of the Lord's saving death ("Go to dark Gethsemane," LBW 109), and the wood of peace that transforms weapons of violence ("Weary of all trumpeting," WOV 785).

What color is the cross? Early Christians carved or incised the cross in stone, terra-cotta, silver, ivory, and gold. They created green and gold mosaics of the cross as a huge tree of life spreading its branches over the walls of the church. Medieval Christians painted green crosses flowering with blossoms and carved crosses into the dark brown wood of their church doors. A scarlet-colored cross became popular in the Renaissance while Luther placed a black cross on a deep red rose in his seal. In places as distant from each other as the Philippines and Poland, nineteenth-century Christians perfected the art of weaving green Palm Sunday branches into elaborate crosses which they placed in their homes until the following Ash Wednesday.

Perhaps the early Christians were reluctant to display the cross publicly because it was a frightening instrument of torture and injustice in their world. Yet they did not hesitate to use the sign of the cross in their worship, a practice that has guided Christians for some two thousand years. At the beginning of life in Christ, the cross is traced over the head or the body in baptism ("This is the Spirit's entry now," LBW 195). And at the end of this earthly life, a cross or pall may be placed over the coffin.

In the ancient and contemporary church, adults who are coming to faith through the adult catechumenate may have their eyes, ears, mouth, shoulders, feet, and arms marked with the cross, each "cross" a claiming of the whole person for Christ ("Take up your cross," LBW 398, and *Welcome to Christ: Lutheran Rites for the Catechumenate*, AFP 3-142). Tertullian, an early Christian teacher, notes that newly baptized adults join the worshiping assembly in extending their arms "in the sign of the Lord's cross" as they pray the Lord's Prayer. The cross is incised in bread baked for the eucharist. Those who participate in healing services have the cross traced over their foreheads or palms. The penitent receives the forgiveness of sins as the sign of the cross is made. And, each worship service begins and ends with the sign of the cross ("God is here," WOV 719).

In the gospel reading for Sunday, September 17 (proper 19), the worshiping assembly will hear Jesus ask this question: "Who do people say that I am?" (Mark 8:27). The disciples offer various responses. Mark continues, "Then he began to teach them that the Son of Man must undergo great suffering." Finally Jesus announces that those who would be his disciples must take up their crosses and follow him (Mark 8:34). Perhaps Mark is alluding to the practice of tracing a Tau cross *T* on the foreheads of Gentile converts to Judaism as a sign of their conversion to the one God of Abraham, Isaac, and Jacob (keep in mind that the Tau cross was believed to have been the style of pole lifted up by Moses in the wilderness; Num. 21:4b-9). In Mark's gospel, this text is a turning point: Jesus will proceed up to Jerusalem, the place of death and resurrection (see proper 29, Christ the King).

On September 14, a few days before this Sunday, the church celebrates Holy Cross Day (see the appointed prayer of the day, scripture readings, and hymn suggestions in *Indexes for Worship Planning*, AFP 3-400). In the context of this gospel and its significance for a theology of the cross, would it not be appropriate to gather for a brief order of evening prayer on this lesser festival? Those who are charged with care for the environment may want to use this week to bring some subtle changes to the worship space, the movement from summer to autumn.

If the congregation possesses a second set of green vestments and paraments or hangings in a darker shade, it would be the time to introduce them. Take note that some shades of green will complement each other while other shades will clash. Be careful, then, about mixing hangings of different shades.

An obvious focus during the autumn season is the cross. Two options present themselves. If worship begins with a procession of ministers following a processional cross, the cross itself can be adorned with a simple wreath of local greens or seasonal flowers (e.g., sunflowers, asters, marigolds, small chrysanthemums). For a prominent, stationary cross in place, decorate with a wreath appropriate to the cross's size, but do not allow the wreath to overwhelm the cross.

A healthy principle to follow is to minimize or eliminate the duplication of central symbols in worship. Thus, only one cross—processional or stationary—is needed. Because congregations use a cross, water, candles, bread, wine, and words in worship, seek to go beyond images of these things on banners or worship folders. For images to use on bulletins, stained glass, service folders, or additional artwork, consider the natural images that appear in scripture: fish, lambs, lions, birds. Few things seem more redundant than to gaze on a burning candle with a picture or banner of a burning candle fastened to the wall behind it!

The worshiping assembly is a "work of art" in the making, and their actions in worship are an integral element in the environment. Use the bulletin to invite parents and their children to trace the cross over their foreheads with water from the baptismal font in thanksgiving for baptism. This is a concrete way in which the assembly can participate in an action that links the lectionary focus of this period with their lives.

In one congregation, the people bring favorite crosses from home (properly labeled on the back), which will form a display in the narthex (or parish hall) from Holy Cross Day to All Saints. People are interested in the variety of crosses, many of which represent different cultures from around the world.

As you look ahead to the festival of All Saints, you may want to read the section on environment and art for the season of November. There you will find suggestions for preparing people to celebrate the memory of the faithful departed. Part of this preparation may take place in October.

AUTUMN

PREACHING with the SEASON

Once more we return to the river. The first reading on the first Sunday in September comes from the book of Deuteronomy, and Deuteronomy always brings us back to the river. Written centuries after the people of Israel crossed the Jordan into the promised land, this last book of the Torah returns to the river as though for the first time. We hear many of the same things written in Exodus, Leviticus, and Numbers: the Ten Commandments, God's strong reminder to open your hand to those in need, and at the end of the book, the choice to be made before crossing into the promised land: "I call heaven and earth to witness against you today that I have set before you life and death, blessings and curses. Choose life so that you and your descendants may live" (Deut. 30:19).

Notice the sense of urgency at the river. Will you remember who has brought you this far? Will you be faithful to the covenant once Mt. Sinai is far from view? Before you go beyond the river, stop long enough to remember who and whose you are. For Christians, every Sunday is a time of returning to the river—the baptismal river that flows in the heart of the sanctuary—even if we can't hear the water running. We come, young, old, and in-between, to be reminded of who and whose we are. Long after the water on our foreheads has dried, we commit ourselves again to the covenant God made with us.

Our Jewish sisters and brothers will begin a new year (Rosh Hashanah) in September. The sound of the ram's horn (shofar) will be heard as in ancient times, urgently calling people to remember the covenant before crossing over into a new year. Perhaps we, too, need a dramatic sound to call us back to the river, back from vacation, back from places of travel, back from the days of summer. Why not invite a trumpeter to sound the call inviting everyone to gather at the baptismal font as we hear the words of the first reading on September 3? If Sunday school is beginning on the first Sunday of September children could lead the procession. Even if Sunday school won't begin until later, children will be going back to weekday school, and the Deuteronomy lesson reminds us of the importance of handing on the stories of faith to our children and our children's children.

A possible theme for these autumn Sundays is "Return to the River," introduced by the Deuteronomy lection for September 3: "But take care and watch yourselves closely, so as neither to forget the things that your eyes have seen nor to let them slip from your mind all the days of your life; make them known to your children and your children's children" (Deut. 4:9). The theme for September 10 could well be "Water Is Thicker Than Blood" as the Syrophoenician woman receives her place at the table. On September 17, "Cross as Watermark" could connect Jesus' words about cross-bearing with the baptismal sign on our foreheads. Like the word written on door post and gate (Deut. 6:8-9), we bear the sign of the cross in our going out and our coming in. The gospel for September 24 sets a child in our midst; at the river we are given "Power to Become Children of God" no matter how old we are. The theme of returning to the river of baptism could continue through Reformation Sunday tying the new covenant written on our hearts with the covenant affirmed at the river.

Another possibility is to preach a series of sermons on the texts from James beginning on September 3 and continuing through October 1. Though Luther called James an "epistle of straw" *(Preface to the New Testament)*, these lections offer down-to-earth help for being Christ to our neighbor. Gerhard Forde's question: "What do you do when you find out you don't have to do anything?" could introduce such a series, reminding us that being "doers of the word" does not earn us salvation, but helps us live in response to God's grace. These readings from James speak of discipleship in earthy ways: dealing with anger, honoring the poor, bridling your tongue, handling conflicts, praying and anointing for healing. This last reading, for October 1, has a central place in the life of African American worship. As the Rev. James Forbes said, "No church building is ever finished until there is a bottle of olive oil in the sanctuary!" (Fosdick Convocation workshop, April 4, 1997).

The five October Sundays could be treated as a separate unit moving toward Reformation Sunday. Those drawn to thematic titles might begin with "Repentance" on October 1; Jesus' hyperbolic words about eye, foot, and hand causing us to sin call for serious amendment of life. The October 8 gospel reading on divorce and welcoming children could focus on "Relationship." On October 15, "Return" could pick up Jesus' desire for the rich man to come back and follow him, or the theme of "Redistribution" could focus on scripture's deep concern about use of wealth. The gospel for October 22 focuses on the theme of "Reversals," which permeates many of the Mark readings for the season. "Reformation" would bring the series to a close, calling us to be reshaped by the truth of Christ that sets us free.

Other October dates can be kept in mind when planning for this month. October 4 (St. Francis) is often marked by the blessing of animals and the calling to care for the earth. The Sunday nearest October 18 (St. Luke, Evangelist) may be observed as a day of prayer for healing, including prayers for people living with AIDS. In some communities October is also the time of harvest festivals as corn, soybeans, and other crops are gathered in, a theme celebrated by Jewish congregations in the festival of Sukkoth. In some parts of the country, October brings a changing landscape of colors as dying leaves make sure we notice them before they bid farewell. In other places, the landscape will remain almost unchanged as summer passes into fall. But in every place, God calls us again to return to the river.

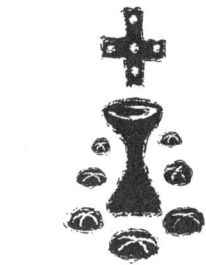

SHAPE OF WORSHIP FOR THE SEASON

BASIC SHAPE OF THE EUCHARISTIC RITE IN AUTUMN

- Confession and Forgiveness: see alternate worship text for autumn in *Sundays and Seasons*

GATHERING

- Greeting: see alternate worship text for autumn in *Sundays and Seasons*
- Omit the Kyrie during autumn (except for Reformation Day)
- Omit or use the hymn of praise during autumn (use for Reformation Day)

WORD

- Use the Apostles' Creed (Nicene Creed for Reformation Day)
- Prayers: see alternate forms and responses for autumn in *Sundays and Seasons*

MEAL

- Offertory prayer: see alternate worship text for autumn in *Sundays and Seasons*
- Use the proper preface for the Sundays after Pentecost (see *LBW* Ministers edition, and *WOV* Leaders edition for each musical setting of the liturgy)
- Eucharistic prayer: in addition to four main options in *LBW*, see "Eucharistic Prayer H: Autumn" in *WOV* Leaders edition, p. 72
- Invitation to communion: see alternate worship text for autumn in *Sundays and Seasons*
- Post-communion prayer: see alternate worship text for autumn in *Sundays and Seasons*

SENDING

- Benediction: see alternate worship text for autumn in *Sundays and Seasons*
- Dismissal: see alternate worship text for autumn in *Sundays and Seasons*

OTHER SEASONAL POSSIBILITIES

- Blessing of Teachers and Students
- See "Recognition of Ministries in the Congregation" in *Occasional Services*, pp. 143–46

DISTRIBUTION OF BIBLES

- If Bibles are distributed publicly to young readers, consider having their parents and/or sponsors involved in physically handing over the Bibles (as a follow-up to promises made in the order for baptism)

BLESSING OF ANIMALS

- Traditionally celebrated on or near October 4 (Francis of Assisi, renewer of the church, 1226). See a possible order for this celebration in the seasonal rites section.

HARVEST FESTIVAL OR HARVEST HOME

- Many congregations celebrate the harvest sometime each fall. While readings are appointed for the occasion of harvest on p. 39 of *LBW*, days when the lectionary also speaks to this theme are proper 17 on September 3 (second reading) and proper 23 on October 15 (gospel).

REFORMATION DAY

- One way to resolve the dilemma between celebrating lesser festivals when they occur on Sundays, or observing the complete cycle of the Revised Common Lectionary, would be to use lectionary readings for proper 25 on October 29, but use the prayer of the day for both proper 25 and Reformation Day. While much of the music and the prayers could reflect the lectionary for proper 25, one or more of the hymns could be chosen to reflect the Reformation festival. The color for the day could also be red.

LECTIONARY OPPORTUNITY FOR HEALING SERVICE

- Proper 21 on October 1 (second reading)

ASSEMBLY SONG FOR THE SEASON

Autumn, a time of harvest in the natural world, can be for the church and its worship a time of planting. Congregations ready for fall beginnings may also be more receptive to receiving and nurturing the new song.

GATHERING

When learning new service music or hymns, a pre-service rehearsal is not only a learning opportunity but a chance to extend hospitality to visitors who often appear at this time. Such practice, better led from the front by an energetic voice than from a keyboard, can include music we tend to assume people know, but isn't sung very confidently. Some background information or a story to associate with the song can help increase the desire to learn. Be sure to allow some time for silence and/or an instrumental prelude to help the assembly focus upon the worship to follow.

WORD

Learn several new hymns in September and October by featuring them for four weeks in a row. Consider "Oh, praise the gracious power" (WOV 750), with its focus on expansive images for Christ centered in the cross, for September. October's recurring themes of Christian service, the first becoming last, are echoed in Brian Wren's text, "Great God, your love has called us here" (WOV 666).

MEAL

The time of harvest invites particular attention to the music at the offering and presentation of the gifts. "Let the vineyards be fruitful" is a natural offertory song. Or, learn a new offertory song for this season that highlights similar themes. See the stewardship section of *With One Voice,* "As the grains of wheat" (WOV 705), and "We plow the fields" (LLC 492), set to a new Hispanic tune.

SENDING

Themes of thanksgiving are appropriate, either in the standard post-communion canticle or another song sung consistently throughout the season, such as "Give thanks with a grateful heart" (TFF 292, W&P), "Thank you, Lord" (TFF 293), "Praise to you, O God of mercy" (WOV 790), or "Let all things now living" (LBW 557).

MUSIC FOR THE SEASON

VERSE AND OFFERTORY

Cherwien, David. *Verses for the Fall Festivals.* MSM 80-880. U/SATB, opt brass, org.

Cherwien, David. *Verses for the Season of Pentecost, set 3.* MSM 80-543. Mxd vcs, org.

Hillert, Richard. *Verses and Offertories, Lesser Festivals, vol. 2.* AFP 11-9543.

Pelz, Walter/arr. Richard Wienhorst. *Verses and Offertory Sentences, part VIII.* CPH 97-5508. U/pt.

Powell, Robert. *Verses and Offertory Sentences, part VI.* CPH 97-5506. U/pt.

CHORAL MUSIC FOR THE SEASON

Ashdown, Franklin D. "Jesus, the Very Thought of Thee." AFP 11-10886. SATB, org, opt C inst.

Brahms, Johannes. "Let Nothing Ever Grieve Thee," Op. 30 (Lass dich nur nichts nicht dauren). PET 6093. SATB, org. Eng/Ger.

Damon, Dan. "Many and Great O God." GIA G-4350. SATB, pno, drm, rec, fl.

Haydn, Franz Joseph/ed. Robert Scholz. "God of Life." AFP 11-10741. Choral score. 11-10740. Complete score, inst pts.

Hobby, Robert. "Open Your Ears, O Faithful People." AFP 11-10752. U, opt desc, fl, fc, tamb, hb.

Kosche, Kenneth T. "When All Your Mercies, O My God." CPH 98-3445. SAB, kybd.

Marshall, Jane. "Sing to God." HWG GCMR03548. SATB, org.

Proulx, Richard. "Strengthen for Service." AFP 12-400005. Also in *The Augsburg Choirbook.* 11-10817. SATB.

Williams, Julius P. "He Is My Strength and Power." AFP 11-10773. SATB, pno.

CHILDREN'S CHORAL MUSIC FOR THE SEASON

Bedford, Michael. "Come Worship God This Holy Day." CG CGA816. U, kybd, opt fl, opt tamb.

Christopherson, Dorothy. "O Praise the Lord, Hallelujah." AFP 11-10550. U/2 pt, cl, tamb, snare drm, pno 4 hands; 2 kybds/kybd, glock.

Ferguson, John. "Hallelujah, Praise the Lord." SEL 241-189. U/2 pt, Orff inst/kybd.

Wold, Wayne. "Build New Bridges." AFP 11-10879. SA, kybd.

Ziegenhals, Harriet. "You Shall Have a Song." HOP A577. 2 pt, fl, kybd.

INSTRUMENTAL MUSIC FOR THE SEASON

Bitgood, Roberta. "Rejoice, Give Thanks." HOP 333. Org, brass.

Harbach, Barbara. "Fantasy and Fugue on 'Swing Low, Sweet Chariot.' " VIV 338. Org.

Joseph, Michael. "Toccata Brevis." WAR GSTC9812. Org.

Manz, Paul. "Reprise." MSM 10-950. Org.

Mathews, Peter. "Autumn Nocturne." MSM 20-959. Org, vc.

McIver, Robert H. "Fantasia on 'Marion.' " WAR GSTC9805. Org.

Porter, Emily Maxson. *Five Hymn Preludes for the Fall.* MSM 10-713. Org.

HANDBELL MUSIC FOR THE SEASON

Helman, Michael. "Processional in C." AFP 11-10768. 3-5 oct, opt tpt.

Kinyon, Barbara. "Lead On O King Eternal." HOP 1409. 2-3 oct.

Lichlyter, Mary. "By the Rivers of Babylon." BEC HB165. 3-5 oct.

Linker/McFadden. "Great Is Thy Faithfulness." HOP 1868. 3-5 oct, opt brass/timp.

Mann, Terry. "Old Hundredth Fanfare." AMSI HB-15. 3 oct.

McChesney, Kevin. "When We Are Living/Somos del Señor." AFP 11-10631. 3-5 oct, opt ch.

McKechnie, D. Linda. "Music for a Beginning Handbell Choir." CG CGB57. 3 oct.

AUTUMN

ALTERNATE WORSHIP TEXTS

CONFESSION AND FORGIVENESS
In the name of the Father, and of the ☩ Son,
and of the Holy Spirit.
Amen

Calling to mind the frailty of our human condition,
let us confess our sin to God.
Silence for reflection and self-examination.

Good and loving God,
you made your abundant creation
for the use and enjoyment of all people.
We confess that we have held
the things you have given us too closely,
and have not shared freely with all in need.
Help us to receive your gracious word
and to practice generosity in our daily lives. Amen

God calls us to seek good
and to turn away from evil.
To those who have faith in Jesus Christ,
God grants forgiveness of sin,
strength in our weakness,
and the promise of eternal salvation.
Amen

GREETING
The waters shall break forth in the wilderness.
The thirsty ground shall become a flowing spring.
The grace of our Lord Jesus Christ, the love of God,
and the communion of the Holy Spirit be with you all.
And also with you.

PRAYERS
As we await the full harvest of the Spirit, let us offer our prayers to
God who is abundant in every good gift.
A brief silence.

Each petition ends:
Hear us, O God;
your mercy is great.

Concluding petition
Teach us to pray, O God, and grant us wisdom in our asking,
in the name of Jesus Christ our Lord.
Amen

OFFERTORY PRAYER
Kind and gracious God,
by Christ's death on the cross
you have given new life to us.
Receive these gifts as tokens of our love for you,
that we might give thanks for the fullness of your salvation
in Jesus Christ our Lord. Amen

INVITATION TO COMMUNION
Let all who seek the gifts of Christ
receive the bounty of this meal.

POST-COMMUNION PRAYER
Gracious God,
through the gift of this meal
you heal our brokenness
and strengthen our spirits.
Increase our faith in you,
that the power of this holy sacrament
might bring us to new life in
Jesus Christ our Lord.
Amen

BENEDICTION
May the gracious gifts of the Lord God be upon you,
and increase the work of your hands.
Almighty God, Father, ☩ Son, and Holy Spirit,
bless you now and forever.
Amen

DISMISSAL
Go in peace.
Welcome others as Christ has welcomed you.
Thanks be to God.

Permission is granted for congregations to reproduce the Alternate Worship Texts, provided copies are for local use only and the following copyright notice appears: From *Sundays & Seasons*, copyright © 1999 Augsburg Fortress. May be reproduced by permission for use only between November 28, 1999 and December 2, 2000.

SEASONAL RITES

BLESSING OF TEACHERS AND STUDENTS

HYMN
LBW 558   Earth and all stars!

If used on a Sunday morning the following prayer may be used during or following the prayers.

Let us pray for all who are beginning a new school year,
that both students and teachers will be blessed in their academic endeavors.

Almighty God,
you give wisdom and knowledge.
Grant teachers the gift of joy and insight,
and students the gift of diligence and openness,
that all may grow in what is good and honest and true.
Support all who teach and all who learn,
that together we may know and follow your ways;
through Jesus Christ our Lord.
Amen

BLESSING OF ANIMALS

This service may be used entirely on its own, perhaps for an observance on or near the commemoration of Francis of Assisi, renewer of the Church, 1226 (October 4). Various elements of this order may also be incorporated into another worship service (though this material is not intended to replace the customary Sunday worship of the congregation). Care should be used in adapting the service to the occasion and to the physical setting in which it is used. For practical reasons this service may be conducted outdoors or in a facility other than a congregation's primary worship space.

The grace of our Lord Jesus Christ, the love of God, and the communion of the Holy Spirit be with you all.
Amen

Let us pray.
O merciful Creator, your hand is open wide to satisfy the needs of every living creature. Make us always thankful for your loving providence; and grant that we, remembering the account that we must one day give, may be faithful stewards of your good gifts; through your Son, Jesus Christ our Lord.
Amen

or

Almighty God, in giving us dominion over things on earth, you made us fellow workers in your creation: Give us wisdom and reverence so to use the resources of nature, that no one may suffer from our abuse of them, and that generations yet to come may continue to praise you for your bounty; through Jesus Christ our Lord.
Amen

Book of Common Prayer, prayer 41, p. 827

READINGS
Genesis 1:1, 20-28
Genesis 6:17-22
Psalm 8
Psalm 148

Other readings about God's creation and the care of animals may be used. A sermon or an address appropriate to the occasion may also be included.

HYMN OR CANTICLE
LBW 18   All you works of the Lord
LBW 409   Praise and thanksgiving
LBW 527   All creatures of our God and King
LBW 554   This is my Father's world
LBW 560   Oh, that I had a thousand voices
WOV 767   All things bright and beautiful
Song of the Three Young Men *(see below* or Psalter for Worship, Cycle C, *Vigil of Easter, response 12)*

The leader may ask all who have brought pets/animals to the celebration to come forward for the following prayer.

The Lord be with you.
And also with you.
Let us pray.
Gracious God, in your love you created us in your image and made us stewards of the animals that live in the skies, the earth, and the sea. Bless us in our care for our pets and animals (names of pets may be added here). Help us recognize your power and wisdom in the variety of creatures that live in our world, and hear our prayer for all that suffer over work, hunger, and ill-treatment. Protect your creatures and guard them from all evil, now and forever.
Amen

THE LORD'S PRAYER

The Lord almighty order our days and our deeds in his peace.
Amen

CANTICLE OF THE SUN

All creatures, worship God most high!
Sound every voice in earth and sky: Alleluia! Alleluia!
Sing, brother sun, in splendor bright;
sing, sister moon and stars of night:
Alleluia, alleluia, alleluia, alleluia, alleluia!

Sing, brother wind; with clouds and rain
you grow the gifts of fruit and grain: Alleluia! Alleluia!
Dear sister water, useful, clear,
make music for your Lord to hear:
Alleluia, alleluia, alleluia, alleluia, alleluia!

O fire, our brother, mirthful, strong,
drive far the shadows, join the song: Alleluia! Alleluia!
O earth, our mother, rich in care,
praise God in colors bright and rare:
Alleluia, alleluia, alleluia, alleluia, alleluia!

All who for love of God forgive,
all who in pain or sorrow grieve: Alleluia! Alleluia!
Christ bears your burdens and your fears;
in mercy rest, sing through the tears:
Alleluia, alleluia, alleluia, alleluia, alleluia!

Come, sister death, your song release
when you enfold our breath in peace: Alleluia! Alleluia!
Since Christ our light has pierced your gloom,
fair is the night that leads us home.
Alleluia, alleluia, alleluia, alleluia, alleluia!

O sisters, brothers, take your part,
and worship God with humble heart: Alleluia! Alleluia!
All creatures, bless the Father, Son,
and Holy Spirit, Three in One:
Alleluia, alleluia, alleluia, alleluia, alleluia!

Text: based on a hymn of Francis of Assisi
Tune: LASST UNS ERFREUEN (LBW 143)

SERVICE OF THE WORD FOR HEALING

This service may be celebrated at any time. It may be especially appropriate on or near the festival of St. Luke, Evangelist (October 18).

Stand
HYMN
LBW 360   O Christ, the healer, we have come
WOV 716   Word of God, come down on earth

GREETING AND WELCOME
The grace of our Lord Jesus Christ, the love of God, and the communion of the Holy Spirit be with you all.
And also with you.

We gather to hear the word of God, pray for those in need, and ask God's blessing on those who seek healing and wholeness through Christ our Lord.

PRAYER OF THE DAY
The proper prayer of the day may be used, or the prayer for St. Luke (October 18), p. 118 in WOV Leaders edition, or the following:

Great God, our healer,
by your power, the Lord Jesus healed the sick
and gave hope to the hopeless.
As we gather in his name,
look upon us with mercy and
bless us with your healing Spirit.
Bring us comfort in the midst of pain,
strength to transform our weakness,
and light to illuminate our darkness.
We ask this in the name of Jesus Christ,
our crucified and risen Lord,
who lives and reigns with you and the Holy Spirit,
one God, now and forever.
Amen

Sit
READINGS
These readings, the readings listed for St. Luke, Evangelist (p. 118 in WOV Leaders edition), or the readings listed on pp. 96–97 of Occasional Services may be used.

Isaiah 61:1-3a
Psalm 23
   The Lord is my shepherd; I shall not be in want.
Luke 17:11-19

SERMON

HYMN
LBW 423   Lord, whose love in humble service
WOV 738 Healer of our every ill
WOV 798 Bless the Lord, O my soul

Stand
THE PRAYERS
This litany, or the prayers in Occasional Services *(pp. 91–93) may be used.*

God the Father, you desire the health and salvation of all people.
We praise you and thank you, O Lord.
God the Son, you came that we might have life,
and might have it more abundantly.
We praise you and thank you, O Lord.
God the Holy Spirit,
you make our bodies the temples of your presence.
We praise you and thank you, O Lord.
Holy Trinity, one God,
in you we live and move and have our being.
We praise you and thank you, O Lord.
Lord, grant your healing grace to all who are sick, injured,
or disabled, that they may be made whole;
hear us, O Lord of life.
Grant to all who are lonely, anxious, or despondent,
the awareness of your presence;
hear us, O Lord of life.
Mend broken relationships, and restore those in emotional distress
to soundness of mind and serenity of spirit;
hear us, O Lord of life.
Bless physicians, nurses, and all others who minister to the suffering;
grant them wisdom and skill, sympathy and patience;
hear us, O Lord of life.
Grant to the dying a peaceful, holy death,
and with your grace strengthen those who mourn;
hear us, O Lord of life.
Restore to wholeness whatever is broken in our lives,
in this nation, and in the world;
hear us, O Lord of life.
Hear us, O Lord of life:
heal us, and make us whole.

Gracious God, in baptism you anointed us with the oil of salvation,
and joined us to the death and resurrection of your Son. Bless all
who seek your healing presence in their lives. In their suffering
draw them more deeply into the mystery of your love, that following Christ in the way of the cross they may know the power of his
resurrection; who lives and reigns forever and ever.
Amen

Sit
LAYING ON OF HANDS AND ANOINTING
*Those who wish to receive the laying on of hands (and anoint-
ing) come to the altar and, if possible, kneel. The minister lays
both hands on each person's head in silence, after which he/she
may dip a thumb in the oil and make the sign of the cross on
the person's forehead, saying:*

(Through this holy anointing) may God's love and mercy uphold
you by the grace and power of the Holy Spirit.
Amen

*During the anointing, the assembly may sing various hymns and
songs, instrumental music may be played, or a simple interval of
silence may be observed.*

Stand
PRAYER
After all have returned to their places, the minister may say:

As you are anointed with this oil,
may God bless you with the healing power of the Holy Spirit.
May God forgive you your sins,
release you from suffering,
and restore you to wholeness and strength.
May God deliver you from all evil,
preserve you in all goodness,
and bring you to everlasting life,
through Jesus Christ our Lord.
Amen

CONCLUDING RITE

THE LORD'S PRAYER

BLESSING AND DISMISSAL

HYMN
LBW 263   Abide with us, our Savior
WOV 721 Go, my children, with my blessing
WOV 737 There is a balm in Gilead

SATURDAY, SEPTEMBER 2
NIKOLAI FREDERIK SEVERIN GRUNDTVIG, BISHOP, RENEWER OF THE CHURCH, 1872

Grundtvig sought to restore orthodoxy to the Danish church by attacking rationalism and state domination of religion. He challenged the notion that Christianity was a philosophical idea rather than God's revelation made known to us in Christ and in the sacraments.

Grundtvig wrote five volumes of hymns, his most famous being "Built on a rock" (LBW 365). Consider commemorating Grundtvig at a meeting of the worship or education committees, and discuss the ways in which our lives of faith are transformed.

SEPTEMBER 3, 2000
TWELFTH SUNDAY AFTER PENTECOST
PROPER 17

INTRODUCTION

In the liturgy, we pray to God who is the giver of every good and perfect gift. We ask God to bring to fruition the word of truth sown in our hearts by Christ, so that we will live the law of love. It is this liberating law that judges all other laws of human origin. It is this gracious command that is sealed with Christ's blood. In this supper Christ forgives us and strengthens us to be communal witnesses to his love.

PRAYER OF THE DAY

O God, we thank you for your Son who chose the path of suffering for the sake of the world. Humble us by his example, point us to the path of obedience, and give us strength to follow his commands; through your Son, Jesus Christ our Lord.

READINGS

Deuteronomy 4:1-2, 6-9
The Israelites believed the Law was a divine gift that provided guidelines for living out the covenant. According to Moses, the people are to obey the Law and neither add to nor subtract from it.

Psalm 15
LORD, who may dwell in your tabernacle? (Ps. 15:1)

James 1:17-27
The letter of James was intended to provide first-century Christians with instruction in godly behavior. Here, Christians are encouraged to listen carefully and to act on what they hear.

Mark 7:1-8, 14-15, 21-23
Mark's gospel depicts Jesus as challenging traditional ways in which religious people determine what is pure or impure. For Jesus, the observance of religious practices cannot become a substitute for godly words or deeds that spring from the faithful heart.

ALTERNATE FIRST READING/PSALM

Song of Solomon 2:8-13
Though using language and images of a tender love story, the Song of Solomon has long inspired the tradition of allegorical interpretation. Jewish lore sees its meaning as a depiction of the love of the Lord with the covenant people. Furthermore, Christian interpretation has often seen this work as a depiction of the love of Christ and his church.

Psalm 45:1-2, 7-10 (Psalm 45:1-2, 6-9 [NRSV])
God has anointed you with the oil of gladness. (Ps. 45:8)

COLOR   Green

THE PRAYERS

As we await the full harvest of the Spirit, let us offer our prayers to God who is abundant in every good gift.
A BRIEF SILENCE.

Let us pray for the church, that God's word would not be crowded out by human traditions, and that right teaching would be coupled always with right living. Hear us, O God;
your mercy is great.

Let us pray for the world, that laborers would be treated fairly, and that opportunities for employment and income would abound in all places. Hear us, O God;
your mercy is great.

Let us pray that the orphaned and widowed would be supported, and that God's people would respond in mercy and with compassion to all in need (especially . . .). Hear us, O God;
your mercy is great.

Let us pray for this congregation, that all who are preparing for the resumption of activities this fall will be invigorated by the Spirit to carry out their tasks with joy and strength. Hear us, O God;
your mercy is great.

HERE OTHER INTERCESSIONS MAY BE OFFERED.

Let us pray for those in sorrow, that they will be met in the valley of their grief by the Comforter and have their hope in the resurrection restored. Hear us, O God;
your mercy is great.

Teach us to pray, O God, and grant us wisdom in our asking, in the name of Jesus Christ our Lord.
Amen

IMAGES FOR PREACHING

Don't go to Mark without taking Deuteronomy along! Christian preaching is often susceptible to the danger of anti-Semitism. That danger is magnified today as Jesus chastises the Pharisees and scribes for abandoning God's commandments and holding to human tradition. We have too often taught that the Old Testament is law while the New Testament is gospel. The danger is not only that we teach disparaging things about the Jews, but we safely distance ourselves from Jesus' words—the problem is always with someone else, not with me!

Deuteronomy's plea to teach the Law "to your children and your children's children" is particularly important as a new school year begins. Today can be a time to affirm the congregation's and larger community's ministry with children in the prayers or in a communal blessing. The Deuteronomy reading affirms the life-giving goodness of the Law, an important reminder alongside Jesus' chastisement of the religious leaders in Mark. The heart of the Law is the great commandment:

"Hear, O Israel: The LORD is our God, the LORD alone. You shall love the LORD your God with all your heart, and with all your soul, and with all your might" (Deut. 6:4). Jesus lifts up these words when he is asked which commandment is first of all (Mark 12:28-29).

With Deuteronomy in our ears, we ask questions not about someone else but about ourselves. Have any of our traditions become more important than God? Are we as passionate about reaching out to our neighbors as we are about the new carpet and remodeling the church kitchen? Do we spend more time getting ready for our annual fall fair than we spend in Bible study? Jesus comes to us in this gospel to call us back to the river, back to the promises of baptism, back to the heart of God.

WORSHIP MATTERS

This day's Old Testament reading focuses on obedience. Christian worship is itself rooted in faithful obedience to God. How obedient are the worship practices of your congregation? Is baptism administered in the name of the triune God? Is it administered with significant amounts of water in order to "symbolize God's power over sin and death" (*The Use of the Means of Grace: A Statement on the Practice of Word and Sacrament*, principle 26)? Are the appointed readings used and the psalm sung each Sunday? Is the sermon based on the readings rather than favorite scriptural passages of the preacher? Does the music illumine the readings and the sacraments? Is the eucharist celebrated weekly and is it the main service, rather than an appended service for a few people?

LET THE CHILDREN COME

Children and other people love attention. Often an older person can provide some kindly companionship and help a child to learn and worship. A child can provide an older person with a renewed sense of vibrancy, wonder, and joy, as well as a sense of being needed. Consider inviting a child to "adopt" an older person during worship.

MUSIC FOR WORSHIP

GATHERING

LBW 561	For the beauty of the earth
WOV 782	All my hope on God is founded

PSALM 15

Bengtson, Bruce. PW, cycle B.

Gelineau, Joseph. "Psalm 15" in *RitualSong*. GIA.

Haas, David/arr. Jeanne Cotter. "They Who Do Justice" in *PCY*, vol. III.

Proulx, Richard/arr. Gelineau. TP.

Pulkingham, Betty. *Celebrate the Church Year with Selected Psalms and Canticles.* PLY MB 94218. Cong, choir, kybd, gtr, inst.

HYMN OF THE DAY

LBW 511   Renew me, O eternal Light
              HERR JESU CHRIST, MEINS

INSTRUMENTAL RESOURCES

Bender, Jan. "Herr Jesu Christ, meins" in *Hymn Preludes and Free Accompaniments, vol. 1.* AFP 11-9397. Org/kybd.

Mahnke, Allen. "Herr Jesu Christ, meins" in *Fourteen Pieces for Treble Instrument and Organ.* CPH 97-6547. Org, inst.

Manz, Paul. "Renew Me, O Eternal Light" in *Improvisations on General Hymns.* MSM 10-830. Org.

ALTERNATE HYMN OF THE DAY

WOV 713   Lord, let my heart be good soil
LBW 504   O God, my faithful God

COMMUNION

LBW 513   Come, my way, my truth, my life
WOV 732   Create in me a clean heart

SENDING

LBW 480   Oh, that the Lord would guide my ways
LBW 503   O Jesus, I have promised

ADDITIONAL HYMNS AND SONGS

H82 681   O God, to whom we turn
NCH 465   Teach me, O Lord, your holy way
TFF 113   Have you got good religion?
W&P   Create in me

MUSIC FOR THE DAY

CHORAL

Harwood, Basil. "I Am the Living Bread." OXF A75. SATB, org.

Moger, Peter. "Teach Me, O Lord." GIA G 4201. SATB, org.

Rachmaninoff, Sergei. "To Thee We Sing" in *The Liturgy of St. John Chrysostom.* GAL 1.3170. S, SATB.

Scott, K. Lee. "Jesus, My Breath, My Life, My Lord." CPH. SATB.

Scott, K. Lee. "So Art Thou to Me" in *Rejoice Now My Spirit, Vocal Solos for the Church Year.* AFP 11-10228. MH. 11-10229. ML.

CHILDREN'S CHOIRS

Honoré, Jeffrey. "All Good Gifts." CG CGA593. U/SATB, kybd, opt 1 oct hb, opt cong.

Sleeth, Natalie. "Blessed Shall They Be." AMSI 386. 2 pt, kybd.

KEYBOARD/INSTRUMENTAL

Carter, John. "Variants on 'For the Beauty of the Earth' " in *Keys of the Kingdom: Piano Arrangements for Worship.* ABI. Pno.

Powell, Robert J. "All Things Bright and Beautiful" in *Ten Seasonal Hymntune Preludes for the Church Year.* GIA G-3829. Org.

HANDBELL

Rodriguez, Rudy. "Short-Handed Pieces for 5 to 10." AGEHR AG34013. 3-4 oct.

Wilson, John F. "Kum Ba Yah." AG 1650. 2-3 oct.

PRAISE ENSEMBLE

Butler, Terry. "Cry of My Heart" in *Maranatha! Music Praise Chorus Book, 3rd ed.* WRD/MAR.

Dearman, Kirk. "We Choose the Fear of the Lord" in *Maranatha! Music Praise Chorus Book, 3rd ed.* WRD/MAR.

Leavitt, John. "All Things Bright and Beautiful." HAL 08595443. 2 pt, pno.

Mitchell, Tom. "All Things Bright and Beautiful." CG CGA-492. SATB, kybd.

Ylvisaker, John. "Who Shall Live on That Holy Mountain" in *Borning Cry.* NGP.

MONDAY, SEPTEMBER 4
ALBERT SCHWEITZER, MISSIONARY TO AFRICA, 1965

Albert Schweitzer was a theologian, philosopher, musician, and missionary doctor. He believed that the solution to the world's problems was simple: have reverence for life. This conviction led him to warn against the atomic bomb and to speak out against racial injustice.

If your congregation honors the vocations of its members in relation to Labor Day, Schweitzer could be held up as a model of someone who wisely used his gifts and was creatively involved in many aspects of life in the world.

SATURDAY, SEPTEMBER 9
PETER CLAVER, PRIEST, MISSIONARY TO COLOMBIA, 1654

Peter Claver was a Jesuit missionary who served in Cartagena (in what is now Colombia) by teaching and caring for the slaves. The slaves arrived in ships where they were penned up like cattle in dehumanizing conditions. Claver met them and attended to their needs, baptizing children who had been born on the voyage.

Claver's advocacy on behalf of the rights of slaves is a witness to a gospel that is for all people. How are we called to work for the dignity and equality of all God's children? Pray for examples of contemporary ministries that offer care and compassion to people living in substandard living conditions.

SEPTEMBER 10, 2000

THIRTEENTH SUNDAY AFTER PENTECOST
PROPER 18

INTRODUCTION

In today's gospel Jesus heals a deaf and mute man using the word *ephphatha*, which means "be opened." The author of James exhorts the community of faith to guard against favoritism among its members. In baptism we have died to any distinctions that would separate us from each other. Likewise, in the eucharist each one receives the free gift of Christ equally and without discrimination. Through word and sacrament God opens our minds and hearts to the healing and liberating gospel of Christ.

PRAYER OF THE DAY

Almighty and eternal God, you know our problems and our weaknesses better than we ourselves. In your love and by your power help us in our confusion and, in spite of our weakness, make us firm in faith; through your Son, Jesus Christ our Lord.

READINGS

Isaiah 35:4-7a

These verses arise as a word of hope to the exiles in Babylon. Chapter 34 portrays God's vengeance on Edom, Israel's age-old enemy, which makes the path from Babylon to Zion safe for the exiles' return. This chapter concludes with a description of the highway home, the holy way of God's people, blossoming with God's glory.

Psalm 146

I will praise the LORD as long as I live. (Ps. 146:1)

James 2:1-10 [11-13] 14-17

The epistle of James is written to Christians who may have misunderstood the teaching that salvation comes by faith rather than by doing good works. James insists that true faith shows itself in action.

Mark 7:24-37

In Mark's gospel, encounters with women usually signify turning points in Jesus' ministry. Here, a conversation with a Syrophoenician woman marks the beginning of his mission to the Gentiles.

ALTERNATE FIRST READING/PSALM

Proverbs 22:1-2, 8-9, 22-23

This section of material from Proverbs deals with the binary sets of rich and poor, wealth and poverty. The wisdom imparted from these particular verses is that those who are blessed by God will honor the poor, for they are within God's special care.

Psalm 125

Those who trust in the LORD stand fast forever. (Ps. 125:1)

COLOR   Green

THE PRAYERS

As we await the full harvest of the Spirit, let us offer our prayers to God who is abundant in every good gift.
A BRIEF SILENCE.

Let us pray that all people be welcomed without reserve to the community of faith gathered around word and sacrament. Hear us, O God;

your mercy is great.
Let us pray that relief would come to places where extreme weather has caused damage, and that those suffering from any sickness or adversity would find comfort (especially . . .). Hear us, O God;
your mercy is great.
Let us pray that God's inclusive love might be the standard by which the needs of all people are addressed. Hear us, O God;
your mercy is great.
Let us pray that children and adults alike might be drawn to love God's word and holy supper as they are proclaimed by faithful teachers and leaders in our congregation. Hear us, O God;
your mercy is great.
HERE OTHER INTERCESSIONS MAY BE OFFERED.

Let us pray that we may be kept in communion with those who have died and who now rest from their labors in your own eternal place. Hear us, O God;
your mercy is great.
Teach us to pray, O God, and grant us wisdom in our asking, in the name of Jesus Christ our Lord.
Amen

IMAGES FOR PREACHING

For centuries, African people were carried to America as slaves in ships with names like *John the Baptist, Jesus*, and *Mary*. Sometime along the way, their white masters taught the slaves stories from a book called the Bible. They heard those same names—John the Baptist, Jesus, Mary—along with the story of God rescuing the Hebrew people from slavery in Egypt. How could the stories in the book be true when they were brought to this land in chains? By some miracle these slaves came to believe that the God of Moses was their God and Jesus was their Savior, even though his name was painted on a slave ship! They took the slave owners' words and turned them upside down, daring to believe God would set them free. And they begin to sing, "Oh, Mary, don't you weep, don't you mourn!"

Who can explain why Jesus said such cruel words to the Syrophoenician woman? (We have convinced ourselves he must have been testing her faith, though the text never says.) But it seems apparent that she had heard good news preached to others and had the audacity to believe it was also for her. This woman is feisty, determined, and desperate. She will not be turned aside. She takes Jesus' demeaning words and tosses them back on behalf of her daughter. She dared to believe that the kingdom of God had come near her and her little girl.

Did she pass Jesus' test? Or did she open his eyes? Mark provides no clear answer in his text. One thing is clear: she received far more than crumbs. Jesus made sure everyone understood—no matter how unlikely it seemed—she was undeniably part of the commonwealth of God.

WORSHIP MATTERS

The reading from James challenges any attempt to show partiality toward the wealthy in the worshiping assembly. Ultimately, James invites us to practice hospitality in worship. How hospitable is the worship of your congregation? Are visitors warmly greeted without being overwhelmed? Are they invited to register their names and addresses so that they might receive a follow-up contact later in the week? Is the bulletin easy to read, and does it give clear instructions? Are different areas in the church building clearly marked or even mapped? Does a brief written or oral statement invite baptized visitors to commune?

LET THE CHILDREN COME

The Syrophoenician girl had an unclean spirit. Children in our congregations sometimes behave as though they have unclean spirits. How do we deal with disruptive behavior? How do we set limits on behavior that distracts others from worship so that we do not alienate the children and their families? How do we encourage parents in the difficult task of raising and disciplining children? How can we bring all people to the place where they can encounter Jesus, the Savior?

MUSIC FOR WORSHIP

GATHERING
LBW 400   God, whose almighty word
WOV 797   O God beyond all praising

PSALM 146
Comer, Marilyn. PW, cycle B.
Cooney, Rory and Gary Daigle. "Praise the Lord, My Soul" in PCY, vol. IV.

Dobry, Wallace. "A Trio of Psalms." MSM 80-706. U/2pt, cong, kybd.
Haugen, Marty. "Lord, Come and Save Us" in PCY, vol. 2.
Stewart, Roy James. "Praise the Lord" in PCY, vol. 5.
Wellicome, Paul. "Maranatha, Alleluia!" in PS, vol. 2.

LBW 538 Oh, praise the Lord, my soul (paraphrase)
LBW 539 Praise the Almighty (paraphrase)

HYMN OF THE DAY

LBW 419 Lord of all nations, grant me grace
BEATUS VIR

INSTRUMENTAL RESOURCES

Busarow, Donald. "Beatus vir" in *All Praise to You, Eternal God*. AFP 11-9076. Org/kybd.
Gehring, Philip. "Beatus vir" in *Hymn Preludes and Free Accompaniments, vol. 3*. AFP 11-9399. Org.
Sensmeier, Randall. "Lord of All Nations, Grant Me Grace" in *The Concordia Hymn Prelude Series, vol. 20*. CPH 97-5711. Org.

ALTERNATE HYMN OF THE DAY

LBW 426 O Son of God, in Galilee
WOV 716 Word of God, come down on earth

COMMUNION

LBW 212 Let us break bread together
WOV 738 Healer of our every ill
WOV 737 There is a balm in Gilead

SENDING

LBW 559 Oh, for a thousand tongues
WOV 755 We all are one in mission

ADDITIONAL HYMNS AND SONGS

DATH 94 Someone in need of your love
H82 700 O love that casts out fear
TFF 134 O Lord, open my eyes
W&P He who began a good work in you

MUSIC FOR THE DAY

CHORAL

Fleming, Larry L. "Humble Service." AFP 11-2294. SATB.
Hassell, Michael. "What a Friend We Have in Jesus." AFP 11-10919. SATB, sop/ten solo, pno.
Purcell, Henry. "Rejoice in the Lord Always" in *A Purcell Anthology*. OXF ISBN 0-19-353351-0. SATB, str, cont.
Scott, K. Lee. "Giver of Every Perfect Gift." CPH 98-3466. SATB, opt cong, opt C inst, org.
Telemann, George Philipp/arr. Susan Palo Cherwien. "I Want to Praise the Lord All of My Life." CPH 98-3350. 2-3 vcs/2-3 pt choir, kybd, opt solo inst.

CHILDREN'S CHOIRS

Handel, G. F./arr. Jane McFadden. "Let My Heart and Soul Praise the Lord." CG CGA650. U, kybd.
Wold, Wayne L. "Build New Bridges." AFP 11-10879. U/2 pt, kybd.

KEYBOARD/INSTRUMENTAL

Cherwien, David. "Healer of Our Every Ill" in *Six Organ Preludes*. GIA G-4291. Org.
Handel, G. F. "Andante" in *Music for a Celebration, Set I*. MSM 10-940. Org.

HANDBELL

Dobrinski, Cynthia. "Canticle of Faith." AG 1932. 3-5 oct.
Handley, Andrea. "Procession and Hymn" (Lobe den Herren). Red River Music BL5008. 3-5 oct.

PRAISE ENSEMBLE

Angerman, David. "Creation Will Dance And Rejoice!" ALF 16136. SATB, kybd.
Davis, Greg and Greg Fisher/arr. Innes. "Honor the Lord." HOP WT1522. SATB, kybd.
Harlan, Benjamin. "Open Thou Mine Eyes." GS A-6722. SATB, acc.
Kendrick, Graham. "We Declare That the Kingdom of God Is Here" in *Praise Worship, vol 4*. INT HMSB04.
Kilpatrick, Bob. "In My Life, Lord, Be Glorified" in *Songs For Praise and Worship*. WRD.

WEDNESDAY, SEPTEMBER 13
JOHN CHRYSOSTOM, BISHOP OF CONSTANTINOPLE, 407

John Chrysostom was trained in law and theology, and he used his oratorical gifts in preaching, which gave him the title "golden-mouthed" (or "Chrysostom"). He was skilled at the exposition of scripture, able to relate both the author's meaning as well as the practical application, opposing the allegorical interpretation common at the time. He was made patriarch of Constantinople against his wishes, and in that office he reformed the city, court, and clergy.

Share a conversation about the tasks and challenges of preaching today. Ask parishioners to relate particularly memorable sermons, and to discuss the ways that preaching impacts their lives of faith. Pastors may gain insights for their homiletical preparation.

THURSDAY, SEPTEMBER 14
HOLY CROSS DAY

The observance of this day dates from 335 in which a basilica was built by Constantine on the sight believed to be the place of the crucifixion. The cross is one of the primary symbols of Christianity. This festival became very popular, being observed in both the East and West.

Congregations might make mention of Holy Cross Day on Sunday and sing "Lift high the cross" (LBW 377) as an entrance hymn. Meetings or services during the week might focus on the readings and themes of the festival. Does the cross have central place in the life of your congregation in its worship, education, evangelism, and social ministry? Do you teach children (and adults) to make the sign of the cross in remembrance of their baptism into Jesus' death and resurrection?

SEPTEMBER 17, 2000

FOURTEENTH SUNDAY AFTER PENTECOST
PROPER 19

INTRODUCTION

Those who confess Jesus as Messiah are called to deny themselves, take up their cross, and follow Christ. As we face the suffering of the world and the brokenness of our own lives, we learn the meaning of losing our lives for the sake of the gospel. Each time we make the sign of the cross, and share the broken bread and the cup of salvation, we remember the good news that our baptism into Christ's death is also the promise of the resurrection.

PRAYER OF THE DAY

O God, you declare your almighty power chiefly in showing mercy and pity. Grant us the fullness of your grace, that, pursuing what you have promised, we may share your heavenly glory; through your Son, Jesus Christ our Lord.

READINGS

Isaiah 50:4-9a

This reading gives good advice to sufferers: trust in God even (and especially) in the midst of pain. The servant remains faithful throughout trials, knowing that God is with and for the sufferer in the midst of pain.

Psalm 116:1-8 (Psalm 116:1-9 [NRSV])

I will walk in the presence of the LORD. (Ps. 116:8)

James 3:1-12

The author of James warns against the power of human speech and the difficulties of controlling the tongue. With our mouths we have the capacity both to bless God and to curse.

Mark 8:27-38

This story provides the turning point in the Markan gospel. Peter is the first human being in the narrative to acknowledge Jesus as the Messiah, but he cannot accept that as the Messiah Jesus will have to suffer. Moreover, Jesus issues a strong challenge to all by connecting discipleship and the cross.

ALTERNATE FIRST READING/PSALM

Proverbs 1:20-33

In these verses Wisdom is personified as a woman. Here wisdom is a gift of the Lord, rather than human achievement. Though Wisdom offers her hand to those who scoff at her, they have spurned all such counsel. That they come to ruin is predictable.

Psalm 19

The statutes of the LORD are just and rejoice the heart. (Ps. 19:8)

or Wisdom of Solomon 7:26—8:1

COLOR Green

THE PRAYERS

As we await the full harvest of the Spirit, let us offer our prayers to God who is abundant in every good gift.
A BRIEF SILENCE.

Let us pray for the church, that its ministries of educa-

tion would be carried out by faithful teachers. Hear us, O God;
your mercy is great.
Let us pray for the leaders of the world, that in their dealings with one another they may be gentle of speech and wise in heart. Hear us, O God;
your mercy is great.
Let us pray for those who have been verbally or emotionally abused, that they may be healed from the evil words that have broken their spirits. Hear us, O God;
your mercy is great.
Let us pray for those struggling with ill health (especially . . .), that they would know God's healing strength. Hear us, O God;
your mercy is great.
Let us pray for all who teach in this congregation, that they would be strengthened in your word, and that their efforts would be used to sustain the weary and instruct the wise. Hear us, O God;
your mercy is great.

HERE OTHER INTERCESSIONS MAY BE OFFERED.

Let us pray for those whose hearts are heavy with sorrow (especially . . .), that they may know the consolation of God's love and the hope of heaven. Hear us, O God;
your mercy is great.
Teach us to pray, O God, and grant us wisdom in our asking, in the name of Jesus Christ our Lord.
Amen

IMAGES FOR PREACHING

"The Lord GOD has given me the tongue of a teacher, that I may know how to sustain the weary with a word." Isaiah's words about the suffering servant can be a powerful prayer for the preacher: "O God, send your Spirit upon me that I may sustain the weary with a word." On some days it is the preacher who is the weariest of all, especially in the crush to get everything up and running in September! It is a good time to invite Sunday school children and teachers to gather around the baptismal font for a blessing, to be marked again with the sign of the cross.

Most of us have some memories of our days in school no matter how many years have passed. Do you remember sliding down in your desk after the teacher asked a question, hoping someone else's name would be called? Jesus began with an easy question: "Who do people say that I am?" The disciples could have answered that all afternoon for lots of different people had different answers; however, Jesus didn't stop with that question. "But who do you say that I am?" It's a question that can make you slide way down in your seat hoping Jesus will call on Andrew or Philip. Peter had his hand up first; his answer was bold and confident. Yet it soon became clear that knowing the right answer wasn't enough.

Again and again we must go back to the river, the baptismal river, where once again we take up the cross, Jesus' sign upon our forehead. Like the ancient word written on doorpost and gate, this sign on our foreheads marks our going out and our coming in forevermore.

WORSHIP MATTERS

The message of this day's gospel from Mark 8 is simple: Christ must suffer! Paradoxically, the one who comes as the embodiment of God must descend to the depths of human existence through suffering pain and death. The paradox is not lost on Peter who attempts to divert Jesus from his path of suffering.

Frequently the temptation in worship is to avoid images of pain and suffering. Our fear is that images of suffering, pain, and hardship might repel worshipers. But this fear recedes once we recognize that the church is not merely a cult of suffering and death. We proclaim the suffering of the cross in juxtaposition to the triumph of Easter. We affirm a risen Christ who comes to us even in the depths of our humanity. Does our *liturgy* of service to those who are poor, sick, and downtrodden also reflect a Christ who is present with us in our sufferings?

LET THE CHILDREN COME

Elementary-aged children are new readers and delight in using the worship book. As they struggle to read, however, they can become frustrated, and even things they know by heart, such as the Lord's Prayer, can be challenging for them to decipher. The congregation that rushes through the liturgy at breakneck speed will leave these greatly frustrated children behind. Better for all is to slow down the pace of congregational speaking to a deliberate, unison response, so that people may reflect on the word and children can keep up. Why not let an early reader lead the psalm, Kyrie, or creed occasionally?

MUSIC FOR WORSHIP
GATHERING
LBW 270	God of our life, all-glorious Lord
WOV 752	I, the Lord of sea and sky

PSALM 116
Brown, Teresa. "The Blessing Cup" in PS, vol. 2.
Comer, Marilyn. PW, cycle B.
Daigle, Gary and Rory Cooney. "Psalm 116: I Will Walk in the Presence of God" in *Gather Comprehensive*. GIA. U.
Fabing, Bob. "Be Like the Sun" in *Rise Up and Sing*. OCP 9391. U.
Glynn, John. "Lord, How Can I Repay" in PS, vol. 2.
Mahnke, Allan. *Psalms for Cantor and Congregation*. CPH 97-6093.
Roberts, Leon C. "I Will Call upon the Name of the Lord" in *This Far by Faith*.
Schalk, Carl. "Ps 116" in *Sing Out! A Children's Psalter*. WLP 7191.
Stewart, Roy James. "I Will Walk in the Presence of God" in PCY, vol. 5.

HYMN OF THE DAY
LBW 537	O Jesus, king most wonderful!
	HIDING PLACE

INSTRUMENTAL RESOURCES
Busarow, Donald. "O Jesus, King Most Wonderful" in *The Concordia Hymn Prelude Series, vol. 27*. CPH 97-5742. Org.

ALTERNATE HYMN OF THE DAY
WOV 750	Oh, praise the gracious power
LBW 377	Lift high the cross

COMMUNION
LBW 218	Strengthen for service, Lord
WOV 777	In the morning when I rise

OTHER SUGGESTIONS
Keesecker, Thomas. "I Am the Living Bread." AFP 11-10684. SATB, kybd, opt cong, opt sop sax/C inst.

SENDING
LBW 221	Sent forth by God's blessing
WOV 721	Go, my children, with my blessing

ADDITIONAL HYMNS AND SONGS
H82 634	I call on thee, Lord Jesus Christ
CW 448	In you, O Lord, I put my trust
TFF 237	Must Jesus bear the cross alone
W&P	Will you come and follow me

MUSIC FOR THE DAY
CHORAL
Hassler, Hans. "Agnus Dei." SHW A1482. SATB. Lat/Eng.
Haugen, Marty. "I Will Walk in the Presence of God." GIA G-4282. Inst pts G-428INST. 3 pt choir, cant, cong, gtr, 2 C ww.
Hobby, Robert A. "Take My Life, That I May Be." MSM 50-8820. SATB, fl, org.
Schubert, Franz. "O Jesus, Crucified for Man" (Begrabt dem leib in Seinen Gruft). NMP CH-10. SATB, org. Ger/Eng.

CHILDREN'S CHOIRS
Glover, Rob. "Embrace My Way and Cross." GIA G-4594. U, assembly, org, pno.
Sleeth, Natalie. "The Kingdom of the Lord." AMSI 301. 2 pt, fl, kybd.

KEYBOARD/INSTRUMENTAL
Billingham, Richard. "Give Me Jesus" in *Seven Reflections on African American Spirituals*. AFP 11-10762. Org.
Organ, Anne Krentz. "The Ash Grove" in *Reflections on Hymn Tunes for Holy Communion*. AFP 11-10621. Pno.

HANDBELL
Moklebust, Cathy. "Oh, for a Thousand Tongues to Sing" in *Hymn Stanzas for Handbells*. AFP 11-10722. 4-5 oct.
Sherman, Arnold. "Acclamation on 'Azmon.'" AG 1363. 3-5 oct.

PRAISE ENSEMBLE
Althouse, Jay. "Come Follow Me." ALF 4255. SAB, acc.
Boltz, Ray. "Take Up Your Cross" in *The Ray Boltz Anthology*. Diadem Music.
Marks. "Meet Us Here" in *Maranatha! Music Praise Chorus Book, 3rd ed.* WRD/MAR.
Ross, Joel A. "Give Me Jesus." CFI CM8490. SSATB, kybd.
Schreiner, John. "Be Thou My Vision" in *Favorite Hymns of Promise Keepers*." MAR 3010133367. 3 pt, kybd.

MONDAY, SEPTEMBER 18
DAG HAMMARSKJÖLD, PEACEMAKER, 1961

Dag Hammarskjöld was a Swedish diplomat and humanitarian who served as Secretary General of the United Nations. He was killed in a plane crash on this day in 1961 while on his way to negotiate a cease fire between the United Nations and Katanga forces. It was not until after Hammarskjöld's death that the publications of his personal journal, *Markings*, revealed his deep Christian faith. The book revealed that his life was a unique combination of diplomatic service with a personal spirituality.

Through word and sacrament we nurture our congregations to bear witness in their daily lives. Our actions often speak louder than our words. How can we deepen the sense that all of us share a baptismal vocation? Does your congregation find ways to honor the many occupations and various "callings" of its members? Pray today for your congregation's vocation.

THURSDAY, SEPTEMBER 21
ST. MATTHEW, APOSTLE AND EVANGELIST

Matthew was a tax collector for the Roman government in Capernaum. He is called Levi in the accounts of his call to discipleship, although in the lists of the Twelve he is always called Matthew. Being a tax collector, Matthew was considered a social outcast in his day. Jesus' associations with tax collectors and sinners were considered a scandal to the religious leaders of that time.

This commemoration could lead your worship, social ministry, and evangelism committees to consider whether your congregation is a welcoming place for those considered outcasts in our society. Is your church building and worship bulletin hospitable towards strangers and guests? Do you provide ways to welcome diversity, or does it appear as though the congregation values uniformity?

SEPTEMBER 24, 2000

FIFTEENTH SUNDAY AFTER PENTECOST
PROPER 20

INTRODUCTION

In worship we learn the reversals in the kingdom of God: greatness is not defined by wealth, power, or prestige. Rather, all people are welcomed in the name of Christ. The children in our midst are a sign of the hospitality that God offers to all persons regardless of their status in the world. We go forth from the liturgy to be servants who find greatness in humble service on behalf of those who are often forgotten or rejected in society.

PRAYER OF THE DAY

Lord God, you call us to work in your vineyard and leave no one standing idle. Set us to our tasks in the work of your kingdom, and help us to order our lives by your wisdom; through your Son, Jesus Christ our Lord.

READINGS

Jeremiah 11:18-20

Today's reading tells of the suffering of a just man, the prophet Jeremiah, who announced God's message of impending doom only to receive opposition. The common idea of the just sufferer seems to have influenced the early Christians as they sought to understand the sufferings and death of Jesus.

or Wisdom of Solomon 1:16—2:1, 12-22

Psalm 54

God is my helper; it is the L<small>ORD</small> *who sustains my life. (Ps. 54:4)*

James 3:13—4:3, 7-8a

James contrasts the wisdom from above, with all its good characteristics, with the desire to "have things," which leads to conflicts and disputes in the community. Meaning in life does not come from cravings for possessions or pleasure, which only breed competition.

Mark 9:30-37

Jesus' teaching and action in this text are directed to the church whenever it is seduced by the world's definition of greatness: prestige, power, influence, and money. The antidote to such a concern for greatness is servanthood.

ALTERNATE FIRST READING/PSALM

Proverbs 31:10-31

The good wife portrayed in these verses provides a view of someone who is equally diligent in household matters as well as those of the commercial arena. Not only does she care for the needs of her family, but she also reaches out to the poor.

Psalm 1

Their delight is in the law of the L<small>ORD</small>*. (Ps. 1:2)*

COLOR Green

THE PRAYERS

As we await the full harvest of the Spirit, let us offer our prayers to God who is abundant in every good gift.

A BRIEF SILENCE.

God of love, give to your church such a spirit of servanthood, that our fears would give way to childlike trust and gentle regard for all people. Hear us, O God;
your mercy is great.

God of peace, conflicts and disputes are many among the nations of the world. In places of turmoil and terror, bring a harvest of righteousness and reconciliation, sown in justice and peace. Hear us, O God;
your mercy is great.

God of hope, all the woes of those in need are completely known by you. Let your compassion rest on those who are terminally ill, and on all who are sick who look for your healing (especially . . .). Hear us, O God;
your mercy is great.

God of grace, bless the children of our congregation and all who minister among them, that we would seek to pattern our faith after their simple trust in you. Hear us, O God;
your mercy is great.

HERE OTHER INTERCESSIONS MAY BE OFFERED.

God of comfort, be near to all who grieve (especially . . .). Strengthen all of us to commend our beloved dead to your eternal and loving home. Hear us, O God;
your mercy is great.

Teach us to pray, O God, and grant us wisdom in our asking, in the name of Jesus Christ our Lord. .
Amen

IMAGES FOR PREACHING

"We've taken in more than 100 members so far this year," the pastor said. "We've pretty much peaked in our membership," said another, "but giving is up 60 percent over last year." We don't say anything because we remember the meeting last night in our church basement, with the newsprint at the front of the room, the upside-down pyramid charting the age groups in our congregation. We knew what it meant: too few children age zero to five and too many over seventy. It would be hard for Jesus to find a little child to set in our midst. We will never be on one of those lists of fastest-growing congregations.

"What were you arguing about on the way?" Jesus asked. They were silent, but it was the kind of silence that spoke louder than words. Jesus must have known how often his followers would be tempted toward greatness rather than servanthood for he talks about it so many times. We find ourselves asking, "Didn't he already say that?" Yes. He said something very similar in last week's gospel. It seems clear that Jesus wants us to pay attention so he will keep speaking of the kingdom's reversals, changing the words slightly, hoping at last to get through to us. The first will be last. The greatest will be a servant. What will it profit you to gain the world and forfeit your life? Last Sunday. This Sunday. Who knows how many more times?

Worship is like that. We hear the same words Sunday after Sunday. The pastor turns to the congregation and proclaims the mercy of almighty God, then these words: "To those who believe in Jesus Christ he gives the power to become the children of God." It is strange power—not the power of lording-it-over nor the power of greater-than-others, but power to become the children of God. Sunday after Sunday, Jesus sets a child in the midst of the sanctuary. The child is each one of us. Who can believe it?

WORSHIP MATTERS

In today's gospel Jesus states that "whoever wants to be first, must be last of all and servant of all." Lavishly decorated liturgical furnishings can belie the church's servant role to the poor. Admittedly, however, furnishings that are too common and ordinary hardly evoke the wonder and awe that befit our experience of worshiping in the presence of God. Choosing furnishings for a worship space requires careful consideration. How can the worship space reflect the servant role of the church in the world? Can our furnishings inspire awe and reverence without suggesting a preference for wealth and luxury? Can our furnishings possess a "noble simplicity"? Can liturgical art lift heart and mind to God without denying the presence of God in everyday life?

LET THE CHILDREN COME

What stops us from welcoming children into full participation in the body of Christ? Do we fear they do not understand enough? Is it concern for reverence? If Jesus, with no prior preparation for the child, takes a child into his arms, how does that inform and guide us in welcoming children? How might Jesus' actions help us to wrestle with questions of young children being brought for baptism and receiving communion? How might Jesus' example help us to examine our own attitudes, so that we become more welcoming of the children among us, great and small?

MUSIC FOR WORSHIP

GATHERING

LBW 363   Christ is alive! Let Christians sing
WOV 719   God is here!

PSALM 54

Comer, Marilyn. PW, cycle B.

Guimont, Michel. "Psalm 54: The Lord Upholds My Life" in *Gather Comprehensive*. GIA.

Haas, David/arr. Jeanne Cotter. "The Lord Upholds My Life" in *PCY*, vol. III.

HYMN OF THE DAY

LBW 423   Lord, whose love in humble service
BEACH SPRING

VOCAL RESOURCES

Wienhorst, Richard. "Lord, Whose Love in Humble Service." MSM 50-9059. SATB, kybd.

INSTRUMENTAL RESOURCES

Albrecht, Mark. "Beach Spring" in *Early American Hymns and Tunes for Flute and Piano*. AFP 11-10830.

Held, Wilbur. "Beach Spring" in *Seven Settings of American Folk Hymns*. CPH 97-5829. Org.

Hyslop, Scott. "Beach Spring" in *Six Chorale Fantasias for Solo Instrument and Piano*. AFP 11-10799. Pno, sax, vc, ob/solo inst.

Manz, Paul. "Lord, Whose Love in Humble Service" in *Three Hymns for Flute, Oboe, and Organ*. MSM 20-871. Fl, ob, org.

Porter, Rachel Trelstad. "Beach Spring" in *Day by Day*. AFP 11-10772. Pno.

Sedio, Mark. "Beach Spring" in *Dancing in the Light of God*. AFP 11-10793. Pno.

ALTERNATE HYMN OF THE DAY

WOV 683   Loving Spirit
LBW 474   Children of the heavenly Father

COMMUNION

LBW 226   Draw near and take the body of the Lord
WOV 741   Thy holy wings

SENDING

LBW 262   Savior, again to your dear name
WOV 801   Thine the amen, thine the praise

ADDITIONAL HYMNS AND SONGS

NCH 509   How deep the silence of the soul
H82 478   Jesus, our mighty Lord
TFF 42/43   Come by here, my Lord
W&P   For God so loved the world

MUSIC FOR THE DAY

CHORAL

Ferguson, John. "Be Thou My Vision." AFP 11-10925. SATB, org.

Hirten, John. "The Harvest of Justice." Chantry 12-105. SAB, org.

Johengen, Carl. "Go to the World!" GIA G-4395. Choir, cant, cong, gtr, kybd, opt trp.

Nelson, Ronald A. "Whoever Would Be Great Among You." AFP 11-1638. Also in *The Augsburg Choirbook*. 11-10817. SAB, gtr/kybd.

Rutter, John. "Open Thou Mine Eyes." HIN HMC-467. SATB.

CHILDREN'S CHOIRS

Hruby, Dolores. "Help Us Accept Each Other." CG CGA713. U, kybd, opt fl, opt gtr.

Scott, K. Lee. "Best of All Friends." MSM 50-9003. 2 pt trbl, pno.

KEYBOARD/INSTRUMENTAL

Callahan, Charles. "Prelude on the Tune 'Faith.'" RME. Org.

Vivaldi, Antonio/ed. S. Drummond Wolff. "Music from *The Four Seasons*, Set 1-Autumn." MSM 10-934. Org.

HANDBELL

Hopson, Hal H. "Simple Gifts." AG 1736. 3-5 oct.

Moklebust, Cathy. "O, God, Our Help in Ages Past" in *Hymn Stanzas for Handbells*. AFP 11-10722. 4-5 oct.

PRAISE ENSEMBLE

Gaither, William J. "I Will Serve Thee" in *The Other Songbook*. Fellowship Publications.

Kee, Ed and Brian Carr. "Heart of a Servant" in *Sing & Rejoice*. BRM BK-3041.

Moen, Don. "I Want to Be Where You Are" in *Come & Worship*. INT.

Schreiner, John. "Be Thou My Vision" in *Favorite Hymns of Promise Keepers*. MAR 3010133367. 3pt, kybd.

Ylvisaker, John. "I Will Offer You My Life" in *Borning Cry*. NGP.

MONDAY, SEPTEMBER 25
SERGIUS OF RADONEZH, ABBOT OF HOLY TRINITY, MOSCOW, 1392

Sergius is the most beloved of Russian saints. He renewed monasticism in Russia, and he was known for his peacemaking skills, his kindness to the poor, and his wise, gentle spirit. Sergius turned down being a bishop, preferring the simple life of a monk. He became abbot of Holy Trinity monastery, from which more than seventy-five monasteries were founded.

The commemoration of Sergius is an opportunity to consider the Russian church. How much do we know of the rich traditions of Russian orthodoxy? What is the role of icons in their worship and spirituality? What do we have in common with Orthodox Christians? Consider these topics in an adult class or forum, or by a visit to an Orthodox liturgy.

THURSDAY, SEPTEMBER 28
JEHU JONES, THE FIRST AFRICAN AMERICAN LUTHERAN PASTOR IN NORTH AMERICA, 1852

Jehu Jones was a missionary among urban African Americans in the North during the decades before the Civil War. In 1834 he formed St. Paul's Evangelical Lutheran Church in Philadelphia, the first African American Lutheran congregation in the United States. Unable to gain needed financial help from the Ministerium of Pennsylvania, Jones lost the church in 1839, but he remained faithful to missionary work until the end of his life.

Jones is remembered for his faithfulness to the teachings of the Lutheran church, and his missionary calling among African Americans. Is your synod establishing new mission congregations in its territory? Are members of your congregation supporting these endeavors? Have you reviewed the new African American worship supplement, *This Far by Faith*, as a resource for your congregation?

FRIDAY, SEPTEMBER 29
ST. MICHAEL AND ALL ANGELS

In the book of Revelation, Michael the archangel fights in a cosmic battle against Satan. In the book of Daniel, Michael is portrayed as the heavenly being who leads the faithful dead to God's throne on the day of resurrection. This day is popular in northern Europe and England, and Michaelmas still marks the beginning of the fall term in some law courts and academic institutions in England.

Angels play an important role in both the Old and New Testaments. Observe St. Michael and All Angels at congregational events today or during the week. Think of biblical stories that include angels, and sing "Ye watchers and ye holy ones" (LBW 175), or a Christmas or Easter hymn that mentions angels. Surround your gatherings today with pictures and images of angels.

SATURDAY, SEPTEMBER 30
JEROME, TRANSLATOR, TEACHER, 420

Jerome is known for his translation of the scriptures from Hebrew and Greek into Latin, the common language at that time. The word for his translation, the "Vulgate," comes from the Latin word for the common people. This translation remained the standard Latin version for fifteen centuries.

What translation of the Bible is used in your worship service? The New Revised Standard Version is probably the most common translation used in mainline churches today. Do you give your parishioners help in selecting a translation for themselves? Explain the difference between a translation and a paraphrase. Why is there a need for new translations of the scriptures? Plan a Bible selection and origin workshop or forum.

OCTOBER 1, 2000

SIXTEENTH SUNDAY AFTER PENTECOST
PROPER 21

INTRODUCTION

The disciples ask Jesus how to deal with those who are doing good in his name, but are not a part of their company. The Lord's response assures them that the reign of God can be served in many and diverse ways. Such words invite the contemporary church to be attentive to those who serve Christ in new or unexpected ministries. Even as Jesus encourages us to be seasoned with salt and to be at peace with one another, James urges us to confess our sins and to pray for the healing of all who are sick.

PRAYER OF THE DAY

God of love, you know our frailties and failings. Give us your grace to overcome them; keep us from those things that harm us; and guide us in the way of salvation; through your Son, Jesus Christ our Lord.

READINGS

Numbers 11:4-6, 10-16, 24-29

What constitutes legitimate need and legitimate leadership is the focus of this reading. While in the wilderness, God provides sustenance as manna, yet the people crave meat. What is truly needful? God bestows the spirit on seventy elders in order to provide leadership for the people, yet complaints are heard when two men not designated as leaders prophesy in the power of God's spirit. What constitutes real leadership?

Psalm 19:7-14

The commandment of the LORD gives light to the eyes. (Ps. 19:8)

James 5:13-20

The epistle of James is a letter offering advice to the church concerning a variety of common problems. In these verses, however, the author concludes with an uplifting picture of what the church can be: a community of prayer and praise, restoration and healing.

Mark 9:38-50

On the way to Jerusalem, Jesus teaches his disciples about ministry that involves service and sacrifice. His disciples are slow to realize these words apply to them as well as to others.

ALTERNATE FIRST READING/PSALM

Esther 7:1-6, 9-10; 9:20-22

As the book of Esther demonstrates, the Persian king, Ahasuerus, enjoyed banquets and courtly ceremony. A Jewish woman named Esther won the king's favor and was crowned queen. Though the king subsequently decreed that all Jews should die, Esther succeeded in convincing the king not to carry out the decree, thereby marking the occasion for even more feasting.

Psalm 124

We have escaped like a bird from the snare of the fowler. (Ps. 124:7)

COLOR Green

THE PRAYERS

As we await the full harvest of the Spirit, let us offer our prayers to God who is abundant in every good gift.
A BRIEF SILENCE.

Let us pray that the church would be seasoned with the Spirit, and that all the baptized would proclaim God's promises to the world. Hear us, O God;
your mercy is great.

Let us pray that the world's fields would yield an abundant harvest, and that many would be fed by the produce of the land God has blessed. Hear us, O God;
your mercy is great.

Let us pray that those who are sick and suffering will be anointed with the healing oil of God's presence (especially . . .), that they will be restored to wholeness. Hear us, O God;
your mercy is great.

Let us pray that the diversity of spiritual gifts in this congregation would be celebrated, and that each gift would be embraced by this community in humility and thankfulness. Hear us, O God;
your mercy is great.

HERE OTHER INTERCESSIONS MAY BE OFFERED.

Let us pray that our memories would be blessed by the living testimonies of all God's saints (especially . . .), that we would be held in communion with them until we are called to join them in eternal light. Hear us, O God;

your mercy is great.
Teach us to pray, O God, and grant us wisdom in our asking, in the name of Jesus Christ our Lord.
Amen

IMAGES FOR PREACHING

It's not easy to say "Praise to you, O Christ" at the end of this gospel reading. We hope people will remember the last lines about being "at peace with one another" and forget the middle. Of course, these images are not easily put aside and we see people wincing as the gospel is read. We console ourselves and say it is hyperbole, an exaggeration intentionally used to make a point. Jesus doesn't expect people to maim themselves, nor does he want us to be drowned in the sea, a great millstone dragging us to the bottom.

Then why did Jesus say such terrible things? Was he making a mountain out of a molehill? Maybe. Maybe he was trying to get us to *see* the molehill, to take seriously those things that cause us and others to stumble. Though Jesus' words seem directed at individuals, his first warning is a communal concern: don't put a stumbling block before one of these little ones who believe in me. These "little ones" aren't only children, but disciples and others who are followers.

We have become serious about accessibility in church buildings: ramps and elevators, infrared hearing systems and sign language, large-print hymnals and braille Bibles. These efforts have removed tangible stumbling blocks that have denied people access to Christian community. Do we see other stumbling blocks that need to be removed? Years ago in a Lutheran church, an usher stood at the edge of the sidewalk leading to the church doors. If a person of color came along, the usher politely directed him or her to the church down the street. That Lutheran church had an accessibility problem. What stumbling blocks are we putting in front of people today? Jesus might have been exaggerating when he talked about that millstone, but he was absolutely serious when he talked about accessibility to the commonwealth of God.

WORSHIP MATTERS

Today's second reading raises up the healing ministry by reminding us that the Christian community must pray for the sick. *Occasional Services* contains a Service of the Word for Healing (pp. 89–98). The service notes list several occasions when it may be appropriate to use this liturgy. One such time is the festival of St. Luke (October 18). This service might also be celebrated once a month (or with some other frequency) on a designated week day.

LET THE CHILDREN COME

"Are any among you sick?" (James 5:14a). It is expected that when older members become sick and homebound, they will receive the visitation ministry of the congregation, but what about children? Is their sickness any less an occasion for the prayers and ministrations of the church than for someone older? What makes an "elder" an "elder"? Is it not the repeated experience over time that God indeed delivers his people from suffering? Who better to visit a sick child or young person, for whom it seems that the "bad times" will never end!

MUSIC FOR WORSHIP

GATHERING

| LBW 415 | God of grace and God of glory |
| WOV 719 | God is here! |

PSALM 19

Bell, John L. *Psalms of Patience, Protest and Praise*. GIA G-4047. U/choir.

Comer, Marilyn. PW, cycle B.

Dohms, Ann Celeen. "Psalm 19" in *Sing Out! A Children's Psalter*. WLP 7191.

Haas, David. "Psalm 19: Lord, You Have the Words" in *Gather Comprehensive*. GIA. U.

Ogden, David. "You, Lord, Have the Message of Eternal Life" in PS, vol. 2.

OTHER SUGGESTIONS

Hruby, Dolores M. *Seasonal Psalms for Children*. WLP 7102. U.

Walker, Christopher. "Your Law, O God" in *Rise Up and Sing*. OCP 939. U. 9391GC. Acc book.

HYMN OF THE DAY

| LBW 508 | Come down, O Love divine |
| | DOWN AMPNEY |

VOCAL RESOURCES

Leavitt, John. "Come Down, O Love Divine." MSM 50-5401. SATB, inst, org.

Wolff, S. Drummond. "Come Down, O Love Divine." MSM 50-5500. SAB, tpt, org.

INSTRUMENTAL RESOURCES

Fruhauf, Ennis. "Down Ampney" in *Ralph Vaughan Williams and the English School: Six Settings for Organ.* AFP 11-10826. Org/kybd.

Langlois, Kristina. "Down Ampney" in *Eight Miniatures for the Seasons of Lent, Easter and Pentecost.* MSM 10-345. Org.

Sedio, Mark. "Down Ampney" in *Music for the Paschal Season.* AFP 11-10763. Org.

Wasson, Laura E. "Down Ampney" in *A Piano Tapestry.* AFP 11-10821. Pno.

ALTERNATE HYMN OF THE DAY

| WOV 684 | Spirit, Spirit of gentleness |
| LBW 429 | Where cross the crowded ways of life |

COMMUNION

| LBW 487 | Let us ever walk with Jesus |
| WOV 737 | There is a balm in Gilead |

OTHER SUGGESTIONS

Landrey, Carey and Larry Theiss. "Feed Us, Lord." OCP 10665. 2 pt, kybd, cong, rec I, II

SENDING

| LBW 261 | On what has now been sown |
| WOV 753 | You are the seed |

ADDITIONAL HYMNS AND SONGS

PH 419	How clear is our vocation, Lord
H82 541	Come, labor on
TFF 241	Every time I feel the spirit
W&P	Bring forth the Kingdom

MUSIC FOR THE DAY

CHORAL

Ashdown, Franklin D. "Jesus, the Very Thought of Thee." AFP 11-10886. SATB, org, opt C inst.

Mathias, William. "Rejoice in the Lord." OXF A359. SATB, org.

Proulx, Richard. "Christ Has Called Us to New Visions/Lord, Whose Love in Humble Service." GIA G-4220. SATB, cong, org, brass qnt, timp.

Proulx, Richard. "Strengthen for Service." Chantry 12-400005. SATB.

Schulz-Widmar, Russell. "God Remembers." AFP 11-10882. SATB, kybd.

Shepperd, Mark. "Balm in Gilead." AFP 11-10923. SATB, kybd.

CHILDREN'S CHOIRS

Agnestig, Carl-Bertil. "Help Me to Pray." AFP 11-10377. U, opt desc, kybd.

Lovelace, Austin C. "Let Us Talents and Tongues Employ." CG CGA619. 2 pt mxd, kybd, opt gtr, opt bng.

Marshall, Jane. "For Hard Things." CG CGA618. U and 2 pt mxd/SAB versions, kybd.

KEYBOARD/INSTRUMENTAL

Bender, Jan. "Four Variations for Organ on Down Ampney." AFP 11-0807. Org.

Cherwien, David. "The Spirit Sends Us Forth to Serve" in *Organ Music for the Seasons.* AFP 11-10859. Org.

HANDBELL

Marcello/arr. Hornibrook. "Psalm 19." Prism 49442014. 3-5 oct.

McKlveen, Paul A. "A Psalm of Praise." Lake State Publications HB93034. 3-5 oct.

PRAISE ENSEMBLE

Hassell, Michael. "Spirit, Spirit of Gentleness." AFP 11-10850. SATB, pno, sax.

Klein, Laurie/arr. Jack Schrader. "I Love You, Lord." HOP GC936. SATB, pno.

Medema, Ken. "Like a River That Overflows." HOP GC995. SATB, pno.

Pink. "Ephesians 6:18" (Keep on Praying) in *Maranatha! Music Praise Chorus Book, 3rd ed.* WRD/MAR.

Smith, Henry. "Give Thanks" in *Songs for Praise and Worship.* WRD.

WEDNESDAY, OCTOBER 4
FRANCIS OF ASSISI, RENEWER OF THE CHURCH, 1226;
THEODORE FLIEDNER, RENEWER OF SOCIETY, 1864

Francis left behind a life of pleasure and riches, and embraced a way of life marked by simplicity, poverty, and care for the poor and needy. He associated with lepers and acted as a peacemaker between towns at war. Though Francis embraced a rigid asceticism that devalued earthly possessions, he had a spirit of gladness and gratitude for all God's creation. The commemoration of Francis has been a traditional time to bless pets and animals, as Francis called the animals his brothers and sisters.

Theodore Fliedner revived the order of deaconesses, and founded a motherhouse in Kaiserswerth, Germany. His work and his writing encouraged women to care for the sick, the poor, and the imprisoned. Inspired by his work, Lutherans all over the world commissioned deaconesses to serve in parishes, schools, hospitals, or prisons.

Both Francis and Fliedner call the church to take its work seriously among the most vulnerable of our society.

What are the ways your parish, synod, or denomination continue to embody the same concerns for the poor and needy? Do you remember these agencies and ministries by name in the prayers at your Sunday eucharist?

FRIDAY, OCTOBER 6
WILLIAM TYNDALE, TRANSLATOR, MARTYR, 1536

Tyndale is remembered for his English translation of the Bible. The style of his translation influenced English versions of the Bible, such as the Authorized Version and the Revised Standard Version, for four centuries.

The reading of the scriptures is at the heart of the liturgy of the word. Many congregations value Bible study as part of their adult education program. Has your parish considered offering a study of the readings for each upcoming Sunday? It could take place during the week, or during the Sunday morning educational hour. Such an offering not only deepens the participants' knowledge and experience of scripture, but also prepares them for the coming Sunday liturgy. Several church publishers offer studies based on the lectionary, including Life Together, a new series of educational resources published by Augsburg Fortress in 1999 that coordinates with the Revised Common Lectionary.

THURSDAY, OCTOBER 7
HENRY MELCHIOR MUHLENBERG, MISSIONARY TO NORTH AMERICA, 1787

Muhlenberg was prominent in setting the course for Lutheranism in the United States. He helped Lutherans make the transition from the state churches of Europe to the independent churches of this country. Among other things, he established the first Lutheran synod in North America, and developed a Lutheran liturgy. His liturgical principles became the basis for the *Common Service* of 1888 used in many North American service books for a majority of this century. *Lutheran Book of Worship* was an attempt to produce a common service book for Lutherans in North America.

Do you remember some of the Lutheran mergers during the past forty years? Do you believe our Lutheran presence and witness is stronger because we are no longer divided along ethnic lines?

OCTOBER 8, 2000

SEVENTEENTH SUNDAY AFTER PENTECOST
PROPER 22

INTRODUCTION

The psalmist sings that human beings are the crown of God's creation. Our loving human relationships, though marred by sin, are a sign of the kingdom of God among us. In their mutual respect and love, they symbolize the wholeness intended for all life. Yet neither husband nor wife nor the creation itself is the property of humans to do with as they will. The world, and all that lives within it, belongs to God, who transforms all things through Christ.

PRAYER OF THE DAY

Our Lord Jesus, you have endured the doubts and foolish questions of every generation. Forgive us for trying to be judge over you, and grant us the confident faith to acknowledge you as Lord.

READINGS

Genesis 2:18-24

Genesis 2 stresses that people are not meant to live in isolation but in relationship. While speaking of the unity of a man and a woman, the focus of this reading is on human community more broadly considered. Ultimately what unites the man and the woman is their common humanity.

Psalm 8

You adorn us with glory and honor. (Ps. 8:6)

Hebrews 1:1-4; 2:5-12

Hebrews, an early Christian sermon, emphasizes that Jesus became so fully human that he shared our experience of death. The one, through whom all things exist, is the one who calls us brother and sister.

Mark 10:2-16

Jesus announced and enacted in history the new reality of God's surprising activity. These two Markan stories demonstrate this new reality: women and children are accepted and valued, not dismissed as inferior to adult men.

ALTERNATE FIRST READING/PSALM

Job 1:1, 2:1-10

Job was a man of wealth and status who came upon horrible reversals of fortune without complaint. No matter the calamity, Job remains the picture of profound faith in God.

Psalm 26

Your love is before my eyes; I have walked faithfully with you. (Ps. 26:3)

COLOR   Green

THE PRAYERS

As we await the full harvest of the Spirit, let us offer our prayers to God who is abundant in every good gift.

A BRIEF SILENCE.

Faithful God, guide your church in the ways of faithfulness and deeper trust, that we may put aside fear-filled divisiveness and exclusivity. Hear us, O God;
your mercy is great.

All powers and dominions are under your subjection, mighty God. Grant that the leaders of the nations would rule justly and deal wisely in all their governing. Hear us, O God;
your mercy is great.

Our joys and sorrows are fully known to you, compassionate God. Heal those who have experienced broken relationships, or who stand in need of physical healing (especially . . .). Hear us, O God;
your mercy is great.

Watch over the young people from this congregation who are away from home at school or in military service. Guide them and keep them in your care. Hear us, O God;
your mercy is great.

HERE OTHER INTERCESSIONS MAY BE OFFERED.

Comfort those grieving the loss of loved ones (especially . . .), that they may be consoled in your tender and merciful arms. Hear us, O God;
your mercy is great.

Teach us to pray, O God, and grant us wisdom in our asking, in the name of Jesus Christ our Lord.
Amen

IMAGES FOR PREACHING

"Sisters and brothers, today's gospel brings some good news and some bad news." But even before the sermon begins, some have heard only bad news. Those who are divorced, particularly those divorced and remarried, feel a clear and specific word of judgment against them. We *can* rightly point out that Jesus calls men and women to the same standard: a man couldn't dismiss his wife even if the written law permitted it.

But the good news of equality also means that *both* women and men feel equally condemned. We can't say that Jesus didn't say what he said. What would we want Jesus to say, "Divorce is fine. In fact, it's often the best option"? Even when divorce is necessary, those effected know the pain of love grown cold or even abusive. John Vannorsdall believes we need Jesus' words though we often fall short: "I want to know Christ's vision. I want to know what's good and worthy; I want to be drawn by it, challenged by it—even if for now the vision judges my failures" (*The Protestant Hour*, February 15, 1987).

Perhaps the problem is not with Jesus but with those who have taught that divorce is a sin greater than others. Next Sunday, Jesus will tell a rich man to sell his possessions and give to the poor. Jesus is clear in this point. But people are seldom turned away from communion for failure to give to the poor. Over the years, many divorced people have been forced outside the embrace of Christian community and sacramental life.

But the last word of today's gospel comes in the graceful pairing of this story with another. Though others were indignant, Jesus welcomed the children saying, "Let them come to me; do not stop them." Does not Jesus say this same word to those who are divorced?

WORSHIP MATTERS

In the Old Testament reading from Genesis 2, God takes the initiative to provide a fitting mate for the man. The first man and woman owed their lives and their relationship to the goodness of God. Today we also acknowledge that marriage and the family are gifts from the God who established marriage and who "continues still to bless it with his abundant and ever-present support" (*LBW*, p. 203). Although the exchange of vows and bestowal of blessings form a vital part of the marriage service, it is nevertheless a God-centered event. In the liturgy of marriage we give thanks *to God* for the new relationship, acknowledge *God's* faithfulness in supporting the family, and pray that *God* enables the couple to become living examples of *Christ's* love for his church.

LET THE CHILDREN COME

Let the church speak clearly the word concerning God's good and gracious gift of marriage and children and the word concerning the hard-heartedness of sin. Let the church finally speak clearly the word that reconciles God's broken family. It is, ultimately, not our sins that exclude us from God's kingdom, but the sin that is failure to trust in Christ as our Savior. The children clamoring around Jesus are no less sinful than we, but they trust Jesus implicitly. They are not interested in clinging to themselves and their sin, but to Jesus, whose very presence forgives and saves them.

MUSIC FOR WORSHIP

GATHERING

LBW 561	For the beauty of the earth
WOV 799	When long before time

PSALM 8

Bell, John T. *Psalms of Patience, Protest and Praise.* GIA G-4047.

Comer, Marilyn. PW, cycle B.

Cooney, Rory/arr. Gary Daigle. "How Glorious Is Your Name" in PCY.

Dykes/arr. Hal H. Hopson. *Eighteen Psalms for the Church Year.* HOP HH-3941.

Geary, Patrick. "Your Name Is Praised" in PS, vol. 3.

Pulkingham, Betty. *Celebrate the Church Year with Selected Psalms and Canticles.* PLY MB 94218. Cong, choir, kybd, inst.

HYMN OF THE DAY

WOV 735	God! When human bonds are broken
	MERTON

INSTRUMENTAL RESOURCES

Bassett, Anita Denniston. "Merton" in *Nine Hymn-Tune Preludes.* LUD 0-08. Org.

Haan, Raymond. "Merton." NPH MC27N0009. Org.

Meyer, Edward. "Merton" in *Easy Hymn Accompaniments for Organ or Piano.* CPH 97-6608. Kybd/org.

Wood, Dale. "Merton" in *New Settings of Twenty Well-Known Hymn Tunes.* AFP 11-9292. Org.

ALTERNATE HYMN OF THE DAY

WOV 749	When love is found
LBW 357	Our Father, by whose name

COMMUNION

LBW 203	Now we join in celebration
WOV 703	Draw us in the Spirit's tether

OTHER SUGGESTIONS

Wetzler, Robert. "Take of the Wonder." AFP 11-10570. SATB, kybd, opt cong, opt gtr, opt fl.

SENDING

LBW 259	Lord, dismiss us with your blessing
WOV 748	Bind us together

ADDITIONAL HYMNS AND SONGS

H82 631	Book of books
H82 480	When Jesus left his Father's throne
TFF 221	We are one in Christ
W&P	Beauty for brokenness

MUSIC FOR THE DAY

CHORAL

Bender Jan. "Whoever Does Not Receive the Kingdom" in *A Baptism Cantata.* Chantry. U, org.

Bonnemere, Edward V. "Suffer the Little Children" in *Suffer the Little Children.* AFP 11-10180. U.

Goemanne, Noel. "The Song of Children" CG CGA-285. Bar, SA, kybd.

Hassell, Michael. "How Exalted Is Your Name." AFP 11-10854. SATB, pno.

Hayes, Mark. "Day by Day." AFP 11-10962. SATB, kybd.

CHILDREN'S CHOIRS

Cox, Joe. "Blessed to Be a Blessing." MSM 50-9409. U/2 pt, pno.

Marcello/arr. Richard Wienhorst. "O Lord, Our Governor." CPH 98-1045. U/2pt, kybd.

KEYBOARD/INSTRUMENTAL

Powell, Robert J. "O Waly, Waly" in *Sing a New Song*. AFP 11-10766. Org.

Willan, Healey. "Matins" in *Two Pieces for Organ*. CFP 6358. Org.

HANDBELL

Larson, Katherine Jordahl. "Praise Him, Praise Him" and "Jesus Loves Me." AFP 11-10352. 3 oct.

McFadden, Jane. "Children of the Heavenly Father" in *Two Swedish Melodies*. AFP 11-10806. 3-4 oct.

Moklebust, Cathy. "Go, My Children, with My Blessing" in *Hymn Stanzas for Handbells*. AFP 11-10722. 4-5 oct.

PRAISE ENSEMBLE

Hanson, Handt. "Psalm 8" in *Spirit Touching Spirit*. CCF.

Root, George F. "Jesus Loves the Little Children" in *The Other Songbook*. Fellowship Publications.

Smith, Michael W./arr. Marsh. "How Majestic Is Your Name." MEA MTM-105. SATB. pno.

Smith, Michael W. and Deborah D./arr. Lojeski. "Great Is the Lord." HAL 08307232. SAB/SATB/SSA, pno, gtr, perc.

Traditional. "He Is Lord" in *Songs for Praise and Worship*. WRD.

OCTOBER 9, 2000

DAY OF THANKSGIVING (CANADA)

INTRODUCTION

As autumn darkness crosses the land, the nation takes time to offer thanks for the harvest and the abundant resources of this land. While this holiday witnesses many households gathering for a festive meal, Christians recognize that the source of all good things is the God who feeds the birds and clothes the grass of the field. Gathered at Christ's supper, we offer thanksgiving for the bread of life and the cup of blessing. And here, as we share these gifts, we are knit together into a community whose mission is among those who are poor and in need. We offer thanks to God for the bounty of the land and seek to share these riches with all in need.

PRAYER OF THE DAY

Almighty God our Father, your generous goodness comes to us new every day. By the work of your Spirit lead us to acknowledge your goodness, give thanks for your benefits, and serve you in willing obedience; through your Son, Jesus Christ our Lord.

READINGS

Joel 2:21-27

The prophecy of Joel comes from the period of 500 to 350 B.C. He views a locust plague that ravaged the country as God's judgment on the people, whom he then calls to repentance. Today's reading points beyond the judgment of the Day of the Lord, when the Lord will repay "the years that the swarming locust has eaten."

Psalm 126

The LORD has done great things for us, and we are glad indeed. (Ps. 126:4)

1 Timothy 2:1-7

The letter to Timothy was written at a time when kings and rulers persecuted those who believed in Christ. Still, the writer calls upon Christians to pray for these rulers and offer thanksgiving on their behalf.

Matthew 6:25-33

In the Sermon on the Mount, Jesus taught his disciples about the providence of God so that they would regard life with thanksgiving and trust rather than anxiety.

COLOR White

THE PRAYERS

In communion with all the saints, let us pray to God who is our eternal home.

SILENCE IS KEPT.

We give you thanks, O God, for your church and for the wondrous ways in which you have dealt with your people. Continue to inspire the church to be a blessing in our communities and in the society at large. Lord, in your mercy,

hear our prayer.

We give you thanks, O God, for the diversity of the world's people, for all nations and their leaders. Grant to all your wisdom and grace, that a quiet and peaceable life would be possible for all people. Lord, in your mercy,
hear our prayer.

We give you thanks, O God, for your abundant blessings to us and for the bounty of the world's resources. Help us to share of our plenty with those in need. Lord, in your mercy,
hear our prayer.

We give you thanks, O God, for this congregation and for the praises you have put in our mouths and in our hearts. Help us work to insure that people in our community have sufficient food, clothing, and shelter. Lord, in your mercy,
hear our prayer.

HERE OTHER INTERCESSIONS MAY BE OFFERED.

We give you thanks, O God, for bringing the promise of comfort to those who grieve. We remember with praise and thanksgiving all who have died and who now rest at peace in your eternal harvest home. Lord, in your mercy,
hear our prayer.

Your reign, O God, endures forever, and in Christ we are free to be your saints and servants. Hear our prayers for the sake of him who died and rose again, and lives with you in the company of all your saints in light.
Amen

IMAGES FOR PREACHING

Thanksgiving seems easier in the country than in the city. People can *see* the words they're singing: "All is safely gathered in ere the winter storms begin." It is not as easy to see Thanksgiving in the city where most everything seems manufactured rather than created. Although we can trace skyscrapers and subways back to the steel mill, then back to the ore in the ground, it takes a long time and it's harder to see God there. Factories don't elicit thankful hearts as readily as grain in the corncrib and jam in the fruit cellar.

Perhaps the prophet Joel knew that people can be forgetful or even reluctant in giving thanks. He doesn't even begin with human beings! First, he talks to the soil, then to the animals of the field, and finally to the children of Zion. It's a wonderful scene as we imagine the soil rejoicing and the animals perking up their ears at news of green pastures in the wilderness. The prophet sees and hears with the eyes and ears of his God-given imagination.

God invites us to reclaim the gift of imagination. Encourage people in the parish to give thanks for what they see where they are: the rainbow of colors in the fruit stands, the vacant lot reclaimed as a garden, curb cuts at the corner for wheelchairs, the fire trucks polished and ready, the nurses working the night shift. Invite children to create psalms and prayers of thanksgiving. Write new words to familiar hymns—and don't worry if they're sung only once! Invite people to bring tangible signs of their daily work for a table of thanksgiving; be sure to include the gifts of children, retired people, and those whose work is unpaid. Then call the whole earth to sing God's praise: "Do not fear, O soil—O parks, O towering buildings, O bus stops, O fruit stands, O neon lights, O newly painted playground—be glad and rejoice, for the Lord has done great things!" (paraphrase of Joel 2:21).

LET THE CHILDREN COME

Children readily grasp the language of creation and its variety of creatures and plants. Children should hear and speak the word that all creation is God's work and the preservation of creation is also God's work (compare the Small Catechism, first article of the creed). Speak directly to the children in reading the gospel today. Let them hear that God feeds the birds, God clothes the grass, and God feeds and clothes them.

MUSIC FOR WORSHIP

GATHERING

LBW 407	Come, you thankful people, come
WOV 797	O God beyond all praising

PSALM 126

Beckstrand, William. PW, cycle B.
Foley, John. "Psalm 126" in PCY, vol. 7.
Haas, David. "Psalm 126" in PCY, vol. 8.
Roff, Joseph. "Psalm 126" in PCY, vol. 3.
Smith, Alan. "The Lord Has Done Great Things" in PS, vol. 1.

HYMN OF THE DAY

LBW 241	We praise you, O God
	KREMSER

VOCAL RESOURCES

Jennings, Carolyn. "We Praise You, O God." AFP 11-10948. SATB, cong, opt tpt.

INSTRUMENTAL RESOURCES

Bernthal, John. "We Praise You, O God" in *Lift High the Cross: Hymn Introductions and Descants for Organ and Trumpet*. AFP 11-10867. Org, tpt.

Callahan, Charles. "Kremser" in *Thanksgiving Suite*. MSM 10-600. Org.

Callahan, Charles. "Kremser" in *Thanksgiving Music for Manuals*. MSM 10-601. Kybd.

Page, Anna Laura. "Kremser" in *Glad Tidings We Raise*. Van Ness Press 4180-04. Org.

ALTERNATE HYMN OF THE DAY

| LBW 407 | Come, you thankful people, come |
| WOV 760 | For the fruit of all creation |

COMMUNION

| LBW 409 | Praise and thanksgiving |
| WOV 705 | As the grains of wheat |

SENDING

| LBW 274 | The day you gave us, Lord has ended |
| WOV 771 | Great is thy faithfulness |

ADDITIONAL HYMNS AND SONGS

H82 432	O praise ye the Lord!
OBS 64	In sacred manner
TFF 293	Thank you, Lord
W&P	I will sing, I will sing

MUSIC FOR THE DAY

CHORAL

Aguiar, Ernani. "Psalm 150" (Salmo 150). Earthsongs. SATB (SSA). Lat.

Bach, J. S. "Alles was odem hat" in *Singet dem Herrn*. MFS 259. SATB.

Ferguson, John. "A Song of Thanksgiving." AFP 11-10505. SATB, org.

Hopson, Hal. "Come, Christians, Join to Sing." MSM 50-7027. SATB, kybd.

Mozart, Wolfgang Amadeus. "Laudate Dominum" in *Sing Solo Sacred*. OXF 0-19-345785-7.

Pachelbel, Johann. "Now Thank We All Our God" (Nun danket alle Gott). Barenreiter 2873. SATB/SATB, SATB/brass. Ger/Eng.

Palestrina, G. P. "Exultate Jubilate." CHE 8794. SAATB.

Pickard, John. "Make a Joyful Noise." AFP 11-10926. SATB, kybd.

Rowan, William. "Praise God from Whom All Blessings Flow." GIA G-4398. SATB.

Young, Jeremy. "Praise God with the Trumpet." AFP 11-10893. SAB, kybd, opt brass/cong.

CHILDREN'S CHOIRS

Heck, Lyle. "Make a Joyful Noise unto the Lord." AFP 11-10601. 2 pt, fl, kybd.

Hobby, Robert. "Offertory for Day of Thanksgiving." MSM 80-600. 2 pt, org.

Pooler/arr. Kemp. "Thanks to God" in *Let's Sing*. AFP 11-7210. U, kybd.

Pooler/arr. Kemp. "Thanksgiving" in *Let's Sing*. AFP 11-7210. U, kybd.

KEYBOARD/INSTRUMENTAL

Cherwien, David. "Now Thank We All Our God" in *Postludes on Well Known Hymns*. AFP 11-10795. Org.

Powell, Robert J. "Pastorale on 'Kremser'" in *Nine Service Pieces for the Church Year for Organ*. FLA HF-5194. Org.

HANDBELL

Rogers, Sharon Elery. "Now Thankful People, Come." (St. George's Windsor, Nun danket alle Gott). AFP 11-10804. 2-3 oct.

PRAISE ENSEMBLE

Chambers, Brent. "How Good It Is" in *Come & Worship*. INT.

Martin, Joseph M. "A Thanksgiving Garden." SHW 10/1653M. SA(T)B, pno.

Perry, Dave & Jean. "Kuimba Asante." (Sing Thanks!) ALF 16109. SATB, kybd, perc. Also available 3 pt (16110); 2 pt (16111).

Smith, Henry/arr. Wilson. "Give Thanks." HOP GC972. SAB, kybd.

Thompson and Scruggs. "Sanctuary" in *Come & Worship*. INT.

Order next year's resources now!

Sundays and Seasons 2001
WORSHIP PLANNING GUIDE, CYCLE C

Order your copies today and you'll be ready for the next church year! The next edition of *Sundays and Seasons* will continue to supply you with all of the information you need to plan worship, dated specifically for Advent through Christ the King Sunday.
ISBN 0-8066-3627-0 · 3-1205 · $30.00
Three or more $25.00 each

Worship Planning Calendar 2001
CYCLE C

You will find this calendar an inseparable complement to *Sundays and Seasons*! Use this worship planning guide, daily devotional, and appointment calendar as your workbook. Each two-page spread includes propers, hymns, liturgical colors, and general rubrics for the Sunday, principal festivals, lesser festivals, and commemorations that occur during the week. You'll wonder how you managed without it!
ISBN 0-8066-3828-1 · 23-2010 · $20.00

Words for Worship 2001
CYCLE C

This CD-ROM contains resources for use with the Revised Common Lectionary, Cycle C. These easy-to-use text and graphic files are organized by calendar date. Includes readings, prayers, introductions to the day, psalm refrains and tones, seasonal rites and texts, and the LBW Symbol font.
ISBN 0-8066-4029-4 · 3-4029
CD-ROM AND COPYRIGHT LICENSE · $139.00

Living and Learning 2000–2001
CYCLE B/C

This educational and seasonal planning guide is part of the new RCL-based resources and curriculum, Life Together. The guide provides an overview of how seasonal and weekly themes—connected to daily life and the lectionary—link across resources, activities, and age levels within parish life. Includes children's worship and story time activities, and connections to the practice of faith in daily life. This handy companion volume to the worship planning guide *Sundays and Seasons* adds another dimension to worship. This guide begins with fall 2000 and goes through summer 2001 to coincide with the beginning of the educational year.
ISBN 0-8066-4200-9 · 15-6050 · $30.00

**See back for more worship planning resources.
All prices are in U.S. dollars.**

Shipping and Handling

Note: Prices and availability are subject to change without notice. **Shipping Charges:** Shipping charges are additional on all orders. For orders up through $10.00 add $2.50; $10.01–$20.00 add $4.00; $20.01–$35.00 add $5.50; $35.01 and above add $6.50. Actual shipping charges will be assessed for all orders over 35 lbs. in weight (bulk), and for expedited shipping service. Promotion orders are shipped separately from other orders. Additional shipping charges for international shipments. For Canadian orders, actual shipping costs will be charged. This policy is subject to change without notice. **Sales Tax:** Add appropriate state/province and local taxes where applicable. Tax exempt organizations must provide tax exempt numbers on all orders.
Return Policy: All U.S. mail, fax and telephone order returns must be shipped postage prepaid to the Augsburg Fortress Distribution Center, 4001 Gantz Road, Suite E, Grove City, Ohio 43123-1891. Permission is not required for returns. Non-dated, in-print product in saleable condition may be returned for up to 60 days after the invoice date. Defective products, products damaged in shipment, or products shipped in error may be returned at any time and postage will be reimbursed. Special order or clearance items may not be returned. Canadian orders must be returned to the location from which the order was shipped.

Order Form

Worship Planning Resources 2001, Cycle C
Just complete this order card, affix postage, and drop it in the mail.
To order by phone: 1-800-328-4648 By fax: 1-800-722-7766

Send to: _____
Address: _____
City: _____ State: _____ Zip: _____
Phone: _____

Bill to: _____
Address: _____
City: _____ State: _____ Zip: _____

Method of Payment *(check one)*
☐ Augsburg Fortress Acct # _____
☐ Credit Card # _____
Exp. Date: _____
(Must be valid for Sept. 1999. Products ship August 1999.)
Signature: _____
(Required on all credit card orders.)
☐ Check *(Place check and order card in envelope and mail to address on reverse. Include proper shipping charges and sales tax.)*

Please refer to Keycode B32C, Group Code 09 when ordering.

Qty.	Title	ISBN	Price
____	Sundays and Seasons	ISBN 0-8066-3627-0	$ 30.00
____	Worship Planning Calendar	ISBN 0-8066-3828-1	$ 20.00
____	Words for Worship	ISBN 0-8066-4029-4	$139.00
____	Living and Learning	ISBN 0-8066-4200-9	$ 30.00
____	Liturgical Wall Calendar	ISBN 0-8066-3831-1	$ 6.95
____	Church Year Calendar	ISBN 0-8066-3809-5	$ 1.95

**Thank you for your order!
Prices valid through April 15, 2000.**

Liturgical Wall Calendar 2001
CYCLE C

This beautiful full-color wall calendar will keep you on track at a glance. Identifies church festivals, and U.S. and Canadian holidays. Large date blocks note Bible readings from the Revised Common Lectionary for Sundays and church festivals and identify the seasonal or festival color. Makes a great gift with custom imprinting available. Create a reference tool for each household, or staff and committee members! 10 ⅞ x 8 ⅜. Spiral bound, punched for hanging. 28 pages. Call for details regarding custom imprinting.

ISBN 0-8066-3831-1 · 23-2013 · $6.95

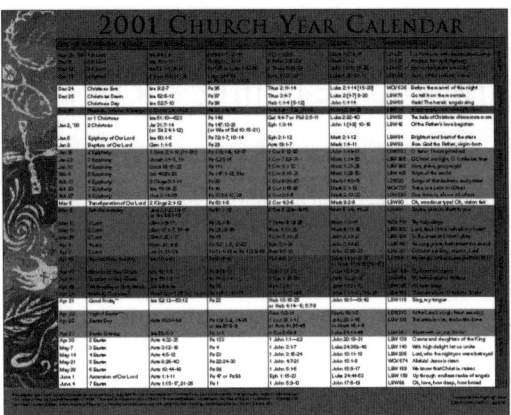

Church Year Calendar 2001
CYCLE C

This simple sheet is a useful tool for anyone in your church: committee members, choir members, worship planners, the altar ghild, teachers, and pastors. The full-color calendar gives dates, Bible readings, hymn of the day, and liturgical color for each Sunday and festival of the church year.
Two sides, 11 x 8 ½.
ISBN 0-8066-3809-5 . 23-2016 . $1.95

Place Stamp Here

AUGSBURG FORTRESS PUBLISHERS
ATTN MAILING CENTER
PO BOX 59303
MINNEAPOLIS, MN 55459-0303

OCTOBER 15, 2000

EIGHTEENTH SUNDAY AFTER PENTECOST
PROPER 23

INTRODUCTION

Jesus knows our weaknesses, especially the weakness of clinging to those things that could be given away or shared for the good of others. In the gospel reading, Jesus states that it will be difficult for those who pursue wealth to enter the reign of God. Living in a culture that seems driven by the pursuit of money and comfort, we may find these words difficult to hear. Yet Jesus announces that nothing is impossible with God who is our life, our treasure, and our salvation.

PRAYER OF THE DAY

Almighty God, source of every blessing, your generous goodness comes to us anew every day. By the work of your Spirit lead us to acknowledge your goodness, give thanks for your benefits, and serve you in willing obedience; through your Son, Jesus Christ our Lord.

READINGS

Amos 5:6-7, 10-15

Amos was a herdsman by profession and a prophet by God's call. During a time of great prosperity in the Northern Kingdom, the prophet speaks of poverty, corruption, and oppression to the wealthy upper class. He warns his listeners that fulfilling God's demand for justice brings blessing, while corruption and evil bring curse.

Psalm 90:12-17

So teach us to number our days that we may apply our hearts to wisdom. (Ps. 90:12)

Hebrews 4:12-16

The letter to the Hebrews teaches that God knows all our failings and understands our struggles. Christ reveals to us that we need not hide from God in shame. We can draw near to receive mercy.

Mark 10:17-31

Jesus has been teaching his disciples about what is most valued in God's eyes. Now, a conversation with a rich man brings his message home to the disciples in a way that is surprising but unforgettable.

ALTERNATE FIRST READING/PSALM

Job 23:1-9, 16-17

Having experienced much personal loss and tragedy, Job expressed his anger about God, even though he was unable to locate God directly. Yet through all this, Job did not doubt God's existence.

Psalm 22:1-15

My God, my God, why have you forsaken me? (Ps. 22:1)

COLOR   Green

THE PRAYERS

As we await the full harvest of the Spirit, let us offer our prayers to God who is abundant in every good gift.
A BRIEF SILENCE.

Let us pray for the church, and especially for all mission congregations and their pastor-developers, that the gospel would be firmly planted in all communities. Hear us, O God;
your mercy is great.

Let us pray for a fruitful harvest of grain from the fields and for a healthy global economy, that a fair and just distribution of the world's goods would be accomplished. Hear us, O God;
your mercy is great.

Let us pray for justice to prevail in our community, that those in need would be cared for, the oppressed be freed from abuse, and the courts be governed with truth. Hear us, O God;
your mercy is great.

Let us pray for the healing of all who suffer with pain and illness (especially . . .), that they may be restored to good health and well-being. Hear us, O God;
your mercy is great.

Let us pray for those who are on the fringes of this congregation and have many questions of faith. May they find a hospitable welcome and experience God's presence in their inquiry. Hear us, O God;
your mercy is great.

HERE OTHER INTERCESSIONS MAY BE OFFERED.

Let us pray in thanksgiving for the faithful departed,

that we might be inspired by their love and faithfulness, and remain united with them in God's eternal community. Hear us, O God;
your mercy is great.
Teach us to pray, O God, and grant us wisdom in our asking, in the name of Jesus Christ our Lord.
Amen

IMAGES FOR PREACHING

In recent years, people begging for money have stationed themselves near cash machines. It might be helpful if the beggar carried a big sign that said, "It is easier for a camel to go through the eye of a needle than for someone who is rich to enter the kingdom of God." It might surprise a few people into making a donation.

But sooner or later, a minister or seminary professor or an active church member would come along and say, "Jesus didn't mean a sewing needle. He was talking about a small gate in the wall of Jerusalem called 'The Eye of a Needle.' And the word translated 'camel' might be 'cable'—a cable could go through the eye of a large needle!" After that encounter, the beggar might pray that religious people would use a different cash machine.

How do we take Jesus' words about possessions seriously without leaving people where the disciples were—thinking that no one can be saved? If we say the text is about *anything* that separates us from God, we mute Jesus' strong words about possessions. But a strong word about wealth may cause people to argue defensively saying, "I'm not wealthy!" or close their ears completely. Still we must try to say something, for few themes are as dominant in scripture as God's concern about wealth and poverty. We cannot preach this text without talking about money.

The sermon can be an invitation to a study series on wealth and poverty. Excellent resources are available such as the statement on economic life from the ELCA's Division for Church and Society and the working group on Women and Children in Poverty. The sermon is a beginning, a call to take seriously one of the most urgent themes in the Bible. Who knows? We might see Jesus the next time we go to the cash machine.

WORSHIP MATTERS

The second reading reminds us of the power and importance of the word of God. Well-trained lectors should read from a lectionary or Bible that is "of appropriate size and dignity" (*The Use of the Means of Grace*, application 7B), and not from a lectionary insert that seems unsuitable for this task. At each reading's conclusion, the lector may pause briefly and then say, "The word of the Lord," to which the assembly responds, "Thanks be to God."

How is the liturgy of the word treated in your congregation? Is it done with dignity and solemnity? Do the lectors receive adequate training? Are they instructed on how to project their voices, and on how to use pauses effectively?

LET THE CHILDREN COME

Jesus addresses the disciples as children in today's gospel. It may be surprising to the children of our congregations to hear that even those closest to Jesus had a hard time understanding why money and riches aren't the highest good. Take advantage of the literal comprehension of children this age and allow them to wrestle with the image of a camel going through the eye of a needle, without trying to rationalize it. Leave them with the announcement of God as the one for whom all things are possible.

MUSIC FOR WORSHIP

GATHERING

LBW 522	Come, thou almighty King
WOV 782	All my hope on God is founded

PSALM 90

Comer, Marilyn. PW, cycle B.
Folkening, John. *Six Psalm Settings with Antiphons*. MSM 80-700. U, SATB, opt cong, kybd.
Hallock, Peter/arr. Carl Crosier. *The Ionian Psalter*. ION. U/SATB, org.
Stewart, Roy James. "Psalm 90: Fill Us With Your Love, O Lord" in *Gather Comprehensive*. GIA.
Walker, Christopher. "Fill Us, Lord, With Your Love" in PS, vol. 3.
LBW 320   O God, our help in ages past (paraphrase)

HYMN OF THE DAY

LBW 408	God, whose giving knows no ending
	RUSTINGTON

INSTRUMENTAL RESOURCES

Bouman, Paul. "God, Whose Giving Knows No Ending" in *The Concordia Hymn Prelude Series, vol. 36*. CPH 97-5751. Org.
Wolff, S. Drummond. "Rustington" in *Hymn Descants, Set III*. CPH 97-6197. Org, inst.

ALTERNATE HYMN OF THE DAY
- WOV 783 — Seek ye first the kingdom of God
- LBW 364 — Son of God, eternal Savior

COMMUNION
- LBW 205 — Now the silence
- WOV 704 — Father, we thank you

OTHER SUGGESTIONS

Armstrong, Matthew. "Take My Life and Let It Be." CPH 98-3455. SATB, kybd.

SENDING
- LBW 433 — The Church of Christ, in every age
- WOV 790 — Praise to you, O God of mercy

ADDITIONAL HYMNS AND SONGS
- DATH 96 — Give it away
- H82 633 — Word of God, come down on earth
- TFF 236 — Some folk would rather have houses
- W&P — The church song

MUSIC FOR THE DAY

CHORAL

Bell, John L. "Lord, You Have Been Our Refuge." GIA G-4297. SATB, desc, cong.

Ferguson, John. "Be Thou My Vision." AFP 11-10925. SATB, org.

Proulx, Richard. "Weary of All Trumpeting." AFP 11-10897. SAB, org, opt cong, brass qnt.

Purcell, Henry. "Thy Word Is a Lantern" in *A Purcell Anthology*. OXF ISBN 0-19-353351-0. SATB, org.

Vaughan Williams, Ralph. "He That Is Down Need Fear No Fall." OXF E138. S(Bar), SATB, fl/ob.

CHILDREN'S CHOIRS

Gieseke, Richard W. "God's Own Time." MSM 50-8000. U, kybd.

Handel/arr. Hal H. Hopson. "Lord, Lead Us Day by Day." AG HH3908. U, kybd.

KEYBOARD/INSTRUMENTAL

Barr, John G. "Jubilation on 'Bunessan.'" HWG GSTC 01096. Org.

Manz, Paul. "Aria." MSM 10-906. Org.

HANDBELL

McFadden, Jane. "Thy Holy Wings" in *Two More Swedish Melodies*. AFP 11-10871. 3-4 oct, opt 2-4 oct hc.

McKechnie, Linda D. "O God, Our Help in Ages Past." GVX 3197-12. 3-5 oct, kybd, opt tpt, cong.

PRAISE ENSEMBLE

Garratt, Childers, Pink, and Burt. "Romans 16:19" in *Hosanna! Music Songbook 8*. INT.

Larson, Lloyd. "Lord, You Have Been Our Dwelling Place." PP152. SATB, kybd, brass.

Pote, Allen. "A Jubilant Song." HOP F979. SATB, kybd, brass, hb.

Tunney, Dick, Melody Tunney, and Paul Smith. "How Excellent Is Thy Name" in *The Other Songbook*. Fellowship Publications.

Unknown. "Into Thy Presence" in *Sing & Rejoice*. BRM BK-3041.

SUNDAY, OCTOBER 15

TERESA OF JESUS (SAME AS TERESA OF AVILA, RENEWER OF THE CHURCH, 1582)

See December 14 for commemoration along with John of the Cross.

TUESDAY, OCTOBER 17

IGNATIUS, BISHOP OF ANTIOCH, MARTYR, C. 115

Ignatius was bishop of Antioch in Syria where the name Christian was first used to describe the followers of Jesus. He is known as a martyr who died for refusing to worship the gods of the state religion. Ignatius believed that in his death he was imitating the passion of Christ. Even as he awaited his own death, his letters encouraged Christians to live in harmony and serve those in need. Reflect together on the cruciform shape of the Christian life.

WEDNESDAY, OCTOBER 18

ST. LUKE, EVANGELIST

Luke was the author of both Luke and Acts, and Paul calls him the "beloved physician." Little else is known of his life. He is commemorated by both the Eastern and Western cultures on this day, and his symbol is the winged ox.

Some congregations use the day of St. Luke to remember and honor those in healing professions. The Service of the Word for Healing in *Occasional Services* may be used. When we define healing to include the emotional, spiritual, and physical dimensions of our lives, we all stand in need of God's healing presence. The gestures of laying on of hands and/or anointing with oil give witness to the church's care for the whole person—body and soul.

OCTOBER 22, 2000

NINETEENTH SUNDAY AFTER PENTECOST
PROPER 24

INTRODUCTION

Baptism into Christ is our entrance into the Lord's mission. This calling is made abundantly clear at the end of the liturgy when the assembly is charged to go in peace and serve the Lord. Such service cannot avoid the cup of suffering. Indeed, the good news is that, in Christ, God has embraced us in love where we are most weak and frail. How shall we do this for each other and for those who are in need?

PRAYER OF THE DAY

Almighty and everlasting God, in Christ you have revealed your glory among the nations. Preserve the works of your mercy, that your Church throughout the world may persevere with steadfast faith in the confession of your name; through your Son, Jesus Christ our Lord.

READINGS

Isaiah 53:4-12

This reading is a section from the last of four passages in Isaiah that are often called "servant songs." Christians are most familiar with the various New Testament interpretations of this passage. In light of Christian faith, the servant's healing ministry and redemptive suffering are brought to fullness in the life and death of Christ.

Psalm 91:9-16

You have made the LORD your refuge, and the Most High your habitation. (Ps. 91:9)

Hebrews 5:1-10

Using imagery borrowed from Jewish worship, the letter to the Hebrews describes Jesus as a great high priest who offers himself as a sacrifice for our sins.

Mark 10:35-45

On the way to Jerusalem, the disciples ask Jesus to grant them seats of honor. Jesus responds by announcing that he and his followers will "rule" through self-giving service.

ALTERNATE FIRST READING/PSALM

Job 38:1-7 [34-41]

Confronted with great suffering, Job attempts to prove his innocence to God. God speaks from the whirlwind, and speaks of the power of the sea and its waves. A series of ironical questions shows that Job, as a finite human, is incapable of judging the Creator.

Psalm 104:1-9, 24, 35c

O LORD, how manifold are your works! In wisdom you have made them all. (Ps. 104:25)

COLOR Green

THE PRAYERS

As we await the full harvest of the Spirit, let us offer our prayers to God who is abundant in every good gift.

A BRIEF SILENCE.

God of suffering service, grant to your church faithful leaders who have the hearts of servants, and who will gently lead your people into love for you and service to their neighbors. Hear us, O God;

your mercy is great.

God of gentle justice, raise up righteous leaders in every nation who will govern with truth and guide their people with fairness and equity. Hear us, O God;

your mercy is great.

God of tender compassion, hear the cries of all who suffer and who are contending with sickness and disease (especially . . .). Lay upon them your gentle hand of healing. Hear us, O God;

your mercy is great.

God of all goodness, guide the work of the congregation council and committees of this parish, that a unity of purpose would prevail over all their decision making. Hear us, O God;

your mercy is great.

HERE OTHER INTERCESSIONS MAY BE OFFERED.

God of comforting hope, tend to those who are grieving, that their mourning would be turned into dancing, and their grieving into gladness. Bring us at length, with all our blessed dead, to the joy of your heavenly realm. Hear us, O God;

your mercy is great.

Teach us to pray, O God, and grant us wisdom in our asking, in the name of Jesus Christ our Lord.

Amen

IMAGES FOR PREACHING

Church bulletin boards often announce the sermon theme for the coming Sunday to generate interest. One sermon title posted outside a city church tried to lure people inside with this promise: "Following Jesus Can Be Loving and Practical." It sounds good, but it's false advertising. Following Jesus doesn't offer "Ten Steps for Success in Business" (or much of anything).

These last Sundays of the season after Pentecost are filled with impractical, almost impossible teachings. No wonder that the inner circle of disciples try to turn Jesus' words around! Peter refuses to hear "suffering" as a word that goes with "Messiah." Now James and John insist that Jesus grant them places at his side in glory. If the inner circle of disciples didn't get it, it's not surprising that we have a hard time. Following Jesus is not very practical.

Then why follow? James and John were looking for something when they left their fishing boat. They saw and heard something in Jesus that compelled them to follow. They weren't sure what it was, but they sensed that making a living was not the same as finding your life. So they got up and went. Things didn't always turn out the way they wanted. They got it wrong more than once, and Jesus corrected them more than once. But they're still here.

And we're still here in this impractical community called the church. Frederick Buechner was close to the truth when he said, "We want to know who [Jesus] is before we follow him, and that is understandable enough except that the truth of the matter is that it is only by first following him that we can begin to find out who he is" (*The Magnificent Defeat*, p. 98).

WORSHIP MATTERS

In today's gospel reading, Jesus intimates that the twelve disciples will share in his sufferings. In the sacrament of baptism, we all become sharers in Christ's sufferings by being joined to his death and resurrection. The early architecture of baptism bespoke the Christian's union with Christ in his sufferings. Rectangular fonts, which imitated ancient sarcophagi and burial niches, as well as cross-shaped fonts, both suggested that baptism is a death and burial with Christ.

The church today is renewing its baptismal practice by returning to older styles of baptismal fonts that permit the immersion of the candidate. If the construction of a new font is not possible, a temporary fixture such as a portable children's wading pool or washtub can be used. The adult candidate simply steps into the pool and the water is poured over him or her. Plants or wooden frames can surround the pool to give a more dignified look. How well does the font in your worship space reflect the imagery of death and burial? Is there a way to renew your baptismal space and furnishings in order to reflect this imagery more adequately?

LET THE CHILDREN COME

It is by baptism that we gain access to the ministry of Jesus, our great high priest. Let the prayers today reflect our baptismal relation to God and others. Examples might be the following prayers: *LBW*, p. 200; prayers 199 and 200 on p. 47; 272 and 255 on p. 195; or the litany beginning on p. 168.

MUSIC FOR WORSHIP

GATHERING

LBW 244	Lord our God, with praise we come
WOV 736	By gracious powers

PSALM 91

Bell, John L. *Psalms of Patience, Protest and Praise*. GIA G-4047. U/SATB.

Comer, Marilyn. PW, cycle B.

Glynn, John. "Song of Blessing" in PS, vol. 2.

Haugen, Marty/arr. David Haas. PCY.

Marshall, Jane. "Psalm 91" in *Psalms Together II*. CGC-21. U, cong.

WOV 779 You who dwell in the shelter of the Lord (paraphrase)

HYMN OF THE DAY

LBW 529	Praise God. Praise him
	TANDANEI

VOCAL RESOURCES

Fleming, Larry L. "Praise God, Praise Him" in *Embellisments for Choir (General)*. AFP 11-10654. SATB.

INSTRUMENTAL RESOURCES

Bisbee, B. Wayne. "Tandanei" in *From the Serene to the Whimsical*. AFP 11-10561. Org.

Burkhardt, Michael. "Praise God, Praise Him" in *Eight Improvisations on 20th Century Hymn Tunes*. MSM 10-707. Org.

Manz, Paul. "Praise God, Praise Him" in *Three Hymns for Flute, Oboe, and Organ*. MSM 20-871. Fl, ob, org.

McChesney, Kevin. "Praise God. Praise Him." AFP 11-10630. Hb.

ALTERNATE HYMN OF THE DAY

WOV 785 Weary of all trumpeting
LBW 433 The Church of Christ, in every age

COMMUNION

LBW 201 O God of life's great mystery
WOV 779 You who dwell in the shelter of the Lord
WOV 765 Jesu, Jesu, fill us with your love

SENDING

LBW 462 God the omnipotent!
WOV 787 Glory to God, we give you thanks

ADDITIONAL HYMNS AND SONGS

OBS 76 Rise, O church, like Christ arisen
H82 160 Cross of Jesus, cross of sorrow
TFF 172 If when you give the best of your service
W&P Sing out, earth and skies

MUSIC FOR THE DAY

CHORAL

Bach, J. S. "Domine Deus" in *Mass in G Major*. B&H OCTB6552. SA, org, opt vlns.

Joncas, Michael. "On Eagle's Wings." OCP 9493. 2 pt, cong, pno, gtr, solo inst, vln.

Proulx, Richard. "Weary of All Trumpeting." AFP 11-10897. SAB, org, opt cong, brass qnt.

Roth, John D. "I Am Trusting You, Lord Jesus" in *Let Light Shine*. CPH 98-3318. SA, C inst, kybd.

Victoria, T. L. "Vere langoures nostros." AMC AE 359. SATB.

CHILDREN'S CHOIRS

Nelson, Ronald A. "Whoever Would Be Great Among You." AFP 11-1638. SAB, gtr/kybd.

Nystedt, Knut. "Teach Me, O Lord." MSM 50-9400. 2 pt trbl, pno, opt perc.

KEYBOARD/INSTRUMENTAL

Albrecht, Mark. "Communion Meditation on Three Tunes" in *Three for Piano and Sax*. AFP 11-10929.

Welch, James. "Jerusalem" in *Two Regal Settings by English Composers*. MSM 10-946. Org.

HANDBELL

Joncas/arr. Honore. "On Eagle's Wings." CPH 97-6429. 3-5 oct.

Wiltse, Carl. "God the Omnipotent." SCM SGM-114. 5 oct, org, opt tpt.

PRAISE ENSEMBLE

Colvin, Tom/arr. Young. "Fill Us with Your Love." AG AG7256. SATB, kybd.

Joncas, Michael/arr. Mark Hayes. "On Eagle's Wings." ALF 16104. SATB. 16105. SAB. 16106. 2 pt. Orch also available.

Kendrick. Graham. "Meekness and Majesty" in *Maranatha! Music Praise Chorus Book, 3rd ed*. MAR/WRD.

Rouse, Jay/arr. Kirkland and Rouse. "He Obeyed unto Death." Sparrow AO82222. SATB, orch.

Vogels, J. "Victory Chant" in *Worship Team, vol. 1*. MAR.

MONDAY, OCTOBER 23
JAMES OF JERUSALEM, MARTYR

James became a leader of the early church in Jerusalem. He is identified as a brother of the Lord, though disagreement remains as to whether Jesus actually had brothers. In Mark, Jesus says that "whoever does the will of God is my brother and sister and mother."

How does your congregation define "family"? When trying to understand the will of God for our lives, do we consider the ways we serve Christ as revealed in our sisters and brothers in need? If we are going to talk of family values, then Jesus' words invite us to reach beyond the ties of blood, and beyond the walls of our congregation.

THURSDAY, OCTOBER 26
PHILIPP NICOLAI, 1608; JOHANN HEERMANN, 1647; PAUL GERHARDT, 1676; HYMNWRITERS

Lutherans are known for music, especially their robust singing of hymns. One of our unique treasures is the chorale, which refers to both the text and tune of German hymns, especially those of the Reformation era. The Lutheran chorale is known for its unique combination of praise and strong proclamation.

Consider holding an October hymn festival, and include both classic Lutheran chorales as well as recent hymns in *WOV*. The three hymnwriters commemorated on October 26 could be featured. Nicolai is especially known for both the text and tune of "Wake, awake, for night is flying" (LBW 31) and "O Morning Star, how fair and bright" (LBW 76). Heerman's most famous hymn text is "Ah, holy Jesus" (LBW 123). Gerhardt has ten hymn texts in *LBW* (see p. 941).

SATURDAY, OCTOBER 28
ST. SIMON AND ST. JUDE, APOSTLES

We know little of either Simon or Jude, two men on the lists of Jesus' apostles. Simon is called a zealot in Luke, and the prayer of the day says "that, as they were faithful and zealous in their mission, so we may with ardent devotion make known the love and mercy" of Christ.

We are usually skeptical of people who are overly zealous about their faith. The Sunday assembly around word and meal nourishes us that we might go into the world to serve. It will take a certain Spirit-filled energy to meet the tasks and challenges we encounter there. Maybe we need to be more zealous! Has your congregation council considered the level of commitment and enthusiasm among your members? Do your members look forward to worship as the place where they are strengthened and inspired for service in the world?

OCTOBER 29, 2000
REFORMATION SUNDAY

INTRODUCTION

By the end of the seventeenth century, many Lutheran churches celebrated a festival commemorating Martin Luther's posting of the Ninety-five Theses, a summary of abuses in the church of his time. At the heart of the reform movement was the gospel, the good news that it is by grace through faith that we are justified and set free. As we observe the Reformation today the church prays for renewal and reconciliation among all Christians, that we may more faithfully witness to the world.

PRAYER OF THE DAY

Almighty God, gracious Lord, pour out your Holy Spirit upon your faithful people. Keep them steadfast in your Word, protect and comfort them in all temptations, defend them against all their enemies, and bestow on the Church your saving peace; through your Son, Jesus Christ our Lord, who lives and reigns with you and the Holy Spirit, one God, now and forever.

READINGS

Jeremiah 31:31-34

After the fall of Jerusalem to the Babylonian army, Jeremiah's message changes from doom to comfort. This reading presents the prophet's vision of the restored community of Israel. The new covenant will fulfill the original intention of the covenant with Moses—God and humanity living in harmonious relationship. The difference between then and now is that the people's response to the liberating God will come naturally.

Psalm 46

The LORD of hosts is with us; the God of Jacob is our stronghold. (Ps. 46:4)

Romans 3:19-28

Martin Luther and other leaders of the Reformation believed the heart of the gospel was found in these words of Paul written to the Romans. All people have sinned, but God offers forgiveness through Christ Jesus. We are justified, or put right with God, by grace through faith in Jesus.

John 8:31-36

Here Jesus promises that true freedom—the freedom to serve our loving God—comes through the truth of the gospel. It is this truth that is revealed in the life of the Lord Jesus.

COLOR   Red

THE PRAYERS

As we await the full harvest of the Spirit, let us offer our prayers to God who is abundant in every good gift.
A BRIEF SILENCE.

O mighty God, give your church an unswerving trust in the great heritage of your word, that it may boldly and freely proclaim the forgiveness of sins with joy. Hear us, O God;
your mercy is great.

O God of all, strengthen those who bring in the abundance of fruit and grain from the fields, that the work of their hands will feed many who hunger for physical nourishment. Hear us, O God;
your mercy is great.
O God our shield, be the protector of the powerless and the hope for those on the margins of society. Touch those who are sick with your tender, healing hand (especially . . .). Hear us, O God;
your mercy is great.
O God our rock, let your sure grace have free course in this congregation, that we would be strong in faith and bold to give witness to the great heritage passed on to us. Hear us, O God;
your mercy is great.

HERE OTHER INTERCESSIONS MAY BE OFFERED.

O God our redeemer, you are our heritage from one generation to another. We praise you for the saints and reformers who have paved the way for us, and who cheer us on toward our eternal home. Hear us, O God;
your mercy is great.
Teach us to pray, O God, and grant us wisdom in our asking, in the name of Jesus Christ our Lord.
Amen

IMAGES FOR PREACHING

"What do you mean by saying, 'You will be made free'?" This timeless question is not only the protest of those who traced their bloodline back to Abraham. It is the unexpressed thought of many who hear these words on Reformation Sunday. We have been freed by God's grace through faith (we say, knowing the verse by heart). We have been freed from allegiance to the pope and other earthly rulers (we may say if we're still celebrating Reformation as Lutheran Pride Sunday). We live in the land of the free (we say, believing that living in the United States means you are free). This gospel must be about somebody else.

Yet we don't feel especially free. We often live in the land of "if only": if only I had gotten in the stock market sooner, if only I'd chosen a different career, if only I could find a good relationship, if only I had more time, more friends, more money. We may be free from outward constraints, yet bound by internalized chains not easily broken. "What will the neighbors think?" can keep us bound for a lifetime. Many are bound by the chains of poverty in a free country. Others are caught up in a market mania in which having more always means wanting more, and more is never enough.

"You will know the truth, and the truth will make you free." How can this glorious Reformation gospel reach us if we don't acknowledge that we, too, are bound? We may even be bound by our own rigid rendition of dogma, which keeps us from hearing anything new in the gospel. Perhaps on this day we need the wisdom attributed to Flannery O'Connor when she paraphrased this Reformation gospel saying, "You will know the truth, and the truth will make you odd."

WORSHIP MATTERS

Lutherans have traditionally believed that the church of the Reformation is always reforming. Perhaps this principle of continual reformation needs to be realized in your ministry of worship. Does your congregation's sense of sacramentality need to be reformed? Can ways be found to highlight the centrality of baptism, such as using an architecturally significant font and regularly celebrating affirmations of baptism? Does your congregation need education about the benefits of weekly communion?

Does the way music is integrated into worship in your congregation need to be reformed? Do people in your congregation need help understanding that the purpose of music in worship is to support the ministry of word and sacrament? Do they need to move beyond the understanding that selecting music for worship is merely a matter of choosing everyone's favorites?

LET THE CHILDREN COME

Consider using or adapting articles one through seven of the Augsburg Confession as a confession of faith today. Children and adults alike are well prepared to celebrate this day when the focus is not on Martin Luther, but on the Christian faith and the one, holy, catholic, and apostolic church that proclaims it.

MUSIC FOR WORSHIP

GATHERING

LBW 369	The Church's one foundation
WOV 750	Oh, praise the gracious power

PSALM 46

Burkhardt, Michael. *Three Psalm Settings*. MSM 80-705. U, cong, opt inst.

Cherwien, David. "Psalm 46: God Is Our Refuge." MSM 80-800. U, cong, org.

Folkening, John. *Six Psalm Settings with Antiphons*. MSM 80-700. U, SATB, cong, kybd.

Hallock, Peter/arr. Carl Crosier. *The Ionian Psalter*. ION. U/choir, org.

Harbor, Rawn. "The Lord of Hosts Is with Us" in *This Far by Faith*.

Wood, Dale. PW, cycle B.

LBW 228/9   A mighty fortress is our God (paraphrase)

HYMN OF THE DAY

LBW 365   Built on a rock
               KIRKEN DEN ER ET GAMMELT HUS

VOCAL RESOURCES

Fedak, Alfred V. "Built on a Rock." SEL 241-503. 2 pt, kybd, opt hb.

INSTRUMENTAL RESOURCES

Albrecht, Mark. "Built on a Rock." Live Oak House 445-1136 SET. Brass.

Behnke, John. "Kirken den er et gammelt Hus" in *Variations for Seven Familiar Hymns*. AFP 11-10702. Org.

McFadden, Jane. "Built on a Rock." AFP 11-10714. Hb, cong, org, opt tpt.

Oliver, Curt. "Built on a Rock" in *Built on a Rock: Keyboard Seasons*. AFP 11-10620. Pno.

ALTERNATE HYMN OF THE DAY

WOV 712   Listen, God is calling
LBW 230   Lord, keep us steadfast in your Word

COMMUNION

LBW 214   Come, let us eat
WOV 680   O Spirit of life

SENDING

LBW 228/9   A mighty fortress is our God
WOV 755   We all are one in mission

ADDITIONAL HYMNS AND SONGS

TFF 290   Praised be the rock
TFF 197   We've come this far by faith
W&P   Rock of my salvation
W&P   What a mighty word

MUSIC FOR THE DAY

CHORAL

Bertalot, John. "I Stand on the Rock." AFP 11-10852. SAB, org.

Buxtehude, Dietrich. "Lord Keep Us Steadfast in Your Word." CPH 97-6331. SATB, 2 vln, vc, cont.

Ferguson, John. "The Church's One Foundation." AFP 11-10965. SATB, opt cong, brass, org.

Grieg, Edvard/arr. Oscar Overby. "God's Son Has Made Me Free" in *The Augsburg Choirbook*. AFP 11-10817. SATB.

Olson, Howard. "Set Free, Set Free" in *Set Free*. AFP 3-420. SATB.

Schultz, Timothy P. "God Is Our Refuge and Strength." CPH 98-3156. SATB.

CHILDREN'S CHOIRS

Bertalot, John. "God Is Our Hope." CG CGA444. 2 pt, kybd.

Larson, Lloyd. "Take Up the Tambourine." CG CGA819. U/2 pt, kybd.

KEYBOARD/INSTRUMENTAL

Albrecht, Timothy. "A Mighty Fortress Is Our God" in *Grace Notes VI*. AFP 11-10825. Org.

Organ, Anne Krentz. "A Mighty Fortress" in *Keys of the Kingdom: Piano Arrangements for Weddings and Funerals*. ABI. Pno.

HANDBELL

Luther/arr. Benton. "A Mighty Fortress Is Our God." AGEHR AG3075. Full score, inst pts. AG5049. 3 oct, opt kybd, brass, timp. AG35103. 4-5 oct. AG301182. Org/kybd.

PRAISE ENSEMBLE

Gustafson, G. "Only by Grace" in *Come & Worship*. INT.

Lojeski, Ed. "Amazing Grace." HAL 08300531. SATB, pno, gtr, perc.

Makeever, Ray. "Write Your Law upon Our Hearts" in DATH.

Moen, Don. "All We Like Sheep" in *Come & Worship*. INT.

Nystrom, Martin J. "He Whom the Son Sets Free" in *Hosanna! Music Songbook, vol 6*. INT HMSB06.

OCTOBER 29, 2000

TWENTIETH SUNDAY AFTER PENTECOST
PROPER 25

INTRODUCTION

Bartimaeus, a blind beggar, beseeches Jesus with these words, "Son of David, have mercy on me." We too seek God's mercy on behalf of the world, the church, and all those in need. In the words of the ancient Kyrie, we sing, "Lord, have mercy." Gathered as God's people, we pray for a faith that will enable us to see the signs of God's merciful presence among us even as we become signs of healing in the world.

PRAYER OF THE DAY

Almighty and everlasting God, increase in us the gifts of faith, hope, and charity; and, that we may obtain what you promise, make us love what you command; through your Son, Jesus Christ our Lord.

READINGS

Jeremiah 31:7-9
> Part of a poem celebrating the return from exile, this passage makes it clear that those who are blind and lame are among those who receive God's gracious consolation.

Psalm 126
> Those who sowed with tears will reap with songs of joy. (Ps. 126:6)

Hebrews 7:23-28
> Jesus is our great high priest, who not only offers us salvation through his sacrificial death, but lives to make intercession on our behalf.

Mark 10:46-52
> In contrast to the disciples who seek after glory in last Sunday's gospel, Bartimaeus comes to Jesus with faith, asking that he might see again. Recognizing Jesus' identity, Bartimaeus is the first person to call him "Son of David" in the Gospel of Mark.

ALTERNATE FIRST READING/PSALM

Job 42:1-6, 10-17
> In these verses we read of Job's period of prolonged suffering coming to an end. Though the end of the book sees Job's fortunes restored to an even greater level than they had been before his string of adversities, the overarching message of the book is that the righteous are not always prosperous.

Psalm 34:1-8 [19-22]
> Taste and see that the LORD is good. (Ps. 34:8)

COLOR Green

THE PRAYERS

As we await the full harvest of the Spirit, let us offer our prayers to God who is abundant in every good gift.
A BRIEF SILENCE.

Let us pray for the church, that its leaders would see God's vision and would encourage the faithful to proceed without fear into the uncertainties of the future. Hear us, O God;
your mercy is great.

Let us pray for the nations of the world and for our own country, that God's peace-giving Spirit would rest upon all who govern and guide us. Hear us, O God;
your mercy is great.

Let us pray for those in need, especially expectant mothers, that their pregnancy would be without complication, and their delivery a day of rejoicing. Hear us, O God;
your mercy is great.

Let us pray for those who are sick, that they might be touched by God's tender, healing hand (especially . . .). Hear us, O God;
your mercy is great.
HERE OTHER INTERCESSIONS MAY BE OFFERED.

Let us pray for all who are dying, and all who have died. Give us a glimpse of the life of the world to come, and grant your comfort to all who grieve. Hear us, O God;
your mercy is great.

Teach us to pray, O God, and grant us wisdom in our asking, in the name of Jesus Christ our Lord.
Amen

IMAGES FOR PREACHING

Many times the disciples saw what Jesus was doing, but they failed to understand him. The gospel reading for today illustrates this gap clearly. Many who had been following Jesus tried to keep the blind beggar Bartimaeus away. Yet this man called Jesus "Son of David." No one else had yet used this phrase to call Jesus in the Gospel of Mark.

When asked what he wanted Jesus to do for him, Bartimaeus responded, "My teacher, let me see again." This plea stands in sharp contrast to the previous passage in which James and John argued about which of them would be first in Jesus' kingdom. With Bartimaeus we find an outsider who has a greater clue into what Jesus' true mission was than do some of his closest followers.

In this episode, Jesus praises the blind man's faith. Yet the disciples' eyes, in contrast, remain clouded, because they come to Jesus filled with their own importance and their desire to sit in high places with him.

When we read the Gospel of Mark closely, we may discover that it communicates something disturbing. It is possible for people who are closest to Jesus, and claim to know him best of all, to be farthest from the truth.

Following Jesus means to deny self, to serve and suffer willingly for others. Such a radical form of following Jesus is a challenge to even the most loyal church member. A genuine follower needs to step apart from family, community, and even church loyalties in order to be able to see things as they really are.

WORSHIP MATTERS

Is God glad when we worship? To ask this question is to presume that our relationship with God is a quid pro quo: we do "X" and God responds by doing "Y." In fact worship has nothing to do with trying to please God. We worship out of awe and wonder before God's eternal being and in gratitude for God's saving deeds on our behalf. We worship God because it is the right thing to do.

It might be tempting to suggest that worship is a favor we do God, and that God will consequently reward us. Perhaps we feel that this approach will encourage people to worship with us and to continue doing so. Yet we do nobody a favor by suggesting that our worship gains God's favor. Such a position contradicts the understanding of grace as God's gift to us. The gospel is the reassuring message that God gives God's self to us solely out of love. It is always in response to this love that we worship God. We thwart this understanding if we preach or sing hymns that suggest worship is a way of earning God's favor.

LET THE CHILDREN COME

In preparation for worship, give children an opportunity to be blindfolded and experience loss of sight. Try this exercise: Blindfold one child and turn him or her around three times. Place a chair at least 20–30 feet away. Have another child give verbal instructions to the "blind" child to get to the chair and sit down. What was easy? What was hard? Bartimaeus trusted Jesus' word and leapt up to go to him. Such faith is difficult, whether or not our eyes see, but Jesus' word makes all the difference.

MUSIC FOR WORSHIP

GATHERING

| LBW 543 | Praise to the Lord, the Almighty |
| WOV 718 | Here in this place |

PSALM 126

Beckstrand, William. PW, cycle B.
Smith, Alan. "The Lord Has Done Great Things." PS, vol. 1.

HYMN OF THE DAY

| LBW 296 | Just as I am, without one plea |
| | WOODWORTH |

INSTRUMENTAL RESOURCES

Beck, Theodore. "Just as I Am" in *76 Offertories*. CPH 97-5207. Org.
Biester, Allen. "Just As I Am" in *Organ Music for the Seasons*. AFP 11-10859. Org.
Bisbee, B. Wayne. "Woodworth" in *From the Serene to the Whimsical*. AFP 11-10561. Org.
Farlee, Robert Buckley. "Just as I Am" in *Deep Waters: Three Hymns of Faith Arranged for Saxophone or Other Instrument and Organ*. AFP 11-10792.
Wetzler, Robert. "Meditation on Woodworth." AMSI MED. Org.

ALTERNATE HYMN OF THE DAY

| WOV 718 | Here in this place |
| LBW 400 | God, whose almighty word |

COMMUNION

| LBW 448 | Amazing grace |
| WOV 766 | We come to the hungry feast |

SENDING

| LBW 559 | Oh, for a thousand tongues to sing |
| WOV 673 | I'm so glad Jesus lifted me |

ADDITIONAL HYMNS AND SONGS

H82 672 O very God of very God
TFF 134 O Lord, open my eyes
W&P I will sing of the mercies of the Lord

MUSIC FOR THE DAY

CHORAL

Bach, J. S. "God, the Lord Is Sun and Shield" (Gott, der herr, ist Sonn' und Schild) in *Cantata 79*. Various ed.

Bertalot, John. "Amazing Grace." AFP 11-10020. Also in *The Augsburg Choirbook*. 11-10817. SATB, org.

Copland, Aaron. "Help Us, O Lord." B&H OCTB6018. SATB. Barenreiter BA 50671. Ger/Eng.

Manalo, Ricky. "Spirit of Truth and Life." GIA G-3909. 2 pt, cong, gtr, pno, C inst.

Proulx, Richard. "Weary of All Trumpeting." AFP 11-10897. SAB, org, opt brass.

Reger, Max. "Our Lady's Vision." PET 6601. SATB.

CHILDREN'S CHOIRS

Beck, Theodore. "Safe in His Love." CPH 98-2752. 2 pt mxd, org.

Forman, Bruce H. "Hear Me, O Lord!" CG CGA578. SATB, cant, cong, kybd, opt gtr.

Hobby, Robert. "Psalm 34: I Will Bless the Lord." MSM 80-707. U, cong, org.

Leaf, Robert. "Come Today with Jubilant Singing." GIA G-2325. U, kybd.

KEYBOARD/INSTRUMENTAL

Cotter, Jeanne. "Gather Us In" in *After the Rain*. GIA G-3390. Pno.

Peeters, Flor. "Aria." Heuwekemeijer ed. Org.

Wellman, Samuel. "Ein feste Burg" in *Keyboard Hymn Favorites*. AFP 11-10820. Pno.

HANDBELL

Larson, Katherine Jordahl. "Be Thou my Vision." AFP 11-10484. 3-4 oct.

PRAISE ENSEMBLE

Cymbala. "Everlasting" in *Songs for Praise and Worship*. WRD.

Haugen, Marty. "Gather Us In." GIA G-2651. SATB, kybd, gtr, ww.

Lojeski, Ed. "Amazing Grace." HAL 08300531. SATB, pno, gtr, perc.

Pethel, Stan. "He Is Exalted" (with O For a Thousand Tongues to Sing) in *The Sunday Celebration Choir Kit*. WAR 08741317. 2 pt mxd, kybd.

TUESDAY, OCTOBER 31
REFORMATION DAY

WEDNESDAY, NOVEMBER 1
ALL SAINTS DAY

SUMMER

AUTUMN

NOVEMBER

NOVEMBER

Rejoice in what is here,
but rejoice as well in what will yet be

IMAGES OF THE SEASON

What kind of a liturgical season is November? It doesn't seem to be part of the year of the Lord, when we follow the life of Jesus from birth through ministry to Passion and resurrection. Nor does it quite seem to fit with what we call the Sundays of ordinary time, when the lectionary readings tend to move us through gospel or epistle in a continuous fashion, without much regard for theme or season.

But then, what kind of a season is November on the secular calendar? There too it seems unsure of its own character. Technically, of course, it's part of autumn. And yet, it doesn't really seem to fit. Where are the bright colors, the refreshing nip in the air? For many parts of the Northern Hemisphere, at least, all of that has come and gone. The predominant color is more likely to be brown, and the novelty of cooler air may have worn off. In some areas, snow may already have arrived. No, it doesn't feel like fall anymore. But it isn't really winter yet, is it? Even Thanksgiving (in the United States) seems not quite sure of itself. It's frequently late for a harvest festival. So we try to rush things a bit, and make it the kickoff of the Christmas season.

November seems to be less of a season than a time in between, a period getting ready for a real season. It has its pleasures, of course, but somehow it's just not the real thing. If it has a theme of its own, perhaps it is the notion of promise, of something yet to come.

The liturgical calendar seems to do something similar with this month that doesn't quite fit. It begins with death, which to some may seem like a strange beginning. All Saints Sunday traditionally is the day for recalling those who have died in the past year. For many in our midst it is a difficult day, a day of recalling a grief still all too recent. But the images of All Saints are not mournful ones. They are images not of what was and is no more but of what will yet be. They are images of hope, of feasts shared and tears wiped away.

The following Sundays also look to a time to come. The writer of the letter to the Hebrews tells of a time when Christ will come again, not to die for sin but to save the faithful. The prophet Daniel describes the coming of Michael, the archangel, to defeat evil and bring in deliverance. Jesus speaks of signs of the end times. Finally the month ends with the festival of Christ the King, with its images of fiery thrones, of Alpha and Omega, of a kingdom not of this world.

November is about promises. It is a time in between, moving us from now to then. As the calendar turns from one season to another, the church points us from one world to another. November says the old is passing away, true, but more is to come. While the calendar holds out the promise of December, of the turn of a new year, faith promises a new world, a new king, a new life.

But even more than that, November is about reality, about what matters most. The place of this month in the calendar seems to suggest that what went before was important, and what is to come is more important yet, but the time in between is not quite real. In a similar way the liturgical calendar creates this nonseason of November. It serves as bridge from the activities of summer, of the life of faith lived fully, to the season of Advent, of awaiting the ultimate. Look, it says, the real is yet to come. Rejoice in what is here, but rejoice as well in what will yet be!

ENVIRONMENT AND ART FOR THE SEASON

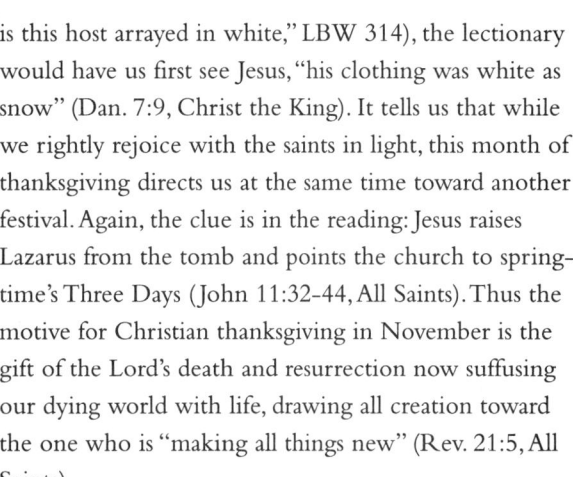

"The Lord will permit us to gather in joy and gladness to celebrate the day of death as a birth day in memory of those athletes who have gone before, and to train and make ready those who come hereafter" *(The Martyrdom of Bishop Polycarp).*

In the words of this second-century letter, we hear the distant origins of a thanksgiving festival for the saints. As the myrrh-bearing women came to the tomb of Jesus, so early Christians would gather at the tombs of their beloved dead—witnesses to Christ—and hold a thanksgiving meal to celebrate their true birthday, the day of their entrance into eternal life.

Ancient Christian cemeteries throughout the Mediterranean world reveal the images and colors that surrounded those who gathered to celebrate this great harvest into heaven. We see garlands of pale green leaves and russet or gold flowers, olive trees bearing ripe olives, large bowls filled to overflowing with apples, pears, oranges, pineapples, grape clusters, and nuts, doves with olive branches in their mouths, peacocks spreading their deep, iridescent green plumage, angels holding wreaths of laurel leaf, shepherds carrying sheep on their shoulders, and Jonah popping out of the sea monster's mouth.

Yet the image that appears repeatedly is the banquet scene in which the people at table are clothed in white robes. "On this mountain the LORD of hosts will make for all peoples a feast of rich food, a feast of well-aged wines . . . [and] he will swallow up death forever" (Isa. 25:6, 7, All Saints). The irony should be obvious: a great meal is prepared at which death itself is swallowed up. So, in the cemetery—a place of death—Christians have praised the one who promises the end of death. Here, then, is the vision the church celebrates in November: the communion of all the saints—living and dead—welcomed to a great banquet and surrounded by images and colors of the resurrection.

At the end of harvesttime, when the land looks like a place of death in many parts of North America, November is clothed in white. While we might think of that great and numberless host dressed in robes ("Who is this host arrayed in white," LBW 314), the lectionary would have us first see Jesus, "his clothing was white as snow" (Dan. 7:9, Christ the King). It tells us that while we rightly rejoice with the saints in light, this month of thanksgiving directs us at the same time toward another festival. Again, the clue is in the reading: Jesus raises Lazarus from the tomb and points the church to springtime's Three Days (John 11:32-44, All Saints). Thus the motive for Christian thanksgiving in November is the gift of the Lord's death and resurrection now suffusing our dying world with life, drawing all creation toward the one who is "making all things new" (Rev. 21:5, All Saints).

The logic of this one-month "season" begins with All Saints and ends with the festival of Christ the King. The color for these two festivals is white, the two intervening Sundays (November 12 and 19) returning to green. A strict interpretation of the calendar might lead one to conclude: a white, two greens, and a white. But why not clothe the entire month in white and thus maintain a visual unity as the church moves from All Saints to Christ the King? Why not add the darker shades of late autumn to this white foundation? If your space will allow for such colors, consider russet (a brownish red), deep gold, pale ochre, yellow (but hold the mustard), darker shades of green, and maroon. These autumnal colorings will set off this month of thanksgiving for the great harvest into heaven's barn.

If you incorporate "harvest" elements into your worship space, consider these three points. First, the church celebrates thanksgiving for many different kinds of harvests each week when it gathers for the eucharist (Greek for thanksgiving). While we rejoice in the harvest of the land, our understanding of that harvest is shaped by the meaning of the church's thanksgiving meal (not the other way around). Thus, any harvest decoration will appear in a secondary fashion to the table, the gifts of bread and wine, and food for the poor.

Second, what constitutes the harvest in your neck of the woods? Pumpkins, corn, and gourds are not indigenous to every region of the country. What fruits, vegetables, grains, vines, or trees are sources for arrangements, garlands, or wreaths in your part of the world? In other words, use your own elements, not imports, and certainly nothing artificial. For instance, sheaves of wheat or autumn vines may adorn the processional cross for the month of November. Tie the wheat bundles or vines with gold or white ribbons. Third, widen your vision of what merits "decoration." Massing corn stalks and overflowing cornucopia around a chancel, altar, or font simply reinforces the notion that the space is a performance hall. What of the space surrounding the people themselves (where they enter, where they sit, where they gather for hospitality)?

Few acts of pastoral care are more needed today than attentiveness to those who mourn the loss of loved ones. Our society offers virtually no places where one can speak honestly about death and loss within the context of Christian hope other than the church (and even in the churches it can be difficult at times). The opportunity to acknowledge this reality in the liturgy is a crying need. November is one month in which people can be drawn to a context in which their deepest sadness and hope can be recognized with no need to fix everything.

Some congregations have begun a practice that has received a grateful and enthusiastic response. In late October, perhaps the two weeks before All Saints Sunday, a new and handsome memorial book is placed on a solid and simple stand in the narthex, next to the baptismal font, or at the crossing. Either the paschal candle or two burning torches/candles are placed to the sides of the stand. Worshipers are encouraged in the monthly newsletter, worship service folder, and with the occasional announcement to write the names of their beloved dead in the book. If a small number of names appear in the book, they may be read during the prayers on All Saints Sunday ("We offer thanksgiving to God for the lives of the faithful departed: [names]"). If the book holds quite a few names, they may be read in sections throughout the Sundays of November.

In some congregations, the people are invited to bring framed photographs (usually no larger than 4"-by-6") of their beloved dead on the Saturday before All Saints Sunday. These photographs may be arranged on an unused "high" altar, in a side chapel, or on a white cloth-covered table or stands next to the baptismal font. Small pictures or icons of the saints may be interspersed among the photographs. Invite the people to spend time looking at the faces of this community's saints.

One way in which we honor the memory of the dead is by caring for their graves. Some congregations were established with a parish cemetery, many times right next door to the church building. Others have a cemetery at some distance from the church. In either case, this season of November is the opportunity to decorate the cemetery entryway with evergreen wreaths or garlands, to hold a brief memorial service at the graves, and to place appropriate psalm texts, prayers from the funeral liturgy, and a few well-known hymn texts in weatherproof holders so that people can use them when they visit the graves.

In one congregation, as people leave the All Saints worship services, small bundles of spring bulbs, wrapped in tissue and tied with bright ribbons, are handed out to everyone: just in time to plant them for spring, a fitting sign of the resurrection and an obvious link between November's festivals and the Three Days.

NOVEMBER

PREACHING with the SEASON

"Sunday morning is the practice of a counter life through counter speech."

With this sentence, Walter Brueggemann describes preaching and worship within the Christian community (*Finally Comes the Poet: Daring Speech for Proclamation*, Fortress Press, p. 3). These words offer an apt description for preaching on these last Sundays of the liturgical year, filled with odd texts that run counter to the texts of the culture. By now we have learned to write the year 2000 on our checks. All the zeroes give us the sense of open-ended time stretching out before us. But the readings for this season point us beyond the new millennium to the end of time. The picture of Christian discipleship in these November readings could be described in words attributed to Flannery O'Connor in her paraphrase of John 8: "You will know the truth, and the truth will make you odd."

The odd truth of the gospel might well be the theme for these last days of the liturgical year. Departing from the rhythm of the long Pentecost season, the first Sunday of November gathers us all in the communion of saints. "Ordinary time" is suspended as past, present, and future are held together in one piece. It is easy to forget how odd these familiar All Saints texts are! We hear extravagant promises of life in the midst of the reality of death. Isaiah, Revelation, and the gospel of John paint pictures of the odd truth we say by heart in the words of the Apostles' Creed: "I believe in the holy catholic Church, the communion of saints, the forgiveness of sins, the resurrection of the body, and the life everlasting." As Martin Luther wrote in his explanation to the creed: "This is most certainly true." Or, as the seer of Revelation dared to say, "these words are trustworthy and true"—in spite of evidence to the contrary. Readings for November 12 dare to call *empty full* when two widows share center stage as witnesses to the oddness of God's abundant life. On November 19, Jesus startles the disciples and us by calling signs of the end "birth pangs!" November 26 brings the liturgical year to an end as we stand before Pilate with Jesus. The Sunday we name Christ the King focuses on the one who refused to be king on this world's terms. These texts are indeed counterspeech calling us to a counterlife in Christ.

This season might also focus on the *countertruth* of the gospel. Such a series might move back a week to begin with Reformation Sunday (October 29), then continuing through the end of November. Thus, we would begin and end with John's gospel, with passages about truth. Jesus' words in John 8 are the starting point: "You will know the truth and the truth will set you free." The series ends with Jesus' words to Pilate: "For this I was born, and for this I came into the world, to testify to the truth. Everyone who belongs to the truth listens to my voice" (John 18:37b). John's gospel can be a resource for reviewing the whole church year. We move back to the gospel for Christmas Day: "And the Word became flesh and lived among us . . . full of grace and truth . . ." (John 1:14). The Greek philosophers thought it odd indeed that the eternal cosmic *logos* would condescend to pitch a tent among mortals. Jesus' lively encounter with the Samaritan woman in John 4 points to another facet of truth: "God is spirit, and those who worship God must worship in spirit and truth." Isn't it odd that a Samaritan woman became one of the first to invite others to see the Messiah? It is also odd that Jesus' strong declaration of the truth on Reformation Sunday comes in the same chapter as the woman accused of adultery. Though her accusers had the facts on their side, Jesus bent down to be with the woman in the vicious circle (John 8: 6-7). Knowing the truth is not the same as having the facts.

These November Sundays are framed by readings from the book of Revelation. We turn to the end of Revelation at the beginning of November: "I saw a new heaven and a new earth. . . . I am the Alpha and the Omega, the beginning and the end" (Rev. 21:1, 6). At the end of November, we go back to the first chapter and hear God's wondrous promise at the end of the church year: " 'I am the Alpha and the Omega,' says the Lord

God, who is and who was and who is to come, the Almighty" (Rev. 1:8). No doubt, the book of Revelation has been in the spotlight as we entered this new millennium. The counterspeech of Revelation has often been misused and misinterpreted as a word of judgment on *our* enemies—whether those enemies are the former USSR, the present-day Cuba, or certain people we think God ought to condemn. These appointed readings from Revelation offer an opportunity to relate the themes for the end of the liturgical year to the millennium that has opened before us. What word does the seer of Revelation speak to us as we near the end of the year 2000?

We cannot escape the end time in these last days of the liturgical year—even though the new millennium seems to stretch endlessly before us. The counterspeech of the gospel proclaims that we should not try to escape. Jesus tells his disciples that the signs of the end times—wars and rumors of wars, nation rising against nation and kingdom against kingdom—are "but the beginning of the birth pangs" (Mark 13:8b). It is such an odd thing to say! But Christian teaching about last things (eschatology) is odd; it is counterspeech at its finest. Theologian Jürgen Moltmann talks about different ways of looking at the future. He notes a distinction between *extrapolation* and *anticipation* (lecture, Pennsylvania Conference of Churches, November 7, 1995). *Extrapolation* means studying current realities in order to plan into the future: how many hospitals or schools will be needed in 2020? Where do new highways need to be built? How will this drought effect crop yields and hungry people over the next ten years? Extrapolation is a valid enterprise. But when the church speaks of eschatology, our witness is not based on extrapolation. Christians move toward the end of time in *anticipation*: God's promises are trustworthy and will someday be fulfilled. These promises, already breaking into the present, will be completed in God's good time. We cannot fully know these promises by extrapolating from demographic data or deciphering clues in the symbol system of Revelation. Eschatology *anticipates* God's surprise of a new heaven and a new earth. As the first liturgical year of this millennium ends, we rest secure in God who is and who was and who is to come. We trust the counterspeech of the gospel expressed in the words of Hebrews (proper 28): "Let us hold fast to the confession of our hope without wavering, for [the one] who has promised is faithful" (Heb. 10:23).

This odd, hopeful word is desperately needed in this new millennium. As Walter Brueggemann reminds us, "The church on Sunday morning, or whenever it engages in its odd speech, may be the last place left in our society for imaginative speech that permits people to enter into new worlds of faith and to participate in joyous, obedient life" (*Finally Comes the Poet*, p. 3).

SHAPE OF WORSHIP FOR THE SEASON

BASIC SHAPE OF THE EUCHARISTIC RITE IN NOVEMBER

- Confession and Forgiveness: see alternate worship text for November in *Sundays and Seasons*

GATHERING

- Greeting: see alternate worship text for November in *Sundays and Seasons*
- Omit the Kyrie during November (except on the festivals of All Saints and Christ the King)
- Use the hymn of praise throughout November (or use "This is the feast" just for the festivals of All Saints and Christ the King)

WORD

- Use the Nicene Creed for the festivals of All Saints and Christ the King. Use the Apostles' Creed for the remainder of the month.
- Prayers: see alternate forms and responses for November in *Sundays and Seasons*
- Incorporate the names of those who have died into one of the prayer petitions on All Saints Sunday

BAPTISM
- Consider observing All Saints Sunday (November 5) as a baptismal festival

MEAL
- Offertory prayer: see alternate worship text for November in *Sundays and Seasons*
- Use the proper preface for Sundays after Pentecost (see *LBW* Ministers edition, and *WOV* Leaders edition for each musical setting of the liturgy); for the festival of All Saints, use the proper preface for All Saints
- Eucharistic prayer: in addition to four main options in *LBW*, see "Eucharistic Prayer I: November" in *WOV* Leaders edition, p. 73
- Invitation to communion: see alternate worship text for November in *Sundays and Seasons*
- Post-communion prayer: see alternate worship text for November in *Sundays and Seasons*

SENDING
- Benediction: see alternate worship text for November in *Sundays and Seasons*
- Dismissal: see alternate worship text for November in *Sundays and Seasons*

ASSEMBLY SONG FOR THE SEASON

In November we open our ears to the song of the assembly: those from every people, nation, and language, gathered forever around the throne of the Lamb. How can we, here and now, echo in some way the depth and breadth of that sonority?

GATHERING
Music of the gathering rite may continue the post-Pentecost pattern of using the hymn of praise but not the Kyrie (except on Christ the King). Or, in light of the movement toward the end time and the approach of Advent, using the Kyrie alone may help to make the bridge. Choose entrance hymns that raise the sights of the assembly to their participation in the greater song of all creation and of the whole company of heaven.

WORD
Since both All Saints Day and Christ the King include an Alpha and Omega text, Donald Busarow's verse setting for Christ the King (AFP 11-9540) might be used throughout the month, with choir or cantor singing the proper section (Rev. 21:6) and the assembly joining on the alleluias. The practice of remembering with thanksgiving the names of the faithful departed might be framed with music. Let the names be interspersed with the singing of the Taizé refrain "Beati in domo Domini" (*Music from Taizé*, vol. 1, GIA Publications).

MEAL
Continue the use of "Let the vineyards be fruitful" as the offertory song, or learn a grand Finnish folk song, "Arise, my soul, arise!" (LBW 516) for this procession. (Stanza 2, with its reference to "the great amen," might be saved to be sung as an acclamation at the conclusion of the eucharistic prayer.) An exciting contemporary alternative for the offertory is Graham Kendrick's "The trumpets sound" (W&P). Consider also the eucharistic acclamations set to the music of LAND OF REST (WOV 616). For the communion, select from the many hymns and songs that revel in the imagery of the eschatological banquet.

SENDING
"Thine the amen, thine the praise" (WOV 801) ties together many of the images of November and could well be used each week as a sending hymn; because of this hymn's expansiveness it may be best to omit the post-communion canticle.

MUSIC FOR THE SEASON

VERSE AND OFFERTORY

Busarow, Donald J. *Verses and Offertories, Pentecost 21–Christ the King.* AFP 11-9540.

Cherwien, David. *Verses for the Fall Festivals.* MSM 80-880. U/SATB, opt brass, org.

CHORAL MUSIC FOR THE SEASON

Bengtson, Bruce. "There'll Be Something in Heaven." AFP 12-113. SATB.

Broege, Timothy. "Four Motets of the Revelation." BRN B238261-358. SATB.

Burkhardt, Michael. "Like the Murmur of the Dove's Song." MSM 60-5000. 2 pt mxd, cong, ob, org.

Chepponis, James J. "Let Nations Sing Your Praise." GIA G-4226. Cant, cong, kybd, gtr, opt SATB, C/B-flat inst, hb.

Hassler, Hans. "Lord, Let at Last Thine Angels Come." CPH 98-1026. SATB/SATB.

Marcello, Benedetto, ed/arr. Dale Grotenhuis. "O God, Creator." MSM 50-9420. 2 pt vcs, kybd.

Parker, Alice, arr. "Hark, I Hear the Harps Eternal." LAW 51331. SATB.

Powell, Robert J. "My Heart Is Steadfast, O God." CPH 98-3352. SATB, org.

Schalk, Carl. "I Saw a New Heaven and a New Earth." AFP 11-10813. Also in *The Augsburg Choirbook.* 11-10817. SATB.

Trinkley, Bruce. "Do, Lord, Remember Me." AFP 11-10727. SATB, pno.

CHILDREN'S CHORAL MUSIC FOR THE SEASON

Gallagher, Barbara. "As We Worship You, O Lord." GIA G-4512. U/2 pt, kybd.

McIver, Robert. "Shall We Gather at the River?" CG CGA688. Combined U and SATB, pno, opt trbl inst.

Pooler, Marie. "Sing to the Lord of Harvest" in *Unison and Two-Part Anthems.* AFP 11-9517. U/2 pt, kybd.

Wood, Dale. "Jubilate Deo." AFP 11-1646. SA, org, opt perc.

INSTRUMENTAL MUSIC FOR THE SEASON

Bach, J. S. "Pièce d'Orgue." Various ed. Org.

Cherwien, David. "Partita on 'For All the Saints.'" CPH 97-9139. Org.

Lachenauer, George. "Cantad Al Señor" in *Three Hispanic Carols.* GIA G-4494. Org.

Lachenauer, George. "Con Que Pagaremos?" in *Three Hispanic Carols.* GIA G-4494. Org.

Langlois, Kristina. "Cantad Al Señor" in *Five Hymns of Praise.* MSM 10-722. Org.

Lovelace, Austin. "Variations on 'Holy, Holy, Holy.'" SEL 160-727. Org.

Reger, Max. "Benedictus." PET 3114. Org.

HANDBELL MUSIC FOR THE SEASON

Fauré, G./arr. McChesney. "Pavane." AFP 11-10318. 3 oct.

Hopson, Hal. "Psalm 100." AFP 11-10524. 3-5 oct.

Kinyon, Barbara. "Rejoice, the Lord Is King." HOP 1931. 3-6 oct.

Loiacono. "Carry Me Home." CG CGB 180. 3 oct.

Moklebust, Cathy and David. "Lift High the Cross." CG CGB192/193/194. 3-5 oct, brass, org, cong.

Wagner, Douglas. "Sine Nomine." HOP 1271. 3-5 oct.

NOVEMBER

ALTERNATE WORSHIP TEXTS

CONFESSION AND FORGIVENESS

In the name of the Father, and of the ☩ Son,
and of the Holy Spirit.
Amen

Let us approach God with a true heart,
in full assurance of God's power
to heal and to forgive.
Silence for reflection and self-examination.

Merciful God,
**you have loved your people
from the beginning of time,
desiring that we also love you
and our neighbor with fullness of heart.
We confess that we have often sought wealth
or betterment for ourselves,
without acting generously toward others.
Redirect our commitments,
that they might reflect your will for us
and your creation. Amen**

God has promised that everyone who calls
on the name of the Lord shall be saved.
As an ordained minister of the church of Christ,
and by his authority, I declare to you pardon,
forgiveness, and remission of all your sins.
Amen

GREETING

God is Alpha and Omega, the first and the last,
the one who is, and who was, and who is to come.
The grace of our Lord Jesus Christ, the love of God,
and the communion of the Holy Spirit be with you all.
And also with you.

PRAYERS

In communion with all the saints,
let us pray to God who is our eternal home.
A brief silence.

Each petition ends:
Lord, in your mercy,
hear our prayer.

Concluding petition
Your reign, O God, endures forever, and in Christ we are free to be your saints and servants. Hear our prayers for the sake of him who died and rose again, and lives with you in the company of all your saints in light.
Amen

OFFERTORY PRAYER

Generous God,
**your jar of meal will not be emptied,
and your heavenly banquet will last for eternity.
Through the gift of this sacrament,
transform us to be servants
of your humble and eternal reign. Amen**

INVITATION TO COMMUNION

The Lord of hosts makes for all peoples
a feast of rich food, a feast of well-aged wines.
**This is the Lord for whom we have waited;
let us be glad and rejoice in God's salvation.**

POST-COMMUNION PRAYER

By your word and sacraments, O God,
you have given us a foretaste of
the new heaven and new earth
that will be ours forever.
Strengthen us in this vision
that we might draw others to believe
in the hope that is ours,
through Jesus Christ our Lord.
Amen

BENEDICTION

May almighty God,
who makes all things new in Jesus Christ,
uphold you by the Spirit in times of trial
and bring you at last to the heavenly Jerusalem.
Amen

DISMISSAL

Go in peace to love God and serve your neighbor.
Thanks be to God.

SUNDAYS & SEASONS

SEASONAL RITES

VIGIL OF ALL SAINTS
This order of worship may be used on All Hallows' Eve, October 31, or the evening before All Saints Sunday.

SERVICE OF LIGHT
A lit paschal candle may be processed during the versicles and placed in its stand near the altar.

VERSICLES
These versicles may be sung to the tones given in evening prayer, LBW, p. 142.

In the new Jerusalem there will be no need of | sun or moon,
for the glory of God will be its | light.
Before the Lamb is a multitude from | every nation,
and they worship God night and | day.
Surely he is | coming soon.
Amen. Come, Lord | Jesus.

HYMN OF LIGHT
The principal hymn of light is given on p. 143 of LBW. Other hymns that may be sung in its place include "Oh, gladsome light" (LBW 279), "Christ, mighty Savior" (WOV 729), and "That Easter day with joy was bright" (LBW 154). The last hymn mentioned may also be sung to PUER NOBIS (LBW 36) if the "Alleluia" is omitted at the end of each stanza.

THANKSGIVING FOR LIGHT
Set to music on p. 144 of LBW.

The Lord be with you.
And also with you.
Let us give thanks to the Lord our God.
It is right to give our thanks and praise.
Blessed are you, O Lord our God, king of the universe,
who led your people Israel by a pillar of cloud by day
and a pillar of fire by night:
Enlighten our darkness by the light of your Christ;
may his Word be a lamp to our feet and a light to our path;
for you are merciful, and you love your whole creation,
and we, your creatures, glorify you, Father, Son, and Holy Spirit.
Amen

Sit

LITURGY OF THE WORD

FIRST READING
Genesis 12:1-8
Response: Psalm 113

SECOND READING
Daniel 6:(1-15)16-23
Response: Psalm 116

THIRD READING
Hebrews 11:32—12:2
Response: Psalm 149

FOURTH READING
Revelation 7:2-4, 9-17

Stand
CANTICLE OF PRAISE
Worthy is Christ (This is the Feast)
Several settings of this hymn are available.

GOSPEL READING
Matthew 5:1-12

Sit
SERMON

Stand
HYMN OF THE DAY
LBW 194   All who believe and are baptized
LBW 358   Glories of your name are spoken
WOV 690   Shall we gather at the river
WOV 695   O blessed spring

THANKSGIVING FOR BAPTISM

If possible, the people may gather around the font. After the prayer all worshipers may dip their hands in the font, making the sign of the cross in remembrance of baptism.

The Lord be with you.
And also with you.
Let us give thanks to the Lord our God.
It is right to give our thanks and praise.
Holy God and mighty Lord, we give you thanks
for you nourish and sustain us and all living things
with the gift of water.
In the beginning your Spirit moved over the waters
and you created heaven and earth.
By the waters of the flood you saved Noah and his family.
You led Israel through the sea out of slavery
into the promised land.
In the waters of the Jordan
your Son was baptized by John and anointed with the Spirit.
By the baptism of his death and resurrection
your Son set us free from sin and death
and opened the way to everlasting life.
We give you thanks, O God,
that you have given us new life in the water of baptism.
Buried with Christ in his death,
you raise us to share in his resurrection
by the power of the Holy Spirit.
Through it we are united to your saints of every time and place,
who proclaim your reign
and surround our steps as we journey
toward the new and eternal Jerusalem.
May all who have passed through the water of baptism
continue in the risen life of our Savior.
To you be all honor and glory, now and forever.
Amen

Sit

LITURGY OF THE EUCHARIST

After all have returned to their places, the Holy Communion continues with the preparation of the altar and the presentation of the gifts.

Notes on the service:
   - The psalm responses to the readings may be sung or spoken by the assembly.
   - The Canticle of Praise is sung.
   - If the people cannot gather at the font, the worship leaders may process there during the singing of the hymn of the day.
   - If this vigil liturgy is not to conclude with the liturgy of the eucharist, it may conclude in a manner similar to evening prayer, as indicated on p. 152 of LBW Ministers edition.

NOVEMBER 5, 2000

ALL SAINTS SUNDAY

INTRODUCTION

All Saints Sunday celebrates the baptized people of God, living and dead, who make up the body of Christ. With thanksgiving we remember all the faithful departed, especially those most dear to us who have died. Today's readings are filled with rich images of the eternal life promised to all the saints. The holy meal is a foretaste of that great and promised feast where death or pain will be no more. Even in the midst of loss and grief God wipes away the tears from our eyes and makes all things new.

PRAYER OF THE DAY

Almighty God, whose people are knit together in one holy Church, the body of Christ our Lord: Grant us grace to follow your blessed saints in lives of faith and commitment, and to know the inexpressible joys you have prepared for those who love you; through your Son, Jesus Christ our Lord, who lives and reigns with you and the Holy Spirit, one God, now and forever.

READINGS

Isaiah 25:6-9

This reading focuses on the future day when the Lord will fully manifest sovereignty over the universe. On that day, the Lord will host a banquet for God's faithful subjects. This banquet symbolizes the establishment of the Lord's dominion on earth. It symbolizes the joy, companionship, and prosperity that will characterize the Lord's reign.

or Wisdom of Solomon 3:1-9

Psalm 24

They shall receive a blessing from the God of their salvation. (Ps. 24:5)

Revelation 21:1-6a

In the book of Revelation, John describes his vision of heaven, where the saints of God will live in light and glory. Of all the blessings found there, none will exceed that of simply being with God.

John 11:32-44

Through the raising of Lazarus, Jesus offers the world a vision of the life to come, when death and weeping will be no more.

COLOR White

THE PRAYERS

In communion with all the saints, let us pray to God who is our eternal home.

SILENCE IS KEPT.

O God our Alpha and our Omega, empower your church to remain faithful to you and to proclaim your salvation from day to day. Lord, in your mercy,

hear our prayer.

O Ruler of earth and heaven, strengthen all who seek to serve in offices of government, and guide all citizens who participate in the political process. Lord, in your mercy,

hear our prayer.

O Comforter of priceless worth, bless those who look to you for comfort in time of illness (especially . . .). Lord, in your mercy,

hear our prayer.

O Lover of our souls, we remember all those who are at rest in your great love and whose names we call to mind in this moment *(names of those who have recently died are mentioned)*. As they blessed us in life, we give you thanks for the blessing of their memory in death. Lord, in your mercy,

hear our prayer.

HERE OTHER INTERCESSIONS MAY BE OFFERED.

O Hope of the world to come, strengthen our hope that one day we will dwell with you in that new Jerusalem, where our every tear will be dried and our mourning will be turned into dancing. Lord, in your mercy,

hear our prayer.

Your reign, O God, endures forever, and in Christ we are free to be your saints and servants. Hear our prayers for the sake of him who died and rose again, and lives with you in the company of all your saints in light.

Amen

IMAGES FOR PREACHING

Today we have a feast of readings from the rich food and aged wines of Isaiah's mountain to the vision of a new heaven and a new earth in Revelation. And in the midst of these cosmic visions is the tender touch of God's hand wiping the tears from our faces, wiping away even Jesus' tears at the grave of his friend Lazarus. It's hard to choose one and leave the others behind. It may be a day to give ourselves permission to weave all three together in a tapestry for all the saints.

Some at worship will not hear anything but the name of their loved one who died within the year past. But as much as they can hear, and for those whose sorrow is not so close at hand, let the images in these texts be unleashed! Invite people up to the mountain of God. Spread the table before them filled with a feast more sumptuous than the best church potluck. (You know what your congregation would want to see there!) While everyone is eating and drinking, don't miss the light breaking in, for the shroud that covered everything is gone. The deep despair we thought would never go away is lifting. Then look, another vision comes from the far end of time. Let it come in both mystery and certainty: death will be no more; mourning and crying will be no more. This word is trustworthy and true.

And in the midst of these grand visions, go with Jesus to the cemetery. It is the earth-bound place of weeping and blaming: "Lord, if you had been here, my brother would not have died." The smell of death is in the air and visions seem far away. But Lazarus comes forth from the grave, the first of many to be raised up. Past and present and future swirl together beyond our comprehension. "See, I am making all things new," says God. This is the word of the Lord.

WORSHIP MATTERS

All Saints Day reminds us of two important realities. First, it reminds us that all of the baptized die into the fellowship of the saints. We affirm as much when we state that we believe in the "communion of saints." Hence, in death we are neither cut off from God nor from the church. Second, All Saints Day reminds us that we celebrate the eucharist in fellowship with all the saints on earth and in heaven. For this reason the eucharistic prayer asks God to "join our prayers with those of your servants of every time and every place and unite them with the ceaseless petitions of our great high priest until he comes as victorious Lord of all."

In worship we can affirm our unity with the saints in heaven in a number of ways. Those who have died into Christ during the week can and should be remembered in the Sunday intercessions. All of those who died during the previous year may be remembered in one petition on All Saints Sunday. In many churches the names of the faithful departed are entered into a special book and are read at this petition.

Does your congregation recognize the contributions of its faithful departed? Does it remember its saints in the Sunday liturgy?

LET THE CHILDREN COME

If baptisms are scheduled for today, why not have the children of the congregation bring forward the water, oil, garments, and candles for those being baptized? Have a crucifer lead the baptismal party to the font and back again into the congregation. Let Lazarus make an appearance in these newborn Christians and let them be clothed in the white robes of the saints who have been washed in the blood of the Lamb. The presiding minister should give careful attention to the actions of baptism so that they are done reverently and are visible and audible for all.

MUSIC FOR WORSHIP

GATHERING

LBW 352	I know that my Redeemer lives!
WOV 690	Shall we gather at the river

PSALM 24

Comer, Marilyn. PW, cycle B.
Gieseke, R. "Lift Up Your Heads." CPH 98-2959. U/2pt, cong.
Harbor, Rawn. "Lift Up Your Heads" in *This Far by Faith*.
Mahnke, Allen. "Fling Wide the Gates." CPH 98-2983. U, cong.
Smith, Geoffrey Boulton. "Stretch Towards Heaven" in PS, vol. 1.
WOV 631   Lift up your heads, O gates (paraphrase)

HYMN OF THE DAY

LBW 175   Ye watchers and ye holy ones
            Lasst uns erfreuen

VOCAL RESOURCES

Powell, Robert J. "Ye Watchers and Ye Holy Ones." GIA G-2427. SATB, brass, timp.

INSTRUMENTAL RESOURCES

Burkhardt, Michael. "From All That Dwell Below the Skies" in *Five Psalm Hymn Improvisations*. MSM 10-511. Org.
Porter, Rachel Trelstad. "Lasst uns erfreuen" in *Day by Day: Hymn Arrangements for Piano*. AFP 11-10772. Pno.

Sedio, Mark. "Lasst uns erfreuen" in *Music for the Paschal Season*.
AFP 11-10763. Org.

Tryggestad, David. "Lasst uns erfreuen" in *Deo Gracias*. AFP 11-10471.
Org.

ALTERNATE HYMN OF THE DAY

| LBW 369 | The Church's one foundation |
| WOV 764 | Blest are they |

COMMUNION

| LBW 330 | In heaven above |
| WOV 702 | I am the Bread of life |

OTHER SUGGESTIONS

Young, Jeremy. "Taste and See." AFP 11-10895. 2 pt, kybd, opt cong.

SENDING

| LBW 337 | Oh, what their joy |
| WOV 801 | Thine the amen, thine the praise |

ADDITIONAL HYMNS AND SONGS

DATH 102	Death be never last
H82 545	Lo! what a cloud of witnesses
TFF 180	Oh, when the saints go marching in
W&P	The trumpets sound, the angels sing

MUSIC FOR THE DAY

CHORAL

Bainton, Edgar. "And I Saw a New Heaven." NOV 15431. SATB, org.

Fauré, Gabriel. "In Paradisum" in *Requiem*. KAL 6166. SATB, org.

Jenkins, Steve. "Around the Throne." MSM 50-8102. SATB, fl, opt hb, org.

Lassus, Orlando. "Justorum animae" (The souls of the righteous). ION CH-1024 SSATB.

Mathias, William. "O How Amiable Are Thy Dwellings." OXF A342. SATB, org.

Schalk, Carl. "I Saw a New Heaven and a New Earth." AFP 11-10803. Also in *The Augsburg Choirbook*. 11-10817. SATB.

Shute, Linda. "Who Are These Like Stars Appearing." AFP 11-10946. SATB, org.

Svedlund, Karl-Erik/ed. Bruce Bengston. "There'll Be Something in Heaven." AFP 12-113. SATB.

Young, Jeremy. "Taste and See." AFP 11-10895. U/2 pt, kybd, opt cong.

CHILDREN'S CHOIRS

Christopherson, Dorothy. "Still Small Voice." AFP 11-10453. U/2 pt, pno, fl, perc.

Exner, Max. "Saints of God." AFP 11-2356. U, kybd.

Hassell, Michael. "I Sing a Song of the Saints of God." 2 pt treb, pno, fl.

Hobby, Robert. "Verse for All Saints Day." MSM 80-810. 2 pt mxd, org.

Hopson, Hal H. "Open the Gates." CG CGA621. U, kybd, opt desc, opt cong, opt 3 oct hb.

KEYBOARD/INSTRUMENTAL

Biery, Marilyn. "Lazarus" in *Meditations on the Love of God*. MSM 10-949. Org.

Cherwien, David. "For All the Saints" in *Postludes on Well Known Hymns*. AFP 11-10795. Org.

Haas, David. "Trio on 'Blest Are They'" in *Laudate, vol. 2*. CPH 97-6508. Org.

Proulx, Richard. "Variations on 'Sine Nomine.'" MSM 10-810. Org.

HANDBELL

Afdahl, Lee J. "Rejoice in God's Saints." AFP 11-10808. 3-5 oct, opt perc.

Vaughan Williams/arr. Betty Garee. "Sine Nomine" (For all the Saints). AGEHR AG46003. 4-6 oct; AGC 021. Full score; AGC 028. Choral pt; AGC 028. Org, opt SATB, cong.

PRAISE ENSEMBLE

Crouch, Andrae. "My Tribute." in *All God's People Sing!* CPH.

Crouch, Andrae/arr. Jack Schrader. "Soon and Very Soon." HOP GC952. SATB, pno. Also available SAB (GC984), TTBB (GC976).

Gaither, William. "Because He Lives" in *Hymns for the Family of God*. Paragon Associates, Inc.

Mason. "All Rise" in *With All My Heart Songbook*. WRD.

McRae, Shirley. "The King of Glory Comes" in *Lift Up Your Voices.*" CG CGA622. U/2pt, Orff.

Tunney, Dick and Melodie/arr. Wilson. "God's Love Never Changes." HOP GC961. SATB, kybd.

NOVEMBER 5, 2000

TWENTY-FIRST SUNDAY AFTER PENTECOST
PROPER 26

INTRODUCTION

In today's gospel Jesus speaks of the two great commandments—love of God, and love of neighbor—yet how difficult it is to observe them diligently. A well-known prayer of confession includes these words: "We have not loved you with our whole heart; we have not loved our neighbors as ourselves." As we hear the word and share the meal we receive the forgiveness, strength, and courage to offer our lives in God's service, loving God through our gracious acts of mercy and kindness.

PRAYER OF THE DAY

Stir up, O Lord, the wills of your faithful people to seek more eagerly the help you offer, that, at the last, they may enjoy the fruit of salvation; through our Lord Jesus Christ.

READINGS

Deuteronomy 6:1-9
> As Israel enters the promised land, the people are bid to keep the Law in future generations. Verses 4-5 are called the Shema, which is used in Jewish daily prayer.

Psalm 119:1-8
> Happy are they who seek the LORD with all their hearts. (Ps. 119:2)

Hebrews 9:11-14
> The sacrifice of Christ, the high priest, not only cleanses from ritual impurity, but brings about forgiveness and thus the worship of the living God.

Mark 12:28-34
> When a scribe asks Jesus which commandment is first of all, Jesus answers that love of God and love of neighbor are interconnected and define the heart of the kingdom of God.

ALTERNATE FIRST READING/PSALM

Ruth 1:1-18
> In this reading, Ruth, a foreign (Moabite) woman, goes beyond duty to stay with her Israelite mother-in-law and expose herself to life in a strange land by accompanying Naomi to live in Bethlehem.

Psalm 146
> The LORD lifts up those who are bowed down. (Ps. 146:7)

COLOR Green

THE PRAYERS

In communion with all the saints, let us pray to God who is our eternal home.
SILENCE IS KEPT.

Guide your church, O God, and give it courage to proclaim your gospel in a culture of change and doubt. Lord, in your mercy,
hear our prayer.

(U.S.)
In this week of national elections, O God, keep this nation in your care. Guide the president, all elected officials, and any who serve in public office. Lord, in your mercy,
hear our prayer.

Care for those who are overlooked, have compassion on those who are forgotten, and grant your gift of healing to all who struggle with ill health (especially . . .). Lord, in your mercy,
hear our prayer.

Guide those who are making inquiry into the faith, and all who wish to explore the baptized life among us. Give them strength in their exploration, and keep them in the nurture of this community. Lord, in your mercy,
hear our prayer.

HERE OTHER INTERCESSIONS MAY BE OFFERED.

Sanctify the memory of all your saints, and especially those who have recently died. Keep us in fellowship with them always in your eternal love. Lord, in your mercy,
hear our prayer.

Your reign, O God, endures forever, and in Christ we are free to be your saints and servants. Hear our prayers for the sake of him who died and rose again, and lives with you in the company of all your saints in light.
Amen

IMAGES FOR PREACHING

It was out of concern for tradition that one of the scribes asked Jesus in today's gospel, "Which commandment is the first of all?" The questioner wanted to know whether Jesus stood within the teachings of Israel or opposed them.

The scene is really a set-up, and has all of the characteristics of a good legal debate. But Jesus rises above the debating game by going to the heart of Jewish tradition. "You shall love the Lord your God with all your heart, and with all your soul, and with all your mind, and with all your strength." Jesus went on, of course, also quoting a section of the law in Leviticus dealing with the proper conduct towards a neighbor. "You shall love your neighbor as yourself."

It is without question more difficult to practice an ethic of love than it is to treat well only those who have obeyed all of the rules. It is easier for us to have rules that clearly define who is good and who is not, so that we don't have to make any judgment calls ourselves.

Rule-bound forms of religion tell us that if you do things *right*, everything will work out. But of course we don't always do things right. In this day and age many of us understand that no one system, no one set of customs or rules will serve us in every situation. We live in an increasingly complex world where the simple tried-and-true ways don't always work.

But the bottom line for all of the commandments is to love God and to love our neighbor. If all our actions are based on love, then the rest of the commandments will take care of themselves.

WORSHIP MATTERS

For the people of Israel, all life revolved around obedience to and remembrance of God's law. The people were even commanded to wear the law on their bodies and to inscribe it on their door posts. These measures reminded the people that they were continually in the presence of God.

We Christians similarly place our lives within the context of God's presence through our daily acts of worship. Morning and evening prayers, prayers at meal time, and the celebration of baptismal anniversaries are good not only because it is our duty to worship God, but because such practices renew our sense of living in God's presence. We sometimes mistakenly believe we are in the presence of God only during the Sunday worship service. The Sunday liturgy, among other things, should remind us that all of life is spent worshiping God.

Do we train the people to worship in their daily lives? Or do we give the impression that God is present and worshiped only on Sunday mornings?

LET THE CHILDREN COME

The Hebrew *Shema* (Deut. 6:4-5) plays an important role in both the Jewish and Christian faith, since it is a summary of God's law. Help the children to learn it and encourage them to commit it to memory.

MUSIC FOR WORSHIP
GATHERING

| LBW 524 | My God, how wonderful thou art |
| WOV 762 | O day of peace |

PSALM 119

Beckstrand, William. PW, cycle B.
Walker, Christopher. "Teach Me, O God" in PS, vol. 3.

HYMN OF THE DAY

| LBW 502 | Thee will I love, my strength |
| | ICH WILL DICH LIEBEN |

INSTRUMENTAL RESOURCES

Beck, Theodore. "Ich will dich lieben" in *Thee Will I Love*. CPH 97-5207. Org.
Krapf, Gerhard. "Ich will dich lieben" in *Hymn Preludes and Free Accompaniments, vol. 13*. AFP 11-9409. Org.
Peeters, Flor. "Ich will dich lieben" in *Hymn Preludes for the Liturgical Year, opus 100, vol. XVI*. CFP 6416. Org.

ALTERNATE HYMN OF THE DAY

| WOV 797 | O God beyond all praising |
| LBW 315 | Love divine, all loves excelling |

COMMUNION

| LBW 486 | Spirit of God, descend upon my heart |
| WOV 703 | Draw us in the Spirit's tether |

OTHER SUGGESTIONS

Young, Jeremy. "Nothing Can Come between Us." AFP 11-10848. SAB, kybd, opt cong

SENDING

| LBW 480 | Oh, that the Lord would guide my ways |
| WOV 748 | Bind us together |

ADDITIONAL HYMNS AND SONGS

DATH 93	Around the Great Commandment
H82 697	My God, accept my heart this day
TFF 224	Help me, Jesus
W&P	I love you, Lord

MUSIC FOR THE DAY

CHORAL

Busarow, Donald. "Lord, Thee I Love with All My Heart."
CPH 98-3429. SATB/2 pt mxd, opt cong, ob/tpt (cl), org.

Hopson, Hal. "Canticle of Love." AFP 11-10911. SATB, org.

Marcello, Benedetto/ed. Dale Grotenhuis. "Teach Me Now, O Lord."
MSM 50-9418. 2 pt, kybd.

Scott, K. Lee. "The Call" in *Sing a Song of Joy, Vocal Solos for Worship*.
AFP 11-8194 (MH); 11-8195 (ML).

Stanford, Charles. "Beati quorum via." B&H OCTB 5318. SSATBB.

Willan, Healey. "Behold the Tabernacle of God." Composer's Forum
CM 427. SATB.

CHILDREN'S CHOIRS

Bedford, Michael. "I Will Love the Lord." CG CGA419.
U/2 pt, kybd.

Davis, Sid. "Love Divine, All Loves Excelling." MSM 50-9408. SA, kybd.

KEYBOARD/INSTRUMENTAL

Cherwien, David. "O God, Beyond All Praising" in *O God Beyond All Praising*. AFP 11-10860. Org.

Hobby, Robert A. "Where Charity and Love Prevail" in *Three Lenten Hymn Settings, Set I*. MSM 10-311. Org.

HANDBELL

Starks, Howard. "Praise to Our Creator." FLA HP 5363. 3-5 oct.

Tucker, Margaret. "Dance Rondo." BEC HB63. 2-3 oct.

PRAISE ENSEMBLE

Colvin, Tom/arr. Young. "Fill Us with Your Love." AG AG7256.
SATB, kybd.

Cymbala and Gilbert. "Make Us One" and "I Love You with the Love of the Lord" medley in *Songs for Praise and Worship*. WRD.

Fitts, Bob. "One God" in *Maranatha! Music Praise Chorus Book, 3rd ed*.
WRD/MAR.

Kendrick, Graham/arr. Jack Schrader. "Such Love." HOP GC987.
3 pt mxd, pno.

Lowry, Robert/arr. Schreiner. "Here Is Love" in *Favorite Hymns of Promise Keepers*. MAR 3010133367. 3pt, kybd.

TUESDAY, NOVEMBER 7
JOHN CHRISTIAN FREDERICK HEYER, MISSIONARY TO INDIA, 1873

Heyer did mission work in India, but he also served as an evangelist and teacher in the United States. He valued Christian education and helped establish Sunday schools in Lutheran parishes.

When our congregations consider their mission, they usually look both inward and outward. How do we teach, preach, and care for our own members? How do we reach out to the needs of our communities, especially to those in need or on the fringes of society? How do we share the good news with people who have not heard the gospel, or who live with the everyday realities of poverty or injustice? Does your congregation include all these elements in its overall ministry? Could the commemoration of Heyer invite you to review your mission statement?

SATURDAY, NOVEMBER 11
MARTIN, BISHOP OF TOURS, 397

Martin became a hermit, and was known for his care for the poor. In time he was elected bishop of Tours in France. Martin is also remembered as a saint for peace, since earlier in his life he had been a soldier who left the army because he was unable to reconcile killing someone in battle with his Christian faith.

This day, sometimes called "Martinmas," was chosen to commemorate the end of the First World War. Veterans Day now honors United States citizens who fought in wars during this century. How can congregations follow in Martin's steps and work tirelessly for peace in the world? We pray for peace in our liturgies, but in what other ways can we practice peacemaking in our families, congregations, and nation?

SØREN AABYE KIERKEGAARD, TEACHER, 1855

Kierkegaard is not only the founder of modern existentialism, he also was a theologian whose writings reveal his Lutheran heritage and his commitment to a faith that is experienced rather than merely intellectualized. He invites our congregations to consider whether doubters and questioners would feel comfortable in our communities of faith. Does your congregation see doubt as an important part of faith? Do we provide opportunities for persons who struggle honestly with issues of faith? Do pastors make themselves available to those who are questioning what they believe? This dimension of pastoral care is important within the life of the congregation.

NOVEMBER 12, 2000

TWENTY-SECOND SUNDAY AFTER PENTECOST
PROPER 27

INTRODUCTION

All that we have—our lives, families, possessions, labor, and talents—comes from God and belongs to God. From the Christian perspective, we are not owners but stewards of all that the Creator has given us. And all that we have is given to us for the good of others. The divine economy works with equity for all, a hand always open to the poor, the outcast, and the forgotten ones. God's bounty gives us the grace to hold nothing back in serving God.

PRAYER OF THE DAY

Lord, when the day of wrath comes we have no hope except in your grace. Make us so to watch for the last days that the consummation of our hope may be the joy of the marriage feast of your Son, Jesus Christ our Lord.

READINGS

1 Kings 17:8-16

The books of Joshua, Judges, Samuel, and Kings present a theological perspective derived from the book of Deuteronomy. One of the basic themes of this theological perspective is that faithful obedience to God's Law brings blessing while disobedience brings curse. Today's reading dramatizes God's power over nature to reward obedience to the Law (survival) and to punish disobedience (drought).

Psalm 146

The LORD lifts up those who are bowed down. (Ps. 146:7)

Hebrews 9:24-28

The letter to the Hebrews describes Christ as a high priest who offers himself as a sacrifice for our sin. Christ does not die again and again each year. He has died once, is alive with God, and will reveal himself on the last day.

Mark 12:38-44

After engaging in a series of public arguments with religious leaders in the temple, Jesus contrasts the proud and evil ways of those leaders with the sacrificial humility and poverty of the widow.

ALTERNATE FIRST READING/PSALM

Ruth 3:1-5; 4:13-17

Naomi has lost her husband and both her sons, but has the support of her widowed daughter-in-law Ruth. Naomi is resourceful in arranging the marriage of Ruth to a wealthy kinsman who, in marrying Ruth, also "redeems" by purchasing a small plot of land that had belonged to Naomi's husband.

Psalm 127

Children are a heritage from the LORD. (Ps. 127:4)

COLOR Green

THE PRAYERS

In communion with all the saints, let us pray to God who is our eternal home.

SILENCE IS KEPT.

Let us pray for the church, that it would always seek to welcome those disregarded or misunderstood by society at large. Lord, in your mercy,

hear our prayer.

Let us pray for the world, that leaders of the nations would be diligent in making policy that is sensitive to those who are poor and in need. Lord, in your mercy,

hear our prayer.

Let us pray for those whose spouses have died and whose income is limited. May they be provided for by caring family, friends, and neighbors. Lord, in your mercy,

hear our prayer.

Let us pray for those who are ill (especially . . .), that they would know God's love in the midst of their sickness, and that healing strength would be theirs. Lord, in your mercy,

hear our prayer.

Let us pray for all who give of their abundance of resources in this congregation, that generosity would increase and our congregation's mission be extended. Lord, in your mercy,

hear our prayer.

HERE OTHER INTERCESSIONS MAY BE OFFERED.

Let us pray for the faithful departed and those who mourn their absence (especially . . .), that the comfort of the Spirit would keep them in the resurrection's hope. Lord, in your mercy,

hear our prayer.

Your reign, O God, endures forever, and in Christ we

are free to be your saints and servants. Hear our prayers for the sake of him who died and rose again, and lives with you in the company of all your saints in light.
Amen

IMAGES FOR PREACHING

As we move ever closer to the end of the church year, today's gospel takes us to the last days of Jesus' life. This journey may not be evident because the reading makes no mention of the time or place. If the previous Sunday was marked as All Saints Sunday, we missed the reading from Mark 12:28-34 (proper 26). Thus, we didn't hear Jesus' summary of the law, and we missed meeting the faithful scribe.

These two stories present two different portraits of faith: a scribe, usually depicted as an enemy of Jesus, and a poor widow, usually portrayed as needing alms. Why not bring the faithful scribe and the faithful widow together in the sermon? Today's reading begins with a warning against the scribes who "devour widows' houses." Jesus doesn't want us to miss the irony that the widow was made poor by people like the scribes and others who give large offerings!

As we watch the widow, let us also remember the scribe to whom Jesus said, "You are not far from the kingdom of God" (Mark 12:34). Jesus' last days are filled with many people: crowds cheering as he enters the city, crowds jeering at the trial, disciples who betray, deny, and run away. Two people emerge as signs of faithfulness: a learned scribe and a poor widow. Those written off as Jesus' enemies step forward testifying to the truth. Those who are needy, who seem empty, give more than we can imagine.

From the beginning, Jesus has been preparing us for these latter days. The first will be last and the last first. The greatest must be servant of all. What will it profit you to gain the world and forfeit your life? This kingdom is strange indeed. Who can believe it? At least two did.

WORSHIP MATTERS

At the offertory procession we place bread and wine on the altar-table, and God uses these elements to feed hungry souls with the body and blood of Christ. Ironically, while we "offer" gifts to God, God is really giving these things to us.

If monetary gifts are presented with the bread and wine, then the former should also be given away to those in need. Gordon Lathrop has suggested that all money received at the offering be given to the poor and hungry, while money for institutional maintenance be received by means of a dues system. Additionally, he suggests that in order to maintain a connection between money offering and food offering, we should consider never collecting money at a service that is not a celebration of the Lord's supper, and never collecting money without collecting food. (See *Worship* 71 [1997], p. 554.) Such practices would help us to realize that we cannot give to God, but only to the poor.

Does your congregation connect God's gift in the eucharist with our acts of giving to those who are poor and in need?

LET THE CHILDREN COME

God surprises us by coming to us when we least expect and in ways we cannot foresee. Encourage family members to share their faith by telling stories of times when they had reached the end of a rope and God delivered them. What examples can we be in taking the widows' risk of faith and entrusting our very lives to God?

MUSIC FOR WORSHIP

GATHERING

LBW 383	Rise up, O saints of God!
WOV 760	For the fruit of all creation

PSALM 146

Beckstrand, William. PW, cycle B.
Cooney/arr. Daigle. "Praise the Lord, My Soul" in PCY, vol. 4.
Stewart, Roy James. "Praise the Lord" in PCY, vol. 5.
Wellicome, Paul. "Maranatha, Alleluia!" in PS, vol. 1.

LBW 538	Oh, praise the Lord, my soul! (paraphrase)
LBW 539	Praise the Almighty (paraphrase)

HYMN OF THE DAY

LBW 406	Take my life, that I may be
	PATMOS

INSTRUMENTAL RESOURCES

Gabrielsen, Stephen. "Patmos" in *Hymn preludes and Free Accompaniments, vol. 20.* AFP 11-9418. Org.
Mahnke, Allen. "Patmos" in *Thirteen Pieces for Treble Instrument and Organ.* CPH 97-6030. Org, inst.
Peeters, Flor. "Patmos" in *Hymn preludes for the Liturgical Year, vol. XVI.* CFP 6416. Org.

Zimmer, Dennis. "Take My Life, O Lord, Renew" in *The Concordia Hymn Prelude Series, vol. 35*. CPH 97-5750. Org/kybd.

ALTERNATE HYMN OF THE DAY
WOV 746 Day by day
LBW 336 Jesus, thy boundless love to me

COMMUNION
LBW 222 O Bread of life from heaven
WOV 761 Now we offer

OTHER SUGGESTIONS
Wetzler, Robert. "Take of the Wonder." AFP 11-10647. SATB, kybd, opt gtr, opt fl, opt cong

SENDING
LBW 408 God, whose giving knows no ending
WOV 699 Blessed assurance

ADDITIONAL HYMNS AND SONGS
H82 656 Blest are the pure in heart
PH 375 Lord of all good
TFF 233 I'd rather have Jesus
W&P We are an offering

MUSIC FOR THE DAY
CHORAL
Ashdown, Franklin. "Jesus, the Very Thought of You." AFP 11-10886. SATB, opt C inst.
Bell, John. "We Will Lay Our Burden Down." GIA G-4221. SATB, solo/cong, fl.
Rutter, John. "O Be Joyful in the Lord." OXF A346. SATB, org.
Sedio, Mark. "Take My Life That It May Be" (Toma, oh Dios, mi voluntad). AFP 11-10967. SAB, kybd.
Svedlund, Karl-Erik. "There'll Be Something in Heaven." AFP 12-113. SATB.
Victoria, T. L. "Jesu, Dulcis Memoria" (Jesus, the Very Thought Is Sweet). BRN ES48. SATB.

CHILDREN'S CHOIRS
Kosche, Kenneth T. "God's Angels." MSM 50-9401. 2 pt trbl, kybd.
Wold, Wayne L. "God's Loving Call." CG CGA649. U, kybd.

KEYBOARD/INSTRUMENTAL
Kolander, Keith. "Praise and Thanksgiving" in *Hymn Tune Preludes in Trio Style*. CPH 97-6614. Org.
Mathews, Peter. "Autumn Nocturne." MSM 20-959. Vc, org.
Porter, Rachel Trelstad. "Day By Day" in *Day by Day*. AFP 11-10772. Pno.

HANDBELL
Beck, Theodore/arr. John Muschick. "Offertory." BEC HB166. 4-5 oct.

PRAISE ENSEMBLE
Davis, Greg and Greg Fisher/arr. John Innes. "Honor the Lord." HOP WT1522. SATB, kybd.
Harlan, Benjamin. "Open Thou Mines Eyes." GS A-6722. SATB, acc.
Jones and Kenoly. "Use Me" in *God Is Able Performance Series*. INT.
Makeever, Ray. "Sing Unto the Lord" in DATH.

FRIDAY, NOVEMBER 17
ELIZABETH OF THURINGIA, PRINCESS OF HUNGARY, 1231

Elizabeth is remembered for her care for the sick, the elderly, and the poor. She founded two hospitals, and many hospitals have been named after her. The commemoration of Elizabeth might be a time for congregations to sponsor forums or classes related to issues of health care. What is the church's role in ensuring that the poor and elderly receive adequate health care? How might we as a community of faith promote wholistic health and preventative medicine? Perhaps your congregation could gather a panel to discuss such issues and include a physician, nurse, social worker, nursing home administrator, and family members.

NOVEMBER 19, 2000

TWENTY-THIRD SUNDAY AFTER PENTECOST
PROPER 28

INTRODUCTION

During November the lectionary leads the worshiping assembly to visions of the last day, to a reflection on the resurrection of the body and life everlasting. Some religious people see only panic and doom in the future. They dwell in the land of fear. The conclusion to the Lord's Prayer offers another view: the kingdom, the power, and the glory are yours, now and forever. It is a bold confession of faith in God, who is our refuge and our strength. Such a hope, according to Hebrews, leads us to encourage one another in love and good deeds.

PRAYER OF THE DAY

Lord God, so rule and govern our hearts and minds by your Holy Spirit that, always keeping in mind the end of all things and the day of judgment, we may be stirred up to holiness of life here and may live with you forever in the world to come, through your Son, Jesus Christ our Lord.
or
Almighty and ever-living God, before the earth was formed and even after it ceases to be, you are God. Break into our short span of life and let us see the signs of your final will and purpose, through your Son, Jesus Christ our Lord.

READINGS

Daniel 12:1-3

The book of Daniel represents a kind of literature called "apocalyptic," which is full of bizarre visions, strange symbolism, and supernatural happenings. Arising during times of great persecution, apocalyptic literature employs a vivid language that prevents outsiders to the faith from understanding its content. Overall, it is concerned with God's revelation about the end-time and the coming kingdom of God, when God will vindicate the righteous who have been persecuted.

Psalm 16

My heart is glad and my spirit rejoices; my body shall rest in hope. (Ps. 16:9)

Hebrews 10:11-14 [15-18] 19-25

The letter to the Hebrews presents an extended discussion of how Christ offered himself as a sacrifice so that sinners, cleansed by his blood, might have life. Therefore, the writer concludes, our life together should be marked by confidence, assurance, hope, and encouragement.

Mark 13:1-8

In the last week of his life, Jesus warned his disciples concerning trials that were to come upon them and upon the world. He exhorts the listener: Do not be alarmed.

ALTERNATE FIRST READING/PSALM

1 Samuel 1:4-20

This story explains the circumstances leading to the birth of Samuel in a pious Israelite family. It exhibits the familiar Israelite motif of the devout barren wife who eventually conceives a son with the help of God.

1 Samuel 2:1-10

My heart exults in the LORD; my strength is exalted in my God. (1 Sam. 2:2)

COLOR Green

THE PRAYERS

In communion with all the saints, let us pray to God who is our eternal home.
SILENCE IS KEPT.
Almighty God, keep your church expectant and ready for that day when you will bring to completion your plan for earth and heaven, making all things new. Lord, in your mercy,
hear our prayer.
Lord of the nations, violence and war threaten to devour the well-being of your people throughout the world. Come to the assistance of all who seek to bring an end to fighting and unrest. Lord, in your mercy,
hear our prayer.
God of the lowly, draw near to all who are imprisoned in body or mind. Restore them to wholeness, and bring to health all who struggle with sickness (especially . . .). Lord, in your mercy,
hear our prayer.
God of grace, help the worship of this congregation to

provide nourishment to all, that we might serve you together in the confession of our faith without wavering. Lord, in your mercy,
hear our prayer.

HERE OTHER INTERCESSIONS MAY BE OFFERED.

Holy God, give us joy as we remember the loved ones who are now at rest in your blessed peace (especially . . .). Bring us one day to be reunited with them in your new Jerusalem. Lord, in your mercy,
hear our prayer.

Your reign, O God, endures forever, and in Christ we are free to be your saints and servants. Hear our prayers for the sake of him who died and rose again, and lives with you in the company of all your saints in light.
Amen

IMAGES FOR PREACHING

What would happen to our congregation if we lost our building? Many African American congregations had to find an answer to that very question when their churches were destroyed by arson a few years ago. Thankfully, many of those churches have been rebuilt by the generous outpouring of labor and money from around the country. But the days without a building no doubt reshaped each congregation in powerful ways. When the soaring spire of Christ Church at Gustavus Adolphus College, St. Peter, Minnesota, was toppled by a tornado in the spring of 1998, the cross atop the spire was torn off and twisted. Just days after the tragedy that twisted cross was carried in procession as people gathered to give thanks for life and to pray for God's help in the face of devastating loss.

This Sunday is a preview of the end of the church year a week from now. It's a good time to talk about God's call to the particular band of disciples gathered in this church building, even if it's not stewardship month. Jesus doesn't call us to make predictions about the end-time, but to remain faithful in this time. As the church year moves to a close in this new millennium we would do well to read the letter to the Hebrews as though it is addressed to our congregation: "Let us hold fast to the confession of our hope without wavering, for the one who has promised is faithful" (even when steeples are falling). "Let us consider how to provoke one another to love and good deeds." This calling is far more intentional than random acts of kindness! Let us not neglect to meet together, though some say it doesn't make any difference and God doesn't need a building! We're the ones who need the building, or at least we need each other as the letter to the Hebrews reminds us: encourage one another now and all the more as you see the day approaching.

WORSHIP MATTERS

Times of national crisis or rejoicing should be occasions for the people of God to gather for prayer. At the end of the Second World War, many congregations of all faiths held special services to give thanks for the end of conflict and to pray for the safe return home of military personnel. In times of national crisis today, such as the outbreak of war, a congregation could gather to pray for the avoidance or cessation of conflict, and to ask for healing and protection for victims. Times of national crisis might also call us to examine our consciences and motivations, in which case a service of corporate confession and forgiveness could be appropriate. Does the worship leadership of your congregation recognize the need for these types of corporate worship experiences?

LET THE CHILDREN COME

As we listen to today's scriptures, can we hear the rumblings in earth and in heaven? Something big is afoot. It is so big that earth cannot contain it; and yet, this event in its entirety is contained within a baby born in Bethlehem. The Omega sneaks up on the Alpha as we move toward a new year in the church. In Jesus, the cosmic battle is waged and won. Jesus lives! Let us remember at what great cost our life has been won and what overwhelming forces we face apart from Christ our Lord and Savior.

MUSIC FOR WORSHIP

GATHERING

LBW 415	God of grace and God of glory
WOV 742	Come, we that love the Lord

PSALM 16

Beckstrand, William. PW, cycle B.

Foley, John. "Psalm 16" in PCY, vol. 7.

Haas, David. "Psalm 16" in PCY, vol. 8.

Howard, Julie. *Sing for Joy: Psalm Settings for God's Children.* Liturgical Press 81462078-7.

Inwood, Paul. "Centre of My Life" in PS, vol. 2.

Marshall, Jane. *Psalms Together.* CG CGC 18. U, cong.

HYMN OF THE DAY

WOV 691   Sing with all the saints in glory
                MISSISSIPPI

VOCAL RESOURCES

Roberts, William Bradley. "In All These You Welcomed Me/Sing with All the Saints in Glory." AFP 11-10661. U/org, opt ob/inst.

INSTRUMENTAL RESOURCES

Biery, James. "Sing with All the Saints in Glory" in *Tree of Life: Hymn Preludes for Organ*. AFP 11-10701. Org.

Hassell, Michael. "Mississippi" in *More Folkways: Hymn Arrangements for Solo Instrument and Piano*. AFP 11-10866. Kybd, inst.

Keesecker, Thomas. "On the Mississippi" in *Together Again: Piano Music*. AFP 11-10717. Kybd.

ALTERNATE HYMN OF THE DAY

LBW 323   O Lord of light, who made the stars
LBW 355   Through the night of doubt and sorrow

COMMUNION

LBW 486   Spirit of God, descend upon my heart
WOV 702   I am the Bread of life

OTHER SUGGESTIONS

Keesecker, Thomas. "Remember." AFP 11-10743. SATB, kybd, 2 trbl inst, opt cong.

SENDING

LBW 495   Lead on, O King eternal!
WOV 744   Soon and very soon

ADDITIONAL HYMNS AND SONGS

DATH 104   For to this end
H82 600/1   O day of God, draw nigh
TFF 174   Deep river
W&P   Blessing, honor and glory

MUSIC FOR THE DAY

CHORAL

Fleming, Larry L. "Blessed Are They." MSM 50-8106. SATB div, cong, opt inst/hb.

Mendelssohn, Felix. "He that shall endure" in *Elijah*. GSCH 10713. SATB, kybd.

Meyer, Daniel C. "You Are Worthy." GIA G-4144. SAB, pno.

Schütz, Heinrich. "I Go My Way to Jesus Christ" (So fahr ich hin zu Jesu Christ). Chantry (Carus-Verlag 20.379). SATB, cont.

Tyler, Edward. "St. Teresa's Bookmark." AFP 11-10964. SSATB.

CHILDREN'S CHOIRS

Leaf, Robert. "Come with Rejoicing." CFP 11-1598. U/2 pt, kybd.

Marshall, Jane. "Psalm 16" in *Psalms Together*. CG CGC18. U antiphonal, kybd.

KEYBOARD/INSTRUMENTAL

Hassell, Michael. "Sing with All the Saints in Glory" in *More Folkways*. AFP 11-10866. Trbl inst, pno.

Janson, PJ. "Partita on 'The Day Is Surely Drawing Near'" in *Organ Music for the Seasons*. AFP 11-10859. Org.

HANDBELL

Afdahl, Lee J. "If Thou But Suffer God to Guide Thee." AFP 11-10574. 3-4 oct.

Behnke, John A. "The Church's One Foundation." CPH 97-6750. 3-5 oct; 97-6743. Full score, inst pts.

Dobrinski, Cynthia. "Hope Eternal." AG 1553. 3-5 oct, opt fl.

PRAISE ENSEMBLE

Baloche, Cueller, Hoffman, and Kerr. "Deeper in Love" in *Let Your Glory Fall Choral Collection*. INT.

Baloche, Paul and Ed Kerr. "I Love to Be in Your Presence" in *Hosanna! Music Songbook, vol 7*. INT HMSB07.

Knapp, Phoebe P./arr. Whaley and Clevenger. "Blessed Assurance." PLY SHS9705. SATB, pno.

Paris, Twila. "We Bow Down" in *Songs for Praise and Worship*. WRD.

Wolfe, Lanny. "Surely the Presence of the Lord Is in This Place" in *Maranatha! Music Praise Chorus Book, 2nd ed*. MAR BK06140.

NOVEMBER 23, 2000

DAY OF THANKSGIVING (U.S.)

INTRODUCTION

As winter darkness crosses the land, the nation takes time to offer thanks for the harvest and the abundant resources of this land. While this holiday witnesses many households gathering for a festive meal, Christians recognize that the source of all good things is the God who feeds the birds and clothes the grass of the field. Gathered at Christ's supper, we offer thanksgiving for the bread of life and the cup of blessing. And here, as we share these gifts, we are knit together into a community whose mission is among those who are poor and in need. We offer thanks to God for the bounty of the land and seek to share these riches with all in need.

PRAYER OF THE DAY

Almighty God our Father, your generous goodness comes to us new every day. By the work of your Spirit lead us to acknowledge your goodness, give thanks for your benefits, and serve you in willing obedience; through your Son, Jesus Christ our Lord.

READINGS

Joel 2:21-27

The prophecy of Joel comes from the period of 500 to 350 B.C. He views a locust plague that ravaged the country as God's judgment on the people, whom he then calls to repentance. Today's reading points beyond the judgment of the Day of the Lord, when the Lord will repay "the years that the swarming locust has eaten."

Psalm 126

The LORD has done great things for us, and we are glad indeed. (Ps. 126:4)

1 Timothy 2:1-7

The letter to Timothy was written at a time when kings and rulers persecuted those who believed in Christ. Still, the writer calls upon Christians to pray for these rulers and offer thanksgiving on their behalf.

Matthew 6:25-33

In the Sermon on the Mount, Jesus taught his disciples about the providence of God so that they would regard life with thanksgiving and trust rather than anxiety.

COLOR White

THE PRAYERS

In communion with all the saints, let us pray to God who is our eternal home.

SILENCE IS KEPT.

We give you thanks, O God, for your church and for the wondrous ways in which you have dealt with your people. Continue to inspire the church to be a blessing in our communities and in the society at large. Lord, in your mercy,

hear our prayer.

We give you thanks, O God, for the diversity of the world's people, for all nations and their leaders. Grant to all your wisdom and grace, that a quiet and peaceable life would be possible for all people. Lord, in your mercy,

hear our prayer.

We give you thanks, O God, for your abundant blessings to us and for the bounty of the world's resources. Help us to share of our plenty with those in need. Lord, in your mercy,

hear our prayer.

We give you thanks, O God, for this congregation and for the praises you have put in our mouths and in our hearts. Help us work to insure that people in our community have sufficient food, clothing, and shelter. Lord, in your mercy,

hear our prayer.

HERE OTHER INTERCESSIONS MAY BE OFFERED.

We give you thanks, O God, for bringing the promise of comfort to those who grieve. We remember with praise and thanksgiving all who have died and who now rest at peace in your eternal harvest home. Lord, in your mercy,

hear our prayer.

Your reign, O God, endures forever, and in Christ we are free to be your saints and servants. Hear our prayers for the sake of him who died and rose again, and lives with you in the company of all your saints in light.

Amen

IMAGES FOR PREACHING

Thanksgiving seems easier in the country than in the city. By November most of the corn has been picked and the wire bins are bulging with golden ears. People can *see* the words they're singing: "All is safely gathered in ere the winter storms begin." It is not as easy to see Thanksgiving in the city where most everything seems manufactured rather than created. Although we can trace skyscrapers and subways back to the steel mill, then back to the ore in the ground, it takes a long time and it's harder to see God there. Factories don't elicit thankful hearts as readily as grain in the corncrib and jam in the fruit cellar.

Perhaps the prophet Joel knew that people can be forgetful or even reluctant in giving thanks. He doesn't even begin with human beings! First, he talks to the soil, then to the animals of the field, and finally to the children of Zion. It's a wonderful scene as we imagine the soil rejoicing and the animals perking up their ears at news of green pastures in the wilderness. The prophet sees and hears with the eyes and ears of his God-given imagination.

God invites us to reclaim the gift of imagination. Encourage people in the parish to give thanks for what they see where they are: the rainbow of colors in the fruit stands, the vacant lot reclaimed as a garden, curb cuts at the corner for wheelchairs, the fire trucks polished and ready, the nurses working the night shift. Invite children to create psalms and prayers of thanksgiving. Write new words to familiar hymns—and don't worry if they're sung only once! Invite people to bring tangible signs of their daily work for a table of thanksgiving; be sure to include the gifts of children, retired people, and those whose work is unpaid. Then call the whole earth to sing God's praise: "Do not fear, O soil— O parks, O towering buildings, O bus stops, O fruit stands, O neon lights, O newly painted playground—be glad and rejoice, for the Lord has done great things!" (paraphrase of Joel 2:21).

LET THE CHILDREN COME

Children readily grasp the language of creation and its variety of creatures and plants. Children should hear and speak the word that all creation is God's work and the preservation of creation is also God's work (compare the Small Catechism, First Article of the creed).

Speak directly to the children in reading the gospel today. Let them hear that God feeds the birds, God clothes the grass, and God feeds and clothes them.

MUSIC FOR WORSHIP

GATHERING

| LBW 407 | Come, you thankful people, come |
| WOV 797 | O God beyond all praising |

PSALM 126

Beckstrand, William. PW, cycle B.
Foley, John. "Psalm 126" in PCY, vol. 7.
Haas, David. "Psalm 126" in PCY, vol. 8.
Roff, Joseph. "Psalm 126" in PCY, vol. 3.
Smith, Alan. "The Lord Has Done Great Things" in PS, vol. 1.

HYMN OF THE DAY

LBW 241   We praise you, O God
          KREMSER

VOCAL RESOURCES

Jennings, Carolyn. "We Praise You, O God." AFP 11-10948. SATB, cong, opt tpt.

INSTRUMENTAL RESOURCES

Bernthal, John. "We Praise You, O God" in *Lift High the Cross: Hymn Introductions and Descants for Organ and Trumpet.* AFP 11-10867. Org, tpt.
Callahan, Charles. "Kremser" in *Thanksgiving Suite.* MSM 10-600. Org.
Callahan, Charles. "Kremser" in *Thanksgiving Music for Manuals.* MSM 10-601. Kybd.
Page, Anna Laura. "Kremser" in *Glad Tidings We Raise.* Van Ness Press 4180-04. Org.

ALTERNATE HYMN OF THE DAY

| LBW 407 | Come, you thankful people, come |
| WOV 760 | For the fruit of all creation |

COMMUNION

| LBW 409 | Praise and thanksgiving |
| WOV 705 | As the grains of wheat |

SENDING

| LBW 274 | The day you gave us, Lord has ended |
| WOV 771 | Great is thy faithfulness |

ADDITIONAL HYMNS AND SONGS

H82 432	O praise ye the Lord!	
OBS 64	In sacred manner	
TFF 293	Thank you, Lord	
W&P	I will sing, I will sing	

MUSIC FOR THE DAY

CHORAL

Aguiar, Ernani. "Psalm 150" (Salmo 150). Earthsongs. SATB (SSA). Lat.

Bach, J. S. "Alles was odem hat" in *Singet dem Herrn*. MFS 259. SATB.

Ferguson, John. "A Song of Thanksgiving." AFP 11-10505. SATB, org.

Hopson, Hal. "Come, Christians, Join to Sing." MSM 50-7027. SATB, kybd.

Mozart, Wolfgang Amadeus. "Laudate Dominum" in *Sing Solo Sacred*. OXF 0-19-345785-7.

Pachelbel, Johann. "Now Thank We All Our God" (Nun danket alle Gott). Barenreiter 2873. SATB/SATB, SATB/brass. Ger/Eng.

Palestrina, G. P. "Exultate Jubilate." CHE 8794. SAATB.

Pickard, John. "Make a Joyful Noise." AFP 11-10926. SATB, kybd.

Rowan, William. "Praise God from Whom All Blessings Flow." GIA G-4398. SATB.

Young, Jeremy. "Praise God with the Trumpet." AFP 11-10893. SAB, kybd, opt brass/cong.

CHILDREN'S CHOIRS

Heck, Lyle. "Make a Joyful Noise Unto the Lord." AFP 11-10601. 2 pt, fl, kybd.

Hobby, Robert. "Offertory for Day of Thanksgiving." MSM 80-600. 2 pt, org.

Pooler/arr. Kemp. "Thanks to God" in *Let's Sing*. AFP 11-7210. U, kybd.

Pooler/arr. Kemp. "Thanksgiving" in *Let's Sing*. AFP 11-7210. U, kybd.

KEYBOARD/INSTRUMENTAL

Cherwien, David. "Now Thank We All Our God" in *Postludes on Well Known Hymns*. AFP 11-10795. Org.

Powell, Robert J. "Pastorale on 'Kremser'" in *Nine Service Pieces for the Church Year for Organ*. FLA HF-5194. Org.

HANDBELL

Rogers, Sharon Elery. "Now Thankful People, Come." (St. George's Windsor, Nun danket alle Gott). AFP 11-10804. 2-3 oct.

PRAISE ENSEMBLE

Chambers, Brent. "How Good It Is" in *Come & Worship*. INT.

Martin, Joseph M. "A Thanksgiving Garden." SHW 10/1653M. SA(T)B, pno.

Perry, Dave and Jean. "Kuimba Asante" (Sing Thanks!) ALF 16109. SATB, kybd, perc. Also available 3 pt (16110); 2 pt (16111).

Smith, Henry/arr. Wilson. "Give Thanks." HOP GC972. SAB, kybd.

Thompson and Scruggs. "Sanctuary" in *Come & Worship*. INT.

THURSDAY, NOVEMBER 23
CLEMENT, BISHOP OF ROME, C. 100

Clement was a bishop of Rome during the first century. Little is known of his life, but he is remembered for his letters, one of which challenges the divisions in the Corinthian community. He offered pastoral counsel by urging a spirit of peace and kindness.

It is not surprising that the church of our day continues to face disagreement, division, and occasionally mean-spiritedness. Clement reminds us that a pastoral love for people must be present amid our differing views of authority, scripture, or social ministry. Can we be united in the central affirmations of our faith, and still embrace diversity in other matters? How does your congregation deal with disagreement or conflict?

MIGUEL AGUSTÍN PRO, PRIEST, MARTYR, MEXICO, 1927

Miguel Pro grew up among oppression in Mexico where revolutionaries accused the church of siding with the rich. After studying for the priesthood in Belgium, he returned to Mexico to work on behalf of the poor and homeless. Living amid constant danger, eventually Miguel and his two brothers were shot, falsely accused of throwing a bomb at the car of a government official.

Reflect on the widening gap between the rich and the poor. How do those who live with abundance share with those living in poverty?

SATURDAY, NOVEMBER 25
ISAAC WATTS, HYMNWRITER, 1748

Watts is one of the most well-known writers of English hymn texts, and was important in establishing hymn singing in the English church. Many of his hymns are based on psalms, and they reflect a strong and serene faith.

Lutheran Book of Worship includes thirteen of his texts. Several especially appropriate for the season are: "From all that dwell below the skies" (LBW 550), "Before Jehovah's awesome throne" (LBW 531), or "Come, let us join our cheerful songs" (LBW 254).

NOVEMBER 26, 2000

CHRIST THE KING
LAST SUNDAY AFTER PENTECOST
PROPER 29

INTRODUCTION

We proclaim Christ our king as he goes to the throne of the cross. We acclaim him our ruler as he sheds his blood. We acknowledge him as our Lord as he gives himself to us in bread and cup. Christ is our king as he reigns from the tree, sharing our fears and experiencing our frailties. In the reign of God, the powerful one does not intimidate the weak, but cares for them. In the reign of God, the person of authority does not use others, but seeks them out and crowns them with mercy.

PRAYER OF THE DAY

Almighty and everlasting God, whose will it is to restore all things to your beloved Son, whom you anointed priest forever and king of all creation: Grant that all the people of the earth, now divided by the power of sin, may be united under the glorious and gentle rule of your Son, our Lord Jesus Christ, who lives and reigns with you and the Holy Spirit, one God, now and forever.

READINGS

Daniel 7:9-10, 13-14

To the community for whom this passage was written, it seemed as though the oppression they (God's people) were experiencing would never end. Daniel's message is: Indeed, it shall end. The Ancient One who is judge will call all nations to account and will give dominion to God's people who are represented by "one like a human being."

Psalm 93

Ever since the world began, your throne has been established. (Ps. 93:3)

Revelation 1:4b-8

The book of Revelation begins with a series of messages addressed to seven churches. John's greeting to these churches extols God as one who controls their past, present, and future.

John 18:33-37

In John's gospel, the story of Jesus and Pilate presents two different ways of exercising power: through force or with love.

ALTERNATE FIRST READING/PSALM

2 Samuel 23:1-7

This passage is a song that aims to give theological and moral legitimacy to the ongoing dynasty of David that endured over four hundred years until the destruction of Jerusalem in 587 B.C.

Psalm 132:1-13 [14-19] (Psalm 132:1-12 [13-18] [NRSV])

Let your faithful people sing with joy. (Ps. 132:9)

COLOR White

THE PRAYERS

In communion with all the saints, let us pray to God who is our eternal home.

SILENCE IS KEPT.

Let us pray that the church would always lift high the cross from which Christ our king rules and reigns. Lord, in your mercy,

hear our prayer.

Let us pray that all people, nations, and languages would be brought into the peace of Christ's eternal dominion of love. Lord, in your mercy,

hear our prayer.

Let us pray that all who have been victims and all who have been mistreated by injustice would be comforted by the one who endured the shame of the cross. Lord, in your mercy,

hear our prayer.

Let us pray that this congregation would identify with the suffering, the sorrowing, and the sick of the community (especially . . .). May we always seek avenues to reach out in tangible and loving ways. Lord, in your mercy,

hear our prayer.

HERE OTHER INTERCESSIONS MAY BE OFFERED.

Let us pray for those who have died (especially . . .), that we, with all your saints will be brought one day to rejoice in your eternal kingdom, there to sing your praises for all eternity. Lord, in your mercy,

hear our prayer.

reign, O God, endures forever, and in Christ we are free to be your saints and servants. Hear our prayers for the sake of him who died and rose again, and lives with you in the company of all your saints in light.
Amen

IMAGES FOR PREACHING

A dissonance characterizes this day. Most of the appointed hymns are regal, fit for a king, yet Jesus stands before Pilate refusing the title. The dissonance needs to be heard: some songs in minor keys, some gentle hymns alongside the mighty choruses. For this king will not be lifted high upon a royal throne, but upon a criminal's cross. A crown of thorns will make a mockery of every claim of royalty. How can the dissonance of this day be honored? How can we remember the king who refused to be king?

Staying with John's gospel, we can return to the very beginning and relive the church year: "And the Word became flesh and lived among us . . . full of grace and truth" (John 1: 14). Hymns from the Advent season such as "My Lord, what a morning" (WOV 627) or "Light one candle to watch for Messiah" (WOV 630) lift up themes of the end time and expectant waiting. The Christmas carol "Once in royal David's city" (WOV 643) connects Jesus' lowly birth with his place at God's side forever. "My song is love unknown" (LBW 94) relives the last days of Jesus' life from the hosannas of Passion Sunday to Good Friday's "crucify!" These hymns might frame portions of the sermon as the congregation moves through the seasons of the church year remembering the life of this peculiar servant king.

Theologian Delores Williams talks about growing up in a small church in the South. Every Sunday the minister asked, "Who is Jesus?" and the choir would sing out the refrain, "King of kings and Lord Almighty." Then the minister asked the question again and little Miss Huff answered in a voice almost too soft to be heard: "Poor little Mary's boy." The choir responded, then Miss Huff, back and forth until it was clear that this king was always poor little Mary's boy. "It was the Black church doing theology," said Williams. They made sure the dissonance of king Jesus was never forgotten. (Paraphrased from Delores Williams's speech at the *Re-Imagining* conference, Minneapolis, November, 1993).

WORSHIP MATTERS

The second reading from Revelation states that the church is a kingdom of priests who serve God. The priesthood of all Christians is exercised in the liturgy. Assisting ministers, lectors, acolytes, crucifers, communion assistants, and musicians all fulfill their priestly callings by using their talents and abilities in the liturgy. All members of the worshiping assembly fulfill the priestly role by singing the canticles and hymns, and by joining in various responses, especially those during the intercessions and the eucharistic prayer. Each Christian exercises her or his priesthood when she or he prays for others, witnesses to her or his faith, and aids those suffering from poverty, disease, and infirmity.

As the liturgical year concludes, your congregation's worship and music committee might want to evaluate how well your worship enables people to fulfill their priestly callings. Do lay people have ample opportunities to serve in assisting minister roles in the liturgy? Does your liturgy avoid the impression that the only "priest" is the presiding minister?

LET THE CHILDREN COME

An aspect of kingship often overlooked by children taken up with power is that of benevolent government. Jesus' kingly rule is not one of tyranny, but of authority for the sake of our life. His chariot, to our vision, is a donkey, and his throne a cross; his crown is made of thorns and his robe a burial cloth. Let the children take part in the acclamation of faith in the hymns and the liturgy: "Christ is king! He reigns forever!"

MUSIC FOR WORSHIP
GATHERING

LBW 377	Lift high the cross
WOV 787	Glory to God, we give you thanks

PSALM 93

Beckstrand, William. PW, cycle B.
Bridges. "O Come and Sing unto the Lord." CPH 98-2927. U, hb.
Hopson, Hal H. *Psalm Refrains and Tones for the Common Lectionary.* HOP 425. U, cong.
Wellicome, Paul. "The Lord Is King" in PS, vol. 2.

HYMN OF THE DAY

LBW 27   Lo! He comes with clouds descending
               HELMSLEY

VOCAL RESOURCES

Boehnke, Paul. "Lo! He Comes with Clouds Descending." MSM 50-8300. SATB, kybd

INSTRUMENTAL RESOURCES

Callahan, Charles. "Helmsley" in *Advent Music for Manuals, set 2.* MSM 10-011. Kybd.

Held, Wilbur. "Helmsley" in *Four Advent Hymn Preludes, set 1.* MSM 10-010. Org.

Lind, Robert. "Helmsley" in *Organ Music for Advent.* CPH 97-6192. Org.

Osterland, Karl. "Helmsley" in *I Wonder as I Wander: Seasonal Hymn Preludes.* AFP 11-10858. Org.

ALTERNATE HYMN OF THE DAY

WOV 744   Soon and very soon
LBW 179   At the name of Jesus

COMMUNION

LBW 198   Let all mortal flesh keep silence
WOV 740   Jesus, remember me

SENDING

LBW 315   Love divine, all loves excelling
WOV 631   Lift up your heads, O gates

ADDITIONAL HYMNS AND SONGS

OBS 50   Blessing be and glory
H82 542   Christ is the world's true Light
TFF 267   All hail the power of Jesus' name
W&P   Lift up your heads

MUSIC FOR THE DAY

CHORAL

Boulanger, Lili. "Psalm XXIV" (Psaume XXIV). DUR 10,481. T, SATB, org, pn/orch. Fr/Eng.

Busarow, Donald. "O Lord, You Are My God and King." AFP 11-10892. SAB, org, tpt, hb, opt cong.

Gabrielli, Giovanni/arr. Engle. "Lift Up Your Heads." AFP 11-0690. SATB/SATB, SATB/brass.

Marshall, Jane. "How Lovely Is Your Dwelling Place." AFP 11-10884. SATB, org.

Rowan, William P. "The Threefold Truth." HOP 410-321. SATB, org, opt cong.

Schulz-Widmar, Russell. "Song of the Advents." AFP 11-10947. SA(T)B, kybd.

Wood, Dale. "Jubilate Deo" in *The Augsburg Choirbook.* AFP 11-10817. 2 pt mxd, org. Also available in SATB, org, 3 tpt, 2 hrn, perc. AFP 11-1603.

CHILDREN'S CHOIRS

Handel, G. F./arr. Patrick Liebergen. "Celebration Song." GIA G-4454. U/2 pt, kybd.

Leaf, Robert. "To the Glory of Our King." CG CGA173. U, kybd.

KEYBOARD/INSTRUMENTAL

Cherwien, David. "Processional on 'Praise, My Soul, the King of Heaven.'" CPH 97-6727. Org, opt tpt.

Schulz-Widmar, Russell. "Procession." SEL 160-626. Org.

HANDBELL

Smith, Vicki. "Crown Him with Many Crowns." CG CGB160. Full score. CGB161. 3-5 oct.

Wagner, Douglas. "Festival Piece on 'Coronation'" (All Hail the Power of Jesus' Name). BEC HB64A. 3-4 oct. HB64. Full score, org. HB64B. Opt brass.

PRAISE ENSEMBLE

Elvey, George/arr. Sterling. "Crown Him with Many Crowns" in *Songs in the Key of Love.* WRD 301034001X. SATB, kybd.

Hayford, Jack W. "Majesty" in *Praise Hymns & Choruses, 4th ed.* MAR.

Moody, Dave and Michael W. Smith. "All Hail King Jesus" and "Our God Reigns" medley in *Songs for Praise and Worship.* WRD.

Paris, Twila. "We Will Glorify" in *Praise & Worship Collection.* MAR BK06008.

Tunney, Dick and Melodie/arr. Wilson. "God's Love Never Changes." HOP GC961. SATB, kybd.

Vader, Randy and Jay Rouse/arr. Kirkland. "Honored, Glorified, Exalted." Sparrow AO8116. SATB, orch.

Zchech, Darlene. "Shout to the Lord" in *Hosanna! Music Songbook 11.* INT.

THURSDAY, NOVEMBER 30
ST. ANDREW, APOSTLE

For the festival of St. Andrew, Apostle, see page 48 of *Sundays and Seasons.*

BIBLIOGRAPHY

CHOIRBOOKS

Augsburg Choirbook, The (1998). Kenneth Jennings, ed. AFP 11-10817. Sixty-seven anthems primarily from twentieth-century North American composers.

Bach through the Church Year. (1999). Richard Erickson and Mark Bighley, eds. AFP 3-5854. Offers movements from cantatas and oratorios presented with carefully reconstructed keyboard parts and fresh English texts.

European Sacred Music (1997). John Rutter, ed. OXF 0-19-343695-7. Fifty choral masterworks primarily from continental European composers of the sixteenth to nineteenth centuries.

Motettenbuch (1959). Hans Holliger, ed. BA 3451. Forty-two classic German motets from the sixteenth to twentieth centuries.

New Church Anthem Book, The (1992). Lionel Dakers, ed. OXF 0-19-353109-0. One hundred favorite anthems for mixed voices from the sixteenth to twentieth centuries.

New Novello Anthem Book, The (1996). Philip Brunelle, ed. NOV 0-85360-705-2. Forty-one anthems primarily from English composers of the nineteenth to twentieth centuries.

100 Carols for Choirs (1987). David Willcocks and John Rutter, eds. OXF 0-19-353227-1. One hundred classic choral settings of traditional Christmas carols.

Oxford Easy Anthem Book, The (1957). OXF 0-19-353321-9. Fifty anthems for a variety of voices primarily from English composers of the sixteenth to twentieth centuries.

COMPUTER RESOURCES

Lutheran Resources for Worship Computer Series. *Lutheran Book of Worship Liturgies; With One Voice Liturgies; Words for Worship: 2000, Cycle B; Graphics for Worship.* Minneapolis: Augsburg Fortress, 1997 and ongoing. These CD-ROM resources enable worship planners to prepare weekly, seasonal, or occasional worship folders.

DAILY PRAYER RESOURCES

Book of Common Worship: Daily Prayer. Louisville: Westminster/John Knox Press, 1993. Presbyterian.

For All the Saints. 4 vols. Frederick Schumacher, ed. Delhi, N.Y.: American Lutheran Publicity Bureau, 1994.

Haugen, Marty. *Holden Evening Prayer.* Chicago: GIA Publications, Inc., 1990.

Weber, Paul. *Music for Morning Prayer.* Augsburg Fortress, 1999. Setting of liturgical music for morning prayer.

Welcome Home: Year of Mark. Augsburg Fortress, 1996. Scripture, prayers, and blessings for the household.

ENVIRONMENT AND ART

Chinn, Nancy. *Spaces for Spirit: Adorning the Church.* Chicago: Liturgy Training Publications, 1998. Imaginative thinking about ways to treat visual elements in the worship space.

Clothed in Glory: Vesting the Church. Edited by David Philippart. Chicago: Liturgy Training Publications, 1997. Photos and essays about liturgical paraments and vestments.

Huffman, Walter C., S. Anita Stauffer, and Ralph R. Van Loon. *Where We Worship.* Minneapolis: Augsburg Publishing House, 1987. Written by three Lutheran worship leaders, this volume sets forth the central principles in understanding and organizing space for worship. Study book and leader guide.

Mauck, Marchita. *Shaping a House for the Church.* Chicago: Liturgy Training Publications, 1990. The author presents basic design principles for worship space and the ways in which the worship space both forms and expresses the faith of the worshiping assembly.

Mazar, Peter. *To Crown the Year: Decorating the Church through the Seasons.* Chicago: Liturgy Training Publications, 1995. A contemporary guide for decorating the worship space throughout the seasons of the year.

Stauffer, S. Anita. *Altar Guild Handbook.* Philadelphia: Fortress Press, 1985. Guidelines for worship preparation.

HYMN AND SONG COLLECTIONS

Borning Cry: Worship for a New Generation. Compiled by John Ylvisaker. Waverly, Iowa: New Generation Publishers, 1992.

Dancing at the Harvest: Songs by Ray Makeever. Minneapolis: Augsburg Fortress, 1997. Songbook 11-10738. Acc ed. 11-10739.

El Himnario. New York: Church Publishing Inc., 1998. An ecumenical Spanish language hymn collection.

Lead Me, Guide Me: A Hymnal for African American Parishes. Chicago: GIA Publications, Inc., 1987. A broad range of hymns, songs, and liturgical music often inspired by African American musical traditions. A Roman Catholic collection.

Lift Every Voice and Sing II: An African American Hymnal. New York: The Church Hymnal Corporation, 1993. An Episcopal collection.

Mil Voces para Celebrar: Himnario Metodista. Nashville: The United Methodist Publishing House, 1996.

O Blessed Spring: Hymns of Susan Palo Cherwien. Minneapolis: Augsburg Fortress, 1997. AFP 11-10818. New hymn texts set to both new and familiar hymn tunes.

Sound the Bamboo. Manila: Asian Institute for Liturgy and Music, 1990. Hymns from Asia.

Wonder, Love, and Praise. New York: Church Publishing, Inc., 1997. A supplement to *The Hymnal 1982*.

Worship & Praise. Minneapolis: Augsburg Fortress, 1999. A collection of songs in various contemporary and popular styles, with helps for their use in Lutheran worship.

LEADING WORSHIP

Adams, William Seth. *Shaped by Images: One Who Presides*. New York: Church Hymnal Corporation, 1995. An excellent review of the ministry of presiding at worship.

Hovda, Robert. *Strong, Loving and Wise: Presiding in Liturgy*. Collegeville: The Liturgical Press, 1981. Sound, practical advice for the worship leader from a beloved advocate of social justice and liturgical renewal.

Huck, Gabe. *Liturgy with Style and Grace*, rev. ed. Chicago: Liturgy Training Publications, 1984. The first three chapters offer a practical, well-written overview of the purpose of worship, the elements of worship, and liturgical leadership.

Huffman, Walter C. *Prayer of the Faithful: Understanding and Creatively Leading Corporate Intercessory Prayer*, rev. ed. Minneapolis: Augsburg Fortress, 1992. A helpful treatment of communal prayer, the Lord's Prayer, and the prayers of the people.

Singing the Liturgy: Building Confidence for Worship Leaders. Audiocassette. Chicago: Evangelical Lutheran Church in America, 1996. A demonstration recording of the chants assigned to leaders in *LBW* and *WOV*.

LECTIONARIES

Lectionary for Worship, Cycle B. Minneapolis: Augsburg Fortress, 1996. The Revised Common Lectionary. Includes first reading, psalm citation, second reading, and gospel for each Sunday and lesser festival. Each reading is "sense-lined" for clearer proclamation of the scriptural texts. New Revised Standard Version.

Lectionary for Worship, Ritual Edition. Minneapolis: Augsburg Fortress, 1996. Large print, illustrated, hardbound edition that includes the complete three-year Revised Common Lectionary and lesser festival scriptural readings.

Readings and Prayers: The Revised Common Lectionary. Minneapolis: Augsburg Fortress, 1995.

Readings for the Assembly, Cycle B. Gordon Lathrop and Gail Ramshaw, eds. Minneapolis: Augsburg Fortress, 1996. The Revised Common Lectionary. Emended NRSV with inclusive language.

LECTIONARY-BASED LEARNING RESOURCES

Life Together. A new, comprehensive series of Revised Common Lectionary resources that integrates the primary activities of congregational life: worship, proclamation, and learning. Minneapolis: Augsburg Fortress, 1999.

FaithLife. Reproducible weekly handouts to guide conversations, prayer, and activities in the home.

LifeSongs (children's songbook, leader book, and audio CDs). A well-rounded selection of age-appropriate songs, hymns, and liturgical music that builds a foundation for a lifetime of singing the faith.

Life Together: Faith Nurturing Resources for Children. Quarterly teaching and learning resources for three age levels: pre-elementary, lower elementary, upper elementary.

Living and Learning. A comprehensive educational and seasonal planning guide, and a companion volume to the worship planning guide *Sundays and Seasons*.

Word of Life. Weekly devotional studies for adults based on the lectionary texts.

PERIODICALS

Assembly. Notre Dame Center for Pastoral Liturgy. Chicago: Liturgy Training Publications. Published five times a year. Each issue examines a particular aspect of worship practice. (800) 933-1800.

Catechumenate: A Journal of Christian Initiation. Chicago: Liturgy Training Publications. Published bimonthly with articles on congregational preparation of older children and adults for the celebration of baptism and eucharist. (800) 933-1800.

Cross Accent. Journal of the Association of Lutheran Church Musicians. Semi-annual publication for church musicians and worship leaders in North America. (800) 624-ALCM.

Faith & Form. Journal of the Interfaith Forum on Religion, Art and Architecture. Editorial office, (617) 965-3018.

Grace Notes. Newsletter of the Association of Lutheran Church Musicians. (708) 272-4116.

Liturgy. Quarterly journal of The Liturgical Conference, Washington, D.C. Each issue explores a worship-related issue from an ecumenical perspective. (800) 394-0885.

Plenty Good Room. Chicago: Liturgy Training Publications. Published bimonthly. A magazine devoted to African American worship within a Roman Catholic context. Helpful articles on the enculturation of worship. (800) 933-1800.

Worship. Collegeville: The Order of St. Benedict. Published through The Liturgical Press six times a year. Since the early decades of this century, the primary promoter of liturgical renewal among the churches. (800) 858-5450.

Worship 2000. Published periodically by the Office of Worship of the Evangelical Lutheran Church in America. Articles and annotated bibliographies on a range of worship topics. (800) 638-3522.

PLANNING TOOLS

Church Year Calendar (2000). A one-sheet calendar of lectionary citations and liturgical colors for each Sunday and festival of the liturgical year. Appropriate for bulk purchase and distribution.

Indexes for Praise. Minneapolis: Augsburg Fortress, forthcoming.

Indexes for Worship Planning: Revised Common Lectionary, Lutheran Book of Worship, With One Voice. Minneapolis: Augsburg Fortress, 1996. Contains many valuable indexes of hymns and psalms for Sundays, principal and lesser festivals, and occasions. A brief summary of each biblical reading with prayer of the day, scriptural verse, and offertory provide a handy guide to the primary biblical, liturgical, and hymn texts for each Sunday.

Liturgical Wall Calendar (2000). Date blocks note Revised Common Lectionary readings for Sundays and festivals and identify seasonal or festival color. A reference tool for home, sacristy, office.

Worship Planning Calendar (2000). A two-page per week calendar helpful for worship planners, with space to record appointments and notes for each day. Specially designed to complement *Sundays and Seasons*.

PREPARING MUSIC FOR WORSHIP

Cherwien, David. *Let the People Sing!: A Keyboardist's Creative and Practical Guide to Engaging God's People in Meaningful Song*. St. Louis: Concordia Publishing House, 1997. A practical and pedagogical approach to leading congregational singing and improvising at the organ.

Cotter, Jeanne. *Keyboard Improvisation for the Liturgical Musician*. Chicago: GIA Publications, Inc. Practical approach to keyboard improvisation.

Handbells in the Liturgy: A Practical Guide for the Use of Handbells in Liturgical Worship Traditions. St. Louis: Concordia Publishing House, 1996. Includes historical information on handbells in worship, ideas for structuring a bell program, and specific segments on the use of bells in the church year.

Haugen, Marty. *Instrumentation and the Liturgical Ensemble*. Chicago: GIA Publications, Inc., 1991. A resource for instrumental ensembles in liturgical settings.

Hopson, Hal H. *The Creative Use of Handbells in Hymn Singing*. Carol Stream: Hope Publishing Co. Resource contains specific handbell techniques to be used in accompanying congregational singing.

Leading the Church's Song. Robert Buckley Farlee, gen. ed. Minneapolis: Augsburg Fortress, 1998. Articles by various contributors, with musical examples and CD recording, giving guidance on the interpretation and leadership of various genres of congregational song.

Rose, Richard. *Hymnal Companion for Woodwind, Brass and Percussion*. St. Louis: Concordia Publishing House, 1997.

Rotermund, Donald. *Intonations and Alternative Accompaniments for Psalm Tones*. St. Louis: Concordia Publishing House, 1997. (*LBW* and *LW* versions available separately.)

Weidler, Scott, and Dori Collins. *Sound Decisions*. Chicago: ELCA, 1997. Theological principles for the evaluation of contemporary worship music.

Westermeyer, Paul. *The Church Musician*, rev. ed. Minneapolis: Augsburg Fortress, 1997. Foundational introduction to the role and task of the church musician as the leader of the people's song in worship.

———. *Te Deum: The Church and Music*. Minneapolis: Fortress Press, 1998. An historical and theological introduction to the music of the church.

Wilson-Dickson, Andrew. *The Story of Christian Music*. Minneapolis: Fortress Press, 1996. An illustrated guide to the major traditions of music in worship.

Wold, Wayne. *Tune My Heart to Sing: Devotions for Choirs Based on the Three-Year Revised Common Lectionary*. Minneapolis: Augsburg Fortress, 1997.

PROCLAIMING THE WORD

Brown, Raymond E. *The Birth of the Messiah*. A volume in *The Anchor Bible Reference Library*. New York: Doubleday, 1993.

Brown, Raymond. *The Death of the Messiah*. Two volumes in *The Anchor Bible Reference Library*. New York: Doubleday, 1994.

Brueggemann, Walter, et al. *Texts for Preaching: A Lectionary Commentary Based on the NRSV*. Cycles A, B, C. Louisville: Westminster John Knox Press, 1993–95.

Craddock, Fred, et al. *Preaching through the Christian Year*. 3 vols. for Cycles A, B, C. Valley Forge, Pa.: Trinity Press International, 1992, 1993. In three volumes, various authors comment on the Sunday readings and psalms as well as various festival readings.

Days of the Lord: The Liturgical Year. 7 vols. Collegeville: The Liturgical Press, 1991–94. Written by French biblical and liturgical experts, this series provides helpful commentary on the readings and seasons. Readily adapted to the Revised Common Lectionary.

Homily Service: An Ecumenical Resource for Sharing the Word. Silver Spring, Md.: The Liturgical Conference. A monthly publication with commentary on Sunday readings (exegesis, ideas and illustrations, healing aspects of the word, a preacher's reflection on the readings).

New Proclamation, Series B. 1999–2000. Various authors. A sound and useful series of commentaries on Cycle B readings.

Reading the Lessons: A Lector's Guide to Pronounciation. Minneapolis: Augsburg Fortress, 1993.

PSALM COLLECTIONS

Anglican Chant Psalter, The. Alec Wyton, ed. New York: Church Hymnal Corporation, 1987.

Basilica Psalter, The. Jay Hunstiger. Collegeville: Liturgical Press.

Grail Gelineau Psalter, The. Chicago: GIA Publications, Inc., 1972. One hundred fifty psalms and eighteen canticles.

Daw, Carl P. and Kevin R. Hackett.

Plainsong Psalter, The. James Litton, ed. New York: Church Hymnal Corporation, 1988.

Psalm Songs. David Ogden and Alan Smith, eds. Minneapolis: Augsburg Fortress, 1998.
  Psalm Songs 1 for Advent–Christmas–Epiphany. AFP 11-10903.
  Psalm Songs 2 for Lent–Holy Week–Easter. AFP 11-10904.
  Psalm Songs 3 for Ordinary Time. AFP 11-10905.

Psalms for the Church Year. Various volumes by different composers. Chicago: GIA Publications, Inc., 1983–present.

Psalter, The. International Commission on English in the Liturgy (ICEL). Chicago: Liturgy Training Publications, 1995. A faithful and inclusive rendering from the Hebrew into contemporary English poetry, intended primarily for communal song and recitation.

Psalter for Worship. (1996–98) Martin Seltz, ed. Minneapolis: Augsburg Fortress, 1995 and continuing. Settings of psalm antiphons by various composers with *LBW* and other psalm tones. Psalm texts included. Prepared for psalms appointed in the Revised Common Lectionary for Sundays and festivals.
  Psalter for Worship, Cycle A. AFP 3-556.
  Psalter for Worship, Cycle B. AFP 3-554.
  Psalter for Worship, Cycle C. AFP 3-555. (Includes all lesser festivals.)

The Psalter: Psalms and Canticles for Singing. Louisville: Westminster/John Knox Press, 1993. Various composers.

Singing the Psalms. Various volumes with various composers represented. Portland: Oregon Catholic Press, 1995–present.

REFERENCE WORKS

Concordance to Hymn Texts: Lutheran Book of Worship. Robbin Hough, compiler. Minneapolis: Augsburg Publishing House, 1985.

New Dictionary of Sacramental Worship, The. Peter Fink, ed. Collegeville: Michael Glazier/Liturgical Press, 1990.

New Westminster Dictionary of Liturgy and Worship, The. J. G. Davies, ed. Philadelphia: Westminster, 1986.

Praying Together. English Language Liturgical Consultation. Nashville: Abingdon Press, 1988. Core ecumenical liturgical texts with annotation and commentary.

Promise of a New Millennium, The. Reflections by the Presiding Bishop and Conference of Bishops of the Evangelical Lutheran Church in America (October 31, 1998).

Pfatteicher, Philip. *Festivals and Commemorations*. Minneapolis: Augsburg Publishing House, 1980.

———. Commentary on *Occasional Services*. Philadelphia: Fortress Press, 1983.

———. Commentary on *Lutheran Book of Worship*. Minneapolis: Augsburg Fortress, 1990.

Pfatteicher, Philip, and Carlos Messerli. *Manual on the Liturgy: Lutheran Book of Worship*. Minneapolis: Augsburg Publishing House, 1979.

Stulken, Marilyn Kay. *Hymnal Companion to the Lutheran Book of Worship*. Philadelphia: Fortress Press, 1981.

———. *With One Voice: A Reference Companion*. Minneapolis: Augsburg Fortress, forthcoming.

Van Loon, Ralph, and S. Anita Stauffer. *Worship Wordbook*. Minneapolis: Augsburg Fortress, 1995.

Welcome to Christ: A Lutheran Introduction to the Catechumenate. Augsburg Fortress, 1997.

Year of Our Lord 2000, The. A Pastoral Letter from the Presiding Bishop and Conference of Bishops of the Evangelical Lutheran Church in America. (October 31, 1998)

SEASONS AND LITURGICAL YEAR

Huck, Gabe. *The Three Days: Parish Prayer in the Paschal Triduum*, rev. ed. Chicago: Liturgy Training Publications, 1992. For worship committees, it is an excellent introduction to worship during the Three Days: Maundy Thursday, Good Friday, and Holy Saturday/Easter Sunday.

Hynes, Mary Ellen. *Companion to the Calendar*. Chicago: Liturgy Training Publications, 1993. An excellent overview of the seasons, festivals and lesser festivals, and many commemorations. Written from an ecumenical/Roman Catholic perspective, including commemorations unique to the Lutheran calendar.

Promise of His Glory: Services and Prayers for the Season from All Saints to Candlemas, The. Collegeville: The Liturgical Press, 1991. And: Perham, Michael, et al., comps. *Enriching the Christian Year*. (Services and prayers from Lent through Pentecost). Collegeville: The Liturgical Press, 1993. New liturgical texts, prayers, litanies, and complete services for congregational use.

WORSHIP BOOKS

Libro de Liturgia y Cántico. Minneapolis: Augsburg Fortress, 1998. A complete Spanish-language worship resource including liturgies and hymns, some with English translations.

Lutheran Book of Worship. Minneapolis: Augsburg Publishing House; Philadelphia: Board of Publication, Lutheran Church in America, 1978.

Lutheran Book of Worship, Ministers edition. Minneapolis: Augsburg Publishing House; Philadelphia: Board of Publication, Lutheran Church in America, 1978.

Occasional Services: A Companion to Lutheran Book of Worship. Minneapolis: Augsburg Publishing House; Philadelphia: Board of Publication, Lutheran Church in America, 1982.

This Far by Faith. Minneapolis: Augsburg Fortress, 1999. A supplement of worship orders, psalms, service music, and hymns representing African American traditions and developed by African American Lutherans.

Welcome to Christ: Lutheran Rites for the Catechumenate. Minneapolis: Augsburg Fortress, 1997.

With One Voice: A Lutheran Resource for Worship. Minneapolis: Augsburg Fortress, 1995. Pew, leader, and accompaniment editions; instrumental parts, organ accompaniment for the liturgy, and cassette.

WORSHIP STUDIES

Foley, Edward. *From Age to Age: How Christians Have Celebrated the Eucharist*. Chicago: Liturgy Training Publications, 1991. An excellent survey of Christian worship, music, environment, and theological concerns.

Gathered and Sent: An Introduction to Worship. Participant book by Karen Bockelman. Leader guide by Roger Prehn. Minneapolis: Augsburg Fortress, 1999. Basic worship study course for inquirers and general adult instruction in congregations.

Inside Out: Worship in an Age of Mission. Minneapolis: Fortress Press, forthcoming. Multiple authors writing on the mission of the church as it pertains to various aspects of worship.

Open Questions in Worship. Gordon Lathrop, gen. ed. Minneapolis: Augsburg Fortress.

What are the essentials of Christian worship? vol. 1 (1994). The scriptural, historical, and ecumenical consensus on essential elements of Christian worship.

What is "contemporary" worship? vol. 2 (1995). Contemporary church music, multiple services and diverse worship styles, and the meaning of the word "contemporary."

How does worship evangelize? vol. 3 (1995). Evangelism in American culture, liturgical leadership in evangelism, and the inclusive nature of the liturgy.

What is changing in baptismal practice? vol. 4 (1995). New developments in bringing adults to the faith, issues in infant baptism, and the relationship between baptism and life stages.

What is changing in eucharistic practice? vol. 5 (1995). Preaching, the eucharistic prayer, and admission to the eucharist.

What are the ethical implications of worship? vol. 6 (1996). Liturgy serving social justice, worship and the cosmos/environment, and liturgy in a secular world.

What does "multicultural" worship look like? vol. 7 (1996). Worship in North American culture, racial/ethnic-specific worship, and culturally diverse worship.

How does the liturgy speak of God? vol. 8 (1996). Images and names for God in worship, women and men preaching, and the trinitarian name invoked in the liturgy.

Ramshaw, Gail. *Every Day and Sunday, Too*. Minneapolis: Augsburg Fortress, 1996. An illustrated book for parents and children. Daily life is related to the central actions of the liturgy.

———. *1-2-3 Church*. Minneapolis: Augsburg Fortress, 1996. An illustrated rhyming primer and number book. For parents with young children, this book presents the fundamental actions of worship through numbered rhymes. A song for singing at home or in church school is included.

———. *Sunday Morning*. Chicago: Liturgy Training Publications, 1993. A book for children and adults on the primary words of Sunday worship.

Senn, Frank. *Christian Liturgy: Catholic and Evangelical*. Minneapolis: Fortress Press, 1997. A comprehensive historical introduction to the liturgy of the Western church with particular emphasis on the Lutheran traditions.

Use of the Means of Grace: A Statement on the Practice of Word and Sacrament, The. Chicago: ELCA; Minneapolis: Augsburg Fortress, 1997.